ACCA

STUDY TEXT

Certificate Paper 8

Managerial Finance

New in this June 1998 edition

This Study Text has been thoroughly updated for all examinable topic developments up to 1 June 1998.

- Many new exam focus points, giving you vital exam hints
- Sharper focus in the coverage of various topics
- New material on activity based costing
- Updating on economic changes

FOR DECEMBER 1998 AND JUNE 1999 EXAMS

BPP Publishing
June 1998

First edition 1993
Sixth edition June 1998

ISBN 0 7517 0132 7 (Previous edition 0 7517 0072 X)

British Library Cataloguing-in-Publication Data
A catalogue record for this book is available from the British Library

Published by

BPP Publishing Limited
Aldine House, Aldine Place
London W12 8AW

http://www.bpp.co.uk

Printed by Ashford Colour Press, Gosport, Hants

We are grateful to the Association of Chartered Certified Accountants for permission to reproduce in this text the syllabus and teaching guide of which the Association holds the copyright.

We are also grateful to the Association of Chartered Certified Accountants for permission to reproduce past examination questions in our Exam Question Bank. The Exam Answer Bank has been prepared by BPP Publishing Limited.

Page

HOW TO USE THIS STUDY TEXT

Aims of this Study Text

To provide you with the knowledge and understanding, skills and applied techniques required for passing the exam

The Study Text has been written around the ACCA's Official Syllabus and the ACCA's Official 1998-9 Teaching Guide (reproduced below, and cross-referenced to where in the text each topic is covered).

- It is **comprehensive**. We do not omit sections of the syllabus as the examiner is liable to examine any angle of any part of the syllabus - and you do not want to be left high and dry.
- It is **up-to-date as at 1 June 1998**, which means that it fulfils the requirement for the December 1998 exams that students should be up-to-date as at 1 June 1998.
- And it is **on-target** - we do not include any material which is not examinable. You can therefore rely on the BPP Study Text as the stand-alone source of all your information for the exam, without worrying that any of the material is irrelevant.

To allow you to study in the way that best suits your learning style and the time you have available, by following your personal Study Plan (see below)

You may be studying at home on your own until the date of the exam, or you may be attending a full-time course. You may like to (and have time to) read every word, or you may prefer to (or only have time to) skim-read and devote the remainder of your time to question practice. Wherever you fall in the spectrum, you will find the BPP Study Text meets your needs in designing and following your personal Study Plan.

To tie in with the other components of the BPP Effective Study Package to ensure you have the best possible chance of passing the exam

Recommended period of use	Elements of BPP Effective Study Package
3-12 months before exam	**Study Text** Acquisition of knowledge, understanding, skills and applied techniques
↓	
1-6 months before exam	**Practice and Revision Kit** Tutorial Questions and helpful checklists of the key points lead you into each area. There are then numerous exam questions to try, graded by topic area, along with realistic suggested solutions prepared by BPP's own authors in the light of the Examiner's Reports. June 1999 examinees will find the 1999 edition of the Kit invaluable for bringing them up-to-date as at 1 December 1998, the cut-off date for the June 1999 examinable material
↓	
last minute - 3 months before exam	**Passcards** Short, memorable notes focused on what is most likely to come up in the exam you will be sitting

Settling down to study

By this stage in your career you are probably a very experienced learner and taker of exams. But have you ever thought about *how* you learn? Let's have a quick look at the key elements required for effective learning. You can then identify your learning style and go on to design your own approach to how you are going to study this text - your personal Study Plan.

Key element of learning	Using the BPP Study Text
Motivation	You can rely on the comprehensiveness and technical quality of BPP. You've chosen the right Study Text - so you're in pole position to pass your exam!
Clear objectives and standards	Do you want to be a prizewinner or simply achieve a moderate pass? Decide.
Feedback	Follow through the examples in this text and do the questions and the Quick Quizzes. Evaluate your efforts critically - how are you doing?
Study plan	You need to be honest about your progress to yourself - do not be over-confident, but don't be negative either. Make your Study Plan (see below) and try to stick to it. Focus on the short-term objectives - completing two chapters a night, say - but beware of losing sight of your study objectives
Practice	Use the Quick Quizzes and Chapter Roundups to refresh your memory regularly after you have completed your initial study of each chapter

These introductory pages let you see exactly what you are up against. However you study, you should:

- **read through the syllabus and teaching guide** - this will help you to identify areas you have already covered, perhaps at a lower level of detail, and areas that are totally new to you
- **study the examination paper section**, where we show you the format of the exam (how many and what kind of questions etc) and analyse all the papers set so far under the syllabus.

Key study steps

The following steps are, in our experience, the ideal way to study for professional exams. You can of course adapt it for your particular learning style (see below).

Tackle the chapters in the order you find them in the Study Text. Taking into account your individual learning style, follow these key study steps for each chapter.

Key study steps	Activity
Step 1 *Chapter topic list*	Study the list. Each numbered topic denotes a numbered section in the chapter
Step 2 *Introduction*	Read it through. It is designed to show you *why* the topics in the chapter need to be studied - how they lead on from previous topics, and how they lead into subsequent ones
Step 3 *Knowledge brought forward boxes*	In these we highlight information and techniques that it is assumed you have 'brought forward' with you from your earlier studies. If there are matters which have changed recently due to legislation etc then these topics are explained in full. Do not panic if you do not feel instantly comfortable with the content - it should come back to you as we develop the subject for this paper. If you are really unsure, we advise you to go back to your previous notes
Step 4 *Explanations*	Proceed methodically through the chapter, reading each section thoroughly and making sure you understand. Where a topic has been examined, we state the month and year of examination against the appropriate heading. You should pay particular attention to these topics
Step 5 *Key terms* and *Exam focus points*	• **Key terms** can often earn you *easy marks* if you state them clearly and correctly in an appropriate exam answer (and they are indexed at the back of the text so you can check easily that you are on top of all of them when you come to revise) • **Exam focus points** give you a good idea of how the examiner tends to examine certain topics - and also pinpoint *easy marks*
Step 6 *Note taking*	Take brief notes if you wish, avoiding the temptation to copy out too much
Step 7 *Examples*	Follow each through to its solution very carefully
Step 8 *Case examples*	Study each one, and try if you can to add flesh to them from your own experience - they are designed to show how the topics you are studying come alive (and often come unstuck) in the real world
Step 9 *Questions*	Make a very good attempt at each one
Step 10 *Answers*	Check yours against ours, and make sure you understand any discrepancies
Step 11 *Chapter roundup*	Check through it very carefully, to make sure you have grasped the major points it is highlighting

Key study steps	Activity
Step 12 *Quick quiz*	When you are happy that you have covered the chapter, use the **Quick quiz** to check your recall of the topics covered. The answers are in the paragraphs in the chapter that we refer you to
Step 13 *Examination question(s)*	Either at this point, or later when you are thinking about revising, make a full attempt at the **Examination question(s)** suggested at the very end of the chapter. You can find these at the end of the Study Text, along with the **Answers** so you can see how you did. We highlight for you which ones are introductory, and which are of the full standard you would expect to find in an exam

Developing your personal Study Plan

Preparing a Study Plan (and sticking closely to it) is one of the key elements in learning success.

First you need to be aware of your style of learning. There are four typical learning styles. Consider yourself in the light of the following descriptions and work out which you fit most closely. You can then plan to follow the key study steps in the sequence suggested.

Learning styles	Characteristics	Sequence of key study steps in the BPP Study Text
Theorist	Seeks to understand principles before applying them in practice	1, 2, 3, 4, 7, 8, 5, 9/10, 11, 12, 13 (6 continuous)
Reflector	Seeks to observe phenomena, thinks about them and then chooses to act	
Activist	Prefers to deal with practical, active problems; does not have much patience with theory	1, 2, 9/10 (read through), 7, 8, 5, 11, 3, 4, 9/10 (full attempt), 12, 13 (6 continuous)
Pragmatist	Prefers to study only if a direct link to practical problems can be seen; not interested in theory for its own sake	9/10 (read through), 2, 5, 7, 8, 11, 1, 3, 4, 9/10 (full attempt), 12, 13 (6 continuous)

Next you should complete the following checklist.

Am I motivated? (a) ☐

Do I have an objective and a standard that I want to achieve? (b) ☐

Am I a theorist, a reflector, an activist or a pragmatist? (c) ☐

How much time do I have available per week, given: (d) ☐

- the standard I have set myself
- the time I need to set aside later for work on the Practice and Revision Kit and Passcards
- the other exam(s) I am sitting, and (of course)
- practical matters such as work, travel, exercise, sleep and social life?

Now:

- take the time you have available per week for this Study Text (d), and multiply it by the number of weeks available to give (e). (e) [ ]
- divide (e) by the number of chapters to give (f) (f) [ ]
- set about studying each chapter in the time represented by (f), following the key study steps in the order suggested by your particular learning style.

This is your personal Study Plan.

Short of time?

Whatever your objectives, standards or style, you may find you simply do not have the time available to follow all the key study steps for each chapter, however you adapt them for your particular learning style. If this is the case, follow the Skim Study technique below (the icons in the Study Text will help you to do this).

Skim Study technique

Study the chapters in the order you find them in the Study Text. For each chapter, follow the key study steps 1-3, and then skim-read through step 4. Jump to step 11, and then go back to step 5. Follow through steps 7 and 8, and prepare outline Answers to Questions (steps 9/10). Try the Quick Quiz (step 12), following up any items you can't answer, then do a plan for the Examination Question (step 13), comparing it against our answers. You should probably still follow step 6 (note-taking), although you may decide simply to rely on the BPP Passcards for this.

Moving on...

However you study, when you are ready to embark on the practice and revision phase of the BPP Effective Study Package, you should still refer back to this Study Text:

- as a source of **reference** (you should find the list of key terms and the index particularly helpful for this)
- as a **refresher** (the Chapter Roundups and Quick Quizzes help you here)

And remember to keep careful hold of this Study Text when you move on to the next level of your exams - you will find it invaluable.

ACCA OFFICIAL SYLLABUS

Introduction

Paper 8 examines two related subjects, Management Accounting (weighting of 40%) and Financial Management (weighting of 60%).

The paper builds on the overview of cost accounting from Paper 3 and covers:

- the application of the management accounting techniques used in planning, control and decision making and the interpretation of information available from their use
- the preparation, organisation, summarisation and presentation of management information/reports.

The paper introduces financial management areas, including:

- the understanding of current practical methods used in making financial management decisions and the influence of the environment on such decisions
- the appreciation of the workings of the financial system, the evaluation of alternative sources of finance and the assessment of investment possibilities
- the communication of the consequences of financial management decisions to accountants and non-accountants.

Management accounting	**Covered in Chapter**
1 Cost and management accounting methods	
(a) Determining and allocating/apportioning costs of activities and outputs through the use of appropriate concepts, methods and techniques	
(i) absorption, marginal and opportunity cost approaches to the accumulation of costs for specific orders (job, batch, contract) or operations (process, service)	2, 3, 4
(ii) activity based costing; use of cost drivers and activities.	2
(b) Consideration and application of information required in relation to	
(i) costing of products and services	3, 4
(ii) preparing plans	5, 13
(iii) monitoring/controlling performance	5, 13
(iv) decision making.	13
2 Information for planning and control	
(a) Budgeting and budgetary control	
(i) identify objectives of budgetary planing and control systems (including an introduction to behavioural influences)	6, 7
(ii) identify/evaluate budgetary systems such as fixed and flexible, zero based and incremental, periodic and continuous	7, 9
(iii) developing/implementing budgeting systems: functional/subsidiary and master budgets (including cash budgeting)	6, 7
(iv) monitoring and controlling performance: calculation of variances; determination of cause of variances	6

	Covered in Chapter
(v) quantitative aids in budgeting: least squares regression; scatter diagram with correlation; forecasting with regression; introduction to time series and seasonality to analyse time related data.	8
(b) Standard costing	
(i) uses and limitations of standard costing	10
(ii) determination of standards	10
(iii) identification and calculation of variances; sales variances (including quantity and mix), cost variances (including mix and yield); absorption and marginal approaches	11, 12
(iv) identify significance and inter-relationship of variances	11
(v) relevance to business performance measurement and control.	7
(c) Cost allocation/apportionment/absorption	
(i) absorption and marginal costing: impact on profit reporting; relevance in planning and control	2
(ii) activity based costing: use in costing of products and services; use as a planning and control device.	2

3 The costing/pricing of products and services

(a) Consideration and application of information requirements in relation to (i) job costs (ii) process costs (iii) service industries (iv) internal services	3, 4

Financial management

4 Financial objectives

(a) The nature, purpose and scope of financial management	14
(b) The relationship between financial management, management accounting and financial accounting	1
(c) The relationship of financial objectives to organisational strategy and ethos and to other organisational objectives. The constraints/conflicts which different objectives may put upon each other.	14
(d) The nature, scope and form (long term and short term) of financial objectives of different types of organisation, including not-for-profit organisations.	14
(e) The roles, responsibilities and relationships of key personnel involved in and with organisations (shareholders, lenders, managers, employees, customers, suppliers, government).	14

		Covered in Chapter
5	**Financial management framework**	
(a)	The commercial and financial environment in which organisations operate (the nature and function of the money and capital markets including banks and other financial intermediaries, the Stock Exchange, the Unlisted Securities Market [now replaced by the Alternative Investment Market] and Over the Counter markets).	15, 18
(b)	The economic environment in which organisations operate	
	(i) application of macro-economic theory as a basis for understanding the key economic variables affecting the business environment	16
	(ii) fiscal policy, its nature, effectiveness of fiscal policy	17
	(iii) money and interest rates, the role of money in the economy, the supply and demand for money	15, 17, 27
	(iv) monetary policy, attitudes to monetary policy, problems of monetary policy	17
	(v) supply side policies, supply side problems, policies to improve supply side	19
	(vi) policies towards monopolies and oligopolies, privatisation and deregulation	19
	(vii) green policies; implications for management of the economy and the firm	19
	(viii) the significance of corporate securities (share capital, debt and preference shares) to commercial organisations and the markets in which they operate, and the influence of markets on organisations.	14, 15
6	**Management of working capital**	
(a)	The nature and scope of working capital management.	20
(b)	The importance of effective working capital management to corporate survival.	20
(c)	Cash: selection of appropriate cash balances, managing cash surpluses and deficits. The nature and functions of the short-term money market.	15, 20, 21
(d)	The management of debtors (including those overseas) involving credit evaluation, terms of credit, cash discounts, debt collection techniques, credit management monitoring and evaluation, factoring and invoice discounting.	21
(e)	Creditors: advantages and disadvantages of alternative methods of paying suppliers (including those overseas), the dangers of trading on credit.	21
(f)	Stock: alternative stock management systems and models including Total Quality Management (TQM), Just in Time (JIT), Economic Order Quantity (EOQ) etc	21

	Covered in Chapter
7 Sources of finance	
(a) Sources and relative costs (including issue costs but not calculations of the cost of capital) of various types of finance and their suitability to different circumstances and organisations (both large and small companies, listed and unlisted) including	
(i) the nature and importance of internally generated funds	22
(ii) capital markets (types of share capital, new issues, rights issues, loan capital, convertibles, warrants)	22
(iii) the effect of dividend policy on financing needs	22
(iv) bank finance (the various forms of short, medium and long term finance that are available, including leasing)	21, 24, 30
(v) trade credit	21
(vi) government sources: grants, regional and national aid schemes, tax incentives etc	19, 27
(vii) venture capital and financial sources particularly suited to the small company	22
(viii) international money and capital markets, including an introduction to international banking, and the finance of foreign trade.	15, 19
(b) Determining requirements for finance (how much, for how long, for what purpose) in relation to a client's operational and strategic objectives. The importance of the choice of capital structure to an organisation.	24
(c) Calculating financial gearing and other key financial ratios and analysing their significance to the organisation.	24
(d) Determining appropriate sources of finance by identifying and evaluating appropriate sources, taking into account such factors as (i) cost of finance including its servicing (ii) timing of cash payments (iii) effect on gearing and other ratios (iv) effect on the company's existing investors	24

	Covered in Chapter
8 Capital expenditure and investment	
(a) Identifying potential investment opportunities.	25
(b) Appraising capital investments (domestic) for commercial and non commercial organisations through the use of appropriate methods and techniques	
(i) return on capital employed and payback	25
(ii) discounting based methods, including the importance of the cost of capital to investment appraisal (but not the calculation of cost of capital)	26
(iii) internal rate of return	26
(iv) net present value	26
(v) capital rationing (single and multi-period)	29
(vi) lease or buy decisions	30
including the effects of taxation and inflation on investment decisions, the handling of risk and uncertainty, eg through the use of probabilities, sensitivity analysis and simulations.	27, 28

ACCA OFFICIAL 1998-1999 TEACHING GUIDE

This is the official Teaching Guide for the December 1998 and June 1999 exams.

	Syllabus reference
Session 1 Management accounting - cost accumulation	1a(i), 4b

- discuss the role of the management accounting function in meeting the needs of management
- outline the nature and scope of management accounting
- explain why the management accountant can be described as a 'gatekeeper' and 'information manager'
- describe the relationship between management accounting, financial management and financial accounting
- evaluate the absorption and marginal cost approaches to the accumulation of costs for specific orders, jobs, batches, contracts or operations

Session 2 A critical review of product costing	1a(i),b(i) 3a(i),(ii)

- compute costs using an opportunity cost accumulation approach
- make a critical evaluation of the absorption, marginal and opportunity approaches to cost accumulation
- discuss the costing/pricing and information requirements of job and process costs

Session 3 Internal services & service industry: Activity based costing	1a(ii) 3a(iii),(iv)

- discuss the costing/pricing and information requirements of internal services and service industries
- outline the differences between activity based costing and traditional absorption costing systems
- prepare product cost computations using activity based costing
- evaluate the validity of the cost drivers which are used

Session 4 Absorption v marginal revisited: An introduction to cost control	1b(ii),(iii) 2c(i)

- illustrate and explain the impact on profit reporting of using absorption costing and marginal costing
- consider the information requirements for the planning process associated with:
  - cost control, including feedback
  - monitoring and controlling performance
- highlight the advantages of predetermined system of cost control over historic costing systems
- assess the suitability of cost control techniques across a range of organisations

Session 5 Budgetary control 1	2a(i),(ii),(iii), 2b(v)

- identify the objectives of budgetary planning and control systems
- draft and/or review and/or explain a budget preparation timetable
- construct and/or evaluate and/or discuss the functional, subsidiary and master budgets
- consider the development and implementation aspects

Syllabus reference

Session 6 Budgetary control 2 — 2a(i),(ii),(iii),(iv)

- prepare and discuss cash budgets (cash flow forecasts)
- compute and evaluate fixed and flexible budgets
- explain ways in which the control phase and the budgets themselves can be evaluated
- appreciate and identify the reason/s for variances
- assess the behavioural implications of budgeting (at an introductory level)

Session 7 Quantitative aids in budgeting — 2a(v)

- in relation to budgeting make use of and discuss:
  - least squares and regression
  - scatter diagrams and correlation
  - forecasting with regression
  - time series and seasonality to analyse time related data

  to compute/construct as appropriate

Session 8 Alternative budget systems: Standard costing 1 — 2a(ii), 2b(i),(ii)

- describe the main features of zero based budgeting systems
- specify the areas/organisations in which zero based budgeting may be applied
- discuss incremental budgeting v zero based budgeting
- identify and evaluate periodic and continuous budgetary systems
- outline the uses, features and limitations of standard costing systems
- explain how standards are determined

Session 9 Standard costing 2 — 2b(iii)

- compute and discuss:
  - material variances (including mix and yield)
  - labour variances
  - overhead variances (including production overhead expenditure, capacity and efficiency variances)

Session 10 Standard costing 3 — 2b(iii),(iv)

- compute and discuss sales variances (including quantity and mix)
- demonstrate an understanding of the inter-relationships between variances
- prepare reconciliations using operating statements which:
  - reconcile the budgeted and actual profit figures, and/or
  - reconcile the actual sales less the standard cost of sales, with the actual profit
- show how the absorption and marginal approaches can be used in standard costing

Session 11 Decision making — 1a(i), 1b(ii),(iii),(iv)

- consider the information required in relation to preparing plans, monitoring and controlling performance and decision making
- know how to present information to management (including reports)
- solve decision making type problems which involve an integration of Paper 8 subjects and knowledge gained from earlier studies
- evaluate performance and interpret information provided

(note: relevant costs are examined in depth in PAPER 9)

Syllabus reference

Session 12 The nature and scope of financial management

4a, c, d, e
5b(viii),

- discuss the nature and scope of financial objectives for private sector companies
- assess the role of social and non-financial objectives and their financial impact (including "green" policies)
- discuss the issue of corporate social responsibility towards other stakeholders
- consider how the objectives of "not-for-profit" organisations differ from those of "commercial" concerns
- discuss the problem of conflict of objectives and justify the primacy of the profit motive for commercial organisations
- consider appropriate indicators to measure corporate financial performance and calculate appropriate ratios from a company's financial statements
- discuss the case for presenting environmental reports as part of the regular financial reporting process

Session 13 The financial management framework

5a, b(viii)
7a(viii)

- discuss the general roles of financial intermediaries
- explain the role of commercial banks, as providers of funds (including the creation of credit)
- explain the functions of a stock market
- outline the Efficient Markets Hypothesis, and assess its implications for corporate policy and financial management
- identify the general factors which determine money market interest rates and rates of return
- discuss the risk-return trade-off
- identify the key features of different types of security in terms of the risk-return trade-off
- discuss the links between the money and capital markets as sources of funds for companies
- identify the international money and capital markets and outline their operation

Session 14 The economic environment: Macro-economic policy 1

5b(i),(ii)

Macro-economic objectives

- specify the main macro-economic policy targets
- examine the recent record of the UK in relation to other G7 countries
- discuss the interdependence of national economies
- consider how government economic policy affects planning and decision-making in both service and manufacturing industries

Fiscal policy

- explain how public expenditure is financed
- explain the PSBR/PSDR and how it may be funded
- explain how the PSBR may interact with other economic indicators
- explain the wider functions of fiscal policy
- identify the main tools of fiscal policy
- discuss the problems associated with fiscal policy especially that of "crowding-out"

Syllabus reference

Session 15 The economic environment: Macro-economic policy 2 — 5b(iii)

- define and explain the role of monetary policy
- discuss the alternative measures of the money stock
- outline the variables which influence the demand for money by households and firms
- explain the relationship between the money stock and rates of interest
- explain how the money stock may be controlled
- discuss the problems associated with monetary policy
- explain the Monetarist "Golden Rule"
- examine the relationship between fiscal and monetary policy

Session 16 Inflation — 5a, b

- explain the alternative ways of measuring inflation
- explain why inflation is a problem for households and firms, especially lenders and borrowers
- explain the impact of inflation on international competitiveness
- explain the effect of inflation on interest rates and exchange rates (Fisher Effect and Law of One Price)
- explain and evaluate the main theories of increases in the price level, especially the role of expectations
- consider how economic agents can protect themselves against inflation
- examine the impact of inflation on company cash flows and profits
- explain how inflation may distort the assessment of company performance

Session 17 Government intervention in industries and markets — 5b, b(vi) 7b(vi),(vii)

Competition policy

- explain the role of the government in ensuring fair competition
- identify barriers to fair competition and outline UK policies designed to control them
- discuss the case for privatisation
- explain the term "de-regulation" and its impact on the UK financial and economic system

Official aid schemes

- explain the role of government as a provider of finance via regional and EU aid schemes
- discuss the effect of tax incentives on financial flows

Green policies

- discuss the case for and against greater "green" intervention
- discuss alternative ways of controlling pollutants and identify their effects on company activity

Supply side policies

- discuss "supply side policies" and their macro-economic significance
- identify contemporary supply side problems, and suggest policies to resolve them

Syllabus reference

Session 18 Working capital management 1

6a, b, d

General issues

- explain what is meant by "working capital", and "working capital management"
- distinguish between cash flow and profits
- identify the need for adequate cash flow information
- explain the function of treasury management
- identify the need for effective working capital management
- explain the importance of corporate liquidity to survival

Control of debtors

- explain how the credit-worthiness of customers may be assessed
- explain how to balance the risks and costs of customer default against the profitability of marginal business
- explain the role of factoring and invoice discounting in assisting the credit manager
- explain the role of settlement discounts in credit management
- discuss the particular problems of managing accounts receivable from overseas including foreign exchange risk

Session 19 Working capital management 2

6c, e, f
7a(iv)

Control of creditors

- identify the various forms of bank finance available to both small and large companies
- explain the availability of credit and the role of the guarantee
- highlight the risks of taking increased credit and buying under extended credit terms
- explain how methods of paying suppliers may influence cash flows of both parties (eg) bank giro, direct debit and cheques, etc

Inventory management

- explain and calculate stock ratios
- explain the possible relationships between sales and stocks
- calculate the EOQ under conditions of certain and uncertain demand
- explain how JIT affects stock control

Control of cash

- calculate optimal cash balances, etc using formal models of cash management
- consider the drawbacks of such models
- outline how centralised cash control and treasury management procedures can be applied by national and multinational organisations

Session 20 Long-term finance 1

5a
7a(i),(iii),(vii)

- describe ways in which a company may obtain a stock market listing
- describe sources of venture capital for the smaller company
- explain the requirements of stock market investors in terms of returns on investment
- show how indicators such as EPS, PE ratio, yield and cover can be used to assess past, current and future investor returns
- outline the Dividend Valuation Model, with and without growth
- explain the importance of internally-generated funds
- explain the pros and cons of making a rights issue, especially when a dividend is also paid
- calculate the price of rights
- explain the purpose and impact of a bonus issue
- explain the purpose and impact of scrip dividends
- explain the purpose and impact of a stock split
- explain why share prices are affected by future dividend policy
- describe and explain how stock markets operate (including AIM)

Syllabus reference

Session 21 Long-term finance 2

7a(ii)

- explain the essential features of different types of preference shares
- consider the reasons why companies issue preference shares
- explain the rights of preference shareholders
- explain the essential features of different types of long-term debt security
- explain the impact of tax-deductibility of debt interest on the cost of debt finance
- explain the essential features of convertible debt
- explain the reasons why convertibles may be issued and their attractions to both companies and investors
- explain the essential features of warrants and why they are issued
- assess the effect on EPS of conversion and option rights

Session 22 Long-term finance 3 - the capital structure decision

7a(iv), b, c, d

- explain and calculate the level of financial gearing using alternative measures of gearing
- distinguish between operational gearing and financial gearing
- explain the advantages of gearing for shareholders
- explain the possible effects of gearing on the value of shares, company risk and required return
- explain how a company may determine its capital structure considering: interest charges, dividend policy, risk and redemption requirements
- explain the role of short-term financing in a firm's capital structure
- discuss the relationship between the management of working capital and the long-term capital structure decision

Session 23 Investment decisions

8a, b(ii)

- explain the meaning of investment, distinguishing between capital and revenue expenditure
- distinguish between investment expenditure on fixed assets and investment expenditure on working capital
- explain the importance of different types of investment to commercial and not-for-profit organisations
- discuss the ways in which firms identify potential investment opportunities (ie) strategic analysis
- consider the impact of investment projects on accounting statements
- explain the payback method of appraisal and examine its drawbacks
- explain the ROCE method and examine its drawbacks
- consider why organisations use "crude" methods like payback and ROCE

Session 24 Investment appraisal using DCF methods

8b(ii),(iii),(iv)

- explain the importance of the time value of money in choosing between alternatives
- calculate present values to derive the NPV and IRR measures of investment worth
- pinpoint the advantages of DCF methods over other approaches
- assess the relative merits of IRR and NPV as ranking criteria when projects are mutually exclusive
- apply incremental analysis in a ranking situation
- examine the problems presented by multiple sign changes in a cash flow profile
- assess the relative merits of the IRR and NPV methods
- apply DCF principles to asset replacement decisions

	Syllabus reference
Session 25 Project appraisal allowing for inflation and taxation	5b(iii) 7a(vi)

Allowing for inflation

- explain the relationship between inflation and interest rates, distinguishing between real and nominal rates
- discuss the impact of inflation on project cash flows, distinguishing between generalised and specific inflation
- evaluate capital projects on a "real terms" basis
- evaluate capital projects on a "money terms" basis

Allowing for tax

- calculate the effect of capital allowances and Corporation Tax on project cash flows
- assess the impact of tax relief on the cost of borrowed finance
- calculate the profitability of capital investments on a post-tax basis

Session 26 Project appraisal under risk — 8b

- distinguish between risk and uncertainty
- identify the sources of risk affecting project profitability
- compute the sensitivity of project NPV to specified changes in key variables
- apply probability analysis to calculate the expected NPV of a project, and the associated standard deviation
- undertake a simple decision tree analysis
- appreciate how a simulation can generate a probability distribution for the NPV of a project
- consider ways of reducing the riskiness of a project

Session 27 Capital rationing — 7,8b(v)

- explain the reasons why a firm may suffer from a shortage of capital resources, distinguishing between internal factors and external factors (eg) government credit policy
- evaluate the single-period rationing problem, using the profitability index, and analyse the source of possible conflict between the PI and NPV methods
- set up and solve by graphical LP means a multi-period rationing problem
- consider ways of relaxing the capital constraints

Session 28 Leasing decisions — 7a(iv) 8b(vi)

- distinguish between operating and finance leases
- assess the relative advantages and disadvantages of different types of lease, contrasting leasing with other methods of credit finance (eg) HP
- consider the impact of leasing on company gearing
- identify the cash flow costs and benefits ensuing from a decision to lease an asset
- evaluate the lease versus borrow-to-buy alternatives for acquiring assets
  (i) for non-taxpayers
  (ii) for companies with taxable capacity

THE EXAMINATION PAPER

Format of the paper

		Number of marks
Section A:	Compulsory mini-case study	40
Section B:	1 (out of 2) questions on financial management	20
Section C:	2 (out of 3) questions on management accounting	40
		100

Section A will be primarily on financial management but may draw upon some management accounting concepts to a limited degree.

Present value, annuity and normal distribution tables will be reproduced in the paper as required.

Formulae will be provided in the exam 'where relevant'.

Time allowed: 3 hours.

Analysis of past papers

Below is an analysis of the topics included in past examination papers.

Note that the format of the paper changed with effect from June 1997. Before then, Section A (case study) and section B (short questions) integrated management accounting and financial management topics, Section C contained management accounting topics and Section D concentrated on financial management.

December 1997

Section A

1 Debtors: factoring and discounts; just-in-time arrangement; hedging of foreign currency risk

Section B

2 Calculation of dividend payout ratios and dividend cover; uses of surplus cash

3 Financial and non-financial appraisal of pollution control project

Section C

4 Activity-based costing versus absorption costing; the advantages and limitations of an activity-based approach for management accounting information

5 Budget and actual profit reconciliation using variances (including mix); commentary on results; sales variances

6 Absorption costing; pricing decisions; impact of capacity on product costs

June 1997

Section A

1 Case study of retail chain: calculation of net cash flow; report on financial performance; financing of proposed investment programme; uses for cash balances

Section B

2 Investment appraisal, involving taxation; identify errors and restate appraisal

3 New stock ordering system: calculation of change in EOQ; payback period

Section C

4 Calculation of break even point, and budgeted profit/loss; variances including profit and loss account reconciliation

5 Preparation of a management report covering cost allocation, budgeted net profit calculations; regression analysis

6 Use of budgets (performance evaluation, resource allocation, authorisation); zero base budgeting.

December 1996

Section A

1 Cash flow budget and investment appraisal; gearing and EPS

Section B

2 Five out of six to be attempted

(a) Cartels
(b) Share warrants
(c) Term loans *versus* overdraft
(d) Public sector budget deficit
(e) Yields on different types of security
(f) Performance measures for public sector services

Section C

3 Fixed production overhead variances and variance inter-relationships

4 Absorption costing and marginal costing and the use of different stock valuation methods

Section D

5 Financing policies and early payment discounts; cash management model

6 Net present value and internal rate of return; sensitivity and break-even analysis

June 1996

Section A

1 Operating and financial gearing; linear regression models and their use in decision making; payback period; cost-volume-profit analysis;

Section B

2 Five out of six to be attempted

(a) Policy on short-term money supply variations
(b) Rights issues
(c) Behavioural aspects of budgeting
(d) Calculation of sales variances using standard marginal costing
(e) The valuation of work in progress in a process costing environment
(f) The use and benefits of idle production capacity

Section C

3 Methods of apportionment of service department costs: bases of apportionment of the cost of internal services: apportionment of service department costs using different methods

4 Calculation of absorption rates; analysis of product profitability and interpretation of results

Section D

5 Importance of trade credit; evaluation of a discount on purchases

6 Sale and leaseback; hire purchase; leasing; evaluation of leasing from lessor's and lessee's viewpoints

December 1995

Section A

1 Problems of rapid growth; stockholding period; managing debtors and creditors; cash budget and budgeted p&l account; conversion to a plc

Section B

2 Five out of six to be attempted

(a) The forward foreign exchange market
(b) Financial intermediation
(c) The payback method of project appraisal
(d) Just-in-time purchasing
(e) The use of fiscal policy
(f) The importance of forecasting; sales forecasting

Section C

3 Variance analysis (including mix and yield variances)

4 Minimum pricing; profit-maximising pricing; overcoming limiting factor analysis

Section D

5 Calculation of financing requirement and evaluation of sources of finance

6 Privatisation and a firm's objectives; performance of regulated privatised company

June 1995

Section A

1 Government budgetary policy; required return for public sector investment decisions compared with private sector; appraisal and methods of finance for a public sector project

Section B

2 Five out of six to be attempted

(a) Credit creation by commercial banks
(b) Zero base budgeting
(c) Variance analysis
(d) The use of statistical information within a management accounting function
(e) Change in credit policy
(f) Capital expenditure budgeting

Section C

3 Flexible budgeting and operating statements

4 Absorption costing and ABC

Section D

5 Appraisal of a capital investment using an accounting rate of return method; extending credit and assessing creditworthiness

6 Reasons for seeking a stock market listing; assessment of company performance; restructuring prior to flotation; consequences of flotation for company policy

December 1994

Section A

1 Budgeting (including cash budget, budgeted profit and loss account and budgeted balance sheet)

Section B

2 Five out of six to be attempted

(a) Factors influencing market value of convertible stocks
(b) Methods to obtain a Stock Exchange quotation
(c) Advantages of scrip dividends
(d) Factoring and invoice discounting
(e) Economic objectives of privatisation
(f) Elasticity of demand

Section C

3 Over and under absorption of overheads; absorption costing versus marginal costing; absorption costing and decision making

4 Problems associated with process costing

Section D

5 Gearing ratios; policies to lower capital gearing and improve interest cover

6 Capital rationing; sharing of projects and raising external finance

June 1994

Section A

1 Appraisal of factory closure and restructuring; efficient markets hypothesis; rights issue; impact of project on earnings per share; operating risks of the project

Section B

2 Five out of six to be attempted:

(a) Supply side economics
(b) Realisation of surplus assets
(c) Process costing
(d) Management accounting and the external environment
(e) Zero base budgeting
(f) Time series analysis

Section C

3 Standard costing and variance analysis

4 Performance appraisal and the use of information for planning, control and decision making

Section D

5 Overtrading and relevant performance and liquidity ratios; policies to reduce debtors

6 Inflation and rates of return on projects; project appraisal with inflation; impact of inflation on analysis of financial decisions

Further guidance from the ACCA

The ACCA provides the following further guidance on the examination paper for Paper 8 *Managerial Finance.*

The objective of the Certificate Stage

This stage continues the introduction of the new subject areas, develops students' analytical skills and introduces students to the problems and situations that they will meet at work.

The Certificate Stage tests the application of the theory in the context of recognisable problems and conceptual understanding. It will consolidate knowledge of current principles, practices and techniques and begin to develop students' ability to criticise current practices. Questions will present practical scenarios requiring students to select the best answer from a range of available solutions in order to achieve the specified objective.

This stage will establish links between subjects, for example coverage of mathematical topics will be wholly in the context of their use in management accounting or financial management.

Skills to be tested in the Certificate Stage

Students should be able to demonstrate the ability to:

- analyse and evaluate information
- apply concepts and principles flexibly in a variety of circumstances
- identify, define and rank problems
- interpret results
- criticise proposed solutions or practices

Aim of Paper 8

To facilitate decision making by developing the management accounting techniques for planning and control and introducing the financial management methods used for analysing the benefits of various sources of finance and capital investment opportunities.

On completion of this paper students should be able to:

- apply management accounting techniques in planning, control and decision making situations and interpret information available from their use
- explain practical methods used in making financial management decisions and the influence of the environment on such decisions
- appreciate the nature and scope of working capital management
- identify appropriate sources of finance for particular situations and assess the impact upon capital structure
- appraise capital investment using appropriate methods and techniques and allow for the effects of tax, inflation, risk and uncertainty

Management accounting

In addition to the above, the paper aims to:

(i) develop and test comprehension skills. Students could be set open-ended questions which require them to apply principles and also to think about the principles they are applying;

(ii) develop analytical skills. Students must be able to make a critical evaluation of some of the techniques they have learned in Paper 3, ie to be able to state how a task could have been performed better;

(iii) assess the ability to make critical evaluations;

(iv) help students to integrate knowledge in preparation for the professional stage examinations.

Financial management

In addition to the above, the paper aims to:

(i) show how financial decisions are made and under what constraints. A key aspect of the syllabus with respect to this is the issue of environmental constraints. The role of the Economics in this paper is to emphasise to students the fact that financial decisions are usually far less simple than they appear in textbooks;

(ii) support a more detailed analysis of strategic and financial planning found in Paper 14.

Prerequisite knowledge for paper 8

Students must have a thorough knowledge of the material in Paper 3 *Management Information* and a good general knowledge of other relevant Foundation and Certificate Stage Papers.

Paper 8 extends the coverage of costing from Paper 3 by:

- providing a more critical review of costing methods (including activity based costing) for different manufacturing processes or services
- evaluating absorption and marginal costing in greater depth
- introducing the preparation and evaluation of budgets (including cash budgets) for performance measurement
- outlining the uses, features and limitations of a standard costing system and applying variance analysis for decision making.

Paper 8 will also draw upon and extend the basic understanding of economic analysis acquired in Paper 4 the *Organisational Framework* in order to examine how the economic environment and changes in it affects the financial decision-making of an organisation.

No further prerequisite knowledge is required for the FM section other than the basic accounting principles from Paper 1 *The Accounting Framework* although students are urged to listen to and or read current financial and economic news.

Development of Paper 8 topics in subsequent papers

The MA section is developed in Paper 9 *Information for Control and Decision Making* where a more critical analysis of management accounting techniques is expected. The introduction to FM is examined in more depth in Paper 14 *Financial Strategy*.

Extent of integration of other studies

Paper 8 will demand an application of the quantitative techniques covered in Paper 3 *Management Information*. These techniques will be examined in the context of MA and/or FM situations, for example discounted cash flow and net present value calculations to appraise capital investments.

Paper 8 discusses how the commercial and financial environment impinges on organisations and relates the significance of economic policy to individual firms. As stated earlier, students would be advised to revise areas from Paper 4 *The Organisational Framework*, for example fiscal and monetary policy, inflation, in preparation for the study of the economic and financial environment in this syllabus.

The sections on performance indicators and investment ratios will refer to the calculation of ratios tested in Paper 1 *The Accounting Framework*.

The impact of capital allowances and corporation tax on capital investment appraisal is examinable. This tax knowledge should be familiar to students from Paper 7 *The Tax Framework*.

Tackling case study questions

The following points on how to tackle case study questions were made in an article in the *Students Newsletter* (November 1994) written by CW Neale.

The Association recognises that accountants need the ability to think across narrow subject boundaries, Paper 8 being a good example here with its 'amalgam' of economics, management accounting and financial management. Longer case study questions test this ability as well as preparing candidates for the style of questions met later, particularly in Papers 9 and 14.

The June 1994 sitting showed that students were having special problems in addition to the usual problems of examination technique. To avoid these problems note the following general principles.

(a) The case study is the largest single source of marks. Therefore, acknowledge the importance of the case study question and allow the appropriate time for it (40 marks × 1.8 mins = 72 mins).

(b) The sections of the question will centre on issues raised in the case. Your answers to the different sections should be related to the company concerned, even if the requirement does not stipulate this directly.

(c) The sections of the question will typically be related. Students often panic when they realise their answer to one section is incorrect and then abandon the question. This is unnecessary, as mistakes will not be penalised twice where a wrong answer is carried forward to a later section.

(d) As always, it is essential to answer the question which is set. A sketchy answer roughly along the lines required will usually earn more marks than a voluminous answer which is barely on the point.

If you are in any doubt about the interpretation which should be made of the question, state your assumptions clearly. They will gain credit, provided that they are reasonable. Most case study questions are capable of different interpretations and approaches: this can present difficulties for the examiner, but it also allows knowledgeable students to demonstrate the breadth and depth of their understanding.

Part A
Dealing with costs

Chapter 1

THE MANAGEMENT ACCOUNTANT

Chapter topic list		Syllabus reference
1	Management accounting and management	Introduction
2	Management accounting	Introduction
3	Management accounting, financial accounting and financial management	5(b)
4	Some basic cost accounting concepts	Introduction

Introduction

Welcome to **Managerial Finance**. As you will already be aware if you have read through the introduction to this Study Text (and if you have not you are strongly advised to do so before going any further), Managerial Finance examines two related subjects, **management accounting** and **financial management**. We will be studying management accounting in the first thirteen chapters of this Study Text, financial management, including some aspects of economics, being the main subject of the remaining part of the text.

This chapter serves as an introduction both to management accounting and the role of the management accountant.

In the following chapters we will be looking at the methods and techniques employed by the management accountant to fulfil that role.

1 MANAGEMENT ACCOUNTING AND MANAGEMENT 6/94

The role of management

1.1 Have you ever wondered what those elevated beings do? You know who I mean don't you? Elevated beings. Managers. So, what do they do? Difficult question? Particularly difficult if you are under their control. Easier, of course, if you just happen to be one of those elevated beings.

1.2 If you are under their control you probably think managers take long lunches in expensive restaurants, spend long holidays in exotic places, spend a long time on personal telephone calls, do little work, make little effort and treat you with little more than contempt.

1.3 If, on the other hand, you are a manager, you probably think that you work very hard, that you do little else but work very hard and that nobody who works for you works very hard at all.

1.4 If you are having trouble defining the role of management, think about your management role. 'What role?', you may be thinking. Well, we are all managers in one sense - managers of our lives. So what do we do (or what should we do) to be effective managers of our lives?

You as a manager

1.5 Imagine your normal working day. There is little point in you waking up each weekday and just hoping that you will find some washed and ironed clothes in your wardrobe, that some milk will have magically appeared in your fridge, that a bus which might happen to pass will get you to the office on time or that you will be able to fly off to the Caribbean on holiday. **You have to plan** for these things. They don't just happen. You have to plan to ensure that you have the appropriate resources (milk, clean and ironed clothes and timely transport) to enable you to conduct your daily life. You have to **plan** to ensure that you have sufficient cash and enough time off work to go on holiday.

1.6 What else do you do while managing your daily life? Very few of us are lucky enough to be able to afford to jump in a helicopter every morning to go to work. Most of us are stuck with the bus, tube, train or car. What would happen if you decided to be extremely extravagant and chartered a helicopter every Monday morning to take you to work. This might mean that your dream holiday to the Caribbean was out of the window. A lack of control over expenditure means that plans you might have made (for a dream holiday to the Caribbean) never come to fruition. As manager of your life **you have to control what you do** to ensure that you can stick to your plans.

1.7 Suppose that you share a house with three other friends. What would happen if you made no decision as to who would do the hoovering, who would clean the toilet and who would put the bin bags out for the dustmen to collect. There would be chaos (as there is in lots of shared houses). Unless all of you like living in chaos, some sort of organisation is necessary to ensure that household duties are shared out equally so that your house does not end up resembling the camel house at London Zoo. If you want to be able to walk around your home barefoot without worrying about what you might step in, **you need to organise yourself and others.**

1.8 Imagine it is 5.00 pm on Friday afternoon and you really fancy a few drinks in the pub after work. Your work colleagues are totally apathetic about the idea. They would rather go home and watch Coronation Street. How do you get them to do what you want them to do? You entice them with thoughts of good company, tomato juice and packets of crisps. You attempt to make them see that it really would be much better for them to accompany you to the pub than to slump in front of the television. You tell them not to be boring. In short **you motivate them**.

1.9 There is one common activity running through the various aspects of managing your life, however. You have to decide what mode of transport to take to work, where to go on holiday, who cleans the toilet and who washes up and what drink to have in the pub. A great part of managing your life obviously involves making decisions. Indeed, **it is difficult to plan, control, organise or motivate without making decisions**.

1.10 What does managing your life therefore involve?

- Planning
- Controlling
- Organising
- Motivating
- Decision making

1.11 This is exactly what those elevated beings have to do to manage you, your organisation's products, your organisation's financial position and your organisation's public image.

- **Planning**

  Management have to **plan for both the short term and the long term**. A long-range plan is necessary in order to anticipate any future needs or opportunities that require action to be taken either now or in the near future. For example, management may need to consider building a new factory to meet future anticipated increased demand for a product. Management should constantly be **thinking ahead**. They should **never be surprised by any gradual developments**. The organisation's long-term objectives (such as building a new factory or developing into a new market) are converted into a succession of short-term plans of action in the form of annual budgets.

- **Controlling**

  Control enables management to see whether the organisation's long-term objectives are achievable. Control is exercised by **comparing actual performance with the short-term plans** so that deviations from these short-term plans can be identified and corrective action taken to ensure that the long-term objectives are possible. If the control process indicates that the long-term objectives are not achievable, the objectives can be changed before any serious damage to the company's future occurs.

- **Organising**

  Organising is the establishment of a **framework within which necessary activities can be performed**, the designation of a member of staff to be responsible for a particular activity and the **definition of managers' responsibilities and lines of authority**. It requires the breakdown of the organisation into manageable sections such as departments and the **coordination of activities** in these sections if the organisation's objectives are to be met.

- **Motivating**

  Managers need to **influence employees to act in such a manner that the employees' objectives and the organisation's objectives are one and the same thing.**

- **Decision making**

  Management is decision taking. Managers of all levels within an organisation take decisions.

  - Decisions taken at the **strategic level set or change the objectives or strategic targets of an organisation**. They include decisions about the selection of products and markets, the required levels of company profitability, the purchase or disposal of subsidiary companies or major fixed assets, whether there should be an employee share of company profits and so on.

  - **Tactical-level decisions** are concerned with the **efficient and effective use of an organisation's resources** (sometimes referred to as the '4Ms': men, materials, machines and money). Tactical-level decisions therefore include setting budgets for the next period for sales, production, stock levels and so on and setting measures of performance by which departmental results can be gauged.

  - **Operational-level decisions** are concerned with **ensuring that specific tasks are carried out effectively and efficiently**. They might include decisions concerning the allocation of particular staff to particular tasks and jobs or the action to take over customer complaints.

Meeting the needs of management

1.12 Just as you manage your life to ensure that you get what want (your objectives), managers manage the organisation to ensure that the organisations' objectives are achieved.

Having considered how the manager manages, let us look at how the management accountant can assist the manager to manage.

- **Assistance in planning**

  The management accountant assists planning **by providing information**. This information may be about pricing, capital expenditure projects, product costs or competition. In the short-term planning process of budgeting, the management accountant provides invaluable information on past costs and revenues which may be used as guidance for the budgets. The management accountant is also deeply involved in the budgeting process itself. He establishes budget procedures, provides a budget timetable, coordinates and ensures the harmonisation of all subsidiary budgets and uses the subsidiary budgets to prepare the master budget which is presented to management for approval.

- **Assistance in controlling**

  The management accountant provides invaluable assistance with the controlling process. He **supplies performance reports which compare actual performance with planned performance and which therefore highlight those activities which are not conforming to plan.**

- **Assistance in organising**

  By **ensuring that the accounting system is tailored to the organisational structure**, the management accountant reinforces the objectives of the organisational framework.

- **Assistance in motivating**

  Budgets prepared by the management accountant serve to motivate managers and subordinates to attempt to achieve the organisation's objectives since formalised targets are more likely to motivate than vague and uncertain comments.

  Performance reports produced by the management accountant for the control process are also intended to motivate individual performances by communicating performance information in relation to the targets which have been set.

  The management accountant also assists the motivation process by **identifying potential managerial problem areas** and highlighting those items which require investigation. Despite the help given by management accountants, it should be borne in mind that budgets and performance reports can cause serious behavioural problems and can be demotivating if used without knowledge of the problems which can occur.

- **Assistance in decision making**

  The management accountant is a vital cog in the organisation's decision-making process, as we will see later in the chapter. The **management accountant collects data about the various options available and analyses that data into information so that management can make an informed decision about the most appropriate course of action.**

  For example, suppose a component that an organisation currently manufactures in-house can now be purchased from a supplier. The management accountant provides information about the various costs and benefits associated with each option so that management can choose whether to buy-in the component or manufacture it in-house.

We will be examining decision making in great detail and so you will have a much fuller understanding of how the management accountant provides assistance with decision making by the time you have completed the text.

Question 1

Have a chat with some managers in your organisation. What do they do? Do they plan, control, organise, motivate and make decisions? How do they do this? Why do they do this? Are they successful in what they are doing and if not, why not?

2 MANAGEMENT ACCOUNTING 6/94, 6/95

Exam focus point

In 6/95, there were 5 marks to be gained for explaining the importance of statistical information to the operation of the management accounting function of an organisation.

2.1 Having looked at the role of management accounting in terms of how it can meet the needs of management, we will now look at the discipline in more general terms. There are many definitions of management accounting but the following CIMA definition from the 1996 edition of *Official Terminology* is generally acceptable.

KEY TERM

Management accounting is the process of identification, measurement, accumulation, analysis, preparation, interpretation and communication of information used by management to plan, evaluate and control within an entity and to assure appropriate use of and accountability for its resources. Management accounting also comprises the preparation of financial reports for non-management groups such as shareholders, creditors, regulatory agencies and tax authorities.

2.2 The *Official Terminology* also describes the core activities of management accounting.

- 'Participation in the planning process at both strategic and operational levels. This involves the establishment of policies and the formulation of plans and budgets which will subsequently be expressed in financial terms.
- The initiation of and the provision of guidance for management decisions. This involves the generation, analysis, presentation and interpretation of appropriate relevant information.
- Contributing to the monitoring and control performance through the provision of reports on organisational (and organisational segment) performance, including comparisons of actual with planned or budgeted performance, and their analysis and interpretation.'

The information manager

2.3 Management accounting therefore deals principally with the following to assist with management planning, control and decision making.

- **Gathering of data** from both internal and external sources
- **Analysing the resulting information**
- **Processing the resulting information**
- **Interpreting the resulting information**
- **Communicating the resulting information**

The management accountant therefore effectively acts as an information manager.

The gatekeeper

2.4 The management accountant is traditionally the sole or primary supplier of management information but there is little point in the management accountant passing all information onto management. **Only relevant information which is valuable to the recipient should be passed on.** The personnel manager does not need to know that the organisation's principal competitors have increased their prices to £10 per kilogram. Similarly the sales manager does not need to know that the average pay of office staff last year was £15,000. As well as sifting information on this general level, the management accountant can sift more specifically and highlight, for example, areas in which actual activity is not on line with planned activity or potential trouble spots, rather than reporting the results of all areas.

2.5 This **management-by-exception approach** frees management from concern about those areas of the organisation's activities which are performing to plan but makes them aware of those areas which would lead to the firm's objectives not being met.

2.6 The **management accounting system should be designed so that recipients of information obtain the information they require**. If the information required is the average purchase cost of material A during the last quarter of the year, the information produced should not be the average cost per delivery during the first six months of the year.

2.7 Not only does the **management accountant control the type of information** that is supplied, he also controls the **direction of the flow of information**. Information can flow from the management accountant in a number of directions.

- **Upwards** to senior management
- **Downwards** to his subordinates
- **Sideways** to his fellow managers
- **Outwards** to external individuals and organisations

2.8 This **filtering, sifting and directing of information** has led the management accountant to be called the **gatekeeper**. By allowing only appropriate information through to the appropriate person/people, he ensures that time is not wasted, decisions are not taken on the basis of erroneous or unsuitable information and that attention is given to potential trouble spots.

Question 2

What one word best describes the type of information that the management accountant should provide?

Answer

Relevant

Cost accounting

KEY TERM

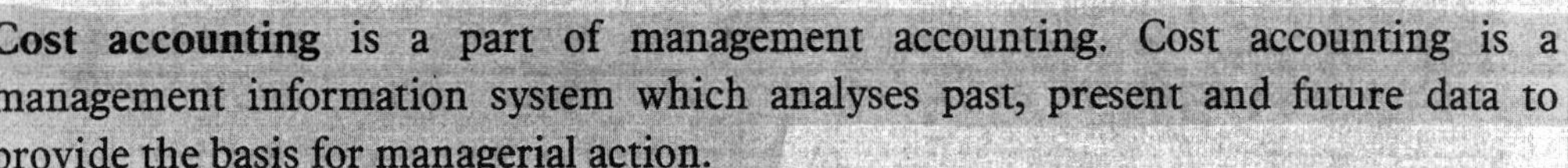

Cost accounting is a part of management accounting. Cost accounting is a management information system which analyses past, present and future data to provide the basis for managerial action.

2.9 In particular, cost accounting **establishes budgets, standard costs** and **actual costs** for operations, processes, departments and products.

These are then used to **analyse variances** between expected and actual results, whether these deal with the cost or profitability of the particular products or services.

The **relationship between cost accounting and management accounting can be summarised as** follows.

Cost accounting provides a bank of data for the management accountant to use.

2.10 Cost accounts **aim to provide the answers to** the following types of questions.

(a) (i) **What has been the cost** of goods produced or services provided?
(ii) **What have revenues** been?

Knowing about costs and revenues that are being/have been incurred and earned **enables management** to do the following.

(i) **Assess the profitability** of a product, a service, a department, or the organisation.

(ii) **Set selling prices** with some regard for the costs of sale.

(iii) Put a **value to stocks of goods** (raw materials, work in progress, finished goods) that are still held in store at the end of a period, thereby aiding the preparation of a balance sheet of the company's assets and liabilities.

(b) **What are the future costs of goods and services** (and operations and so on) likely to be?

Costing is an integral part of budgeting (planning) for the future.

(c) **How do actual costs compare with budgeted costs?** If an organisation plans for its revenues and costs to be a certain amount, but they actually turn out differently, the differences can be measured and reported. Management can use these reports as a guide to whether corrective action (or 'control' action) is needed to sort out a problem revealed by these differences between budgeted and actual results. This system of control is often referred to as budgetary control.

(d) **What information does management need in order to make sensible decisions about profits and costs?**

2.11 **Originally** cost accounting dealt with ways of accumulating historical costs and of charging these costs to units of output, or to departments, in order to establish **stock valuations, profits** and **balance sheets** (item (a) in Paragraph 2.9 above). It has since **been extended** into areas (b), (c) and (d), **planning**, **control** and **decision making**, where it is indistinguishable from management accounting.

3 MANAGEMENT ACCOUNTING, FINANCIAL ACCOUNTING AND FINANCIAL MANAGEMENT

Financial accounting

3.1 Of course, it is not just people *within* an organisation who require information. Those external to the organisation such as banks, shareholders, the Inland Revenue, creditors and government agencies all desire information too.

3.2 **Management accountants provide internally-used information. The financial accounting function is the provider of information to parties external to an organisation.** The management accountant is not concerned with the calculation of earnings per share. On the other hand, the financial accountant is not concerned with the variances between budgeted and actual expenditure on labour.

3.3 **Management information provides a common source from which are prepared financial accounts and management accounts.** The **differences** between the two types of accounts **arise in the manner in which the common source of data is analysed.**

Financial accounts	Management accounts
Financial accounts **detail the performance of an organisation over a defined period and the state of affairs at the end of that period.**	Management accounts are **used to aid management record, plan** and **control activities and to help the decision-making process.**
Limited companies must, **by law,** prepare financial accounts.	There is **no legal requirement** to prepare management accounts.
The **format** of published financial accounts is **determined by law,** by SSAPs and by FRSs. In principle the accounts of different organisations can therefore be easily compared.	The **format** of management accounts is entirely at management discretion: **no strict rules** govern the way they are prepared or presented. Each organisation can devise its own management accounting system and format of reports.
Financial accounts **concentrate on the business as a whole,** aggregating revenues and costs from different operations, and are an end in themselves.	Management accounts can **focus on specific areas** of an organisation's activities. Information may aid a decision rather than be an end product of a decision.
Most financial accounting information is of a **monetary** nature.	Management accounts incorporate **non-monetary** measures.
Financial accounts present an essentially **historic** picture of **past** operations.	Management accounts are both a **historical** record and a **future** planning tool.

Financial management

3.4 Financial management is **the management of finance**. Finance (that is, the ability to purchase things) is used by an organisation just as, for example, labour and material are used by an organisation. Finance therefore needs management in a similar way to labour and material. The management accounting function provides information to ensure the effective management of labour and material and, in the same way, the financial management function provides information on, for example, the costs and profitability of projects and projected cash flows to aid the effective management of finance.

4 SOME BASIC COST ACCOUNTING CONCEPTS

4.1 We end this chapter with a brief reminder of the fundamentals of cost accounting which were introduced in Paper 3 *Management Information* and which provide the foundation for the management accounting concepts and techniques covered in Paper 8.

Knowledge brought forward from Paper 3

Cost accounting

- A **direct cost** is a cost that can be traced in full to the product, service or department that is being costed. The total of direct costs (direct material, direct labour and direct expenses) is known as **prime cost**. An **indirect cost/overhead** is a cost that is incurred in the course of making a product, providing a service or running a department but which cannot be traced directly and in full to the product, service or department. Indirect costs can be sub-divided into indirect material costs, indirect labour costs and indirect expenses. Overheads are often classified as production, administration, distribution or selling overhead.
- **Classification by function** involves dividing costs into production, administration, selling and distribution, research and development and financing costs. A commonly found build up of costs using such a system of classification is as follows.

Direct production costs: Direct material	X	
Direct labour	X	
Direct expenses	X	
Prime cost		X
Production overheads		X
Full factory cost		X
Administration/selling and distribution costs		X
Full cost of sales		X

- A **fixed cost** is a cost which is incurred for a particular period of time and which, within certain activity levels, is unaffected by changes in the level of activity. A variable cost, on the other hand, tends to vary with the level of output.
- **Product costs** are costs identified with goods produced or purchased for resale. Such costs are initially identified as part of the value of stock. These become expenses (in the form of cost of goods sold) only when the stock is sold. In contrast, period costs are costs that are deducted as expenses during the current period without ever being included in the value of stock held.
- **Avoidable costs** are specific costs of, say, an activity or business, which would be avoided if the activity or business did not exist. Costs which would be incurred whether or not an activity or business existed are known as unavoidable costs.
- A **normal cost** is an expected cost whereas an abnormal cost is not expected either in terms of its occurrence or in terms of its value.
- A **controllable cost** is a cost which can be influenced by management decisions and actions. An **uncontrollable cost** cannot be affected by management within a given time span.
- A **relevant cost** is a future cash flow which will be changed as the result of a decision. **Non-relevant costs** are unaffected by the outcome of a decision.
- A **notional cost** is a hypothetical cost charged in the cost accounts in order to give a more realistic picture of the true cost of, for example, an activity. **Real costs** cause actual cash flows.
- In general, for cost accounting purposes, an organisation's departments are termed **cost centres** and the product produced by the organisation is termed the **cost unit**.

Question 3

Wilton, MacDonald, Pearce & Co, a medium-sized firm of architects, are about to absorb Butcher, Fowler & Partners, a similar sized firm. They have engaged you as management accountant. Part of your duties will be to review the cost and management accounting function of the combined practice and to recruit an assistant. You have an appointment tomorrow morning with the senior partner to discuss these issues.

Required

Jot down notes to use in tomorrow's meeting which cover the following points.

(a) The functions of cost and management accounting, with particular reference to Wilton, MacDonald, Pearce & Co

(b) The personal attributes you would expect the assistant management accountant to possess

Answer

(a) The functions of cost and management accounting

Cost and management accounting involve providing and interpreting internal accounting information for managers to use for the following purposes.

(i) Planning the organisation's activities in the short, medium and long term.

For example, the management accounting system should provide information which will allow management to plan the future activities of the new, larger business.

(ii) Controlling the activities of the organisation

Management will have to learn to control a larger business. They will therefore need control reports so that they can compare actual results against plans or budgets. Action can then be taken to correct any differences between actual and plan (variances) and to help the organisation to continue in the direction set out by the plans.

(iii) Making decisions

For example, information will be needed for pricing architectural contracts for tendering purposes.

(iv) Performance appraisal, both financial and non-financial

For example, information on the percentage of jobs completed on time, percentage of successful tenders and so on should be provided.

(b) The personal attributes of the assistant management accountant

(i) Be training for or already possess a professional qualification in management accountancy both because he/she will have to deal with professionals and for technical reasons.

(ii) Be highly numerate.

(iii) Have excellent knowledge of the cost and management accounting information requirements of a large architects' business.

(iv) Be able to critically appraise the existing systems and information to ensure their relevance to the future.

(v) Have excellent communication skills. This is particularly important because of the uncertainty caused by the major changes taking place. He or she must be able to explain and interpret management accounting information for those architects and other employees who have little or no financial background.

(vi) Be flexible and self-motivating. For example he/she must be willing to leave their office desk and visit sites when necessary.

(vii) Possess management perspective as well as being technically competent.

Of course you may have thought of completely different points to those noted above. The purpose of this question was to get you thinking about management accounting.

Exam focus point

In the first paper that he set (12/97), the examiner advised candidates to take note of the marks for each question and for each part of it and to allocate time accordingly. He also stressed the importance of identifying what is required in each part of the question (such as calculate, explain, discuss, comment, analyse and so on) and of following these instructions carefully.

Chapter roundup

- **Management accounting** deals principally with the gathering of data from both internal and external sources and analysing, processing, interpreting and communicating the resulting information within the organisation to aid the management processes of planning, controlling, organising and motivating.
- The management accounting function **provides internally-used information**. The financial accounting function is the provider of information to parties **external** to an organisation.
- **Cost accounting** provides a bank of data for the management accountant to use.

Quick quiz

1. How is control exercised by management? (see para 1.10)
2. Why is the management accountant known as the gatekeeper? (2.3 - 2.7)
3. What is cost accounting? (key terms)
4. List six differences between financial accounts and management accounts. (3.3)
5. What is financial management? (3.4)

Question to try	Level	Marks	Time
1	Examination	5	9 mins

Chapter 2

METHODS OF COST ACCUMULATION

Chapter topic list		Syllabus reference
1	The problem of overheads	1(a)(i)
2	Absorption costing	1(a)(i), 2(c)(i)
3	Marginal costing	1(a)(i), 2(c)(i)
4	The relative merits of absorption costing and marginal costing	1(a)(i), 2(c)(i)
5	Opportunity costing	1(a)(i)
6	Activity based costing	1(a)(ii), 2(c)(ii)
7	Merits and criticisms of ABC	1(a)(ii), 2(c)(ii)

Introduction

You should now have an idea about what a management accountant is and what a management accountant does. Many of the tasks to which the management accountant must apply himself require, as you will see in later chapters, the ascertainment of the cost of a product, job or service (whatever the organisation happens to be involved in). Such costs have to be built up using a process known as **cost accumulation.**

In your studies for Paper 3 you will have learnt how to accumulate the various cost elements which make up total cost. If you have forgotten, the following diagram of an **absorption costing** cost accumulation system should jog your memory.

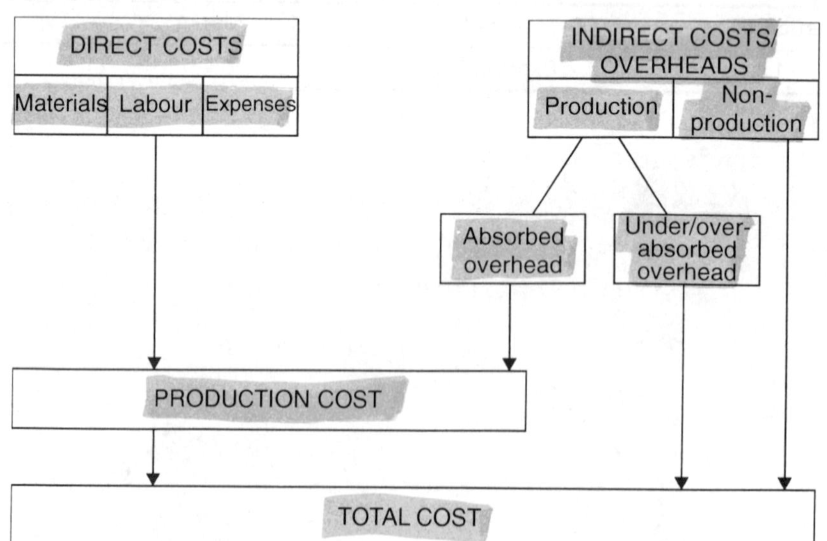

Remember that under a **marginal costing** system the production overhead absorbed would be variable production overhead only.

The **collection and analysis of direct costs** was covered in detail for Paper 3 and will be revisited briefly in Chapters 3 and 4 of this Study Text. As far as **overheads** are concerned, in this chapter we will be both building on your Paper 3 knowledge and seeing how the techniques which you have already learnt can be applied in more complex situations. This is a long chapter but much of what we cover will be familiar to you so working through it won't be too arduous.

1 THE PROBLEM OF OVERHEADS

1.1 If a company manufactures a product, the cost of the product will include the following.

- The cost of the raw materials and components used in it
- The cost of the labour effort required to make it

These are **direct costs** of the product. The company would, however, incur many other costs in making the product, which are not directly attributable to a single product, but which are incurred generally in the process of manufacturing a large number of product units. These are **indirect costs** or **overheads**. Such costs include the following.

- Factory rent and rates
- Machine depreciation
- Supervision costs
- The costs of control checks and inspections
- Design costs
- Heating and lighting

KEY TERMS

A **direct cost** is a cost that can be traced in full to the product, service or department that is being costed.

An **indirect cost** or **overhead** is a cost that is incurred in the course of making a product, providing a service or running a department, but which cannot be traced directly and in full to the product, service or department.

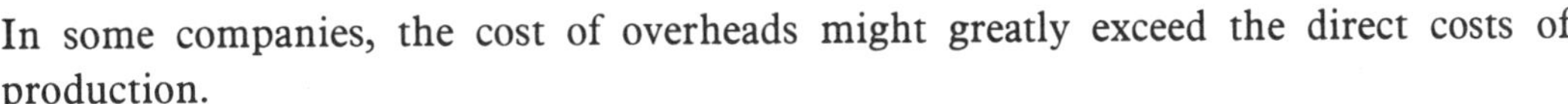

In some companies, the cost of overheads might greatly exceed the direct costs of production.

1.2 It might seem unreasonable to ignore indirect costs entirely when accumulating the costs of making a product, and yet there **cannot be a completely satisfactory way of sharing out indirect costs** between the many different items of production which benefit from them. We therefore need to **decide whether**, when accumulating the costs of an item, the **overhead costs should be added to the direct costs of production to arrive at** a **total product cost**.

- Traditionally, the view has been taken in cost accounting that a fair share of overheads should be added to the cost of units produced. This fair share will **include a portion of all production overhead expenditure** and possibly administration and marketing overheads too. This is the view embodied in the principles of **absorption costing.**
- Advocates of **marginal costing** take the view that it is sufficient to identify the variable costs of making and selling a product or service. **Fixed costs should be dealt with separately** and treated as a lump sum cost of the accounting period rather than shared out somehow or other between units produced and sold. Some overhead costs are, however, variable costs which increase as the total level of activity rises. Strictly speaking, therefore, the marginal cost of production and sales should include an amount for variable overheads.

2 ABSORPTION COSTING 12/94, 6/95, 6/96, 12/96, 6/97, 12/97

KEY TERM

Absorption costing is a method of product costing which aims to include in the total cost of a product (unit, job, process and so on) an appropriate share of an organisation's total overhead. An appropriate share is generally taken to mean an amount which reflects the amount of time and effort that has gone into producing a unit or completing a job.

Exam focus point

Absorption costing has been heavily examined in the past. In some exams, it has been examined as part of a longer question on another topic, in others there have been whole questions testing the subject in more depth. In 6/96 there were 20 marks to be gained by those students having a thorough understanding of absorption costing.

2.1 You should have covered absorption costing in your earlier studies. We will therefore summarise the simpler points of the topic but will go into some detail on the more complex areas to refresh your memory.

Knowledge brought forward from Paper 3

Absorption costing

- Product costs are built up using absorption costing by a process of **allocation**, **apportionment** and **overhead absorption**.
- **Allocation** is the process by which whole cost items are charged directly to a cost unit or cost centre. **Direct costs** are allocated directly to cost units. **Overheads** clearly identifiable with cost centres are allocated to those cost centres but costs which cannot be identified with one particular cost centre are allocated to general overhead cost centres. The cost of a warehouse security guard would therefore be charged to the warehouse cost centre but heating and lighting costs would be charged to a general overhead cost centre.
- The **first stage of overhead apportionment** is the identification of all overheads as production, service, administration or selling and distribution overheads. Overheads within **general overhead cost centres** therefore have to be shared out (or apportioned) between the other cost centres using a fair basis of apportionment (such as volume of space/floor area occupied by each cost centre for heating and lighting costs).
- The **second stage of overhead apportionment** is to apportion the costs of **service cost centres** (both directly allocated and apportioned costs) to production cost centres. One method by which service cost centre costs can be apportioned is to share out the costs of each service cost centre to production cost centres only.
- Costs allocated and apportioned to administrative and selling and distribution cost centres are not usually included as part of a product cost (and hence are not included in the value of stock) and are deducted from the full cost of production to arrive at the cost of sales.
- The final stage in absorption costing is the **absorption** into product costs (using overhead absorption rates) of the overheads which have been allocated and apportioned to the production cost centres.

Question 1

Briefly discuss the type of factors which could affect the choice of the bases an organisation can use to apportion service department costs.

Answer

(a) The type of service being provided
(b) The amount of overhead expenditure involved
(c) The number of departments benefiting from the service
(d) The ability to be able to produce realistic estimates of the usage of the service
(e) The resulting costs and benefits

Question 2

A company is preparing its production overhead budgets and determining the apportionment of those overheads to products. Cost centre expenses and related information have been budgeted as follows.

	Total	*Machine shop A*	*Machine shop B*	*Assembly*	*Canteen*	*Mainten-ance*
	£	£	£	£	£	£
Indirect wages	78,560	8,586	9,190	15,674	29,650	15,460
Consumable materials (incl. maintenance)	16,900	6,400	8,700	1,200	600	-
Rent and rates	16,700					
Buildings insurance	2,400					
Power	8,600					
Heat and light	3,400					
Depreciation of machinery	40,200					
Value of machinery	402,000	201,000	179,000	22,000	-	-
	Total	*Machine shop A*	*Machine shop B*	*Assembly*	*Canteen*	*Mainten-ance*
	£	£	£	£	£	£
Other information:						
Power usage - technical estimates (%)	100	55	40	3	-	2
Direct labour (hours)	35,000	8,000	6,200	20,800	-	-
Machine usage (hours)	25,200	7,200	18,000	-	-	-
Area (sq ft)	45,000	10,000	12,000	15,000	6,000	2,000

Required

Using the direct apportionment to production departments method and bases of apportionment which you consider most appropriate from the information provided, calculate overhead totals for the three production departments.

Answer

	Total	A	B	Assembly	Canteen	Maintenance	Basis of apportionment
	£	£	£	£	£	£	
Indirect wages	78,560	8,586	9,190	15,674	29,650	15,460	Actual
Consumable materials	16,900	6,400	8,700	1,200	600	-	Actual
Rent and rates	16,700	3,711	4,453	5,567	2,227	742	Area
Insurance	2,400	533	640	800	320	107	Area
Power	8,600	4,730	3,440	258	-	172	Usage
Heat and light	3,400	756	907	1,133	453	151	Area
Depreciation	40,200	20,100	17,900	2,200	-	-	Val of mach
	166,760	44,816	45,230	26,832	33,250	16,632	
Reallocate	-	7,600	5,890	19,760	(33,250)	-	Direct labour
Reallocate	-	4,752	11,880	-	-	(16,632)	Mach usage
Totals	166,760	57,168	63,000	46,592	-	-	

Second stage of overhead apportionment

2.2 In Question 2 above the costs of the canteen were allocated only to production departments, and not to maintenance, even though employees working in maintenance are as likely to use the canteen as anyone else and it is quite possible for the ovens and other machines in the kitchen to require maintenance.

2.3 It could therefore be argued that a **fair sharing** of service department costs is not possible unless consideration is given to the work done by each service department for other service departments, that is unless any **reciprocal services are taken into account.**

2.4 For example, suppose a company called Hover and Hover Ltd has two production and two service departments (stores and maintenance). The following information about activity in the recent costing period is available.

	Production departments *A*	*B*	*Stores department*	*Maintenance department*
Overhead costs	£10,030	£8,970	£10,000	£8,000
Number of material requisitions	300	500	-	200
Maintenance hours needed	8,000	1,000	1,000	

If service department overheads were apportioned directly to production departments, the apportionment would be as follows.

Service department	*Basis of apportionment*	*Total cost*		*A*		*B*
		£		£		£
Stores	Material requisitions	10,000	(3/8)	3,750	(5/8)	6,250
Maintenance	Maintenance hours	8,000	(8/9)	7,111	(1/9)	889
		18,000		10,861		7,139
Overheads of departments A and B		19,000		10,030		8,970
		37,000		20,891		16,109

If, however, recognition is made of the fact that the stores and maintenance department do work for each other, and the basis of apportionment remains the same, we ought to apportion service department costs as follows.

	Dept A	*Dept B*	*Stores*	*Maint-enance*
Stores (100%)	30%	50%	-	20%
Maintenance (100%)	80%	10%	10%	-

2.5 This may be done using one of the following methods.

(a) **The repeated distribution method**
(b) **The simultaneous equation (algebraic) method**
(c) **The step-wise (elimination) method**

Repeated distribution method

2.6

	Production Dept A	*Production Dept B*	*Stores*	*Mainten-ance*
	£	£	£	£
Overhead costs	10,030	8,970	10,000	8,000
Apportion stores costs * (30%/50%/20%)	3,000	5,000	(10,000)	2,000
			0	10,000
Apportion maintenance costs (80%/10%/10%)	8,000	1,000	1,000	(10,000)
			1,000	0
Repeat: Apportion stores	300	500	(1,000)	200
Repeat: Apportion maintenance	160	20	20	(200)
Repeat: Apportion stores	6	10	(20)	4
Repeat: Apportion maintenance **	4	-	-	(4)
	21,500	15,500	0	0

* The first apportionment could have been the costs of maintenance, rather than stores; there is no difference to the final results.

** When the repeated distributions bring service department costs down to small numbers (here £4) the final apportionment to production departments is an approximate rounding.

Simultaneous equation (algebraic) method

2.7 (a) Let S be the total stores department overhead for apportionment, after it has been apportioned overhead from Maintenance.

(b) Let M be the total of maintenance department overhead after it has been apportioned overhead from Stores.

We can set up our equations as follows.

$$S = 0.1M + £10{,}000 \quad (1)$$
$$M = 0.2S + £8{,}000 \quad (2)$$

Multiplying (2) by 5 gives us

$$5M = S + £40{,}000 \quad (3)$$, which can be rearranged so that
$$S = 5M - £40{,}000 \quad (4)$$

Subtracting (1) from (4)

$$S = 5M - £40{,}000 \quad (4)$$
$$S = 0.1M + £10{,}000 \quad (1)$$
$$0 = 4.9M - £50{,}000$$
$$M = \frac{£50{,}000}{4.9} = £10{,}204$$

Substituting in (1)

$$S = 0.1 \times (£10{,}204) + £10{,}000$$
$$S = £11{,}020$$

These overheads can be apportioned as follows, using the percentages in Paragraph 4.11.

	Production dept A	*Production dept B*	*Stores*	*Maintenance*
	£	£	£	£
Overhead costs	10,030	8,970	10,000	8,000
Apportion stores total	3,306	5,510	(11,020)	2,204
Apportion maintenance total	8,164	1,020	1,020	(10,204)
	21,500	15,500	-	-

This is the same result as the one we got using repeated distribution.

Step-wise (elimination) method

2.8 In examination questions you will be told which service department overheads to apportion first. We will start with stores.

	Production depts		*Service depts*	
	A	*B*	*Stores*	*Maintenance*
	£	£	£	£
Overhead costs	10,030	8,970	10,000	8,000
Apportion stores (30%/50%/20%)	3,000	5,000	(10,000)	2,000
	13,030	13,970	-	10,000
Apportion maintenance (8/9, 1/9)	8,889	1,111		(10,000)
	21,915	15,081		-

As you can see, the service department **overheads apportioned first** (stores) **are apportioned across all the other departments,** both production and service. The **other service department's overheads** (maintenance) (which now include an apportionment of those of the stores department) are **apportioned to the production departments only in the ratio of use by the production departments.** In our example the ratio is 80% to 10% or 8:1 or 8/9:1/9 (the denominator of 9 coming from 8 + 1). If the usage percentages had been 30% and 40% (with stores usage at 30%), the ratio would have been 3:4 or 3/7:4/7.

2.9 **Apportioning service department overheads is only useful if the resulting product costs reflect accurately the amounts expended by service departments.** If, however, the apportionment is arbitrary or ill-considered, the absorption of service department costs into product costs may be misleading.

Question 3

You are the cost accountant of an industrial concern and have been given the following budgeted information regarding the four cost centres within your organisation.

	Dept 1	*Dept 2*	*Maintenance dept*	*Canteen*	*Total*
	£	£	£	£	£
Indirect labour	60,000	70,000	25,000	15,000	170,000
Consumables	12,000	16,000	3,000	10,000	41,000
Heating and lighting					12,000
Rent and rates					18,000
Depreciation					30,000
Supervision					24,000
Power					20,000
					315,000

You are given the following information.

	Dept 1	Dept 2	Maintenance dept	Canteen	Total
Floor space in sq. metres	10,000	12,000	5,000	3,000	30,000
Book value of machinery (£)	150,000	120,000	20,000	10,000	300,000
Number of employees	40	30	10		80
Kilowatt hours	4,500	4,000	1,000	500	10,000

You are also told the following.

(a) The canteen staff are outside contractors.

(b) Departments 1 and 2 are production cost centres and the maintenance department and canteen are service cost centres.

Required

(a) Provide an overhead cost statement showing the allocation of overheads and the apportionment of general overheads to the four cost centres, clearly showing the basis of apportionment.

(b) Using the fact that the maintenance department provides 4,000 service hours to department 1, 3,000 service hours to department 2 and 1,000 hours for the canteen, apportion the overheads of the two service departments using the algebraic method.

(c) List the factors which should be considered when choosing which bases of apportionment should be used when apportioning the overheads of the maintenance department and the canteen.

Answer

(a)

	Basis of apportionment	Dept 1	Dept 2	Maintenance dept	Canteen	Total
		£	£	£	£	£
Indirect labour	-	60,000	70,000	25,000	15,000	170,000
Consumables	-	12,000	16,000	3,000	10,000	41,000
Heat and light	Space	4,000	4,800	2,000	1,200	12,000
Rent and rates	Space	6,000	7,200	3,000	1,800	18,000
Depreciation	Book value	15,000	12,000	2,000	1,000	30,000
Supervision	Employees	12,000	9,000	3,000	-	24,000
Power	Kilowatt hrs	9,000	8,000	2,000	1,000	20,000
		118,000	127,000	40,000	30,000	315,000

(b) Let C = canteen overhead including apportioned maintenance overhead.

Let M = maintenance overhead including apportioned canteen overhead.

$C = 30,000 + {}^1/_8\,M$ (1)

$M = 40,000 + {}^1/_8\,C$ (2)

$8(M - 40,000) = C$ (3) (from (2))

$8(M - 40,000) = 30,000 + {}^1/_8\,M$ (4) (sub (1) into (3))

$8M - 320,000 = 30,000 + {}^1/_8\,M$

$7\,{}^7/_8\,M = 350,000$

M = £44,444

$C = 30,000 + {}^1/_8\,(44,444)$

C = £35,556

	Dept 1	Dept 2	Maintenance	Canteen
	£	£	£	£
Overheads	118,000	127,000	40,000	30,000
Apportion maintenance	22,222	16,666	(44,444)	5,556
Apportion canteen	17,778	13,334	4,444	(35,556)
Total	158,000	157,000	-	-

(c) (i) Services which the maintenance department and the canteen provide to each other, and to departments 1 and 2.

(ii) Selecting an appropriate basis of apportionment eg space, book value, employees, kilowatt hours.

(iii) The ability to produce accurate estimates about the usage of the maintenance department and the canteen by each other and by departments 1 and 2.

(iv) The cost of implementing the overhead apportionment as compared with the benefit to be had.

(v) The value of the overhead expenditure incurred by the service and production departments, and how many departments used the service departments.

Overhead absorption

2.10 Having allocated and/or apportioned all **overheads**, the next stage in absorption costing is to **add them to, or absorb them into**, the cost of production or sales.

Use of a predetermined absorption rate

Knowledge brought forward from Paper 3

Step 1. The overhead likely to be incurred during the coming year is estimated.

Step 2. The total hours, units or direct costs on which the overhead absorption rates are based (activity levels) are estimated.

Step 3. The estimated overhead is divided by the budgeted activity level to arrive at an absorption rate.

Choosing the appropriate absorption base

Question 4

List as many possible bases of absorption (or 'overhead recovery rates') which you can think of.

Answer

(a) A percentage of direct materials cost
(b) A percentage of direct labour cost
(c) A percentage of prime cost
(d) A rate per machine hour
(e) A rate per direct labour hour
(f) A rate per unit
(g) A percentage of factory cost (for administration overhead)
(h) A percentage of sales or factory cost (for selling and distribution overhead)

2.11 The choice of an absorption basis is a **matter of judgement and common sense**. There are no strict rules or formulae involved. What is required, however, is an absorption basis which realistically reflects the characteristics of a given cost centre and which avoids undue anomalies.

2.12 In theory, each basis of absorption would be possible, but the company should choose a basis for its own costs which seems to be 'fairest'. This **choice will be significant in determining the cost of individual products, but the total cost of production overheads is the budgeted overhead expenditure, no matter what basis of absorption is selected**. It is the relative share of overhead costs borne by individual products and jobs which is affected by the choice of overhead absorption basis.

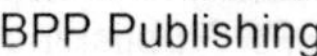

Question 5

Using the information in and the results of Question 2, determine budgeted overhead absorption rates for each of the production departments using bases of absorption which you consider most appropriate from the information provided.

Answer

Absorption rates

Machine shop A: $\frac{£57,168}{7,200}$ = £7.94 per machine hour

Machine shop B: $\frac{£63,000}{18,000}$ = £3.50 per machine hour

Assembly: $\frac{£46,592}{20,800}$ = £2.24 per direct labour hour

Over and under absorption of overheads

2.13 The rate of overhead absorption is based on estimates (of both numerator and denominator) and it is quite likely that either one or both of the estimates will not agree with what actually occurs. Actual overheads incurred will probably be either greater than or less than overheads absorbed into the cost of production.

- **Over absorption** means that the **overheads charged to the cost of sales are greater than the overheads actually incurred.**
- **Under absorption** means that **insufficient overheads have been included in the cost of sales.**

It is almost inevitable that at the end of the accounting year there will have been an over absorption or under absorption of the overhead actually incurred.

2.14 Suppose that the budgeted overhead in a production department is £80,000 and the budgeted activity is 40,000 direct labour hours, the overhead recovery rate (using a direct labour hour basis) would be £2 per direct labour hour.

Actual overheads in the period are, say £84,000 and 45,000 direct labour hours are worked.

	£
Overhead incurred (actual)	84,000
Overhead absorbed (45,000 × £2)	90,000
Over-absorption of overhead	6,000

2.15 In this example, the cost of produced units or jobs has been charged with £6,000 more than was actually spent and so the cost of production that is recorded will be too high. An adjustment to reconcile the overheads charged to the actual overhead is necessary and the over-absorbed overhead will be written as an adjustment to the profit and loss account at the end of the accounting period.

Question 6

The total production overhead expenditure of the company in Questions 2 and 5 was £176,533 and its actual activity was as follows.

	Machine shop A	*Machine shop B*	*Assembly*
Direct labour hours	8,200	6,500	21,900
Machine usage hours	7,300	18,700	-

Required

Using the information in and results of Questions 2 and 5, calculate the under- or over-absorption of overheads.

Answer

		£	£
Actual expenditure			176,533
Overhead absorbed			
Machine shop A	7,300 hrs × £7.94	57,962	
Machine shop B	18,700 hrs × £3.50	65,450	
Assembly	21,900 hrs × £2.24	49,056	
			172,468
Under-absorbed overhead			4,065

The reasons for under- /over-absorbed overhead

2.16 The overhead absorption rate is predetermined from budget estimates of overhead cost and the expected volume of activity. Under or over recovery of overhead will occur in the following circumstances.

- Actual overhead costs are different from budgeted overheads
- The actual activity level is different from the budgeted activity level
- Both actual overhead costs and actual activity level are different from the budgeted costs and level.

Question 7

Elsewhere Ltd has a budgeted production overhead of £180,000 and a budgeted activity of 45,000 machine hours.

Required

Calculate the under-/over-absorbed overhead, and note the reasons for the under-/over-absorption in the following circumstances.

(a) Actual overheads cost £170,000 and 45,000 machine hours were worked.
(b) Actual overheads cost £180,000 and 40,000 machine hours were worked.
(c) Actual overheads cost £170,000 and 40,000 machine hours were worked.

Answer

The overhead recovery rate is £180,000/45,000 = £4 per machine hour.

		£
(a)	Actual overhead	170,000
	Absorbed overhead (45,000 × £4)	180,000
	Over-absorbed overhead	10,000

The reason for the over-absorption is that although the actual and budgeted machine hours are the same, actual overheads cost less than expected. There is therefore an expenditure variance.

		£
(b)	Actual overhead	180,000
	Absorbed overhead (40,000 × £4)	160,000
	Under-absorbed overhead	20,000

The reason for the under-absorption is that although budgeted and actual overhead costs were the same, fewer machine hours were worked than expected. There is therefore an activity variance.

		£
(c)	Actual overhead	170,000
	Absorbed overhead (40,000 × £4)	160,000
	Under-absorbed overhead	10,000

The reason for the under-absorption is a combination of the reasons in (a) and (b) and there are therefore expenditure and activity variances.

Overhead absorption rates and cost control

Exam focus point

Four marks were available in the 12/97 exam for demonstrating understanding of product costs based on maximum capacity.

2.17 Absorption costing has received bad press in recent years but Inman (*ACCA Students' Newsletter*, December 1994) argues that the use of overhead absorption rates makes a valuable contribution to the control process. He claims that the **amount under/over absorbed indicates whether spending is in line with the level of activity**. An under absorption may indicate that activity is below a viable level given the existing cost structure or that costs are out of control.

2.18 Moreover, it is claimed that **serious under absorption might direct management to go out and get extra orders** so that production levels increase and the under absorption disappears. And the attention-directing and action-motivating impact of under/over absorption could be further increased if the overhead absorption rate were to be based on maximum capacity levels rather than normal capacity terms. Chalos (*Managing Cost in Today's Manufacturing Environment*, 1992) is also critical of the use of normal levels of activity in calculating the absorption rate. Management should ask themselves why maximum capacity is *not* normal capacity.

2.19 On the other hand, if **product full costs are based on maximum capacity** rather than annual budget volume, **costs are not representative of the average actual product cost achieved during the year**, unless current volumes are the same as maximum capacity level.

3 MARGINAL COSTING   12/94, 12/95, 6/96, 12/96, 6/97

Exam focus point

Marginal costing was an important examination topic for Paper 3. It is also examined heavily in the Managerial Finance exam. For Paper 8, however, you need to be able to apply the basic principles to more complex situations than those encountered in Paper 3.

KEY TERMS

Marginal cost is the cost of one unit of a product/service which could be avoided if that unit were not produced/provided.

Contribution is the difference between sales revenue and variable (marginal) cost of sales.

Marginal costing is an alternative method of costing to absorption costing. In marginal costing, *only* variable costs (marginal costs) are charged as a cost of sales. Fixed costs are treated as period costs and are charged in full against the profit of the period in which they are incurred.

Knowledge brought forward from Paper 3

Marginal costing

- In **marginal costing**, closing **stocks are valued at marginal (variable) production cost** whereas, in **absorption costing**, stocks are **valued at their full production cost** which includes absorbed fixed production overhead.
- If the opening and closing stock levels differ, the **profit reported** for the accounting period **under the two methods** of cost accumulation **will be different** because the two systems value stock differently.
- **In the long run, total profit for a company will be the same** whether marginal costing or absorption costing is used because, in the long run, total costs will be the same by either method of accounting. Different accounting conventions merely affect the profit of individual accounting periods.

Question 8

A company makes and sells a single product. At the beginning of period 1, there are no opening stocks of the product, for which the variable production cost is £4 and the sales price £6 per unit. Fixed costs are £2,000 per period, of which £1,500 are fixed production costs. Normal output is 1,500 units per period.

	Period 1	*Period 2*
	Units	Units
Sales	1,200	1,700
Production	1,500	1,400

Required

Prepare profit statements for each period and for the two periods in total using both absorption costing and marginal costing.

Answer

It is important to notice that although production and sales volumes in each period are different (therefore the profit for each period by absorption costing will be different from the profit by marginal costing), over the full period, total production equals sales volume. The total cost of sales is the same and therefore the total profit is the same by either method of accounting. Differences in profit in any one period are merely timing differences which cancel out over a longer period of time.

(a) *Absorption costing.* The absorption rate for fixed production overhead is £1,500/1,500 units = £1 per unit. The fully absorbed cost per unit = £(4+1) = £5.

		Period 1		Period 2		Total	
		£	£	£	£	£	£
Sales			7,200		10,200		17,400
Production costs							
Variable		6,000		5,600		11,600	
Fixed		1,500		1,400		2,900	
		7,500		7,000		14,500	
Add opening stock b/f	(300×£5)	–		1,500		1,500	
		7,500		8,500		16,000	
Less closing stock c/f	(300×£5)	1,500		-		1,500	
Production cost of sales		6,000		8,500		14,500	
Under-absorbed o/hd		-		100		100	
Total costs			6,000		8,600		14,600
Gross profit			1,200		1,600		2,800
Other costs			(500)		(500)		(1,000)
Net profit			700		1,100		1,800

(b) *Marginal costing*

The marginal cost per unit = £4.

		Period 1		Period 2		Total	
		£	£	£	£	£	£
Sales			7,200		10,200		17,400
Variable production cost		6,000		5,600		11,600	
Add opening stock b/f	(300×£4)	-		1,200		1,200	
		6,000		6,800		12,800	
Less closing stock c/f	(300×£4)	1,200		-		1,200	
Variable production cost of sales			4,800		6,800		11,600
Contribution b/f			2,400		3,400		5,800
Contribution c/f			2,400		3,400		5,800
Fixed costs			2,000		2,000		4,000
Profit			400		1,400		1,800

Question 9

RH Ltd makes and sells one product, the standard production cost of which is as follows for one unit.

		£
Direct labour	3 hours at £6 per hour	18
Direct materials	4 kilograms at £7 per kg	28
Production overhead	Variable	3
	Fixed	20
Standard production cost		69

Normal output is 16,000 units per annum and this figure is used for the fixed production overhead calculation.

Costs relating to selling, distribution and administration are as follows.

Variable	20 per cent of sales value
Fixed	£180,000 per annum

The only variance is a fixed production overhead volume variance. There are no units in finished goods stock at 1 October 19X2. The fixed overhead expenditure is spread evenly throughout the year. The selling price per unit is £140.

For the two six-monthly periods detailed below, the number of units to be produced and sold are budgeted as follows.

	Six months ending 31 March 19X3	*Six months ending 30 September 19X3*
Production	8,500	7,000
Sales	7,000	8,000

Required

Prepare statements for management showing sales, costs and profits for each of the six-monthly periods, using the following methods of costing.

(a) Marginal costing
(b) Absorption costing

Answer

(a) *Profit statements for the year ending 30 September 19X3*
Marginal costing basis

	Six months ending 31 March 19X3		*Six months ending 30 September 19X3*	
	£'000	£'000	£'000	£'000
Sales at £140 per unit		980		1,120
Opening stock	-		73.5	
Standard variable production cost (at £49 per unit)	416.5		343.0	
	416.5		416.5	
Closing stock (W1)	73.5		24.5	
		343		392
		637		728
Variable selling, distribution and administration costs		196		224
Contribution		441		504
Fixed costs: production (W2)	160		160	
selling and so on	90		90	
		250		250
Net profit		191		254

(b) *Profit statements for the year ending 30 September 19X3*
Absorption costing basis

	Six months ending 31 March 19X3		*Six months ending 30 September 19X3*	
	£'000	£'000	£'000	£'000
Sales at £140 per unit		980		1,120
Opening stock	-		103.5	
Standard cost of production (at £69 per unit)	586.5		483.0	
	586.5		586.5	
Closing stock (W1)	103.5		34.5	
	483.0		552.0	
(Over-)/under-absorbed overhead	(10.0)		20.0	
		473		572
Gross profit		507		548
Selling, distribution and administration costs				
Variable	196		224	
Fixed	90		90	
		286		314
Net profit		221		234

Workings

1

	Six months ending 31 March 19X3	*Six months ending 30 September 19X3*
	Units	Units
Opening stock	-	1,500
Production	8,500	7,000
	8,500	8,500
Sales	7,000	8,000
Closing stock	1,500	500

	Six months ending 31 March 19X3	Six months ending 30 September 19X3
Marginal cost valuation (× £49)	£73,500	£24,500
Absorption cost valuation (× £69)	£103,500	£34,500

2 Budgeted fixed production overhead = 16,000 units × £20
= £320,000 per annum
= £160,000 per six months

3

	Six months ending 31 March 19X3	Six months ending 30 September 19X3
Normal output (16,000 ÷ 2)	8,000 units	8,000 units
Budgeted output	8,500 units	7,000 units
Difference	500 units	1,000 units
× standard fixed production overhead per unit	× £20	× £20
(Over-)/under-absorbed overhead	(£10,000)	£20,000

Reconciling the profit figures given by the two methods

3.1 The **difference in profits** reported under the two costing systems is due to the **different stock valuation methods** used.

3.2 **If stock levels increase** between the beginning and end of a period, **absorption costing will report the higher profit** because some of the fixed production overhead incurred during the period will be carried forward in closing stock (which reduces cost of sales) to be set against sales revenue in the following period instead of being written off in full against profit in the period concerned.

3.3 However, **if stock levels decrease, absorption costing will report the lower profit** because as well as the fixed overhead incurred, fixed production overhead which had been carried forward in opening stock is released and is also included in cost of sales.

3.4 EXAMPLE: RECONCILING PROFITS

The profits reported under absorption costing and marginal costing for period 1 in Question 8 would be reconciled as follows.

	£
Marginal costing profit	400
Adjust for fixed overhead in stock:	
Stock increase of 300 units × £1 per unit	300
Absorption costing profit	700

Question 10

Reconcile the profits reported under the two systems for period 2 of the example in Question 8.

Answer

	£
Marginal costing profit	1,400
Adjust for fixed overhead in stock:	
Stock decrease of 300 units × £1 per unit	(300)
Absorption costing profit	1,100

4 THE RELATIVE MERITS OF ABSORPTION COSTING AND MARGINAL COSTING 12/94, 6/96

Exam focus point

The effect on profit of using the two different costing methods is a popular exam topic. Remember that if opening stock values are greater than closing stock values, marginal costing shows the greater profit.

4.1 Absorption costing and marginal costing may be **compared** in three ways.

(a) As costing methods for reporting to management, for the purposes of **profit monitoring and control.**

(b) As costing methods for reporting profits and inventory values in **externally published accounts.**

(c) As costing methods for **providing information** for decision making to management.

Marginal versus absorption costing: reporting to management

4.2 We have already seen that, because of differences in inventory valuations, the reported profit in any period is likely to differ according to the costing method used. Presumably, however, one method might be said to provide a more reliable guide to management about the organisation's profit position.

4.3 **With marginal costing, contribution** (sales minus variable costs) **varies in direct proportion to the volume of units sold.** Profits will increase as sales volume rises, by the amount of extra contribution earned. Since fixed cost expenditure does not alter, it can be argued that marginal costing gives an accurate picture of how a firm's cash flows and profits are affected by changes in sales volumes.

4.4 **With absorption costing,** in contrast, **there is no clear relationship between profit and sales volume,** and as sales volume rises the total profit will rise by the sum of the gross profit per unit plus the amount of overhead absorbed per unit. Arguably this is a confusing and unsatisfactory method of monitoring profitability.

4.5 If sales volumes are the same from period to period, marginal costing will report the same profit each period (given no change in selling prices or costs). In contrast, using absorption costing, profits can vary with the volume of production, even when the volume of sales is constant. **Absorption costing is therefore often criticised because of the possibility of manipulating profit, simply by changing output and inventory levels.**

4.6 EXAMPLE: MANIPULATING PROFITS

Gloom Ltd budgeted to make and sell 10,000 units of its product in 19X1. The selling price is £10 per unit and the variable cost £4 per unit. Fixed production costs were budgeted at £50,000 for the year.

The company uses absorption costing and budgeted an absorption rate of £5 per unit.

During 19X1, it became apparent that sales demand would only be 8,000 units. The management, concerned about the apparent effect of the low volume of sales on profits, decided to increase production for the year to 15,000 units. Actual fixed costs were still expected to be £50,000 in spite of the significant increase in production volume.

Required

Calculate the profit at an actual sales volume of 8,000 units, using the following methods.

(a) Absorption costing
(b) Marginal costing

4.7 SOLUTION

(a) *Absorption costing*

	£	£
Sales (8,000 × £10)		80,000
Cost of production (15,000 × £9)	135,000	
Less: over-absorbed overhead	(25,000)	
		(110,000)
		(30,000)
Closing stock (7,000 × £9)		63,000
Profit		33,000

(b) *Marginal costing*

	£	£
Sales		80,000
Cost of sales		
Cost of production (15,000 × £4)	60,000	
Closing stock (7,000 × £4)	28,000	
		32,000
Contribution		48,000
Fixed costs		50,000
Loss		(2,000)

4.8 The difference in profits of £35,000 is explained by the difference in the increase in stock values (7,000 units × £5 of fixed overhead per unit). With absorption costing, the expected profit will be higher than the original budget of (10,000 units × (£10 – 9)) £10,000 simply because £35,000 of fixed overheads will be carried forward in closing stock values. By producing to absorb overhead rather than to satisfy customers, stock levels will, of course, increase. Unless this stock is sold, however, there may come a point when production has to stop and the inventory has to be sold off at lower prices.

Marginal costing would report a contribution of £6 per unit, or £48,000 in total for 8,000 units, which fails to cover the fixed costs of £50,000 by £2,000.

4.9 This argument is not conclusive, however, because **marginal costing is not so useful when sales fluctuate from month to month because of seasonal variations in sales demand,** but production per month is held constant in order to arrange for an even flow of output (and thereby prevent the cost of idle resources in periods of low demand and overtime in periods of high demand).

Consider the following example.

4.10 EXAMPLE: SEASONAL VARIATIONS IN SALES DEMAND

High Scream Ltd budgets to make and sell 3,600 units of its product during 19X2 at a selling price of £5. Production variable costs are £3 per unit and fixed costs for the year are budgeted as £5,400 (divisible equally between the 12 months of the year). Sales demand in the first six months of the year will be only 200 units per month, but demand will double in the second six months to 400 per month. In order to save unnecessary production costs, the company has budgeted to spread production evenly over the year by producing 300 units per month.

Required

Calculate the profits each month using the following costing methods.

(a) Absorption costing

(b) Marginal costing

4.11 SOLUTION

(a) *Absorption costing*

The fixed overhead absorption rate is $\frac{£5{,}400}{3{,}600 \text{ units}} = £1.50$ per unit

For each of the first six months of the year, profit per month would be as follows.

	£
Sales (200 units × £5)	1,000
Less full cost of sales (200 units × £4.50)	900
	100
Under-/over-absorbed overhead	0
Profit (£0.50 per unit)	100

For each of the second six months of the year, profit per month would be as follows.

	£
Sales (400 units × £5)	2,000
Less full cost of sales (400 units × £4.50)	1,800
	200
Under-/over-absorbed overhead	0
Profit (£0.50 per unit)	200

Total profit for the year would be 3,600 units × £0.50 = £1,800

(b) *Marginal costing*

For each of the first six months of the year, there would be a loss.

	£
Sales (200 units × £5)	1,000
Less variable cost of sales (200 units × £3)	600
Contribution (£2 per unit)	400
Less fixed costs	450
Loss	(50)

For each of the second six months of the year there would be a profit.

	£
Sales (400 units × £5)	2,000
Less variable cost of sales (400 units × £3)	1,200
Contribution (£2 per unit)	800
Less fixed costs	450
Profit	350

Total profit for the year would be £1,800

4.12 In this example it might be argued that in view of the deliberate policy of producing goods for stock in the first half of the year, and selling out of stock in the second half absorption costing would provide a better method of reporting profits month by month. At a profit of £0.50 per unit, total monthly profits double when sales double, which would conform to the expectations of the management of High Scream Ltd.

4.13 In contrast, marginal costing would report a loss in each of the first six months (which might cause unnecessary concern to management) and a misleadingly large jump into profitability in the second half of the year.

4.14 Other **arguments in favour of absorption costing for internal profit reporting** are as follows.

- **Marginal costing fails to recognise the importance of working to full capacity**. With absorption costing, the effect of higher production volumes is to reduce unit costs (because the fixed cost per unit is lower) and if sales prices are based on the 'cost-plus' method, the relevance of output capacity to cost, price and sales demand should be apparent.
- **Selling prices based on marginal costing** might enable the firm to make a contribution on each unit of product it sells, but the **total contribution earned might be insufficient to cover all fixed costs**.
- **In the long run, all costs are variable**, and inventory values based on **absorption costing will give recognition to these long-run variable costs**.

4.15 There are also further **arguments in favour of marginal costing for internal profit reporting**.

- **Separating fixed and variable costs helps management to make short-run pricing decisions concerning incremental profits.**
- **Fixed costs** (such as depreciation, rent or salaries) **relate to a period of time and should be charged against the revenues of the period in which they are incurred.**

Marginal versus absorption costing: external reporting

4.16 It **might be argued that absorption costing is preferable** to marginal costing in management accounting, **in order to be consistent with the requirement of SSAP 9** to include production overhead in inventory values in published accounts. This argument might be especially relevant when a firm has an integrated or combined accounting system for its financial and management accounts.

4.17 The argument is, however, an unimportant one because it is quite easy for a firm to maintain its accounts on a marginal costing basis, and when financial accounts are prepared, to convert its stock values into fully absorbed costs.

Marginal versus absorption costing: decision making information

4.18 Suppose that a sales manager has an item of product which he is having difficulty in selling. Its historical full cost is £80, made up of variable costs of £50 and fixed costs of £30. A customer offers £60 for it.

(a) If there is no other customer for the product, £60 would be better than nothing and the product should be sold to improve income and profit by this amount.

(b) If the company has spare production capacity which would otherwise not be used, it would be profitable to continue making more of the same product, if customers are willing to pay £60 for each extra unit made. This is because the additional costs are only £50 so that the profit would be increased marginally by £10 per unit produced.

(c) In absorption costing terms, the product makes a loss of £20, which would discourage the sales manager from accepting a price of £60 from the customer. His decision would be a bad one.

(i) If the product is not sold for £60, it will presumably be scrapped eventually, so the choice is really between making a loss in absorption costing terms of £20, or a loss of £80 when the stock is written off, whenever this happens.

(ii) If there is demand for some extra units at £60 each, the absorption costing loss would be £20 per unit, but at the end of the year there would be an additional contribution to overheads and profit of £10 per unit. In terms of absorption costing the under-absorbed overhead would be reduced by £30 (the fixed cost part of the product's full cost) for each extra unit made and sold.

4.19 **Absorption costing information** about unit profits is therefore **irrelevant in short-run decisions in which fixed costs do not change** (such as short-run tactical decisions seeking to make the best use of existing facilities). In such circumstances the decision rule is to choose the alternative which maximises contribution.

Summary

4.20 No recommendation of the costing method which should be used can be given. **Although any technique can be used for internal purposes, absorption costing must be used for external reporting.** It would appear that the use of marginal costing in an organisation for cost accumulation is rare. This does not mean, however, that marginal costing techniques are unimportant. An understanding of the behaviour of cost and the implications of contribution is vital for accountants and managers, and the use of marginal costing for planning and decision making is universal. Dopuch, Birnberg and Demski provide the most appropriate conclusion: 'In short, we continue to regard a firm's best cost reporting system as a situation-specific question'.

5 OPPORTUNITY COSTING

KEY TERM

The **opportunity cost** is the benefit foregone by choosing one opportunity instead of the next best alternative.

5.1 A common feature of both absorption costing and marginal costing is that the costs of the jobs or products or services are built up from the 'purchase' costs of the resources that are used up in making them.

5.2 For example, suppose that a company manufactures a product at each of two sites, one in London and one in North East England. The factory rental in London is very cheap by London standards, because the company has occupied the premises for many years. The actual rental in London is £40,000 pa, which is exactly the same as for the similar-sized factory in the North East, where a full commercial rental is being paid. The company could sub-let the London factory, if it wished, for £100,000 pa.

(a) If absorption costing were used to cost the output from each factory, the rental cost allocated to production overhead would be £40,000 pa for each factory.

(b) If marginal costing were used instead, the rental cost of £40,000 pa at each factory would be charged as a period cost against profits.

5.3 **Neither method of costing recognises the opportunity cost of the London factory, which is the revenue that could be earned from sub-letting the factory**. There is an argument that £100,000 should be charged as the cost of the London factory, to reflect the true value to the company of the resource - factory space - that it is using in London.

5.4 In our example, the benefit from sub-letting the London factory has been sacrificed in favour of using the factory to make the company's own product. The value of the benefit is £100,000 pa.

In a system of opportunity costing, the cost of factory rental in London would be £100,000 pa, not £40,000 pa.

5.5 In a system of cost accumulation using **opportunity costing**, the **costs of resources consumed are valued at their opportunity cost rather than at the amount it actually costs to acquire them**.

- **If no alternative use for a resource exists then the opportunity cost is zero.**
- **If a resource is not scarce, no sacrifice exists from using the resource and so the opportunity cost is zero.**

5.6 **The main argument in favour of opportunity costing** is that management are made more aware of how well they are using resources to make products, and whether resources could be used better in other ways, to make bigger profits or produce more valuable output.

5.7 **The main drawback to opportunity costing** is a practical one. It is not always easy to recognise alternative uses for certain resources, nor to put an accurate value on opportunity cost. It is only likely to be accurate in situations where resources have an alternative use which can be valued at an external market price. This would be factory rental in the example above, or staff time in the case of professional firms of accountants or solicitors, and so on.

5.8 EXAMPLE: OPPORTUNITY COSTING

An information technology consultancy firm has been asked to do an urgent job by a client, for which a price of £2,500 has been offered. The job would require the following.

(a) 30 hours' work from one member of staff, who is paid on an hourly basis, at a rate of £20 per hour, but who would normally be employed on work for clients where the charge-out rate is £45 per hour. No other member of staff is able to do the member of staff in question's work.

(b) The use of 5 hours of mainframe computer time, which the firm normally charges out to external users at a rate of £50 per hour. Mainframe computer time is currently used 24 hours a day, 7 days a week.

(c) Supplies and incidental expenses of £200.

The opportunity cost of the job would be calculated as follows.

	£
Labour (30 hours × £45)	1,350
Computer time opportunity cost (5 hours × £50)	250
Supplies and expenses	200
	1,800

The opportunity cost of labour and computer time is the normal charge-out rate, of £45 and £50 per hour respectively.

A further addition to cost might be added for 'general overhead' depending on the system of costing being used.

The opportunity cost of the job shows that the firm would increase profits by accepting the job, by £(2,500 - 1,800) = £700.

Imputed interest (notional interest)

5.9 **There is a view that costs should include an interest charge which is based on the opportunity cost of the capital value of resources tied up**. For example, if a production department employs assets valued at £100,000, and the company's cost of borrowing is 12% pa, it might be considered appropriate to charge interest of £12,000 pa to the department, to reflect the cost of the assets.

5.10 Another reason for charging jobs or services with notional interest is to assist comparability. Suppose that there are two departments, A and B, each producing the same finished product with the same item of machinery. However, A has purchased its machine, whereas B leases its machine. Costs for period 1 of 19X1 are as follows.

	Dept A	*Dept B*
Output (units)	10,000	10,000
	£	£
Variable costs	10,000	10,000
Depreciation	2,000	-
Lease charge	-	2,500
Other fixed costs	8,000	8,000
	20,000	20,500

5.11 The costs in each department are identical, except that Dept A is charged with depreciation (a share of the original capital cost) whereas Dept B's lease charge will include an element for capital cost and an element for the finance or interest charge in the lease. To make the costs of the two departments properly comparable, it could be argued that Dept A ought to be charged a notional amount for interest on the capital value of its machine.

6 ACTIVITY BASED COSTING 6/95, 6/97, 12/97

Exam focus point

In the 6/95 exam, there were 10 marks to be gained for preparing and presenting a profit statement using activity based costing.

The reasons for the development of ABC

6.1 The **absorption costing approach** to dealing with overheads which we have been looking at were **developed in a time** when most organisations produced only a narrow range of products and **when overhead costs were only a very small fraction of total**

costs, direct labour and direct material costs accounting for the largest proportion of the costs. Errors made in attributing overheads to projects were therefore not too significant.

6.2 Nowadays, however, the situation is different. With the advent of advanced manufacturing technology (AMT), overheads are likely to be far more important.

- Direct labour may account for as little as 5% of a product's cost.
- The accessibility of information technology now allows for more sophisticated overhead allocation methods than in the past.

In today's business environment it therefore appears difficult to justify the use of direct labour or direct material as the basis for allocating overheads or to believe that errors made in attributing overheads will not be significant. It is against this background that **activity based costing (ABC)** has emerged.

6.3 The traditional methods accurately allocate to products the costs of those resources that are used in proportion to the number of units produced of a particular product. Such resources include labour, materials and machine-related costs such as power and lubricants. Many resources, however, are used in non-volume related support activities, (which have increased due to AMT), such as setting-up, production scheduling, first item inspection and data processing. These support activities assist the efficient manufacture of a wide range of products and are not, in general, affected by changes in production volume. They tend to vary in the long term according to the range and complexity of the products manufactured rather than the volume of output.

6.4 The wider the range and the more complex the products, the more support services will be required. Consider, for example, factory X which produces 10,000 units of one product, the Alpha, and factory Y which produces 1,000 units each of ten slightly different versions of the Alpha. Support activity costs in the factory Y are likely to be a lot higher than in factory X but the factories produce an identical number of units. Take setting-up. Factory X will only need to set-up once whereas Factory Y will have to set-up the production run at least ten times for the ten different products. Factory Y will therefore incur more set-up costs.

6.5 **Traditional costing systems, which assume that all products consume all resources in proportion to their production volumes, tend to allocate too great a proportion of overheads to high volume products (which cause relatively little diversity and hence use fewer support services) and too small a proportion of overheads to low volume products (which cause greater diversity and therefore use more support services).** ABC attempts to overcome this problem.

6.6 The **major ideas behind activity based costing** are as follows.

- **Activities cause costs.** Activities include ordering, materials handling, machining, assembly, production scheduling and despatching.
- **Producing products creates demand** for the activities.
- **Costs are assigned to a product on the basis of the product's consumption of the activities.**

KEY TERM

Activity based costing (ABC) involves the identification of the factors which cause the costs of an organisation's major activities. Support overheads are charged to products on the basis of their usage of the factor causing the overheads.

Calculating product costs using ABC

6.7 An ABC costing system operates as follows.

Step 1. **Identify** an organisation's **major activities**.

Step 2. **Identify** the factors which determine the size of the costs of an activity/cause the costs of an activity. These are known as **cost drivers**.

KEY TERM

A **cost driver** is the factor which causes the costs of an activity.

Look at the following examples.

Activity	Cost driver
Ordering	Number of orders
Materials handling	Number of production runs
Production scheduling	Number of production runs
Despatching	Number of despatches

(a) For **short-term variable overhead costs, cost drivers will be volume of activity,** such as machine hours operated or direct labour hours.

(b) For **long-term variable overhead costs, cost drivers** will not be related to output volume, and Kaplan and Cooper argue that these costs are **related to the transactions undertaken by the support departments where the costs are incurred.**

- **Logistical transactions** are those activities concerned with organising the flow of resources throughout the manufacturing process.
- **Balancing transactions** are those activities which ensure that demand for and supply of resources are matched.
- **Quality transactions** are those activities which relate to ensuring that production is at the required level of quality.
- **Change transactions** are those activities associated with ensuring that customers' requirements (delivery date, changed design and so on) are met.

These transactions in the support departments are the appropriate cost drivers to use.

> 'There are no simple rules that pertain to the selection of cost drivers. The best approach is to identify the resources that constitute a significant proportion of the product costs and determine their cost behaviour. If several are long-term variable costs, a transaction-based cost system should be considered.' (Cooper)

Step 3. **Collect the costs of each activity** into what are known as **cost pools** (equivalent to cost centres under more traditional costing methods).

Step 4. **Charge support overheads to products on the basis of their usage of the activity. A product's usage of an activity is measured by the number of the activity's cost driver it generates.**

Suppose, for example, that the cost pool for the ordering activity totalled £100,000 and that there were 10,000 orders (the cost driver). Each product would therefore be charged with £10 for each order it required. A batch requiring five orders would therefore be charged with £50.

6.8 Professor Kaplan has commented ('Relevance Regained', *Management Accounting*, September 1988) as follows.

> 'Our task is to dissect these (overhead) activities, find out how much is being spent on them and come up with a quantity measure that can be related to a finished product. These measures will be things like how many items are being inspected, how many purchase orders are being produced, how many engineering changes are being processed, how much material is being moved, how many set-up hours are being delivered, how many customer calls are being made.
>
> Remarkably, the old traditional methods of cost accounting never had quantity measures related to overhead. We had quantity measures for labour, we had quantity measures for direct material, but overhead was always a big glob of money to be allocated. That's exactly the wrong way to think about it. The goal is to think about what are the quantities of overhead that are being delivered.'

6.9 The following example illustrates the point that traditional cost accounting techniques result in a misleading and inequitable division of costs between low-volume and high-volume products, and that ABC can provide a more meaningful allocation of costs.

6.10 EXAMPLE: ABC

Suppose that Cooplan Ltd manufactures four products, W, X, Y and Z. Output and cost data for the period just ended are as follows.

	Output	*Number of production runs in the period*	*Material cost per unit*	*Direct labour hours per unit*	*Machine hours per unit*
	Units		£		
W	10	2	20	1	1
X	10	2	80	3	3
Y	100	5	20	1	1
Z	100	5	80	3	3
		14			

Direct labour cost per hour is £5. Overhead costs are as follows.

	£
Short run variable costs	3,080
Set-up costs	10,920
Expediting and scheduling costs	9,100
Materials handling costs	7,700
	30,800

Required

Calculate product costs using the following approaches.

(a) Absorption costing
(b) ABC

6.11 SOLUTION

(a) Using a conventional absorption costing approach and an absorption rate for overheads based on either direct labour hours or machine hours, the product costs would be as follows.

	W	*X*	*Y*	*Z*	*Total*
	£	£	£	£	£
Direct material	200	800	2,000	8,000	11,000
Direct labour	50	150	500	1,500	2,200
Overheads ★	700	2,100	7,000	21,000	30,800
	950	3,050	9,500	30,500	44,000
Units produced	10	10	100	100	
Cost per unit	£95	£305	£95	£305	

★ £30,800 ÷ 440 hours = £70 per direct labour or machine hour.

(b) Using activity based costing and assuming that the number of production runs is the cost driver for set-up costs, expediting and scheduling costs and materials handling costs and that machine hours are the cost driver for short-run variable costs, unit costs would be as follows.

	W	*X*	*Y*	*Z*	*Total*
	£	£	£	£	£
Direct material	200	800	2,000	8,000	11,000
Direct labour	50	150	500	1,500	2,200
Short-run variable overheads (W1)	70	210	700	2,100	3,080
Set-up costs (W2)	1,560	1,560	3,900	3,900	10,920
Expediting, scheduling costs (W3)	1,300	1,300	3,250	3,250	9,100
Materials handling costs (W4)	1,100	1,100	2,750	2,750	7,700
	4,280	5,120	13,100	21,500	44,000

	W	*X*	*Y*	*Z*
	£	£	£	£
Units produced	10	10	100	100
Cost per unit	£428	£512	£131	£215

Workings

1	£3,080 ÷ 440 machine hours	=	£7 per machine hour
2	£10,920 ÷ 14 production runs	=	£780 per run
3	£9,100 ÷ 14 production runs	=	£650 per run
4	£7,700 ÷ 14 production runs	=	£550 per run

Summary

Product	*Conventional costing Unit cost*	*ABC Unit cost*	*Difference*
	£	£	£
W	95	428	+ 333
X	305	512	+ 207
Y	95	131	+ 36
Z	305	215	- 90

6.12 The figures in the previous example suggest that the traditional volume-based absorption costing system is flawed.

- It under-allocates overhead costs to low-volume products (here, W and X with ten units of output) and over-allocates overheads to higher-volume products (here Z in particular).
- It under-allocates overhead costs to less complex products (here W and Y with just one hour of work needed per unit) and over-allocates overheads to more complex products (here X and particularly Z).

ABC versus absorption costing

Exam focus point

In the 12/97 exam, candidates could have earned eight marks for describing how ABC is different to absorption costing and for explaining why it was developed.

Allocation and apportionment of overheads

6.13 Absorption costing allocates overheads to production departments (cost centres) whereas ABC systems assign overheads to each major activity (cost pools). With ABC systems, lots of activity-based cost pools are established whereas with absorption costing, overheads tend to be pooled by departments. This can result in many reapportionments of service department costs to ensure that all overheads are allocated to production departments. **ABC** establishes separate cost pools for support activities such as despatching. As the costs of these activities are assigned directly to products through cost driver rates, **reapportionment of service department costs is avoided.**

Absorption of overheads

6.14 The principal difference between the two systems is the way in which overheads are absorbed into products.

- **Absorption costing** uses usually **two absorption bases** (labour hours and/or machine hours) to charge overheads to products.
- **ABC uses many cost drivers as absorption bases** (number of orders, number of dispatches and so on).

Absorption rates under ABC should therefore be more closely linked to the causes of overhead costs and hence ABC should produce more realistic product costs.

Cost drivers and absorption rates

6.15 The principal idea of ABC is to focus attention on what causes costs to increase, the cost drivers. Just as there are no rules for what to use as the basis for absorbing costs in absorption costing, there are also difficulties in choosing cost drivers.

- Those **costs that do vary with production volume**, such as power costs, should be **traced to products using production volume-related cost drivers** as appropriate, such as direct labour hours or direct machine hours.
- **Overheads which do not vary with output** but with some other activity should be **traced to products using transaction-based cost drivers**, such as number of production runs and number of orders received.

6.16 Focusing attention on what actually causes overheads and tracing overheads to products on the basis of the usage of the cost drivers ensures that a greater proportion of overheads are product related, whereas traditional costing systems allow overheads to be related to products in rather more arbitrary ways. It is this feature of ABC which produces, it is claimed, greater accuracy.

Case example

Wavin is a Dutch subsidiary of Shell engaged in the manufacture of plastic pipe systems. The following table shows areas where Wavin has identified strong relationships between activities and costs.

Activity pools	*Cost drivers*
Extrusion production	Product weights Number of runs
Injection moulding	Cycle times Set-ups Number of pieces
Finishing	Standard times Number of pieces
Maintenance	Production volumes Planned maintenance programme
Warehousing	Number of locations Number of lanes Number of products Demand levels
Activity pools	*Cost drivers*
Order entry	Customer groups Number of customers Number of order lines
Selling costs	Number of salesmen's calls
Finance	Number of customers Number of suppliers Number of transactions

Source: Brent Marshall, 'Activity-based costing at Wavin', *Management Accounting*, May 1995

Question 11

A company manufactures two products, L and M, using the same equipment and similar processes. An extract of the production data for these products in one period is shown below.

	L	*M*
Quantity produced (units)	5,000	7,000
Direct labour hours per unit	1	2
Machine hours per unit	3	1
Set-ups in the period	10	40
Orders handled in the period	15	60

Overhead costs	£
Relating to machine activity	220,000
Relating to production run set-ups	20,000
Relating to handling of orders	45,000
	285,000

Required

Calculate the production overheads to be absorbed by one unit of each of the products using the following costing methods.

(a) A traditional costing approach using a direct labour hour rate to absorb overheads
(b) An activity based costing approach, using suitable cost drivers to trace overheads to products

Answer

(a) *Traditional costing approach*

	Direct labour hours
Product L = 5,000 units × 1 hour	5,000
Product M = 7,000 units × 2 hours	14,000
	19,000

∴ Overhead absorption rate = $\frac{£285,000}{19,000}$

= £15 per hour

Overhead absorbed would be as follows.

Product L	1 hour × £15	=	£15 per unit
Product M	2 hours × £15	=	£30 per unit

(b) *ABC approach*

		Machine hours
Product L	= 5,000 units × 3 hours	15,000
Product M	= 7,000 units × 1 hour	7,000
		22,000

Using ABC the overhead costs are absorbed according to the *cost drivers*.

	£			
Machine-hour driven costs	220,000	÷	22,000 m/c hours	= £10 per m/c hour
Set-up driven costs	20,000	÷	50 set-ups	= £400 per set-up
Order driven costs	45,000	÷	75 orders	= £600 per order

Overhead costs are therefore as follows.

		Product L		*Product M*
		£		£
Machine-driven costs	(15,000 hrs × £10)	150,000	(7,000 hrs × £10)	70,000
Set-up costs	(10 × £400)	4,000	(40 × £400)	16,000
Order handling costs	(15 × £600)	9,000	(60 × £600)	36,000
		163,000		122,000
Units produced		5,000		7,000
Overhead cost per unit		£32.60		£17.43

These figures suggest that product M absorbs an unrealistic amount of overhead using a direct labour hour basis. Overhead absorption should be based on the activities which drive the costs, in this case machine hours, the number of production run set-ups and the number of orders handled for each product.

7 MERITS AND CRITICISMS OF ABC

Further merits of ABC

7.1 As you will have discovered when attempting the question above, there is nothing difficult about ABC. Once the necessary information has been obtained it is similar to traditional absorption costing. This simplicity is part of its appeal. Further merits of ABC are as follows.

- Because of the financial accounting requirement to value stocks at full cost, management accounting has not given sufficient priority to the need to provide meaningful product costs and has simply used absorption costing to produce costs.

  ABC, on the other hand, focuses attention on the nature of cost behaviour and **attempts to provide meaningful product costs.**

- ABC uses multiple cost drivers to allocate overhead costs to activities and then to products, and does not use a meaningless direct labour hour recovery rate or machine hour recovery rate, that assumes overhead costs are related to volume of activity only. Only **ABC recognises that many overhead costs arise out of the diversity and complexity of operations.**

- **The complexity of manufacturing has increased,** with wider product ranges, shorter product life cycles, a greater importance being attached to quality and more complex production processes. **ABC recognises this complexity with its multiple cost drivers.**
- In a more competitive environment, companies must be able to assess **product profitability** realistically. **ABC facilitates a good understanding of what drives overhead costs.**
- In modern manufacturing systems, overhead functions include a lot of non-factory-floor activities such as product design, quality control, production planning, sales order planning and customer service. **ABC is concerned with all overhead costs,** including the costs of these functions, and so it takes management accounting beyond its 'traditional' factory floor boundaries.
- ABC can give valuable insights into the following.
  - Product design
  - Product mix
  - Processing methods
  - Administration
  - Pricing

> 'If this new product cost attribution were the end of the story, then it would just be a mildly interesting exercise. What changes this from being mildly interesting to being incredibly interesting is that you can now set about reversing the process. Because a company is able to see clearly where the majority of its indirect expenses are going, it can make changes to its processes so that these expenses can be minimised. Going back to the purchasing department example again, if we can see that the costs of purchasing are directly related to the number of vendors and the lack of component commonality, then we can change the way we design products and purchase material so that purchasing costs are significantly reduced.
>
> Pricing decisions, product mix decisions, design decisions and production decisions can all be much better understood when the background analysis and modelling from ABC is available. Many companies are selling products at a loss, subsidising their customers, because they do not understand the true cost of a product owing to the distortion of the costing system. The ABC approach gives them a better way of making that kind of assessment.'
>
> (RS Kaplan, 'Relevance Regained', *Management Accounting,* September 1988)

Customer profitability analysis and ABC

7.2 In certain circumstances a useful approach to performance evaluation may be the analysis of profitability by customer or customer group. **Profitability can vary widely between different customers because various overhead costs** (including the following) **are, to some extent, variable and 'customer-driven'.**

- Discounts
- Sales force (telesales are cheaper and more time-efficient than a field sales force)
- Quality control (some customers demand higher quality)
- Merchandising
- Distribution (full-pallet transactions are cheaper than breaking bulk)
- Promotions
- Financing costs
- Enquiries

7.3 Customer profitability analysis (CPA) can be used to **relate these variabilities in cost to individual customers or customer groups**. Managers can use this information to **check whether individual customers are actually profitable to sell to**, and to assess whether profitability can be improved for any customer by switching effort from one type of overhead activity to another, or by reducing spending on some overhead activities.

7.4 CPA therefore provides valuable management accounting information.

(a) It helps a firm to identify unprofitable customers as well as unprofitable products.

(b) It draws attention to the three ways of improving profitability, both for individual customers and so for products in total. These are:

- productivity improvements to reduce product costs;
- higher sales volumes to customers, to increase total contribution;
- more efficient use of 'overhead' resources to improve customer profitability.

Because of its abilities to deal with support costs, ABC is ideally suited to this analysis.

ABC and non-value-added activities

7.5 ABC might be useful in contributing towards the **control of non-value-added activities**. These activities, which do not augment the customer's perception of a product's value and are therefore undesirable, include the following.

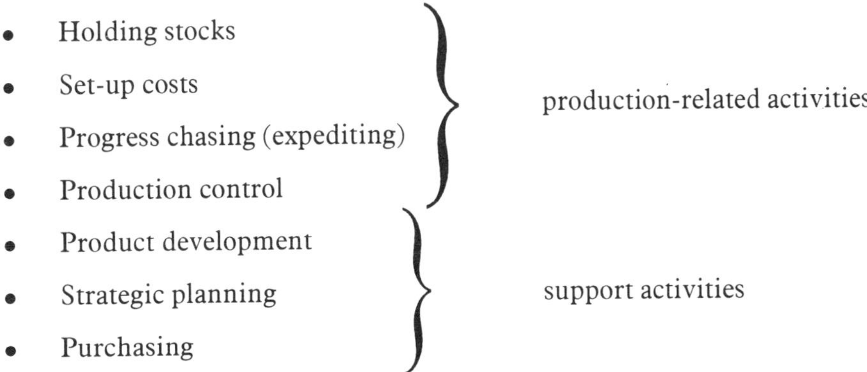

- Holding stocks
- Set-up costs
- Progress chasing (expediting)
- Production control

} production-related activities

- Product development
- Strategic planning
- Purchasing

} support activities

To **control, reduce** or perhaps even **eliminate** if possible, **non-value-added activities,** management need to **understand what are the cost drivers** that cause the costs to happen.

Other uses of ABC

7.6 The information provided by analysing activities can support the management functions of planning, control and decision making, provided it is used carefully and with full appreciation of its implications.

Planning

7.7 Before an ABC system can be implemented, management must:

(a) analyse the organisation's activities;
(b) determine the extent of their occurrence; and
(c) establish the relationships between activities, products/services and their cost.

7.8 The **information database** produced from such an exercise can then be **used as a basis for forward planning and budgeting**. For example, once an organisation has set its budgeted production level, the database can be used to determine the number of times that activities will need to be carried out, thereby establishing necessary departmental staffing and machine levels.

7.9 Financial budgets can be drawn up by multiplying the budgeted activity levels by cost per activity.

7.10 This activity-based approach may not produce the final budget figures but it can **provide the basis for different possible planning scenarios.**

Control

7.11 The information database also provides an **insight into the way in which costs are structured and incurred in service and support departments.**

Traditionally it has been difficult to control the costs of such departments because of the lack of relationship between departmental output levels and departmental cost. With ABC, however, it is possible to **control or manage the costs by managing the activities which underlie them** by monitoring a number of key performance measures.

Decision making

7.12 Many of ABC's supporters claim that it can assist with decision making in a number of ways.

- It **provides accurate and reliable cost information.**
- It establishes a long-run product cost.
- It provides data which can be used to evaluate different possibilities of delivering business.

It is therefore particularly suited for the following types of decision.

- Pricing
- Promoting or discontinuing products or parts of the business
- Developing and designing changed products, new products or new ways to do business

7.13 Note, however, that an ABC cost is **not a true cost**, it is **simply an average cost** because some costs such as depreciation are still arbitrarily allocated to products. An ABC cost is therefore **not a relevant cost** for all decisions.

7.14 The traditional cost behaviour patterns of fixed cost and variable cost are felt by advocates of ABC to be unsuitable for longer-term decisions, when resources are not fixed and changes in the volume or mix of business can be expected to have an impact on the cost of all resources used, not just short-term variable costs. A **five-level hierarchy** has therefore been suggested to facilitate the analysis of costs.

Level	Basis	Cost are dependent on ...	Example
1	Unit	volume of production	Machine power
2	Batch	number of batches	Set-up costs
3	Process	existence of a process	Quality control
4	Product	existence of a product group/line	Product management
5	Facility	existence of a production facility or plant	Rent and rates

7.15 As Innes and Mitchell (*Activity Based Costing: A Review with Case Studies*, CIMA 1990) say, 'This analysis of cost highlights the decision level at which each element of cost can be influenced. For example, the reduction of production cost levels will not simply depend on a general reduction in output volumes, but also on reorganising production to perhaps increase *batch* size and reduce batch volume, on eliminating or modifying a *process*, on cutting out or merging product lines or on altering or removing *facility* capacity'.

7.16 Raiborn *et al* explain how a product cost is determined using such an analysis.

> 'Traditionally, accounting has assumed that if costs did not vary until changes in production at the unit level, those costs were fixed rather than variable. Such an assumption is not true. Batch level, product level, and organizational level costs are all variable, but these types of costs vary for reasons other than changes in production volume. For this reason, to determine an accurate estimate of product or service cost, **costs should be accumulated at each successively higher level of costs**. Because unit, batch and product level costs are all related to units of products (merely at different levels), these **costs can be gathered together at the product level to match with the revenues generated by product sales. Organisational level costs**, however, are not product related and, thus, should **only be subtracted in total from net product revenues**.'

Such an analysis provides an alternative method of determining product profitability which may be used for management decision making.

Criticisms of ABC

7.17 It has been suggested by critics that **activity based costing has some serious flaws.**

- It should not be introduced unless it can provide additional information for management to use in planning or control decisions.
- Some measure of (arbitrary) cost apportionment may still be required at the cost pooling stage for items like rent, rates and building depreciation. If an ABC system has many cost pools the amount of apportionment needed may be greater than ever.
- The ability of a single cost driver to explain fully the cost behaviour of all items in its associated pool is questionable.
- To have a usable cost driver, a cost must be caused by an activity that is measurable in quantitative terms and which can be related to production output. But not all costs can be treated in this way. For example, what drives the cost of the annual external audit?
- Because it is often easier to measure what is easily quantifiable, quantitative cost drivers are often readily identified and applied while qualitative cost drivers are ignored. For example, the number of purchase orders may be identified as a cost driver and the more crucial negotiating ability of different purchase officers may be ignored.
- One of the fundamental assumptions of ABC is that activity causes cost. It could be argued, however, that **decisions** cause cost or the passage of **time** causes cost or that there may be no one clear cause of cost.

Adoption of ABC

7.18 The findings of a recent study by *Management Accounting* and Ernst and Young provide a useful summary of the current state of ABC adoption.

> '... whilst some 41 per cent of companies are considering implementing activity-based techniques, only 21 per cent have actually done something. Of the latter, 28 per cent claim to

have it "embedded" into the organisation. Whilst it is acknowledged that activity-based techniques are not the only option to supplement traditional management accounting approaches, they are widely recognised as an increasingly important addition.'

(H Evans and G Ashworth, 'Survey conclusion: wake up to the competition', *Management Accounting,* May 1996)

The benefits of ABC in practice

7.19 Lyne and Friedman set out the main findings from their CIMA-funded research project into the benefits of ABC in practice in a July/August 1996 *Management Accounting* article.

(a) A **wide variety of uses for AB techniques** was found, eg pricing bids; supply chain analysis; understanding process, cost or quality; flexible budgets; capital expenditure; product range decisions; and eliminating non-value adding activities. Many firms did not emphasise costing.

(b) **Activity-based data** was perceived as **more relevant** both by accountants and managers and as a result was used more widely.

(c) Implementation of AB techniques **encouraged greater interaction between management accountants and operational managers.**

(d) The study spoke of two breeds of accountant: 'beancounters' who did not understand the business and viewed everything in terms of accounting numbers, and 'new management accountants' who had a clear understanding of business imperatives and prided themselves on the useful information they provided. The **implementation of AB techniques** seemed to **encourage operational managers to view their management accountants as 'new management accountants' rather than 'beancounters'.**

Conclusion

7.20 The examiner provided a useful conclusion to the ABC debate in a recent article. [Bullet points and emphasis are BPP's own.]

- 'It can offer considerable benefits to some companies but a **decision to adopt ABC should not be taken lightly**. The staff time involved in developing and getting the system into operation is conservatively estimated at two person years, costs are at least £100,000 though it depends on the system being implemented and the size of the company.
- It requires **serious commitment of resources** and top management support.
- It is not a system that the accountant can do in his/her spare time.
- Indeed it is **not a system that should focus exclusively on the accountant**. It is common for a project team to develop the ABC system on which the accountant can play a part, but not necessarily a dominating part.
- Its **implementation** is not easy but is **made easier by the availability of IT support** within the organisation. Existing IT facilities can make it possible, at little extra cost, to obtain useful cost driver data. There is now a range of PC based packages on which to develop stand alone ABC systems, or they can be integrated with existing systems, though the former seem advisable at the prototype stage.
- There are cases of companies claiming significant benefit from adopting ABC (changing the way they do business) but also **examples of companies trying but rejecting the activity-based approach**.
- To be effective, cost management must be based on a sound knowledge of an organisation's cost structure, the proportion of its overheads, the degree of competition, its information needs within the organisation, an appreciation of how costs are determined and how they may be influenced. Only after **consideration of these factors can a judgement be made on the potential for an organisation of ABC**.'

Evaluating the Potential of Activity-Based Costing, Mike Tayles, ACCA Students' Newsletter

Chapter roundup

- The traditional approach to dealing with overheads is **absorption costing**, the three stages of which are **allocation**, **apportionment** and **absorption**. Apportionment has two stages, general overhead apportionment and service department cost apportionment (either directly, using algebra or using the repeated distribution method). After apportionment, overheads are absorbed into products using an appropriate absorption rate based on budgeted costs and budgeted activity levels. **Under-/over-absorbed overhead** occurs when overheads incurred do not equal overheads absorbed.
- In **marginal costing**, **stocks are valued at variable production cost** whereas in **absorption costing** they are valued at their **full production cost** and hence, if the opening and closing stock levels differ, the profit reported for the accounting period under the two methods will be different. In the long run, however, total profit will be the same whatever method is used.
- The balance of the arguments for one costing method or the other have been summarised by Dopuch, Birnberg and Demski as follows.

  'Fundamentally, we can offer no preference for either absorption costing or direct costing [marginal costing] for profit reporting. Direct costing reveals more of the cost structure, but absorption costing, with its charge for fixed overhead per unit, may provide a useful estimate of the long-run opportunity cost of using capacities - at least a closer estimate than direct costing, which inputs a zero opportunity cost for capacities. On the other hand, absorption costing may provide too high an estimate in the short run, when available capacities could be used for special orders, increased output levels and additional products. There is utility in reporting variable and fixed costs separately. (There is also an added cost) .... In short, we continue to regard a firm's best cost reporting system as a situation-specific question.'
- An **opportunity cost** is the value of the benefit sacrificed by not carrying out an alternative course of action. **Opportunity costing** is perhaps most useful for costing services which are provided to production departments by non-revenue-earning service departments. It can also be used to cost processes. We will return to this area in Chapter 4.
- An alternative to the traditional methods of accounting for costs is **activity based costing**. **ABC** involves the identification of the factors (**cost drivers**) which cause the costs of an organisation's major activities. Support overheads are charged to products on the basis of their usage of an activity.
- When using ABC, for costs that vary with production levels in the short term, the cost driver will be volume related (labour or machine hours). Overheads that vary with some other activity (and not volume of production) should be traced to products using transaction-based cost drivers such as production runs or number of orders received.

Quick quiz

1. What is the problem of overheads? (see para 1.2)
2. List three reasons for under-/over-absorbed overhead. (2.16)
3. If stock levels increase between the beginning and end of a period, does absorption costing or marginal costing show the higher profit? (3.2)
4. In what three ways may marginal costing and absorption costing be compared? (4.1)
5. What are the main arguments in favour of and against an opportunity cost approach to cost accumulation? (5.6, 5.7)
6. What are the major ideas of ABC? (6.6)
7. What is the advantage of using cost drivers instead of traditional absorption bases? (6.16)
8. What criticisms of ABC have been suggested? (7.17)

Question to try	Level	Marks	Time
2	Examination	20	36 mins

Chapter 3

SPECIFIC ORDER COSTING

Chapter topic list		Syllabus reference
1	Job costing	1(a)(i), (b)(i), 3(a)(i)
2	Batch costing	1(a)(i), (b)(i)
3	Contract costing	1(a)(i), (b)(i)
4	Pricing specific orders	1(a)(i), (b)(i)
5	Decisions and specific order costing	1(b)(i),(iv)

Introduction

In Chapter 2 we learnt how to accumulate costs in order to determine the cost of a product or service produced/provided by an organisation. This chapter describes how costs, once accumulated using one of the methods covered in Chapter 2, are attributed to **specific orders (jobs, batches and contracts)**. This attribution is carried out using a costing method.

As you should know from your Paper 3 studies, a **costing method** is a method of costing which is designed to suit the way goods are processed or manufactured or the way that services are provided. Each organisation's costing method will therefore have unique features, but it is more than likely that costing methods of firms in the same line of business will have features in common. On the other hand, organisations involved in completely different activities, such as hospitals and car part manufacturers, will use very different costing methods.

The principal costing methods are **job** and **batch costing**, **contract costing**, **process costing** and **service costing**. In this chapter we will examine job, batch and contract costing (collectively known as specific order costing) in detail. Process costing and service costing are dealt with in the next chapter. You have already encountered all of these costing methods in Paper 3 but where necessary we have included 'Knowledge Brought Forward' boxes to remind you of important points.

1 JOB COSTING

KEY TERMS

- A **job** is a cost unit which consists of a single order or contract.
- **Job costing** is a costing method applicable where work is undertaken to customers' special requirements and each order is of comparatively short duration.

Knowledge brought forward from Paper 3

Job costing and batch costing

- Features of job costing include the following.
  - Jobs move through processes and operations as a continuously identifiable unit.
  - Each job usually differs in one or more respects from every other job and therefore a separate record must be maintained to show the details of a particular job.
- The procedure adopted in jobbing concerns is as follows.
  - The prospective customer states his requirements.
  - A responsible official agrees the details of the job.
  - The estimating department prepares an estimate for the job.
- Job costs are collected on a **job cost sheet/card**.
- Information for the following cost elements must be gathered for each job.
  - Direct material cost
  - Direct labour cost
  - Direct expenses
  - Production overheads
  - Administration, selling and distribution overheads
- At the year end, work in progress is the sum of the costs incurred on incomplete work (provided that this is lower than the net realisable value of the job).
- **Rectification costs** (costs of rectifying substandard work) can be either charged as a direct cost of the job concerned if not a frequent occurrence or treated as production overhead if regarded as a normal part of the work carried out generally.
- In general, the procedures for costing a **batch** (a cost unit which consists of a separate, readily identifiable group of units) are very similar to those for costing jobs. The batch is treated as a job during production. Once the batch is completed, the cost per unit is calculated as total batch cost ÷ number of units in the batch.

1.1 An example will be the best way of reminding ourselves of the principles involved in job costing.

1.2 EXAMPLE: JOB COSTING

In order to identify the costs incurred in carrying out a range of work to customer specification in its factory, a company has a job costing system. This system identifies costs directly with a job where this is possible and reasonable. In addition, production overhead costs are absorbed into the cost of jobs at the end of each month, at an actual rate per direct labour hour for each of the two production departments.

One of the jobs carried out in the factory during the month just ended was Job No 123. The following information has been collected relating specifically to this job.

(a) 400 kilos of Material Y were issued from stores to Department A.

(b) 76 direct labour hours were worked in Department A at a basic wage of £4.50 per hour. Six of these hours were classified as overtime at a premium of 50%.

(c) 300 kilos of Material Z were issued from stores to Department B.

(d) Department B returned 30 kilos of material Z to the storeroom being excess to requirements for the job.

(e) 110 direct labour hours were worked in Department B at a basic wage of £4.00 per hour. 30 of these hours were classified as overtime at a premium of 50%. All overtime worked in Department B in the month is a result of the request of a customer for early completion of another job which had been originally scheduled for completion in the month following.

(f) Department B discovered defects in some of the work, which was returned to Department A for rectification. Three labour hours were worked in Department A on rectification (these are additional to the 76 direct labour hours in Department A noted above). Such rectification is regarded as a normal part of the work carried out generally in the department.

(g) Department B damaged five kilos of material Z which then had to be disposed of. Such losses of material are not expected to occur.

(h) Total costs incurred during the month on all jobs in the two production departments were as follows.

	Dept A	*Dept B*
	£	£
Direct materials issued from stores (note (i))	6,500	13,730
Direct materials returned to stores	135	275
Direct labour, at basic wage rate (note (ii))	9,090	11,200
Indirect labour, at basic wage rate	2,420	2,960
Overtime premium	450	120
Lubricants and cleaning compounds	520	680
Maintenance	720	510
Other	1,200	2,150

Notes

(i) This includes, in Department B, the scrapped Material Z. This was the only material scrapped in the month.

(ii) All direct labour in Department A is paid a basic wage of £4.50 per hour, and in Department B £4.00 per hour. Department A direct labour includes a total of 20 hours spent on rectification work.

(i) Materials are priced at the end of each month on a weighted average basis. Relevant information of material stock movements during the month, for Material Y and Z, is as follows.

	Material Y	*Material Z*
Opening stock	1,050 kilos (value £529.75)	6,970 kilos (value £9,946.50)
Purchases	600 kilos at £0.50 per kilo	16,000 kilos at £1.46 per kilo
	500 kilos at £0.50 per kilo	
	400 kilos at £0.52 per kilo	
Issues from stores	1,430 kilos	8,100 kilos
Returns to stores	-	30 kilos

Required

Prepare a list of the costs that should be assigned to Job No 123. Provide an explanation of your treatment of each item.

1.3 SOLUTION

Job 123: Costs

Materials	£	*Explanation*
Material Y (W1)	202.00	The question states that this specifically relates to Job No 123.
Material Z (W2)	391.50	As above. The figure takes account of the fact that of the 300 kilos initially issued to the job, 30 kilos were returned and are therefore not included. The lost five kilos are discussed in W2.
Department A 76 hrs × 4.50 per hr	342.00	As material Y
Department B 110 hrs × £4 per hr	440.00	As material Y. (Overtime is not a consideration at this stage.) In neither the case of dept A or dept B was the overtime worked specifically at the request of the Job 123 customer and so the overtime premium should not be a direct cost of Job 123.
Overheads		
Department A 76 hrs × £2.70 per hour (W3)	205.20	The explanation of items included in overheads, and the calculation of absorption rates, are shown at W3.
Department B 110 hrs × £2.25 per hour (W3)	247.50	

Workings

1 *Cost of material Y issued to Job 123*

This is priced at the month-end weighted average.

	kg	£
Balance b/f	1,050	529.75
plus, at 50p per kg	600	300.00
plus, at 50p per kg	500	250.00
plus, at 52p per kg	400	208.00
	2,550	1,287.75

Hence weighted average is $\frac{£1,287.75}{2,550 \text{ kg}} = 50\frac{1}{2}$p per kg

So cost of stock issued to Job 123 is 400 kg × 50½p per kg

= £202

2 *Cost of material Z issued to Job 123*

Also priced at the month-end weighted average

	kg	£
Balance b/f	6,970	9,946.50
plus, at £1.46 per kg	16,000	23,360.00
	22,970	33,306.50

Hence weighted average is $\frac{£33{,}306.50}{22{,}970}$ = £1.45 per kg

So cost of stock issued to Job 123 is (300 – 30)kg × £1.45 per kg
= £391.50

It is assumed that the five kilos damaged in Department B will be charged to Job 123, just as any adverse material usage would be charged to the job in hand. An alternative approach would be to regard the loss of the five kilos as an exceptional item and charge it as an overhead cost to an appropriate overhead cost centre (eg abnormal wastage in Department B).

3 *Rates of overhead absorption*

(a) *Departmental costs*

Department	*A* £	*B* £	*Explanation*
Rectification work 20 hrs × £4.50 per hr	90	-	Rectification is *normal* and part of work carried out *generally* in the dept.
Indirect labour	2,420	2,960	Their time is not allocated to any particular job, but all jobs benefit indirectly.
Overtime premium	450	-	The inclusion of over-time premium in over-heads ensures that all jobs bear the same direct wage rate, regardless of whether they were performed in what is classified as overtime, or not. All overtime in Dept B, however, is specifically attributable to another job because the over-time was incurred at the specific request of the customer for the job.
Lubricants	520	680	Each job benefits from
Maintenance	720	510	these in a general way.
Other	1,200	2,150	
	5,400	6,300	

(b)

Departmental direct labour hours	$\frac{9{,}090}{£4.50 / hr}$	$\frac{11{,}200}{£4 / hr}$	
Hours worked	2,020 hrs	2,800 hrs	
Less			
Rectification work	(20) hrs	-	Included in overheads
Direct labour hrs	2,000 hrs	2,800 hrs	
Hence absorption rates =	$\frac{£5{,}400}{2{,}000 \text{ hrs}}$	$\frac{£6{,}300}{2{,}800 \text{ hrs}}$	
=	£2.70 per hr	£2.25 per hr	

Question 1

Discuss briefly how information concerning the cost of individual jobs can be used.

Answer

The cost of an individual job can be used in four principal ways.

Firstly, such costs may be *used to establish a price* which the customer should be charged for the job, in situations where the customer agrees to pay a price based on 'actual cost plus'. Because the job's share of fixed and variable production overhead has been included in the cost (in addition to, of course, the direct costs of the job), a selling price set in excess of total costs will ensure that all expenses have been covered, provided of course that the organisation works at budgeted capacity.

Secondly, the information may be *used in budgeting for future periods*. If the work to customer specification forms any sort of a pattern, an analysis of previous years' jobs will provide a useful basis for the production of future periods' work.

Thirdly, job costs can be *used for control purposes*. If an estimated cost for a job is produced, actual costs can be compared with estimate. Excess costs can be investigated with a view to control action.

Fourthly, in cases where a customer is quoted a firm price before a job begins, actual job costs can be *used to measure the actual profit or loss on each job*.

Job costing for internal services

1.4 It is possible to use a job costing system to control the costs of an internal service department, such as the maintenance department or the printing department. If a job costing system is used it is possible to **charge the user departments for the cost of specific jobs carried out, rather than apportioning the total costs of these service departments** to the user departments using an arbitrarily determined apportionment basis.

1.5 An internal job costing system for service departments will have the following advantages.

Advantages	Comment
Realistic apportionment	The identification of expenses with jobs and the subsequent charging of these to the department(s) responsible means that costs are borne by those who incurred them.
Increased responsibility and awareness	User departments will be aware that they are charged for the specific services used and may be more careful to use the facility more efficiently. They will also appreciate the true cost of the facilities that they are using and can take decisions accordingly.
Control of service department costs	The service department may be restricted to charging a standard cost to user departments for specific jobs carried out or time spent. It will then be possible to measure the efficiency or inefficiency of the service department by recording the difference between the standard charges and the actual expenditure.
Planning information	This information will ease the planning process, as the purpose and cost of service department expenditure can be separately identified.

2 BATCH COSTING

KEY TERM

A **batch** is a group of similar articles which maintains its identity during one or more stages of production and is treated as a cost unit.

2.1 As we said in the 'Knowledge Brought Forward' box at the beginning of the chapter, costs are collected for batches in much the same way as they are collected for jobs.

Question 2

The management of a company manufacturing electrical components is considering introducing an historical batch costing system into their factory.

Required

(a) Outline the information and procedures required in order to obtain the actual direct material cost of each batch of components manufactured.

(b) Identify the elements which could make up a direct operative's gross wage and for each element explain, with supporting reasons, whether it should be regarded as part of the prime cost of the components manufactured.

Answer

(a) The necessary information and procedures are set out below.

(i) A batch card must be set up for each batch, carrying a unique identifying number. This card will be used to collect information on the costs of the batch.

(ii) Quantities of materials issued to each batch should be documented by some form of materials requisition document. This will be a record of materials issued from stores. A similar document should be used to record materials returned to stores.

(iii) The materials issued from stores need to be priced in some way. One method is to maintain a perpetual inventory system on ledger cards. The cards would be updated for material receipts from goods inward notes, which would have to be priced at actual cost. The materials requisition document would be the source for updating the cards for material issues. A decision would have to be taken on the basis for pricing such issues; possible bases include LIFO, FIFO and average cost.

(b) Elements included in an operative's gross wage are basic wage, overtime earnings, shift premium, and bonus payments.

(i) Basic wage is remuneration for the operative's ordinary working hours. To the extent that these hours are occupied directly with manufacturing, the related wage should be regarded as prime cost, since it can be directly related to particular components. Any wage in respect of idle time or time spent on non-manufacturing activities is not part of prime cost.

(ii) Overtime earnings frequently arise because a company is seeking to increase production. The amount of overtime premium should be spread over production generally rather than charged solely to those units produced during the overtime hours. The basic wage earned during overtime hours should be treated as in (i) above: it should be regarded as prime cost if it is related to time spent on manufacturing activities.

(iii) Shift premium would not normally be related to specific units of production and so should not be regarded as prime cost. Even if it could be so related, the same argument as for overtime premium would suggest that it should be spread over all units produced.

(iv) Bonus payments arising under a piece work scheme can usually be related very easily to specific units of production and are therefore part of prime cost. Other bonus payments, for example payments under a group bonus scheme, are not traceable in the same way and should be regarded as overhead.

Economic batch quantity

2.2 If an organisation produces its products in batches a **decision has to be made about the quantity to produce in each batch.** The following factors will affect the decision as to the production batch size.

- The rate of consumption
- Storage costs
- Setting up/taking down (production line) costs
- Resource availability

2.3 Just as an economic order quantity can be determined by graphical, tabular or formula methods (as we saw in Paper 3), so too can the economic batch quantity (EBQ).

FORMULA TO LEARN

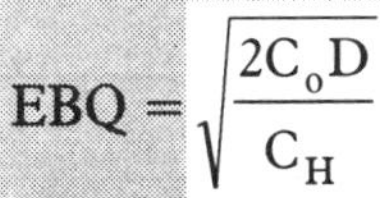

$$EBQ = \sqrt{\frac{2C_oD}{C_H}}$$

where D = annual demand
C_o = setting up/taking down costs
C_H = annual storage costs

3 CONTRACT COSTING

KEY TERMS

A **contract** is a cost unit or cost centre which is charged with the direct costs of production and an apportionment of head office overheads.

Contract costing is the name given to a method of job costing where the job to be carried out is of such magnitude that a formal contract is made between the customer and supplier. It applies where work is undertaken to customers' special requirements and each order is of long duration (compared with the time to which job costing applies). The work is usually constructional and *in general* the method is similar to job costing, although there are, of course, a few differences.

Knowledge brought forward from Paper 3

Contract costing

- Each contract is separately identifiable and is usually of a non-standard nature.
- Costs will need to be collected and charged to the contract's job/work in progress account.
- Retention monies are released by the customer when the contract is fully completed and is accepted by him/her.
- Much work may be done by subcontractors, the cost of which is treated as a direct expense.
- Progress payments are likely to be made by the customer throughout the course of the contract work.

Question 3

Describe three methods of accounting for company-owned plant used in a contract.

Answer

(a) The contract may be charged depreciation on the plant.

(b) The contract may be charged with the current book value of the plant. On the receipt of the plant the contract account is debited with the current book value of the plant. At the end of an accounting period or when plant is returned from the site to head office (or another contract site) the contract account is credited with the written down value of the plant. The difference between the values on the debit and credit side of the account at the end of the year is the cost of the equipment to the contract for the year.

(c) A third method of accounting for plant costs is to open a *plant account*, which is debited with the depreciation costs and the running costs (repairs, fuel and so on) of the equipment. A notional hire charge is then made to contracts using the plant, at a rate of £x per day.

3.1 The problems which may arise in contract costing are as follows.

Problem	Comment
Identifying direct costs	Because of the large size of the job, many cost items which are usually thought of as production overhead are charged as direct costs of the contract (for example supervision, hire of plant, depreciation or loss in value of plant which is owned, sub-contractors' fees or charges and so on).
Low indirect costs	Because many costs normally classed as overheads are charged as direct costs of a contract, the absorption rate for overheads should only apply a share of the cost of those cost items which are not already direct costs. For most contracts the only item of indirect cost would be a charge for head office expenses.
Difficulties of cost control	Because of the size of some contracts and some sites, there are often cost control problems (material usage and losses, pilferage, labour supervision and utilisation, damage to and loss of plant and tools, vandalism and so on).
Dividing the profit between different accounting periods	When a contract covers two or more accounting periods, how should the profit (or loss) on the contract be divided between the periods? This problem is, fortunately, outside the scope of your syllabus.

Profits on contracts

3.2 Progress payments do not necessarily give rise to profit immediately because of retentions.

3.3 If a **contract is started and completed in the same accounting period**, the calculation of the **profit** is straightforward, **sales minus the cost of the contract.**

3.4 A more difficult problem emerges when a **contract is incomplete at the end of an accounting period**. The contractor may have spent considerable sums of money on the work, and received substantial progress payments, and even if the work is not finished, the **contractor will want to claim some profit on the work done so far**.

3.5 To make this point clearer, suppose that a company starts four new contracts in its accounting year to 31 December 19X1, but at the end of the year, none of them has been completed. All of the contracts are eventually completed in the first few months of 19X2 and they make profits of £40,000, £50,000, £60,000 and £70,000 respectively, £220,000 in total. If **profits are not taken until the contracts are finished**, the company would make no profits at all in 19X1, when most of the work was done, and £220,000 in 19X2. Such **violent fluctuations in profitability** would be confusing not only to the company's management, but also to shareholders and the investing public at large.

3.6 The **problem arises because contracts are for long-term work**, and it is a **well-established practice that some profits should be taken in an accounting period, even if the contract is incomplete.** Let us look at an example.

3.7 EXAMPLE: PROFITS AND INCOMPLETE CONTRACTS

One of the building contracts currently engaged in by a construction company, which it commenced ten months ago, remains unfinished at the end of the accounting year. At the year end costs of £33,500 had been incurred, certificates had been issued for work valued at £50,000 and the contractee had made progress payments of £45,000.

It would appear that £50,000 should be recognised as turnover and £33,500 as cost of sales, leaving £16,500 as net profit. However it is often considered imprudent to claim this full amount of profit, and it is commonly argued that the profit taken should be a more conservative figure (in our example, less than £16,500, so that amounts taken to turnover and cost of sales relating to the contract should be less than £50,000 and £33,500 respectively).

Estimating the size of the profit

The method of calculating profit on an incomplete contract may vary, and you should check any examination question carefully to find out whether a specific method is stated in the text of the question. The **concept of prudence should be applied**, and it is suggested that the following guidelines should be followed for calculating profit on an incomplete contract.

(a) If the contract is in its **early stages, no profit should be taken**. Profit should only be taken when the outcome of the contract can be assessed with reasonable accuracy.

(b) For a contract on which substantial costs have been incurred, but which is **not yet near completion** (that is, it is in the region of **35% to 85% complete**) a formula which has often been used in the past is as follows.

FORMULAE TO LEARN

Profit taken = $^2/_3$ (or $^3/_4$) of the notional profit

where **notional profit** = (the value of work certified to date) – (the cost of the work certified).

In the example above, the notional profit for the contract is £16,500 (£(50,000 – 33,500)) and the profit taken for the period using the above formula would be calculated as follows.

$^2/_3$ of £16,500 = £11,000 (or $^3/_4$ of £16,500 = £12,375)

(c) If the contract is **nearing completion**, the size of the eventual profit should be foreseeable with reasonable certainty and there is no need to be excessively prudent.

FORMULAE TO LEARN

The profit taken may be calculated by one of three methods.

(i) Value of work certified to date minus the cost of work certified.

(ii) $\dfrac{\text{Cost of work done}}{\text{Estimated total cost of contract}} \times$ estimated total profit on contract

(iii) $\dfrac{\text{Value of work certified}}{\text{contract price}} \times$ estimated total profit

(i) In our example, this would be the full £16,500.

(ii) In our example, if the estimated total cost of the contract is £64,000 and the estimated total profit on the contract is £18,000, the profit taken would be:

$$\frac{£33,500}{£64,000} \times £18,000 = £9,422$$

(iii) This is perhaps the most-favoured of the three methods. In our example, if the final contract price is £82,000 and the estimated total profit is £18,000 the profit taken would be:

$$\frac{£50,000}{£82,000} \times £18,000 = £10,976$$

Losses on incomplete contracts

3.8 At the end of an accounting period, it may be that instead of finding that the contract is profitable, a loss is expected. When this occurs, **the total expected loss should be taken into account as soon as it is recognised, even if the contract is not yet complete**. The contract account should be debited with the anticipated future loss (the total loss expected to arise over the entire life of the contract – loss to date) and the profit and loss account debited with the total expected loss (final cost of contract – full contract price).

This means that in the next accounting period, the contract should break even, making neither a profit nor a loss, because the full loss has already been charged to the profit and loss account.

4 PRICING SPECIFIC ORDERS

4.1 An organisation basically has two choices when setting selling prices.

- Cost-plus pricing
- Market-based pricing

Cost-plus pricing

4.2 With this pricing method, **costs are estimated and then a profit margin is added in order to set the price**. This does ensure that a profit is made but it has a number of **weaknesses**.

- It offers no incentive to control costs as a profit is guaranteed.

- There is no motive to tackle inefficiencies or waste.
- It takes no account of the demand curve for a product (the way in which the selling price affects the demand).
- It takes no account of any significant differences between the actual and estimated volumes of activity used in the calculation of the overhead absorption rate, which may lead to large under or over absorbed overhead balances.
- The arbitrary nature of the basis of apportionment of overhead costs can lead to over and under pricing.

Nevertheless, **the cost plus system is often adopted where one-off jobs are carried out to customers' specifications**. It is widely used in the defence industries where the Government will determine an appropriate return for companies contracted to do particular tasks.

4.3 **Different margin figures can be applied under absorption costing** as follows.

- The profit margin may be calculated as a percentage of production cost which gives a **gross profit margin**.
- The profit margin may be calculated as a percentage of total cost which gives a **net profit margin**.
- Likewise, the profit margin may be a percentage of the selling price, the cost being based on production cost, to give a **gross profit on selling price**.
- Alternatively, the profit margin may be a percentage of the selling price, the cost being based on total cost, to give a **net profit margin on selling price.**

4.4 **Under marginal costing**, the calculations follow the same principle as for absorption costing but are based on variable cost rather than production or total cost, **using the contribution to sales ratio as a basis** (rather than a gross/net profit margin). For example, if the variable cost of a job is £100 and the organisation usually achieves a C/S ratio of 40%, the price quoted for the job should be £100/(100 – 40)% = £100/0.6 = £166.67.

4.5 There is always a **danger of underpricing when basing prices on contribution**, however ('any contribution towards fixed costs is better than nothing'). In the long run prices must cover fixed costs and offer an acceptable return.

4.6 Prices can be agreed before the job or contract is carried out or after the work has been completed. In the first instance the organisation carrying out work is at risk that actual costs may be greater than those on which the price is based. The customer carries the risk if the price is agreed after the work since he/she has no guarantee of the final price.

Market-based pricing

4.7 The price charged for a contract or job may be **determined by market forces**. Competitors may charge particular prices or labour may have a certain hourly rate. Such an approach avoids the absorption cost versus marginal costing problem set out in the paragraphs above.

5 DECISIONS AND SPECIFIC ORDER COSTING

5.1 An organisation can face any number of decisions relating to specific order costing.

- Product mixes have to be decided.
- An organisation may decide to add to or drop a product from its product range.
- A decision may have to be made as to whether to make or by-in a particular component.
- Joint products may be produced. The organisation may have to decide whether to sell the products at their split off point or process them further.
- An organisation may need to decide whether or not to undertake a particular order.

Such decisions **require the application of relevant costing**, a topic covered in Chapter 13.

Exam focus point

The costing of specific orders was covered in detail in Paper 3. A Paper 8 question on the topic might incorporate Paper 3 techniques and knowledge along with the more advanced Paper 8 aspects of absorption costing, stock valuation and decision making.

Chapter roundup

- You should be aware of the basics of job, batch and contract costing from your earlier studies but the main points are summarised below.
- **Job costing** is the costing method used where each cost unit is separately identifiable. The work is undertaken to customers' special requirements, is of comparatively short duration, is usually carried out within a factory or workshop and moves through processes and operations as a continuously identifiable unit.
- Costs for each job are collected on a **job cost sheet** or job card. Material costs for each job are determined from material requisition notes. Labour times on each job are recorded on a job ticket, which is then costed and recorded on the job cost sheet. Some labour costs, such as overtime premium or the cost of rectifying sub-standard output, might be charged either directly to a job or else as an overhead cost, depending on the circumstances in which the costs have arisen. Overhead is absorbed into the cost of jobs using the predetermined overhead absorption rates.
- **Batch costing** is similar to job costing in that each batch of similar articles is separately identifiable. The cost per unit manufactured in a batch is the total batch cost divided by the number of units in the batch.
- **Contract costing** is the form of job costing which applies where the job is of a large scale and long duration. The majority of costs for a contract are direct costs.
- A customer is likely to be required to make **progress payments** which are calculated as the value of work done and certified by the architect or engineer minus a retention minus the payments made to date.
- The long duration of a contract usually means that an estimate must be made of the profit earned on each incomplete contract at the end of the accounting period. There are several different ways of calculating contract profits, but the overriding consideration must be the application of the prudence concept. If a loss is expected on a contract, the total expected loss should be taken into account as soon as it is recognised, even if the contract is not complete.
- Prices can be set using **cost-plus pricing** or **market-based pricing**.

Quick quiz

1. What are the advantages of an internal job costing system for service departments? (see para 1.5)
2. What factors affect the decision as to production batch size? (2.2)
3. Why will a contractor want to claim some profit at the end of an accounting period, even if a contract is not finished? (3.4 - 3.6)
4. How is the anticipated future loss on a contract calculated? (3.8)
5. What are the disadvantages of cost-plus pricing? (4.2)

Question to try	Level	Marks	Time
3	Examination	5	9 mins

i) Value of work certified / Contract Price x estimated Total Profit.

(ii) Value of Work certified - Cost of Work certified ÷ 1/3 or 3/4.

(iii) Cost of Work Done / Est. Total Cost of Contract x Est Total Profit.

Chapter 4

PROCESS COSTING AND SERVICE COSTING

Chapter topic list		Syllabus reference
1	A framework for dealing with process costing questions	1(a)(i), b(i), 3(a)(ii)
2	Losses in process	1(a)(i), b(i), 3(a)(ii)
3	Valuing opening and closing work in progress	1(a)(i), b(i), 3(a)(ii)
4	Joint products and by-products	1(a)(i), b(i), 3(a)(ii)
5	Process costing and cost control	1(a)(i), b(i), 3(a)(ii)
6	Process costing and opportunity costing	1(a)(i), b(i), 3(a)(ii)
7	Process costing in practice	1(a)(i), b(i), 3(a)(ii)
8	Service industry costing	1(a)(i), b(i), 3(a)(iii)
9	Service department costing	1(a)(i), b(i), 3(a)(iv)

Introduction

In the previous chapter we looked at the three specific order costing methods. In this chapter we are going to consider process costing and service costing.

We begin the chapter with **process costing**, which you have already covered at an introductory level in Paper 3. However, it is a topic which does seem to give students problems (although once you get the basic principles sorted out in your mind it is very straightforward) and so we make no apologies for covering most aspects of the subject again rather than assuming any prior knowledge. Of course, we will also be **building on your Paper 3 knowledge and considering some more complex applications of process costing**. This is the line favoured by the examiner, who commented in his report on the 6/94 exam that 'The definition of normal loss and its accounting treatment is covered in Paper 3. This question was an attempt to build on that knowledge ...'.

In the second part of the chapter we turn our attention to **service costing** which is concerned with **establishing the costs,** not of items of production, but **of services rendered**. It is used by organisations operating in a service industry that wish to cost their services, and by organisations wishing to establish the cost of services carried out by some of their own departments. Basic service costing was also covered in Paper 3 but for Paper 8 we need to look at higher-level issues.

This is another long chapter but don't worry because you've covered most of it at an introductory level in Paper 3. You will probably be surprised by how much of it you already know.

Chapter 5 provides an introduction to Parts B and C of this Study Text with an examination of control. Parts B and C cover specific control systems, budgetary control and standard costing.

KEY TERM

Process costing is a costing method used where it is not possible to identify separate units of production, or jobs, usually because of the continuous nature of the production processes involved.

Knowledge brought forward from Paper 3

Process costing

- It is common (but not essential) to **identify process costing with continuous production** such as oil refining, or the manufacture of soap, paint, textiles, paper, foods and drinks, many chemicals and so on. Process costing may also be associated with the continuous production of large volumes of low-cost items, such as cans or tins and with mass production industries such as car manufacturing.
- The **features** of process costing which make it different from job or batch costing are as follows.
  - The continuous nature of production in many processes means that there will usually be **opening and closing work in progress which must be valued**. In process costing it is not possible to build up cost records of the cost per unit of output or the cost per unit of closing stock because **production in progress is an indistinguishable homogeneous mass.**
  - There is often a **loss in process** due to spoilage, wastage, evaporation and so on.
  - Output from production may be a single product, but there may also be a **by-product** (or by-products) and/or **joint products**.
- The basic idea behind process costing is that, where a series of separate processes is required to manufacture the finished product, **the output of one process becomes the input to the next** until the final output is made in the final process. For example, if two processes are required the accounts would look like this.

PROCESS 1 ACCOUNT

	Units	£		Units	£
Direct materials	1,000	50,000	Output to process 2	1,000	90,000
Direct labour		20,000			
Production overhead		20,000			
	1,000	90,000		1,000	90,000

PROCESS 2 ACCOUNT

	Units	£		Units	£
Materials from process 1	1,000	90,000	Output to finished goods	1,500	150,000
Added materials	500	30,000			
Direct labour		15,000			
Production overhead		15,000			
	1,500	150,000		1,500	150,000

  - Direct labour and production overhead may be treated together in an examination question as **'conversion cost'**.
  - Added materials, labour and overhead in process 2 are added gradually throughout the process. Materials from process 1, in contrast, will be introduced in full at the start of process 2.
  - The 'units' columns in the process accounts are for memorandum purposes only and help you to ensure that you do not miss out any entries.

Exam focus point

In the 12/94 exam, there were 20 marks to be gained for preparing a report for management explaining the problems associated with process costing.

1 A FRAMEWORK FOR DEALING WITH PROCESS COSTING QUESTIONS

Exam focus point

To date, Paper 8 process costing questions have been narrative rather than computational. In order to answer such questions, it is *essential* that you fully understand the techniques involved in setting up a process account.

1.1 Process costing is centred around four key steps. The exact work done at each step will depend on whether there are losses, opening stock, closing stock and so on, but this four-step approach can be adopted in any question.

Step 1. *Determine output and losses.*

- Determine expected output.
- Calculate normal loss and abnormal loss and gain.
- Calculate equivalent units if there is closing or opening work in progress.

Step 2. *Calculate cost per unit of output, losses and WIP.*

- Calculate cost per unit or cost per equivalent unit.

Step 3. *Calculate total cost of output, losses and WIP.*

- In some examples this will be straightforward
- If there is closing and/or opening work-in-progress a **statement of evaluation** will have to be prepared.

Step 4. *Complete accounts.*

- Complete the process account.
- Write up the other accounts required by the question such as abnormal loss/gain accounts.

2 LOSSES IN PROCESS 6/94, 12/94

2.1 Losses during processing can happen through evaporation of liquids, wastage, or rejected units, and so the quantity of materials output from a process might be less than the quantities input. How would any losses be costed?

Three different ways of costing losses

2.2 Suppose that input to a process consists of 100 litres of material. Total process costs are £85,652. What is the cost per litre if output is as follows?

(a) 92 litres
(b) 98 litres

2.3 One way of costing the output is to say that the **cost per unit should be based on actual units produced (output), so that any lost units have no cost at all.**

	Cost per unit		
(a) If output is 92 litres	$\frac{£85,652}{92}$	=	£931 per litre
(b) If output is 98 litres	$\frac{£85,652}{98}$	=	£874 per litre

You should see that the **cost per litre varies according to the actual loss in the period.** This means that if some loss in process is unavoidable, and if the amount of loss varies a little from period to period, this approach to costing will result in fluctuations in unit costs.

It might be more satisfactory to take a longer-term view of loss, and calculate average unit costs on the basis of average loss over a longer period of time. This would give greater stability and consistency to unit costs of production between one period (eg one month) and the next.

2.4 A second way of costing the output is to say that **lost units have a cost, which should be charged to the P & L account whenever they occur**. The cost per unit would then be **based on units of *input* rather than units of output.**

		Cost per unit		*Cost of output*	*Cost of loss*
			£	£	£
(a)	If output is 92 litres	$\frac{£85,652}{100}$	856.52	(× 92) 78,799.84	(× 8) 6,852.16
(b)	If output is 98 litres	$\frac{£85,652}{100}$	856.52	(× 98) 83,938.96	(× 2) 1,713.04

The cost of the loss would be written off directly to the P & L account.

The main drawback to this method of costing is that **if some loss in processing is unavoidable** and to be expected, there would be **some cost of production unavoidably written off to the P & L account** in every period, and this is an unsatisfactory method of costing.

2.5 The third method of costing loss (described below) is a **compromise system**, which is based on the following view.

- **If some loss is to be expected, it should not be given a cost.**
- **If there is some loss that 'shouldn't happen', it ought to be given a cost.**

Normal loss and abnormal loss/gain

KEY TERMS

- **Normal loss** is the loss expected in the normal course of operations for unavoidable reasons.
- **Abnormal loss** is the loss resulting when actual loss is greater than the normal or expected loss.
- **Abnormal gain** is the gain resulting when actual loss is less than the normal or expected loss.

2.6 • Normal loss is not given a cost.

• Abnormal loss is given a cost.

• Abnormal gain is given a 'cost', which is debited rather than credited to the process cost account: it is a 'negative' cost and so an item of gain.

2.7 EXAMPLE: NORMAL AND ABNORMAL LOSSES

Using the information in Paragraph 2.2, and the fact that normal output is 95% of input, draw up the process account if actual output is:

(a) 92 litres; and
(b) 98 litres.

2.8 SOLUTION

(a) If actual output is 92 litres, the steps are as follows.

Step 1. *Determine output and losses.*

Normal or expected output is 95 (100 × 95%) litres, and so there is an abnormal loss of 3 litres (95 – 92).

Step 2. *Calculate cost per unit of output, losses and WIP.*

$$\text{Cost per unit} = \text{Costs} \div \text{expected output} = \frac{£85{,}652}{95} = £901.60 \text{ per litre}$$

Step 3. *Calculate total cost of output and losses.*

	£
Cost of actual output (92 litres × £901.60)	82,947.20
Normal loss (given no cost)	0.00
Abnormal loss (3 litres × £901.60)	2,704.80
	85,652.00

Step 4. *Complete accounts.*

PROCESS ACCOUNT

	Units	£		Units	£
Costs	100		Finished goods	92	82,947.20
		85,652	Normal loss	5	0.00
			Abnormal loss	3	2,704.80
	100	85,652		100	85,652.00

ABNORMAL LOSS A/C

	£		£
Process a/c	2704.80	P & L account	2704.80

(b) If actual output is 98 litres, the steps are as follows.

Step 1. *Determine output and losses.*

Normal output is 95 litres, and normal loss is 5 litres and so there is an abnormal gain of (98 – 95) = 3 litres.

Step 2. *Calculate cost per unit of output and losses.*

This will be £901.60 as above. Whether there is abnormal loss or gain does not affect the valuation of units of output since the valuation is based on expected output. The figure of £901.60 is exactly the same no matter what the actual output.

Step 3. *Calculate total cost of output and losses.*

	£
Cost of actual output (98 × £901.60)	88,356.80
Normal loss	0.00
	88,356.80
Abnormal gain (3 litres × £901.60)	(2,704.80)
	85,652.00

Step 4. *Complete accounts.*

PROCESS ACCOUNT

	Units	£		Units	£
Cost	100	85,652.00	Finished goods	98	88,356.80
Abnormal gain	3	2,704.80	Normal loss	5	0.00
	103	88,356.80		103	88,356.80

ABNORMAL GAIN A/C

	£		£
P & L account	2704.8 0	Process a/c	2704.80

Scrap value of loss

2.9 Loss or spoilage may have a scrap value.

- **The scrap value of normal loss is usually deducted from the cost of materials in the process.**
- **The scrap value of abnormal loss (or abnormal gain) is usually set off against its cost, in an abnormal loss (abnormal gain) account.**

2.10 As the question that follows will show, the three steps to remember are these.

Firstly Separate the scrap value of normal loss from the scrap value of abnormal loss or gain.

Secondly In effect, subtract the scrap value of normal loss from the cost of the process, by crediting it to the process account (as a 'value' for normal loss).

Thirdly ***Either*** subtract the value of abnormal loss scrap from the cost of abnormal loss, by crediting the abnormal loss account.

or subtract the cost of the abnormal gain scrap from the value of abnormal gain, by debiting the abnormal gain account.

Question 1

Navigator Ltd has a factory which operates two production processes. Normal spoilage in each process is 10%, and scrapped units out of process 1 sell for 50p per unit whereas scrapped units out of process 2 sell for £3. Output from process 1 is transferred to process 2: output from process 2 is finished output ready for sale.

Relevant information about costs for period 5 are as follows.

	Process 1		*Process 2*	
	Units	£	Units	£
Input materials	2,000	£8,100		
Transferred to process 2	1,750			
Materials from process 1			1,750	
Added materials			1,250	£1,900
Labour and overheads		£10,000		£22,000
Output to finished goods			2,800	

Required

Prepare the following cost accounts.

(a) Process 1
(b) Process 2
(c) Abnormal loss
(d) Abnormal gain
(e) Scrap

Answer

(a) *Process 1*

Step 1. *Determine output and losses*

The normal loss is 10% of 2000 units = 200 units, and the actual loss is (2000 - 1750) = 250 units. This means that there is abnormal loss of 50 units.

Actual output	1,750 units
Abnormal loss	50 units
Expected output (90% of 2,000)	1,800 units

Step 2. *Calculate cost per unit of output and losses*

(i) The total value of scrap is 250 units at 50p per unit = £125. We must split this between the scrap value of normal loss and the scrap value of abnormal loss.

	£
Normal loss	100
Abnormal loss	25
Total scrap (250 units × 50p)	125

(ii) The scrap value of normal loss is first deducted from the materials cost in the process, in order to calculate the output cost per unit and then credited to the process account as a 'value' for normal loss. The cost per unit in process 1 is calculated as follows.

	Total cost		*Cost per expected unit of output*
	£		£
Materials	8,100		
Less normal loss scrap value *	100		
	8,000	(÷ 1,800)	4.44
Labour and overhead	10,000	(÷ 1,800)	5.56
Total	18,000	(÷ 1,800)	10.00

* It is usual to set this scrap value of normal loss against the cost of materials.

Step 3. *Calculate total cost of output and losses*

		£
Output	(1,750 units × £10)	17,500
Normal loss	(200 units × £0.50)	100
Abnormal loss	(50 units × £10)	500
		18,100

Step 4. *Complete accounts*

Now we can put the process 1 account together.

PROCESS 1 ACCOUNT

	Units	£		Units	£
Materials	2,000	8,100	Output to process 2*	1,750	17,500
Labour and overhead		10,000	Normal loss (scrap a/c)	200	100
			Abnormal loss a/c	50	500
	2,000	18,100		2,000	18,100

* At £10 per unit.

(b) *Process 2*

Step 1. *Determine output and losses*

The normal loss is 10% of the units processed = 10% of (1,750 + 1,250) = 300 units. The actual loss is (3,000 - 2,800) = 200 units, so that there is abnormal gain of 100 units. These are *deducted* from actual output in arriving at the number of expected units (normal output) in the period.

Expected units of output

	Units
Actual output	2,800
Abnormal gain	(100)
Expected output (90% of 3,000)	2,700

Step 2. *Calculate cost per unit of output and losses*

(i) The total value of scrap is 200 units at £3 per unit = £600. We must split this between the scrap value of normal loss and the scrap value of abnormal gain. Abnormal gain's scrap value is 'negative'.

		£
Normal loss scrap value	300 units × £3	900
Abnormal gain scrap value	100 units × £3	(300)
Scrap value of actual loss	200 units × £3	600

(ii) The scrap value of normal loss is first deducted from the cost of materials in the process, in order to calculate a cost per unit of output, and then credited to the process account as a 'value' for normal loss. The cost per unit in process 2 is calculated as follows.

	Total cost		*Cost per expected unit of output*
	£		£
Materials:			
Transferred from process 1	17,500		
Added in process 2	1,900		
	19,400		
Less scrap value of normal loss	900		
	18,500	(÷ 2,700)	6.85
Labour and overhead	22,000	(÷ 2,700)	8.15
	40,500	(÷ 2,700)	15.00

Step 3. *Calculate total cost of output and losses*

		£
Output	(2,800 units × £15)	42,000
Normal loss	(300 units × £3)	900
		42,900
Abnormal gain	(100 units × £15)	(1,500)
		41,400

Step 4. *Complete accounts*

PROCESS 2 ACCOUNT

	Units	£		Units	£
From process 1	1,750	17,500	Finished output *	2,800	42,000
Added materials	1,250	1,900			
Labour and overhead		22,000	Normal loss (scrap a/c)	300	900
	3,000	41,400			
Abnormal gain a/c	100*	1,500			
	3,100	42,900		3,100	42,900

* At £15 per unit

(c) and (d)

Abnormal loss and abnormal gain accounts

For each process, one or the other of these accounts will record three items.

(i) The cost/value of the abnormal loss/gain. This is the corresponding entry to the entry in the process account.

(ii) The scrap value of the abnormal loss or gain, to set off against it.

(iii) A balancing figure, which is written to the P&L account as an adjustment to the profit figure.

ABNORMAL LOSS ACCOUNT

	Units	£		£
Process 1	50	500	Scrap a/c (scrap value of abnormal loss)	25
			Profit and Loss a/c (balance)	475
		500		500

ABNORMAL GAIN ACCOUNT

	£		Units	£
Scrap a/c (scrap value of abnormal gain units)	300	Process 2	100	1,500
Profit & Loss a/c (balance)	1,200			
	1,500			1,500

(e) *Scrap account*

This is credited with the cash value of actual units scrapped. The other entries in the account should all be identifiable as corresponding entries to those in the process accounts, and abnormal loss and abnormal gain accounts.

SCRAP ACCOUNT

	£		£
Normal loss:		Cash: sale of	
Process 1 (200 × 50p)	100	process 1 scrap (250 × 50p)	125
Process 2 (300 × £3)	900	Cash: sale of	
Abnormal loss a/c	25	process 2 scrap (200 × £3)	600
		Abnormal gain a/c	300
	1,025		1,025

Losses with a disposal cost

2.11 As well as being able to deal with questions in which scrap or loss units are worthless or have a scrap value, you must also be able to deal with losses which have a disposal cost.

2.12 The **basic calculations required** in such circumstances are as follows.

- Increase the process costs by the cost of disposing of the units of normal loss and use the resulting cost per unit to value good output and abnormal loss/gain.
- The normal loss is given no value in the process account.
- Include the disposal costs of normal loss on the debit side of the process account.
- Include the disposal costs of abnormal loss in the abnormal loss account and hence in the transfer of the cost of abnormal loss to the profit and loss account.

2.13 Suppose that input to a process was 1,000 units at a cost of £4,500. Normal loss is 10% and there are no opening and closing stocks. Actual output was 860 units and loss units had to be disposed of at a cost of £0.90 per unit.

Normal loss = 10% × 1,000 = 100 units

∴ Abnormal loss = 900 – 860 = 40 units

$$\text{Cost per unit} = \frac{£4,500 + (100 \times £0.90)}{900} = £5.10$$

2.14 The relevant accounts would be as follows.

PROCESS ACCOUNT

	Units	£		Units	£
Cost of input	1,000	4,500	Output	860	4,386
Disposal cost of			Normal loss	100	-
normal loss		90	Abnormal loss	40	204
	1,000	4,590		1,000	4,590

ABNORMAL LOSS ACCOUNT

	£		£
Process a/c	204	Profit and loss a/c	240
Disposal cost (40 × £0.90)	36		
	240		240

3 VALUING OPENING AND CLOSING WORK IN PROGRESS 12/94, 6/96

3.1 Suppose that we have the following process account for period 13.

PROCESS ACCOUNT

	Units	£		Units	£
Opening WIP	300	800			
Materials	700	5,400	Finished goods	800	?
Labour and overhead		2,850	Closing WIP	200	?
	1,000	9,050		1,000	9,050

How do we value the finished goods and closing work in process?

3.2 With any form of process costing involving closing WIP, we have to apportion costs between output and closing WIP. To apportion costs 'fairly' we make use of the concept of **equivalent units of production**.

Equivalent units

KEY TERM

Equivalent units are whole units of complete work equivalent to units of incomplete work. They are used in process costing to value opening and closing work in progress.

3.3 Let's suppose that in the example above the degree of completion is as follows.

(a) *Direct materials*. These are added in full at the start of processing, and so any opening WIP or closing WIP have 100% of their direct material content. (This is not always the case. Materials might be added gradually throughout the process, in which case opening stock will only be a certain percentage complete as to material content.)

(b) *Direct labour and production overhead*. These are usually assumed to be incurred at an even rate through the production process, so that when we refer to a unit that is 50% complete, we mean that it is half complete for labour and overhead, although it might be 100% complete for materials.

3.4 Continuing with the example, let us also make the following suppositions.

(a) The opening WIP is 100% complete for materials, and one-third complete for labour and overhead.

(b) The opening WIP's total cost of £800 consists of £550 direct materials and £250 labour and overhead.

(c) The closing WIP is 100% complete for materials and 25% complete for labour and overhead.

3.5 How would we now put a cost to the finished output and the closing WIP?

These 'actual' costs now depend on the stock pricing method used, either FIFO or weighted average cost.

Equivalent units and FIFO

3.6 With **FIFO**, we take the following view.

(a) **Opening WIP is finished first.** It is part-costed at the start of the period (in our example, at £800). We must therefore calculate how much it has cost to complete the units during the current period. The total cost to completion of these units of opening stock is the sum of the following.

(i) Cost brought forward as opening stock value
(ii) Cost in the current period to complete the units

(b) **Some units are started and finished in the period**, and so are 100% produced during the period. In our example, the total finished output in the period is 800 units, of which 300 units were opening stock, finished first, and so 500 units must have been started and finished in the period.

(c) **Some units are started and only part-completed**. These are the units of closing WIP.

3.7 Let's now use our four step approach.

Step 1. *Determine output and losses*

We know what the output is and there are no losses, but we need to calculate equivalent units.

		Equivalent units of work in the current period	
	Total units	*Materials*	*Labour and overhead*
Opening WIP	300	0 (note (a))	200 (note (b))
Units started and finished in the period	500	500 (note (c))	500 (note (c))
Total finished output	800		
Closing WIP	200	200 (note (d))	50 (note (e))
	1,000	700	750

Notes

(a) Opening WIP already 100% complete for materials, so no more cost to add this period

(b) Opening WIP one-third complete at the start of the period, and so two-thirds of work (labour and overhead) needed to complete in this period. Equivalent units = $^2/_3 \times 300 = 200$

(c) Units started and completed in this period are 1 equivalent unit each

(d) Closing WIP: 100% complete for materials

(e) Closing WIP: equivalent units of labour and overhead = 25% of 200 = 50

Step 2. *Calculate cost per unit of output, losses and WIP*

Having worked out the number of equivalent units of work done this period, we can calculate an average cost per equivalent unit.

	Materials	*Labour and overhead*
Costs incurred in the period	£5,400	£2,850
Equivalent units of work done	700	750
Cost per equivalent unit (approx)	£7.715	£3.80

Step 3. *Calculate total cost of output, losses and WIP*

These costs can now be used to build up the total costs of finished output and closing WIP.

	Materials			*Labour and overhead*		*Total cost*
	Units		£	Units	£	£
Opening WIP cost b/f			550		250	800
Cost to complete			-	200 × £3.80	760	760
Total	300		550		1,010	1,560
Other finished units	500	× £7.715	3,857	500 × £3.80	1,900	5,757
Total finished output	800		4,407		2,910	7,317
Closing WIP	200	× £7.715	1,543	50 × £3.80	190	1,733
	1,000		5,950		3,100	9,050

Step 4. *Complete accounts*

PROCESS ACCOUNT

	£		£
Opening WIP	800	Finished goods	7,317
Materials	5,400		
Labour and overhead	2,850	Closing WIP	1,733
	9,050		9,050

Previous process costs

3.8 A common mistake made by students is to forget to include the costs of the previous process as an input cost in a subsequent process when dealing with production that passes through a number of processes (such as in the example in the 'knowledge brought forward' box).

3.9 Note that the **costs of the previous process** (Process 1 in the aforementioned box) are **combined together into a single cost of input in Process 2** and that we always **assume that the transfers into Process 2 are 100% complete with respect to Process 1 costs.** The cost of any additional materials added in Process 2 is treated separately from Process 1 costs.

Equivalent units and weighted average costing

3.10 If weighted average costing is used instead of FIFO, the equivalent units rules are the same, **except that** the **cost of opening WIP is not kept distinct from costs incurred in the current period.** We **add the costs brought forward in opening WIP to the costs incurred in the period,** and **treat all finished output as a full equivalent unit.**

3.11 Returning for a last time to our example, if we used weighted average costing instead of FIFO, our four-step approach would be as follows.

Step 1. *Determine output and losses*

		Equivalent units	
	Total units	*Materials*	*Labour and overhead*
Finished output	800	800	800
Closing WIP	200	200	50
Total	1,000	1,000	850

Step 2. *Calculate cost per unit of output, losses and WIP*

	Materials	*Labour and overhead*
Costs incurred in the period	£5,950*	£3,100**
Equivalent units of work done	1,000	850
Cost per equivalent unit (approx)	£5.95	£3.647

* £(550 + 5,400) **£(250 + 2,850)

Step 3. *Calculate total cost of output, losses and WIP*

	Units	*Materials* £	*Labour and overheads* £	*Total* £
Finished output	800	*4,760	**2,918	7,678
Closing WIP	200	1,190	182	1,372
	1,000	5,950	3,100	9,050

* 800 × £5.95 ** 800 × £3.647

Step 4. *Complete accounts*

PROCESS ACCOUNT

	£		£
Opening WIP	800	Finished output	7,678
Materials	5,400		
Labour and overhead	2,850	Closing WIP	1,372
	9,050		9,050

Which to use - FIFO or weighted average

3.12 **FIFO stock valuation is more common than the weighted average method, and should be used unless an indication is given to the contrary**. You may find that you are presented with limited information about the opening stock, which forces you to use either the FIFO or the weighted average method. The rules are as follows.

(a) If you are **told the degree of completion of each element in opening stock**, but not the value of each cost element, then you must use the **FIFO method**.

(b) If you are not given the degree of completion of each cost element in opening stock, but you are **given the value of each cost element**, then you must use the **weighted average method**.

Equivalent units, normal loss, abnormal loss, abnormal gain

3.13 When there is loss during processing, and so normal loss and abnormal loss/gain, the equivalent units of cost for loss will depend on when during processing the loss occurs. If (as is often the case) we assume that loss occurs at the end of the processing, then:

- a unit of normal loss counts as **no equivalent units;**
- a unit of abnormal loss counts as **one equivalent unit extra;**
- a unit of abnormal gain counts as **minus one equivalent unit.**

3.14 We calculate a cost per equivalent unit in the same way as already shown, and use the cost per equivalent unit to put a total cost to finished output, closing WIP, abnormal loss and abnormal gain.

Losses in process: gradual loss

3.15 When the loss during process occurs continuously the calculation of equivalent units of production is a little more tricky if we want the apportionment of the process costs to be as 'fair' as possible.

3.16 If it is possible physically to distinguish opening work in progress from material input in a period, and to distinguish output from closing work in progress, then these **items can be treated separately in the equivalent units calculations.**

(a) For example, in a continuous process (such as a chemical process) the 20 kg loss may be the result of evaporation, so that work in progress may be of a significantly higher concentration than input (and kept in different tanks).

(b) Alternatively, if work in progress and output have undergone a chemical reaction, leading to weight loss (for example if waste material is skimmed from the surface of a tank) this too distinguishes them from raw materials.

(c) Again, if a large number of small objects (like confectionery) is produced in a process then objects at the end of the process may be more advanced (for example if chocolate has been moulded or shaped) than at the beginning.

Therefore, the fact that loss is continuous does not mean that work in progress at the beginning of a period, and materials input during the period need to be aggregated either physically, or in the calculation of equivalent units.

3.17 EXAMPLE: LOSSES

Suppose that a company manufactures X in a continuous process. Every 120 kgs of input produces 100 kg of output, and loss during the process is gradual.

On 1 March 19X5, there were 5,500 kg of unfinished work in process, which was 50% complete. During March, 16,000 kg of output were finished and transferred to finished goods store. At the end of March, there were 4,240 kg of unfinished work in process, 70% complete. Opening WIP can be separately identified from materials introduced, as it is at a further stage of processing.

The normal loss for each kg of input occurs at the rate of the amount of conversion work done (eg 25% of the normal loss occurs after 25% of the conversion work is done).

There was no abnormal loss during the month.

Required

Calculate the equivalent units of work during the month for both materials and labour and overheads, given that materials are all introduced at the start of processing.

3.18 SOLUTION

The problem here is that if loss occurs gradually, both opening and closing WIP will have suffered some but not all of its loss already, and the calculation of equivalent units ought to take this into consideration in order to be 'fair'.

For every 120 kg input, 100 kg of output is produced, giving a total loss in processing of 20 kg per 120 kg input and per 100 kg output.

(a) Opening stock was 50% complete, and so for every 120 kg input, loss of 10 kg would have already occurred. Opening stock equals:

(i) $\frac{110 \text{ kg}}{120 \text{ kg}}$ of input; and (ii) $\frac{110 \text{ kg}}{100 \text{ kg}}$ of expected output

Expected output from this opening stock is:

$$\frac{100}{110} \times 5{,}500 = 5{,}000 \text{ kg of finished work}$$

(The input for 5,000 kg output is therefore 120/100 × 5,000 = 6,000 kg, but we do not need to know this in this example.)

(b) Total finished work was 16,000 kg, consisting of

	kg
Opening stock finished	5,000
Work started and finished in March (balance)	11,000
	16,000

(c) Closing stock is 70% complete and so for every 120 kg input, 70% of 20 kg = 14 kg of loss should have occurred already. The closing stock therefore represents:

$$\frac{120 - (70\% \text{ of } 20)}{100} = \frac{106}{100} \text{ of expected output.}$$

Expected output from this closing stock will be:

$$\frac{100}{106} \times 4{,}240 \text{ kg} = 4{,}000 \text{ kg of finished work (equivalent units of output)}$$

Check the arithmetic of this: it can be a bit confusing

As for labour and overhead, 50% of the total conversion costs per output kg need to be spent in the period on the opening WIP to complete it, and 70% of the output kg of closing WIP are to be spent during the period. The equivalent units are determined by applying these percentages to the figures calculated above.

Summary: Equivalent units of work in March, expressed in units of finished output.

	Total finished units equivalent	*Equivalent units of work in March* Materials *		*Labour and overhead*
Opening stock finished	5,000	0	(50% × 5,000)	2,500
Other finished work	11,000	11,000		11,000
Closing stock	4,000	4,000	(70% × 4,000)	2,800
Total		15,000		16,300

* Materials are introduced in full at the start of processing.

The cost per equivalent unit could then be calculated. (Remember, **equivalent units are notional units of expected output, calculated for accounting purposes. They are not supposed to represent actual physical quantities.)**

Exam focus point

Do not waste time in the exam. Every second counts! Candidates in the 6/97 exam demonstrated poor use of time by carrying out lots of repetitive calculations.

4 JOINT PRODUCTS AND BY-PRODUCTS 12/94

KEY TERMS

- **Joint products** are two or more products which are output from the same processing operation, but which are indistinguishable from each other (that is, they are the same commonly processed materials) up to their point of separation. Joint products have a substantial sales value (or a substantial sales value after further, separate, processing has been carried out to make them ready for sale).
- A **by-product** is a product which is similarly produced at the same time and from the same common process as the 'main product' or joint products. The distinguishing feature of a by-product is its relatively low sales value in comparison to the large value of the main product.

Knowledge brought forward from Paper 3

- Joint products are not separately identifiable until the **separation point** or **split-off point** is reached.
- Costs incurred before this point are **common** or **joint costs** and must be apportioned in some manner to the various joint products.
- There are four principal methods of apportioning the joint costs.
  - **Physical measurement** (common costs are apportioned on the basis of the proportion that the output of each joint product bears by weight or volume to total output)
  - **Sales value at split-off point** (common costs are apportioned according to each product's ability to produce income)
  - **Sales value where no market value at split-off point** exists (common costs are apportioned according to each product's residual sales value (final sales value less post-separation processing and selling costs))
  - **Weighted average** (common costs are apportioned using units of each joint product multiplied by a weighting factor as the basis)
- By-products are not costed but there are three alternative approaches to dealing with by-product net realisable income (sales value less post-separation costs).
  - Treat as a separate, incidental source of income
  - Deduct from the total cost of sales
  - Deduct from the cost of production (thereby affecting stock valuation)

  The third method is arguably the most 'correct' but the choice of method will be influenced by practicality as well as by conceptual correctness.

Question 2

Three products are produced from a single process. During one period in which the process costs are expected to be £200,000, the following outputs are expected.

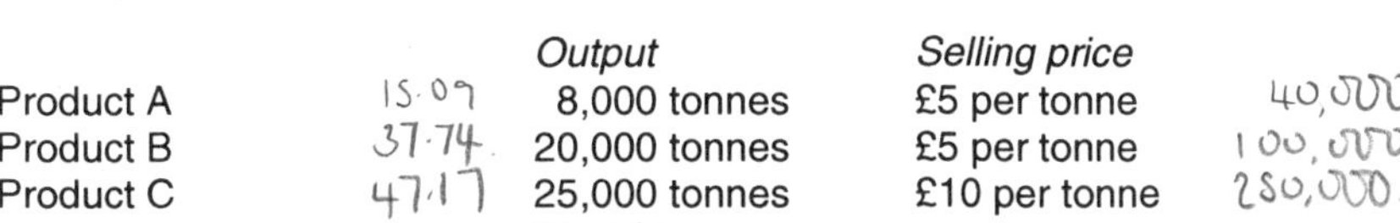

	Output	*Selling price*
Product A	8,000 tonnes	£5 per tonne
Product B	20,000 tonnes	£5 per tonne
Product C	25,000 tonnes	£10 per tonne

Required

(a) Calculate the apportionment of joint costs using the physical measurement method
(b) Calculate the apportionment using the relative sales value apportionment method.
(c) Why might the sales value method be considered fairer of the two?

Answer

(a) *Physical measurement*

Product	*A*	*B*	*C*	*Total*
Output (tonnes)	8,000	20,000	25,000	53,000
Proportion of joint cost allocated	8/53	20/53	25/53	
Joint costs	£30,188	£75,472	£94,340	

(b) *Relative sales value apportionment*

Product	*A*	*B*	*C*	*Total*
Sales value	(8,000 × £5) £40,000	(20,000 × £5) £100,000	(25,000 × £10) £250,000	£390,000
Proportion of joint cost allocated	4/39	10/39	25/39	
Joint costs	£20,513	£51,282	£128,205	

(c) A comparison of the gross profit margins resulting from the application of the two methods would illustrate that the relative sales value apportionment method could be regarded as the 'fairer' of the two, by ensuring that each joint product makes the same gross profit margin after deducting the product's share of the common costs. In contrast, the physical measurement basis of apportionment could result in high gross profits for some joint products and low gross profits - even losses - for others.

Question 3

John Tellymade Ltd has a factory where four products are originated in a common process. During period 4, the costs of the common process were £16,000. Output was as follows.

	Units made	*Units sold*	*Sales value per unit*
Product P1	600		
Product Q1	400		
Product R	500	400	£ 7
Product S	600	450	£10

Products P1 and Q1 are further processed, separately, to make end-products P2 and Q2.

	Units processed	*Units sold*	*Cost of further processing*	*Sales value per unit*
Product P1/P2	600	600	£1,000	(P2) - £10
Product Q1/Q2	400	300	£2,500	(Q2) - £20

Required

Calculate the costs of each joint product and the profit from each in period 4. There were no opening stocks.

Answer

(a)

	P2	*Q2*
	£	£
Sales value of production	6,000	8,000
Less further processing costs	1,000	2,500
Assumed sales value for P1 and Q1	5,000	5,500

(b) *Joint products*

	Sales va.		*Allocation of joint costs*
	£	%	£
P1	5,000	25	4,000
Q1	5,500	27½	4,400
R	3,500	17½	2,800
S	6,000	30	4,800
	20,000	100	16,000

(c) *Profit statement*

	P1/2	*Q1/2*	*R*	*S*	*Total*
	£	£	£	£	£
Joint costs	4,000	4,400	2,800	4,800	16,000
Further processing	1,000	2,500	-	-	3,500
Cost of production	5,000	6,900	2,800	4,800	19,500
Less closing stock	0	1,725	560	1,200	3,485
Cost of sales	5,000	5,175	2,240	3,600	16,015
Sales	6,000	6,000	2,800	4,500	19,300
Profit	1,000	825	560	900	3,285
Profit/sales ratio	17%	14%	20%	20%	

Question 4

Three joint products are made from a common process costing £24,000. Output of JP1 is 2,000 kilograms, JP2 is 5,000 litres and JP3 is 14,000 litres. Weightings of 6, 4 and 2 are given to JP1, JP2 and JP3 respectively.

Required

Determine the costs of each joint product.

Answer

Output	*Product*	*Weighting*	*Weighted output*		*Share of joint costs*
	Units		Units	%	£
JP1	2,000 kg	6	12,000	20	4,800
JP2	5,000 litres	4	20,000	33 1/3	8,000
JP3	14,000 litres	2	28,000	46 2/3	11,200
			60,000	100	24,000

4.1 Note that we will be looking at joint product decisions in Chapter 13.

5 PROCESS COSTING AND COST CONTROL

5.1 Process costing is often just a system for apportioning common costs, in order to find a way of establishing the following.

- How to share costs between closing stocks and finished output
- How to put a cost, if any, to wastage and scrap in process
- How to share common costs between joint products

5.2 The **costs that are established** have no real use except for calculating closing stock values and profit figures for the end products.

(a) The costs are **not helpful for control**, because they do not identify whether resources are being used as efficiently as they could be, nor whether there is overspending.

(b) The costs **do not help with decision making**, in particular deciding whether a product should be sold after one stage of processing, or whether it would be more profitable to process the product one stage further, and sell it in a more complete form. (This is the so-called 'further processing decision' that sometimes occurs with process manufacturing and which we consider in Chapter 13.)

5.3 EXAMPLE: PROCESS COSTING AND COST CONTROL

Suppose that Ruffage Ltd manufactures two products, T42 and 24T. These products are made jointly in process A, and then processed further, separately, with the manufacture of T42 completed in process B and 24T in process C.

Costs and revenues for September 19X1 were as follows:

		£
Process A	Materials (2,000 tonnes)	36,000
	Labour and overhead	24,000
		60,000

		£
Process B	Added materials (500 tonnes)	5,000
	Labour and overhead	20,000
		25,000

		£
Process C	Added materials (1,000 tonnes)	8,000
	Labour and overhead	25,000
		33,000

Output from process A was 1,000 tonnes of part-finished T42 and 1,000 tonnes of part-finished 24T. At this stage in processing the sales value of T42 is £26 per tonne and of 24T is £39 per tonne.

All completed output was sold in the month, as follows.

	Revenue
	£
T42 (1,500 tonnes)	£66,000
24T (2,000 tonnes)	£66,000

Required

(a) Calculate the profitability of each product in the month, assuming that joint costs in process A are apportioned using the following methods.

(i) On a physical units basis

(ii) On the basis of sales value at the point of separation

(b) Comment on what these figures suggest about the following.

(i) Whether either product makes losses and ought not to be manufactured

(ii) Whether either product should be sold partially-finished on output from process A, instead of processed further in process B or C

5.4 SOLUTION

(a) (i) *Units basis of apportionment*

	Product T42	*Product 24T*	*Total*
	£	£	£
Process A costs (apportioned 1:1)	30,000	30,000	60,000
Process B costs	25,000	-	25,000
Process C costs	-	33,000	33,000
Total costs	55,000	63,000	118,000
Revenue	66,000	66,000	132,000
Profit	11,000	3,000	14,000

(ii) *Sales revenue basis of apportionment*

	Product T42	*Product 24T*	*Total*
Sales Value	£	£	£
Process A costs (apportioned 26:39)	24,000	36,000	60,000
Process B costs	25,000	-	25,000
Process C costs	-	33,000	33,000
Total costs	49,000	69,000	118,000
Revenue	66,000	66,000	132,000
Profit	17,000	(3,000)	14,000

(b) *Discussion points.* Product 24T makes a loss when the sales revenue basis of apportionment is used, but not when the units basis of apportionment is used.

The difference between profit and loss is due simply to how the common costs in Process A are shared between the two products.

Although product 24T makes a loss by one method, it would be wrong to conclude that it should not be made at all. If the company continues to make T42, it has got to make 24T as well, at least in process A, since the products are output jointly from a common process. And if product 24T does make some contribution towards covering fixed overheads, it is worth making and selling, if no better alternative exists.

In this situation, there is some choice. Product 24T can either be sold as part-finished output from process A, for £39 per tonne, or processed further in process C. The relevant analysis of this decision would be:

	£
Revenue from process C output	66,000
Revenue obtainable from sale of process A output (1,000 × 39)	39,000
Extra revenue from further processing	27,000
Costs of process C	33,000
Possible loss in process C	(6,000)

Not all of the £33,000 of process C costs might be avoidable. If there are some fixed and unavoidable costs charged to process C, there would be a smaller loss incurred by operating process C instead of selling part-finished product 24T. It might even be profitable to run process C, for example if avoidable costs were only £25,000, say, out of the £33,000 total costs for process C.

Even so, the possibility ought to be drawn to management's attention that it might be more profitable to close down process C and sell product 24T in its part-complete form. Neither method of cost apportionment that we used brings out this information for management's attention, and so both methods of costing are inadequate in this respect.

6 PROCESS COSTING AND OPPORTUNITY COSTING

6.1 The final conclusion from the previous example should lead us on to ask whether it would be more appropriate to use a system of opportunity costing for process costing.

(a) **Opportunity costing would provide more useful control information,** by drawing management's attention to situations where it might be better to sell products at an earlier stage in processing.

(b) In the case of process costing, **opportunity costs would commonly be the sales value** of the materials input to a process.

(c) **Each stage** in processing can be made more directly **accountable for its contribution towards company profits.**

6.2 EXAMPLE: COSTING MATERIALS AT SALES VALUE

In the previous example in Paragraph 5.3, the opportunity cost of the materials transferred from process A to processes B and C would be their sales value at the point of separation after process A - that is, £26 per tonne for product T42 and £39 per tonne for product 24T.

Here are the process accounts, using this method.

PROCESS A

	£		£
Materials	36,000	Output T42: process B	
Labour and overhead	24,000	(1,000 × £26)	26,000
Process A profit		Output 24T: process C	
(P&L account)	5,000	(1,000 × £39)	39,000
	65,000		65,000

PROCESS B

	£		£
Process A: T42	26,000	P&L account	
Added materials	5,000	(T42 costs)	51,000
Labour and overhead	20,000		
	51,000		51,000

PROCESS C

	£		£
Process A: 24T	39,000	P&L account	
Added materials	8,000	(24T costs)	72,000
Labour and overhead	25,000		
	72,000		72,000

PROFIT AND LOSS ACCOUNT

	Process B	*Process C*	*Total*
	£	£	£
Sales revenue	66,000	66,000	132,000
Costs	51,000	72,000	123,000
Profit/(loss)	15,000	(6,000)	9,000
Profit, process A			5,000
Total profit			14,000

Process costing and profit centre accounting

6.3 The important features of opportunity costing in process costing are as follows.

(a) Each **process becomes** a separate **profit centre**. Here, Process A as well as Processes B and C become profit centres. Profit centre accounting is a feature of **responsibility accounting** - ie making managers accountable for operations over which they have control and responsibility.

(b) It is the **process**, rather than the product, that **makes a profit or loss**.

(c) The resulting figures draw management attention to the **possibility** that it might be **more profitable to close down certain processes**. In this example, the possible saving of up to £6,000 from closing down Process C becomes a feature of the reporting system.

Note. With opportunity costing, the 'costs' of each process are not suitable for putting a value to closing stocks, because there will be a profit element in material costs. A stock value adjustment would be necessary to make the accounts suitable for external profit reporting.

6.4 The main weakness of opportunity costing in process costing is the same as for opportunity costing in general - **the difficulty in practice of establishing opportunity costs**. Not all part-finished output has a sales value!

7 PROCESS COSTING IN PRACTICE

7.1 There have been numerous surveys, both in the past and more recently, into the use of process costing. The use of equivalent units and/or the valuation of work in progress, in theory such integral parts of a system of process costing, are, according to surveys, little used in practice. Short production cycles were claimed by a 1970 survey as the reason for no work in progress. With the emphasis in today's AMT environment on shorter production runs to meet customers' specific orders, twenty years on this claim can only be even more relevant. The survey also found that in the food industry, a typical process costing industry, processes were cleaned down at the end of a shift or period for reasons of hygiene, removing the possibility of work in progress.

7.2 In the brewing industry, work in progress in each of the distinct processes between maturation stages is valued at the standard cost up to the end of each distinct stage, in contrast to the highly subjective estimates required under traditional process costing. During distillation, raw spirit is valued at the cost of raw materials. To anticipate profit during the 10 to 20 years of maturity would be incorrect.

7.3 Research in 1992 highlighted the scant use of traditional process costing. Of the manufacturing companies which took part in the survey, 9% were from the food industry and 26% from the chemicals and plastics industry (traditional process costing industries) but none used traditional process costing methodology. Fairly constant levels of inventory were kept by 58% of companies which reinforces the view that traditional process costing should perhaps only be used where there are significant fluctuations in work in progress.

7.4 One possible solution involved establishing accounting check-points when production orders reach objective identifiable stages of completion where costs can be allocated. Critics claimed the emphasis in such a system was on production just to absorb overhead, however. By moving the emphasis to output, however, overhead can only be absorbed when *saleable* output is produced.

7.5 For your examination you must be prepared to deal with process costing techniques but you should also give consideration to the shortcomings and problems associated with its use.

8 SERVICE INDUSTRY COSTING

What are service organisations?

8.1 **Service organisations do not make or sell tangible goods**. Profit-seeking service organisations include accountancy firms, law firms, management consultants, transport companies, banks, insurance companies and hotels. Almost all non-profit-making organisations - hospitals, schools, libraries and so on - are also service organisations.

8.2 **Service costing** (also termed **operating costing**) **differs from the other costing methods** (product costing methods) for a number of reasons.

(a) With many services, the **cost of direct materials** consumed will be **relatively small** compared to the labour, direct expenses and overheads cost. In product costing the direct materials are often a greater proportion of the total cost.

(b) The **output** of most service organisations is **difficult to define** and hence a **unit cost is difficult to calculate**.

(c) The service industry includes such a **wide range of organisations** which provide such different services and have such **different cost structures** that costing will vary considerably from one to another.

8.3 Tom Sheridan, in his article 'Costing in the service sector' (*Management Accounting*, May 1996), expands on these differences between service costing and product costing.

> 'Britain has a powerful service economy but nonetheless costing has only become a talking point in the service sector in the last decade. The service sector is wide-ranging. It not only covers a whole variety of business areas but also includes the head office administrative element of manufacturing companies...
>
> **In theory costing should be easier in the service sector**: there are **no stocks** or work-in-progress to be valued while, secondly, being a Johnny-come-lately in costing, it has been possible to ... **take advantage of the new concepts** ... Not a few new businesses in the service sector have been able to introduce ABC or incorporate ABC concepts, right from the start without going through the trauma and expense of dismantling their previous costing systems.
>
> **But there are disadvantages too**. The products are so **subjective**. **Simultaneity** and **perishability** are also key factors. One cannot build for stock. A lawyer without clients loses billable time for ever, a hotel with rooms unoccupied or an airline with seats unsold cannot recoup the costs after the event...
>
> If management's bottom-line objective is - as it usually is - cost management through cost understanding and traceability, the task is not made any easier because in most service industries one is dealing with intangibles. Everything is **intangible**. You cannot touch the product as you can in manufacturing. So, how do you measure it? How does one define a product or service? How does one cost IT? Everything seems to be an overhead and therefore, try as one will, one cannot get away from that bugbear of the management accountant's life - allocations ...
>
> A key to unravelling the complexities is to **take an ABC approach** ...'

Unit cost measures

8.4 We mentioned above that the output of most service organisations is difficult to define. This is a particular problem with service costing: the difficulty in defining a realistic cost unit that represents a suitable measure of the service provided. Frequently, a **composite cost unit may be deemed more appropriate** if the service is a function of two activity variables. Hotels, for example, may use the 'occupied bed night' as an appropriate unit for cost ascertainment and control.

8.5 Typical cost units used by companies operating in a service industry are shown as follows.

Service	**Cost unit**
Road, rail and air transport services	Passenger/mile or kilometre, ton/mile, tonne/kilometre
Hotels	Occupied bed-night
Education	Full-time student
Hospitals	Patient
Catering establishments	Meal served

8.6 Each organisation will need to ascertain the cost unit most appropriate to its activities. If a number of organisations within an industry use a common cost unit, valuable comparisons can be made between similar establishments. This is particularly applicable to hospitals, educational establishments and local authorities. Unit costs are also useful control measures as we shall see in the examples that follow.

8.7 The following examples will illustrate the principles involved in service industry costing and the further considerations to bear in mind when costing services.

Management accounting in service industries

8.8 The difficulties of costing service businesses set out in Paragraph 8.2 means that attention should be directed on to other measures rather than the traditional 'cost per unit'.

(a) **Competitive performance** should focus on factors such as sales growth and market share.

(b) Like any other business, a service business needs to monitor its **financial performance** and to plan, and its short-term plans can be drawn up for service activities in the form of a budget. (We will be considering budgeting in more detail in Chapters 6 to 8.)

   (i) There might be a budgeted expenditure limit for individual activities within the business.

   (ii) Standard performance measures can be established as targets for efficiency.

(c) **Service quality** is measured principally by qualitative measures, as you might expect, although some quantitative measures are used by some businesses. If it were able to obtain the information, a retailer, for example, might use number of lost customers in a period as an indicator of service quality. Lawyers use the proportion of time spent with clients.

(d) **Flexibility** has three aspects: speed of delivery, response to customer specifications and ability to cope with fluctuations in demand.

   (i) **Speed of delivery** in the sense of punctuality is vital in some service industries like passenger transport: indeed punctuality is currently one of the most widely-publicised performance measures in the UK, because organisations like British Rail and London Underground are making a point of it. Measures include waiting time in queues, as well as late trains.

   (ii) The **ability** of a service organisation **to respond to customers' specifications** is vital in a professional service such as legal advice where assistance must be tailored exactly to the customers' needs.

   (iii) **Coping with demand** is clearly measurable in quantitative terms in a mass service like British Rail which can ascertain the extent of overcrowding. It can also be very closely monitored in service shops: customer queuing time can be measured for example, and this is highly relevant for banks and retailers. Professional services can measure levels of overtime worked: excessive amounts indicate that the current demand is too great for the organisation to cope with in the long term without obtaining extra human resources.

(e) **Resource utilisation** is usually measured in terms of productivity, which is the ratio of inputs to outputs. As usual, the ease with which this may be measured varies according to the service being delivered.

(i) The main resource of a firm of accountants, for example, is the *time* of various grades of staff. The main output of an accountancy firm is chargeable hours.

(ii) In a restaurant it is not nearly so straightforward. Inputs are the ingredients for the meal, the chef's time and expertise, the waiter's time and expertise, the surroundings, the music, the other customers, and the customers' own likes and dislikes. A customer attitude survey might show whether or not a customer enjoyed the food, but it could not ascribe the enjoyment or lack of it to the quality of the ingredients, say, rather than the skill of the chef, the speed of the waiter, or customer idiosyncrasy.

(f) Companies do not have to **innovate** to be successful, but it helps! Others will try to steal their market, and so others' innovations must at least be matched. In a modern environment in which product quality, product differentiation and continuous improvement are the order of the day, a company that can find innovative ways of satisfying customers' needs has an important competitive advantage.

Management accounting and not-for-profit service organisations

8.9 Not-for-profit organisations include private sector organisations like **charities** and **churches** and much of the **public sector**. Commercial organisations generally have market competition and the profit motive to guide the process of managing resources economically, efficiently and effectively. However, non-profit-making organisations **cannot by definition be judged by profitability nor do they generally have to be successful against competition**. Moreover, **outputs can seldom be measured in a way that is generally agreed to be meaningful.**

Universities

8.10 The 'outputs' of universities are not readily measured in accounting or financial terms, and outputs might be measured in terms of the following.

Broader performance measures

- Proportion of total undergraduate population attending the university (by subject)
- Proportion of students graduating and classes of degrees obtained
- Numbers of post-graduate students
- Amount of private sector research funds attracted
- Quality of teaching
- Number of students finding employment after graduation, and types of jobs they go into
- Number of publications/articles produced by teaching staff

Operational performance measures

- Unit costs for each operating 'unit'
- Staff: student ratios; staff workloads
- Class sizes
- Availability of computers; good library stock
- Courses offered

8.11 By **judging how well each university has performed**, perhaps using a point scoring system, it is possible for the University Grants Committee to make decisions about

sharing the allocation of government funds to university education among the individual universities. A **system of budgetary control** can then be applied with **individual budget centres (the universities)** being given the delegated authority for deciding how to carry out its budget plan and for budget spending.

8.12 It is not clear, however, how this system can be extended into motivating individual teachers, for example by rewarding successful teachers more than not-so-successful ones. In an article on management accounting in British universities, G Keenleside (*Management Accounting in the Public Sector*, ed Pendlebury) commented as follows.

> The University Grants Committee system of allocating resources among universities according to performances achieved has helped to **stimulate a competitive environment and to reward good performance.**
>
> However, individual universities have not yet got round to using the same system of rewarding performance for allocating funds between individual departments within the university.

8.13 He concluded, however, that the role of management accounting in the universities will expand in the 1990s. 'The **emphasis on revenue earnings** from research grants and contracts, consultancies, industrial units, technology transfer and contract management **will require a clear definition of direct costs and overhead recovery.**'

8.14 The key findings of Paul Cropper and Professor Colin Drury's recent survey of management accounting practices within UK university management are as follows.

(a) 'The costing method considered the most appropriate for determining the cost of running *degree courses* was identified as the calculation of '**full costs**' (35 per cent of institutions favoured this method). A significant number of institutions (27 per cent) stated that they believed '**activity-based costing**' was the most appropriate method. 'Direct cost plus a fixed percentage overhead' was preferred by only 21 per cent of institutions despite the fact that 56 per cent of respondents said they currently used this method 'often or always'.

These findings indicate that institutions would like to move towards a **more accurate basis for costing their principal activities**.'

(b) '... 100 per cent of higher-education institutions indicating that they operated a system of **budgetary control** ... in cases where the cost estimates submitted by managers were perceived to be excessive, 57 per cent of respondents indicated that budgets were reduced through negotiation. A further 9 per cent said that a reduction was achieved through a combination of negotiation and cuts deemed appropriate by upper management. ... Of the budgetary control methods available, by far the most popular were '**previous year plus inflation**' and '**incremental budgeting**'.'

(c) 'The majority of respondents (73 per cent) do place a strong emphasis on a manager's ability to attain the budget as a major factor in judging performance ... **non-financial measures** are used [to measure performance] and that institutions do attempt to measure student/customer satisfaction and student achievement on a regular basis ... Most respondents placed an emphasis on **measuring and evaluating their performance relative to that of other institutions**.'

('Management Accounting Practices in Universities', *Management Accounting*, February 1996)

Retailing

8.15 The following extract from an article by Rosemary Thorne (finance director of J Sainsbury) in *Accountancy Age* illustrates the information that management accountants need to provide the management of a retailing organisation.

> 'The management accountant's job is to provide management with the knowledge that will best enable them to plan and control the operation of the enterprise. That is why we have developed Sainsbury's general ledger system to manipulate huge amounts of data to provide information that can be used effectively.

Some 200,000 transactions are entered every month, and a similar number of cost centre and account code combinations are used to organise that data.

Sales are the cornerstone of our business. So it is not enough for us to be able to determine our sales on a monthly, weekly, or even daily basis. The opening of a new store or a promotional bull's-eye ... can throw into confusion orders simply based upon the previous day's sales.

Our scanning system enables branch managers to monitor sales on a real-time basis. Sales are budgeted hourly in the case of new stores to enable comparison with expectations. And sales for groups of stores or for product types are analysed.

Our monthly management accounts now go well beyond what we might call "traditional" accounting information. They provide, among other things, **details of our price position compared with our competitors, average queue lengths throughout the chain, and the number of packers available in our stores.**

Sales are the key to success in any business. In ours, there is little that we can do immediately to influence them other than ensure that goods are available for customers to purchase. What we can and do **control** is the **level of wastage and costs** throughout the business.

Cost centre managers are expected to **take personal responsibility for spending in the areas they control. A detailed budgeting process provides a benchmark against which managers are expected to perform.**

Regular **profit forecasts** throughout the year are used to **update management's expectations of the financial result.** They are also used to **revise our plans in the light of the prevailing conditions.**

The management accounting system is also used to **communicate to our more senior management reasons for departing from agreed plans.**'

8.16 EXAMPLE: COSTING AN EDUCATIONAL ESTABLISHMENT

A university offers a range of degree courses. The university organisation structure consists of three faculties each with a number of teaching departments. In addition, there is a university administrative/management function and a central services function.

(a) The following cost information is available for the year ended 30 June 19X3.

(i) *Occupancy costs*
Total £1,500,000

Such costs are apportioned on the basis of area used which is as follows.

	Square metres
Faculties	7,500
Teaching departments	20,000
Administration/management	7,000
Central services	3,000

(ii) *Administrative/management costs*

Direct costs: £1,775,000
Indirect costs: an apportionment of occupancy costs

Direct and indirect costs are charged to degree courses on a percentage basis.

(iii) *Faculty costs*

Direct costs: £700,000
Indirect costs: an apportionment of occupancy costs and central service costs

Direct and indirect costs are charged to teaching departments.

(iv) *Teaching departments*

Direct costs: £5,525,000
Indirect costs: an apportionment of occupancy costs and central service costs plus all faculty costs

Direct and indirect costs are charged to degree courses on a percentage basis.

(v) *Central services*

Direct costs: £1,000,000

Indirect costs: an apportionment of occupancy costs

(b) Direct and indirect costs of central services have, in previous years, been charged to users on a percentage basis. A study has now been completed which has estimated what user areas would have paid external suppliers for the same services on an individual basis. For the year ended 30 June 19X3, the apportionment of the central services cost is to be recalculated in a manner which recognises the cost savings achieved by using the central services facilities instead of using external service companies. This is to be done by apportioning the overall savings to user areas in proportion to their share of the estimated external costs.

The estimated external costs of service provision are as follows.

	£'000
Faculties	240
Teaching departments	800
Degree courses:	
Business studies	32
Mechanical engineering	48
Catering studies	32
All other degrees	448
	1,600

(c) Additional data relating to the degree courses is as follows.

		Degree course	
	Business studies	*Mechanical engineering*	*Catering studies*
Number of graduates	80	50	120
Apportioned costs (as % of totals)			
Teaching departments	3.0%	2.5%	7%
Administration/management	2.5%	5.0%	4%

Central services are to be apportioned as detailed in (a)(v) above.

The total number of undergraduates from the university in the year to 30 June 19X3 was 2,500.

Required

(a) Calculate the average cost per undergraduate for the year ended 30 June 19X3 and discuss the relevance of this information to the university management.

(b) Calculate the average cost per undergraduate for each of the degrees in business studies, mechanical engineering and catering studies, showing all relevant cost analysis.

(c) Suggest reasons for any differences in the average cost per undergraduate from one degree to another, and discuss briefly the usefulness of such information to the university management.

8.17 SOLUTION

(a) The average cost per undergraduate is as follows.

	Total costs for university
	£'000
Occupancy	1,500
Admin/management	1,775
Faculty	700
Teaching departments	5,525
Central services	1,000
	10,500
Number of undergraduates	2,500
Average cost per undergraduate for year ended 30 June 19X3	£4,200

The average cost per undergraduate is not particularly relevant for the university management. It is a figure that can be monitored from year to year. If it become too high then control action needs to be taken to bring costs down.

(b) Average cost per undergraduate for specified course is as follows.

	Business studies	*Mechanical engineering*	*Catering studies*
	£	£	£
Teaching department costs (W1 and using % in question)	241,590	201,325	563.710
Admin/management costs (W1 and using % in question)	51,375	102,750	82,200
Central services (W2)	22,400	33,600	22,400
	315,365	337,675	668,310
Number of undergraduates	80	50	120
Average cost per undergraduate for year ended 30 June 19X3	£3,942	£6,754	£5,569

Workings

1 Cost allocation and apportionment

Cost item	*Basis of apportionment*	*Teaching departments*	*Admin/ management*	*Central services*	*Faculties*
		£'000	£'000	£'000	£'000
Direct costs	allocation	5,525	1,775	1,000	700
Occupancy costs	area used	800	280	120	300
Central services reapportioned	(W2)	560	-	(1,120)	168
Faculty costs reallocated	allocation	1,168	-	-	(1,168)
		8,053	2,055	-	-

2 Apportioning savings to user areas on the basis given in the question gives the same result as apportioning internal costs in proportion to the external costs.

	External costs	*Apportionment of internal central service costs*
	£'000	£'000
Faculties	240	168.0
Teaching	800	560.0
Degree courses:		
Business studies	32	22.4
Mechanical engineering	48	33.6
Catering studies	32	22.4
All other degrees	448	313.6
	1,600	1,120.0

(c) **Possible reasons for the differences in the average cost per undergraduate**

(i) Some of the courses may require lecturers of greater skill, who command higher rates of pay.

(ii) Teaching methods may be different on the various courses. Some may be split into small groups, each needing a separate tutor. Others may be taught by one lecturer in a large group, or two or more lecturers simultaneously.

(iii) Teaching aids in use will vary from course to course. Both mechanical engineering and catering studies require specialist equipment.

(iv) Some courses may take longer to complete than others.

(v) Some courses may feature intensive one-to-one tuition as a matter of routine, whereas others will operate on the basis of seminars or lectures.

(vi) Management and administration charges will vary from course to course. Catering studies is likely to require extensive space for kitchens.

(vii) The students for each course may be drawn from different years. The overall size of each year may be different.

Usefulness of the information

(i) The information on the average cost per graduate from one degree to another is far more useful than that about the average cost per graduate for the year. Although there is little control information to be gained from comparing the average cost per graduate for one degree with that of another, the monitoring of the cost per graduate for each degree course on a year by year basis will prove useful. Such information will allow an assessment of how well the costs relating to particular disciplines are being controlled.

(ii) Consideration should be given to the costs actually included in the analysis. The management should consider whether unavoidable costs (costs which would not be avoided if the degree course ceased) should be incorporated.

(iii) The information may prove more useful if it is used in conjunction with qualitative information such as pass rates and student satisfaction with the course.

Question 5

Gramsci Vans is a distribution business. It operates a fleet of five vans, all of which run on lead free petrol. The practical capacity of the business is 12,000 hours per year, which is equivalent to 180,000 kilometres. However, practical capacity usage is never 100%. For 60% of the time capacity usage is 90%. For the remainder of the time, capacity usage is 50%.

Gramsci Vans employs five fulltime drivers.

Typical costs, on an annual basis, are given below.

Drivers' wages (each)	£3,834 per annum
Drivers' expenses (each)	£3,578 per annum
Depreciation per vehicle	£3,284 per annum
Maintenance per vehicle	£714 per annum
General administration	£17,760 per annum
Licence fee per vehicle	£140 per annum
Insurance per vehicle	£410 per annum
Tyres, per van every 30,000 km	£400 per set
Lead-free petrol	£0.40 per litre
Spares, oil etc per vehicle	£20 per '000 km
Average kilometres per litre	4.0

General administration costs are absorbed into the cost of jobs at 20% of the total costs (other than general administration costs).

Required

(a) Briefly describe cost units that are appropriate to a transport business.

(b) Draw a graph which shows the total cost per kilometre (calculated to three decimal places) as practical capacity usage increases from 50% to 100%. (Plot costs at 9,000 kilometre intervals.)

(c) Calculate the extent of the fixed overhead over- or under-absorbed if jobs are costed in unit costs per kilometre (in £ to three decimal places) at 90% of practical capacity.

(d) For a job that requires one vehicle to drive 100 kilometres, calculate the total and variable costs that would be charged to the job.

Answer

(a) The cost unit is the basic measure of control in an organisation, used to monitor cost and activity levels. The cost unit selected must be measurable and appropriate for the type of cost and activity. Possible cost units which could be suggested are as follows.

Cost per kilometre

(i) Variable cost per kilometre
(ii) Fixed cost per kilometre

This is not particularly useful for control purposes because it will tend to vary with the kilometres run.

(iii) Total cost of each vehicle per kilometre
(iv) Maintenance cost of each vehicle per kilometre

Cost per tonne-kilometre

This can be more useful than a cost per kilometre for control purposes, because it combines the distance travelled and the load carried, both of which affect cost.

Cost per operating hour

Once again, many costs can be related to this cost unit, including the following.

(i) Total cost of each vehicle per operating hour
(ii) Variable costs per operating hour
(iii) Fixed costs per operating hour

(b) Data for graph

Annual fixed costs for five vans

		£
Vehicle depreciation	£3,284 × 5	16,420
Basic maintenance	£714 × 5	3,570
Vehicle licence	£140 × 5	700
Vehicle insurance	£410 × 5	2,050
Tyres	£400 × 5	2,000
Drivers' wages	£3,834 × 5	19,170
Drivers' expenses	£3,578 × 5	17,890
		61,800

Variable costs

		£ per km
Spares/replacement parts	(£20 × 5) ÷ 1,000 km	0.10
Lead free petrol	£0.40 per litre ÷ 4 km per litre	0.10
		0.20

Capacity utilisation %	'000 km	Annual fixed costs £/km	+ £0.20 variable cost = total cost £/km	20% Admin £/km	Total cost £/km
50	90	0.686 (W1)	0.886	0.177 (W2)	1.063
55	99	0.624	0.824	0.165	0.989
60	108	0.572	0.772	0.154	0.926
65	117	0.528	0.728	0.146	0.874
70	126	0.490	0.690	0.138	0.828
75	135	0.458	0.658	0.132	0.790
80	144	0.429	0.629	0.126	0.755
85	153	0.404	0.604	0.121	0.725
90	162	0.381	0.581	0.116	0.697
95	171	0.361	0.561	0.112	0.673
100	180	0.343	0.543	0.109	0.652

Workings

1 $\frac{£61{,}800}{90{,}000\text{km}} = £0.686$

2 £0.886 × 20% = £0.177

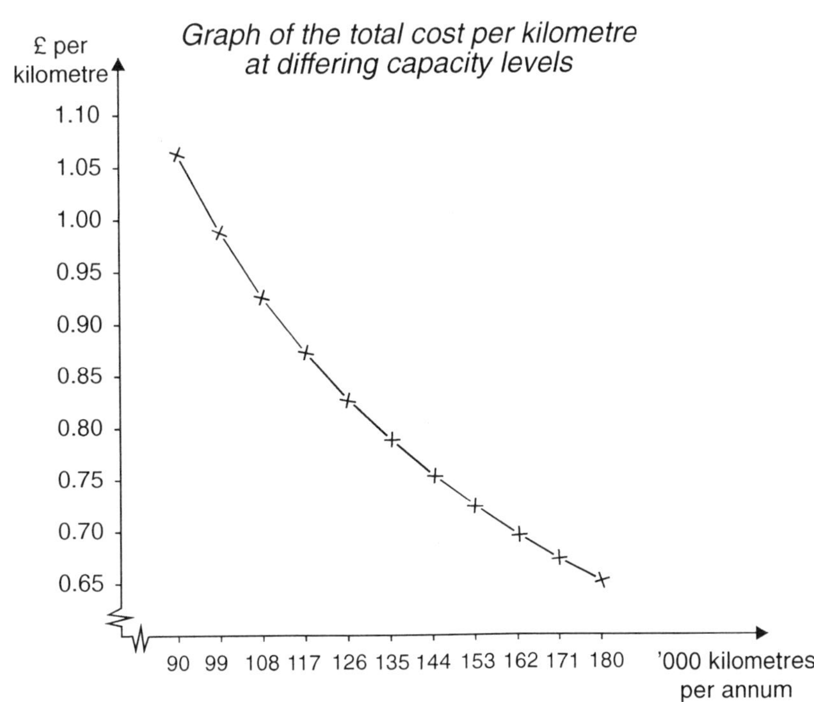

(c)

	£
Operating costs, from (b)	61,800
General administration costs (per question)	17,760
Fixed overhead incurred	79,560

90% × 180,000 km practical capacity = 162,000 kilometres

∴ Fixed overhead absorption rate $= \frac{£79{,}560}{162{,}000} = £0.491$ per kilometre

Fixed overhead absorbed

	£
60% × 162,000 km × 0.491	47,725
40% × 90,000 km × 0.491	17,676
Fixed costs absorbed	65,401
Fixed costs incurred	79,560
∴ Fixed costs under-absorbed	14,159

(d) For fixed overheads, the absorption rate of £0.491 per kilometre would be used.

			Cost charged to job
			£
Variable cost	=	100 km × £0.20	20.00
Fixed cost	=	100 km × £0.491	49.10
			69.10

Charging customers for services

8.18 The procedure for charging customers for services is similar to that which applies in job costing. A **mark up will be added to the cost per unit to give a selling price** which will provide the required level of profit.

8.19 The choice of the cost unit by the organisation is important to ensure that an equitable charge is made to the users of the service. Consider a transport company which has the choice between the following cost units.

- Cost per tonne
- Cost per kilometre
- Cost per tonne kilometre

8.20 The cost unit based on tonne kilometres will be by far the most equitable since it will take account of both the distance travelled and the tonnage carried. Job costs using the other two cost unit measures are likely to vary widely.

9 SERVICE DEPARTMENT COSTING

9.1 Service department costing is used to establish a **specific cost for an 'internal service'** which is a service provided by one department for another, rather than sold externally to customers. Service departments therefore include canteens and data processing departments.

The purposes of service department costing

9.2 Service department costing will be a waste of time unless it has a purpose, and it has two basic purposes.

(a) **To control the costs and efficiency in the service department.**

If we establish a distribution cost per tonne/km, a canteen cost per employee, a maintenance cost per machine hour, job cost per repair, or a mainframe computer operating cost per hour, we can do the following in order to establish control measures.

(i) Compare actual costs against a target or standard.

(ii) Compare actual costs in the current period against actual costs in previous periods.

(b) **To control the costs of the user departments, and prevent the unnecessary use of services.**

If the costs of services are charged to the user departments in such a way that the charges reflect the use actually made by each user department of the service department's services then the following will occur.

(i) The overhead costs of user departments will be established more accurately. Some service department variable costs might be identified as costs which are directly attributable to the user department.

(ii) If the service department's charges for a user department are high, the user department might be encouraged to consider whether it is making an excessively costly and wasteful use of the service department's service.

(iii) The user department might decide that it can obtain a similar service at a lower cost from an external service company and so the service department will have priced itself out of the market. This is clearly not satisfactory from the point of view of the organisation as a whole.

9.3 Service costing also provides a **fairer basis for charging service costs to user departments**, instead of charging service costs as overheads on a broad direct labour hour basis, or similar arbitrary apportionment basis. This is because service **costs are related more directly to use**.

9.4 Two examples may be given.

(a) If repair costs in a factory are costed as jobs with each bit of repair work being given a job number and costed accordingly, repair costs can be charged to the departments on the basis of repair jobs actually undertaken, instead of on a more generalised basis, such as apportionment according to machine hour capacity in each department. Departments with high repair costs could then consider their high incidence of repairs, the age and reliability of their machines, or the skills of the machine operators.

(b) If mainframe computer costs are charged to a user department on the basis of a cost per hour, the user department would make the following assessment.

(i) Whether it was getting good value from its use of the mainframe computer.

(ii) Whether it might be better to hire the service of a computer bureau, or perhaps install a stand-alone microcomputer system in the department.

The bases for charging service costs to user departments 6/96

9.5 The 'cost' of support services charged to user departments could be based on any of the following.

(a) **No charge at all**

If service costs are not charged directly to the user departments, they will be either apportioned on a more arbitrary basis between production departments, in a system of absorption costing or charged against profit as a period charge in a system of marginal costing, without any attempt to recognise that some departments might be using services more than others.

(b) **Total actual cost**

By this method, the total costs of the service department are accumulated over a period of time. No distinction is made between fixed and variable costs in the department. The charge to the user departments will then be:

$$\frac{\text{Total actual cost}}{\text{Total activity (eg hours worked)}} \times \text{work done for user department}$$

For example, a distribution department might charge production departments for road haulage (carriage inwards). If actual distribution costs are £200,000 per month and 400,000 tonne/miles are delivered, the charge to the production departments would be £0.50 per tonne mile.

This method might be suitable if it is difficult to separate fixed and variable costs or if it is difficult to establish standard costs. There are several problems associated with it, however.

(i) If actual service costs are charged to user departments, then user departments will be charged for any overspending and inefficiency in the service departments. The user departments 'suffer' from poor cost control in the service departments.

(ii) If the service department is not working at full capacity, the charge per unit of service would be higher than if the department is more busy. This might discourage user departments from using the service, to avoid high service charges.

(iii) These fluctuating charges which can result from the use of actual costs would make it difficult for the user departments to plan and control costs.

(c) **Standard absorption cost**

By this method, the charge to user departments for support services is based on a standard, predetermined cost for the service. This service cost will consist of variable costs plus a share of fixed costs for the service department.

Standard cost has an advantage over actual cost. Standard cost is based on:

$$\frac{\text{Standard total costs}}{\text{Standard (budgeted) service activity}}$$

The user departments would therefore *not* be penalised for either overspending and inefficiency or under-capacity in the service department. There are, however, two problems with using standard absorption costs for services.

(i) It is necessary to review the standard cost regularly and frequently, so that user departments do not get a false impression of the cost of the service.

(ii) There is a problem in deciding what the standard activity level ought to be.

(d) **Variable cost**

By this method of charging, support services are costed at marginal or variable cost only. This could be either standard or actual variable cost.

The advantage of this method is that user departments are charged for the extra costs incurred by using more of the service, which would help to provide better costing information within a system of marginal costing. There are, however, a number of weaknesses or problems with this system.

(i) The user departments would be under a false impression as to the true full cost of the service that they are using, because they would be charged with just the marginal costs.

(ii) If actual variable costs are used, there would be no control of overspending and inefficiency in the service department because the service department would simply 'pass on' its overspending in higher charges to the user department.

(iii) If standard variable costs are used it will be necessary to revise the standard regularly.

(e) **Opportunity cost**

This method would be appropriate where the service department is working at full capacity and is also providing services outside the company. This means that profit is forgone every time the service department provides a service internally, which should be reflected in an opportunity cost charge. The main problem associated with this method is that it is difficult to establish the opportunity cost.

Establishing service departments as profit centres

9.6 It might be argued that instead of charging user departments just for service department costs, a charge should be made which includes an element of 'profit' on top of the actual cost. The **reasons** for turning a service department into a 'profit centre' by allowing it to earn 'profits' on the work that it does are, broadly, as follows.

- When service cost centres are treated as ordinary cost centres instead of ordinary profit centres there are problems which profit centre accounting would help to overcome.
  - It is **difficult to establish whether the service department is operating efficiently**. If the service department is made an ordinary cost centre with a budgeted fixed expenditure:

    'at times of financial stringency, the output of the service department may be restricted as a way of reducing costs. This may not be desirable if it restricts or downgrades the performance of revenue-producing departments that would be willing to pay for additional amounts of the service' (Kaplan, *Advanced Management Accounting*).
  - If the service department's work is not priced, there will be **no indication as to whether the firm should continue to supply the service internally**, or whether it might be less costly to obtain the service from an external supplier or contractor.
  - In the absence of a pricing system for charging service department time, there is **no easy way to determine the quality of service** that the department should provide. Unless user departments are aware of the cost to them of service department work, there would be 'little opportunity for a user department to communicate its preference on the price-versus-quality dimension'.
- In addition Kaplan argued that charging user departments for the output of service departments would **help in making resource-allocation decisions when service departments resources are in scarce supply.**

  'Prices ... can be set above the actual cost of service departments so as to ration the excess demand to those user departments who most value the service. If enough user groups are willing to pay a high price for a service, the firm can use this clearing price to determine whether it pays to invest in additional (and costly) capacity for the service department.'

Question 6

Identify three different reasons for the charging of service department costs to user departments and comment on the charging methods which may be relevant in the case of maintenance, computer services, and health, safety and welfare service departments.

Answer

Service department costs are charged to user departments for the following reasons.

(a) User departments which use most of the services are made responsible for them.

(b) Service costs are included in production costs, where appropriate. Overheads related to production are included in many stock valuations.

(c) The 'true' cost of each user department is known to management.

(d) User departments are encouraged to use the service (if they are being charged for it) as opposed to external contractors.

Maintenance might be easy to allocate. The machines are in definite locations, and there is a distinct chain of responsibility. Maintenance costs could be charged out in the budget as part of production overhead at a predetermined rate, or in an activity based costing system. This would be for budgetary purposes only. In practice, during the budget period, maintenance jobs could be charged out on an individual basis, directly to user departments.

Computer services cost would be charged on the basis of computer time for normal processing, and any computer projects which are directly attributable to user departments would be charged directly. Some estimate would be needed of any system enhancements required during the year.

The health, safety and welfare department's cost will be allocated to user departments on a basis of employee numbers in the case of nursing care, or floorspace in the case of fire prevention equipment, alarm systems and so forth. Both the number of employees and the floor area might therefore be a means of allocating the cost.

Exam focus point

Candidates frequently fail to pick up marks in the Paper 8 exam because of poor or insufficient explanation, comment and discussion. You must be as competent at producing written answers as you are at producing numerical solutions.

9.7 Not all service departments can be costed using the approach laid out in this chapter. For example, it would be difficult to work out a job cost or service unit cost for the accounting department, personnel department or general administration work at head office. These service costs would be charged as general overheads and then apportioned between user departments on a suitable basis.

Chapter roundup

- This was a long chapter which covered a lot of ground. The majority of the points covered should not, however, have been new to you and your memory should now be fully refreshed.
- Losses may occur in process. If a certain level of loss is expected, this is known as **normal loss**. If losses are greater than expected, the extra loss is **abnormal loss**. If losses are less than expected, the difference is known as **abnormal gain.**
- It is conventional for the **scrap value of normal loss to be deducted from the cost of materials** before a cost per equivalent unit is calculated.
- **Abnormal losses and gains never affect the cost of good units of production**. The scrap value of abnormal losses is not credited to the process account, and abnormal loss and gain units carry the same full cost as a good unit of production.
- When units are partly completed at the end of a period, it is necessary to calculate the **equivalent units of production** in order to determine the cost of a completed unit.
- Stocks in process can be valued using either the **FIFO** method or the **weighted average cost method**.
- **Joint products** are two or more products separated in a process, each of which has a significant value compared to the other. A **by-product** is an incidental product from a process and has an insignificant value compared to the main product.
- The point at which joint and by-products become separately identifiable is known as the **split-off point** or **separation point**. Costs incurred up to this point are called **common costs** or **joint costs**.
- There are four methods of apportioning joint costs, each of which can produce significantly different results. These methods are as follows.
    - **Physical measurement**
    - **Relative sales value apportionment method; sales value at split-off point**
    - **Relative sales value apportionment method; sales value of end product less further processing costs after split-off point**
    - **Weighted average method**
- The most common method of **accounting for by-products** is to deduct the net realisable value of the by-product from the cost of the main products.
- **Service costing** can be used by companies operating in a service industry or by companies wishing to establish the cost of services carried out by some of their departments.
- **Service costing for internal services** adds to the administrative burdens of an organisation because it costs time and money. The benefits of the system should therefore exceed the costs of its operation.
- A problem faced in both service costing situations is the selection of an appropriate cost unit. The unit will often be a two part one, such as the tonne/kilometre. Whatever cost unit is decided upon, the calculation of a **cost per unit** will be the total costs for the period divided by the number of service units in the period.
- Service costing differs from process costing in that it does not operate within rigid rules. You will therefore have to use your common sense in service cost analysis situations.

Quick quiz

1 What are the three steps to remember when accounting for scrap in process costing? (see para 2.10)

2 What is the principal difference between weighted average costing and FIFO for valuing closing stock of equivalent units in process costing? (3.10)

3 Describe the difference between a joint product and a by-product. (key terms)

4 What are the three approaches to accounting for by-products? (Section 4)

5 What are the four methods of accounting for joint processing costs? (Section 4)

6 List three advantages to using a system of opportunity costing for costing processes. (6.1)

7 What other measures apart from 'cost per unit' should be considered when costing service businesses? (8.8)

8 Suggest ten performance measures for universities. (8.10)

9 What are the two basic purposes of service department costing? (9.2)

10 Describe three weaknesses of using variable cost as a method of charging service costs to user departments. (9.5)

Question to try	Level	Marks	Time
4	Examination	20	36 mins

Chapter 5

CONTROL

Chapter topic list		Syllabus reference
1	The need for control over a system	1(b)(ii),(iii)
2	Control systems	1(b)(ii),(iii)
3	The role of the management accountant in control systems	1(b)(ii),(iii)
4	Control in different businesses	1(b)(ii),(iii)
5	The practical application of control theory	1(b)(ii),(iii)
6	Budgeting and responsibility accounting	1(b)(ii),(iii),2(a)

Introduction

Chapters 2, 3 and 4 looked at the ways in which the management accountant accumulates costs so as to arrive at the costs of jobs, contracts, processes and so on.

This chapter serves as an introduction to another role of the management accountant, that of **controller**. The management accountant is deeply involved with two main control systems, **budgetary control** and **standard costing**, which are dealt with in Chapters 6 to 9 and Chapters 10 to 12. This chapter, however, looks at **control in general and cost control in particular**. It explains how control is achieved and looks in detail at control information, which is termed feedback. The role of the management accountant in control systems and the exercise of control in various businesses is also examined as well as the practical application of control theory.

1 THE NEED FOR CONTROL OVER A SYSTEM

Systems

1.1 There is no universally accepted definition of a system, but one which applies to **business systems** is 'a **collection of men, machines and methods organised to accomplish a set of specific functions**' (Davis, *Systems Analysis and Design*).

The need for control

1.2 **A system must be controlled to keep it steady or enable it to change safely** and therefore each system must have its control system. Control is required **because unpredictable disturbances arise and enter the system, so that actual results** (outputs of the system) **deviate from the expected results or goals**. Examples of disturbances in a business system include the following.

- The entry of a powerful new competitor into the market
- An unexpected rise in labour costs
- The failure of a supplier to deliver promised raw materials
- The tendency of employees to stop working in order to chatter or gossip.

A control system must ensure that the business is capable of surviving these disturbances by dealing with them in an appropriate manner.

1.3 To have a control system, there **has to be a plan, standard, budget, rule book** or any other sort of **target** or **guideline** towards which the system as a whole should be aiming. The two main accounting control systems are **budgetary control** and **standard costing**.

2 CONTROL SYSTEMS

Open and closed loop control

KEY TERM

An **open loop control system** is a system where control is exercised regardless of the output produced by the system.

2.1 Since information from within the organisation is not used for control purposes with an **open loop control system, control must be exercised by external intervention**. The output of the system is not coupled to the input for measurement. Mechanical examples of open loop system include automatic light switches and traffic lights.

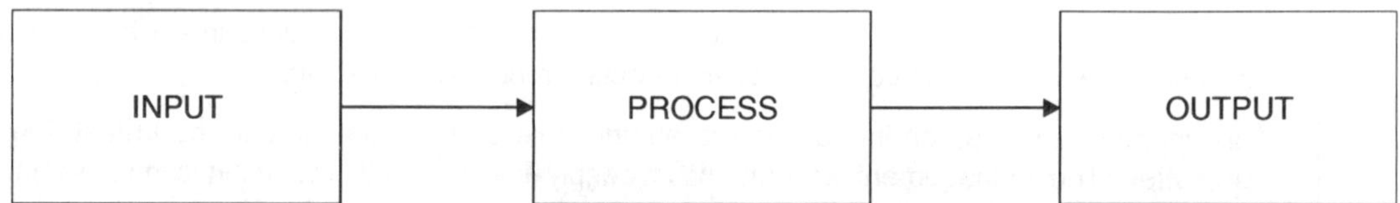

KEY TERM

A **closed loop control system** is a system where part of the output is 'fed back', so that the output can initiate control action to change either the activities of the system or the system's input.

2.2 In a closed loop control system, a feedback system or a **feedback loop** carries output back to be compared with the input.

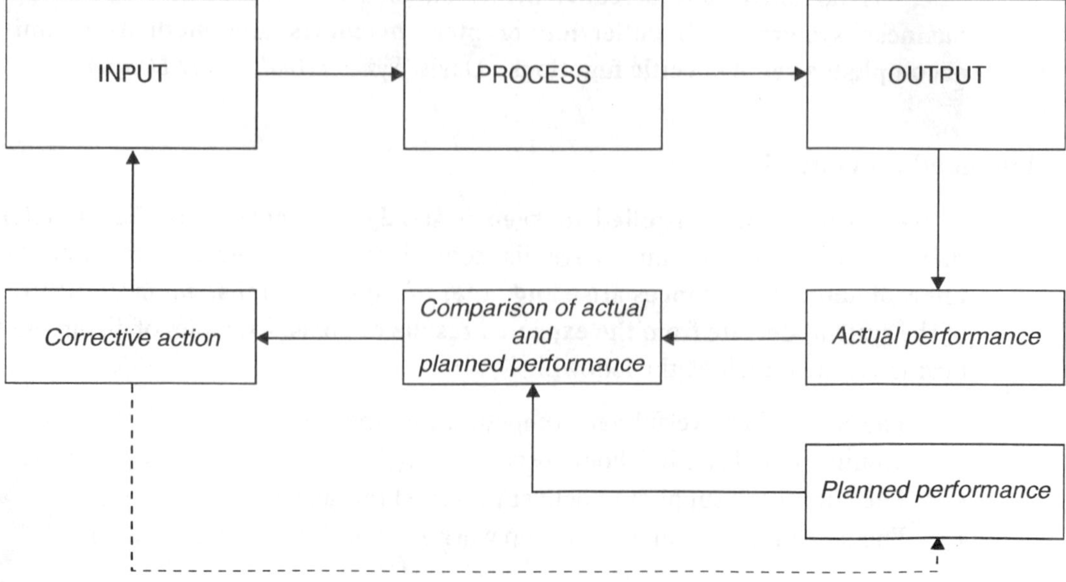

2.3 A **business organisation uses feedback for control**, and therefore has a **closed loop control system**; however, external influences are not ignored. A management information system must be designed to provide proper feedback (information from internal sources) as well as environmental information to optimise the control system.

The control cycle

2.4 Control is achieved through what is known as a control cycle. The elements in the control cycle, illustrated in the diagram, are as follows.

Step 1. **Plans and targets are set for the future**. These could be long-term, medium-term or short-term plans. Examples of plans include budgets, profit targets and standard costs (cost targets).

Step 2. **Plans are put into operation**. As a consequence, materials and labour are used, and other expenses are incurred.

Step 3. **Actual results are recorded and analysed.**

Step 4. **Information about actual results is fed back** to the management concerned, often in the form of accounting reports. This reported information is **feedback**.

Step 5. **The feedback is used by management to compare** actual results (what is being or has been achieved) with the plan or targets (what should be or should have been achieved).

Step 6. By comparing actual and planned results, management can then do one of three things, depending on how they see the situation.

- **They can take control action.** By identifying what has gone wrong, and then finding out why, corrective measures can be taken.
- **They can decide to do nothing.** This could be the decision when actual results are going better than planned, or when poor results were caused by something which is unlikely to happen again in the future.
- **They can alter the plan or target.** This should be the decision when actual results are different from the plan or target, and there is nothing that management can do (or nothing, perhaps, that they want to do) to correct the situation.

Feedback loop in the control cycle

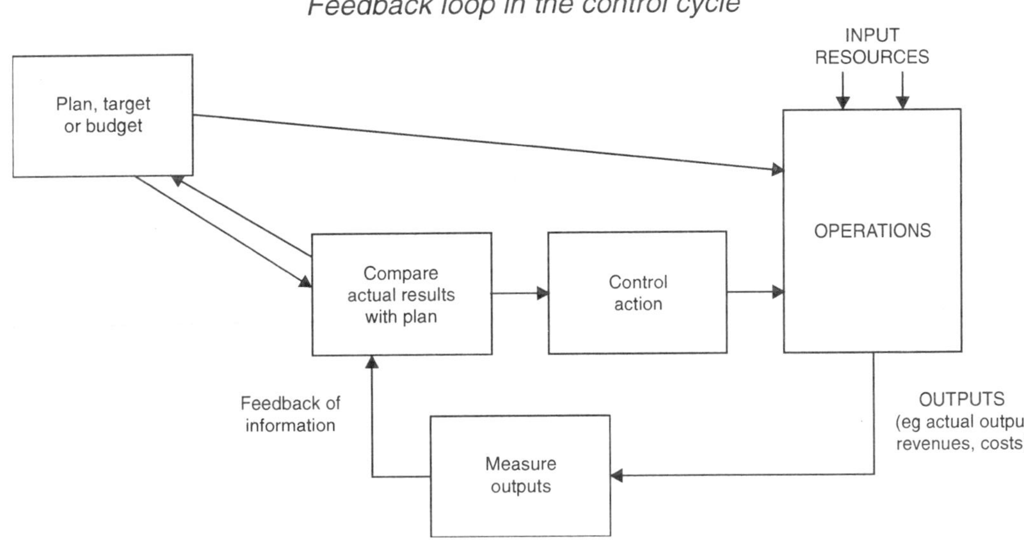

2.5 It may be helpful at this stage to relate the control system to a **practical example, such as monthly sales.**

Step 1. A **sales budget** or plan is prepared for the year.

Step 2. Management **organises the resources** of the business so as to achieve the budget targets.

Step 3. At the end of each month, **actual results** (sales units, revenue and so on) are **reported back to management**. The process of sending reports to the managers responsible provides the feedback loop.

Step 4. Managers **compare actual results against the plan.**

Step 5. Where necessary, they **take corrective action to adjust the workings of the system**, probably by amending the inputs to the system.

- Salesmen might be asked to work longer hours
- More money might be spent on advertising
- Some new price discounts might be decided
- The production department might be asked to increase output of a product in order to reduce delivery periods to customers

Where appropriate the sales plan may be revised, up or down.

2.6 In this example, however, we have **not allowed for several factors**.

- The **influence of the environment** on both plans and system inputs. Environmental influences would include government legislation about safety standards, changing consumer demand, an unexpected rise in raw material prices, or a long strike in a supplier industry.
- **Whether control action is possible**. For example, a sales manager might not be able to do anything to increase sales if the production department can't produce the desired output fast enough.
- **How much information should be measured and compared with planned results.** Not all output is measured, either because it would not have any useful value as information, or because the system does not provide for its measurement. For example, the reasons why customers buy or don't buy from the company might be reported back, but they might not.
- It is also important to bear in mind that the **plan might need to be changed** and a **comparison of actual results against the existing plan might be invalid.** Environmental influences (such as an increase in income tax rates, reducing the spending power of customers) could be responsible for the need to change the sales plan.
- **Not all inputs to the system are controllable**; a rise in raw material prices, or a change in weather conditions which affects sales (such as ice creams or soft drinks) are outside the scope of management control. Other inputs might be controllable, but are **not controlled due to lax or inattentive management** (for example poor labour morale and a high labour turnover amongst sales staff, or difficulties in recruiting staff might be controllable by improving the quality of job content, training or pay).

2.7 It may now be apparent that in the **design of a control system**, factors which should be considered are as follows.

- How much output should be measured, and in what ways should it be reported?
- What is the importance of environmental factors?

- What inputs should be regarded as controllable, and which of these would be worth attempting to control? (*Note.* The cost of one part of a control system might exceed the value of the benefits arising from its implementation).

2.8 To enable the control cycle to function properly, information is essential.

Activity in control cycle	Information required
Make plan	Resources available, value to the company if the plan is successfully carried out compared with alternative plans which could be carried out.
Record the plan	How the plan will fit into the company's operations as a whole, so that other people, departments affected by the plan can be informed.
Carry out the plan	Details of the quantity and quality of resources for the job, specifying time and place.
Comparison of actual against plan	What happens?
Evaluation and control action	Changes which have taken place since the original plan, outside the framework of the plan itself; the goal of the original plan may need to be amended and control action should be adjusted accordingly.

Feedback

KEY TERM

The term **feedback** is used to describe the process of reporting back control information to management and the control information itself.

2.9 In a business organisation, it is information produced from within the organisation (**management control reports**) with **the purpose of helping management and other employees with control decisions.**

2.10 **Single loop feedback,** normally expressed as feedback, is the feedback of relatively small variations between actual and plan in order that corrective action can bring performance in line with planned results. This implies that the existing plans will not change. This type of feedback is **associated with budgetary control** and **standard costing.**

Double loop feedback, also known as **higher level feedback,** ensures that plans, budgets, organisation structures and the control systems themselves are revised to meet changes in conditions.

2.11 Feedback will most often be **negative**: targets were missed and this was *not* what was required. It may, however, be **positive**: targets were missed, but other targets were hit which were better than those we were aiming at. Negative feedback would result in control action to get back onto target. Positive feedback means that the target should be moved.

Control by comparison

2.12 Most control systems make use of a comparison between results of the current period (historical costs) and the planned results. Past events are therefore used as a means of controlling or adjusting future activity.

2.13 Consider, however, a cash budget (which we will be looking at in detail in Chapter 6). This is used to identify likely peaks and troughs in cash balances, and if it seems probable, say, that a higher overdraft facility will be needed later in the year, control action will be taken in advance of the actual need, to make sure that the facility will be available. This is an example of **feedforward control.**

KEY TERM

Feedforward control is control based on comparing original targets or actual results with a forecast of future results.

2.14 The '**information revolution**', which has arisen from computer technology, management information system theory and growing use of quantitative techniques has **widened the scope for the use of this control technique**. Forecasting models can be constructed which enable regular revised forecasts to be prepared about what is now likely to happen in view of changes in key variables (such as sales demand, wage rates and so on).

2.15 If regular forecasts are prepared, managers will have both the current forecast and the original plan to guide their action. The original plan may or may not be achievable in view of the changing circumstances. The current forecast indicates what is expected to happen in view of these circumstances.

2.16 **Control comparisons** which are then possible are as follows.

(a) **Current forecast v plan**. What action must be taken to get back to the plan, given the differences between the current forecast and the plan? Is any control action worthwhile?

(b) If control action is planned, the current forecast will need to be amended to take account of the effects of the control action and a revised forecast prepared.

The next comparison should then be **revised forecast v plan** to determine whether the plan is now expected to be achieved.

(c) A comparison between the **original current forecast and the revised forecast** will show what the expected effect of the control action will be.

(d) At the end of a control period, actual results will be analysed and two comparisons may be made.

- **Actual results v the revised forecast**

  Why did differences between the two occur?

- **Actual results so far in the year v the plan**

  How close are actual results to the plan?

(e) At the same time, a new current forecast should be prepared, and the cycle of comparisons and control action may begin again.

It is in this way that costs are constantly controlled and monitored.

Question

Distinguish 'feedforward' from 'feedback' control, giving two examples of *each* from within management accounting.

Answer

A feedback system operates by comparing actual ('historical') results against a standard or plan, and taking control action where differences between actual and plan have occurred. Events in the past are used to take corrective action for the future. Positive feedback indicates that results were better than planned, and control action is taken to encourage the deviation from what was originally expected. Negative feedback indicates worse results than planned: control action aims to get back to the original plan.

Examples

(a) Variance analysis within a budgetary control system

(b) Profit statements for profit centres; actual profits are compared with target profits for each centre

A *feedforward* system operates by comparing planned results against a current (revised) forecast of what results will be (unless corrective measures are taken). Control action is triggered by differences between *anticipated* and planned results.

Examples [two of]

(a) In budgetary control systems, a revised forecast for the budget period might be produced at regular intervals within the budget period (say, every three months). The revised forecast would be compared with the original budget and significant variances drawn to management's attention.

(b) Project control. Feedforward control can be used within critical path analysis, to monitor and control the anticipated progress of projects to completion, with control action taken when non-critical activities threaten to become critical, or when critical path activities threaten to overrun their scheduled completion date.

(c) Regular cash budgets are used to compare anticipated cash shortages with finance facilities available (eg overdraft limits) so that measures can be taken where necessary to obtain additional finance to meet anticipated needs.

3 THE ROLE OF THE MANAGEMENT ACCOUNTANT IN CONTROL SYSTEMS

3.1 The management accountant's role in an organisation is to **provide information to help with planning and control decisions** by other managers throughout the organisation. Management accounting can provide the basis for much control reporting by doing the following.

- **Recording actual results**
- **Analysing actual results and comparing them with the target, plan or budget**
- **Reporting actual results and the comparisons with plan** to the managers who are responsible for whatever control action might be necessary

3.2 Management accountants are not the only people in an organisation who **provide feedback or feedforward control information**. Within any organisation, there will be many **other feedback loops and feedforward loops** that are **provided by non-accountants.**

- Salespeople or market researchers will provide control information about customers and sales demand.
- Quality controllers will provide control information about product quality.

- Maintenance staff will provide information about the amount of maintenance and repair work, and reasons for breakdowns.
- Research and development staff will provide control information about the progress of product development projects.

3.3 **Such information** tends to be highly **user-specific** and **localised** whereas **management accounting systems** provide feedback on every aspect of an organisation's operations using the common denominator, **money**.

3.4 The diagram below shows the division of responsibilities in a typical system.

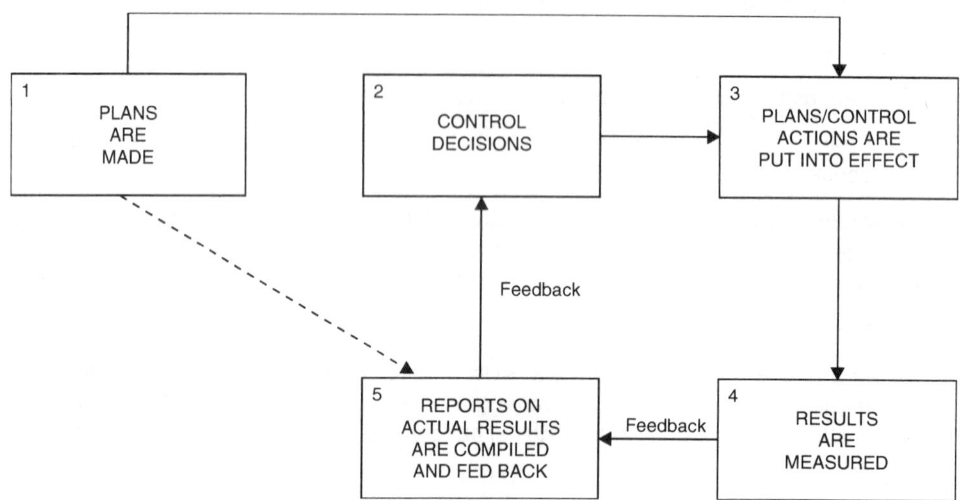

Activities 1, 2, 3, and some of 4 will be done by **line managers and their subordinates.**

Activity 5 and some of 4 will be done by the **management accountant** whose main role is to provide feedback. In budgeting, the management accountant, in the role of budget controller, may be required to coordinate and consolidate the plans of the various departments into a single master budget. The comparison of actual results with plan is a task that is begun by the management accountant (activity 5) but completed by the line manager (activity 2).

3.5 **For as long as budgetary control based on money remains central to the coordination and control of organisations, management accounting information will retain its central place within the overall management information system (MIS).** Financial information will always be extremely important because commercial organisations aim to make profits and even non-profit-making organisations or public sector bodies must break even financially or keep spending within budgeted limits.

3.6 The role of the management accountant and the information he is expected to provide is, however, changing. **Developments in information technology** mean that **almost instant feedback** can, in theory, be obtained **at the touch of a button**. The impact on the traditional management accounting function could be profound.

> 'Departmental and divisional approaches are a thing of the past. Increasingly, successful organisations are those taking a **corporate view of their information needs** and a corporate approach to planning and developing systems to address these needs.
>
> At the same time, **new technologies** - electronic links between companies, electronic data capture, executive information systems - [are] **gradually eliminating the need for account clerks** handling simple clerical transactions, such as processing invoices and usurping the traditional accounting role of providing information.

Taken together, the effect of these new technologies and the **increasing emphasis** on **customer, product and operational performance information**, place a serious question mark over the future of the finance function itself.

This technical environment conspires against the traditional finance function - it eliminates the need for ad-hoc analysis and reporting by accounting staff and effectively it can **cut the finance function out of the loop**.' (*Accountancy Age*, March 1993)

4 CONTROL IN DIFFERENT BUSINESSES

4.1 Cost control as we have described it so far is mainly applicable to manufacturing businesses. We will now look at the suitability of cost control in different businesses.

Service organisations

4.2 The cost control techniques used by manufacturing organisations may not be entirely suitable for service organisations due to the following service organisation characteristics.

Characteristic	Example
Most services are intangible	'... in travelling on a particular airline the customer will be influenced by the comfort of the seat, the meal served, the attitudes and confidence of the cabin staff, the boarding process and so on. This makes managing and controlling the operation complex because it is difficult to establish exactly what an individual customer is buying, is it the journey or the treatment?' (Fitzgerald, Johnston, Silvestro and Steele, 'Management control in service industries', *Management Accounting* (1989))
Service outputs vary from day to day	Services are provided by individuals whose performance can affect the quality of service provided. An example of such a service is that provided by hairdressers.
Production and consumption of many services are inseparable	A plane journey is produced and consumed simultaneously.
Services are perishable and cannot be stored	If an airline seat is unoccupied, the sales opportunity is lost forever and the service is wasted.

4.3 To overcome these differences Fitzgerald *et al* found in their research that the following methods were used for control purposes.

Measure	Example
Satisfaction after the service	Letters of complaint, questionnaires and so on are used by organisations to assess customers' perceptions of quality of service.
During the service	Management may make unannounced visits to ascertain quality levels or dummy customers may be used to report their views.
Tangibles as surrogates for intangibles	Some organisations may use waiting times or conditions of waiting as substitutes for customer satisfaction of service.

4.4 Control measures in service organisations should be **related to the corporate and marketing strategies** of organisations. If quality is a strategy the organisation is following then performance measures should concentrate on quality.

4.5 There is also a greater danger in service organisations of focusing excessively on financial performance measures, which can be easily quantified, thus placing an undue emphasis on maximising short-term performance even if this conflicts with maximising long-term performance. It is therefore more important in service organisations that a range of **non-financial performance indicators** be developed to provide better predictors for the attainment of long-term profitability goals.

4.6 Some service organisations, notably banks, are using **activity-based profitability analysis** to analyse and thus measure profits of different segments of the business.

Not-for-profit organisations

4.7 Control in not-for-profit organisations is particularly difficult because the objectives of the organisation cannot always be expressed in quantitative terms. **Control involves assessing whether objectives have been met.** If a particular objective cannot be expressed in measurable terms it must be stated in some other way so that an assessment of whether the objective has been met can be made.

4.8 Such organisations can therefore **compare planned objectives with actual results** using either the subjective judgement of a person or group of people or using information which is not directly based on human judgement.

4.9 Control in not-for-profit organisations should be **concerned with quantity and quality.** Quantity is usually easier to measure than quality. It is easy to measure the number of graduates from a university but not how well they have been educated. The quantity measure can, however, give some indication of quality. The number of graduates grouped according to degree classification provides an approximate measure of the quality of education.

4.10 Inputs can also provide an indication of quality of output. Amounts spent on education may provide a clue to quality of education if no suitable output measures are available.

4.11 Other techniques that can be used for measuring the performance of both not-for-profit and service organisations include **management audits** and **management by objectives**.

Management audits

KEY TERM

Management audit is an investigation of the entire management control system so as to assist management to do a better job by identifying waste and inefficiency and recommending corrective action.

4.12 **Management audits** investigate the entire management control system and focus on the following aspects of an organisation's performance.

- The **nature** and **functions** of the organisation's managerial systems and procedures
- The **economy** and **efficiency** with which the organisation's services are provided
- The **effectiveness** of the organisation's performance in achieving its objectives

Management by objectives

KEY TERM

Management by objectives is a system of control whereby managers are required to state, as specifically as possible, the objectives that they expect to attain during the year. Actual results are then measured against objectives via a periodic performance appraisal interview and management's progress evaluated.

4.13 The process of management by objectives encourages members of an organisation, by working with each other, to identify appropriate individual objectives, to coordinate their effort towards the achievement of those objectives, and then to evaluate their progress. Management by objectives is therefore particularly appropriate in situations where control by means of formal reports of planned input and output is difficult when outputs cannot easily be measured.

5 THE PRACTICAL APPLICATION OF CONTROL THEORY

5.1 Control theory may sound all well and good in theory, but there are a number of serious problems to overcome in applying theory to practice. The **problems** are as follows.

- **Preparing a standard or plan** in the first place, which is reliable and acceptable to the managers who will be responsible for the achievement of the standard or plan.
- **Measuring actual results** with sufficient accuracy.
- Measuring actual results with **suitable feedback periods**. The reporting cycle time must be kept sufficiently short to give managers a chance to take prompt control action when serious deviations from plan occur.
- **Providing non-accounting** as well as accounting **information** to help with the assessment of plans and results.
- **Identifying the causes of variations** between actual results and the standard or plan, and distinguishing controllable from uncontrollable causes.
- **Drawing the attention of managers to a deviation** between actual results and plan, and persuading them to do something about it.
- **Coordinating** the plans and activities of different departments in the organisation.
- **Informing** everybody who needs to be informed about how results are going.

Reasonableness of the plan

5.2 Feedback information is obtained by comparing actual results against a plan. For the information to have any control value, there must be a reasonable and realistic plan in the first place.

5.3 **Planning is not an easy task.**

- There are a lot of **uncertainties** in forecasting costs and revenues. **Assumptions** might have to be made about sales growth, cost inflation and so on. Planning, although **difficult** to do well, should be done sensibly, and the budget, standard or other plan that is finally adopted should be **realistic** in the context of the organisation's current position and expectations.

- **Different assumptions** can be built into standard costs about the level of efficiency. When control information is reported, the assumptions that are built into the plan or standard should be clearly understood, so that deviations between actual and plan can be judged according to the degree of 'difficulty of attainment' that is in the plan.

5.4 Unless a plan is realistic, managers will not rely on the control information that is produced. It is often hard to persuade managers to use control information that is produced by a management accounting system, and getting them to have trust in the budget or plan is an essential prerequisite to solving the 'behavioural' problem. We will look at this point in more detail later in the Study Text when we consider the behavioural implications of budgeting.

Controllability of events

5.5 When actual results deviate from the budget or plan, the deviation might be one of the following.

(a) Likely to carry on into the future, unless corrective action is taken

(b) Likely to carry on into the future, and not stoppable by any corrective action

(c) A one-off deviation that will not recur again, and which will disappear in the future without anything having to be done about it

Item **(a)** would be a **controllable** event. Items **(b) and (c)** would be **uncontrollable**.

5.6 If a **controllable event** occurs then **control action should be taken**, either to get rid of an adverse deviation between actual results and the plan, or to exploit a favourable deviation.

If an **uncontrollable event** occurs which is likely to carry on into the future, or which has already had a major effect on results, the action that probably ought to be taken is to **alter the plan**, for example by updating the budget or revising the standard. This would mean that a **realistic plan** would be available against which actual performance could be measured. Unless the plan is realistic, remember, measures of performance such as variances would be unrealistic and unhelpful as control information.

Controllability and apportioned costs

5.7 A guiding principle from control theory is that **managers should only be held accountable in control reports for costs over which they have some influence or control.** This may seem quite straightforward in theory, but it is not always so easy in practice to **distinguish controllable from uncontrollable costs. Apportioned overhead costs provide a good example.**

5.8 Suppose that a manager of a production department in a manufacturing company is made responsible for the costs of his department. These costs include directly attributable overhead items such as the costs of indirect labour employed in the department, the cost of metered power units consumed and indirect materials consumed in the department, depreciation costs of items of equipment in the department, and so on. The department's overhead costs also include an apportionment of costs from other cost centres, such as the following.

- Rent and rates for the building which the department shares with other departments

- A share of the costs of the central production planning department
- A share of the costs of the repairs department
- A share of the costs of the central data processing (DP) department

Should the production manager be held accountable for any of these apportioned costs?

5.9 The answer to this question for control purposes is as follows.

(a) **Managers should not be held accountable for costs over which they have no control**. In this example, apportioned rent and rates costs would not be controllable by the production department manager.

(b) **Managers should be held accountable for costs over which they have some influence**. In this example, it is the responsibility of the repairs department manager to keep repair costs within budget and of the DP manager to keep central DP costs within budget. But their costs will be partly variable and partly fixed, and the variable cost element will depend on the volume of demand for their services. If the production department's staff treated their equipment badly, we might expect higher repair costs - and the production department manager should therefore be made accountable for the repair costs that his department makes the repairs department incur on his behalf.

When costs vary with usage, the user as well as the provider of the service should be made accountable. The user's responsibility would be for the amount of usage of the service.

Controllability and dual responsibility

5.10 Quite often a particular cost might be the **responsibility of two or more managers**. For example, raw materials costs might be the responsibility of the purchasing manger (prices) and the production manager (usage). A **reporting system must allocate responsibility appropriately**. The purchasing manager must be responsible for any increase in raw materials prices whereas the production manager should be responsible for any increase in raw materials usage.

Control delay

5.11 As we know, **control delay** could be the **fault of the manager responsible for taking control action**, but it could **also be caused by a failure to inform the manager who should be directly responsible for putting it right**. Feedback might be reported to a manager in a different department, or a man more senior in the organisation's hierarchy. The management accounting system should therefore be built on the principle of **responsibility accounting**, with individual managers held accountable for the costs, revenues, assets or liabilities over which they have some control.

Control reporting

5.12 Some feedback is **continuous**: automated equipment continuously reports back information about what the equipment is doing to its control processor, and office supervisors or factory foremen will keep a more-or-less continual eye on what their staff are doing. Management accounting reports are largely **periodic**, and produced at regular intervals, typically every four weeks or one month, with an overall annual review at the end of each year. However, some management accounting control reports might be '**ad**

hoc' and irregular, for example reports commissioned by the board of directors or the finance director.

5.13 Feedback periods ought to be planned, especially for routine control reporting.

(a) It is important to **avoid excessive reporting**. There is no point in producing control reports weekly if it takes several days to find out the cause of a variance and put it right. There has to be a reasonable interval between control reports so that managers can make a reasonable judgement about the effects of their past control actions. If reports are too frequent, they might well be thrown into the wastepaper basket unread.

(b) It is also important to **avoid unnecessary delays** in control reporting, by making the feedback period too long, or by taking too much time to put a feedback report together.

The most suitable frequency of routine control reporting will vary from operation to operation.

5.14 Control reports should be **clear** and **understandable** to the person receiving them. **Highlighting key results** and **exception reporting** are ways of improving clarity. Several reports will be prepared, all relating in some way to the same actual results. This is because reports will go to managers at different levels in the chain of command.

Designing a control report

5.15 The **format of a control report** should take into account the following.

- What results the report is measuring.
- What amount of detail is required. Lower grades of manager tend to need more detailed information about narrower areas of information.
- What the most suitable measures of performance would be. Ratios are a possibility. Profits and total costs are others.
- What the frequency of the report would be.
- Whether exception reporting would be suitable.
- Whether a report to a more senior manager should inform him of significantly adverse or favourable results in the control reports sent to individual subordinates. (This would tell the manager that the subordinate concerned should be asked to explain to his superior the cause of the variance, and the control action that has been taken).
- Whether some **non-financial information** as well as financial information might help to clarify the report. Accounting figures on their own might not give a complete picture of results, and examples of non-financial information than might give more meaning to costs and revenues include units produced, percentage rejected, units sold, number of transactions processed, number of visits by salesmen to customers, miles travelled, ton/miles of delivery, average miles per gallon, and so on.

5.16 Control reports should have the following features.

Feature	Comment
Relevance	The report must be relevant to the particular budget holder. He/she should not have to search through reams of paper in an attempt to find the information relevant to his/her particular budget centre. Control reports are often based on the principle of 'exception reporting' whereby only those results which differ *significantly* from budget are reported. The segregation of the variances into those that are controllable by the budget holder and those that are uncontrollable is also useful.
Accuracy	The information contained in a budgetary control report should obviously be accurate because using incorrect information could have serious and damaging consequences. However information should aim to be accurate enough for its purpose and there is no need to go into unnecessary detail for pointless accuracy, especially if this puts the speedy delivery of the report at risk.
Timeliness	A budgetary control report should be passed to the budget holder as soon as possible after the end of the control period so that immediate corrective action can be taken.
Communicated to the right person	Budget holders' responsibilities should be clearly defined so that control reports are sent to the appropriate person. If information is communicated to the wrong person its value will be lost and adverse variance trends could continue.

6 BUDGETING AND RESPONSIBILITY ACCOUNTING

6.1 In order to prepare a budget for an organisation as a whole, individual budgets have to be prepared for sub-sections of the organisation, such as individual subsidiaries within the group and individual departments, products or activities within each subsidiary.

KEY TERM

Each section of an organisation for which a budget is prepared is a **budget centre**.

Since budgets will be made for each of these budget centres, control reporting (the comparison of actual results against plan) will also be based on budget centres.

6.2 The selection of budget centres in an organisation is therefore a key first step in setting up a control system. What should the budget centres be? What income, expenditure and/or capital employment plans should each budget centre prepare? And how will measures of performance for each budget centre be made?

6.3 A well-organised system of control should have the following features.

- **A hierarchy of budget centres**, if the organisation is quite large. Subsidiary companies within a group should be budget centres, departments within each subsidiary might be budget centres and work sections within each department might be budget centres too. The budgets of each section would then be consolidated into a departmental budget, departmental budgets in turn would be consolidated into a budget for the subsidiary, and the budgets of each subsidiary would be combined into a master budget for the group as a whole.

- **Clearly identified responsibilities for the achievement of budget targets.** Individual managers should be made responsible for achieving the budget targets of a particular budget centre.

KEY TERM

A **responsibility centre** is a unit of an organisation headed by a manager who has direct responsibility for its performance.

- Responsibility centres should also be budget centres. **Responsibilities for revenues, costs and capital employed.** Budget centres and responsibility centres should be organised so that all the revenues earned by an organisation, all the costs it incurs, and all the capital it employs are made the responsibility of someone within the organisation, at an appropriate level of authority in the management hierarchy.

KEY TERM

Responsibility accounting is a system of accounting that segregates revenue and costs into areas of personal responsibility in order to monitor and assess the performance of each part of an organisation.

Budget centres might be a mixture of cost centres, revenue centres, profit centres and investment centres.

Exam focus point

In 6/94 the examiner commented that there were two common reasons why candidates performed badly on this paper. The reasons are as follows.

- Insufficient preparation for the examination
- Inability to read and answer the question set

Similar comments have been made since this examination. Bear this in mind as you read through this text.

Chapter roundup

- Control is achieved through a **control cycle. Actual performance** is compared with **planned performance** and the appropriate action is taken for those items that are not proceeding according to plan.
- **Feedback** is both the process of reporting back control information to management and the control information itself.
- Feedback can be **positive** or **negative** and **single loop** or **double loop**.
- **Feedforward control** is control based on comparing original targets or actual results with a forecast of future results.
- For as long as budgetary control based on money remains central to the coordination and control of organisations, management accounting information will retain its central place within the overall MIS.
- The **control of not-for-profit organisations** and **service organisations** differs from that of manufacturing businesses.
- There are a number of serious problems to overcome in **applying control theory in practice,** including preparing a reliable and acceptable plan, distinguishing controllable from uncontrollable causes of variation between actual and planned results and coordinating plans and activities of different departments.
- Control reports should be relevant, accurate, timely and communicated to the right person.
- The selection of **budget centres** in an organisation is a key first step in setting up a control system. A system of **responsibility accounting** must be established.

Quick quiz

1. What is a closed loop control system? (see key terms)
2. What is single loop feedback? (2.10)
3. Distinguish between positive and negative feedback. (2.11)
4. What is feedforward control? (2.13)
5. List six control comparisons that are possible using forecasting models. (2.16)
6. What is a management audit? (key terms)
7. List eight problems of applying control theory in practice. (5.1)
8. What are the three features of a well-organised system of control? (6.3)

Question to try	Level	Marks	Time
5	Examination	5	9 mins

Part B
Budgeting

Chapter 6

BUDGETS

Chapter topic list		Syllabus reference
1	The budgeting process in context	2(a)
2	The functions of a budget	2(a)(i)
3	Administration of the budget	2(a)(iii)
4	The budget preparation timetable	2(a)(iii)
5	Functional budgets	2(a)(iii)
6	Cash budgets	2(a)(iii)
7	Budgeted profit and loss account and balance sheet	2(a)(iii)
8	The master budget	2(a)(iii)
9	Capital expenditure budgets	2(a)(iii)

Introduction

In Chapter 5 we looked at control in general. In this chapter we are going to begin our study of a particular control system, **the budgetary control system.** This is a topic which you will meet at all stages of your examination studies and so it is vital that you get a firm grasp of the basics now.

The chapter begins by showing how budgeting fits into the overall organisation plan and then goes on to explain the functions of a budget and provides an overview of the budget process. The process is then broken down and the individual stages looked at in detail. We will see how the **sales budget** and the **production and related budgets** (the functional budgets) are prepared, as well as the **cash budget.** The culmination of the budget process is the **master budget**, which comprises the **budgeted profit and loss account**, **budgeted balance sheet and the cash budget**. You will have the opportunity to see how a master budget is prepared in Section 7 of the chapter.

Chapter 7 builds on the general awareness of budgeting which you will have gained in this chapter and considers the control function of budgets.

1 THE BUDGETING PROCESS IN CONTEXT

1.1 The diagram below represents the planning and control cycle. The first five steps cover the planning process. **Planning** involves making choices between alternatives and is primarily a decision-making activity. The last two steps cover the **control** process, which we looked at in the previous chapter.

The planning and control cycle

Planning process	Identify objectives	Step 1
	Identify alternative courses of action (strategies) which might contribute towards achieving the objectives	Step 2
	Evaluate each strategy	Step 3
	Choose alternative courses of action	Step 4
	Implement the long-term plan in the form of the annual budget	Step 5
Control process	Measure actual results and compare with the plan	Step 6
	Respond to divergences from plan	Step 7

Step 1. **Identify objectives**

Objectives establish the direction in which the management of the organisation wish it to be heading. Typical objectives include the following.

- To maximise profits
- To increase market share
- To produce a better quality product than anyone else

Objectives answer the question: '**where do we want to be?**'.

Step 2. **Identify potential strategies**

Once an organisation has decided 'where it wants to be', the next step is to identify a range of possible courses of action or **strategies that might enable the organisation to get there.**

The organisation must therefore carry out an **information-gathering exercise** to ensure that it has a full **understanding of where it is now.** This is known as a '**position audit**' or '**strategic analysis**' and involves **looking** both **inwards** and **outwards.**

- The organisation must **gather information from all of its internal parts** to find out what resources it possesses: what its manufacturing capacity and capability is, what is the state of its technical know-how, how well it is able to market itself, how much cash it has in the bank, how much it could borrow and so on.
- It must also **gather information externally** so that it can assess its position in the environment. Just as it has assessed its **own strengths and weaknesses**, it must do likewise for its competitors (**threats**). Its market must be analysed (and any other markets that it is intending to enter) to identify possible new **opportunities**. The 'state of the world' must be considered. Is it in recession or is it booming? What is likely to happen in the future?

Having carried out a strategic analysis, alternative strategies can be identified.

An organisation might decide to aim a product or service at a particular buyer group or to be the lowest cost producer in the industry, perhaps by withdrawing from some markets or developing new products for sale in existing markets. This may involve, for example, internal development or some kind of joint venture.

Step 3. **Evaluate strategies**

The strategies must then be evaluated **in terms of suitability, feasibility and acceptability in the context of the strategic analysis**. Management should select those strategies that have the greatest potential for achieving the organisation's objectives. One strategy may be chosen or several.

Step 4. **Choose alternative courses of action**

The next step in the process is to collect the **chosen strategies** together and **co-ordinate them into a long-term plan**, commonly expressed in financial terms.

Typically a long-term financial plan would show the following.

- Projected cash flows
- Projected long-term profits
- Capital expenditure plans
- Balance sheet forecasts
- A description of the long-term objectives and strategies in words

Step 5. **Implement the long-term plan**

The **long-term plan** should then be **broken down into smaller parts**. It is unlikely that the different parts will fall conveniently into successive time periods. Strategy A may take two and a half years, while Strategy B may take five months, but not start until year three of the plan. It is usual, however, to break down the plan as a whole into equal time periods (usually one year). The resulting **short-term plan** is called a **budget**.

2 THE FUNCTIONS OF A BUDGET 6/97

KEY TERM

A **budget** is an organisation's plan for a forthcoming period, expressed in money terms.

2.1 There is, however, little point in an organisation simply preparing a budget for the sake of preparing a budget. A beautifully laid out budgeted profit and loss account filed in the management accountant's file and never looked at again is worthless. The organisation should gain from both the actual preparation process and from the budget once it has been prepared.

2.2 Budgets are therefore not prepared in isolation and then filed away; they actually have a number of very important functions in an organisation.

Function	Detail
Ensure the achievement of the organisation's objectives	Quantified expressions of objectives are drawn up as targets to be achieved within the timescale of the budget plan.
Compel planning	Probably the most important function of a budget. Planning forces management to look ahead, to set out detailed plans for achieving the targets for each department, operation and (ideally) each manager and to anticipate problems.
Communicate ideas and plans	A formal system is necessary to ensure that each person affected by the plans is aware of what he or she is supposed to be doing. Communication might be one-way, with managers giving orders to subordinates, or there might be a two-way dialogue.
Coordinate activities	The activities of different departments need to be coordinated to ensure maximum integration of effort towards common goals. This implies, for example, that the purchasing department should base its budget on production requirements and that the production budget should in turn be based on sales expectations. Coordination is remarkably difficult to achieve, however.
Provide a framework for responsibility accounting	Budgets require that managers of budget centres are made responsible for the achievement of budget targets for the operations under their personal control.
Establish a system of control	Control over actual performance is provided by the comparisons of actual results against the budget plan. Departures from budget can then be investigated and the reasons for the departures can be divided into controllable and uncontrollable factors.
Motivate employees to improve their performance	The interest and commitment of employees can be retained if there is a system which lets them know how well or badly they are performing. The identification of controllable reasons for departures from budget with managers responsible provides an incentive for improving future performance.

2.3 Despite the simple definition of a budget offered at the beginning this section, its preparation and subsequent use have far reaching implications for the organisation concerned.

Exam focus point

There were twelve marks available in the 6/97 exam for demonstrating an understanding of three of the objectives of budgeting in particular circumstances.

The benefits of budgeting

2.4 Provided that the budgeting system is carefully planned, controlled and coordinated, the objectives set out above should be realised and translated into benefits (although, of course, these benefits will not appear overnight).

3 ADMINISTRATION OF THE BUDGET

3.1 Having seen why organisations prepare budgets, we will now turn our attention to the administrative procedures that ensure that the budget process works effectively.

The budget period

KEY TERM

The **budget period** is the time period to which the budget relates.

3.2 Except for capital expenditure budgets, the budget period is commonly the accounting year (sub-divided into 12 or 13 control periods).

Budget documentation: the budget manual

KEY TERM

The **budget manual** is a collection of instructions governing the responsibilities of persons and the procedures, forms and records relating to the preparation and use of budgetary data.

3.3 As one of the functions of the budget is to improve communication, a manual should be produced so that everyone can refer to it for information and guidance about the budgeting process. The budget manual does *not* contain the actual budgets for the forthcoming period; it is more of an **instruction/information manual about the way budgeting operates** in a particular organisation.

3.4 A budget manual will usually be prepared by the management accountant and although its contents will vary from organisation to organisation, it may contain the following.

Content	Detail
Explanation of the objectives of the budgeting process	• The purpose of budgetary planning and control • The objectives of the various stages of the budgeting process • The importance of budgets in the long-term planning and administration of the enterprise
Organisational structures	• An organisation chart • A list of individuals holding budget responsibilities
Outline of the principal budgets	• Relationship between them.
Administrative details	• Membership, and terms of reference, of the budget committee • The sequence in which budgets are to be prepared • A timetable

Content	Detail
Procedural matters	• Specimen forms and instructions for completing them • Specimen reports • Account codes (or a chart of accounts) • The name of the budget officer to whom enquiries must be sent

Responsibility for the preparation of budgets

3.5 **Managers responsible for preparing budgets should ideally be the managers** (and their subordinates) **who are responsible for carrying out the budget**. For example, the sales manager should draft the sales budget and selling overhead cost centre budget and the purchasing manager should draft the material purchases budget.

Budget committee

3.6 The **coordination** and **administration of budgets** is usually the **responsibility of a budget committee** (with the managing director as chairman). The budget committee is **assisted by a budget officer** who is usually an accountant. Every part of the organisation should be represented on the committee, so there should be a **representative from sales, production, marketing** and so on. Functions of the budget committee include the following.

- Coordination of the preparation of budgets, which includes the issue of the budget manual
- Issuing of timetables for the preparation of functional budgets
- Allocation of responsibilities for the preparation of functional budgets
- Provision of information to assist in the preparation of budgets
- Communication of final budgets to the appropriate managers
- Comparison of actual results with budget and the investigation of variances
- Continuous assessment of the budgeting and planning process, in order to improve the planning and control function

4 THE BUDGET PREPARATION TIMETABLE 12/94, 6/97

4.1 Let us now look at the steps involved in the preparation of a budget. The procedures will differ from organisation to organisation, but the step-by-step approach described here is indicative of the steps followed by many organisations. The preparation of a budget may take weeks or months and the budget committee may meet several times before an organisation's budget is finally agreed.

Step 1. **Communicating details of the budget policy and budget guidelines**

The long-term plan is the starting point for the preparation of the annual budget. Managers responsible for preparing the budget must be aware of the way it is affected by the long-term plan so that it becomes part of the process of meeting the organisation's objectives. For example, if the long-term plan calls for a more aggressive pricing policy, the budget must take this into account. Managers should also be provided with important guidelines for wage rate increases, changes in productivity and so on, as well as information about industry demand and output.

Step 2. **Determining the factor that restricts output**

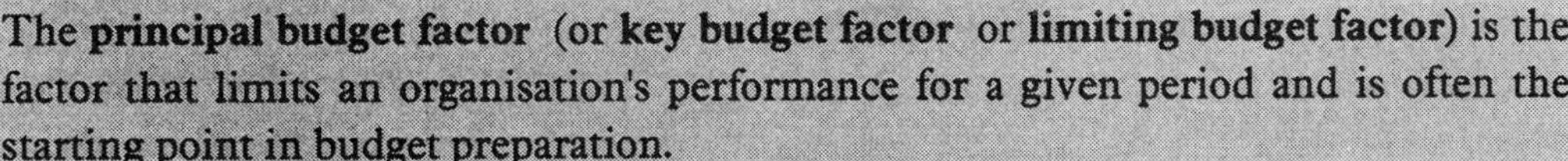

KEY TERM

The **principal budget factor** (or **key budget factor** or **limiting budget factor**) is the factor that limits an organisation's performance for a given period and is often the starting point in budget preparation.

For example, a company's sales department might estimate that it could sell 1,000 units of product X, which would require 5,000 hours of grade A labour to produce. If there are no units of product X already in stock, and only 4,000 hours of grade A labour available in the budget period, then the company would be unable to sell 1,000 units of X because of the shortage of labour hours. Grade A labour would be a limiting budget factor, and the company's management must choose one of the following options.

- Reduce budgeted sales by 20%.
- Try to increase the availability of grade A labour by 1,000 hours (25%) by recruitment or overtime working.
- Try to sub-contract the production of 1,000 units to another manufacturer, but still profit on the transaction.

In most organisations the principal budget factor is sales demand: a company is usually restricted from making and selling more of its products because there would be no sales demand for the increased output at a price which would be acceptable/profitable to the company. The principal budget factor may also be machine capacity, distribution and selling resources, the availability of key raw materials or the availability of cash. Once this factor is defined then the rest of the budget can be prepared. For example, if sales are the principal budget factor then the production manager can only prepare his budget after the sales budget is complete.

Management may not know what the limiting budget factor is until a draft budget has been attempted. The first draft budget will therefore usually begin with the preparation of a draft sales budget.

Step 3. **Preparation of the sales budget**

We have already established that, for many organisations, the principal budget factor is sales volume. The sales budget is therefore often the primary budget from which the majority of the other budgets are derived.

Before the sales budget can be prepared a **sales forecast** has to be made. Sales forecasting is complex and difficult and involves the consideration of a number of factors.

- Past sales patterns
- The economic environment
- Results of market research
- Anticipated advertising
- Competition
- Changing consumer taste
- New legislation
- Distribution
- Pricing policies and discounts offered
- Legislation
- Environmental factors

As well as bearing in mind the above factors, management can use a number of forecasting methods, which we will return to in Chapter 8.

On the basis of the sales forecast and the production capacity of the organisation, a sales budget will be prepared. This may be subdivided, possible subdivisions being by product, by sales area, by management responsibility and so on.

Step 4. **Initial preparation of budgets**

Budget	Detail
Finished goods stock budget	Decides the planned increase or decrease in finished stock levels.
Production budget	Stated in units of each product and is calculated as the sales budget in units plus the budgeted increase in finished goods stocks or minus the budgeted decrease in finished goods stocks.
Budgets of resources for production	**Materials usage budget** is stated in quantities and perhaps cost for each type of material used. It should take into account budgeted losses in production. **Machine utilisation budget** shows the operating hours required on each machine or group of machines. **Labour budget or wages budget** will be expressed in hours for each grade of labour and in terms of cost. It should take into account budgeted idle time.
Overhead cost budgets	**Production overheads** **Administration overheads** **Selling and distribution overheads** **Research and development department overheads**
Raw materials stock budget	Decides the planned increase or decrease of the level of stocks.
Raw materials purchase budget	Can be prepared in quantities and value for each type of material purchased once the raw material usage requirements and the raw materials stock budget are known.
Overhead absorption rate	Can be calculated once the production volumes are planned, and the overhead cost centre budgets prepared.

Step 5. **Negotiation of budgets with superiors**

Once a manager has prepared his draft budget he should submit it to his superior for approval. The superior should then incorporate this budget with the others for which he or she is responsible and then submit this budget for approval to his or her superior. This process continues until the final budget is presented to the budget committee for approval.

At each stage of the process, the **budget** would be **negotiated between the manager who had prepared the budget and his/her superior** until agreed by both parties.

Step 6. **Co-ordination of budgets**

Remember that it is unlikely that the execution of the above steps will be problem-free. The budgets must be reviewed in relation to one another. Such a **review may indicate that some budgets are out of balance with others and need modifying** so that they will be compatible. The budget officer must identify such inconsistencies and bring them to the attention of the manager concerned. The **revision of one budget may lead to the revision of all budgets**. During this process the budgeted profit and loss account and budgeted balance sheet and cash budget should be prepared to ensure that all of the individual parts of the budget combine into an acceptable master budget.

Step 7. **Final acceptance of the budget**

When all the budgets are in harmony with one another they are summarised into a **master budget** consisting of a budgeted profit and loss account, budgeted balance sheet and cash budget.

Step 8. **Budget review**

The budgeting process does not stop once the budgets have been agreed. Actual results should be compared on a regular basis with the budgeted results. The frequency with which such comparisons are made depends very much on the organisation's circumstances and the sophistication of its control systems but it should occur at least monthly. Management should receive a report detailing the differences and should investigate the reasons for the differences. **If the differences are within the control of management, corrective action should be taken** to bring the reasons for the difference under control and to ensure that such inefficiencies do not occur in the future.

The **differences may have occurred, however, because the budget was unrealistic to begin with or because the actual conditions did not reflect those anticipated (or could have possibly been anticipated).** This would therefore invalidate the remainder of the budget.

The **budget committee**, who should meet periodically to evaluate the organisation's actual performance, **may need to reappraise the organisation's future plans in the light of changes to anticipated conditions and to adjust the budget to take account of such changes.**

The important point to note is that the budgeting process does not end for the current year once the budget period has begun: budgeting should be seen as a continuous and dynamic process.

Question 1

A company that manufactures and sells a range of products, with sales potential limited by market share, is considering introducing a system of budgeting.

Required

(a) List (in order of preparation) the functional budgets that need to be prepared.

(b) State which budgets the master budget will comprise.

(c) Consider how the work outlined in (a) and (b) can be coordinated in order for the budgeting process to be successful.

Answer

(a) The sequence of budget preparation will be roughly as follows.

(i) Sales budget

(The market share limits demand and so sales is the principal budget factor. All other activities will depend upon this forecast.)

(ii) Finished goods stock budget (in units)

(iii) Production budget (in units)

(iv) Production resources budgets (materials, machine hours, labour)

(v) Overhead budgets for production, administration, selling and distribution, research and development and so on

Other budgets required will be the capital expenditure budget, the working capital budget (debtors and creditors) and, very importantly, the cash budget.

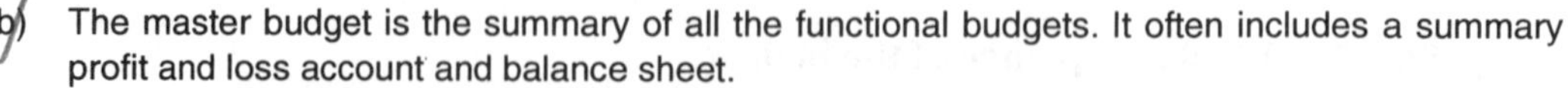

(b) The master budget is the summary of all the functional budgets. It often includes a summary profit and loss account and balance sheet.

(c) Procedures for preparing budgets can be contained in a budget manual which shows which budgets must be prepared when and by whom, what each functional budget should contain and detailed directions on how to prepare budgets including, for example, expected price increases, rates of interest, rates of depreciation and so on.

The formulation of budgets can be coordinated by a budget committee comprising the senior executives of the departments responsible for carrying out the budgets: sales, production, purchasing, personnel and so on.

The budgeting process may also be assisted by the use of a spreadsheet/computer budgeting package.

---

5 FUNCTIONAL BUDGETS 12/94

Exam focus point

You must be able to prepare budgets from information provided in examination questions and comment on those budgets, perhaps giving recommendations about management action required.

KEY TERM

Functional (or **departmental**) **budgets** are the budgets for the various functions and departments of an organisation. They therefore include production budgets, marketing budgets, sales budgets, personnel budgets, purchasing budgets and research and development budgets.

5.1 We will look at the preparation of a number of types of functional budget in this chapter but the general principles covered can be applied in most situations.

Production cost budget

Exam focus point

In the 12/94 exam, there were 3½ marks to be gained for preparing a production cost budget from the information given in the question.

5.2 If the principal budget factor was production capacity then the production cost budget would be the first to be prepared.

5.3 To assess whether production is the principal budget factor, the **production capacity available** must be determined. This should take into account the following factors.

- **Available labour**, including idle time, overtime and standard output rates per hour
- **Availability of raw materials** including allowances for losses during production
- **Maximum machine hours available**, including expected idle time and expected output rates per machine hour

It is, however, normally sales volume that is the constraint and therefore the production budget is prepared after the sales budget and the finished goods stock budget.

5.4 The **production cost budget** will show the **quantities** and **costs** for **each product** and product group and will tie in with the sales and stock budgets. This co-ordinating process is likely to show any shortfalls or excesses in capacity at various times over the budget period. If there is likely to be a shortfall then consideration should be given to overtime, subcontracting, machine hire, new sources of raw materials or some other way of increasing output. A significant shortfall means that production capacity is, in fact, the limiting factor.

5.5 If capacity exceeds sales volume for a length of time then consideration should be given to product diversification, a reduction in selling price (if demand is price elastic) and so on.

5.6 Once the production budget has been finalised, the labour, materials and machine budgets can be drawn up. These budgets will be based on budgeted activity levels, existing stock positions and projected labour and material costs.

5.7 EXAMPLE: THE PREPARATION OF THE PRODUCTION BUDGET AND DIRECT LABOUR BUDGET

Pearson Ltd manufactures two products, P and L, and is preparing its budget for 19X3. Both products are made by the same grade of labour, grade G. The company currently holds 800 units of P and 1,200 units of L in stock, but 250 of these units of L have just been discovered to have deteriorated in quality, and must therefore be scrapped. Budgeted sales of P are 3,000 units and of L 4,000 units, provided that the company maintains finished goods stocks at a level equal to three months' sales.

Grade G labour was originally expected to produce one unit of P in two hours and one unit of L in three hours, at an hourly rate of £2.50 per hour. In discussions with trade union negotiators, however, it has been agreed that the hourly wage rate should be raised by 50p per hour, provided that the times to produce P and L are reduced by 20%.

Required

Prepare the production budget and direct labour budget for 19X3.

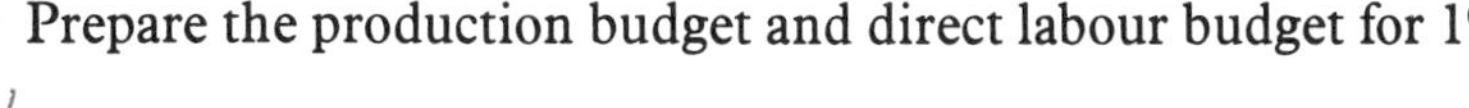

5.8 SOLUTION

The expected time to produce a unit of P will now be 80% of 2 hours = 1.6 hours, and the time for a unit of L will be 2.4 hours. The hourly wage rate will be £3, so that the direct labour cost will be £4.80 for P and £7.20 for L (thus achieving a saving for the company of 20p per unit of P produced and 30p per unit of L).

(a) *Production budget*

		Product P			*Product L*	
		Units	Units		Units	Units
Budgeted sales			3,000			4,000
Closing stocks	(3/12 of 3,000)	750		(3/12 of 4,000)	1,000	
Opening stocks (minus stocks scrapped)		800			950	
(Decrease)/increase in stocks			(50)			50
Production			2,950			4,050

(b) *Direct labour budget*

	Grade G	*Cost*
	Hours	£
2,950 units of product P	4,720	14,160
4,050 units of product L	9,720	29,160
Total	14,440	43,320

It is assumed that there will be no idle time among grade G labour which, if it existed, would have to be paid for at the rate of £3 per hour.

Labour budget

5.9 A useful concept in budgeting for labour requirements is the standard hour.

KEY TERM

A **standard hour** is the quantity of work achievable at standard performance, expressed in terms of a standard unit of work done in a standard period of time.

5.10 Budgeted output of different products or jobs in a period can be converted into standard hours of production, and a labour budget constructed accordingly.

5.11 Standard hours are particularly useful when management wants to monitor the production levels of a variety of dissimilar units. For example product A may take five hours to produce and product B, seven hours. If four units of each product are produced, instead of saying that total output is eight units, we could state the production level as $(4 \times 5) + (4 \times 7)$ standard hours = 48 standard hours.

5.12 EXAMPLE: DIRECT LABOUR BUDGET BASED ON STANDARD HOURS

Canaervon Ltd manufactures a single product, the close, with a single grade of labour. Its sales budget and finished goods stock budget for period 3 of 19X6 are as follows.

Sales	700 units
Opening stocks, finished goods	50 units
Closing stocks, finished goods	70 units

The goods are inspected only when production work is completed, and it is budgeted that 10% of finished work will be scrapped.

The standard direct labour hour content of the close is three hours. The budgeted productivity ratio for direct labour is only 80% (which means that labour is only working at 80% efficiency).

The company employs 18 direct operatives, who are expected to average 144 working hours each in period 3.

Required

(a) Prepare a production budget.

(b) Prepare a direct labour budget.

(c) Comment on the problem that your direct labour budget reveals, and suggest how this problem might be overcome.

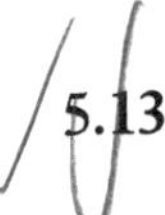

5.13 SOLUTION

(a) *Production budget*

	Units
Sales	700
Add closing stock	70
	770
Less opening stock	50
Production required of 'good' output	720
Wastage rate	10%
Total production required	?

(* Note that the required adjustment is 100/90, not 110/100, since the waste is assumed to be 10% of total production, not 10% of good production.)

(b) Now we can prepare the direct labour budget.

Standard hours per unit	3
Total standard hours required = 800 units × 3 hours	2,400 hours
Productivity ratio	80%
Actual hours required	

(c) If we look at the direct labour budget against the information provided, we can identify the problem.

	Hours
Budgeted hours available (18 operatives × 144 hours)	2,592
Actual hours required	3,000
Shortfall in labour hours	408

The (draft) budget indicates that there will not be enough direct labour hours to meet the production requirements. This problem might be overcome in one, or a combination, of the following ways.

- Reduce the closing stock requirement below 70 units. This would reduce the number of production units required.
- Persuade the workforce to do some overtime working.
- Perhaps recruit more direct labour if long-term prospects are for higher production volumes.
- Discuss with the workforce (or their union representatives) the following possibilities.
  - Improve the productivity ratio, and so reduce the number of hours required to produce the output.
  - If possible, reduce the wastage rate below 10%.

Coordination of functional budgets

5.14 **It is vital that the functional budgets are prepared in the correct order** (for example, the material usage budget should be prepared after the production budget) and that the **overall process is coordinated** to ensure that the budgets are all in balance with each other. There is little point in the material usage budget being based on a budgeted production level of 10,000 units if the budgeted production level specified in the production budget is 15,000 units.

6 CASH BUDGETS 12/94, 12/95, 12/96

KEY TERM

A cash budget is a detailed budget of cash inflows and outflows incorporating both revenue and capital items.

6.1 A cash budget is thus a statement in which estimated future cash receipts and payments are tabulated in such a way as to show the forecast cash balance of a business at defined intervals. For example, in December 19X2 an accounts department might wish to estimate the cash position of the business during the three following months, January to March 19X3. A cash budget might be drawn up in the following format.

	Jan	*Feb*	*Mar*
	£	£	£
Estimated cash receipts			
From credit customers	14,000	16,500	17,000
From cash sales	3,000	4,000	4,500
Proceeds on disposal of fixed assets		2,200	
Total cash receipts	17,000	22,700	21,500
Estimated cash payments			
To suppliers of goods	8,000	7,800	10,500
To employees (wages)	3,000	3,500	3,500
Purchase of fixed assets		16,000	
Rent and rates			1,000
Other overheads	1,200	1,200	1,200
Repayment of loan	2,500		
	14,700	28,500	16,200
Net surplus/(deficit) for month	2,300	(5,800)	5,300
Opening cash balance	1,200	3,500	(2,300)
Closing cash balance	3,500	(2,300)	3,000

6.2 In the example above (where the figures are purely for illustration) the accounts department has calculated that the cash balance at the beginning of the budget period, 1 January, will be £1,200. Estimates have been made of the cash which is likely to be received by the business (from cash and credit sales, and from a planned disposal of fixed assets in February). Similar estimates have been made of cash due to be paid out by the business (payments to suppliers and employees, payments for rent, rates and other overheads, payment for a planned purchase of fixed assets in February and a loan repayment due in January).

6.3 From these estimates it is a simple step to calculate the excess of cash receipts over cash payments in each month. In some months cash payments may exceed cash receipts and there will be a deficit for the month; this occurs during February in the above example because of the large investment in fixed assets in that month.

6.4 The last part of the cash budget above shows how the business's estimated cash balance can then be rolled along from month to month. Starting with the opening balance of £1,200 at 1 January a cash surplus of £2,300 is generated in January. This leads to a closing January balance of £3,500 which becomes the opening balance for February. The deficit of £5,800 in February throws the business's cash position into overdraft and the overdrawn balance of £2,300 becomes the opening balance for March. Finally, the healthy cash surplus of £5,300 in March leaves the business with a favourable cash position of £3,000 at the end of the budget period.

Exam focus point

When preparing budgets, it is vital that your work is clearly laid out, and referenced to workings if necessary.

The usefulness of cash budgets

6.5 The cash budget is one of the most important planning tools that an organisation can use. It shows the cash effect of all plans made within the budgetary process and hence its preparation can lead to a modification of budgets if it shows that there are insufficient cash resources to finance the planned operations.

6.6 It can also **give management an indication of potential problems that could arise and allows them the opportunity to take action to avoid such problems**. A cash budget can show four positions. Management will need to take appropriate action depending on the potential position.

Cash position	Appropriate management action
Short-term surplus	Pay creditors early to obtain discount Attempt to increase sales by increasing debtors and stocks Make short-term investments
Short-term deficit	Increase creditors Reduce debtors Arrange an overdraft
Long-term surplus	Make long-term investments Expand Diversify Replace/update fixed assets
Long-term deficit	Raise long-term finance (such as via issue of share capital) Consider shutdown/disinvestment opportunities

Exam focus point

A cash budgeting question in an examination could ask you to recommend appropriate action for management to take once you have prepared the cash budget. Ensure your advice takes account both of whether there is a surplus or deficit and whether the position is long or short term.

What to include in a cash budget

6.7 A cash budget is prepared to show the **expected receipts of cash and payments of cash** during a budget period.

6.8 Receipts of cash may come from one or more of the following.

- Cash sales
- Payments by debtors (credit sales)
- The sale of fixed assets
- The issue of new shares or loan stock and less formalised loans
- The receipt of interest and dividends from investments outside the business

6.9 **Although all of these receipts would affect a cash budget they would not all appear in the profit and loss account.**

(a) The issue of new shares or loan stock is a balance sheet item.

(b) The cash received from an asset affects the balance sheet, and the profit or loss on the sale of an asset, which appears in the profit and loss account, is not the cash received but the difference between cash received and the written down value of the asset at the time of sale.

6.10 Payments of cash may be for one or more of the following.

- Purchase of stocks
- Payroll costs or other expenses
- Purchase of capital items
- Payment of interest, dividends or taxation

Not all payments are profit and loss account items. The purchase of capital equipment and the payment of VAT affect the balance sheet.

6.11 It should be obvious that the **profit or loss made by an organisation during an accounting period does not reflect its cash flow position for the following reasons.**

- Not all cash receipts affect profit and loss account income.
- Not all cash payments affect profit and loss account expenditure.
- Some costs in the profit and loss account such as profit or loss on sale of fixed assets or depreciation are not cash items but are costs derived from accounting conventions.
- The timing of cash receipts and payments may not coincide with the recording of profit and loss account transactions. For example, a dividend might be declared in the results for 19X6 and shown in the profit and loss account for that year, but paid in 19X7.

6.12 To ensure that there is sufficient cash in hand to cope adequately with budgeted activities, management should therefore prepare and pay close attention to a cash budget rather than a profit and loss account. Cash budgets are most effective if they are treated as rolling budgets. **Rolling budgets** involve a process of continuous budgeting whereby regularly each period (week month, quarter) a new future period is added to the budget whilst the earliest period is deleted. In this way the budget is **constantly revised** to reflect the most up to date position. We consider rolling budgets in Chapter 9.

6.13 EXAMPLE: CASH BUDGET

Peter Blair has worked for some years as a sales representative, but has recently been made redundant. He intends to start up in business on his own account, using £15,000 which he currently has invested with a building society. Peter maintains a bank account showing a small credit balance, and he plans to approach his bank for the necessary additional finance. Peter asks you for advice and provides the following additional information.

(a) Arrangements have been made to purchase fixed assets costing £8,000. These will be paid for at the end of September and are expected to have a five-year life, at the end of which they will possess a nil residual value.

(b) Stocks costing £5,000 will be acquired on 28 September and subsequent monthly purchases will be at a level sufficient to replace forecast sales for the month.

(c) Forecast monthly sales are £3,000 for October, £6,000 for November and December, and £10,500 from January 19X4 onwards.

(d) Selling price is fixed at the cost of stock plus 50%.

(e) Two months' credit will be allowed to customers but only one month's credit will be received from suppliers of stock.

(f) Running expenses, including rent but excluding depreciation of fixed assets, are estimated at £1,600 per month.

(g) Blair intends to make monthly cash drawings of £1,000.

Required

Prepare a cash budget for the six months to 31 March 19X4.

6.14 SOLUTION

The opening cash balance at 1 October will consist of Peter's initial £15,000 less the £8,000 expended on fixed assets purchased in September. In other words, the opening balance is £7,000. Cash receipts from credit customers arise two months after the relevant sales.

Payments to suppliers are a little more tricky. We are told that cost of sales is 100/150 × sales. Thus for October cost of sales is 100/150 × £3,000 = £2,000. These goods will be purchased in October but not paid for until November. Similar calculations can be made for later months. The initial stock of £5,000 is purchased in September and consequently paid for in October.

Depreciation is not a cash flow and so is *not* included in a cash budget.

6.15 The cash budget can now be constructed.

CASH BUDGET FOR THE SIX MONTHS ENDING 31 MARCH 19X4

	Oct	*Nov*	*Dec*	*Jan*	*Feb*	*Mar*
	£	£	£	£	£	£
Payments						
Suppliers	5,000	2,000	4,000	4,000	7,000	7,000
Running expenses	1,600	1,600	1,600	1,600	1,600	1,600
Drawings	1,000	1,000	1,000	1,000	1,000	1,000
	7,600	4,600	6,600	6,600	9,600	9,600
Receipts						
Debtors	-	-	3,000	6,000	6,000	10,500
Surplus/(shortfall)	(7,600)	(4,600)	(3,600)	(600)	(3,600)	900
Opening balance	7,000	(600)	(5,200)	(8,800)	(9,400)	(13,000)
Closing balance	(600)	(5,200)	(8,800)	(9,400)	(13,000)	(12,100)

Cash budgets and an opening balance sheet

6.16 You might be given a cash budget question in which you are required to analyse an opening balance sheet to decide how many outstanding debtors will pay what they owe in the first few months of the cash budget period, and how many outstanding creditors must be paid.

6.17 Suppose that a balance sheet as at 31 December 19X4 shows the following details.

Debtors	£150,000
Trade creditors	£60,000

The following information is relevant.

- Debtors are allowed two months to pay.
- $1^1/_2$ months' credit is taken from trade creditors.
- Sales and materials purchases were both made at an even monthly rate throughout 19X4.

Let's try to ascertain the months of 19X5 in which the debtors will eventually pay and the creditors will be paid.

(a) Since debtors take two months to pay, the £150,000 of debtors in the balance sheet represents credit sales in November and December 19X4, who will pay in January and February 19X5 respectively. Since sales in 19X4 were at an equal monthly rate, the cash budget should plan for receipts of £75,000 each month in January and February from the debtors in the opening balance sheet.

(b) Similarly, since creditors are paid after $1^1/_2$ months, the balance sheet creditors will be paid in January and the first half of February 19X5, which means that budgeted payments will be as follows.

	£
In January (purchases in 2nd half of November and 1st half of December 19X4)	40,000
In February (purchases in 2nd half of December 19X4)	20,000
Total creditors in the balance sheet	60,000

(The balance sheet creditors of £60,000 represent $1^1/_2$ months' purchases, so that purchases in 19X4 must be £40,000 per month, which is £20,000 per half month.)

6.18 EXAMPLE: A MONTH BY MONTH CASH BUDGET

From the following information which relates to George and Zola Ltd you are required to prepare a month by month cash budget for the second half of 19X5 and to append such brief comments as you consider might be helpful to management.

(a) The company's only product, a vest, sells at £40 and has a variable cost of £26 made up as follows.

Material £20	Labour £4	Overhead £2

(b) Fixed costs of £6,000 per month are paid on the 28th of each month.

(c) Quantities sold/to be sold on credit

May	*June*	*July*	*Aug*	*Sept*	*Oct*	*Nov*	*Dec*
1,000	1,200	1,400	1,600	1,800	2,000	2,200	2,600

(d) Production quantities

May	*June*	*July*	*Aug*	*Sept*	*Oct*	*Nov*	*Dec*
1,200	1,400	1,600	2,000	2,400	2,600	2,400	2,200

(e) Cash sales at a discount of 5% are expected to average 100 units a month.

(f) Customers are expected to settle their accounts by the end of the second month following sale.

(g) Suppliers of material are paid two months after the material is used in production.

(h) Wages are paid in the same month as they are incurred.

(i) 70% of the variable overhead is paid in the month of production, the remainder in the following month.

(j) Corporation tax of £18,000 is to be paid in October.

(k) A new delivery vehicle was bought in June. It cost £8,000 and is to be paid for in August. The old vehicle was sold for £600, the buyer undertaking to pay in July.

(l) The company is expected to be £3,000 overdrawn at the bank at 30 June 19X5.

(m) No increases or decreases in raw materials, work in progress or finished goods are planned over the period.

(n) No price increases or cost increases are expected in the period.

6.19 SOLUTION

Cash budget for July 1 to December 31 19X5

	July	*Aug*	*Sept*	*Oct*	*Nov*	*Dec*	*Total*
	£	£	£	£	£	£	£
Receipts							
Credit sales	40,000	48,000	56,000	64,000	72,000	80,000	360,000
Cash sales	3,800	3,800	3,800	3,800	3,800	3,800	22,800
Sale of vehicle	600	-	-	-	-	-	600
	44,400	51,800	59,800	67,800	75,800	83,800	383,400
Payments							
Materials	24,000	28,000	32,000	40,000	48,000	52,000	224,000
Labour	6,400	8,000	9,600	10,400	9,600	8,800	52,800
Variable overhead (W)	3,080	3,760	4,560	5,080	4,920	4,520	25,920
Fixed costs	6,000	6,000	6,000	6,000	6,000	6,000	36,000
Corporation tax				18,000			18,000
Purchase of vehicle		8,000					8,000
	39,480	53,760	52,160	79,480	68,520	71,320	364,720
Receipts less payments	4,920	(1,960)	7,640	(11,680)	7,280	12,480	18,680
Balance b/f	(3,000)	1,920	(40)	7,600	(4,080)	3,200	(3,000)
Balance c/f	1,920	(40)	7,600	(4,080)	3,200	15,680	15,680

Working

Variable overhead

	June	*July*	*Aug*	*Sept*	*Oct*	*Nov*	*Dec*
	£	£	£	£	£	£	£
Variable overhead production cost	2,800	3,200	4,000	4,800	5,200	4,800	4,400
70% paid in month		2,240	2,800	3,360	3,640	3,360	3,080
30% in following month		840	960	1,200	1,440	1,560	1,440
		3,080	3,760	4,560	5,080	4,920	4,520

Comments

(a) There will be a small overdraft at the end of August but a much larger one at the end of October. It may be possible to delay payments to suppliers for longer than two months or to reduce purchases of materials or reduce the volume of production by running down existing stock levels.

(b) If neither of these courses is possible, the company may need to negotiate overdraft facilities with its bank.

(c) The cash deficit is only temporary and by the end of December there will be a comfortable surplus. The use to which this cash will be put should ideally be planned in advance.

Question 2

You are presented with the following budgeted cash flow data for your organisation for the period November 19X1 to June 19X2. It has been extracted from functional budgets that have already been prepared.

	Nov X1	*Dec X1*	*Jan X2*	*Feb X2*	*Mar X2*	*Apr X2*	*May X2*	*June X2*
	£	£	£	£	£	£	£	£
Sales	80,000	100,000	110,000	130,000	140,000	150,000	160,000	180,000
Purchases	40,000	60,000	80,000	90,000	110,000	130,000	140,000	150,000
Wages	10,000	12,000	16,000	20,000	24,000	28,000	32,000	36,000
Overheads	10,000	10,000	15,000	15,000	15,000	20,000	20,000	20,000
Dividends		20,000						40,000
Capital expenditure			30,000			40,000		

You are also told the following.

(a) Sales are 40% cash 60% credit. Credit sales are paid two months after the month of sale.
(b) Purchases are paid the month following purchase.
(c) 75% of wages are paid in the current month and 25% the following month.
(d) Overheads are paid the month after they are incurred.
(e) Dividends are paid three months after they are declared.
(f) Capital expenditure is paid two months after it is incurred.
(g) The opening cash balance is £15,000.

The managing director is pleased with the above figures as they show sales will have increased by more than 100% in the period under review. In order to achieve this he has arranged a bank overdraft with a ceiling of £50,000 to accommodate the increased stock levels and wage bill for overtime worked.

Required

(a) Prepare a cash budget for the six-month period January to June 19X2.

(b) Comment upon your results in the light of your managing director's comments and offer advice.

Answer

(a)

	January	*February*	*March*	*April*	*May*	*June*
	£	£	£	£	£	£
Cash receipts						
Cash sales	44,000	52,000	56,000	60,000	64,000	72,000
Credit sales	48,000	60,000	66,000	78,000	84,000	90,000
	92,000	112,000	122,000	138,000	148,000	162,000
Cash payments						
Purchases	60,000	80,000	90,000	110,000	130,000	140,000
Wages						
75%	12,000	15,000	18,000	21,000	24,000	27,000
25%	3,000	4,000	5,000	6,000	7,000	8,000
Overheads	10,000	15,000	15,000	15,000	20,000	20,000
Dividends			20,000			
Capital expenditure			30,000			40,000
	85,000	114,000	178,000	152,000	181,000	235,000
b/f	15,000	22,000	20,000	(36,000)	(50,000)	(83,000)
Net cash flow	7,000	(2,000)	(56,000)	(14,000)	(33,000)	(73,000)
c/f	22,000	20,000	(36,000)	(50,000)	(83,000)	(156,000)

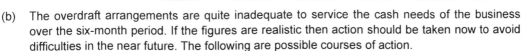

(b) The overdraft arrangements are quite inadequate to service the cash needs of the business over the six-month period. If the figures are realistic then action should be taken now to avoid difficulties in the near future. The following are possible courses of action.

(i) Activities could be curtailed.

(ii) Other sources of cash could be explored, for example a long-term loan to finance the capital expenditure and a factoring arrangement to provide cash due from debtors more quickly.

(iii) Efforts to increase the speed of debt collection could be made.

(iv) Payments to creditors could be delayed.

(v) The dividend payments could be postponed (the figures indicate that this is a small company, possibly owner-managed).

(vi) Staff might be persuaded to work at a lower rate in return for, say, an annual bonus or a profit-sharing agreement.

(vii) Extra staff might be taken on to reduce the amount of overtime paid.

(viii) The stockholding policy should be reviewed; it may be possible to meet demand from current production and minimise cash tied up in stocks.

7 BUDGETED PROFIT AND LOSS ACCOUNT AND BALANCE SHEET

12/94, 12/95

7.1 As well as wishing to forecast its cash position, a business might want to estimate its profitability and its financial position for a coming period. This would involve the preparation of a budgeted profit and loss account and balance sheet, along with the cash budget which form the master budget.

7.2 Just like historical financial statements, **budgeted accounts are based on the accruals concept**. If you keep this point in mind you will often be able to cut through the deliberately confusing detail of examination questions to prepare an answer very quickly. The example of Peter Blair in Paragraph 6.13 will be used to illustrate the procedure.

7.3 EXAMPLE: PREPARING A BUDGETED PROFIT AND LOSS ACCOUNT AND BALANCE SHEET

Using the information in Paragraph 6.13, you are required to prepare Peter Blair's budgeted profit and loss account for the six months ending on 31 March 19X4 and a budgeted balance sheet as at that date.

7.4 SOLUTION

The profit and loss account is straightforward. The first figure is sales, which can be computed very easily from the information in Paragraph 6.13(c). It is sufficient to add up the monthly sales figures given there; for the profit and loss account there is no need to worry about any closing debtor. Similarly, cost of sales is calculated directly from the information on gross margin contained in Paragraph 6.13(d).

FORECAST TRADING AND PROFIT AND LOSS ACCOUNT
FOR THE SIX MONTHS ENDING 31 MARCH 19X4

	£	£
Sales (3,000 + (2 × 6,000) + (3 × 10,500))		46,500
Cost of sales (2/3 × £46,500)		31,000
Gross profit		15,500
Expenses		
Running expenses (6 × £1,600)	9,600	
Depreciation (£8,000 × 20% × 6/12)	800	
		10,400
Net profit		5,100

Items will be shown in the balance sheet as follows.

(a) Stock will comprise the initial purchases of £5,000.

(b) Debtors will comprise sales made in February and March (not paid until April and May respectively).

(c) Creditors will comprise purchases made in March (not paid for until April).

(d) The bank overdraft is the closing cash figure computed in the cash budget.

FORECAST BALANCE SHEET AT 31 MARCH 19X4

	£	£
Fixed assets £(8,000 – 800)		7,200
Current assets		
Stocks	5,000	
Debtors (2 × £10,500)	21,000	
	26,000	
Current liabilities		
Bank overdraft	12,100	
Trade creditors (March purchases)	7,000	
	19,100	
Net current assets		6,900
		14,100
Proprietor's interest		
Capital introduced		15,000
Profit for the period	5,100	
Less drawings	6,000	
Deficit retained		(900)
		14,100

7.5 Budget questions are often accompanied by a large amount of sometimes confusing detail. This should not blind you to the fact that many figures can be entered very simply from the logic of the trading situation described. For example in the case of Blair you might feel tempted to begin a T-account to compute the closing debtors figure. This kind of working is rarely necessary, since you are told that debtors take two months to pay. Closing debtors will equal total credit sales in the last two months of the period.

7.6 Similarly, you may be given a simple statement that a business pays rates at £1,500 a year, followed by a lot of detail to enable you to calculate a prepayment at the beginning and end of the year. If you are preparing a budgeted profit and loss account for the year do not lose sight of the fact that the rates expense can be entered as £1,500 without any calculation at all.

8 THE MASTER BUDGET 12/94, 12/95

KEY TERM

When all the functional budgets have been prepared, they are summarised and consolidated into a **master budget** which consists of the budgeted profit and loss account, budgeted balance sheet and cash budget and which provides the overall picture of the planned performance for the budget period

8.1 EXAMPLE: A MASTER BUDGET

Plagued Engineering Limited produces two products, Niks and Args. The budget for the forthcoming year to 31 March 19X8 is to be prepared. Expectations for the forthcoming year include the following.

(a) PLAGUED ENGINEERING LTD
BALANCE SHEET AS AT 1 APRIL 19X7

	£	£
Fixed assets		
Land and buildings		45,000
Plant and equipment at cost	187,000	
Less accumulated depreciation	75,000	
		112,000
Current assets		
Raw materials	7,650	
Finished goods	23,600	
Debtors	19,500	
Cash	4,300	
	55,050	
Current liabilities		
Creditors	6,800	
		48,250
		205,250
Financed by		
Share capital		150,000
Retained profit		55,250
		205,250

(b) *Finished products*

The sales director has estimated the following.

		Niks	*Args*
(i)	Demand for the company's products units	4,500 units	4,000
(ii)	Selling price per unit	£32	£44
(iii)	Closing stock of finished products at 31 March 19X8 units	400 units	1,200
(iv)	Opening stock of finished products at 1 April 19X7	900 units	200 units
(v)	Unit cost of this opening stock	£20	£28
(vi)	Amount of plant capacity required for each unit of product		
	Machining	15 min	24 min
	Assembling	12 min	18 min
(vii)	Raw material content per unit of each product		
	Material A	1.5 kilos	0.5 kilos
	Material B	2.0 kilos	4.0 kilos
(viii)	Direct labour hours required per unit of each product	6 hours	9 hours

Finished goods are valued on a FIFO basis at full production cost.

(c) *Raw materials*

		Material A	*Material B*
(i)	Closing stock requirement in kilos at 31 March 19X8	600	1,000
(ii)	Opening stock at 1 April 19X7 in kilos	1,100	6,000
(iii)	Budgeted cost of raw materials per kilo	£1.50	£1.00

Actual costs per kilo of opening stocks are as budgeted cost for the coming year.

(d) *Direct labour*

The standard wage rate of direct labour is £1.60 per hour.

(e) *Production overhead*

Production overhead is absorbed on the basis of machining hours, with separate absorption rates for each department. The following overheads are anticipated in the production cost centre budgets.

	Machining department	*Assembling department*
	£	£
Supervisors' salaries	10,000	9,150
Power	4,400	2,000
Maintenance and running costs	2,100	2,000
Consumables	3,400	500
General expenses	19,600	5,000
	39,500	18,650

Depreciation is taken at 5% straight line on plant and equipment. A machine costing the company £20,000 is due to be installed on 1 October 19X7 in the machining department, which already has machinery installed to the value of £100,000 (at cost). Land worth £180,000 is to be acquired in December 19X7.

(f) *Selling and administration expenses*

	£
Sales commissions and salaries	14,300
Travelling and distribution	3,500
Office salaries	10,100
General administration expenses	2,500
	30,400

(g) There is no opening or closing work in progress and inflation should be ignored.

(h) Budgeted cash flows are as follows.

	Quarter 1	*Quarter 2*	*Quarter 3*	*Quarter 4*
Receipts from customers	70,000	100,000	100,000	40,000
Payments:				
Materials	7,000	9,000	10,000	5,000
Wages	33,000	20,000	11,000	15,000
Other costs and expenses	10,000	100,000	205,000	5,000

Required

Prepare the following for the year ended 31 March 19X8 for Plagued Engineering Ltd.

(a) Sales budget
(b) Production budget (in quantities)
(c) Plant utilisation budget (hrs).
(d) Direct materials usage budget
(e) Direct labour budget
(f) Factory overhead budget
(g) Computation of the factory cost per unit for each product
(h) Direct materials purchases budget
(i) Cost of goods sold budget
(j) Cash budget
(k) A budgeted profit and loss account and balance sheet

8.2 SOLUTION

(a) *Sales budget*

	Market demand	*Selling price*	*Sales value*
	Units	£	£
Niks	4,500	32.00	144,000
Args	4,000	44.00	176,000
			320,000

(b) *Production budget*

	Niks	*Args*
	Units	Units
Sales requirement	4,500	4,000
(Decrease)/increase in finished goods stock	(500)	1,000
Production requirement	4,000	5,000

(c) *Plant utilisation budget*

Product		*Machining*		*Assembling*	
	Units	Hours per unit	Total hours	Hours per unit	Total hours
Niks	4,000	0.25	1,000	0.20	800
Args	5,000	0.40	2,000	0.30	1,500
			3,000		2,300

(d) *Direct materials usage budget*

	Material A	*Material B*
	kg	kg
Required for production:		
Niks: 4,000 × 1.5 kilos	6,000	-
4,000 × 2.0 kilos	-	8,000
Args: 5,000 × 0.5 kilos	2,500	-
5,000 × 4.0 kilos	-	20,000
Material usage	8,500	28,000
Unit cost	£1.50 per kilo	£1.00 per kilo
Cost of materials used	£12,750	£28,000

(e) *Direct labour budget*

Product	*Production*	*Hours required per unit*		*Rate per hour*	*Cost*
	Units		Total hours	£	£
Niks	4,000	6	24,000	1.60	38,400
Args	5,000	9	45,000	1.60	72,000
				Total direct wages	110,400

(f) *Production overhead budget*

	Machining dept	*Assembling dept*
	£	£
Production overhead allocated and apportioned (excluding depreciation)	39,500	18,650
Depreciation costs		
(i) Existing plant		
(5% of £100,000 in machining)	5,000	
(5% of £87,000 in assembly)		4,350
(ii) Proposed plant		
(5% of $^6/_{12}$ × £20,000)	500	
Total production overhead	45,000	23,000
Total machine hours (see (c))	3,000 hrs	2,300 hrs
Absorption rate per machine hour	£15	£10

(g) *Cost of finished goods*

			Niks		Args
			£		£
Direct material	A	1.5 kg × £1.50	2.25	0.5 kg × £1.50	0.75
	B	2.0 kg × £1.00	2.00	4.0 kg × £1.00	4.00
Direct labour		6 hrs × £1.60	9.60	9 hrs × £1.60	14.40
Production overhead					
Machining department		15 mins at £15 per hr	3.75	24 min at £15 per hr	6.00
Assembling department		12 mins at £10 per hr	2.00	18 mins at £10 per hr	3.00
Production cost per unit			19.60		28.15

(h) *Direct material purchases budget*

	A	B
	kg	kg
Closing stock required	600	1,000
Production requirements	8,500	28,000
	9,100	29,000
Less opening stock	1,100	6,000
Purchase requirements	8,000	23,000
Cost per unit	£1.50	£1.00
Purchase costs	£12,000	£23,000

(i) *Cost of goods sold budget* (Using FIFO)

	Niks			Args		
	Units		£	Units		£
Opening stocks	900	(× £20.00)	18,000	200	(× £28.00)	5,600
Cost of production	4,000	(× £19.60)	78,400	5,000	(× £28.15)	140,750
	4,900		96,400	5,200		146,350
Less closing stocks	400	(× £19.60)	7,840	1,200	(× £28.15)	33,780
Cost of sales	4,500		88,560	4,000		112,570

Notes

(i) The cost of sales of Niks = 900 units at £20 each plus 3,600 units at £19.60 each.

(ii) The cost of sales of Args = 200 units at £28 each plus 3,800 units at £28.15 each.

(j) MASTER BUDGET

Cash budget for year to 31.3.X8

	Quarter 1	Quarter 2	Quarter 3	Quarter 4	Total
	£	£	£	£	£
Receipts	70,000	100,000	100,000	40,000	310,000
Payments					
Materials	7,000	9,000	10,000	5,000	31,000
Labour	33,000	20,000	11,000	15,000	79,000
Other costs and expenses	10,000	100,000	205,000	5,000	320,000
	50,000	129,000	226,000	25,000	430,000
Receipts less payments	20,000	(29,000)	(126,000)	15,000	(120,000)
Opening cash balance b/f	4,300	24,300	(4,700)	(130,700)	4,300
Closing cash balance c/f	24,300	(4,700)	(130,700)	(115,700)	(115,700)

Budgeted profit and loss account for year to 31.3.X8

	Niks	Args	Total
	£	£	£
Sales	144,000	176,000	320,000
Less cost of sales	88,560	112,570	201,130
Gross profit	55,440	63,430	118,870
Less selling and administration			30,400
Net profit			88,470

Note. There will be no under-/over-absorbed production overhead in the budgeted profit and loss account.

Budgeted balance sheet at 31.3.X8

	£	£	£
Fixed assets			
Land and buildings (W1)			225,000
Plant and equipment at cost (W2)		207,000	
Less accumulated depreciation (W3)		84,850	
			122,150
			347,150
Current assets			
Raw materials (W4)		1,900	
Finished goods (W5)		41,620	
Debtors (W6)		29,500	
		73,020	
Current liabilities			
Creditors (W7)	10,750		
Bank overdraft (W8)	115,700		
		126,450	
Net current liabilities			(53,430)
			293,720
Financed by			
Share capital			150,000
Retained profit (W9)			143,720
			293,720

Workings

1

	£
Opening balance at 1.4.X7	45,000
Addition	180,000
Cost at 31.3.X8	225,000

2

	£
Opening balance at 1.4.X7	187,000
Addition	20,000
Cost at 31.3.X8	207,000

3

	£
Opening balance at 1.4.X7	75,000
Addition in period	5,000
((f)(i) and (ii) of solution)	4,350
	500
Accumulated depreciation at 31.3.X8	84,850

4

	A	*B*	*Total*
Closing stock (kgs)	600	1,000	
Cost per kg	× £1.50	× £1.00	
Value of closing stock	£900	£1,000	£1,900

5

	Niks	*Args*	*Total*
Closing stock (units)	400	1,200	
Cost per unit ((g) of solution)	× £19.60	× £28.15	
	£7,840	£33,780	£41,620

6

	£
Opening balance	19,500
Sales ((a) of solution)	320,000
Receipts (from cash budget)	(310,000)
Closing balance	29,500

7			£	£
	Opening balance at 1.4.X7			6,800
	Land		180,000	
	Machine		20,000	
	Labour		110,400	
	Production overhead	39,500		
		18,650		
			58,150	
	Materials	12,000		
		23,000		
			35,000	
	Expenses		30,400	
				433,950
				440,750
	Cash payments (from cash budget)			(430,000)
	Closing balance at 31.3.X8			10,750

8 From cash budget £115,750 overdrawn

9		£
	Retained profit b/f	55,250
	Profit for year	88,470
	Retained profit c/f	143,720

Exam focus point

In the 12/94 exam, there were 10 marks to be gained for preparing a master budget. You need to be able to transfer **accurate** information **quickly** when building up a master budget, so make sure that you are happy with the techniques covered in this section.

9 CAPITAL EXPENDITURE BUDGETS 6/95

Exam focus point

In 6/95, there were 5 marks to be gained for explaining the principal steps involved in preparing a capital expenditure budget.

9.1 Because of the monetary amounts involved in capital expenditure, the **capital expenditure budget is one of the principal subsidiary budgets**. The steps in the preparation of such a budget are as follows.

Step 1. An **accountant or budget officer should be responsible** for the capital expenditure budget. Their tasks should include communicating between interested parties, providing necessary data to assist in budget preparation, drawing up a time table to ensure that proper consultation takes place and so on.

Step 2. Sales, production and related budgets cover, in general, a 12 month period. A detailed **capital expenditure budget should be prepared for the budget period but additional budgets should be drawn up for both the medium and long term**. This requires an in-depth consideration of the organisation's requirements for land, buildings, plant, machinery , vehicles, fixtures and fittings and so on for the short, medium and long term.

Step 3. The **budget covering the 12 month period** should be **broken down into monthly or quarterly spending**, the details of which can be incorporated into the cash budget.

Step 4. Suitable **financing** must be arranged as necessary.

Step 5. The capital expenditure budget should **taken account of the principal budget factor**. If available funds are limiting the organisation's activities then it will more than likely limit capital expenditure.

Step 6. As part of the overall budget coordination process, the capital expenditure budget must be **reviewed in relation to the other budgets**. Proposed expansion of production may well require significant fixed assets expenditure which should be reflected in the budget.

Step 7. The capital expenditure budget should be **updated on a regular basis** since both the timing and amount of expenditure can change at short notice.

9.2 You will be looking at methods for assessing individual capital expenditure decisions in Part I of this Study Text.

Chapter roundup

- The functions of a **system of budgeting** are as follows.
  - To ensure the achievement of the organisation's objectives
  - To compel planning
  - To communicate ideas and plans
  - To coordinate activities
  - To provide a framework for responsibility accounting
  - To establish a system of control
  - To motivate employees to improve their performance
- A budget is a **quantified plan of action** for a forthcoming accounting period.
- The **budget manual** is a collection of instructions governing the responsibilities of persons and the procedures, forms and records relating to the preparation and use of budgetary data.
- Managers responsible for preparing budgets should ideally be the managers responsible for carrying out the budget.
- The **budget committee** is the coordinating body in the preparation and administration of budgets.
- The **budget preparation process** is as follows.
  - Communicating details of the budget policy and budget guidelines.
  - Determining the factor that restricts output
  - Preparation of the sales budget
  - Initial preparation of budgets
  - Negotiation of budgets with superiors
  - Coordination and review of budgets
  - Final acceptance of the budgets
  - Budget review
- The **principal budget factor** should be identified at the beginning of the budgetary process, and the budget for this is prepared before all the others.
- Once prepared, the **subsidiary budgets** must be reviewed to ensure they are consistent with one another.
- **Cash budgets** show the expected receipts and payments during a budget period and are a vital management control tool, especially during times of recession.
- The profit or loss made by an organisation during an accounting period does not reflect its cash flow position.
- The **master budget** consists of a budgeted profit and loss account, a budgeted balance sheet and a cash budget.

Quick quiz

1 What are the aims of a system of budgetary control? (see para 2.2)
2 What are the functions of a budget committee? (3.6)
3 What is meant by the term *principal budget factor*? (key term)
4 What are the steps in the preparation of a budget? (4.1)
5 Explain the concept of the standard hour. (key terms)
6 What is the appropriate management action if a cash budget shows a long-term surplus? (6.6)
7 What are the steps in the preparation of a capital expenditure budget? (9.1)

Question to try	Level	Marks	Time
6	Examination	20	36 mins

Chapter 7

BUDGETARY CONTROL AND THE BEHAVIOURAL IMPLICATIONS OF BUDGETING

Introduction

Chapter 6 began our study of budgeting. You should now be able to prepare functional budgets and a master budget and have a firm grasp of the budgeting process. This chapter continues the budgeting theme and looks at two particular issues.

Flexible budgets are vital in management planning and control and this chapter shows how they are constructed and their use in the overall budgetary control process. It also provides an introduction to **variance analysis**, which is covered in much greater depth in Chapters 11 and 12.

The chapter then moves on to consider the **behavioural implications** of operating a budgetary control system. Many accountants find it hard to believe that anything as subjective as human behaviour can have any impact on budgeting since they see budgeting as a purely technical, number-crunching process.

There has been a great deal of research into the behavioural implications of budgeting and, as in all studies of human behaviour, it is difficult to draw concrete conclusions. There is, however, one point which is agreed: **budgeting is more than a mathematical technique**.

How can budgeting be simply a mathematical technique? Without the cooperation of its participants, the budgetary process is useless. If managers and the employees make no attempt to achieve budgets, if irresponsible estimates of figures are provided for inclusion in particular budgets, then the budgetary process is doomed.

Chapter 8 details the **quantitative techniques** which the management accountant can use for assistance in the budgeting process.

Chapter 9 examines **alternative budgeting systems** which can be used in particular situations, for example in the public sector.

1 FIXED AND FLEXIBLE BUDGETS 6/95

Fixed budgets

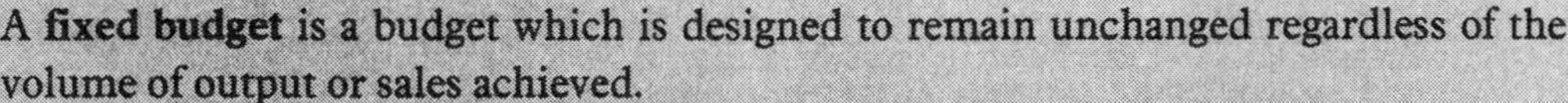

KEY TERM

A **fixed budget** is a budget which is designed to remain unchanged regardless of the volume of output or sales achieved.

1.1 The master budget prepared before the beginning of the budget period is known as the **fixed budget**. The term 'fixed' means the following.

(a) The budget is **prepared on the basis of an estimated volume of production** and an **estimated volume of sales**, but no plans are made for the event that actual volumes of production and sales may differ from budgeted volumes.

(b) When actual volumes of production and sales during a control period (month or four weeks or quarter) are achieved, a fixed budget is **not adjusted (in retrospect) to the new levels of activity.**

1.2 The major purpose of a fixed budget is at the planning stage, when it seeks to define the broad objectives of the organisation.

Flexible budgets

KEY TERM

A **flexible budget** is a budget which, by recognising different cost behaviour patterns, is designed to change as volumes of output change.

1.3 Flexible budgets may be used in one of two ways.

(a) **At the planning stage**. For example, suppose that a company expects to sell 10,000 units of output during the next year. A master budget (the fixed budget) would be prepared on the basis of these expected volumes. However, if the company thinks that output and sales might be as low as 8,000 units or as high as 12,000 units, it may prepare **contingency flexible budgets**, at volumes of, say 8,000, 9,000, 11,000 and 12,000 units. There are a number of advantages of planning with flexible budgets.

- It is possible to find out well in advance the costs of lay-off pay, idle time and so on if output falls short of budget.
- Management can decide whether it would be possible to find alternative uses for spare capacity if output falls short of budget (could employees be asked to overhaul their own machines for example, instead of paying for an outside contractor?).
- An estimate of the costs of overtime, subcontracting work or extra machine hire if sales volume exceeds the fixed budget estimate can be made. From this, it can be established whether there is a limiting factor which would prevent high volumes of output and sales being achieved.

(b) **Retrospectively**. At the end of each month (control period) or year, flexible budgets can be used to compare actual results achieved with what results should have been under the circumstances. Flexible budgets are an essential factor in **budgetary control**.

- Management needs to be informed about how good or bad actual performance has been. To provide a **measure of performance**, there must be a yardstick (budget or standard) against which actual performance can be measured.
- Every business is dynamic, and actual volumes of output cannot be expected to conform exactly to the fixed budget. Comparing actual costs directly with the fixed budget costs is meaningless (unless the actual level of activity turns out to be exactly as planned).
- For **useful control information**, it is necessary to compare actual results at the actual level of activity achieved against the results that should have been expected at this level of activity, which are shown by the flexible budget.

1.4 **Flexible budgeting uses the principles of marginal costing**. In estimating future costs it is often necessary to begin by looking at cost behaviour in the past. For costs which are wholly fixed or wholly variable no problem arises. But you may be presented with a cost which appears to have behaved in the past as a mixed cost (partly fixed and partly variable). A technique for estimating the level of the cost for the future is called the **high-low method**.

Exam focus point

Remember that a fixed budget is not adjusted (in retrospect) to reflect actual activity levels. A flexible budget, however, is one which, by recognising different cost behaviour patterns, changes as activity levels change.

Knowledge brought forward from Paper 3

The high-low method

- Review records of costs in previous periods and select the period with the highest activity level and the period with the lowest activity level.
- If necessary, adjust costs to the same level by means of a price index.
- Total cost of high activity level minus total cost of low activity level = variable cost of difference in activity levels.
- Determine the fixed cost by substitution.

Question 1

Rice and Faull Ltd has recorded the following total costs during the last five years.

Year	*Output volume*	*Total cost*	*Average price level index*
	Units	£	
19X0	65,000	145,000	100
19X1	80,000	179,000	112
19X2	90,000	209,100	123
19X3	60,000	201,600	144
19X4	75,000	248,000	160

Required

Calculate the expected costs in 19X5 if output is 85,000 units and the average price level index is 180. (In other words do not ignore inflation!)

Answer

Price levels should be adjusted to a common basis, say index level 100.

(a)

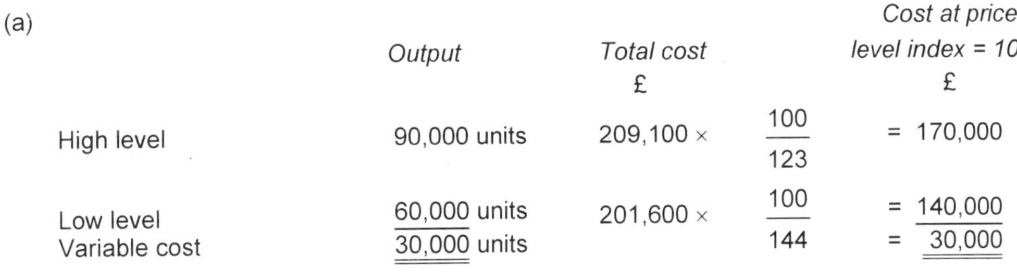

	Output	*Total cost* £		*Cost at price level index = 100* £
High level	90,000 units	209,100 ×	$\frac{100}{123}$	= 170,000
Low level	60,000 units	201,600 ×	$\frac{100}{144}$	= 140,000
Variable cost	30,000 units			= 30,000

The variable cost is therefore £1 per unit.

(b) Use the variable cost to determine the fixed cost.

	£
Total cost of 90,000 units (Index 100)	170,000
Variable cost of 90,000 units (× £1)	90,000
Fixed costs (Index 100)	80,000

(c) Costs in 19X5 for 85,000 units will be as follows.

	£
Variable costs (Index 100)	85,000
Fixed costs (Index 100)	80,000
Total costs (Index 100)	165,000

At 19X5 price levels (Index 180) $= £165{,}000 \times \frac{180}{100}$

$= £297{,}000$

1.5 We can now look at a full example of preparing a flexible budget.

1.6 EXAMPLE: PREPARING A FLEXIBLE BUDGET

(a) Prepare a budget for 19X6 for the direct labour costs and overhead expenses of a production department at the activity levels of 80%, 90% and 100%, using the information listed below.

(i) The direct labour hourly rate is expected to be £3.75.

(ii) 100% activity represents 60,000 direct labour hours.

(iii) Variable costs

Indirect labour	£0.75 per direct labour hour
Consumable supplies	£0.375 per direct labour hour
Canteen and other welfare services	6% of direct and indirect labour costs

(iv) Semi-variable costs are expected to relate to the direct labour hours in the same manner as for the last five years.

Year	*Direct labour hours*	*Semi-variable costs* £
19X1	64,000	20,800
19X2	59,000	19,800
19X3	53,000	18,600
19X4	49,000	17,800
19X5	40,000 (estimate)	16,000 (estimate)

(v) *Fixed costs*

	£
Depreciation	18,000
Maintenance	10,000
Insurance	4,000
Rates	15,000
Management salaries	25,000

(vi) Inflation is to be ignored.

(b) Calculate the **budget cost allowance (ie expected expenditure)** for 19X6 assuming that 57,000 direct labour hours are worked.

1.7 SOLUTION

(a)

	80% level *48,000 hrs* £'000	*90% level* *54,000 hrs* £'000	*100% level* *60,000 hrs* £'000
Direct labour	180.00	202.50	225.0
Other variable costs			
Indirect labour	36.00	40.50	45.0
Consumable supplies	18.00	20.25	22.5
Canteen etc	12.96	14.58	16.2
Total variable costs (£5.145 per hour)	246.96	277.83	308.7
Semi-variable costs (W)	17.60	18.80	20.0
Fixed costs			
Depreciation	18.00	18.00	18.0
Maintenance	10.00	10.00	10.0
Insurance	4.00	4.00	4.0
Rates	15.00	15.00	15.0
Management salaries	25.00	25.00	25.0
Budgeted costs	336.56	368.63	400.7

Working

Using the high/low method:

	£
Total cost of 64,000 hours	20,800
Total cost of 40,000 hours	16,000
Variable cost of 24,000 hours	4,800
Variable cost per hour (£4,800/24,000)	£0.20

	£
Total cost of 64,000 hours	20,800
Variable cost of 64,000 hours (× £0.20)	12,800
Fixed costs	8,000

Semi-variable costs are calculated as follows.

			£
60,000 hours	(60,000 × £0.20) + £8,000	=	20,000
54,000 hours	(54,000 × £0.20) + £8,000	=	18,800
48,000 hours	(48,000 × £0.20) + £8,000	=	17,600

(b) The budget cost allowance for 57,000 direct labour hours of work would be as follows.

		£
Variable costs	(57,000 × £5.145)	293,265
Semi-variable costs	(£8,000 + (57,000 × £0.20))	19,400
Fixed costs		72,000
		384,665

2 FLEXIBLE BUDGETS AND BUDGETARY CONTROL 6/95

KEY TERM

Budgetary control is the practice of establishing budgets which identify areas of responsibility for individual managers (for example production managers, purchasing managers and so on) and of regularly comparing actual results against expected results. The differences between actual results and expected results are called **variances** and these are used to provide a guideline for control action by individual managers

2.1 We will be looking at variances in some detail in Chapters 11 and 12.

2.2 Note that individual managers are held responsible for investigating differences between budgeted and actual results, and are then expected to take corrective action or amend the plan in the light of actual events.

2.3 The wrong approach to budgetary control is to compare actual results against a fixed budget. Consider the following example.

Windy Ltd manufactures a single product, the cloud. Budgeted results and actual results for June 19X2 are shown below.

	Budget	*Actual results*	*Variance*
Production and sales of the cloud (units)	2,000	3,000	
	£	£	£
Sales revenue (a)	20,000	30,000	10,000 (F)
Direct materials	6,000	8,500	2,500 (A)
Direct labour	4,000	4,500	500 (A)
Maintenance	1,000	1,400	400 (A)
Depreciation	2,000	2,200	200 (A)
Rent and rates	1,500	1,600	100 (A)
Other costs	3,600	5,000	1,400 (A)
Total costs (b)	18,100	23,200	5,100
Profit (a) – (b)	1,900	6,800	4,900 (F)

2.4 (a) In this example, the variances are meaningless for purposes of control. Costs were higher than budget because the volume of output was also higher; variable costs would be expected to increase above the budgeted costs in the fixed budget. There is no information to show whether control action is needed for any aspect of costs or revenue.

(b) For control purposes, it is necessary to know the answers to questions such as the following.

(i) Were actual costs higher than they should have been to produce and sell 3,000 clouds?

(ii) Was actual revenue satisfactory from the sale of 3,000 clouds?

2.5 The **correct approach to budgetary control** is as follows.

- **Identify fixed and variable costs.**
- **Produce a flexible budget using marginal costing techniques.**

2.6 In the previous example of Windy Ltd, let us suppose that we have the following estimates of cost behaviour.

(a) Direct materials and maintenance costs are variable.

(b) Although basic wages are a fixed cost, direct labour is regarded as variable in order to measure efficiency/productivity.

(c) Rent and rates and depreciation are fixed costs.

(d) Other costs consist of fixed costs of £1,600 plus a variable cost of £1 per unit made and sold.

2.7 Now that the cost behaviour patterns are known, a budget cost allowance can be calculated for each item of expenditure. This allowance is shown in a flexible budget as the expected expenditure on each item for the relevant level of activity. The budget cost allowances are calculated as follows.

(a) Variable cost allowances = original budgets × (3,000 units/2,000 units)
eg material cost allowance = £6,000 × $^3/_2$ = £9,000

(b) Fixed cost allowances = as original budget

(c) Semi-fixed cost allowances = original budgeted fixed costs + (3,000 units × variable cost per unit)
eg other cost allowances = £1,600 + (3,000 × £1) = £4,600

2.8 The budgetary control analysis should be as follows.

	Fixed budget (a)	*Flexible budget (b)*	*Actual results (c)*	*Budget variance (b) - (c)*
Production & sales (units)	2,000	3,000	3,000	
	£	£	£	£
Sales revenue	20,000	30,000	30,000	0
Variable costs				
Direct materials	6,000	9,000	8,500	500 (F)
Direct labour	4,000	6,000	4,500	1,500 (F)
Maintenance	1,000	1,500	1,400	100 (F)
Semi-variable costs				
Other costs	3,600	4,600	5,000	400 (A)
Fixed costs				
Depreciation	2,000	2,000	2,200	200 (A)
Rent and rates	1,500	1,500	1,600	100 (A)
Total costs	18,100	24,600	23,200	1,400 (F)
Profit	1,900	5,400	6,800	1,400 (F)

Note. **(F) denotes a favourable variance** and **(A) an adverse or unfavourable variance.** Adverse variances are sometimes denoted as (U) for 'unfavourable'.

2.9 We can **analyse** the above as follows.

(a) In selling 3,000 units the expected profit should have been, not the fixed budget profit of £1,900, but the flexible budget profit of £5,400. Instead, actual profit was £6,800 ie £1,400 more than we should have expected. One of the reasons for the improvement is that, **given output and sales** of 3,000 units, **costs were lower than expected** (and sales revenue exactly as expected).

	£
Direct materials cost variance	500 (F)
Direct labour cost variance	1,500 (F)
Maintenance cost variance	100 (F)
Other costs variance	400 (A)
Fixed cost variances	
Depreciation	200 (A)
Rent and rates	100 (A)
	1,400 (F)

Profit was therefore increased by £1,400 because costs were lower than anticipated.

(b) Another reason for the improvement in profit above the fixed budget profit is the **sales volume**. Windy Ltd sold 3,000 clouds instead of 2,000 clouds, with the following result.

	£	£
Sales revenue increased by		10,000
Variable costs increased by:		
direct materials	3,000	
direct labour	2,000	
maintenance	500	
variable element of other costs	1,000	
Fixed costs are unchanged		6,500
Profit increased by		3,500

Profit was therefore increased by £3,500 because sales volumes increased.

(c) A full variance analysis statement would be as follows.

	£	£
Fixed budget profit		1,900
Variances		
Sales volume	3,500 (F)	
Direct materials cost	500 (F)	
Direct labour cost	1,500 (F)	
Maintenance cost	100 (F)	
Other costs	400 (A)	
Depreciation	200 (A)	
Rent and rates	100 (A)	
		4,900 (F)
Actual profit		6,800

2.10 If management believes that any of these variances are large enough to justify it, they will investigate the reasons for them to see whether any corrective action is necessary or whether the plan needs amending in the light of actual events.

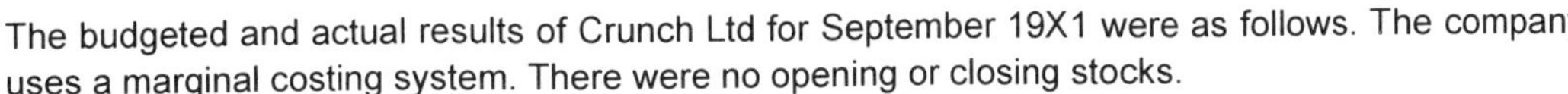

Question 2

The budgeted and actual results of Crunch Ltd for September 19X1 were as follows. The company uses a marginal costing system. There were no opening or closing stocks.

	Fixed budget		*Actual*	
Sales and production	1,000 units		700 units	
	£	£	£	£
Sales		20,000		14,200
Variable cost of sales				
Direct materials	8,000		5,200	
Direct labour	4,000		3,100	
Variable overhead	2,000		1,500	
		14,000		9,800
Contribution		6,000		4,400
Fixed costs		5,000		5,400
Profit/(loss)		1,000		(1,000)

Required

Prepare a budget that will be useful for management control purposes.

Answer

We need to prepare a flexible budget for 700 units.

	Budget		*Flexed budget*	*Actual*	*Variances*
	1,000 units	Per unit	700 units	700 units	
	£	£	£	£	£
Sales	20,000	(20)	14,000	14,200	200 (F)
Variable costs					
Direct material	8,000	(8)	5,600	5,200	400 (F)
Direct labour	4,000	(4)	2,800	3,100	300 (A)
Variable production overhead	2,000	(2)	1,400	1,500	100 (A)
	14,000	(14)	9,800	9,800	
Contribution	6,000		4,200	4,400	
Fixed costs	5,000	(N/A)	5,000	5,400	400 (A)
Profit/(loss)	1,000		(800)	(1,000)	200 (A)

Note that the differences between actual results (what revenues and costs *were* for 700 units) and the flexed budget (what revenues and costs *should* be for 700 units) have been noted in the right hand column as *variances*. (F) denotes a situation where actual results were better than the flexible budget results whereas (A) denotes a situation where actual results were worse than flexible budget results.

2.11 By flexing the budget in the exercise above we removed the effect on sales revenue of the difference between budgeted *sales volume* and actual *sales volume*. But there is still a variance of £200 (F). This means that the actual *selling price* must have been different to the budgeted selling price, resulting in a £200 (F) selling price variance.

We will be looking at variances in much more detail in Chapters 11 and 12.

Factors to consider when preparing flexible budgets

2.12 The mechanics of flexible budgeting are, in theory, fairly straightforward. In practice, however, there are a number of points that must be considered before figures are simply flexed.

(a) The separation of costs into their fixed and variable elements is not always straightforward.

(b) Fixed costs may behave in a step-line fashion as activity levels increase/decrease.

(c) Account must be taken of the assumptions upon which the original fixed budget was based. Such assumptions might include the constraint posed by limiting factors, the rate of inflation, judgements about future uncertainty, the demand for the organisation's products and so on.

3 BEHAVIOURAL IMPLICATIONS OF BUDGETING 6/96, 6/97

Exam focus point

You only need to be able to assess the behavioural implications of budgeting at an introductory level. This topic is examined in more detail in Paper 9.

3.1 The purpose of a budgetary control system is to assist management in planning and controlling the resources of their organisation by providing appropriate control information. The information will only be valuable, however, if it is interpreted correctly and used purposefully by managers *and* employees.

3.2 The correct use of control information therefore depends not only on the content of the information itself, but also on the behaviour of its recipients. This is because control in business is exercised by people. Their attitude to control information will colour their views on what they should do with it. There are a number of behavioural problems which can arise, however.

- The **managers who set the budget** or standards are **often not the managers** who are then made **responsible for achieving budget targets.**
- The **goals of the organisation as a whole**, as expressed in a budget, **may not coincide with the personal aspirations of individual managers.**
- **Control is applied at different stages by different people**. A supervisor might get weekly control reports, and act on them; his superior might get monthly control reports, and decide to take different control action, which may or may not coincide with the efforts of his subordinate. Different managers can get in each others' way, and resent the interference from others.

Motivation

3.3 Motivation is what makes people behave in the way that they do. It comes from individual attitudes, or group attitudes. Individuals will be motivated by personal desires and interests. These may be in line with the objectives of the organisation, and some people 'live for their jobs'. Other individuals see their job as a chore, and their motivations will be unrelated to the objectives of the organisation they work for.

3.4 It is therefore vital that the goals of management and the employees harmonise with the goals of the organisation as a whole. This is known as goal congruence. Although obtaining goal congruence is essentially a behavioural problem, **it is possible to design and run a budgetary control system which will go some way towards ensuring that goal congruence is achieved**. Managers and employees must therefore be favourably disposed towards the budgetary control system so that it can operate efficiently.

3.5 One role of the management accountant is therefore to encourage positive attitudes towards the following aspects of budgeting.

(a) **Setting budgets**
(b) **Implementing budgets** (that is, putting the organisation's plans into practice)
(c) Feedback of results (**control information**)

Poor attitudes when setting budgets

3.6 But poor attitudes or hostile behaviour towards the budgetary control system can begin at the **planning stage. If managers are involved in preparing a budget** the following may happen.

- Managers may **complain that they are too busy** to spend much time on budgeting.
- They may **build 'slack' into their expenditure estimates** and lobby for a high budget expenditure allowance.
- They may argue that **formalising a budget plan on paper is too restricting** and that managers should be allowed flexibility and room for manoeuvre in the operational decisions they take.

- They may set budgets for their budget centre and **not coordinate** their own plans with those of other budget centres.
- They may **base future plans on past results**, instead of using the opportunity for formalised planning to look at alternative options and new ideas.

3.7 On the other hand, **managers may not be involved in the budgeting process**. Organisational goals may not be communicated to them and they might have their budget decided for them by senior management or administrative decision. It is **hard for people to be motivated to achieve targets set by someone else.**

Poor attitudes when putting plans into action

3.8 Poor attitudes also arise **when a budget is implemented**.

- Managers might **put in only just enough effort** to achieve budget targets, without trying to beat targets.
- A formal budget might **encourage rigidity and discourage flexibility**.
- **Short-term planning** in a budget **can draw attention away from the longer-term consequences** of decisions.
- Managers might **tolerate slapdash and inaccurate methods of recording** (classifying and codifying) actual costs.
- There might be **minimal cooperation and communication** between managers.
- Managers will often try to make sure that they **spend up to their full budget allowance, and do not overspend**, so that they will not be accused of having asked for too much spending allowance in the first place.

Poor attitudes and the use of control information

3.9 The **attitude of managers towards the accounting control information** they receive **might reduce the information's effectiveness**.

- Management accounting control reports could well be seen as having a relatively **low priority** in the list of management tasks. Managers might take the view that they have more pressing jobs on hand than looking at routine control reports.
- Managers might **resent control information**; they may see it as **part of a system of trying to find fault with their work**. This resentment is likely to be particularly strong when budgets or standards are imposed on managers without allowing them to participate in the budget-setting process. When managers resent control reports, they are likely to adopt a hostile and defensive attitude.
- If budgets are seen as **pressure devices** to push managers into doing better, control reports will be resented.
- Managers **may not understand the information** in the control reports, because they are unfamiliar with accounting terminology or principles.
- Managers might have a **false sense of what their objectives should be**. A production manager, for example, might consider it more important to maintain quality standards regardless of cost, and a service department manager might similarly think that his department must maintain a certain level of service, regardless of expense. They would then dismiss adverse expenditure variances as inevitable and unavoidable.

- **If there are flaws in the system of recording actual costs**, managers will dismiss control information as unreliable.
- **Control information** might be **received weeks after the end of the** period to which it relates, in which case managers might regard it as out-of-date and no longer useful.
- Managers might be **held responsible for variances outside their control**.

3.10 It is therefore obvious that accountants and senior management should try to implement systems that are acceptable to budget holders and which produce positive effects.

Pay as a motivator

3.11 Many researchers agree that **pay can be an important motivator**, when there is a formal link between higher pay (or other rewards, such as promotion) and achieving budget targets. Individuals are likely to work harder to achieve budget if they know that they will be rewarded for their successful efforts. There are, however, problems with using pay as an incentive.

- A serious problem that can arise is that **formal reward and performance evaluation systems can encourage dysfunctional behaviour**. Many investigations have noted the tendency of managers to pad their budgets either in anticipation of cuts by superiors or to make the subsequent variances more favourable. And there are numerous examples of managers making decisions in response to performance indices, even though the decisions are contrary to the wider purposes of the organisation.
- The targets must be challenging, but fair, otherwise individuals will become dissatisfied. **Pay can be a demotivator as well as a motivator**!

4 PARTICIPATION AND PERFORMANCE EVALUATION 6/96, 6/97

Participation

4.1 Another view is that **participation** in the budgeting process **will improve motivation** and so will improve the quality of budget decisions and the efforts of individuals to achieve their budget targets.

4.2 There are basically two ways in which a budget can be set: from the **top down** (imposed budget) or from the **bottom up** (participatory budget).

Imposed style of budgeting

4.3 In this approach to budgeting, **top management prepare a budget with little or no input from operating personnel** which is then imposed upon the employees who have to work to the budgeted figures.

4.4 The times when imposed budgets are effective are as follows.

- In newly-formed organisations
- In very small businesses
- During periods of economic hardship
- When operational managers lack budgeting skills
- When the organisation's different units require precise coordination

4.5 They are, of course, advantages and disadvantages to this style of setting budgets.

(a) **Advantages**

- They increase the probability that the organisation's strategic plans are incorporated into planned activities.
- They enhance the coordination between the plans and objectives of divisions.
- They use senior management's awareness of total resource availability.
- They decrease the possibility of input from inexperienced or uninformed lower-level employees.
- They decrease the period of time taken to draw up the budgets.

(b) **Disadvantages**

- Dissatisfaction, defensiveness and low morale amongst employees who must work under them can be produced.
- The feeling of team spirit may disappear.
- The acceptance of organisational goals and objectives could be limited
- The feeling of the budget as a punitive device could arise.
- Unachievable budgets for overseas divisions could result if consideration is not given to local operating and political environments.
- Lower-level management initiative may be stifled.

Participative style of budgeting

4.6 In this approach to budgeting, **budgets are developed by lower-level managers who then submit the budgets to their superiors**. The budgets are based on the lower-level managers' perceptions of what is achievable and the associated necessary resources. The extent to which lower-level managers are allowed to participate in the budgeting process will depend on two things: senior management's awareness of participatory budgeting's advantages and their agreement with those advantages.

4.7 **Participative budgets** are effective in the following circumstances.

- In well-established organisations
- In very large businesses
- During periods of economic affluence
- When operational managers have strong budgeting skills
- When the organisation's different units act autonomously

4.8 The **advantages** of participative budgets are as follows.

- Information from employees most familiar with each unit's needs and constraints is included.
- Knowledge spread among several levels of management is pulled together.
- Morale and motivation is improved.
- Acceptance of and commitment to organisational goals and objectives by operational managers is increased.
- In general they are more realistic.
- Co-ordination between units is improved.
- Operating management are able to develop plans which tie in with the organisation's goals and objectives.

- Specific resource requirements are included.
- Senior managers' overview of the organisation is mixed with operational level details.
- An expression of the expectations of both senior management and their subordinates is provided.

4.9 There are, on the other hand, a number of **disadvantages** of participative budgets.

- They consume more time.
- The advantages of managerial participation could be negated by changes implemented by senior management leading to a dissatisfaction similar to that experienced with imposed budgets.
- Managers could be ambivalent about or unqualified to participate and hence the budget may be unachievable.
- They may cause managers to introduce budgetary slack.
- They can support 'empire building' by subordinates.
- An earlier start to the budgeting process could be required when there is more uncertainty about the future.

4.10 Many writers refer to a third style of budgeting, a **negotiated style**.

Negotiated style of budgeting

4.11 At the two extremes, budgets can be dictated from above or simply emerge from below but, in practice, different levels of management often agree budgets by a process of negotiation. In the imposed budget approach, operational managers will try to negotiate with senior managers the budget targets which they consider to be unreasonable or unrealistic. Likewise senior management usually review and revise budgets presented to them under a participative approach through a process of negotiation with lower level managers. **Final budgets are therefore most likely to lie between what top management would really like and what junior managers believe is feasible.** The budgeting process is hence a **bargaining process** and it is this bargaining which is of vital importance, **determining whether the budget is an effective management tool or simply a clerical device**.

Performance evaluation

4.12 A very important **source of motivation to perform well** (to achieve budget targets, perhaps, or to eliminate variances) is, not surprisingly, being **kept informed about how actual results are progressing, and how actual results compare with target.** Individuals should not be kept in the dark about their performance.

The information fed back about actual results should obviously have the qualities of good information.

- Reports should be clear and comprehensive.
- Significant variances should be highlighted for investigation.
- Reports should be timely, which means they must be produced in good time to allow the individual to take control action before any adverse results get much worse.

4.13 It is conventionally assumed that by establishing formal systems of performance measurement and rewarding individuals for their performance they will be encouraged to maximise their contribution towards the organisation's objectives. But research evidence suggests that **all too often accounting performance measures lead to a lack of goal congruence**. Managers seek to improve their performance on the basis of the indicator used, even if this is not in the best interests of the organisation as a whole.

For example, a production manager may be encouraged to achieve and maintain high production levels and to reduce costs, particularly if his or her bonus is linked to these factors. Such a manager is likely to be highly motivated. But the need to maintain high production levels could lead to high levels of slow-moving stock, resulting in an adverse effect on the company's cash flow.

Budgetary slack

KEY TERM

Budgetary slack is the difference between the minimum necessary costs and the costs built into the budget or actually incurred.

4.14 In the process of preparing budgets, managers might **deliberately overestimate costs**, so that they will not be blamed in the future for overspending.

In controlling actual operations, managers must then **ensure that their spending rises to meet their budget**, otherwise they will be 'blamed' for careless budgeting.

4.15 A typical situation is for a manager to waste money on non-essential expenses so that he uses all his budget allowances. The reason behind his action is the fear that unless the allowance is fully spent it will be reduced in future periods thus making his job more difficult as the future reduced budgets will not be so easy to attain. Because inefficiency and slack are allowed for in budgets, achieving a budget target means only that costs have remained within the accepted levels of inefficient spending.

5 THE MANAGEMENT ACCOUNTANT AND MOTIVATION

5.1 **Can performance measures and the related budgetary control system ever motivate managers towards achieving the organisation's goals?**

- Accounting measures of performance **can't provide a comprehensive assessment** of what a person has achieved for the organisation.
- It is usually **impossible to segregate the controllable component of performance from the uncontrollable** component. This can lead to unfairness in evaluating performance.
- Accounting **reports tend to concentrate on short-term achievements**, to the exclusion of the long-term effects.
- Many accounting **reports try to serve several different purposes**, and in trying to satisfy several needs actually satisfy none properly.

5.2 The management accountant does not have the authority to do much on his or her own to improve hostile or apathetic attitudes to control information. There has to be support, either from senior management or from cost and profit centre managers. However, the management accountant can do quite a lot to improve and then maintain the standard of a budgetary control reporting system.

(a) **Senior management can offer support** by doing the following.

- Making sure that a **system of responsibility accounting is adopted** within the organisation, and that individual managers are fully aware of what their areas of responsibility are, and how they will be held accountable for results in these areas.
- Allowing **managers to have a say in formulating their budgets**. The participative approach in budgeting should reduce hostility to control reporting.
- Offering **incentives** (for example bonuses) to managers who meet budget targets.
- **Regarding budgetary control information as a tool** for managers to use constructively, not a way of apportioning blame and punishing managers who fail to achieve a target or standard.

(b) **Cost centre/profit centre managers should accept their responsibilities**. Ideally, they ought to be aware of the benefits of a budgetary control system and welcome the feedback of control information. If necessary, in-house training courses in the budgetary control system could be held to encourage a collective, cooperative and positive attitude amongst managers.

(c) The **management accountant should improve** (or maintain) the **quality of the budgetary control system** by doing the following.

- **Developing a working relationship with operational managers**, for example going out to meet them and discussing the control reports, instead of sitting in isolation in the accounting office, divorced from contact with the people to whom he or she sends the control reports.
- **Explaining the meaning of budgets and control reports**. Explanations can be provided in a budget manual, but managers have to be encouraged to read and use the manual if the message is to get across this way.
- **Keeping accounting jargon in these reports to a minimum.**
- Making **reports clear and to the point**, for example using the principle of reporting by exception.
- Providing control information with a **minimum of delay.**
- **Making control information as useful as possible**, by clearly distinguishing between directly attributable costs over which a manager should have influence and apportioned costs or fixed costs which are unavoidable or uncontrollable.
- Trying to make sure that **actual costs are recorded accurately** at the point of data capture.
- Trying to ensure that **budgets are up-to-date**, either by having a system of rolling budgets, or else by updating budgets or standards as necessary, and ensuring that standards are 'fair' so that control information is realistic.

Question 3

Discuss the behavioural aspects of participation in the budgeting process and any difficulties you might envisage.

Answer

The level of participation in the budgeting process can vary from zero participation to a process of group decision making. There are a number of behavioural aspects of participation to consider.

(a) *Aspiration levels.* It is generally accepted that standards and targets should take account of individual aspiration levels as far as possible. One way of being aware of these aspiration levels is to involve people in the preparation of their own budgets.

(b) *Communication.* Managers cannot be expected to achieve targets if they do not know what those targets are. Communication of targets is made easier if managers have participated in the budgetary process from the beginning.

(c) *Motivation.* Managers are likely to be better motivated to achieve a budget if they have been involved in compiling it, rather than having a dictatorial budget imposed on them.

(d) *Realistic targets.* A target must be achievable and accepted as realistic if it is to be a motivating factor. A manager who has been involved in setting targets is more likely to accept them as realistic. In addition, managers who are close to the operation of their departments may be more aware of the costs and potential savings in running it.

(e) *Goal congruence.* Goal congruence is the state which exists in the budgeting process where the individual's personal goals tally with the goals of the organisation. One of the best ways of achieving goal congruence is to involve managers in the preparation of their own budgets, so that their personal goals can be taken into account in setting targets.

Although participative budgeting has many advantages, difficulties might also arise.

(a) *Pseudo-participation.* Participation may not be genuine, but merely a pretence at involving managers in the preparation of their budgets. Managers may feel that their contribution is being ignored, or that the participation consists of merely obtaining their agreement to a budget which has already been decided. If this is the case then managers are likely to be more demotivated than if there is no participation at all.

(b) *Coordination.* If participative budgeting is well managed it can improve the coordination of the preparation of the various budgets. There is, however, a danger that too many managers will become involved so that communication becomes difficult and the process become complex.

(c) *Training.* Some managers may not possess the necessary skill to make an effective contribution to the preparation of their budgets. Additional training may be necessary, with the consequent investment of money and time. It may also be necessary to train managers to understand the purposes and advantages of participation. They will then accept the need for their own participation and that of their subordinates in the budgeting process.

(d) *Slack.* Budgetary slack is unnecessary expenditure built into a budget. If budgets are used in a punitive fashion for control purposes then managers will be tempted to build in extra expenditure to provide a 'cushion' against overspending. It is easier for them to build in slack in a participative system.

Chapter roundup

- **Fixed budgets** remain unchanged regardless of the level of activity; **flexible budgets** are designed to flex with the level of activity.
- Comparison of a fixed budget with the actual results for a different level of activity is of little use for control purposes. Flexible budgets should be used to show what cost and revenues should have been for the actual level of activity.
- A prerequisite of flexible budgeting is a knowledge of cost behaviour.
- The differences between the components of the fixed budget and the actual results are known as **budget variances**.
- Budgeting is more than a technical, number-crunching process: the **behavioural implications** of budgeting must be considered.
- Used correctly a budgetary control system can **motivate** but it can also produce undesirable **negative reactions**.
- A great deal of research has been done into the effects on motivation of participation in the budgeting process.
- There are basically two ways in which a budget can be set: from the **top down** (imposed budget) or from the **bottom up** (participatory budget). Many writers refer to a third style (**negotiated**).
- Budgetary information can be used to **evaluate performance**.

Quick quiz

1. Distinguish between a fixed budget and a flexible budget. (see paras 1.1 - 1.3)
2. Describe the uses of a flexible budget in planning and as a retrospective control measure. (1.2)
3. Flexible budgets are normally prepared on a marginal cost basis. True or false? (1.3)
4. What is the correct approach to budgetary control? (2.5)
5. What are the two main reasons for differences between a fixed budget profit and an actual profit? (2.8)
6. List five results of an absence of motivation at the planning stage of the budgetary process. (3.6)
7. What are the advantages of participative budgets? (3.23) 4.6
8. What are the three distinct ways of using budgetary information to evaluate managerial performance as identified by Hopwood? (3.32)

Question to try	Level	Marks	Time
7	Introductory	n/a	15 mins

Chapter 8

QUANTITATIVE AIDS IN BUDGETING

Chapter topic list		Syllabus reference
1	Cost forecasting	2(a)(v)
2	Linear regression analysis	2(a)(v)
3	Correlation	2(a)(v)
4	Sales forecasting	2(a)(v)
5	Regression and forecasting	2(a)(v)
6	The components of time series	2(a)(v)
7	Finding the trend	2(a)(v)
8	Finding the seasonal variations	2(a)(v)
9	Time series analysis and forecasting	2(a)(v)
10	Forecasting problems	2(a)(v)

Introduction

In Chapters 6 and 7 we have seen how to prepare budgets but we have not yet looked at where the figures which go into the budgets come from. As we will see in this chapter, to produce a budget calls for the **preparation of forecasts of costs and revenues**.

Various quantitative techniques can assist with these **'number-crunching' aspects of budgeting.** This chapter aims to provide an understanding of those techniques. Note that the techniques will be described within their budgetary context.

It has been said that **budgeting is more a test of forecasting skill than anything else** and there is a certain amount of truth in such a comment. Forecasts need to be made of sales volumes and prices, wage rates and earnings, material availability's and prices, rates of inflation, the cost of bought-in services and the cost of overhead items such as power. However, it is not sufficient to simply add a percentage to last year's budget in the hope of achieving a realistic forecast.

A **forecast** is an estimate of what might happen in the future. It is a **best estimate**, based on certain assumptions about the conditions that are expected to apply. A **budget**, in contrast, is a **plan** of what the organisation is aiming to achieve and what it has set as a target. A budget should be **realistic** and so it will be based to some extent on forecasts prepared. In formulating a budget, however, management will be trying to establish some control over the conditions that will apply in the future.

When a budget is set it will, for a short time, be the same as the forecasts. As actual events progress and the situation develops and changes, however, new forecasts might be prepared that differ from the budget targets. Management might be able to take control action to bring forecasts back into line with the budget; alternatively, management will have to accept that the budget will not be achieved, or it will be exceeded, depending on what the current forecasts indicate.

In the next chapter we will consider budgeting using alternative systems.

1 COST FORECASTING

1.1 There are three basic approaches to cost forecasting.

- The industrial engineering approach
- The account classification method
- Extrapolation of historical costs and data, frequently using statistical analysis of varying degrees of sophistication

Industrial engineering approach

1.2 When there are **no historic data records** because, perhaps, a new product is being launched, or when conditions have changed dramatically, statistical analysis will be of little use and so the industrial engineering approach should be used for estimation purposes. The method uses a detailed approach to **establish the required level of input** (labour, materials, and so on) **for a particular output level**. The inputs are then converted into money values. It is a **lengthy** and **expensive** method of estimation but in the right circumstances **can be fairly accurate**. Such circumstances are when there is a clear, physical relationship between input and output.

1.3 The approach uses work study and production engineering techniques and **attempts to establish what a cost *should* be**. It is the same approach used in the establishment of standard costs.

Account classification method

1.4 This method involves the **examination of each cost item and its classification** as either fixed or variable. Semi-variable costs must be split into their fixed and variable components. Values will then be assigned to each cost item, probably on the basis of data from historical cost accounts.

Although **quick** and **inexpensive**, this method of estimation involves the **use of subjective judgement** and management skill and realism in estimating costs. Considerable difficulty can arise when splitting semi-variable costs into their fixed and variable components. Only **approximate accuracy** can therefore be expected from its use.

Forecasting using historical data

1.5 Numerous techniques have been developed for using past costs incurred as the basis for forecasting future values. These techniques range from simple arithmetic and visual methods to advanced computer-based statistical systems. With all techniques, however, there is the **presumption that the past will provide guidance to the future**. Before using any extrapolation techniques, the **past data** must therefore be critically examined to **assess their appropriateness for the intended purpose**. The following checks should be made.

- The **time period** should be long enough to include any periodically paid costs but short enough to ensure that averaging of variations in the level of activity has not occurred.
- The **data** should be examined to ensure that any non-activity level factors affecting costs were roughly the same in the past as those forecast for the future. Such factors might include changes in technology, changes in efficiency, changes in production

methods, changes in resource costs, strikes, weather conditions and so on. Changes to the past data are frequently necessary.

- The **methods of data collection** and the accounting policies used should not introduce bias. Examples might include depreciation policies and the treatment of by-products.

(d) Appropriate choices of **dependent** and **independent variables** must be made.

1.6 The three methods which we are going to look at (the high-low method, the scattergraph method and linear regression analysis) are based on the assumption that a **linear relationship** links levels of cost and levels of activity.

Knowledge brought forward from Paper 3

Linear relationships

- A **linear relationship** can be expressed in the form of an equation which has the general form $y = a + bx$

  where y is the **dependent** variable, depending for its value on the value of x

  x is the **independent** variable, whose value helps to determine the corresponding value of y

  a is a **constant**, a fixed amount

  b is a constant, being the **coefficient of x** (that is, the number by which the value of x should be multiplied to derive the value of y)

- If there is a linear relationship between total costs and level of activity, y = total costs, x = level of activity, a = fixed cost (the cost when there is no activity level) and b = variable cost per unit.

- The graph of a linear equation is a **straight line** and is determined by two things, the **gradient** (or slope) of the straight line and the point at which the straight line crosses the y axis (the **intercept**).

  - Gradient = b in the equation $y = a + bx = (y_2 - y_1)/(x_2 - x_1)$ where (x_1, y_1), (x_2, y_2) are two points on the straight line
  - Intercept = a in the equation $y = a + bx$

High-low method

1.7 We have already looked at the algebraic approach to the high-low method in Chapter 7. The **graphical approach** involves plotting on a graph the points representing the highest and lowest activity levels and joining them with a **straight line** to **represent total cost**.

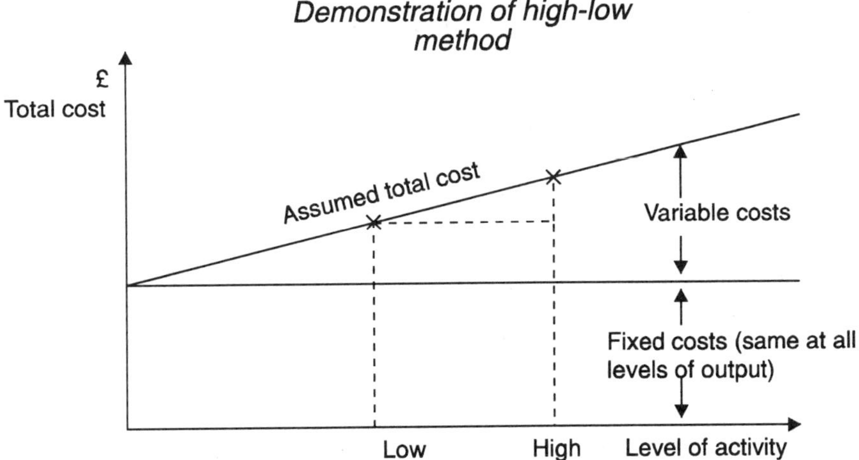

1.8 The slope of the line represents the variable cost per unit and the intercept with the vertical axis the fixed cost. **Forecasts of the total cost** at certain activity levels can be **read directly from the graph** provided the activity level is within the range covered by the graph.

1.9 The major drawback to the high-low method is that **only two historical cost records from previous periods are used** in the cost estimation. Unless these two records are a reliable indicator of costs throughout the relevant range of output, which is unlikely, only a '**loose approximation**' of fixed and variable costs will be obtained. The advantage of the method is its **relative simplicity**.

The scattergraph method

1.10 By this method of cost estimation, cost and activity data are plotted as for the high-low method. A '**line of best fit**' is then drawn. This line should be drawn through the middle of the plotted points as closely as possible so that the distance of points above the line are equal to distances below the line. Where necessary costs should be adjusted to the same indexed price level to allow for inflation.

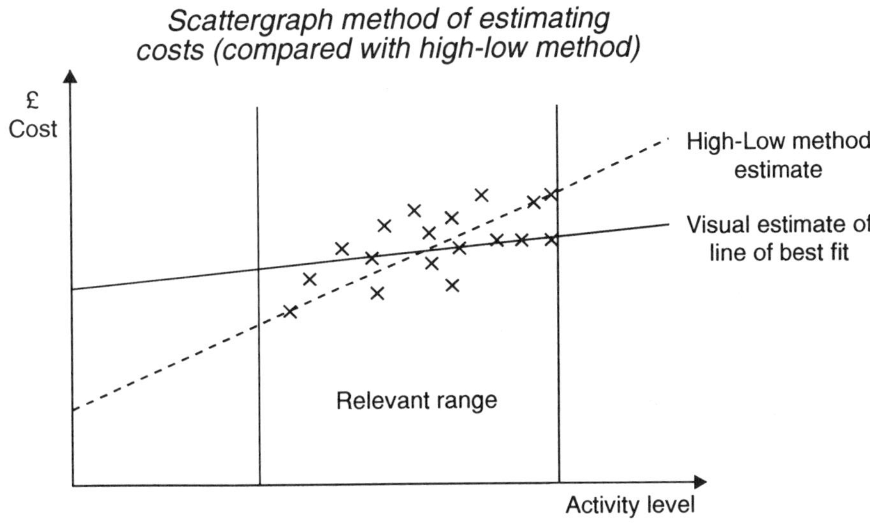

Note how the high-low method would provide a different estimate of fixed and variable costs.

1.11 The fixed cost is the intercept of the line of best fit on the vertical axis. Suppose the fixed cost is £500 and that one of the plotted points (which is very close to the line or actually on it) represents output of 100 units and total cost of £550. The variable cost of 100 units is therefore calculated as £(550 – 500) = £50 and so the variable cost per unit is £0.50. The equation of the line of best fit is therefore *approximately* y = 500 + 0.5x.

1.12 If the company to which this data relate wanted to forecast total costs when output is 90 units, a forecast based on the equation would be 500 + (0.5 × 90) = £545. Alternatively the **forecast could be read directly from the graph using the line of best fit.**

1.13 The advantage of the scattergraph over the high-low method is that a **greater quantity of historical data is used** in the estimation, but its disadvantage is that the cost line is drawn by visual judgement and so is a **subjective approximation**.

2 LINEAR REGRESSION ANALYSIS 12/95, 6/97

Exam focus point

To date, candidates have not been examined on the derivation of linear regression equations. They have, however been asked to explain how regression analysis can be used in certain situations.

2.1 **Linear regression analysis**, also known as the **'least squares technique'**, is a **statistical method** of estimating costs using historical data from a number of previous accounting periods. As a technique it is preferable to the scattergraph because it **avoids the subjectivity of visual judgement** and therefore analyses the historical data more accurately.

2.2 Linear regression analysis is used to derive a **line of best fit which has the general form**

y = a + bx where

y, the dependent variable = total cost
x, the independent variable = the level of activity
a, the intercept of the line on the y axis = the fixed cost
b, the gradient of the line = the variable cost per unit of activity.

2.3 Historical data is collected from previous periods and adjusted to a common price level to remove inflationary differences. This provides a number of readings for activity levels (x) and their associated costs (y). Then, by substituting these readings into the formulae below for a and b, estimates of the fixed cost and variable cost per unit are provided.

FORMULA TO LEARN

If y = a + bx, $b = \frac{n\Sigma xy - \Sigma x\Sigma y}{n\Sigma x^2 - (\Sigma x)^2}$ and $a = \frac{\Sigma y}{n} - \frac{b\Sigma x}{n}$

where n is the number of pair of data for x and y.

An example will help to illustrate this technique.

2.4 EXAMPLE: LEAST SQUARES METHOD

The transport department of the Norwest Council operates a large fleet of assorted vehicles. These vehicles are used as the need arises by the various departments of the Council. Each month a statement is prepared for the transport department comparing actual results with budget.

One of the items in the transport department's monthly statement is the cost of vehicle maintenance. This maintenance is carried out by the employees of the department.

To facilitate control, the transport manager has asked that future statements should show vehicle maintenance costs analysed into fixed and variable costs.

Data from the six months from January to June 19X2 inclusive are given below.

19X2	*Vehicle maintenance cost*	*Vehicle running hours*
	£	
January	13,600	2,100
February	15,800	2,800
March	14,500	2,200
April	16,200	3,000
May	14,900	2,600
June	15,000	2,500

Required

Analyse the vehicle maintenance costs into fixed and variable costs, based on the data given, utilising the least squares method.

2.5 SOLUTION

If y = a + bx, where y represent costs and x represents running hours (since costs depend on running hours) then

$$b = \frac{n\Sigma xy - \Sigma x\Sigma y}{n\Sigma x^2 - (\Sigma x)^2}$$

when n is the number of pairs of data, which is 6 in this problem.

x	*y*	*xy*	x^2
'000 hrs	£'000		
2.1	13.6	28.56	4.41
2.8	15.8	44.24	7.84
2.2	14.5	31.90	4.84
3.0	16.2	48.60	9.00
2.6	14.9	38.74	6.76
2.5	15.0	37.50	6.25
15.2	90.0	229.54	39.10

Variable cost per hour, b $= \frac{6(229.54) - (15.2)(90.00)}{6(39.1) - (15.2)^2}$

$$= \frac{1{,}377.24 - 1{,}368}{234.6 - 231.04} = \frac{9.24}{3.56} = £2.60$$

Fixed costs (in £'000), a $= \frac{\Sigma y}{n} - \frac{b\Sigma x}{n} = \frac{90}{6} - \frac{2.6(15.2)}{6}$

= 8.41 approx, say £8,400

Question 1

You are given the following data for output at a factory and costs of production over the past five months.

Month	Output '000 units x	Costs £'000 y
1	20	82
2	16	70
3	24	90
4	22	85
5	18	73

Required

(a) Calculate an equation to determine the expected level of costs, for any given volume of output.

(b) Prepare a budget for total costs if output is 22,000 units.

Answer

(a) *Workings*

x	*y*	*xy*	x^2	y^2
20	82	1,640	400	6,724
16	70	1,120	256	4,900
24	90	2,160	576	8,100
22	85	1,870	484	7,225
18	73	1,314	324	5,329
Σx = 100	Σy = 400	Σxy = 8,104	Σx^2 = 2,040	Σy^2 = 32,278

n = 5 (There are five pairs of data for x and y values)

$$b = \frac{n\Sigma xy - \Sigma x\Sigma y}{n\Sigma x^2 - (\Sigma x)^2}$$

$$= \frac{(5 \times 8{,}104) - (100 \times 400)}{(5 \times 2{,}040) - 100^2}$$

$$= \frac{40{,}520 - 40{,}000}{10{,}200 - 10{,}000} = \frac{520}{200}$$

$$= 2.6$$

$$a = \bar{y} - b\bar{x}$$

$$= \frac{400}{5} - 2.6 \times (\frac{100}{5})$$

$$= 28$$

$$y = 28 + 2.6x$$

where y = total cost, in thousands of pounds
x = output, in thousands of units.

(b) If the output is 22,000 units, we would expect costs to be

28 + 2.6 × 22

= 85.2 = £85,200.

When should linear regression analysis be used?

2.6 **All of the techniques described so far** are based on the **assumption of linearity** in costs, meaning that a cost item is either a fixed cost, variable cost or a mixed cost (semi-fixed, semi-variable). This is often a sufficiently accurate assumption, although management accountants should nevertheless be aware of the 'step' nature of some costs and of other unusual cost behaviour patterns.

2.7 Perhaps the **most convenient and straightforward technique** of estimating costs is the **account-classification** or **engineering method.** The **high-low method**, however, is a simple and convenient way of estimating fixed and variable costs and it would be more

appropriate than the engineering method for **estimating the total costs of a department, factory or business.** (It avoids the need to build up cost estimates for each cost item individually and is therefore a quicker technique than the engineering method.)

2.8 **Linear regression analysis** is an alternative technique to the high-low and scattergraph methods, and it would be used in the following circumstances.

- **When the high-low and scattergraph methods are thought to be too unreliable** so that they might produce serious inaccuracies in the estimate of costs.
- When there is a **sufficient number of historical records** of cost at different activity levels to make the linear regression method capable of providing a more reliable estimate of costs.

The conditions suited to the use of linear regression analysis

2.9 The conditions which should apply if linear regression analysis is to be used to estimate costs are as follows.

- A **linear cost function should be assumed**. This assumption can be tested by measures of reliability, such as the correlation coefficient and the coefficient of determination (which ought to be reasonably close to 1). We will be looking at these concepts later in the chapter.
- When calculating a line of best fit, there will be a range of values for x. In Question 1, the line y = 28 + 2.6x was predicted from data with output values ranging from x = 16 to x = 24. Depending on the degree of correlation between x and y, we might safely use the estimated line of best fit to forecast values for y, provided that the value of x remains within the range 16 to 24. We would be on less safe ground if we used the equation to predict a value for y when x = 10, or 30, or any other value outside the range 16 to 24, because we would **have to assume that costs behave in the same way outside the range of x values used to establish the line in the first place.**

KEY TERMS

- **Interpolation** means using a line of best fit to predict a value within the two extreme points of the observed range.
- **Extrapolation** means using a line of best fit to predict a value outside the two extreme points.

- The **historical data** for cost and output should be **adjusted to a common price level** (to overcome cost differences caused by inflation) and the historical data should also be **representative of** the following.
  - **Current technology**
  - **Current efficiency levels**
  - **Current operations** (products made)
- As far as possible, **historical data should be accurately recorded** so that variable costs are properly matched against the items produced or sold, and fixed costs are properly matched against the time period to which they relate. For example, if a factory rental is £120,000 per annum, it is important that if data is gathered monthly, these costs should be charged £10,000 to each month instead of £120,000 in full to a single month.

- Management should either be **confident that conditions** which have existed in the past **will continue into the future or amend the estimates** of cost produced by the linear regression analysis to **allow for expected changes** in the future (such as an improvement in labour productivity).
- As with any forecasting process, the **amount of data available is very important**. Even if correlation is high, if we have fewer than about ten pairs of data, we must regard any forecast as being somewhat unreliable.
- It must be assumed that the **value of one variable, y, can be predicted or estimated from the value of one other variable, x.**

Question 2

The relationship between total operating cost and quantity produced (in a manufacturing company) is given by the following linear regression model.

TC = 5,000 + 500Q

where TC = Total operating cost (in £) per annum
Q = Quantity produced per annum (kg)

What reservations might you have about relying on the above model for decision-making purposes?

Answer

(a) The reliability of the model is unknown if we do not know the correlation coefficient. A low correlation would suggest that the model may be unreliable.

(b) The model is probably valid only over a certain range of quantity produced. Outside this range, the relationship between total operating cost and quantity produced may be very different.

(c) The model is based on past data, and assumes that what has happened in the past will happen in the future.

(d) The model assumes that a linear relationship exists between the quantity produced per annum and the total operating costs per annum. It is possible that a non-linear relationship may in fact exist.

(e) The fixed costs of £5,000 per annum may be misleading if they include an element of allocated costs.

3 CORRELATION 6/97

Exam focus point

Be prepared for discursive questions on this topic rather than computational question. For example, in the 6/97 exam candidates could earn 3 marks for explaining how regression analysis and the coefficient of determination (see Paragraph 3.12) could be used in a particular scenario.

3.1 (a)

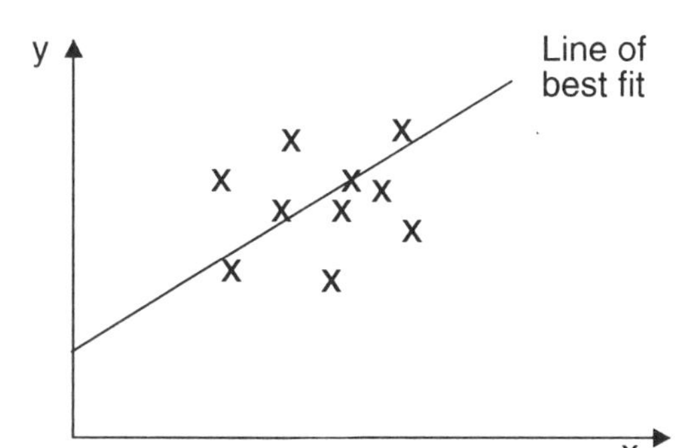

(b)

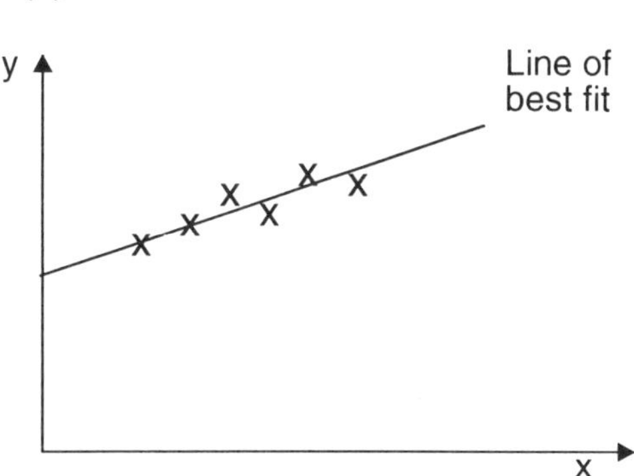

In the diagrams above, you should agree that a line of best fit is more likely to reflect the 'real' relationship between x and y in (b) than in (a). In (b), the pairs of data are all close to the line of best fit, whereas in (a), there is much more scatter around the line.

In the situation represented in (b), forecasting the value of y from a given value for x would be more likely to be accurate than in the situation represented in (a). This is because there would be greater correlation between x and y in (b) than in (a).

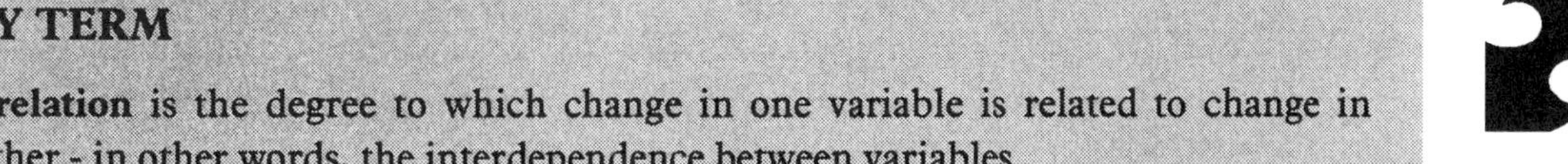

KEY TERM

Correlation is the degree to which change in one variable is related to change in another - in other words, the interdependence between variables.

Degrees of correlation

3.2 Two variables might be **perfectly correlated, partly correlated** or **uncorrelated**.

These differing degrees of correlation can be illustrated by scatter diagrams.

3.3 *Perfect correlation*

(a)

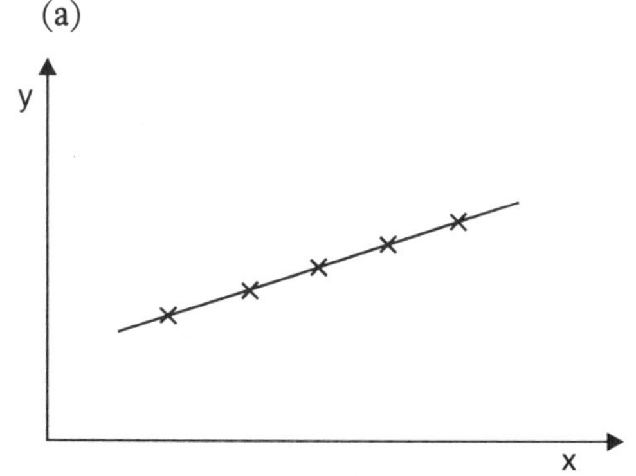

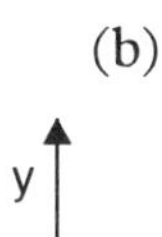

(b)

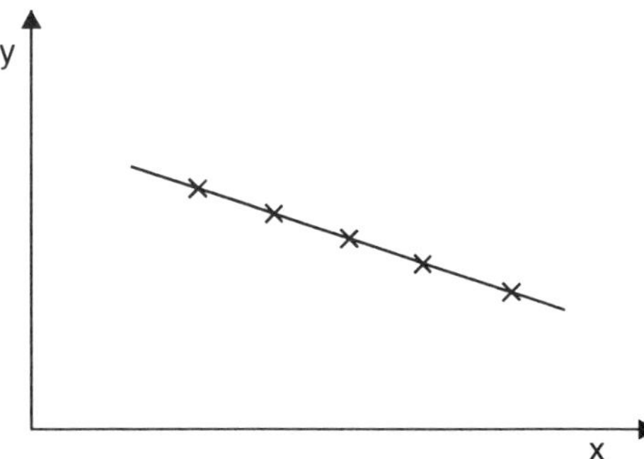

All the pairs of values lie on a straight line. An exact linear relationship exists between the two variables.

3.4 *Partial correlation*

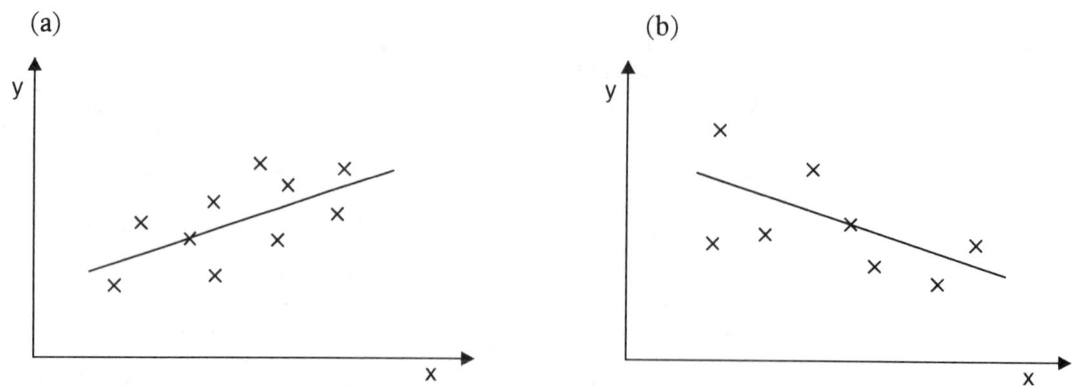

In (a), although there is no exact relationship, **low values of x tend to be associated with low values of y, and high values of x with high values of y.**

In (b) again, there is no exact relationship, but low values of x tend to be associated with high values of y and vice versa.

3.5 *No correlation*

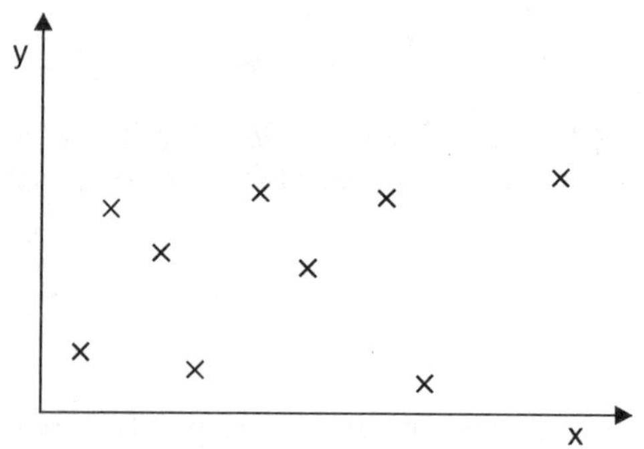

The values of these two variables are not correlated with each other.

3.6 *Non-linear or curvilinear correlation*

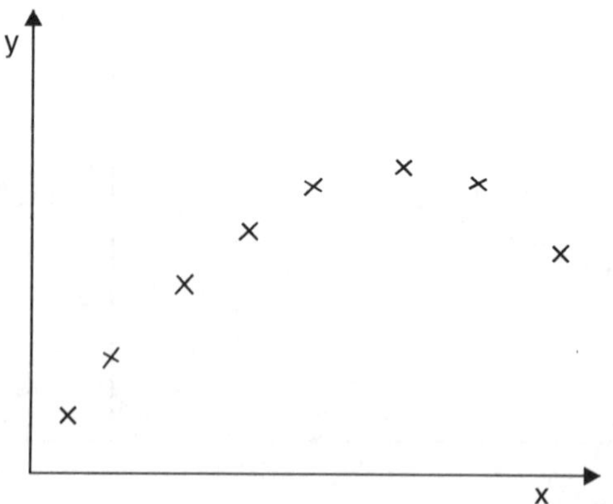

There is a relationship between x and y since the points are on an obvious curve but it is not a linear relationship.

Positive and negative correlation

3.7 Correlation, whether perfect or partial, can be **positive** or **negative**.

KEY TERMS

- **Positive correlation** is the type of correlation where low values of one variable are associated with low values of the other, and high values of one variable are associated with high values of the other.
- **Negative correlation** is the type of correlation where low values of one variable are associated with high values of the other, and high values of one variable with low values of the other.

Question 3

Which of the diagrams in Paragraphs 3.3 and 3.4 demonstrate positive correlation?

Answer

The diagrams in Paragraphs 3.3(a) and 3.4(a).

3.8 There are two measures of correlation.

- Coefficient of correlation, r
- Coefficient of determination, r^2

The coefficient of correlation, r

3.9 The **degree of correlation between two variables** can be measured using the **Pearsonian coefficient of correlation** (also called the **product moment correlation coefficient**).

r has a value between –1 (perfect negative correlation) and +1 (perfect positive correlation). If r = 0 then the variables are uncorrelated.

FORMULA TO LEARN

The **coefficient of correlation**, r, is calculated as follows.

$$r = \frac{n\Sigma xy - \Sigma x\Sigma y}{\sqrt{[n\Sigma x^2 - (\Sigma x)^2][n\Sigma y^2 - (\Sigma y)^2]}}$$

3.10 Look back at the example in Paragraph 2.4. Suppose that we wanted to know the correlation between vehicle maintenance costs and vehicle running hours. We can use a lot of the calculation in Paragraph 2.5 to determine r.

$$r = \frac{6(229.54) - (15.2)(90.0)}{\sqrt{[6(39.1) - (15.2)^2][6\Sigma y^2 - (90.0)^2]}}$$

$$= \frac{1{,}377.24 - 1{,}368}{\sqrt{[(234.6 - 231.04)(6\Sigma y^2 - 8{,}100)]}}$$

All we need to calculate is Σy^2

y	y^2
£'000	
13.6	184.96
15.8	249.64
14.5	210.25
16.2	262.44
14.9	222.01
15.0	225.00
90.0	1,354.30

$$r = \frac{9.24}{\sqrt{(3.56)(6 \times (1{,}354.30) - 8{,}100)}} = 0.96$$

3.11 A **fairly high degree of positive correlation** between x (vehicle running hours) and y (vehicle maintenance cost) is indicated here **because r is quite close to +1**.

The coefficient of determination, r^2

KEY TERM

The **coefficient of determination** is a measure of the proportion of the change in the value of one variable that can be explained by variations in the value of the other variable.

3.12 In our example, $r^2 = (0.96)^2 = 0.9216$, and so 92% of variation in the value of y (cost) can be explained by a linear relationship with x (running hours). This leaves only 8% of variations in y to be predicted from other factors. It is therefore **likely that vehicle** running hours could be used with a high degree of confidence to predict costs during a period.

Correlation and causation

3.13 If two variables are well correlated, either positively or negatively, this may be due to pure chance or there may be a reason for it. The **larger the number of pairs of data** collected, the **less likely it is that the correlation is due to chance**, though that possibility should never be ignored entirely.

3.14 **If there is a reason, it may not be causal**. For example, monthly net income is well correlated with monthly credit to a person's bank account, for the logical (rather than causal) reason that for most people the one equals the other.

3.15 **Even if there is a causal explanation** for a correlation, it **does not follow that variations in the value of one variable cause variations in the value of the other**. For example, sales of ice cream and of sunglasses are well correlated, not because of a direct causal link but because the weather influences both variables.

3.16 Having said this, it is of course possible that where two variables are correlated, there is a direct causal link to be found.

The interactions of r^2 and r with linear regression

3.17 The successful application of linear regression models depends on x and y being closely linearly related. r measures the strength of the linear relationship between two variables but **what numerical value of r is suggestive of sufficient linearity in data to allow one to proceed with linear regression?** The lower the value of r, the less chance of forecasts made using linear regression being adequate.

3.18 If there is a perfect linear relationship between the two variables ($r = \pm 1$), we can predict y from any given value of x with great confidence. If correlation is high (for example $r = 0.9$), the actual values will all be quite close to the regression line and so predictions should not be far out. If correlation is below about 0.7, predictions will only give a very rough guide to the likely value of y.

3.19 If $r = 0.75$, say, you may feel that the linear relationship between the two variables is fairly strong. But $r^2 = 56.25\%$ indicates that only just over half of the variations in the dependent variable can be explained by a linear relationship with the independent variable. The low figure could be because a non-linear relationship is a better model for the data or because extraneous factors need to be considered (and hence multiple regression analysis should be used). It is a **common rule of thumb that $r^2 \geq 80\%$ indicates that linear regression may be applied for the purpose of forecasting.**

4 SALES FORECASTING 12/95

Exam focus point

There were 3 marks to be gained in the 12/95 exam for detailing information which should be considered when producing a sales forecast.

4.1 The sales budget is frequently the first budget prepared since **sales is usually the principal budget factor**, but before the sales budget can be prepared a sales forecast has to be made. Sales forecasting is complex *and* difficult and involves the consideration of a number of factors.

Question 4

In Chapter 6 we looked at the factors which need to be considered when forecasting sales. List as many of the factors as you can remember.

Answer

(a) Past sales patterns
(b) The economic environment
(c) Results of market research
(d) Anticipated advertising during the budget period
(e) Competition
(f) Changing consumer tastes
(g) New technology
(h) Distribution and quality of sales outlets and personnel
(i) Pricing policies and discounts offered
(j) Legislation
(k) Environmental factors

4.2 As well as bearing in mind the above factors, management can use a number of forecasting methods, often combining them to reduce the level of uncertainty.

- **Sales personnel** can be asked to provide estimates.
- **Market research** can be used (especially if an organisation is considering introducing a new product or service).

- **Mathematical** models can be employed. Models are set up so that, after changing one or more factors, repetitive computer simulations can be run which permit managers to review the results that would be obtained in various circumstances.
- Various **mathematical techniques** can be used to estimate sales levels. We will cover these in the remainder of the chapter.

5 REGRESSION AND FORECASTING

5.1 The same regression techniques as those considered earlier in the chapter can be used to **calculate a regression line (a trend line) for a time series.** A time series is simply a series of figures or values recorded over time (such as total annual costs for the last ten years). The calculation of a trend line is particularly useful in forecasting. (We will be looking at time series and trend lines in more detail in the next section.)

5.2 The **years (or days or months) become the x variables in the regression formulae** by **numbering them from 0 upwards.**

5.3 EXAMPLE: REGRESSION AND FORECASTING

Sales of product B over the seven year period from 19X1 to 19X7 were as follows.

Year	*Sales of B*
	'000 units
19X1	22
19X2	25
19X3	24
19X4	26
19X5	29
19X6	28
19X7	30

There is high correlation between time and the volume of sales.

Required

Calculate the trend line of sales, and forecast sales in 19X8 and 19X9.

5.4 SOLUTION

Workings

Year	x	y	xy	x^2
19X1	0	22	0	0
19X2	1	25	25	1
19X3	2	24	48	4
19X4	3	26	78	9
19X5	4	29	116	16
19X6	5	28	140	25
19X7	6	30	180	36
	Σx = 21	Σy = 184	Σxy = 587	Σx^2 = 91

n = 7

Where y = a + bx

$$b = \frac{(7 \times 587) - (21 \times 184)}{(7 \times 91) - (21 \times 21)}$$

$$= \frac{245}{196}$$

$$= 1.25$$

$$a = \frac{184}{7} - \frac{1.25 \times 21}{7}$$

$$= 22.5357, \text{ say } 22.5$$

$$y = 22.5 + 1.25x \text{ where } x = 0 \text{ in 19X1}, x = 1 \text{ in 19X2 and so on.}$$

Using this trend line, predicted sales in 19X8 (year 7) would be

$$22.5 + 1.25 \times 7 = 31.25 = 31{,}250 \text{ units.}$$

Similarly, for 19X9 (year 8) predicted sales would be

$$22.5 + 1.25 \times 8 = 32.50 = 32{,}500 \text{ units.}$$

6 THE COMPONENTS OF TIME SERIES 6/94

Exam focus point

Time series analysis has so far only been examined as a narrative question. The examiner has stated that numerical questions are possible, and are likely to be accompanied by a discussion part as well. Make sure you are happy with the computational techniques covered in this section.

KEY TERM

A **time series** is a series of figures or values recorded over time.

6.1 The following are examples of time series.

- Output at a factory each day for the last month
- Monthly sales over the last two years
- Total annual costs for the last ten years
- The Retail Prices Index each month for the last ten years
- The number of people employed by a company each year for the last 20 years

KEY TERM

A graph of a time series is called a **historigram.**

6.2 (Note the 'ri'; this is not the same as a histogram.) For example, consider the following time series.

Year	*Sales*
	£'000
19X0	20
19X1	21
19X2	24
19X3	23
19X4	27
19X5	30
19X6	28

The historigram is as follows.

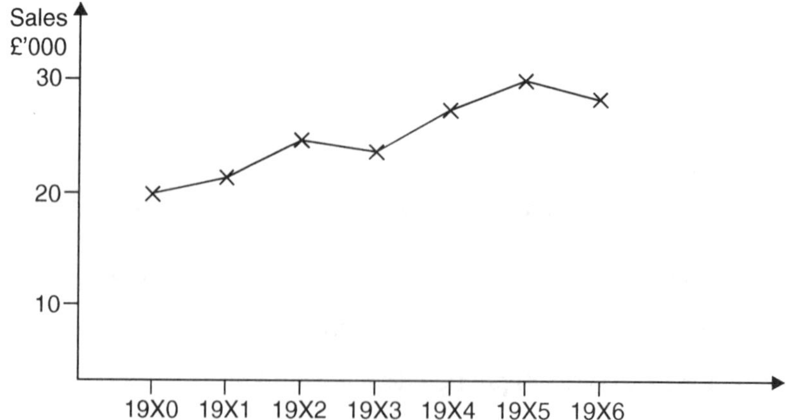

The horizontal axis is always chosen to represent time, and the vertical axis represents the values of the data recorded.

6.3 There are several **components of a time series** which it may be necessary to identify.

- **A trend**
- **Seasonal variations** or fluctuations
- Cycles, or **cyclical variations**
- Non-recurring, **random variations**. These may be caused by unforeseen circumstances, such as a change in the government of the country, a war, the collapse of a company, technological change or a fire.

The trend

KEY TERM

The **trend** is the underlying long-term movement over time in the values of the data recorded.

6.4 In the following examples of time series, there are three types of trend.

	Output per labour hour	*Cost per unit*	*Number of employees*
	Units	£	
19X4	30	1.00	100
19X5	24	1.08	103
19X6	26	1.20	96
19X7	22	1.15	102
19X8	21	1.18	103
19X9	17	1.25	98
	(A)	(B)	(C)

(a) In time series **(A)** there is a **downward trend** in the output per labour hour. Output per labour hour did not fall every year, because it went up between 19X5 and 19X6, but the long-term movement is clearly a downward one.

(b) In time series **(B)** there is an **upward trend** in the cost per unit. Although unit costs went down in 19X7 from a higher level in 19X6, the basic movement over time is one of rising costs.

(c) In time series **(C)** there is **no clear movement** up or down, and the number of employees remained fairly constant around 100. The trend is therefore a static, or level one.

Seasonal variations

> **KEY TERM**
>
> **Seasonal variations** are short-term fluctuations in recorded values, due to different circumstances which affect results at different times of the year, on different days of the week, at different times of day, or whatever.

6.5 Here are two examples of seasonal variations.

- Sales of ice cream will be higher in summer than in winter.
- The telephone network may be heavily used at certain times of the day (such as mid-morning and mid-afternoon) and much less used at other times (such as in the middle of the night).

6.6 'Seasonal' is a term which may appear to refer to the seasons of the year, but its meaning in time series analysis is somewhat broader, as the examples given above show.

6.7 EXAMPLE: A TREND AND SEASONAL VARIATIONS

The number of customers served by a company of travel agents over the past four years is shown in the following historigram.

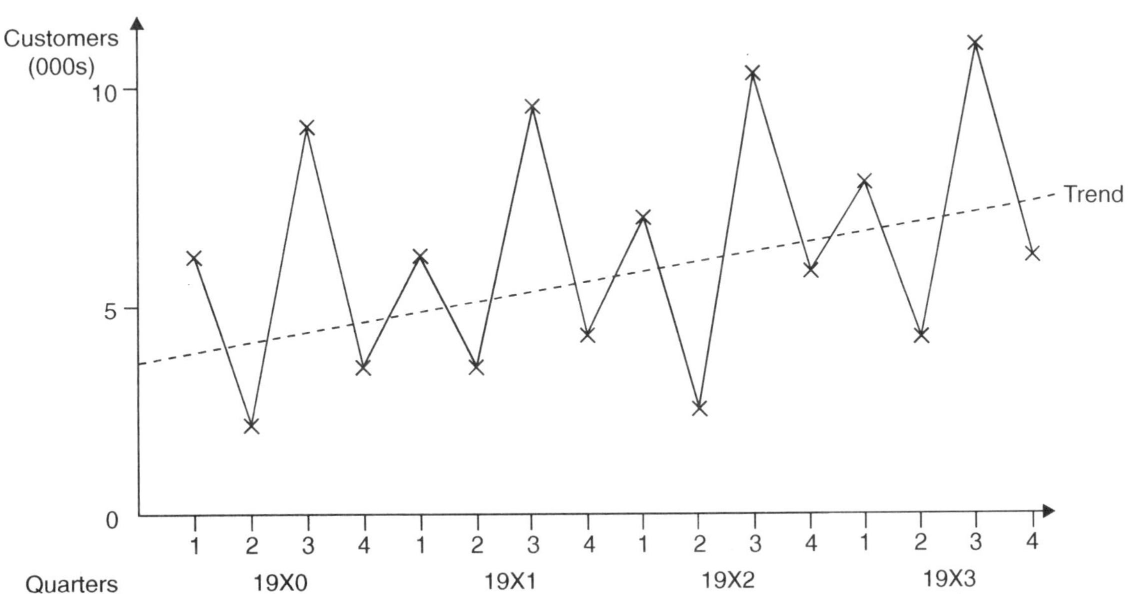

In this example, there would appear to be large seasonal fluctuations in demand, but there is also a basic upward trend.

Cyclical variations

6.8 Cyclical variations are **medium-term changes in results caused by circumstances which repeat in cycles**. In business, cyclical variations are commonly associated with economic cycles, successive booms and slumps in the economy. Economic cycles may last a few years. Cyclical variations are longer term than seasonal variations.

Summarising the components

6.9 In practice a time series could incorporate all of the four features we have been looking at and, to make reasonably accurate forecasts, the four features often have to be isolated. We can begin the process of isolating each feature by summarising the components of a time series as follows.

The **actual time series, Y= T + S + C + R**

where **Y = the actual time series**
T = the trend series
S = the seasonal component
C = the cyclical component
R = the random component

6.10 Though you should be aware of the cyclical component, it is unlikely that you will be expected to carry out any calculation connected with isolating it. The mathematical model which we will use, the **additive model**, therefore excludes any reference to C and is **Y = T + S + R.**

KEY TERM

The **additive model** expresses a time series as Y = T + S + R.

We will begin by looking at how to find the trend in a time series.

7 FINDING THE TREND

7.1 Look at these monthly sales figures.

19X6	*Sales* £'000
August	0.02
September	0.04
October	0.04
November	3.20
December	14.60

7.2 It looks as though the business is expanding rapidly - and so it is, in a way. But when you know that the business is a Christmas card manufacturer, then you see immediately that the January sales will no doubt slump right back down again.

7.3 It is obvious that the business will do better in the Christmas season than at any other time - that is the seasonal variation with which the statistician has to contend. Using the monthly figures, how can he tell whether or not the business is doing well overall - whether there is a rising sales trend over time other than the short-term rise over Christmas?

7.4 One possibility is to compare figures with the equivalent figures of a year ago. However, many things can happen over a period of twelve months to make such a comparison misleading - for example, new products might now be manufactured and prices will probably have changed.

7.5 In fact, there are a number of ways of overcoming this problem of distinguishing trend from seasonal variations. One such method is called **moving averages.** This method attempts to **remove seasonal (or cyclical) variations from a time series by a process of averaging so as to leave a set of figures representing the trend.**

7.6 A **moving average** is an average of the results of a fixed number of periods. Since it is an average of several time periods, it is **related to the mid-point of the overall period**.

7.7 EXAMPLE: MOVING AVERAGES

Year	*Sales*
	Units
19X0	390
19X1	380
19X2	460
19X3	450
19X4	470
19X5	440
19X6	500

Required

Take a moving average of the annual sales over a period of three years.

7.8 SOLUTION

(a) Average sales in the three year period 19X0 – 19X2 were

$$\left(\frac{390+380+460}{3}\right) = \frac{1,230}{3} = 410$$

This average relates to the middle year of the period, 19X1.

(b) Similarly, average sales in the three year period 19X1 – 19X3 were

$$\left(\frac{380+460+450}{3}\right) = \frac{1,290}{3} = 430$$

This average relates to the middle year of the period, 19X2.

(c) The average sales can also be found for the periods 19X2 - 19X4, 19X3 - 19X5 and 19X4 - 19X6, to give the following.

Year	*Sales*	*Moving total of 3 years sales*	*Moving average of 3 years sales (÷ 3)*
19X0	390		
19X1	380	1,230	410
19X2	460	1,290	430
19X3	450	1,380	460
19X4	470	1,360	453
19X5	440	1,410	470
19X6	500		

Note the following points.

(i) The **moving average series has five figures** relating to the years from 19X1 to 19X5. The **original series had seven figures** for the years from 19X0 to 19X6.

(ii) There is an upward trend in sales, which is more noticeable from the series of moving averages than from the original series of actual sales each year.

7.9 The above example averaged over a three-year period. Over what period should a moving average be taken? The answer to this question is that the **moving average which is most appropriate will depend on the circumstances and the nature of the time series.** Note the following points.

(a) A moving average which takes an **average of the results in many time periods will represent results over a longer term** than a moving average of two or three periods.

(b) On the other hand, with a moving average of results in many time periods, the **last figure in the series will be out of date by several periods**. In our example, the most recent average related to 19X5. With a moving average of five years' results, the final figure in the series would relate to 19X4.

(c) When there is a **known cycle** over which seasonal variations occur, such as all the days in the week or all the seasons in the year, the **most suitable moving average would be one which covers one full cycle.**

Moving averages of an even number of results

7.10 In the previous example, **moving averages were taken of the results in an *odd* number of time periods,** and the **average then related to the mid-point of the overall period**.

7.11 If a **moving average** were taken of results in an **even number of time periods**, the basic technique would be the same, but the mid-point of the overall period would not relate to a single period. For example, suppose an average were taken of the following four results.

Spring	120	
Summer	90	
Autumn	180	average 115
Winter	70	

The average would relate to the mid-point of the period, between summer and autumn.

7.12 The trend line average figures need to relate to a particular time period; otherwise, seasonal variations cannot be calculated. To overcome this difficulty, we take a **moving average of the moving average.** An example will illustrate this technique.

7.13 EXAMPLE: MOVING AVERAGES OVER AN EVEN NUMBER OF PERIODS

Calculate a moving average trend line of the following results of Linden Ltd.

Year	*Quarter*	*Volume of sales* '000 units
19X5	1	600
	2	840
	3	420
	4	720
19X6	1	640
	2	860
	3	420
	4	740
19X7	1	670
	2	900
	3	430
	4	760

7.14 SOLUTION

A moving average of four will be used, since the volume of sales would appear to depend on the season of the year, and each year has four quarterly results.

The moving average of four does not relate to any specific period of time; therefore a second moving average of two will be calculated on the first moving averages.

Year	*Quarter*	*Actual volume of sales* '000 units (A)	*Moving total of 4 quarters' sales* '000 units (B)	*Moving average of 4 quarters' sales* '000 units (B ÷ 4)	*Mid-point of 2 moving averages Trend line* '000 units (C)
19X5	1	600			
	2	840			
			2,580	645.0	
	3	420			650.00
			2,620	655.0	
	4	720			657.50
			2,640	660.0	
19X6	1	640			660.00
			2,640	660.0	
	2	860			662.50
			2,660	665.0	
	3	420			668.75
			2,690	672.5	
	4	740			677.50
			2,730	682.5	
19X7	1	670			683.75
			2,740	685.0	
	2	900			687.50
			2,760	690.0	
	3	430			
	4	760			

7.15 By taking a mid point (a moving average of two) of the original moving averages, we can relate the results to specific quarters (from the third quarter of 19X5 to the second quarter of 19X7).

8 FINDING THE SEASONAL VARIATIONS

8.1 Once a trend has been established, by whatever method, we can find the seasonal variations.

8.2 The additive model for time series analysis is Y = T + S + R. We can therefore write Y – T = S + R. In other words, if we deduct the trend series from the actual series, we will be left with the seasonal and residual components of the time series. If we assume that the random component is relatively small, and hence negligible, the **seasonal component can be found as S = Y – T,** the **de-trended series.**

8.3 The actual and trend sales for Linden Ltd (as calculated in Paragraph 7.14) are set out below. The **difference between the actual results for any one quarter (Y) and the trend figure for that quarter (T)** will be the seasonal variation for that quarter.

Year	*Quarter*	*Actual*	*Trend*	*Seasonal variation*
19X5	1	600		
	2	840		
	3	420	650.00	–230.00
	4	720	657.50	62.50
19X6	1	640	660.00	–20.00
	2	860	662.50	197.50
	3	420	668.75	–248.75
	4	740	677.50	62.50
19X7	1	670	683.75	–13.75
	2	900	687.50	212.50
	3	430		
	4	760		

8.4 The variation between the actual result for any one particular quarter and the trend line average is not the same from year to year, but an **average of these variations can be taken.**

	Q_1	Q_2	Q_3	Q_4
19X5			–230.00	62.50
19X6	–20.00	197.50	–248.75	62.50
19X7	–13.75	212.50		
Total	–33.75	410.00	–478.75	125.00
Average (÷ 2)	–16.875	205.00	–239.375	62.50

8.5 Our estimate of the 'seasonal' or quarterly variation is almost complete, but there is one more important step to take. Variations around the basic trend line should cancel each other out, and add up to zero. At the moment, they do not. We therefore **spread the total of the variations** (11.25) **across the four quarters** (11.25 ÷ 4) **so that the final total of the variations sum to zero.**

	Q_1	Q_2	Q_3	Q_4	*Total*
Estimated quarterly variations	– 16.8750	205.0000	–239.3750	62.5000	11.250
Adjustment to reduce variations to 0	–2.8125	–2.8125	–2.8125	–2.8125	–11.250
Final estimates of quarterly variations	–19.6875	202.1875	–242.1875	59.6875	0
These might be rounded as follows	Ql: –20,	Ql: 202,	Ql:-242,	Ql: 60,	Total: 0

Question 5

Calculate a four-quarter moving average trend centred on actual quarters and then find seasonal variations from the following.

	Sales in £'000			
	Spring	*Summer*	*Autumn*	*Winter*
19X7	200	120	160	280
19X8	220	140	140	300
19X9	200	120	180	320

Answer

		Sales (Y)	*4-quarter total*	*8-quarter total*	*Moving average (T)*	*Seasonal variation (Y-T)*
19X7	Spring	200				
	Summer	120				
			760			
	Autumn	160		1,540	192.5	–32.5
			780			
	Winter	280		1,580	197.5	+82.5
			800			
19X8	Spring	220		1,580	197.5	+22.5
			780			
	Summer	140		1,580	197.5	–57.5
			800			
	Autumn	140		1,580	197.5	–57.5
			780			
	Winter	300		1,540	192.5	+107.5
			760			
19X9	Spring	200		1,560	195.0	+5.0
			800			
	Summer	120		1,620	202.5	–82.5
			820			
	Autumn	180				
	Winter	320				

We can now average the seasonal variations.

	Spring	Summer	Autumn	Winter	Total
19X7			–32.5	+82.5	
19X8	+22.5	–57.5	–57.5	+107.5	
19X9	+5.0	–82.5			
	+27.5	–140.0	–90.0	+190.0	
Average variation (in £'000)	+13.75	–70.00	–45.00	+95.00	–6.25
Adjustment so sum is zero	+1.5625	+1.5625	+1.562	+1.5625	+6.25
Adjusted average variations	+15.3125	–68.4375	–43.4375	+96.5625	0

These might be rounded up or down to:

Spring £15,000, Summer –£68,000, Autumn –£43,000, Winter £96,000

Seasonal variations using the proportional model

8.6 The method of estimating the seasonal variations in the above example was to use the differences between the trend and actual data. This is called the **additive model**. This model **assumes that the components of the series are independent** of each other, an increasing trend not affecting the seasonal variations for example.

The alternative is to use the **proportional model** whereby each actual figure is expressed as a proportion of the trend. Sometimes this method is called the **multiplicative model**

KEY TERM

The proportional (multiplicative) model summarises a time series as $Y = T \times S \times R$.

8.7 Note that the **trend component** will be the **same whichever model is used** but the values of the **seasonal and random components** will **vary according to the model being applied.**

8.8 The example in Paragraph 7.13 can be reworked on this alternative basis.

The trend is calculated in exactly the same way as before but we need a different approach for the seasonal variations.

The proportional model is $Y = T \times S \times R$ and, just as we calculated $S = Y - T$ for the additive model (Paragraph 7.13) we can calculate $S = Y/T$ for the proportional model.

Year	*Quarter*	*Actual (Y)*	*Trend (T)*	*Seasonal percentage (Y/T)*
19X5	1	600		
	2	840		
	3	420	650.00	0.646
	4	720	657.50	1.095
19X6	1	640	660.00	0.970
	2	860	662.50	1.298
	3	420	668.75	0.628
	4	740	677.50	1.092
19X7	1	670	683.75	0.980
	2	900	687.50	1.309
	3	430		
	4	760		

8.9 The summary of the seasonal variations expressed in proportional terms is as follows.

	Q_1	Q_2	Q_3	Q_4
	%	%	%	%
19X5			0.646	1.095
19X6	0.970	1.298	0.628	1.092
19X7	0.980	1.309		
Total	1.950	2.607	1.274	2.187
Average	0.975	1.3035	0.637	1.0935

8.10 **Instead of summing to zero**, as **with the additive approach**, the **averages should sum (in this case) to 4.0, 1.0 for each of the four quarters.** They actually sum to 4.009 so 0.00225 has to be deducted from each one.

	Q_1	Q_2	Q_3	Q_4
Average	0.97500	1.30350	0.63700	1.09350
Adjustment	–0.00225	–0.00225	–0.00225	–0.00225
Final estimate	0.97275	1.30125	0.63475	1.09125
Rounded	0.97	1.30	0.64	1.09

Question 6

A company's quarterly sales figures have been analysed into a trend and seasonal variations using moving averages. Here is an extract from the analysis.

Year	*Quarter*	*Actual*	*Trend*
		£'000	£'000
19X1	1	350	366
	2	380	370
	3	400	380
	4	360	394
19X2	1	410	406
	2	430	414
	3	450	418
	4	370	423

Required

Find the average seasonal variation for each quarter, using the proportional model.

Answer

Quarter	*1*	*2*	*3*	*4*
	%	%	%	%
Variation, 19X1	0.956	1.027	1.053	0.914
Variation, 19X2	1.010	1.039	1.077	0.875
Average variation	0.983	1.033	1.065	0.895
Adjustment	0.006	0.006	0.006	0.006
Adjusted average variation	0.989	1.039	1.071	0.901

8.11 Note that the **proportional model is better than the additive model when the trend is increasing or decreasing over time**. In such circumstances, seasonal variations are likely to be increasing or decreasing too. The additive model simply adds absolute and unchanging seasonal variations to the trend figures whereas the proportional model, by multiplying increasing or decreasing trend values by a constant seasonal variation factor, takes account of changing seasonal variations.

9 TIME SERIES ANALYSIS AND FORECASTING 6/94

9.1 By extrapolating a trend and then adjusting for seasonal variations, forecasts of future values can be made.

9.2 Forecasts of future values should be made as follows.

(a) **Calculate a trend line.**

(b) **Use the trend line to forecast future trend line values.**

(c) **Adjust these values by the average seasonal variation applicable to the future period, to determine the forecast for that period.** With the additive model, add (or subtract for negative variations) the variation. With the multiplicative model, multiply the trend value by the variation proportion.

9.3 Extending a trend line outside the range of known data, in this case forecasting the future from a trend line based on historical data, is known as **extrapolation.**

9.4 EXAMPLE: FORECASTING

The sales (in £'000) of swimwear by a large department store for each period of three months are as follows.

Quarter	*19X4*	*19X5*	*19X6*	*19X7*
	£'000	£'000	£'000	£'000
First		8	20	40
Second		30	50	62
Third		60	80	92
Fourth	24	20	40	

Task

(a) Using an additive model, find the centred moving average trend.

(b) Find the average seasonal variation for each quarter.

(c) Predict sales for the last quarter of 19X7 and the first quarter of 19X8, stating any assumptions.

9.5 SOLUTION

	Quarter	*4 quarter moving total*	*Centred moving total*	*Moving average(÷4)*
19X4	4			
19X5	1			
		122		
	2		120	30
		118		
	3		124	31
		130		
	4		140	35
		150		
19X6	1		160	40
		170		
	2		180	45
		190		
	3		200	50
		210		
	4		216	54
		222		
19X7	1		228	57
		234		
	2			
	3			

(a) The centred moving average trend is shown in the right hand column of the table.

(b) *Seasonal variations*

		Quarter			
	1	*2*	*3*	*4*	*Total*
Year 19X5		0.00	+29.00	−15.00	
19X6	−20.00	+5.00	+30.00	−14.00	
19X7	−17.00				
Total	−37.00	+5.00	+59.00	−29.00	
Average	−18.50	+2.50	+29.50	−14.50	−1
Adjust total variation to nil	+0.25	+0.25	+0.25	+0.25	+1
Average seasonal variation	−18.25	+2.75	+29.75	−14.25	

(c) We might guess that the trend line is rising steadily, by (57 – 40)/4 = 4.25 per quarter in the period 1st quarter 19X6 to 1st quarter 19X7 (57 being the prediction in 1st quarter 19X7 and 40 the prediction in 1st quarter 19X6).

Since the trend may be levelling off a little, a quarterly increase of +4 in the trend will be assumed.

		Trend	*Seasonal variation*	*Forecast*
1st quarter	19X7	57		
4th quarter	19X7 (+ (3 × 4))	69	−14.25	54.75
1st quarter	19X8 (+ (4 × 4))	73	−18.25	54.75

Rounding to the nearest thousand pounds, the forecast sales are £55,000 for each of the two quarters.

9.6 Note that you could actually plot the trend line figures on a graph, extrapolate the trend line into the future and read off forecasts from the graph using the extrapolated trend line.

9.7 If we had been using the proportional model, with an average variation for (for example) quarter 4 of 0.8, our prediction for the fourth quarter of 19X7 would have been 69 × 0.8 = 55.2, say £55,000.

Question 7

A company's sales figures for January 19X3 (month 0) to December 19X4 (month 23) have been analysed into a trend and percentage seasonal variations using regression analysis.

The regression line is y = 780 + 4x, where x is the month number and y is sales in thousands of pounds.

The average seasonal variation for March is 106%.

Required

Forecast the sales for March 19X5.

Answer

x = 26

Forecast = 1.06 × [780 + (4 × 26)] = 937.04 = £937,040 or about £937,000.

10 FORECASTING PROBLEMS

10.1 All forecasts are subject to error, but the likely errors vary from case to case.

- The **further into the future** the forecast is for, the **more unreliable** it is likely to be.
- The **less data** available on which to base the forecast, the **less reliable** the forecast.

- The **pattern** of trend and seasonal variations **cannot be guaranteed to continue** in the future.
- There is always the danger of **random variations** upsetting the pattern of trend and seasonal variation.

10.2 There are a number of changes that also may make it difficult to forecast future events.

Type of change	Examples
Political and economic changes	These will create uncertainty. For example changes in interest rates, exchange rates or inflation can mean that future sales and costs are difficult to forecast.
Environmental changes	These can also cause forecasting problems. For example the opening of a high-speed rail link might have a considerable impact on some companies' markets.
Technological changes	These may mean that the past is not a reliable indication of likely future events. For example the availability of faster machinery may make it difficult to use current output levels as the basis for forecasting future production output.
Technological advances	They can also change the nature of production. The advent of advanced manufacturing technology is changing the cost structure of many firms. Direct labour costs are reducing in significance and fixed manufacturing costs are increasing. This causes forecasting difficulties because of the resulting changes in cost behaviour patterns, breakeven points and so on.
Social changes	Alterations in taste and fashion and changes in the social acceptability of different products can cause difficulties in forecasting future sales levels.

Chapter roundup

- This chapter has considered the quantitative methods the management accountant can use to obtain information for inclusion in budgets.
- Simple cost estimation techniques include the **industrial engineering approach**, the **account classification method**, the **high-low method** and the **scattergraph method**.
- **Linear regression analysis** (least squares technique) is a more sophisticated cost estimation method. It involves determining a **line of best fit.** Ensure that you know how to use the formulae to calculate the values of a and b in y = a + bx.
- **Correlation** describes the extent to which the values of two variables are related. Two variables might be **perfectly** correlated, **partly** correlated or **uncorrelated**. The correlation may be **positive** or **negative**. The degree of correlation between two variables can be measured using the **Pearsonian coefficient of correlation**, **r**. The **coefficient of determination** indicates the variations in the dependent variable that can be explained by variations in the independent variable.
- **Regression** techniques can be used in forecasting.
- A **time series** is a series of figures or values recorded over time. A graph of a time series is called a **historigram**. A time series has four components: a **trend**, **seasonal variations**, **cyclical variations** and **random variations**. The **trend** is the underlying long-term movement over time in the values of the data recorded. **Seasonal variations** are short-term fluctuations due to different circumstances which affect results at different points in time. **Cyclical variations** are medium-term change in results caused by circumstances which repeat in cycles.
- **Trend** values can be determined by a process of **moving averages**.
- **Seasonal variations** can be estimated using the **additive** model or the **proportional** (**multiplicative**) model.
- **Forecasts** can be made by calculating a **trend line** (using moving averages or linear regression), using the trend line to forecast future trend line values, and adjusting these values by the **average seasonal variation** applicable to the future period.
- Management should, however, have reasonable confidence in their estimates and forecasts. In particular the assumptions on which the forecasts/estimates are based should be properly understood and the methods used to make a forecast or estimate should be in keeping with the nature, quantity and reliability of the data on which the forecast or estimate will be based. There is no point in using a 'sophisticated' technique with unreliable data; on the other hand, if there is a lot of accurate data about historical costs, it would be a waste of the data to use the high-low method for cost estimating.

Quick quiz

1 In what way is the scattergraph method more reliable than the high-low method of cost estimation? What is its main weakness? (see para 1.13)

2 When would linear regression rather than the high-low method be used? (2.8)

3 What is extrapolation? (key terms)

4 What is positive correlation? (key terms)

5 What does it mean if r, the coefficient of correlation is zero? (3.9)

6 When using regression analysis for forecasting, what are the x variables? (5.2)

7 What is the definition of a time series? (key terms)

8 What are the four components that combine to form a time series? (6.3)

9 Distinguish between the additive model and the proportional (multiplicative) model for estimating time series. (key terms)

10 Describe how the additive model may be used in forecasting (9.2 - 9.5)

11 What types of change make it difficult to forecast future events? (10.2)

Question to try	Level	Marks	Time
8	Introductory	n/a	25 mins

Chapter 9

ALTERNATIVE BUDGET SYSTEMS

	Chapter topic list	Syllabus reference
1	Incremental budgeting and zero base budgeting	2(a)(ii)
2	The main features of zero base budgeting systems	2(a)(ii)
3	The advantages and limitations of zero base budgeting	2(a)(ii)
4	Using zero base budgeting	2(a)(ii)
5	Programme planning and budgeting systems	2(a)(ii)
6	Rolling budgets	2(a)(ii)

Introduction

The system of budgeting which we have looked at so far in this Study Text may not always be appropriate for certain organisations or for certain types of cost and revenue. **Zero base budgeting**, **programme planning and budgeting systems** and **rolling budgets** are alternative budget systems which can be applied in certain circumstances and situations. This chapter looks in detail at these three systems.

This chapter concludes our study of budgeting. Chapter 10 introduces a new subject: standard costing.

1 INCREMENTAL BUDGETING AND ZERO BASE BUDGETING 6/94

KEY TERM

Incremental budgeting involves basing next year's budget on the current year's results plus an extra amount for estimated growth or inflation next year.

1.1 **Incremental budgeting** is so called because it is concerned mainly with the increments in costs and revenues which will occur in the coming period.

1.2 Incremental budgeting is a reasonable procedure if current operations are as effective, efficient and economical as they can be. It is also appropriate for budgeting for costs such as staff salaries, which may be estimated on the basis of current salaries plus an increment for inflation and are hence administratively fairly easy to prepare.

1.3 In general, however, it is an **inefficient form of budgeting** as it **encourages slack** and **wasteful spending** to creep into budgets. Past inefficiencies are perpetuated because cost levels are rarely subjected to close scrutiny.

1.4 To ensure that inefficiencies are not concealed, however, alternative approaches to budgeting have been developed. One such approach is **zero base budgeting (ZBB)**, the use of which was pioneered by P Pyhrr in the United States in the early 1970s.

2 THE MAIN FEATURES OF ZERO BASE BUDGETING SYSTEMS 6/94

Exam focus point

In both the 6/94 and 6/95 examinations, the examiner commented that the question on ZBB was badly answered.

The principles of zero base budgeting

2.1 ZBB rejects the assumption inherent in incremental budgeting that this year's activities will continue at the same level or volume next year, and that next year's budget can be based on this year's costs plus an extra amount, perhaps for expansion and inflation.

KEY TERM

Zero base budgeting involves preparing a budget for each cost centre from a zero base. Every item of expenditure has then to be justified in its entirety in order to be included in the next year's budget.

2.2 In reality, however, managers do not have to budget from zero, but can **start from their current level of expenditure and work downwards**, asking what would happen if any particular aspect of current expenditure and current operations were removed from the budget. In this way, every aspect of the budget is examined in terms of its cost and the benefits it provides and the selection of better alternatives is encouraged.

Implementing zero base budgeting

2.3 The implementation of ZBB involves a number of steps but of greater importance is the **development of a questioning attitude** by all those involved in the budgetary process. Existing practices and expenditures must be challenged and searching questions, such as the following must be asked.

- Does the activity need to be carried out?
- What would be the consequences if the activity was not carried out?
- Does the activity benefit the organisation?
- Is the current level of provision current?
- Are there alternative ways of providing the function?
- How much should the activity cost?
- Is the expenditure worth the benefits achieved?

2.4 The basic approach of ZBB has three steps.

Step 1. *Define decision packages*

A **decision package** is a comprehensive **description of a specific organisational activity which management can use to evaluate the activity and rank it in order of priority against other activities.** Managers prepare decision packages for the activities within the budget centre for which they have responsibility.

There are two types of decision package.

- **Mutually exclusive packages** contain **alternative methods of getting the same job done.** The best option among the packages must be selected by comparing costs and benefits and the other packages are then discarded. For example, an organisation might consider two alternative decision packages for the preparation of the payroll: Package 1 might be in-house preparation of the payroll whereas Package 2 could involve the use of an outside agency.
- **Incremental packages divide one aspect of an activity into different levels of effort.** The 'base' package will describe the minimum amount of work that must be done to carry out the activity and the other packages describe what additional work could be done, at what cost and for what benefits.

Suppose that a cost centre manager is preparing a budget for maintenance costs. He might first consider two mutually exclusive packages. Package A might be to keep a maintenance team of two men per shift for two shifts each day at a cost of £60,000 per annum, whereas package B might be to obtain a maintenance service from an outside contractor at a cost of £50,000. A cost-benefit analysis will be conducted because the quicker repairs obtainable from an in-house maintenance service might justify its extra cost.

If we now suppose that package A is preferred, the budget analysis must be completed by describing the incremental variations in this chosen alternative.

(a) The 'base' package would describe the minimum requirement for the maintenance work. This might be to pay for one man per shift for two shifts each day at a cost of £30,000.

(b) Incremental package 1 might be to pay for two men on the early shift and one man on the late shift, at a cost of £45,000. The extra cost of £15,000 would need to be justified, for example by savings in lost production time, or by more efficient machinery.

(c) Incremental package 2 might be the original preference, for two men on each shift at a cost of £60,000. The cost-benefit analysis would compare its advantages, if any, over incremental package 1.

(d) Incremental package 3 might be for three men on the early shift and two on the late shift, at a cost of £75,000; and so on.

Question 1

What might the base package for a personnel department cover? What might incremental packages cover?

Answer

The base package might cover the recruitment and dismissal of staff. Incremental packages might cover training, pension administration, trade union liaison, staff welfare and so on.

Step 2. *Evaluate and rank packages*

Each activity (decision package) is evaluated and ranked on the basis of its benefit to the organisation.

The ranking process provides managers with a technique to **allocate scarce resources** between different activities. Minimum work requirements (those that are essential to get a job done) will be given high priority and so too will work which meets legal obligations. In the accounting department these would be minimum requirements to operate the payroll, purchase ledger and sales ledger systems, and to maintain and publish a set of accounts which satisfies the external auditors.

The **ranking process can be lengthy** because large numbers of different packages will have been prepared by managers throughout the organisation. In large organisations the number of packages might be so huge that senior management cannot do the ranking unaided. In such circumstances, the following occurs.

(a) Cost centre managers will be asked to rank the packages for their own cost centre.

(b) The manager at the next level up the hierarchy of seniority will consolidate the rankings of his or her subordinates into a single ranking list for the group of cost centres, using the rankings of each cost centre as a guide.

(c) These consolidated rankings will be passed in turn one stage further up the management hierarchy for further consolidation. At higher levels of consolidation, the ranking process might be done by a committee of managers rather than by an individual.

Once a consolidated ranking of packages has been prepared, it should be reviewed to make sure that there is a general agreement that the rankings are reasonable and there are no anomalies in them.

Step 3. *Allocate resources*

Resources in the budget are then **allocated** according to the funds available and the evaluation and ranking of the competing packages. Packages involving small expenditures can be dealt with by junior managers but senior managers must make decisions involving larger amounts of expenditure. The ZBB process must, however, run through the entire management structure.

3 THE ADVANTAGES AND LIMITATIONS OF ZERO BASE BUDGETS 6/94

The advantages of implementing ZBB

3.1 The **advantages** of zero base budgeting are as follows.

- It is possible to identify and **remove inefficient or obsolete operations.**
- It forces employees to **avoid wasteful expenditure**.
- It can **increase motivation**.
- It provides a **budgeting and planning tool** for management which responds to changes in the business environment; 'obsolescent' items of expenditure are identified and dropped.

- The **documentation** required **provides** all management with a coordinated, in-depth **appraisal of an organisation's operations.**
- It **challenges the status quo** and forces an organisation to examine alternative activities and existing expenditure levels.
- In summary, ZBB should result in a **more efficient allocation of resources** to an organisation's activities and departments.

The disadvantages of ZBB

3.2 The major disadvantage of zero base budgeting is the **volume of extra paperwork** created. The assumptions about costs and benefits in each package must be continually updated and new packages developed as soon as new activities emerge. The following problems might also occur.

- **Short-term benefits** might be **emphasised** to the detriment of long-term benefits.
- The **false idea that all decisions have to be made in the budget might be encouraged**. Management must be able to meet unforeseen opportunities and threats at all times, and must not feel restricted from carrying out new ideas simply because they were not approved by a decision package, cost benefit analysis and the ranking process.
- It may be a **call for management skills** both in constructing decision packages and in the ranking process **which the organisation does not possess**. Managers may therefore have to be trained in ZBB techniques so that they can apply them sensibly and properly.
- It may be **difficult to 'sell' ZBB to managers as a useful technique** for the following reasons.
    - Incremental costs and benefits of alternative courses of action are hard to quantify accurately.
    - Employees or trade union representatives may resist management ideas for changing the ways in which work is done.
- The organisation's **information systems may not be capable of providing suitable** incremental cost and incremental benefit **analysis**.
- **The ranking process can be difficult**. Managers face three common problems.
    - A large number of packages may have to be ranked.
    - There is often a conceptual difficulty in having to rank packages which managers regard as being equally vital, for legal or operational reasons.
    - It is difficult to rank completely different types of activity, especially where activities have qualitative rather than quantitative benefits - such as spending on staff welfare and working conditions - where ranking must usually be entirely subjective.

3.3 In summary, perhaps the **most serious drawback to ZBB is that it requires a lot of management time and paperwork**. One way of obtaining the benefits of ZBB but of overcoming the drawbacks is to apply it selectively on a rolling basis throughout the organisation. This year finance, next year marketing, the year after personnel and so on. In this way all activities will be thoroughly scrutinised over a period of time.

4 USING ZERO BASE BUDGETING 6/94, 6/97

4.1 ZBB can be used by both **profit-making** and **non-profit-making** organisations. It is popular in the US and Canada but its adoption has been slow in the UK.

4.2 The procedures of zero base budgeting do not lend themselves easily to direct manufacturing costs where standard costing, work study and the techniques of management planning and control have long been established as a means of budgeting expenditure.

4.3 ZBB is best applied to **support expenses**, that is expenditure incurred in departments which exist to support the essential production function. These support areas include marketing, finance, quality control, repairs and maintenance, production planning, research and development, engineering design, personnel, data processing, sales and distribution. In many organisations, these expenses make up a large proportion of the total expenditure. These activities are less easily quantifiable by conventional methods and are more discretionary in nature.

4.4 ZBB can also be successfully applied to **service industries** and **non-profit-making organisations** such as local and central government departments, educational establishments, hospitals and so on.

4.5 ZBB can be applied in any organisation where alternative levels of provision for each activity are possible and where the costs and benefits are separately identifiable.

4.6 Some particular uses of ZBB are as follows.

- **Budgeting for discretionary cost items**, such as advertising, R & D and training costs. The priorities for spending money could be established by ranking activities and alternative levels of spending or service can be evaluated on an incremental basis. For example, is it worth spending £2,000 more to increase the numbers trained on one type of training course by 10%? If so, what priority should this incremental spending on training be given, when compared with other potential training activities?
- **Rationalisation measures.** 'Rationalisation' is a euphemism for cutting back on production and activity levels, and cutting costs. The need for service departments to operate above a minimum service level or the need for having a particular department at all can be questioned, and ZBB can be used to make rationalisation decisions when an organisation is forced to make spending cuts. (This use of ZBB might explain any unpopularity it might have among managers.)

Question

You work for a large multinational company which manufactures weedkillers. It has been decided to introduce zero base budgeting in place of the more traditional incremental budgeting. The manager of the research and development department has never heard of zero base budgeting.

Required

Write a report to the manager of the research and development department which explains the following.

(a) How zero base budgeting techniques differ from traditional budgeting
(b) How ZBB may assist in planning and controlling discretionary costs
(c) How ZBB will help to control budgetary slack

Answer

REPORT

To: R&D manager
From: Management accountant
Date: 01.01.X3
Subject: Zero base budgeting

(a) Zero base budgeting and traditional budgeting

The traditional approach to budgeting works from the premise that last year's activities will continue at the same level or volume, and that next year's budget can be based on last year's costs plus an extra amount to allow for expansion and inflation. The term 'incremental' budgeting is often used to describe this approach.

Zero base budgeting (ZBB) quite literally works from a zero base. The approach recognises that every activity has a cost and insists that there must be quantifiable benefits to justify the spending. ZBB expects managers to choose the best method of achieving each task on a cost-benefit basis. Activities must be ranked in order of priority.

(b) Discretionary cost is 'expenditure whose value is a matter of policy', that is, it is not vital to the continued existence of an organisation in the way that, say, raw materials are to a manufacturing business. ZBB was developed originally to help management with the difficult task of allocating resources in precisely such areas. Research and development is a frequently cited example; others are advertising and training.

Within a research and development department ZBB will establish priorities by ranking the projects that are planned and in progress. Project managers will be forced to consider the benefit obtainable from their work in relation to the costs involved. The result may be an overall increase in R&D expenditure, but only if it is justified.

It is worth mentioning that when R&D costs are subsequently being monitored care is needed in interpreting variances. A favourable expenditure variance may not be a good thing: it may mean that not enough is being spent on R&D activity.

(c) Budgetary slack may be defined as the difference between the minimum necessary costs and the costs built into the budget or actually incurred. One of the reasons why, under traditional budgeting, an extra amount is added to last year's budget may be because managers are overestimating costs to avoid being blamed in the future for overspending and to make targets easier to achieve. Slack is a protective device and it is self-fulfilling because managers will subsequently ensure that their actual spending rises to meet the (overestimated) budget, in case they are blamed for careless budgeting.

In an R&D department a further incentive to include slack is the nature of the work. Managers may well have 'pet' projects in which their personal interest is so strong that they tend to ignore the benefit or lack of benefit to the organisation which is funding them.

The ZBB approach, as described in (a) above, clearly will not accept this approach: all expenditure has (in theory) to be justified in cost-benefit terms in its entirety in order to be included in next year's budget. In practice it is more likely that managers will start from their current level of expenditure as usual, but ZBB requires them to work *downwards*, asking what would happen if any particular element of current expenditure and current operations were removed from the budget.

5 PROGRAMME PLANNING AND BUDGETING SYSTEMS

5.1 **Non-profit-seeking organisations** such as government departments, schools, hospitals and charities face **three budgeting problems**.

(a) Such organisations usually prepare conventional budgets but frequently their **output levels are difficult to measure**. Flexible budgets are therefore difficult to construct and budgetary control difficult to operate. Actual expenditure is often compared to budgeted expenditure rather than to the level of expenditure which should have occurred given the level of output.

(b) Non-profit-seeking organisations have particular problems with **long-term strategic planning and resource allocation.** Short-term annual budgets are therefore frequently used as the basis for long-term policy planning, a system which has obvious disadvantages.

(c) The problems of **controlling discretionary costs** are particularly acute in non-profit-seeking organisations.

5.2 In an attempt to overcome these problems the **Programme Planning and Budgeting System (PPBS)** was evolved.

5.3 PPBS, a sophisticated concept, was developed in North America and is usually associated with State and Federal government activities although there is absolutely no reason why the principles should not be more widely applied.

5.4 The system is **based**, not on traditional organisational structures and divisions, but **on 'programmes'** which are groupings of activities with common objectives.

5.5 PPBS requires that an organisation prepares a long-term plan relating to the objectives of the organisation, subdivided into programmes. These programmes are expressed in terms of objectives to be achieved over the **medium to long term**, say three to five years. When the various programmes have been agreed they form the organisation's long-term plan. PPBS covers activities spanning several years and conventional annual expenditure budgeting takes place within this framework. Each year the departments contributing to a given programme prepare, and are monitored by, normal expenditure budgets for their share of the programme's activities for the particular year.

5.6 The method of budgeting using PPBS was set down as follows by D R Nichols (in PPBS - A challenge to non-profit accounting, *Management Accounting* (US), November 1969).

> '1 The overall objectives and goals of the organisation and of the various agencies and departments within the organisation are formulated. Priorities are determined for the attainment of the goals and objectives.
>
> 2 The possible alternative programmes which may be used to fulfil the desired objectives are compared based on the effectiveness of each in achieving the organisational objectives.
>
> 3 The total cost of each programme is related to the total benefits that would be derived from the programme to determine the efficiency of the programme.
>
> 4 The most effective and efficient programmes are selected, integrated into a comprehensive programme, and implemented.
>
> 5 The results of this programme, once initiated, are reviewed and judged on the basis of performance. The purposes of this review are control in the implementation of the programme and procurement of information for future decisions and forecasts.'

5.7 Each programme cannot, of course, be reviewed each year but the analytical steps of PPBS call for a **periodic review** of fundamental programme objectives, costs and accomplishments to date.

5.8 Note that **programmes are objectives related** and spread across several conventional departments. The total estimated costs are for the programme as a whole and are not initially expressed in relation to departments.

5.9 A J Cuyler (*The Economics of Social Policy*, Oxford: Martin Robertson, 1973) provides a useful illustration of PPBS with respect to the allocation of expenditure in a police force. Whereas the conventional budget categories (pay, transport, establishment expenses, supplies and so on) bear no relation at all to the *activities* of a police force, it is possible to identify various functions carried out by the police and hence determine suitable programmes. A list of police functions might include the following.

- Maintenance of law and order
- Prevention of crime
- Detection of criminals and interrogation

- Prosecution of offenders
- Road traffic control

5.10 On the basis of such objectives, major police programmes could be grouped as follows.

- Protection of persons and property from:
  - criminal activities
  - traffic hazards
  - miscellaneous hazards
- Treatment of offenders
  - Detection and apprehension
  - Process and trial
  - Training

Advantages of PPBS

5.11 The US National Association of Accountants (*Financial Planning and Evaluation for the Non-profit Organisation*, New York, 1981) cites the following advantages of using a PPBS system.

- It provides a framework for responsibility.
- It provides an opportunity for long-range planning.
- It promotes an optimisation of resources.
- It assists in acquiring government funds.
- It provides opportunities to the programme staff to input into the decision-making process.
- It compels organisational self-study and analysis.
- It promotes rational decisions.

Disadvantages of PPBS

5.12 The disadvantages of PPBS are as follows.

- It may not always be possible to allocate all of the costs meaningfully to a category.
- The development of programme structures can be seen as an additional administrative responsibility rather than as a substitute for previous ones.
- Difficulty can be encountered in defining programmes.

PPBS and information systems

5.13 PPBS **requires** a **sophisticated information system** which is able to monitor progress towards meeting objectives. It should be able to report upon results in terms of the programmes of activities (unlike conventional reporting which is geared to existing organisational sub-divisions and usually deals only with expenditures).

6 ROLLING BUDGETS

6.1 If management need the chance to revise their plans (perhaps because it is suspected that a new competitor will enter the market at the beginning of the year, the effect of which cannot be quantified when the budget is set or perhaps because inflation is very high or is expected to rise or fall by a large amount during the course of the year) management may decide to introduce a system of **rolling budgets** (also called **continuous budgets**).

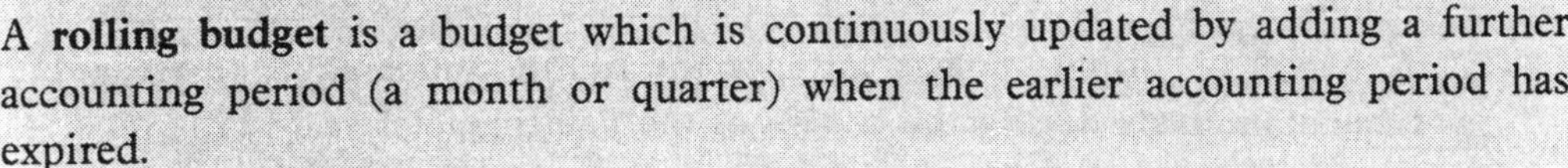

KEY TERM

A **rolling budget** is a budget which is continuously updated by adding a further accounting period (a month or quarter) when the earlier accounting period has expired.

6.2 Rolling budgets are an attempt to prepare targets and plans which are **more realistic and certain,** particularly with a regard to price levels, by **shortening the period between preparing budgets.**

6.3 Instead of preparing a periodic budget annually for the full budget period, there would be **budgets every one, two, three or four months** (three to six, or even twelve budgets each year). **Each of these budgets would plan for the next twelve months** so that the current budget is extended by an extra period as the current period ends: hence the name rolling budgets.

6.4 Suppose, for example, that a rolling budget is prepared every three months. The first three months of the budget period would be planned in great detail, and the remaining nine months in lesser detail, because of the greater uncertainty about the longer-term future.

If a first continuous budget is prepared for January to March in detail and April to December in less detail, a new budget will be prepared towards the end of March, planning April to June in detail and July to March in less detail. Four rolling budgets would be prepared every 12 months on this 3 and 9 month basis, requiring, inevitably, greater administrative effort.

The detail in the first three months would be principally important for the following.

- **Planning working capital and short-term resources** (cash, materials, labour and so on).
- **Control**: the budget for each control period should provide a more reliable yardstick for comparison with actual results.

The advantages and disadvantages of rolling budgets

6.5 The **advantages** are as follows.

(a) They **reduce the element of uncertainty** in budgeting. If a high rate of inflation or major changes in market conditions or any other change is likely which cannot be quantified with accuracy, rolling budgets concentrate detailed planning and control on short-term prospects where the degree of uncertainty is much smaller.

(b) They force managers to reassess the budget regularly, and to **produce budgets which are up to date in the light of current events and expectations.**

(c) **Planning and control will be based on a recent plan** instead of a fixed annual budget that might have been made many months ago and which is no longer realistic.

(d) Realistic budgets are likely to have a **better motivational influence** on managers.

(e) There is **always a budget which extends for several months ahead**. For example, if rolling budgets are prepared quarterly there will always be a budget extending for the next 9 to 12 months. If rolling budgets are prepared monthly there will always be a budget for the next 11 to 12 months. This is not the case when fixed annual budgets are used.

6.6 The **disadvantages** of rolling budgets can be a deterrent to using them.

(a) A system of rolling budgets calls for the routine preparation of a new budget at regular intervals during the course of the one financial year. This involves **more time, effort and money** in budget preparation.

(b) Frequent budgeting might have an **off-putting effect on managers** who doubt the value of preparing one budget after another at regular intervals, even when there are major differences between the figures in one budget and the next.

(c) Revisions to the budget might involve revisions to standard costs too, which in turn would involve revisions to stock valuations. This could mean that a large **administrative effort** is required in the accounts department every time a rolling budget is prepared to bring the accounting records up to date.

Rolling budgets or updated annual budgets

6.7 If the expected changes are not likely to be continuous there is a strong argument that routine updating of the budget is unnecessary. **Instead the annual budget could be updated whenever changes become foreseeable,** so that a budget might be updated once or twice, and perhaps more often, during the course of the year.

6.8 When a fixed budget is updated, a 'rolling' budget would probably not be prepared. For example, if a budget is updated in month 8 of the year, the updated budget would relate to months 8 - 12 and the end of the financial year. It would not be extended to month 7 of the following year.

Chapter roundup

- The traditional approach to budgeting, known as **incremental budgeting**, bases the budget on the current year's results plus an extra amount for estimated growth or inflation next year. It encourages slack and wasteful spending to creep into budgets.
- The principle behind **zero base budgeting** is that the budget for each cost centre should be made from **'scratch'** or **zero**. Every item of expenditure must be justified in its entirety in order to be included in the next year's budget.
- There is a three-step approach to ZBB.
    - Define decision units
    - Evaluate and rank packages
    - Allocate resources
- ZBB is particularly useful for the following.
    - Budgeting for discretionary costs
    - Rationalisation measures
- **PPBS** is a budgeting method which is particularly useful for non profit seeking organisations.
- **Rolling budgets** (continuous budgets) are budgets which are continuously updated by adding a further period (say a month or a quarter) and deducting the earliest period.

Quick quiz

1. What is incremental budgeting? (see key term)
2. What is zero base budgeting? (key term)
3. What are the two types of decision package? (2.4)
4. List four advantages of ZBB. (3.1)
5. Describe two particular uses of ZBB. (4.6)
6. Describe the five steps in PPBS as set out by Nichols. (5.6)
7. List four advantages and four disadvantages of continuous budgets. (6.5, 6.6)

Question to try	Level	Marks	Time
9	Examination	20	36 mins

Part C
Standard costing

Chapter 10

INTRODUCTION TO STANDARD COSTING

Chapter topic list		Syllabus reference
1	Standard costs	2(b)(i)
2	Standard costing	2(b)(i)
3	Budgets and standards compared	2(a), (b)
4	Setting standards	2(b)(ii)
5	Types of standard and their motivational impact	2(b)(ii)
6	Reviewing standards	2(b)(i)(ii)

Introduction

Just as there are standards for most things in our daily lives (cleanliness in hamburger restaurants, educational achievement of nine year olds, number of underground trains running on time) there are standards for the costs of units of products and units of services rendered in a commercial organisation. Moreover, just as the standards in our daily lives are not always met, the standards for the costs of units of products and services rendered are not always met. We will not, however, be considering the cleanliness of hamburger restaurants in this chapter but we will be looking at standard costs and standard costing.

In the next chapter we will see how standard costing forms the basis of a process called variance analysis, a vital management control tool.

1 STANDARD COSTS

1.1 Just as there are standards for most things in our daily lives (cleanliness in hamburger restaurants, educational achievement of nine year olds, number of tubes on the Circle line running on time), there are standards for the costs of products and services.

KEY TERM

A **standard cost** is an estimated unit cost.

1.2 The standard cost of product 12345 is set out below on a **standard cost card.**

STANDARD COST CARD
Product: the Splodget, No 12345

	Cost	*Requirement*	£	£
Direct materials				
A	£2.00 per kg	6 kgs	12.00	
B	£3.00 per kg	2 kgs	6.00	
C	£4.00 per litre	1 litre	4.00	
Others			2.00	
				24.00
Direct labour				
Grade I	£4.00 per hour	3 hrs	12.00	
Grade II	£5.40 per hour	5 hrs	27.00	
				39.00
Variable production overheads	£1.00 per hour	8 hrs		8.00
Fixed production overheads	£3.00 per hour	8 hrs		24.00
Standard full cost of production				95.00

1.3 Notice how it is **built up from standards for each cost element:** standard quantities of materials at standard prices, standard quantities of labour time at standard rates and so on. It is therefore determined by management's estimates of the following.

- The expected prices of materials, labour and expenses
- Efficiency levels in the use of materials and labour
- Budgeted overhead costs and budgeted volumes of activity

We will see how management arrives at these estimates later in the chapter.

1.4 But why should management want to prepare standard costs? Obviously to assist with standard costing, but what is the point of standard costing?

2 STANDARD COSTING

The uses of standard costing

2.1 **Standard costing has a variety of uses** but its two principal ones are as follows.

- **To value stocks and cost production** for cost accounting purposes. It is an alternative method of valuation to methods like FIFO and LIFO which you will have covered in your earlier studies.
- **To act as a control device** by establishing standards (expected costs) and comparing actual costs with the expected costs, thus highlighting areas of the organisation which may be out of control

2.2 Although the use of standard costs to value stocks and cost production should not be overlooked, we will be concentrating on the control aspect of standard costing.

Standard costing as a control technique

> **KEY TERMS**
>
> **Standard costing** involves the establishment of predetermined estimates of the costs of products or services, the collection of actual costs and the comparison of the actual costs with the predetermined estimates. The predetermined costs are known as standard costs and the difference between standard and actual cost is known as a **variance.** The process by which the total difference between standard and actual results is analysed in known as **variance analysis.**

Where standard costing should be used

2.3 Although standard costing can be used in a variety of costing situations (batch and mass production, process manufacture, jobbing manufacture (where there is standardisation of parts) and service industries (if a realistic cost unit can be established)), the **greatest benefit from its use can be gained if there is a degree of repetition in the production process** so that average or expected usage of resources can be determined. It is therefore **most suited to mass production and repetitive assembly work** and less suited to organisations which produce to customer demand and requirements.

3 BUDGETS AND STANDARDS COMPARED

3.1 A **budget** is a **quantified monetary plan** for a future period, which mangers will try to achieve. It is mainly used for communicating plans and coordinating activities within an organisation.

A **standard** is a carefully **predetermined quantity target** which can be achieved in certain conditions.

3.2 Budgets and standards are **similar** in the following ways.

- They both involve **looking to the future** and **forecasting** what is likely to happen given a certain set of circumstances.
- They are both used for **control** purposes. A budget helps with control by setting financial targets or limits for a forthcoming period. Actual achievements or expenditures are then compared with the budgets and action is taken to correct any variances where necessary. A standard also achieves control by comparison of actual results against a predetermined target.

3.3 As well as being similar, budgets and standards are **interrelated**. For example, a standard unit production cost can act as the basis for a production cost budget. The unit cost is multiplied by the budgeted activity level to arrive at the budgeted expenditure on production costs.

3.4 There are, however, important **differences** between budgets and standards.

- A **budget** gives the planned **total costs** for a function or cost centre such as production department A, whereas a **standard** shows the amount of resource that should be used for a **single task**, for example the standard labour hours for a single unit of production.

- The use of **standards** is **limited to situations where repetitive actions are performed and output can be measured. Budgets** can be **prepared for all functions** (such as the personnel department), **even where output cannot be measured.**
- **A standard need not be expressed in money terms**. For example, a standard rate of output (6 units per hour) can be determined for control purposes without the need to put a financial value on it. **In contrast, a budget is expressed in money terms.**
    - **Budgets are revised on a periodic basis** (usually) whereas **standards are revised only when they are no longer appropriate** in current operating conditions.
    - The **accounting treatment** of budgets and standards **differs**. Budgets are memorandum figures and do not form part of the double entry accounting system whereas standards and variances do.

3.5 In summary, **budgets and standards are very similar and interrelated, but there are important differences between them.**

Question 1

What are the possible advantages for the control function of an organisation of having a standard costing system?

Answer

- Carefully planned standards are an aid to more accurate budgeting.
- Standard costs provide a yardstick against which actual costs can be measured.
- The setting of standards involves determining the best materials and methods which may lead to economies.
- A target of efficiency is set for employees to reach and cost-consciousness is stimulated.
- Variances can be calculated which enable the principle of 'management by exception' to be operated. Only the variances which exceed acceptable tolerance limits need to be investigated by management with a view to control action.
- Standard costs and variance analysis can provide a way of motivation to managers to achieve better performance. However, care must be taken to distinguish between controllable and non-controllable costs in variance reporting.

4 SETTING STANDARDS

4.1 A standard cost implies that a standard or target exists for every single element that contributes to the product: the types, usage and prices of materials and parts, the grades, rates of pay and times for the labour involved, the production methods, tools and so on. The standard cost for each part of the product is recorded on a **standard cost card**, an example of which was given earlier in the chapter.

4.2 Standard costs may be **used in both marginal and absorption costing systems**. The card we saw earlier had been prepared under an absorption costing system, with selling and administration costs excluded from the standard.

4.3 The **responsibility for setting standard costs** should be shared between **managers able to provide the necessary information** about levels of expected efficiency, prices and overhead costs.

Setting standards for materials costs

4.4 Direct materials costs per unit of raw material will be estimated by the purchasing department from their knowledge of the following.

- Purchase contracts already agreed
- Pricing discussions with regular suppliers
- The forecast movement of prices in the market
- The availability of bulk purchase discounts
- The quality of material required by the production departments

4.5 The standard cost ought to include an allowance for **bulk purchase discounts**, if these are available on all or some of the purchases, and it may have to be a weighted average price of the differing prices charged for the same product by alternative suppliers.

4.6 A decision must also be taken as to how to deal with price **inflation**. Suppose that a material costs £10 per kilogram at the moment, and during the course of the next 12 months, it is expected to go up in price by 20% to £12 per kilogram. What standard price should be selected: the current price of £10 per kilogram or the average expected price for the year, which might be, for example, £11 per kilogram? Either would be possible, but neither would be entirely satisfactory.

- If the **current price were used in the standard**, the reported price variance would become adverse as soon as prices go up, which might be very early in the year. If prices go up gradually rather than in one big jump, it would be difficult to select an appropriate time for revising the standard.
- If an **estimated mid-year price were used**, price variances should be favourable in the first half of the year and adverse in the second half, again assuming that prices go up gradually. Management could only really check that in any month, the price variance did not become excessively adverse (or favourable) and that the price variance switched from being favourable to adverse around month six or seven and not sooner.

4.7 Standard costing is therefore more difficult **in times of inflation but it is still worthwhile.**

- Usage and efficiency variances will still be meaningful.
- Inflation is measurable: there is no reason why its effects cannot be removed from the variances reported.
- Standard costs can be revised, so long as this is not done too frequently.

Setting standards for labour costs

4.8 Direct labour rates per hour will be set by reference to the payroll and to any agreements on pay rises with trade union representatives of the employees.

(a) A separate hourly rate or weekly wage will be set for each different labour grade/type of employee.

(b) An average hourly rate will be applied for each grade (even though individual rates of pay may vary according to age and experience).

Setting standards for material usage and labour efficiency

4.9 To estimate the materials required to make each product (material usage) and also the labour hours required (labour efficiency), technical specifications must be prepared for each product by production experts (either in the production department or the work study department).

- The **standard product specification** for materials must list the quantities required of each material in the product. The quantities should take into account allowances for breakages and losses. Operators in the production department must know about these standard input quantities so that control action by management to deal with excess material wastage will be understood by them.
- The **standard operation sheet** for labour will specify the expected hours required by each grade of labour in each department to make one unit of product. These standard times must be carefully set and must be understood by the labour force. Where necessary, standard procedures or operating methods should be stated.

Setting standards for overheads

4.10 The overhead absorption rate is usually based on the number of direct labour hours and so the standard overhead cost per unit is usually calculated as follows.

Standard labour hours per unit × standard absorption rate per hour

The **standard absorption rate per hour is the same as the predetermined overhead absorption rate** as calculated for an absorption costing system.

4.11 The standard absorption rate will **depend on the planned production volume** for a period. **Production volume will depend on two factors.**

- **Production capacity** (or '**volume capacity**') measured perhaps in standard hours of output (a concept which we met in Chapter 6), which in turn reflects production direct labour hours.
- **Efficiency of working**, by labour or machines, allowing for rest time and contingency allowances.

4.12 Suppose that a department has a work force of ten men, each of whom works a 36 hour week to make standard units, and each unit has a standard time of two hours to make. The expected efficiency of the work-force is 125%.

(a) Budgeted capacity, in direct labour hours, would be 10 × 36 = 360 production hours per week.

(b) Budgeted efficiency is 125% so that the work-force should take only 1 hour of actual production time to produce 1.25 standard hours of output.

(c) This means in our example that budgeted output is 360 production hours × 125% = 450 standard hours of output per week. At 2 standard hours per unit, this represents production activity or volume of 225 units of output per week.

Output, capacity and efficiency are inter-related items, and you should check your understanding of them by attempting a quick answer to the following problem.

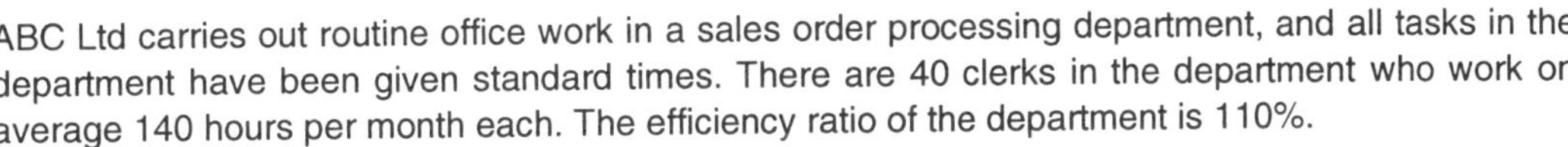

Question 2

ABC Ltd carries out routine office work in a sales order processing department, and all tasks in the department have been given standard times. There are 40 clerks in the department who work on average 140 hours per month each. The efficiency ratio of the department is 110%.

Required

Calculate the budgeted output in the department.

Answer

Capacity	=	40 × 140 = 5,600 hours per month
Efficiency	=	110%
Budgeted output	=	5,600 × 110% = 6,160 standard hours of work per month.

Capacity levels

4.13 Capacity levels are needed to establish a standard absorption rate for production overhead, when standard absorption costing is used. Any one of three capacity levels might be used for budgeting.

- Full capacity
- Practical capacity
- Budgeted capacity

KEY TERMS

- **Full capacity** is the theoretical capacity, assuming continuous production without any stoppages due to factors such as machine downtime, supply shortages or labour shortages. Full capacity would be associated with ideal standards.
- **Practical capacity** is an output level below full capacity, and is associated with attainable standards, since it takes account of known, unavoidable stoppages.
- **Budgeted capacity** is the capacity (labour hours, machine hours) needed to produce the budgeted output. It is associated with current standards, which relate to current conditions but may not be representative of normal practical capacity over a longer period of time.
- **Idle capacity** is the practical capacity in a period less the budgeted capacity measured in standard hours of output. It represents unused capacity that ought to be available, but which is not needed because the budgeted volume is lower than the practicable volume that could be achieved.

4.14 **Capacity ratios** can be calculated. They provide similar information to variances.

Question 3

Given the following information, calculate an idle capacity ratio, a production volume/ratio, a capacity ratio and an efficiency ratio and explain their meanings.

Full capacity	10,000 standard hours
Practical capacity	8,000 standard hours
Budgeted capacity	7500 standard hours
Standard hours produced	6,500
Actual hours worked	7,000

Answer

Idle capacity ratio $= \dfrac{\text{Practical capacity} - \text{budgeted capacity}}{\text{Practical capacity}} \times 100\%$

$= \dfrac{8{,}000 - 7{,}500}{8{,}000} \times 100\% = 6.25\%.$

This means that 6.25% of practical capacity will be unused because budgeted volume is lower than the volume that could be achieved.

Production volume ratio $= \dfrac{\text{Actual output measured in expected or standard hours}}{\text{Budgeted capacity}} \times 100\%$

$= \dfrac{6{,}500}{7{,}500} \times 100\% = 86.67\%$

This means actual output was only 86.67% of budgeted output.

Capacity ratio $= \dfrac{\text{Actual hours worked}}{\text{Budgeted capacity}}$

$= \dfrac{7{,}000}{7{,}500} \times 100\% = 93.33\%$

This means that only 93.33% of budgeted capacity was actually used.

Efficiency ratio $= \dfrac{\text{Actual output measured in standard or expected hours}}{\text{Actual hours worked}} \times 100\%$

$= \dfrac{6{,}500}{7{,}000} \times 100\% = 92.86\%$

This means that the labour force were working at 92.86% efficiency.

4.15 The production volume ratio shows the overall effect of the capacity and efficiency ratio. In the question above we have:

Production volume ratio	=	**capacity ratio**	×	**efficiency ratio**
ie 86.67%	=	93.33%	×	92.86%

Setting standards for sales price and margin

4.16 The **standard selling price** will depend on a number of factors including the following.

- Anticipated market demand
- Competing products
- Manufacturing costs
- Inflation estimates

4.17 The **standard sales margin** is the difference between the standard cost and the standard selling price.

Question 4

What problems do you think could occur when standards are being set?

Answer

The following problems can occur when setting standards.

(a) Deciding how to incorporate inflation into planned unit costs

(b) Agreeing on a performance standard (attainable or ideal)

(c) Deciding on the quality of materials to be used (a better quality of material will cost more, but perhaps reduce material wastage)

(d) Estimating materials prices where seasonal price variations or bulk purchase discounts may be significant

(e) Finding sufficient time to construct accurate standards as standard setting can be a time-consuming process

(f) Incurring the cost of setting up and maintaining a system for establishing standards

5 TYPES OF STANDARD AND THEIR MOTIVATIONAL IMPACT

5.1 How demanding should a standard be? Should the standard represent perfect performance or easily attainable performance? There are four types of standard.

KEY TERMS

- An **ideal standard** is a standard which can be attained under perfect operating conditions: no wastage, no spoilage, no inefficiencies, no idle time, no breakdowns.
- An **attainable standard** is a standard which can be attained if production is carried out efficiently, machines are properly operated and/or materials are properly used. Some allowance is made for wastage and inefficiencies.
- A **current standard** is standard based on current working conditions (current wastage, current inefficiencies).
- A **basic standard** is a long-term standard which remains unchanged over the years and is used to show trends.

5.2 The **different types of standard have a number of advantages and disadvantages.**

- Ideal standards can be seen as long-term targets but are not very useful for day-to-day control purposes.
- Ideal standards cannot be achieved. If such standards are used for budgeting, an allowance will therefore have to be included to make the budget realistic and attainable.
- Attainable standards can be used for product costing, cost control, stock valuation, estimating and as a basis for budgeting.
- Current standards or attainable standards provide the best basis for budgeting, because they represent an achievable level of productivity.
- Current standards do not attempt to improve on current levels of efficiency.
- Current standards are useful during periods when inflation is high. They can be set on a month by month basis.
- Basic standards are used to show changes in efficiency or performance over a long period of time. They are perhaps the least useful and least common type of standard in use.

The impact on employee motivation of the type of standard set.

5.3 The type of standard set can have an impact on the motivation of the employees trying to achieve those standards.

Type of standard	Impact
Ideal	Some say that they provide employees with an **incentive to be more efficient** even though it is highly unlikely that the standard will be achieved. Others argue that they are likely to have an unfavourable effect on employee motivation because the differences between standards and actual results will always be adverse. The **employees may feel that the goals are unattainable** and so **they will not work so hard**.
Attainable	Might be an **incentive to work harder** as they provide a **realistic but challenging target of efficiency**.
Current	**Will not motivate employees to do anything more than they are currently doing**.
Basic	May have an **unfavourable impact** on the motivation of employees. Over time they will discover that they are easily able to achieve the standards. They may become bored and lose interest in what they are doing if they have nothing to aim for.

6 REVIEWING STANDARDS

6.1 Although standards are developed from past and current information, they should reflect technical and current factors expected for the period in which the standards are to be applied. Management should not think that once standards are set they will remain useful for ever. **Standards must evolve to reflect an organisation's changing methods and processes**. Comparing out-of-date standards with actual results will provide misleading information.

6.2 Consider a computer manufacturer. Suppose that the standard price for computer chips was set in 1993 and not changed until 1998. In the five-year period, however, the price of chips would have dramatically decreased. Consistently favourable material price variances would have been reported, giving the appearance that the purchasing department was performing very well, buying chips at well below the standard price. What's more, if stocks are valued at standard cost, the stock value of the chips would have been too high The price reductions occurring since the standard was set would therefore render the standard obsolete and worthless.

6.3 It is therefore vital that management **review standards on a regular basis and revise them if necessary.**

6.4 **Some argue that standards should be revised as soon as there is any change in the basis upon which they were set**. Clearly, for example, if a standard is based on the cost of a material that is no longer available or the use of equipment which has been replaced, it is meaningless to compare actual performance using the new material and equipment with the old standard. Or if an existing standard is discovered to be incorrectly set and there is a significant difference between the incorrect and correct standards, the use of the incorrect standard is pointless.

6.5 **Others people believe that frequent changes in standards make them ineffective as motivators and measures of performance**, since those trying to achieve the targets will believe the target setters are constantly '**moving the goal posts**'. It has also been argued that frequent changes to standards are **too time-consuming** from the point of view of administration, although the introduction of computer systems makes this objection less forceful.

6.6 In practice, standard costs are **usually revised once a year** to allow for the new overheads budget, inflation in prices and wage rates, and any changes in expected efficiency of material usage, labour or machinery. One research study showed that most organisations revise their standards annually. Some revise them more frequently than this: about 7% revise them quarterly.

6.7 The **most suitable approach** would therefore appear to be a policy of **revising the standards whenever changes of a permanent and reasonably long-term nature occur,** but not in response to temporary 'blips' in price or efficiency.

Chapter roundup

- A **standard cost** is an estimated unit cost.
- A standard cost is built up of standards for each cost element (standard resource price and standard resource usage).
- **Standard costing** is principally used to value stocks and cost production and to act as a control device.
- Standard costing is most suited to mass production and repetitive assembly work.
- **Budgets** and standards are very similar and interrelated, but there are important differences between them.
- The responsibility for setting standards should be shared between the managers able to provide the necessary information about levels of expected efficiency, prices and overhead costs.
- There are four **types of standard: ideal, attainable, current** and **basic**. These can have an impact on employee motivation.
- Standards should be revised whenever there are changes of a permanent and reasonably long-term nature.

Quick quiz

1 How does standard costing act as a control device? (see para 2.1)

2 In what circumstances can standard costing be used in service industries? (2.3)

3 In what way are budgets and standards interrelated? (3.3)

4 What problem can arise when setting standards for materials costs? (4.6)

5 What is a current standard? (5.1)

6 What are the arguments against revising standards too frequently? (6.5)

Question to try	Level	Marks	Time
10	Examination	5	9 mins

Chapter 11

BASIC VARIANCE ANALYSIS

Introduction

The **actual results** achieved by an organisation during a reporting period (week, month, quarter, year) will, more than likely, be **different from the expected results** (the expected results being the standard costs and revenues which we looked at in the previous chapter). Such differences may occur between individual items, such as the cost of labour and the volume of sales, and between the total expected profit/contribution and the total actual profit/contribution.

Management will have spent considerable time and trouble setting standards. Actual results have differed from the standards. Have costs been controlled? What does the wise manager do? Ignore the difference and continue trying to attain the standards? Let us hope not. The wise manager will consider the differences that have occurred and use the results of his considerations to assist him in his attempts to attain the standards. The wise manager will use **variance analysis** as a method of cost control.

1 VARIANCES

KEY TERMS

- **A variance** is the difference between an actual result and an expected result.
- **Variance analysis** is the process by which the *total* difference between standard and actual results is analysed.

1.1 When actual results are better than expected results, we have a **favourable variance (F).** If, on the other hand, actual results are worse than expected results, we have an **adverse variance (A).**

1.2 Variances can be divided into three main groups.

- Variable cost variances
- Fixed production overhead variances
- Sales variances

2 DIRECT MATERIAL COST VARIANCES 6/94, 6/95, 12/95

KEY TERMS

- The **direct material total variance** is the difference between what the output actually cost and what it should have cost, in terms of material. It can be divided into the following two sub-variances.
- The **direct material price variance** is the difference between the standard cost and the actual cost for the *actual* quantity of material used or purchased. In other words, it is the difference between what the material did cost and what it should have cost.
- The **direct material usage variance** is the difference between the standard quantity of materials that *should* have been used for the number of units *actually* produced, and the actual quantity of materials used, valued at the standard cost per unit of material. In other words, it is the difference between how much material should have been used and how much material was used, valued at standard cost.

2.1 EXAMPLE: DIRECT MATERIAL VARIANCES

Product X has a standard direct material cost as follows.

10 kilograms of material Y at £10 per kilogram = £100 per unit of X.

During period 4, 1,000 units of X were manufactured, using 11,700 kilograms of material Y which cost £98,600.

Required

Calculate the following variances.

(a) The direct material total variance 1400 F
(b) The direct material price variance 18400F
(c) The direct material usage variance 17000A

2.2 SOLUTION

(a) *The direct material total variance*

This is the difference between what 1,000 units should have cost and what they did cost.

	£
1,000 units should have cost (× £100)	100,000
but did cost	98,600
Direct material total variance	1,400 (F)

The variance is favourable because the units cost less than they should have cost.

Now we can break down the direct material total variance into its two constituent parts: the direct material price variance and the direct material usage variance.

(b) *The direct material price variance*

This is the difference between what 11,700 kgs should have cost and what 11,700 kgs did cost.

	£
11,700 kgs of Y should have cost (× £10)	117,000
but did cost	98,600
Material Y price variance	18,400 (F)

The variance is favourable because the material cost less than it should have.

(c) *The direct material usage variance*

This is the difference between how many kilograms of Y should have been used to produce 1,000 units of X and how many kilograms were used, valued at the standard cost per kilogram.

1,000 units should have used (× 10 kgs)	10,000 kgs
but did use	11,700 kgs
Usage variance in kgs	1,700 kgs (A)
× standard cost per kilogram	× £10
Usage variance in £	£17,000 (A)

The variance is adverse because more material than should have been used was used.

(d) *Summary*

	£
Price variance	18,400 (F)
Usage variance	17,000 (A)
Total variance	1,400 (F)

Materials variances and opening and closing stock

2.3 Suppose that a company uses raw material P in production, and that this raw material has a standard price of £3 per metre. During one month 6,000 metres are bought for £18,600, and 5,000 metres are used in production. At the end of the month, stock will have been increased by 1,000 metres. In variance analysis, the problem is to decide the material price variance. Should it be calculated on the basis of materials purchased (6,000 metres) or on the basis of materials used (5,000 metres)?

2.4 The answer to this problem depends on how **closing stocks** of the raw materials will be valued.

- If they are **valued at standard cost,** (1,000 units at £3 per unit) the **price variance** is **calculated on material purchases** in the period.
- If they are **valued at actual cost** (FIFO) (1,000 units at £3.10 per unit) the **price variance is calculated on materials used in production** in the period.

2.5 A full standard costing system is usually in operation and therefore the price variance is calculated on purchases in the period. The variance on the full 6,000 metres will be written off to the costing profit and loss account, even though only 5,000 metres are included in the cost of production.

2.6 There are two main **advantages** in extracting the material price variance at the time of receipt.

- If variances are extracted at the time of receipt they will be brought to the attention of managers earlier than if they are extracted as the material is used. If it is necessary to correct any variances then management action can be more timely.
- Since variances are extracted at the time of receipt, all stocks will be valued at standard price. This is administratively easier than using FIFO, LIFO or one of the weighted average methods and it means that all issues from stocks can be made at standard price. If stocks are held at actual cost it is necessary to calculate a separate price variance on each batch as it is issued. Since issues are usually made in a number of small batches this can be a time consuming task, especially with a manual system.

2.7 The price variance would be calculated as follows.

	£	
6,000 metres of material P purchased should cost (× £3)	18,000	
but did cost	18,600	
Price variance	600	(A)

2.8 Note that there are **disadvantages** to doing this, however.

- The matching concept requires the matching of costs and revenues in a period but if variances are extracted at the time of receipt, revenues will be matched with the standard cost of the materials used plus the variances on the materials purchased rather than the true cost of sales.
- If variances are extracted at the time of receipt, the usage variance may be calculated on a different amount to that on which the price variance is calculated. The two variances may therefore not sum to the materials total variance.
- SSAP 9 requires that stocks are valued at the lower of cost and net realisable value but by extracting variances upon receipt stocks are valued at standard. This may require an inventory adjustment for financial accounting purposes.

2.9 **In practice**, most organisations calculate materials price variances **when the material is purchased**. As far as your exam is concerned, David Cornes provides the following guidance in 'Variances, variances and more variances', in the June 1996 edition of *ACCA Students' Newsletter*.

> 'In examination questions the wording of the question should make clear what method is to be used. If both variances are to be calculated on the same quantity the examiner may say that the company uses a method of just-in-time purchasing or even that a system of Backflush Accounting ensures that purchases are not accounted for until the materials are used.'

3 DIRECT LABOUR COST VARIANCES 6/94, 12/95, 12/97

Exam focus point

In the 12/95 exam, there were 4 marks to be gained for calculating labour cost, efficiency and rate variances.

KEY TERMS

- The **direct labour total variance** is the difference between what the output should have cost and what it did cost, in terms of labour. It can be divided into two sub-variances.
- The **direct labour rate variance** is the difference between the standard cost and the actual cost for the actual number of hours paid for. In other words, it is the difference between what the labour did cost and what it should have cost.
- The **direct labour efficiency variance** is the difference between the hours that *should* have been worked for the number of units *actually* produced, and the actual number of hours worked, valued at the standard rate per hour. In other words, it is the difference between how many hours should have been worked and how many hours were worked, valued at the standard rate per hour.

3.1 The calculation of labour variances is very similar to the calculation of material variances. The calculation of the labour rate variance is similar to that for the material price variance while the calculation of the labour efficiency variance is similar to that for the material usage variance.

3.2 EXAMPLE: DIRECT LABOUR VARIANCES

The standard direct labour cost of product X is as follows.

2 hours of grade Z labour at £5 per hour = £10 per unit of product X.

During period 4, 1,000 units of product X were made, and the direct labour cost of grade Z labour was £8,900 for 2,300 hours of work.

Required

Calculate the following variances.

(a) The direct labour total variance
(b) The direct labour rate variance
(c) The direct labour efficiency (productivity) variance

3.3 SOLUTION

(a) *The direct labour total variance*

This is the difference between what 1,000 units should have cost and what they did cost.

	£
1,000 units should have cost (× £10)	10,000
but did cost	8,900
Direct labour total variance	1,100 (F)

The variance is favourable because the units cost less than they should have done.

Again we can split this total variance into two parts.

(b) *The direct labour rate variance*

This is the difference between what 2,300 hours should have cost and what 2,300 hours did cost.

	£
2,300 hours of work should have cost (× £5 per hr)	11,500
but did cost	8,900
Direct labour rate variance	2,600 (F)

The variance is favourable because the labour cost less than it should have cost.

(c) *The direct labour efficiency variance*

1,000 units of X should have taken (× 2 hrs)	2,000 hrs
but did take	2,300 hrs
Efficiency variance in hours	300 hrs (A)
× standard rate per hour	× £5
Efficiency variance in £	£1,500 (A)

The variance is adverse because more hours were worked than should have been worked.

(d) *Summary*

	£
Rate variance	2,600 (F)
Efficiency variance	1,500 (A)
Total variance	1,100 (F)

Idle time variance

KEY TERM

The **idle time** variance is the number of hours that labour were idle valued at the standard rate per hour.

3.4 A company may operate a costing system in which any idle time is recorded. Idle time may be caused by machine breakdowns or not having work to give to employees, perhaps because of bottlenecks in production or a shortage of orders from customers. When idle time occurs, the labour force is still paid wages for time at work, but no actual work is done. Time paid for without any work being done is unproductive and therefore inefficient. **In variance analysis, idle time is an adverse efficiency variance.**

3.5 When idle time is recorded separately, it is helpful to provide control information which identifies the cost of idle time separately, and in variance analysis, there will be an idle time variance as a separate part of the total labour efficiency variance. **The remaining efficiency variance will then relate only to the productivity of the labour force during the hours spent actively working.**

3.6 EXAMPLE: LABOUR VARIANCES WITH IDLE TIME

During period 5, 1,500 units of product X were made and the cost of grade Z labour was £17,500 for 3,080 hours. During the period, however, there as a shortage of customer orders and 100 hours were recorded as idle time.

Required

Calculate the following variances.

(a) The direct labour total variance 2500A
(b) The direct labour rate variance 2100A
(c) The idle time variance 500A
(d) The direct labour efficiency variance 100F

3.7 SOLUTION

(a) *The direct labour total variance*

	£
1,500 units of product X should have cost (× £10)	15,000
but did cost	17,500
Direct labour total variance	2,500 (A)

Actual cost is greater than standard cost. The variance is therefore adverse.

(b) *The direct labour rate variance*

The rate variance is a comparison of what the hours paid should have cost and what they did cost.

	£
3,080 hours of grade Z labour should have cost (× £5)	15,400
but did cost	17,500
Direct labour rate variance	2,100 (A)

Actual cost is greater than standard cost. The variance is therefore adverse.

(c) *The idle time variance*

The idle time variance is the hours of idle time, valued at the standard rate per hour.

Idle time variance = 100 hours (A) × £5 = £500 (A)

Idle time is *always* an adverse variance.

(d) *The direct labour efficiency variance*

The efficiency variance considers the hours actively worked (the difference between hours paid for and idle time hours). In our example, there were (3,080 – 100) = 2,980 hours when the labour force was not idle. The variance is calculated by taking the amount of output produced (1,500 units of product X) and comparing the time it should have taken to make them, with the actual time spent *actively* making them (2,980 hours). Once again, the variance in hours is valued at the standard rate per labour hour.

1,500 units of product X should take (× 2 hrs)	3,000 hrs
but did take (3,080 – 100)	2,980 hrs
Direct labour efficiency variance in hours	20 hrs (F)
× standard rate per hour	× £5
Direct labour efficiency variance in £	£100 (F)

(e) *Summary*

	£
Direct labour rate variance	2,100 (A)
Idle time variance	500 (A)
Direct labour efficiency variance	100 (F)
Direct labour total variance	2,500 (A)

3.8 Remember that, if idle time is recorded, the actual hours used in the efficiency variance calculation are the hours worked and not the hours paid for.

4 VARIABLE PRODUCTION OVERHEAD VARIANCES 6/97

4.1 Suppose that the variable production overhead cost of product X is as follows.

2 hours at £1.50 = £3 per unit

During period 6, 400 units of product X were made. The labour force worked 820 hours, of which 60 hours were recorded as idle time. The variable overhead cost was £1,230.

Calculate the following variances.

(a) The variable production overhead total variance
(b) The variable production overhead expenditure variance
(c) The variable production overhead efficiency variance

4.2 Since this **example relates to variable production costs, the total variance is based on actual units of production**. (If the overhead had been a variable selling cost, the variance would be based on sales volumes.)

	£	
400 units of product X should cost (× £3)	1,200	
but did cost	1,230	
Variable production overhead total variance	30	(A)

4.3 In many variance reporting systems, the variance analysis goes no further, and expenditure and efficiency variances are not calculated. However, the adverse variance of £30 may be explained as the sum of two factors.

(a) The **hourly rate of spending on variable production overheads was higher** than it **should have been,** that is there is an **expenditure variance**.

(b) The **labour force worked inefficiently**, and took longer to make the output than it should have done. This means that spending on variable production overhead was higher than it should have been, in other words there is an **efficiency (productivity) variance**. The **variable production overhead efficiency variance is exactly the same, in hours, as the direct labour efficiency variance, and occurs for the same reasons.**

4.4 It is usually **assumed that variable overheads are incurred during active working hours,** but are not incurred during idle time (for example the machines are not running, therefore power is not being consumed, and no direct materials are being used). This means in our example that although the labour force was paid for 820 hours, they were actively working for only 760 of those hours, therefore variable production overhead spending occurred during 760 hours.

KEY TERMS

- **The variable production overhead total variance** is the difference between what the output should have cost and what it did cost, in terms of variable production overhead. It can be divided into two sub-variances.
- **The variable production overhead expenditure variance** is the difference between the amount of variable production overhead that should have been incurred in the actual hours actively worked, and the actual amount of variable production overhead incurred.
- **The variable production overhead efficiency variance** is the difference between the standard number of hours that should have been worked for the number of units actually produced, and the actual number of hours worked, valued at the variable production overhead rate per hour.

4.5 In our example, the expenditure and efficiency variances would be as follows.

		£
(a)	760 hours of variable production overhead should cost (× £1.50)	1,140
	but did cost	1,230
	Variable production overhead expenditure variance	90 (A)
(b)	400 units of product X should take (× 2 hrs)	800 hrs
	but did take (active hours)	760 hrs
	Variable production overhead efficiency variance in hours	40 hrs (F)
	× standard rate per hour	× £1.50
	Variable production overhead efficiency variance in £	£60 (F)
(c)	*Summary*	£
	Variable production overhead expenditure variance	90 (A)
	Variable production overhead efficiency variance	60 (F)
	Variable production overhead total variance	30 (A)

4.6 Note that **if variances change in line with production volume rather than labour hours, only a total variance can be calculated.**

5 FIXED PRODUCTION OVERHEAD VARIANCES 6/94, 12/96, 6/97

5.1 You may have noticed that the method of calculating cost variances for variable cost items is essentially the same for labour, materials and variable overheads. Fixed production overhead variances are very different. In an absorption costing system, they are an **attempt to explain the under or over absorption of fixed production overheads in production costs.**

5.2 The **fixed production overhead total variance may be broken down into two parts** as usual.

- An **expenditure variance**
- A **volume variance. This in turn may be split into two parts.**
  - **A volume efficiency variance**
  - **A volume capacity variance**

5.3 The fixed production overhead volume variance sometimes causes confusion and may need more explanation. The most important point is that the volume variance applies to fixed production overhead costs only and not to variable production overheads.

(a) Variable production overheads incurred change with the volume of activity. Thus, if the master budget is to work for 300 hours and variable production overheads are incurred and absorbed at a rate of £6 per hour, the variable production overhead budget will be £1,800. If, however, actual hours worked turn out to be only 200 hours, the variable production overhead absorbed will be £1,200, but the expected expenditure will also be £1,200, so that there will be no under- or over-absorption of production overhead because of volume changes.

(b) Fixed production overheads are different because the level of expenditure does not change as the number of hours worked varies. Thus if the master budget is to work for 300 hours and fixed production overheads are budgeted to be £2,400, the fixed production overhead absorption rate will be £8 per hour. Now if actual hours worked are only 200 hours, the fixed production overhead absorbed will be £1,600, whereas expected expenditure will be unchanged at £2,400. There is an under-absorption of £800 because of the volume variance of 100 hours shortfall multiplied by the absorption rate of £8 per hour.

5.4 You will find it easier to calculate and understand fixed production overhead variances if you keep in mind the whole time the fact that you are trying to explain the reasons for any under- or over-absorbed production overhead. Remember that the absorption rate is calculated as follows.

$$\text{Overhead absorption rate} = \frac{\text{budgeted fixed production overhead}}{\text{budgeted level of activity}}$$

Generally the level of activity used in the overhead absorption rate will be units of production or hours of activity. More often than not, if just one product is being produced, the level of activity is in terms of units produced. If, however, more than one product is produced, units of output are converted to standard hours.

5.5 As you should remember from your studies of absorption costing, if either the numerator or the denominator or both are incorrect then we will have under- or over-absorbed production overhead.

(a) The fixed production overhead **expenditure variance** measures the under- or over-absorption caused by the **actual production overhead expenditure being different from budget**, that is the numerator being incorrect.

(b) There are two reasons why the actual production or hours of activity may be different from the budgeted production or budgeted number of hours used in calculating the absorption rate.

(i) The **work force may have been working at a more or less efficient rate than standard** to produce a given output. This is measured by the fixed production overhead **volume efficiency variance**, which is similar to the variable production overhead efficiency variance.

(ii) Regardless of the level of efficiency, the **total number of hours worked could have been less or more than was originally budgeted** (employees may have worked a lot of overtime or there may have been a strike and so actual hours worked were less than budgeted). Other things being equal, this could lead to under- or over-absorbed fixed overhead and the effect is measured by the fixed production overhead **volume capacity variance.**

How to calculate the variances

KEY TERMS

- **Fixed production overhead total variance** is the difference between fixed production overhead incurred and fixed production overhead absorbed. In other words, it is the under- or over-absorbed fixed production overhead.
- **Fixed production overhead expenditure variance** is the difference between the budgeted fixed production overhead expenditure and actual fixed production overhead expenditure.
- **Fixed production overhead volume variance** is the difference between actual and budgeted production/volume multiplied by the standard absorption rate per *unit*.
- **Fixed production overhead volume efficiency variance** is the difference between the number of hours that actual production should have taken, and the number of hours actually taken (that is, worked) multiplied by the standard absorption rate per *hour*.

KEY TERMS (cont'd)

- **Fixed production overhead volume capacity variance** is the difference between budgeted hours of work and the actual hours worked, multiplied by the standard absorption rate per *hour*.

5.6 You should now be ready to work through an example to demonstrate all of the fixed production overhead variances.

5.7 EXAMPLE: FIXED PRODUCTION OVERHEAD VARIANCES

Suppose that a company budgets to produce 1,000 units of product E during August 19X3. The expected time to produce a unit of E is five hours, and the budgeted fixed production overhead is £20,000. The standard fixed production overhead cost per unit of product E will therefore be as follows.

5 hours at £4 per hour = £20 per unit

Actual fixed production overhead expenditure in August 19X3 turns out to be £20,450. The labour force manages to produce 1,100 units of product E in 5,400 hours of work.

Required

Calculate the following variances.

(a) The fixed production overhead total variance
(b) The fixed production overhead expenditure variance
(c) The fixed production overhead volume variance
(d) The fixed production overhead volume efficiency variance
(e) The fixed production overhead volume capacity variance

5.8 SOLUTION

All of the variances help to assess the under- or over-absorption of fixed production overheads, some in greater detail than others.

(a) *Fixed production overhead total variance*

	£
Fixed production overhead incurred	20,450
Fixed production overhead absorbed (1,100 units × £20 per unit)	20,000
Fixed production overhead expenditure variance	1,550 (F)
(= under-/over-absorbed overhead)	

The variance is favourable because more overheads were absorbed than budgeted.

(b) *Fixed production overhead expenditure variance*

	£
Budgeted fixed production overhead expenditure	20,000
Actual fixed production overhead expenditure	20,450
Fixed production overhead expenditure variance	450 (A)

The variance is adverse because actual expenditure was greater than budgeted expenditure.

(c) *Fixed production overhead volume variance*

The production volume achieved was greater than expected. The fixed production overhead volume variance measures the difference at the standard rate.

	£
Actual production at standard rate (1,100 × £20 per unit)	22,000
Budgeted production at standard rate (1,000 × £20 per unit)	20,000
Fixed production overhead volume variance	2,000 (F)

The variance is favourable because output was greater than expected.

(i) The labour force may have worked efficiently, and produced output at a faster rate than expected. Since overheads are absorbed at the rate of £20 per unit, more will be absorbed if units are produced more quickly. This *efficiency variance* is exactly the same in hours as the direct labour efficiency variance (and the variable production overhead efficiency variance), but is valued in £ at the standard absorption rate for fixed overhead.

(ii) The labour force may have worked longer hours than budgeted, and therefore produced more output, so there may be a *capacity variance*.

(d) *Fixed production overhead volume efficiency variance*

The volume efficiency variance is calculated in the same way as the labour efficiency variance.

1,100 units of product E should take (× 5 hrs)	5,500 hrs
but did take	5,400 hrs
Fixed overhead production volume efficiency variance in hours	100 hrs (F)
× standard fixed production overhead absorption rate per hour	× £4
Fixed production overhead volume efficiency variance in £	£400 (F)

The labour force has produced 5,500 standard hours of work in 5,400 actual hours and so output is 100 standard hours (or 20 units of product E) higher than budgeted for this reason and the variance is favourable.

(e) *Fixed production overhead volume capacity variance*

The volume capacity variance is the difference between the budgeted hours of work and the actual active hours of work (excluding any idle time).

Budgeted hours of work	5,000 hrs
Actual hours of work	5,400 hrs
Fixed production overhead volume capacity variance	400 hrs (F)
× standard fixed production overhead absorption rate per hour	× £4
Fixed production overhead volume capacity variance in £	£1,600 (F)

Since the labour force worked 400 hours longer than budgeted, we should expect output to be 400 standard hours (or 80 units of product E) higher than budgeted and hence the variance is favourable.

5.9 Do not worry if you find fixed production overhead variances more difficult to grasp than the other variances we have covered. Most students do. Read over this section again and then try the following question.

Question

Brain Ltd produces and sells one product only, the Blob, the standard cost for one unit being as follows.

	£
Direct material A - 10 kilograms at £20 per kg	200
Direct material B - 5 litres at £6 per litre	30
Direct wages - 5 hours at £6 per hour	30
Fixed production overhead	50
Total standard cost	310

The fixed overhead included in the standard cost is based on an expected monthly output of 900 units. Fixed production overhead is absorbed on the basis of direct labour hours.

During April 19X3 the actual results were as follows.

Production	800 units
Material A	7,800 kg used, costing £159,900
Material B	4,300 units used, costing £23,650
Direct wages	4,200 hours worked for £24,150
Fixed production overhead	£47,000

Required

(a) Calculate price and usage variances for each material.

(b) Calculate labour rate and efficiency variances.

(c) Calculate fixed production overhead expenditure and volume variances and then subdivide the volume variance.

Answer

(a) *Price variance - A*

	£
7,800 kgs should have cost (× £20)	156,000
but did cost	159,900
Price variance	3,900 (A)

Usage variance - A

800 units should have used (× 10 kgs)	8,000 kgs
but did use	7,800 kgs
Usage variance in kgs	200 kgs (F)
× standard cost per kilogram	× £20
Usage variance in £	£4,000 (F)

Price variance - B

	£
4,300 units should have cost (× £6)	25,800
but did cost	23,650
Price variance	2,150 (F)

Usage variance - B

800 units should have used (× 5 l)	4,000 l
but did use	4,300 l
Usage variance in litres	300 (A)
× standard cost per litre	× £6
Usage variance in £	£1,800 (A)

(b) *Labour rate variance*

	£
4,200 hours should have cost (× £6)	25,200
but did cost	24,150
Rate variance	1,050 (F)

Labour efficiency variance

800 units should have taken (× 5 hrs)	4,000 hrs
but did take	4,200 hrs
Efficiency variance in hours	200 hrs (A)
× standard rate per hour	× £6
Efficiency variance in £	£1,200 (A)

(c) *Fixed overhead expenditure variance*

	£
Budgeted expenditure (£50 × 900)	45,000
Actual expenditure	47,000
Expenditure variance	2,000 (A)

Fixed overhead volume variance

	£
Budgeted production at standard rate (900 × £50)	45,000
Actual production at standard rate (800 × £50)	40,000
Volume variance	5,000 (A)

Fixed overhead volume efficiency variance

	£
800 units should have taken (× 5 hrs)	4,000 hrs
but did take	4,200 hrs
Volume efficiency variance in hours	200 hrs
× standard absorption rate per hour	× £10
Volume efficiency variance	£2,000 (A)

Fixed overhead volume capacity variance

Budgeted hours	4,500 hrs
Actual hours	4,200 hrs
Volume capacity variance in hours	300 hrs (A)
× standard absorption rate per hour (£50 ÷ 5)	× £10
	£3,000 (A)

6 SALES VARIANCES 6/94, 12/95, 6/96, 12/97

Selling price variance

KEY TERM

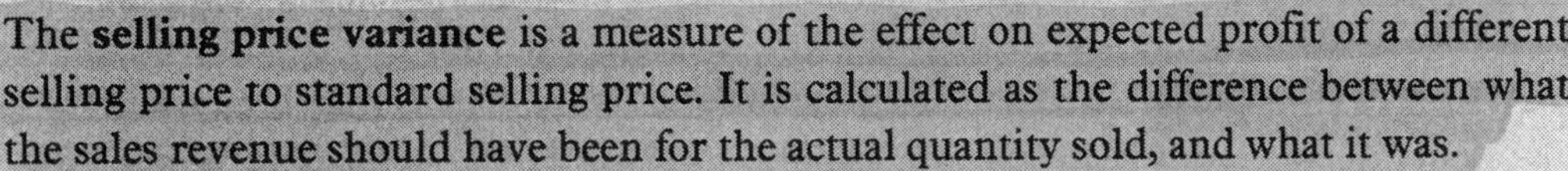

The **selling price variance** is a measure of the effect on expected profit of a different selling price to standard selling price. It is calculated as the difference between what the sales revenue should have been for the actual quantity sold, and what it was.

6.1 Suppose that the standard selling price of product X is £15. Actual sales in 19X3 were 2,000 units at £15.30 per unit. The selling price variance is calculated as follows.

	£
Revenue from 2,000 units should be (× £15)	30,000
but was (× £15.30)	30,600
Selling price variance	600 (F)

The variance is favourable because the price was higher than expected.

Sales volume variance

KEY TERM

The **sales volume variance** is the difference between the actual units sold and the budgeted quantity, valued at the standard profit per unit. In other words, it measures the increase or decrease in expected profit as a result of the sales volume being higher or lower than budgeted.

6.2 Suppose that a company budgets to sell 8,000 units of product J for £12 per unit. The standard full cost per unit is £7. Actual sales were 7,700 units, at £12.50 per unit.

The sales volume variance is calculated as follows.

Budgeted sales volume	8,000 units
Actual sales volume	7,700 units
Sales volume variance in units	300 units (A)
× standard profit per unit (£(12–7))	× £5
Sales volume variance	£1,500 (A)

The variance is adverse because actual sales were less than budgeted.

6.3 EXAMPLE: SALES VARIANCES

Jasper Ltd has the following budget and actual figures for 19X4.

	Budget	*Actual*
Sales units	600	620
Selling price per unit	£30	£29

Standard full cost of production = £28 per unit.

Required

Calculate the selling price variance and the sales volume variance.

6.4 SOLUTION

(a) The selling price variance is calculated as follows.

	£
Sales revenue for 620 units should have been (× £30)	18,600
but was (× £29)	17,980
Selling price variance	620 (A)

(b) The sales volume variance is calculated as follows.

Budgeted sales volume	600 units
Actual sales volume	620 units
Sales volume variance in units	20 units (F)
× standard profit per unit (£(30 – 28))	× £2
Sales volume variance	£40 (F)

7 THE REASONS FOR VARIANCES 6/94, 12/95, 6/96, 12/96

Exam focus point

In an examination, always be prepared to be able to explain the reasons why variances have occurred, and their significance.

7.1 There are many possible reasons for variances arising, including efficiencies and inefficiencies of operations, errors in standard setting and changes in exchange rates. There now follows a list of a few possible causes of variances. This is not an exhaustive list and in an examination question you should review the information given and use your imagination and common sense to suggest possible reasons for variances.

Variance	Favourable	Adverse
Material price	Unforeseen discounts received Greater care taken in purchasing Change in material standard	Price increase Careless purchasing Change in material standard
Material usage	Material used of higher quality than standard More effective use made of material Errors in allocating material to jobs	Defective material Excessive waste Theft Stricter quality control Errors in allocating material to jobs
Labour rate	Use of apprentices or other workers at a rate of pay lower than standard	Wage rate increase
Idle time	*The idle time variance is always adverse.*	Machine breakdown Non-availability of material Illness or injury to worker
Labour efficiency	Output produced more quickly than expected, ie actual output in excess of standard output set for same number of hours because of work motivation, better quality of equipment or materials Errors in allocating time to jobs	Lost time in excess of standard allowed Output lower than standard set because of deliberate restriction, lack of training, or sub-standard material used Errors in allocating time to jobs
Overhead expenditure	Savings in costs incurred More economical use of services	Increase in cost of services used Excessive use of services Change in type of services used
Overhead volume	Production or level of activity greater than budgeted	Production or level of activity less than budgeted
Selling price	Unplanned price increase	Unplanned price reduction
Sales volume	Additional demand	Unexpected fall in demand Production difficulties

8 INVESTIGATING VARIANCES 12/96, 6/97

8.1 Once variances have been calculated management are faced with three options.

- They can investigate every reported variance. This would be extremely time consuming and expensive and could lead to investigations which result in no improvement to operations even if the cause of the variance was determined.
- Alternatively, management could do nothing with the reported variances, making a mockery of the supposed control function arising from variance analysis.
- The best option lies somewhere between the two extremes.

8.2 There are a number of factors which should be taken into account when deciding whether or not to investigate a variance.

- **Materiality**

  A standard cost is really only an *average* expected cost and is not a rigid specification. Small variations either side of this average are therefore bound to occur. The problem is to **decide whether a variation from standard should be considered significant and worthy of investigation. Tolerance limits** can be set and only variances which exceed such limits would require investigating.

- **Controllability**

  Controllability must also influence the decision about whether to investigate. If there is a general worldwide increase in the price of a raw material there is nothing that can be done internally to control the effect of this. If a central decision is made to award all employees a 10% increase in salary, staff costs in division A will increase by this amount and the variance is not controllable by division A's manager. **Uncontrollable variances call for a change in the plan, not an investigation into the past.**

- **The type of standard being used**

  The efficiency variance reported in any control period, whether for materials or labour, will depend on the **efficiency level set**. If, for example, an ideal standard is used, variances will always be adverse.

  A similar problem arises if average price levels are used as standards. If **inflation** exists, favourable price variances are likely to be reported at the beginning of a period, to be offset by adverse price variances later in the period as inflation pushes prices up.

- **Interdependence between variances**

  Individual variances should not be looked at in isolation. One variance might be inter-related with another, and much of it might have occurred only because the other, inter-related, variance occurred too. **When two variances are interdependent (interrelated) one will usually be adverse and the other one favourable.** Here are some examples.

Interrelated variances	Explanation
Materials price and usage	If cheaper materials are purchased for a job in order to obtain a favourable price variance, a possible consequence is that materials wastage will be higher and an adverse usage variance will occur. If the cheaper materials are more difficult to handle, there might be some adverse labour efficiency variance too. If a decision is made to purchase more expensive materials, the price variance will be adverse but the usage variance might be favourable if the material is easier to use or of a higher quality.
Labour rate and efficiency	If employees in a workforce are paid higher rates for experience and skill, using a highly skilled team to do some work might lead to an adverse rate variance and a favourable efficiency variance (experienced staff are less likely to waste material, for example). In contrast, a favourable rate variance might indicate a larger-than-expected proportion of inexperienced workers in the workforce, which could result in an adverse labour efficiency variance, and perhaps poor materials handling and high rates of rejects too (and hence an adverse materials usage variance).

Interrelated variances	Explanation
Selling price and sales volume	The connection between selling price and sales volume is perhaps an obvious one. A reduction in the selling price might stimulate bigger sales demand, so that an adverse selling price variance might be counterbalanced by a favourable sales volume variance. Similarly, a price rise would give a favourable price variance, but possibly at the cost of a fall in demand and an adverse sales volume variance.

Because cost accountants analyse total variances into component elements (materials price and usage, labour rate, idle time, efficiency, and so on) they should not lose sight of the overall 'integrated' picture of events, and any interdependence between variances should be reported whenever it is suspected to have occurred.

- **Costs of investigation**

  The costs of an investigation should be weighed against the benefits of correcting the cause of a variance.

8.3 Bear in mind that it is not only efficient or inefficient operations (controllable or otherwise) which cause differences between standard and actual performance.

- **Measurement errors**

  In examination questions there is generally no question of the information that you are given being wrong. In practice, however, it may be extremely difficult to establish that 1,000 units of product A used 32,000 kg of raw material X. Scales may be misread, the pilfering or wastage of materials may go unrecorded, items may be wrongly classified (as material X3, say, when material X8 was used in reality), or employees may make 'cosmetic' adjustments to their records to make their own performance look better than it really was.

- **Out of date standards**

  Price standards are likely to become out of data quickly when frequent changes to the costs of material, labour and so on occur or in **periods of high inflation**. In such circumstances an **investigation of variances is likely to highlight a general change in market prices** rather than efficiencies or inefficiencies in acquiring resources.

  Standards may also be out of date where operations are subject to **technological development** or if **learning curve effects** have not been taken into account. Investigation of this type of variance will provide feedback on the inaccuracy of the standard and **highlight the need to frequently review and update standards**.

Exam focus point

When asked to provide a commentary on variances you have calculated, make sure that you *interpret* your calculations rather than simply detail them.

Chapter roundup

- **Variances** measure the difference between actual results and expected results.
- The **direct material total variance** can be subdivided into the direct material **price** variance and the direct material **usage** variance.
- **Direct material price variances** are extracted at the time of receipt of the materials, not the time of usage.
- The **direct labour total variance** can be subdivided into the direct labour **rate** variance and the direct labour **efficiency** variance.
- If idle time arises, it is usual to calculate a separate **idle time variance**, and to base the calculation of the **efficiency** variance on active hours (when labour actually worked) only. It is always an adverse variance.
- The **variable production overhead total variance** can be subdivided into the variable production overhead **expenditure** variance and the variable production overhead **efficiency** variance (based on active hours).
- The **fixed production overhead total variance** can be subdivided into an **expenditure** variance and a **volume** variance. The volume variance can be subdivided into an **efficiency** variance and a **capacity** variance.
- The **selling price variance** measures the effect on profit of a different selling price to standard selling price.
- The **sales volume variance** measures the effect on profit of actual sales volume being different to budgeted sales volume.
- Materiality, controllability, the type of standard being used, interdependence and costs should be taken into account when deciding on the significance of a variance.
- Measurement errors and out of date standards, as well as efficient/inefficient operations, can cause differences between standard and actual performance.

Quick quiz

1 Which two variances subdivide the direct material total variance? (see key terms)

2 What are the two main advantages in calculating the material price variance at the time of receipt of materials? (2.6)

3 What does the direct labour rate variance mean? (key terms)

4 Idle time is a favourable efficiency variance. True or false? (key terms)

5 Suggest two reasons for an adverse variable overhead variance. (4.3)

6 Why is the calculation of fixed overhead variances different from that of variable overhead variances? (5.3)

7 What is the sales volume variance? (key terms)

8 Give three possible causes of an adverse material usage variance. (7.1)

9 What is meant by interdependence between variances? (8.2)

Question to try	Level	Marks	Time
11	Examination	20	36 mins

Chapter 12

FURTHER VARIANCE ANALYSIS

Chapter topic list		Syllabus reference
1	Operating statements	2(b)
2	Variances in a standard marginal costing system	2(b)(iii)
3	Materials mix and yield variances	2(b)(iii)
4	Sales mix and quantity variances	2(b)(iii)

Introduction

The objective of the process of basic cost and revenue variance analysis, which we looked at in the previous chapter, is to assist management accountants (and management) in the control role.

In this chapter we build on this knowledge and examine a number of **further variance analysis** topics. We begin by considering the way in which the variances which have been calculated should be presented by the management accountant to management so as to aid control of the organisation in the most effective way.

We then move on to looking at the differences between variances in an absorption costing system (which we have been concentrating on so far) and those in a marginal costing system.

The final two topics of the chapter deal with slightly more complex variance analysis. When a product requires two or more materials in its make-up the materials **usage variance** can be split into a materials **mix variance** and a materials **yield variance**. Likewise, if a company sells more than one product, it is possible to analyse the overall sales volume variance into a sales mix variance and a sales quantity variance.

Don't be put off by these new terms. The basic principles of variance calculation covered in the previous chapter still applies: an actual result is compared with an original standard result.

In the next chapter we look at a new subject, decision making.

1 OPERATING STATEMENTS 6/94, 6/97, 12/97

1.1 So far, we have considered how variances are calculated without considering how they combine to reconcile the difference between budgeted profit and actual profit during a period. This reconciliation is usually presented as a report to senior management at the end of each control period. The report is called an **operating statement** or **statement of variances.**

KEY TERM

An **operating statement** is a regular report for management which compares actual costs and revenues with budgeted figures and shows variances.

1.2 An extensive example will now be introduced, both to revise the variance calculations already described, and also to combine them into an operating statement.

1.3 EXAMPLE: VARIANCES AND OPERATING STATEMENTS

Armoured Kangaroo Ltd manufactures one product, and the entire product is sold as soon as it is produced. There are no opening or closing stocks and work in progress is negligible. The company operates a standard costing system and analysis of variances is made every month. The standard cost card for the product, a boomerang, is as follows.

STANDARD COST CARD - BOOMERANG

		£
Direct materials	0.5 kilos at £4 per kilo	2.00
Direct wages	2 hours at £2.00 per hour	4.00
Variable overheads	2 hours at £0.30 per hour	0.60
Fixed overhead	2 hours at £3.70 per hour	7.40
Standard cost		14.00
Standard profit		6.00
Standing selling price		20.00

Selling and administration expenses are not included in the standard cost, and are deducted from profit as a period charge.

Budgeted output for the month of June 19X7 was 5,100 units. Actual results for June 19X7 were as follows.

Production of 4,850 units was sold for £95,600
Materials consumed in production amounted to 2,300 kilos at a total cost of £9,800
Labour hours paid for amounted to 8,500 hours at a cost of £16,800
Actual operating hours amounted to 8,000 hours
Variable overheads amounted to £2,600
Fixed overheads amounted to £42,300
Selling and administration expenses amounted to £18,000

Required

Calculate all variances and prepare an operating statement for the month ended 30 June 19X7.

1.4 SOLUTION

		£
(a)	2,300 kg of material should cost (× £4)	9,200
	but did cost	9,800
	Material price variance	600 (A)
(b)	4,850 boomerangs should use (× 0.5 kgs)	2,425 kg
	but did use	2,300 kg
	Material usage variance in kgs	125 kg (F)
	× standard cost per kg	× £4
	Material usage variance in £	£ 500 (F)
		£
(c)	8,500 hours of labour should cost (× £2)	17,000
	but did cost	16,800
	Labour rate variance	200 (F)
(d)	4,850 boomerangs should take (× 2 hrs) *	9,700 hrs
	but did take (active hours)	8,000 hrs
	Labour efficiency variance in hours	1,700 hrs (F)
	× standard cost per hour	× £2
	Labour efficiency variance in £	£3,400 (F)

(* 9,700 standard hours were produced)

(e)	Idle time variance 500 hours (A) × £2	£1,000 (A)
		£
(f)	8,000 hours incurring variable o/hd expenditure should cost (× £0.30)	2,400
	but did cost	2,600
	Variable overhead expenditure variance	200 (A)
(g)	Variable overhead efficiency variance is the same as the labour efficiency variance:	
	1,700 hours (F) × £0.30 per hour	£ 510 (F)
		£
(h)	Budgeted fixed overhead (5,100 units × 2 hrs × £3.70)	37,740
	Actual fixed overhead	42,300
	Fixed overhead expenditure variance	4,560 (A)
		£
(i)	Actual production at standard rate (4,850 units × £7.40)	35,890
	Budgeted production at standard rate (5,100 units × £7.40)	37,740
	Fixed overhead volume variance	1,850 (A)
		£
(j)	4,850 boomerangs should have sold for (× £20)	97,000
	but did sell for	95,600
	Selling price variance	1,400 (A)
(k)	Budgeted sales volume	5,100 units
	Actual sales volume	4,850 units
	Sales volume variance in units	250 units
	× standard profit per unit	× £6 (A)
	Sales volume variance in £	£1,500 (A)

There are several ways in which an operating statement may be presented. Perhaps the most common format is one which reconciles budgeted profit to actual profit. In this example, sales and administration costs will be introduced at the end of the statement, so that we shall begin with 'budgeted profit before sales and administration costs'.

Sales variances are reported first, and the total of the budgeted profit and the two sales variances results in a figure for 'actual sales minus the standard cost of sales' as follows.

	£	£
Budgeted profit, before sales and administration costs (5,100 units × £6 profit)		30,600
Selling price variance	1,400 (A)	
Sales volume variance	1,500 (A)	
		2,900 (A)
Actual sales (£95,600) less the standard cost of sales (4,850 × £14)		27,700

The cost variances are then reported, and an actual profit (before sales and administration costs) calculated. Sales and administration costs are then deducted to reach the actual profit for 19X7.

ARMOURED KANGAROO LTD - OPERATING STATEMENT JUNE 19X7

		£	£
Budgeted profit before sales and administration costs			30,600
Sales variances:	price	1,400 (A)	
	volume	1,500 (A)	
			2,900 (A)
Actual sales minus the standard cost of sales			27,700

Cost variances	(F)	(A)	
	£	£	£
Material price		600	
Material usage	500		
Labour rate	200		
Labour efficiency	3,400		
Labour idle time		1,000	
Variable overhead expenditure		200	
Variable overhead efficiency	510		
Fixed overhead expenditure		4,560	
Fixed overhead volume		1,850	
	4,610	8,210	3,600 (A)
Sales and administration costs			18,000
Actual profit, June 19X7			6,100

Check	£	£
Sales		95,600
Materials	9,800	
Labour	16,800	
Variable overhead	2,600	
Fixed overhead	42,300	
Sales and administration	18,000	
		89,500
Actual profit		6,100

1.5 As mentioned earlier, there are several ways in which an operating statement can be presented. Another way is to reconcile the actual sales minus the standard cost of sales with the actual profit. In other words, only the cost variances are shown on the face of the operating statement.

Exam focus point

In the 6/97 exam, there were 9 marks to be gained for preparing an operating statement reconciling budgeted marginal costing profit and actual absorption costing profit, and giving a brief explanation of the results obtained.

2 VARIANCES IN A STANDARD MARGINAL COSTING SYSTEM 6/94, 6/96, 12/97

Exam focus point

Before tackling variances in a standard marginal costing system, it is vital that you are happy with the principles of marginal costing.

2.1 If an organisation uses standard marginal costing instead of standard absorption costing, there will be two differences in the way the variances are calculated.

- In marginal costing, fixed costs are not absorbed into product costs and so there are no fixed cost variances to explain any under- or over-absorption of overheads. There will, therefore, be ***no* fixed overhead volume variance**. There will be a fixed overhead expenditure variance which is calculated in exactly the same way as for absorption costing systems.

- The **sales volume variance will be valued at standard contribution margin, not standard profit margin** (that is, sales price per unit minus variable costs of sale per unit).

2.2 EXAMPLE: MARGINAL COSTING OPERATING STATEMENT

Returning once again to the example of Armoured Kangaroo Ltd, the variances in a system of standard marginal costing would be as follows.

(a) There is no fixed overhead volume variance.

(b) The standard contribution per unit of boomerang is £(20 – 6.60) = £13.40, therefore the sales volume variance of 250 units (A) is valued at (× £13.40) = £3,350 (A).

The other variances are unchanged, therefore an operating statement might appear as follows.

ARMOURED KANGAROO - OPERATING STATEMENT JUNE 19X7

		£	£	£
Budgeted profit before sales and administration costs				30,600
Budgeted fixed production costs				37,740
Budgeted contribution				68,340
Sales variances:	volume		3,350 (A)	
	price		1,400 (A)	
				4,750 (A)
Actual sales (£95,600) minus the standard variable cost of sales (4,850 × £6.60)				63,590
Variable cost variances				
Material price			600	
Material usage		500		
Labour rate		200		
Labour efficiency		3,400		
Labour idle time			1,000	
Variable overhead expenditure			200	
Variable overhead efficiency		510		
		4,610	1,800	
				2,810 (F)
Actual contribution				66,400
Budgeted fixed production overhead			37,740	
Expenditure variance			4,560 (A)	
Actual fixed production overhead				42,300
Actual profit before sales and administration costs				24,100
Sales and administration costs				18,000
Actual profit				6,100

Note. The profit here is the same on the profit calculated by standard absorption costing because there were no changes in stock levels. Absorption costing and marginal costing do not always produce an identical profit figure.

Question 1

Hides of March Ltd manufacture a standard leather walking boot, model number M25, for which the standard unit cost and selling price are as follows.

		£	£
Direct materials			
Leather	3 units at £5 per unit	15	
Other materials		3	
			18
Direct labour	1½ hours at £4 per hour		6
Variable production overheads	1½ hours at £2 per hour		3
Fixed production overheads	1½ hours at £6 per hour		9
Standard cost			36
Selling price			48
Standard profit, before marketing and administrative expenses			12

Budgeted production and sales for period 7 of 19X8 were 3,000 units of M25.

During period 7 of 19X8, actual results were as follows.

Production of M25		3,200 units
Sales of M25		2,850 units
Sales revenue		£141,000
Costs		
Leather purchased:	quantity	9,200 units
	cost	£45,400
Leather used		9,750 units
Other materials purchased and used		£9,500
Direct labour:	hours paid for	5,850 hours
	production time	5,100 hours
	labour cost	£24,100
Variable production overheads		£10,650
Fixed production overheads		£31,500

Stocks of leather are valued at standard cost, and stocks of finished goods are valued at standard full production cost.

Required

Prepare an operating statement for period 7 reconciling budgeted and actual profit and specifying all the relevant variances. Ignore marketing and administration costs.

Answer and discussion

The key test for you here is to establish how readily you can calculate the variances. This solution tries to explain the calculations in case you have any difficulties with them.

Budgeted profit. This is clearly 3,000 units × standard profit of £12 per unit = £36,000.

Direct materials variances

The variance for leather can be divided into a materials price and a materials usage variance.

(a) *Leather: price variance*

Stocks are valued at standard costs, and so price variances must be calculated on quantities purchased, rather than quantities used.

	£
9,200 units of leather were purchased and cost	45,400
but should cost (× £ 5)	46,000
Price variance	600 (F)

(b) *Leather: usage variance*

3,200 units of M25 were made and used	9,750 units of materials
but 3,200 units should use (× 3)	9,600 units of materials
Usage variance in units	150 units (A)
× standard cost per unit of leather	× £5
Usage variance in £	£750 (A)

(c) *Other materials*

We are not given a breakdown into units of material and price per unit of material, and so the only materials variance we can calculate is the total cost variance.

	£
3,200 units of M25 did cost	9,500 in other materials
but should cost (× £3)	9,600
Other materials cost variance	100 (F)

Direct labour variances

Idle time is treated as an indirect labour cost, but the variances for direct labour are as follows.

(a) A rate variance based on total hours paid for, whether idle time or active production time.

Direct labour rate variance

	£	
5,850 hours were paid for and cost	24,100	
but should cost (× £4)	23,400	
Labour rate variance	700	(A)

(b) An efficiency variance based on production hours, excluding idle time. In this example, actual production time was 5,100 hours, leaving 750 hours of idle time.

Direct labour efficiency variance

3,200 units of M25 took	5,100 hours
but should take (× 11/2 hrs)	4,800 hours
Efficiency variance, in hours	300 hours (A)
× standard cost per labour hour	× £4
Efficiency variance in £	£1,200 (A)

Idle time variance

This is the idle time in hours priced at the standard rate per hour.

750 hours × £4 per hr	£3,000 (A)

This is a large variance compared to the others calculated so far, and the existence of this variance would raise control questions about how such a large amount of idle time occurred, and if it is normal downtime, why an allowance for idle time has not been built into the standard cost itself.

Variable production overhead variances

The variable overhead variance might be calculated as a total figure or be sub-analysed into an expenditure variance (a spending per production hour variance) and an efficiency variance (an over- or under-spending variance caused by inefficiency or efficiency in labour times). Variable overhead spending is normally assumed to occur in active production time only, and not in idle time, and so in this example, both the expenditure and efficiency variances would be based on 5,100 hours of working, not 5,850 hours.

(a) *Total variance*

	£	
3,200 units of M25 did cost	10,650	
but should cost (× £3)	9,600	
Total variable overhead variance	1,050	(A)

(b) *Expenditure variance*

	£	
5,100 hours of working did cost	10,650	
but should cost (× £2)	10,200	
Variable overhead expenditure variance	450	(A)

(c) *Efficiency variance* £

This is exactly the same in hours as the direct labour efficiency variance, ignoring idle time hours and is valued at the standard cost per hour for variable overhead.

300 hours (A) × £2 per hour	£600 (A)

		£	
Check	Expenditure variance	450	(A)
	Efficiency variance	600	(A)
	Total variance	1,050	(A)

Fixed production overhead variances

Fixed production overhead variances measure the total under- or over-absorbed production overhead in the period.

In our example, we have a standard fixed overhead cost of £9 per unit and budgeted production of 3,000 units, which means that the budgeted fixed overheads for the period must be £9 × 3,000 units = £27,000. In standard costing, the fixed overhead absorbed is the standard cost per unit, for the actual number of units made: 3,200 units × £9 per unit. This gives us the following.

	£
Actual fixed overheads absorbed (3,200 × £9)	28,800
Actual fixed overheads incurred	31,500
Total fixed overhead variance	2,700 (A)

Variance analysis then goes on to establish why the total under- or over-absorbed fixed overhead occurred.

(a) *Fixed overhead expenditure variance*

This is under- or over-absorption of overhead because actual fixed overhead expenditure differed from budgeted expenditure.

	£
Budgeted fixed overhead	27,000
Actual fixed overhead	31,500
Expenditure variance	4,500 (A)

The expenditure variance also indicates over-spending above budget by £4,500, and a control report should attempt to pinpoint the source of this excessive overhead spending more specifically.

(b) *Fixed overhead volume variance*

This is under- or over-absorbed overhead caused by a difference between actual and budgeted production volume.

	In terms of units	*Alternatively standard hours*
Budgeted production volume of M25	3,000 (× 11)	4,500
Actual production volume	3,200 (× 11)	4,800
Total volume variance, in units or std hours	200 (F)	300 (F)
× standard fixed overhead cost per unit or per std hr	× £9	× £6
Total volume variance in £	£1,800 (F)	£1,800 (F)

Like efficiency and usage variances, a volume variance is a quantity variance, measured in units or standard hours, and converted into money values at standard cost. Producing a bigger quantity than budgeted will create over-absorption of fixed overhead, and so is a favourable variance.

The fixed overhead total volume variance of 300 standard hours (F) means that the company produced 300 standard hours worth of output more than budgeted in period 7. The reason for this must have been either one of the following.

(a) Working more efficiently than expected - a volume efficiency variance
(b) Working more production hours than expected - a volume capacity variance

(c) *Fixed overhead volume efficiency variance*

This is the same variance in hours as the direct labour efficiency variance (ignoring idle time) and is valued in £ at the standard fixed overhead rate per hour.

300 hrs (A) × £6 per hour	£1,800 (A)

(d) *Fixed overhead volume capacity variance*

This is the difference between actual and budgeted production hours.

Budgeted production hours (3,000 units × 11 hrs)	4,500 hours
Actual production hours, ignoring idle time	5,100 hours
Volume capacity variance in hours	600 hours (F)
× standard fixed overhead rate per hour	× £6
Volume capacity variance in £	£3,600 (F)

The capacity and efficiency variances add up to the total volume variance of £1,800(F).

Sales variances

The sales variances tend to be easier to remember and calculate.

(a) *Selling price variance*

	£
2,850 units of M25 should have sold for (× £48)	136,800
but did sell for	141,000
Selling price variance	4,200 (F)

(b) *Sales volume variance*

In a standard full costing system, the sales volume variance is valued in terms of standard profit margin.

Budgeted sales volume of M25	3,000 units
Actual sales volume	2,850 units
Sales volume variance	150 units (A)
× standard profit margin per unit	× £12
Sales volume variance	£1,800 (A)

The variances can now be summarised in an operating statement.

HIDES OF MARCH LTD
OPERATING STATEMENT FOR PERIOD 7 19X8

		£	£	£
Budgeted profit				36,000
Sales variances:	price variance		4,200 (F)	
	volume variance		1,800 (A)	
				2,400 (F)
				38,400
Cost variances		(F)	(A)	
Leather: price		600		
usage			750	
Other materials		100		
Direct labour:	rate		700	
	efficiency		1,200	
Idle time			3,000	
Variable overhead expenditure			450	
Variable overhead efficiency			600	
Fixed overhead expenditure			4,500	
Fixed overhead volume		1,800		
		2,500	11,200	
Total cost variances				8,700 (A)
Actual profit				29,700

Exam focus point
Make sure that you are completely happy with everything covered in Chapters 11 and 12. The examiner concluded that some candidates were clearly not confident with the calculations which are fundamental to this paper when he studied their solutions to a variance analysis question in the 6/97 exam.

3 MATERIALS MIX AND YIELD VARIANCES 6/95, 12/95

Exam focus point
With all variance calculations, it is vital that you do not simply learn formulae. You must have a thorough understanding of what your calculations are showing. This is especially true of the variances we will look at in this section and in Section 4.

3.1 When a product requires two or more raw materials in its make-up, it is often possible to **sub-analyse the materials usage variance into a materials mix and a materials yield variance.**

3.2 Adding a greater proportion of one material (therefore a smaller proportion of a different material) might make the materials mix cheaper or more expensive. For example the standard mix of materials for a product might consist of the following.

	£
(2/3) 2 kg of material A at £1.00 per kg	2.00
(1/3) 1 kg of material B at £0.50 per kg	0.50
	2.50

It may be possible to change the mix so that one kilogram of material A is used and two kilograms of material B. The new mix would be cheaper.

	£
(1/3) 1 kg of material A	1
(2/3) 2 kg of material B	1
	2

3.3 By changing the proportions in the mix, the efficiency of the combined material usage may change. In our example, in making the proportions of A and B cheaper, at 1:2, the product may now require more than three kilograms of input for its manufacture, and the new materials requirement per unit of product might be 3.6 kilograms.

	£
(1/3) 1.2 kg of material A at £1.00 per kg	1.20
(2/3) 2.4 kg of material B at £0.50 per kg	1.20
	2.40

3.4 In establishing a materials usage standard, management may therefore have to balance the cost of a particular mix of materials with the efficiency of the yield of the mix.

3.5 Once the standard has been established it may be possible for management to exercise control over the materials used in production by calculating and reviewing mix and yield variances.

Mix variance

3.6 A mix variance occurs when the materials are not mixed or blended in standard proportions and it is a **measure of whether the actual mix is cheaper or more expensive than the standard mix.** If a greater proportion of cheaper materials is used in the blend, there will be a favourable mix variance, whereas if a greater proportion of the more expensive materials is used, there will be an adverse mix variance.

3.7 The mix variance is calculated as the **difference between the actual total quantity used in the standard mix and the actual quantities used in the actual mix, valued at standard costs.**

Yield variance

3.8 The yield variance **arises because there is a difference between what the input should have been for the output achieved and the actual input**. A yield variance is therefore calculated as the **difference between the standard input for what was actually output, and the actual input, valued at standard costs.**

When to calculate the mix and yield variance

3.9 A mix variance and yield variance have no meaning, and should only be calculated when they are a guide to control action. They are only appropriate in the following situations.

(a) **Where proportions of materials in a mix are changeable and controllable**

(b) Where the **usage variance of individual materials is of limited value because of the variability of the mix**, and a combined yield variance for all the materials together is more helpful for control

3.10 It would be totally inappropriate to calculate a mix variance where the materials in the 'mix' are discrete items. A chair, for example, might consist of wood, covering material, stuffing and glue. These materials are separate components, and it would not be possible to think in terms of controlling the proportions of each material in the final product. The usage of each material must be controlled separately.

3.11 There are two main approaches to calculating mix and yield variances.

(a) Mix and yield variances are **valued at the standard individual price per element of the mix.** If one unit of a product Z is produced from combining 2 kg material A at £2 per kilo and 1 kg material B at £8 per kilo, then the variances will be valued on these prices.

(b) Mix and yield variances can be **valued using a budgeted weighted average price.** The cost of a unit of Z is (2 kg × £2 A) + (1 kg × £8 B) = £4 + £8 = £12. The variances are therefore valued at the weighted average cost of £12/3 kg = £4 per kg.

The worked examples in the following paragraphs will make this clear.

3.12 EXAMPLE: MATERIALS USAGE, MIX AND YIELD VARIANCES

A company manufactures a chemical, Dynamite, using two compounds Flash and Bang. The standard materials usage and cost of one unit of Dynamite are as follows.

		£
Flash	5 kg at £2 per kg	10
Bang	10 kg at £3 per kg	30
		40

In a particular period, 80 units of Dynamite were produced from 500 kg of Flash and 730 kg of Bang.

Required

Calculate the materials usage, mix and yield variances using the following variance valuation bases.

(a) Individual prices per kg
(b) Budgeted weighted average price per kg of input materials

3.13 SOLUTION: INDIVIDUAL PRICES PER KG AS VARIANCE VALUATION BASES

(a) **Usage variance**

	Flash		*Bang*
80 units of Dynamite should have used	400 kgs		800 kgs
but did use	500 kgs		730 kgs
Usage variance in kgs	100 kgs (A)		70 kgs (F)
× standard cost per kg	× £2		× £3
Usage variance in £	£200 (A)		£210 (F)
Total usage variance		£10 (F)	

The total usage variance of £10 (F) can be analysed into a mix variance and a yield variance.

(b) **Mix variance**

To calculate the mix variance, it is first necessary to decide how the total quantity of materials used (500 kg + 730 kg) should have been divided between Flash and Bang. In other words, we need to **calculate the standard mix of the actual quantity of materials used.**

		kg
Total quantity used (500 + 730)		1,230
		kg
Standard mix of actual use:	1/3 Flash	410
	2/3 Bang	820
		1,230

The differences between what should have been used in the mix (as calculated above) and what was actually used is the mix variance (in kg) which should be converted into money values at standard cost.

	Flash		*Bang*
Mix should have been	410 kgs		820 kgs
but was	500 kgs		730 kgs
Mix variance in kgs	90 kgs (A)*		90 kgs (F)
× standard cost per kg	× £2		× £3
Mix variance in £	£180 (A)		£270 (F)
Total mix variance		£90 (F)	

* When actual use exceeds standard use the variance is always adverse.

Note that the **total mix variance in quantity is zero**. This must always be the case since the expected mix is based on the total quantity actually used and hence the difference between the total expected and total actual is zero.

The favourable money variance is due to the greater use in the mix of the relatively cheap material, Flash.

(c) *Yield variance*

This is calculated as the **difference between what the input should have been for the output actually achieved and the actual input in the standard mix**, converted into money values at standard cost.

	Flash		*Bang*
80 units of Dynamite should have used	400 kgs		800 kgs
but actual input in standard mix was	410 kgs		820 kgs
Yield variance in kgs	10 kgs (A)		20 kgs (A)
× standard cost per kg	× £2		× £3
	£20 (A)		£60 (A)
Total yield variance		£80 (A)	

3.14 SOLUTION: BUDGETED WEIGHTED AVERAGE PRICE PER KILO OF INPUT AS VARIANCE VALUATION BASE

(a) **Usage variance**

The total usage variance is the **same under both methods**: £10 (F).

(b) **Mix variance**

The ***total*** **mix variance is also the same, but is analysed differently between the materials.**

We need to **calculate a budgeted weighted average price per kg.**

			£
Each unit of output (Dynamite) requires	5 kg	of Flash, costing	10
	10 kg	of Bang, costing	30
	15 kg		40

The budgeted weighted average price per kg = £40/15 kg = £2.67 per kg.

	Flash		Bang
Usage variance (from Paragraph 3.13)	100 kgs (A)		70 kgs (F)
× **difference between individual price per kg and budgeted weighted average price per kg**			
£(2 – 2.67)	× (£0.67)		
£(3 – 2.67)			× £0.33
	£67 (F)		£23 (F)
Total mix variance		£90 (F)	

The variance for Flash is the product of an adverse variance (in kgs) and a negative price difference and so the resulting money variance is favourable. There is a net increase in contribution from the change of mix because more Flash is used than standard and, since it is a cheaper material, costs are saved.

(c) **Yield variance**

	Flash		Bang
80 units of dynamite should have been used	400 kgs		800 kgs
but did use	500 kgs		730 kgs
Yield variance in kgs	100 kgs (A)		70 kgs (F)
× **budgeted weighted average price per kg**	× £2.67		× £2.67
Yield variance in £	£267 (A)		£187 (F)
Total yield variance		£80 (A)	

Comparison of the two methods

3.15 Textbooks vary in their recommended approach to calculating mix and yield variances. For example, Drury *(Management and Cost Accounting)* uses the standard individual price method for the mix variance and the budgeted weighted average price method for the yield variance.

3.16 As we have seen, **either method, or any combination of the two methods, gives the same overall results**. Below we set out the individual results.

	Mix		*Yield*	
	Standard individual price	*Budgeted weighted average price*	*Standard individual price*	*Budgeted weighted average price*
	£	£	£	£
Flash	180 (A)	67 (F)	20 (A)	267 (A)
Bang	270 (F)	23 (F)	60 (A)	187 (F)
Total	90 (F)	90 (F)	80 (A)	80 (A)

3.17 The mix variance is supposed to measure the effect on cost of changing the proportions used. By using more Flash (the cheaper material) and less Bang (the more expensive material) money has been saved. Logically both variances should be favourable. Thus the budgeted weighted average price method gives the more meaningful result.

3.18 As for the yield variance, under the first method both variances are adverse, but consider whether this is a fair reflection of what has actually happened. The material usage per unit of Dynamite is as follows.

	Actual usage	*Standard usage*
Flash	500 kg/80 = 6.250 kg	5 kg
Bang	730 kg/80 = 9.125 kg	10 kg

More kilograms of Flash per unit of Dynamite have been used, but less kilograms of Bang per unit of Dynamite have been used. Flash has been used less efficiently, Bang more so. Again this is reflected by the budgeted weighted average price method but not by the standard individual price method.

3.19 In summary, **the budgeted weighted average price method appears to give more meaningful results at the level of individual materials.**

Question 2

The standard materials cost of product D456 is as follows.

		£
Material X	3 kg at £2.00 per kg	6
Material Y	5 kg at £3.60 per kg	18
		24

During period 2, the actual costs of producing 500 units of D456 were as follows.

Material X	2,000 kg, cost £4,100
Material Y	2,400 kg, cost £9,600

Required

Calculate the following variances.

(a) Price variances
(b) Mix variances using both methods
(c) Yield variances using both methods

Answer

(a)

	£
2,000 kg of X should cost (× £2)	4,000
but did cost	4,100
Material X price variance	100 (A)

	£
2,400 kg of Y should cost (× £3.60)	8,640
but did cost	9,600
Material Y price variance	960 (A)

Total price variance = £(100 + 960) (A) = £1,060 (A)

(b) *Mix variances*

Individual price

		kg
Total quantity used (2,000 + 2,400) kgs		4,400
		kg
Standard mix for actual use:	3/8 X	1,650
	5/8 Y	2,750
		4,400

	X		*Y*
Mix should have been	1,650 kgs		2,750 kgs
but was	2,000 kgs		2,400 kgs
Mix variance in kgs	350 kgs(A)		350 kgs (F)
× standard cost per kg	× £2		× £3.60
Mix variance in £	£700 (A)		£1,260 (F)
Total mix variance		£560 (F)	

Weighted average price

Each unit of output requires	3 kg of X, costing	£6
	5 kg of Y, costing	£18
	8 kg	£24

The budgeted weighted average price per kg = £24/8 kg = £3 per kg.

	X		Y
500 units should have used	1,500 kgs		2,500 kgs
but did use	2,000 kgs		2,400 kgs
Usage variance in kgs	500 kgs (A)		100 kgs (F)
× difference between individual price per kg and budgeted weighted average price per kg			
£(2.00 – 3.00)	× (£1.00)		
£(3.60 – 3.00)			× £0.60
	£500 (F)		£60 (F)
Total mix variance		£560 (F)	

(c) *Yield variances*

Individual price

	X		Y
500 units should have used	1,500 kgs		2,500 kgs
but actual input in standard mix was			
(3/8 × 4,400 kgs)	1,650 kgs		
(5/8 × 4,400 kgs)			2,750 kgs
Yield variance in kgs	150 kgs (A)		250 kgs (A)
× standard cost per kg	× £2		× £3.60
	£300 (A)		£900 (A)
Total yield variance		£1,200 (A)	

Weighted average price

	X		Y
500 units should have used	1,500 kgs		2,500 kgs
but did use	2,000 kgs		2,400 kgs
Yield variance in kgs	500 kgs (A)		100 kgs (F)
× weighted average price per kg	× £3		× £3
	£1,500 (A)		£300 (F)
Total yield variance		£1,200 (A)	

4 SALES MIX AND QUANTITY VARIANCES 12/97

4.1 Just as it is possible to subdivide the materials usage variance into mix and yield variances, the **sales volume variance** can be subdivided into a **mix variance** and a **quantity variance**.

4.2 If a company sells more than one product, the **volume variance can be caused by two factors**.

(a) The **quantity** of product sold is **different than budgeted**.

For example, Nilats Ltd sells two products, the Trot and the Sky.

	Budget Units	*Actual* Units
Trots	100 (50%)	175 (70%)
Skys	100 (50%)	75 (30%)
	200	250

Notice the following.

(i) The total quantity is 50 greater than budget.

(ii) The relative proportions of the product to the total are also different than budgeted.

(b) The **mix** of products sold can be **different than budgeted.**

If product A earned a standard profit of £10 per unit and product B earned a standard profit of £8 a unit, a change in the relative numbers of each product sold will change the total profit.

	Budgeted sales		*Actual sales*	
	Units	£	Units	£
A	100	1,000	75	750
B	50	400	75	600
	150	1,400	150	1,350

4.3 **If management cannot control the proportions** of products sold then there is **little point in calculating sales mix and sales quantity variances** since their causes are uncontrollable.

4.4 There are two methods of calculating the sales volume, sales quantity and sales mix variances.

(a) The use of **individual product standard profit** as the variance valuation base (the **units method**)

(b) The use of **budgeted weighted average profit** per unit as the variance valuation base

This is similar to the calculation of materials mix and yield variances. Let us look at an example.

4.5 EXAMPLE: SALES QUANTITY AND SALES MIX VARIANCES

Tardis Ltd manufactures three products, the Dalek, the Yeti and the Cyberman. The budget relating to period 1 is given below.

	Sales price per unit	*Full cost of product per unit*	*Profit per unit*	*Budgeted sales*	*Standard mix*
	£	£	£	Units	%
Dalek	5	3	2	500	50
Yeti	7	4	3	300	30
Cyberman	10	6	4	200	20

Actual sales in period 1 were as follows.

	Units	%
Dalek	700	46.7
Yeti	300	20.0
Cyberman	500	33.3
	1,500	100.0

4.6 SOLUTION: STANDARD PROFIT PER PRODUCT (UNITS METHOD)

Using **individual standard profit as the variance valuation base,** the variances are calculated as follows.

(a) *Sales quantity variance*

Product	*Actual sales in standard mix*	*Budgeted sales*	*Variance*	*Standard profit per unit*	*Variance*
	Units	Units	Units	£	£
Dalek	750	500	250 (F)	2	500 (F)
Yeti	450	300	150 (F)	3	450 (F)
Cyberman	300	200	100 (F)	4	400 (F)
	1,500	1,000	500 (F)		1,350 (F)

(b) *Sales mix variance*

Product	*Actual sales in actual mix*		*Actual sales in standard mix*	*Variance*	*Standard profit per unit*	*Variance*
	Units		Units	Units	£	£
Dalek	700	(1,500 × 50%) =	750	(50) (A)	2	(100) (A)
Yeti	300	(1,500 × 30%) =	450	(150) (A)	3	(450) (A)
Cyberman	500	(1,500 × 20%) =	300	200 (F)	4	800 (F)
	1,500		1,500	0		250 (F)

(c) *Total sales volume variance*

			£
Dalek	£500(F) quantity + £100(A) mix	=	400 (F)
Yeti	£450(F) quantity + £450(A) mix	=	0
Cyberman	£400(F) quantity + £800(F) mix	=	1,200 (F)
Total sales volume variance			1,600 (F)

The sales volume variance is basically the difference in profit caused by the actual sales volume differing from the budgeted sales volume.

4.7 SOLUTION: BUDGETED WEIGHTED AVERAGE PROFIT

Using **weighted average profit as the variance valuation base**, the variances are calculated as follows.

We first calculate the budgeted weighted average profit per unit. In effect, **all products are 'lumped together'** for this calculation.

	Budgeted sales		*Standard profit*
	Units	£	£
Daleks	500	2	1,000
Yetis	300	3	900
Cybermen	200	4	800
	1,000		2,700

Budgeted weighted average profit per unit =

(a) *Sales quantity variance*

Product	*Actual sales*	*Budgeted sales*	*Variance*	*Budgeted weighted average profit per unit*	*Variance*
	Units	Units	Units	£	£
Daleks	700	500	200 (F)	2.70	540 (F)
Yetis	300	300	-	2.70	-
Cybermen	500	200	300 (F)	2.70	810 (F)
	1,500	1,000	500 (F)		1,350 (F)

(b) *Sales mix variance*

Product	*Actual sales* Units	*Budgeted sales* Units	*Variance* Units	*Standard profit per unit* £	*Budgeted weighted average profit per unit* £	*Difference* £	*Sales mix variance* £
Dalek	700	500	200	2.00	2.70	(0.70)	(140) (A)
Yeti	300	300	-	3.00	2.70	0.30	-
Cyberman	500	200	300	4.00	2.70	1.30	390 (F)
	1,500	1,000	500				250 (F)

(c) *Total sales volume variance*

		£
Dalek	£540 (F) quantity + £140 (A) mix =	400 (F)
Yeti	Nil quantity =	0
Cyberman	£810 (F) quantity + £390 (F) mix =	1,200 (F)
		1,600 (F)

Exam focus point

According to the examiner, a number of candidates had difficulty with the calculation of a sales mix variance in the 12/97 exam. Make sure you aren't one such candidate if the topic comes up in your exam.

Sales mix and quantity: calculations compared

4.8 We should now compare the results given by the two methods.

	Sales quantity		*Sales mix*		
Product	*Standard profit per product method* £	*Budgeted weighted ave. profit per unit method* £	*Standard profit per product method* £	*Budgeted weighted ave. profit per unit method* £	*Total sales volume variance* £
Dalek	500 (F)	540 (F)	(100) (A)	(140) (A)	400 (F)
Yeti	450 (F)	-	(450) (A)	-	Nil
Cyberman	400 (F)	810 (F)	800 (F)	390 (F)	1,200 (F)
	1,350 (F)	1,350 (F)	250 (F)	250 (F)	1,600 (F)

Notice the following.

- The sales volume variance is the same for each product.
- The **total quantity variance** and the **total mix variance do not differ** whichever method is used.
- The mix and quantity variances differ per product according to which method is used.

4.9 Let us look at each product in turn.

(a) For Daleks, there is not a large difference in the variances calculated by either method.

(b) The actual number of units of Yeti sold and the budget number are the same, yet under the standard product profit method, we are given a quantity variance (favourable) of £450, which is exactly matched by an adverse mix variance of £450. Given that the quantity sold did not change at all, it would make no sense at all to show a quantity variance.

(c) For Cybermen sold, the weighted average profit method gives more emphasis to the quantity variance than the mix variance.

The sales mix variance under this method measures the effect of changes to the budget mix depending on how much a product's **profit** differs from the budgeted average profit. The **use of the average profit per unit** perhaps **enables the total quantity and mix variances to be calculated more appropriately**, as they highlight the substitution of sales of products with greater than average profit for sales of products with less than average profit.

In the examples most of the change in mix was caused by a smaller proportion of Yetis being sold (20% as opposed to 30%) compared to Cybermen (33% as opposed to 20%). At the same time, Cybermen had the highest unit profit, so any increase in the percentage sales would give favourable variances for both quantity and mix.

Exam focus point

Question 13 in the exam question bank should be studied very carefully as it is based upon a sample question which was written by the current examiner. This question is intended to illustrate the style of exam question that candidates can expect in relation to the management accounting part of paper 8.

Chapter roundup

- **Operating statements** show how cost and revenue variances combine to reconcile budgeted profit to actual profit.
- There are two main differences between the variances calculated in an absorption costing system and the variances calculated in a marginal costing system. In a **marginal costing** system the **only fixed overhead variance is an expenditure variance** and the **sales volume variance is valued at standard contribution** margin, not standard profit margin.
- The **materials usage variance** can be subdivided into a materials **mix** variance and a materials **yield** variance.
- The **sales volume variance** can be subdivided into a **mix** variance and a **quantity** variance.
- There are two methods of calculating both the materials mix and yield variances and the sales mix and quantity variances.

Quick quiz

1 What is the most common format of an operating statement? (see para 1.4)

2 In what specific ways do variances in a standard marginal costing system differ from those in a standard absorption costing system? (2.1)

3 When does a materials mix variance occur? (3.6)

4 When should materials mix and yield variances be calculated? (3.9)

5 How is the sales quantity variance calculated using the budgeted weighted average profit per unit method? (4.7)

Question to try	Level	Marks	Time
12	Examination	20	36 mins
13	Examination	16	29 mins

Part D
Decision making

Chapter 13

INFORMATION AND TECHNIQUES FOR DECISION MAKING

Chapter topic list		Syllabus reference
1	Information	1b(ii),(iii),(iv)
2	Relevant and non-relevant costs	1(b)(iv)
3	The assumptions in relevant costing	1(b)(iv)
4	Limiting factor analysis	1(b)(iv)
5	Make or buy decisions	1(b)(iv)
6	Shutdown problems	1(b)(iv)
7	Extra shift decisions and overtime	1(b)(iv)
8	Accepting or rejecting orders	1(b)(iv)
9	Cost-volume-profit analysis	1(b)(iv)
10	Joint product decisions	1(b)(iv)
11	Pricing decisions	1(b)(iv)
12	Qualitative factors in decision making	1(b)(iv)
13	Presentation of information	1(b)(iv)

Introduction

Although **decision making** in general runs throughout the *Managerial Finance* syllabus (for example, in relation to pricing products and services and setting budgets and standards in the chapters you have already covered), we are going to look at the topic in some detail in this chapter.

We begin by looking at information, a topic examined briefly in Chapter 1. The emphasis of the remainder of the chapter is on **information for decision making**, **techniques** which assist in the decision-making process and various **decision-making situations**.

So what is a **decision**? Arising from the existence of a choice about what to do, a decision is **the selection of the choice that seems best** from those available. As a management accountant you may make decisions, but the principal **role of the management accountant** will be in **providing management information**. Your job is to present that information to the decision makers to help them to reach their decisions, and to make recommendations and give advice and suggestions to the decision maker. The provision of this management information is a complex task, decision-making information being unlike the accounting information recorded in the financial accounts and/or conventional cost accounts. It is not, however, a difficult task (once you have read this Study Text). It **relies on the application of the principles of marginal costing** (which you have covered in this Study Text), a **knowledge of cost behaviour** (covered in earlier studies) and **relevant costing**, which we will look at in this chapter.

1 INFORMATION 6/94

1.1 'I want that information and I want it now' is a phrase that we are all familiar with. Your boss may want you to provide him with information on last month's sales; creditors and providers of loan capital may require information on an organisation's ability to meet its financial obligations; the Inland Revenue needs information about a company's taxable profits; shareholders require information on the value of their shareholding; government agencies request information about dividends paid and sales activity; employees demand information about the ability of the firm to meet wage demands.

1.2 **Management therefore need information**. In fact, the successful management of *any* organisation depends on information: non-profit-making organisations such as charities, clubs and local authorities need information just as multinationals do. For example, a tennis club needs to know the cost of undertaking its various activities so that it can determine the amount of annual subscription it should charge its members.

1.3 Having ascertained that all organisations require information we now need to consider the type of information needed.

Planning information

1.4 A plan describes how a thing is to be done. In the case of an organisation the overall plan describes how it intends to achieve its objectives. **Planning information**, therefore, is the information needed to **describe what those objectives should be and how they are** to be **achieved**.

1.5 Objectives answer the question: 'where do we want to be?' This presupposes, however, that the organisation knows where it is now. Before the plan can be drawn up the organisation therefore needs to carry out an information-gathering exercise to ensure that it has full understanding of where it is at present. This is known variously as a '**position audit**' or '**strategic analysis**' and involves **looking both inwards and outwards.**

Internal information

1.6 The organisation must gather information from all its internal parts to find out what resources it possesses.

Type of information	Examples
Production and operational information	Manufacturing capacities and capabilities, lead times and quality standards
Marketing and sales information	Performance, revenues, market share and distribution channels
Financial information	How much cash it has in the bank, how much it could borrow, profits, costs, cash flows and investments
Research and development information	Technical know-how, patents and new products and developments
Personnel information	Labour skills and availability, labour relations and training

1.7 Sources of internal information can be divided into two groups.

- **Formal sources**

  All output of the organisation's management information system including control and monitoring reports, forecasting and enquiry systems, modelling and simulation, investigative reports, budgets, job descriptions, organisation charts, correspondence and video displays.

- **Informal sources**

  Discussions, meetings, social contact, telephone conversations, personal record keeping and correspondence.

External information

1.8 The organisation must also gather information externally on various factors to allow it to assess its position in the environment.

Factor	Details
Market and competitors	Just as it assessed its own strengths and weaknesses, the organisation must do likewise for its competitors. It should analyse its market (and any other markets that it is intending to enter) to identify possible new opportunities.
Economic conditions	The state of the world must be considered. Is it in recession or is it booming? The organisation should gather information on forecasts for growth, inflation, GDP and so on and the effect of developments such as the European Union single market.
Industrial structure	The organisation should determine whether a process of rationalisation or concentration is taking place within the industry, whether there are any privatisation issues to take into consideration and whether many new firms are entering the industry.
Political factors	Any political instability, especially in overseas markets, and any significant political decisions, should be assessed.
Technological change	Information on any new technology of which the organisation might be able to take advantage and its effects on the organisation should be collected.
Demographic trends and social factors	The organisation should assess the effects of any changes in the population structure, the age profile of customers, family patterns, and attitudes to consumption and savings.

1.9 External information also comes from two sources.

- **Formal sources**

  Published reports, government statistics, scientific and technical abstracts, company reports, commercial data banks, trade associations and special investigations.

- **Information sources**

  Discussions, social contact of all types, media coverage, conferences, business and holiday trips (at home and abroad) and correspondence.

1.10 Once these questions have been answered the information is available to decide how to achieve the objectives that have been identified. The paths chosen are called **strategies** and the next step in the process is to **collect** them together and **coordinate** them into a

long-term plan. The long-term plan is then broken down into smaller parts which usually cover equal time periods (more often than not one year). The resulting **short-term plans** are called **budgets**.

Long-term and short-term planning information requirements

1.11 In the light of the above we can list the factors that distinguish long-term planning information requirements from short-term planning information requirements.

(a) **Long-term planning information** is used by **top management** whereas **short-term planning information** is used at a **lower level**, by those who actually implement the plans.

(b) **Long-term planning** is **broad in scope** rather than deep in detail. More **external information** is required for planning in the long term to ensure the survival and success of the organisation.

(c) Long-term planning information is **more descriptive** in nature; short-term planning information needs to be quantified to measure how well the plan is progressing.

(d) Long-term planning information **looks to the future and lacks certainty**; for short-term planning, forecasts need to be replaced, where possible, with definite information such as firm orders, agreed usage rates and so on.

Uncertainty

1.12 **Planning information** might be based on historic data, but it is essentially **forward looking**, and so inevitably, it will be subject to **uncertainty**. When plans depend on environmental information, there is also likely to be some difficulty in obtaining all the relevant information to plan with.

The uncertainty of planning information, and the likelihood that forecasts will turn out to be inaccurate, can make some managers reluctant to plan at all.

Control information

1.13 Control information is the information which provides a comparison between actual results and the plan. Control information cannot exist without a plan or target. **Feedback** is the major element in control information, and it is often very detailed. The value of control information in an organisation will depend largely on the qualities of the information - that is, its **relevance, accuracy** and **reliability, comprehensiveness, timeliness**, who receives it and so on. Frequent criticisms of control information are as follows.

- It arrives too late to be of any use.
- It contains information about matters outside the control of the person who receives it.
- The person receiving it does not rely on it, perhaps because he or she suspects it of being inaccurate or incomplete.

Decision-making information

1.14 Management is decision taking. Managers at all levels within an organisation take decisions. The overriding requirement of the information that should be supplied for decision making is that of **relevance**. Consistency of treatment in the traditional accounting sense is not possible in decision making and so relevancy is all important.

Information for decision making is the topic of the remainder of this chapter. We begin by considering relevant costing.

2 RELEVANT AND NON-RELEVANT COSTS

2.1 The **costs which should be used for decision making** are often referred to as **relevant costs**.

KEY TERM

A **relevant cost** is a future cash flow arising as a direct consequence of a decision.

2.2

- **Relevant costs are future costs.**
  - A decision is about the future; it cannot alter what has been done already. A cost that has been incurred in the past is totally irrelevant to any decision that is being made 'now'.
  - Costs that have been incurred include not only costs that have already been paid, but also **costs that are the subject of legally binding contracts**, even if payments due under the contract have not yet been made. (These are known as **committed costs**.)
- **Relevant costs are cash flows.**
  - The assumption used in relevant costing is that, in the end, profits earn cash. Reported profits and cash flow are not the same in any period for various reasons, such as the timing differences caused by giving credit and the accounting treatment of depreciation. In the long run, however, a profit that is earned will eventually produce a net inflow of an equal amount of cash. Hence when accounting for decision making we look at cash flow as a means of measuring profits.
  - Only cash flow information is required.

    This means that costs or charges which do not reflect additional cash spending should be **ignored** for the purpose of decision making. These include the following.

    - **Depreciation**, as a fixed overhead incurred.
    - **Notional rent or interest**, as a fixed overhead incurred.
    - **All overheads absorbed**. Fixed overhead absorption is always irrelevant since it is overheads to be incurred which affect decisions.
- **Relevant costs are incremental costs.**

  A relevant cost is one which **arises as a direct consequence of a decision**. Thus, only costs which will differ under some or all of the available opportunities should be considered; relevant costs are therefore sometimes referred to as incremental costs. For example, if an employee is expected to have no other work to do during the next week, but will be paid his basic wage (of, say, £100 per week) for attending work and doing nothing, his manager might decide to give him a job which earns only £40. The net gain is £40 and the £100 is irrelevant to the decision because although it is a future cash flow, it will be incurred anyway whether the employee is given work or not.

Relevant costs are therefore future, incremental cash flows.

2.3 Other terms can be used to describe relevant costs.

KEY TERM

Avoidable costs are costs which would not be incurred if the activity to which they relate did not exist.

One of the situations in which it is necessary to identify the avoidable costs is in deciding whether or not to discontinue a product. The only costs which would be saved are the avoidable costs, which are usually the variable costs and sometimes some specific fixed costs. Costs which would be incurred whether or not the product is discontinued are known as unavoidable costs.

KEY TERM

Differential cost is the difference in total cost between alternatives.

If option A will cost an extra £300 and option B will cost an extra £360, the differential cost is £60, with option B being more expensive. A differential cost is the difference between the relevant costs of each option. The differential cost of an extra unit of production is the extra cost required to make that unit: it is the difference in cost between making the unit and not making it. This type of cost is sometimes referred to as an **incremental cost**.

KEY TERM

Opportunity cost is the benefit which could have been earned, but which has been given up, by choosing one option instead of another.

Suppose for example that there are three mutually exclusive options, A, B and C. The net profit from each would be £80, £100 and £70 respectively.

Since only one option can be selected option B would be chosen because it offers the biggest benefit.

	£
Profit from option B	100
Less opportunity cost (ie the benefit from the most profitable alternative, A)	80
Differential benefit of option B	20

The decision to choose option B would not be taken simply because it offers a profit of £100, but because it offers a differential profit of £20 in excess of the next best alternative.

Opportunity costs will never appear in a set of double entry cost accounts.

Non-relevant costs

2.4 A number of terms are used to describe costs that are **irrelevant for decision making** because they are either not future cash flows or they are costs which will be incurred anyway, regardless of the decision that is taken.

KEY TERM

A **sunk cost** is a cost which has already been incurred and hence should not be taken account of in decision making.

The principle underlying decision accounting is that 'bygones are bygones'. What has happened in the past is done, and cannot be undone. Management decisions can only affect the future. In decision making, managers therefore require information about future costs and revenues which would be affected by the decision under review, and they must not be misled by events, costs and revenues in the past, about which they can do nothing. A sunk cost has either been charged already as a cost of sales in a previous accounting period or will be charged in a future accounting period, although the expenditure has already been incurred (or the expenditure decision irrevocably taken). An **example** of this type of cost is **depreciation**. If the fixed asset has been purchased, depreciation may be charged for several years but the cost is a sunk cost, about which nothing can now be done.

KEY TERM

A **committed cost** is a future cash outflow that will be incurred anyway, whatever decision is taken now about alternative opportunities.

Committed costs may exist because of contracts already entered into by the organisation, which it cannot get out of.

KEY TERM

A **notional cost** or **imputed cost** is a hypothetical accounting cost to reflect the use of a benefit for which no actual cash expense is incurred.

Examples in cost accounting systems include the following.

- **Notional rent**, such as that charged to a subsidiary, cost centre or profit centre of an organisation for the use of accommodation which the organisation owns.
- **Notional interest** charges on capital employed, sometimes made against a profit centre or cost centre.

Although **historical costs** are irrelevant for decision making, historical cost data will often provide the best available basis for predicting future costs.

Fixed and variable costs

2.5 Unless you are given an indication to the contrary, you should assume the following.

- **Variable costs will be relevant costs.**
- **Fixed costs are irrelevant to a decision.**

This need not be the case, however, and you should analyse variable and fixed cost data carefully. Do not forget that 'fixed' costs may only be fixed in the short term.

2.6 There might, however, be occasions when a variable cost is in fact a sunk cost. For example, suppose that a company has some units of raw material in stock. They have been paid for already, and originally cost £2,000. They are now obsolete and are no longer used in regular production, and they have no scrap value. However, they could be used in a special job which the company is trying to decide whether to undertake. The special job is a 'one-off' customer order, and would use up all these materials in stock.

In deciding whether the job should be undertaken, the relevant cost of the materials to the special job is nil. Their original cost of £2,000 is a sunk cost, and should be ignored in the decision.

However, if the materials did have a scrap value of, say, £300, then their relevant cost to the job would be the opportunity cost of being unable to sell them for scrap, ie £300.

Attributable fixed costs

2.7 There might be occasions when a fixed cost is a relevant cost, and you must be aware of the distinction between 'specific' or 'directly attributable' fixed costs, and general fixed overheads.

- **Directly attributable fixed costs** are those costs which, although fixed within a relevant range of activity level, or regarded as fixed because management has set a budgeted expenditure level (for example advertising costs are often treated as fixed), would, in fact, do one of two things.
  - **Increase if certain extra activities were undertaken**
  - **Decrease/be eliminated entirely if a decision were taken either to reduce the scale of operations or shut down entirely**
- **General fixed overheads** are those fixed overheads which will be **unaffected** by **decisions to increase or decrease the scale of operations,** perhaps because they are an apportioned share of the fixed costs of items which would be completely unaffected by the decisions. An apportioned share of head office charges is an example of general fixed overheads for a local office or department.

2.8 You should appreciate that whereas **directly attributable fixed costs will be relevant** to a decision in hand, **general fixed overheads will not be**.

Contribution theory

2.9 Contribution theory is the **basis for providing information for decision making.** Managers who are making a decision should focus on those costs and revenues that will change as a result of the decision. Since fixed costs will often remain unaltered it is, as we have discussed, usually the variable costs that are the relevant costs. Revenues will also alter when activity levels change.

Contribution theory **is based on marginal costing principles.** Contribution is the difference between sales revenue and variable cost. By focusing on changes in contribution, managers can identify the net incremental effect of a particular decision. Allowance can then be made for any steps in fixed costs in order to appreciate the overall financial impact of the decision.

THE RELEVANT COST OF MATERIALS

2.10 The relevant cost of raw materials is **generally their current replacement cost**, *unless* the materials have already been purchased and would not be replaced once used.

If materials have already been purchased but will not be replaced, then the relevant cost of using them is the **higher of** the following.

- **Their current resale value**
- **The value they would obtain if they were put to an alternative use**

If the materials have no resale value and no other possible use, then the relevant cost of using them for the opportunity under consideration would be nil.

You should test your knowledge of the relevant cost of materials by attempting the following exercise.

IDENTIFYING RELEVANT COSTS

2.11 It is important that you should be able to identify the relevant costs which are appropriate to a decision. In many cases, this is a fairly straightforward problem, but there are cases where great care should be taken. Consider the following example.

2.12 EXAMPLE: IDENTIFYING RELEVANT COSTS

A company has been making a machine to order for a customer, but the customer has since gone into liquidation, and there is no prospect that any money will be obtained from the winding up of the company.

Costs incurred to date in manufacturing the machine are £50,000 and progress payments of £15,000 had been received from the customer prior to the liquidation.

The sales department has found another company willing to buy the machine for £34,000 once it has been completed.

To complete the work, the following costs would be incurred.

(a) Materials: these have been bought at a cost of £6,000. They have no other use, and if the machine is not finished, they would be sold for scrap for £2,000.

(b) Further labour costs would be £8,000. Labour is in short supply, and if the machine is not finished, the work force would be switched to another job, which would earn £30,000 in revenue, and incur direct costs of £12,000 and absorbed (fixed) overhead of £8,000.

(c) Consultancy fees £4,000. If the work is not completed, the consultant's contract would be cancelled at a cost of £1,500.

(d) General overheads of £8,000 would be added to the cost of the additional work.

Required

Assess whether the new customer's offer should be accepted.

2.13 SOLUTION

(a) Costs incurred in the past, or revenue received in the past are not relevant because they cannot affect a decision about what is best for the future. Costs incurred to date of £50,000 and revenue received of £15,000 are 'water under the bridge' and should be ignored.

(b) Similarly, the price paid in the past for the materials is irrelevant. The only relevant cost of materials affecting the decision is the opportunity cost of the revenue from scrap which would be forgone - £2,000.

(c) *Labour costs*

	£
Labour costs required to complete work	8,000
Opportunity costs: contribution forgone by losing other work £(30,000 – 12,000)	18,000
Relevant cost of labour	26,000

(d) The incremental cost of consultancy from completing the work is £2,500.

	£
Cost of completing work	4,000
Cost of cancelling contract	1,500
Incremental cost of completing work	2,500

(e) Absorbed overhead is a notional accounting cost and should be ignored. Actual overhead incurred is the only overhead cost to consider. General overhead costs (and the absorbed overhead of the alternative work for the labour force) should be ignored.

(f) Relevant costs may be summarised as follows.

		£	£
Revenue from completing work			34,000
Relevant costs			
Materials:	opportunity cost	2,000	
Labour:	basic pay	8,000	
	opportunity cost	18,000	
Incremental cost of consultant		2,500	
			30,500
Extra profit to be earned by accepting the completion order			3,500

3 THE ASSUMPTIONS IN RELEVANT COSTING

3.1 Relevant costs are future costs. Whenever anyone tries to predict what will happen in the future, the predictions could well be wrong. Management accountants have to make the best forecasts of relevant income and costs that they can, and at the same time recognise the assumptions on which their estimates are based. A variety of assumptions will be made, and you ought to be aware of them.

In particular, if you make an assumption in answering an examination question and you are not sure that the examiner or marker will appreciate or recognise the assumption you are making, you should explain it in narrative in your solution.

3.2 Some of the **assumptions** that are typically made in relevant costing are as follows.

- **Cost behaviour patterns are known**; if a department closes down, for example, the attributable fixed cost savings would be known.
- The **amount** of fixed costs, unit variable costs, sales price and sales demand are **known with certainty**.
- The objective of decision making in the short run is to **maximise 'satisfaction'**, which is often regarded as '**short-term profit**'.
- The **information** on which a decision is based is **complete and reliable**.

4 LIMITING FACTOR ANALYSIS 12/95

Exam focus point

In the 12/95 exam, there were 4 marks to be gained for applying 'limiting factor' knowledge to a specific situation.

4.1 One of the more common decision-making problems is a budgeting decision in a situation where there are not enough resources to meet the potential sales demand, and so a decision has to be made about using what resources there are as effectively as possible. These **scarce resources** are known as **key** or **limiting factors**. There might be just one limiting factor (other than maximum sales demand) but there might also be several scarce resources, with two or more of them putting an effective limit on the level of activity that can be achieved.

We shall concentrate on single limiting factor problems and a technique for resolving these.

4.2 A limiting factor could be sales if there is a limit to sales demand but any one of the organisation's resources (labour, materials, manufacturing capacity, financial resources and so on) may be insufficient to meet the level of production demanded.

- If **sales demand** is the factor which **restricts greater production output, profit will be maximised by making exactly the amount required for sales** (and no more) **provided that each product sold earns a positive contribution**.
- If **labour supply, materials availability, machine capacity or cash availability limits production** to less than the volume which could be sold, management is faced with the **problem of deciding what to produce** and what should not be produced because there are insufficient resources to make everything.

4.3 **It is assumed in limiting factor accounting that management wishes to maximise profit and that profit will be maximised when contribution is maximised** (given no change in fixed cost expenditure incurred). In other words, marginal costing ideas are applied.

Contribution will be maximised by earning the biggest possible contribution per unit of limiting factor. Thus if grade A labour is the limiting factor, contribution will be maximised by earning the biggest contribution per hour of grade A labour worked. Similarly, if machine time is in short supply, profit will be maximised by earning the biggest contribution per machine hour worked.

The **limiting factor decision** therefore **involves the determination of the contribution earned by each different product per unit of limiting factor**. In limiting factor decisions, we generally **assume that fixed costs are the same whatever production mix is selected**, so that the **only relevant costs are variable costs**.

4.4 EXAMPLE: LIMITING FACTOR

Desperate Dan Ltd makes two products, the Biff and the Snoot. Unit variable costs are as follows.

	Biff	*Snoot*
	£	£
Direct materials	1	3
Direct labour (£3 per hour)	6	3
Variable overhead	1	1
	8	7

The sales price per unit is £14 per Biff and £11 per Snoot. During July 19X2 the available direct labour is limited to 8,000 hours. Sales demand in July is expected to be 3,000 units for Biffs and 5,000 units for Snoots.

Required

Determine the profit-maximising production levels, assuming that monthly fixed costs are £20,000, and that opening stocks of finished goods and work in progress are nil.

4.5 SOLUTION

Step 1. **Confirm that the limiting factor is something other than sales demand.**

	Biffs	*Snoots*	*Total*
Labour hours per unit	2 hrs	1 hr	
Sales demand	3,000 units	5,000 units	
Labour hours needed	6,000 hrs	5,000 hrs	11,000 hrs
Labour hours available			8,000 hrs
Shortfall			3,000 hrs

Labour is the limiting factor on production.

Step 2. **Identify the contribution earned by each product per unit of scarce resource**, that is per labour hour worked.

	Biffs	*Snoots*
	£	£
Sales price	14	11
Variable cost	8	7
Unit contribution	6	4
Labour hours per unit	2 hrs	1 hr
Contribution per labour hour (= unit of limiting factor)	£3	£4

Although Biffs have a higher unit contribution than Snoots, two Snoots can be made in the time it takes to make one Biff. Because labour is in short supply it is more profitable to make Snoots than Biffs.

Step 3. **Work out the budgeted production and sales.** Sufficient Snoots will be made to meet the full sales demand, and the remaining labour hours available will then be used to make Biffs.

(a)

Product	*Demand*	*Hours required*	*Hours available*	*Priority of manufacture*
Snoots	5,000	5,000	5,000	1st
Biffs	3,000	6,000	3,000 (bal)	2nd
		11,000	8,000	

(b)

Product	*Units*	*Hours needed*	*Contribution per unit*	*Total*
			£	£
Snoots	5,000	5,000	4	20,000
Biffs	1,500	3,000	6	9,000
		8,000		29,000
Less fixed costs				20,000
Profit				9,000

Note that it is *not* more profitable to begin by making as many units as possible with the bigger unit contribution. We could make 3,000 units of Biff in 6,000 hours and 2,000 units of Snoot in the remaining 2,000 hours but profit would be only £6,000. Unit contribution is not the correct way to decide priorities, because it takes two hours to earn £6 from a Biff and one hour to earn £4 from a Snoot. Snoots make more profitable use of the scarce resource, labour hours.

Limiting factors and opportunity costs

4.6 Whenever there are limiting factors, there will be opportunity costs. As we have seen, these are the benefits forgone by using a limiting factor in one way instead of in the next most profitable way.

4.7 For example, suppose that a company manufactures two items X and Y, which earn a contribution of £24 and £18 per unit respectively. Product X requires 4 machine hours per unit, and product Y 2 hours. Only 5,000 machine hours are available, and potential sales demand is for 1,000 units each of X and Y.

4.8 Machine hours would be a scarce resource, and with X earning £6 per hour and Y earning £9 per hour, the profit-maximising decision would be as follows.

	Units	Hours	*Contribution* £
Y	1,000	2,000	18,000
X (balance)	750	3,000	18,000
		5,000	36,000

Priority is given to Y because the **opportunity cost of making Y** instead of more units of X **is £6 per hour (X's contribution per machine hour)**, and since Y earns £9 per hour, the incremental benefit of making Y instead of X would be £3 per hour.

4.9 If extra machine hours could be made available, more units of X (up to 1,000) would be made, and an extra contribution of £6 per hour could be earned. Similarly, if fewer machine hours were available, the decision would be to make fewer units of X and to keep production of Y at 1,000 units, and so the loss of machine hours would cost the company £6 per hour in lost contribution. This £6 per hour, the **marginal contribution-earning potential of the limiting factor at the profit-maximising output level**, is referred to as the **shadow price** (or **dual price**) of the limiting factor.

5 MAKE OR BUY DECISIONS

5.1 A make or buy problem involves a decision by an organisation about **whether it should make a product or carry out an activity with its own internal resources, or whether it should pay another organisation to make the product or carry out the activity.** Examples of make or buy decisions would be as follows.

- Whether a company should manufacture its own components, or else buy the components from an outside supplier.
- Whether a construction company should do some work with its own employees, or whether it should subcontract the work to another company.
- Whether the design and development of a new computer system should be entrusted to in-house data processing staff or whether an external software house should be hired to do the work.

5.2 The **'make' option** should give management **more direct control** over the work, but the **'buy' option** often has the benefit that the external organisation has a **specialist skill and expertise** in the work. Make or buy decisions should certainly not be based exclusively on cost considerations.

5.3 If an organisation has the freedom of choice about whether to make internally or buy externally and has no scarce resources that put a restriction on what it can do itself, the **relevant costs** for the decision will be the **differential costs between the two options.**

5.4 EXAMPLE: MAKE OR BUY

Shellfish Ltd makes four components, W, X, Y and Z, for which costs in the forthcoming year are expected to be as follows.

	W	*X*	*Y*	*Z*
Production (units)	1,000	2,000	4,000	3,000
Unit marginal costs	£	£	£	£
Direct materials	4	5	2	4
Direct labour	8	9	4	6
Variable production overheads	2	3	1	2
	14	17	7	12

Directly attributable fixed costs per annum and committed fixed costs are as follows.

	£
Incurred as a direct consequence of making W	1,000
Incurred as a direct consequence of making X	5,000
Incurred as a direct consequence of making Y	6,000
Incurred as a direct consequence of making Z	8,000
Other fixed costs (committed)	30,000
	50,000

A subcontractor has offered to supply units of W, X, Y and Z for £12, £21, £10 and £14 respectively.

Required

Decide whether Shellfish Ltd should make or buy the components.

5.5 SOLUTION AND DISCUSSION

(a) The **relevant costs** are the **differential costs between making and buying**, and they consist of **differences in unit variable costs plus differences in directly attributable fixed costs**. Subcontracting will result in some fixed cost savings.

	W	*X*	*Y*	*Z*
	£	£	£	£
Unit variable cost of making	14	17	7	12
Unit variable cost of buying	12	21	10	14
	£(2)	£4	£3	£2
Annual requirements (units)	1,000	2,000	4,000	3,000
	£	£	£	£
Extra variable cost of buying (per annum)	(2,000)	8,000	12,000	6,000
Fixed costs saved by buying	1,000	5,000	6,000	8,000
Extra total cost of buying	(3,000)	3,000	6,000	(2,000)

(b) The company would save £3,000 pa by subcontracting component W (where the purchase cost would be less than the marginal cost per unit to make internally) and would save £2,000 pa by subcontracting component Z (because of the saving in fixed costs of £8,000).

(c) In this example, relevant costs are the variable costs of in-house manufacture, the variable costs of subcontracted units, and the saving in fixed costs.

(d) Important **further considerations** would be as follows.

(i) If components W and Z are subcontracted, the company will have spare capacity. How should that **spare capacity be profitably used**? Are there **hidden benefits** to be obtained from subcontracting? Would the company's workforce resent the loss of work to an outside subcontractor, and might such a decision cause an **industrial dispute**?

(ii) Would the subcontractor be **reliable with delivery times**, and would he supply components of the same **quality** as those manufactured internally?

(iii) Does the company wish to be **flexible** and **maintain better control** over operations by making everything itself?

(iv) Are the **estimates** of fixed cost savings **reliable**? In the case of Product W, buying is clearly cheaper than making in-house. In the case of product Z, the decision to buy rather than make would only be financially beneficial if the fixed cost savings of £8,000 could really be 'delivered' by management. All too often in practice, promised savings fail to materialise!

Make or buy decisions and limiting factors

5.6 Where there are limiting factors on production other than sales one way of overcoming the limitation on production is to subcontract work. Where this problem arises, profit is maximised by producing or buying all the components or products at the cheapest cost. The cost of bought in components supplied by subcontractors normally exceeds the marginal cost of making products internally because the supplier's cost includes a contribution/profit margin on his costs. A company would then prefer to make all its own products, but the limiting factor makes this impossible.

5.7 In a situation where a **company must subcontract work to make up a shortfall in its own production capability**, its **total costs are minimised where the extra marginal cost of buying from a subcontractor is least for each unit of limiting factor saved by buying in.**

5.8 EXAMPLE: MAKE OR BUY AND LIMITING FACTORS

Ancient Mariner Ltd manufactures three components, the shotter, the alba and the tross using the same machines for each. The budget for the next year calls for the production and assembly of 4,000 of each component. The variable production cost per unit of the final product, the coal ridge, is as follows.

	Machine hours	*Variable cost*
		£
1 unit of shotter	3	20
1 unit of alba	2	36
1 unit of tross	4	24
Assembly		20
		100

Only 24,000 hours of machine time will be available during the year, and a sub-contractor has quoted the following unit prices for supplying components: Shotter £29; Alba £40; Tross £34. Advise Ancient Mariner Ltd.

5.9 SOLUTION

(a) There is a shortfall in machine hours available, and some products must be sub-contracted.

Product	*Units*		*Machine hours*
Shotter	4,000		12,000
Alba	4,000		8,000
Tross	4,000		16,000
		Required	36,000
		Available	24,000
		Shortfall	12,000

(b) The assembly costs are not relevant costs because they are unaffected by the make-or-buy decision. The **units subcontracted should be those which will add least to the costs** of Ancient Mariner Ltd. Since 12,000 hours of work must be sub-contracted, the cheapest policy is to subcontract work which adds the least extra costs (the least extra variable costs) per hour of own-time saved.

(c)

	Shotter	*Alba*	*Tross*
	£	£	£
Variable cost of making	20	36	24
Variable cost of buying	29	40	34
Extra variable cost of buying	9	4	10
Machine hours saved by buying	3 hrs	2 hrs	4 hrs
Extra variable cost of buying, per hour saved	£3	£2	£2.50

It is cheaper to buy alba than to buy tross and it is most expensive to buy shotters. The priority for making the components in-house will be in the reverse order to the preference for buying them from a subcontractor.

(d)

Component	*Hrs per unit to make in-house*	*Hrs required in total*	*Cumulative hours*
Shotter	3 hrs	12,000	12,000
Tross	4 hrs	16,000	28,000
Alba	2 hrs	8,000	36,000
		36,000	
Hours available		24,000	
Shortfall		12,000	

There are enough machine hours to make all 4,000 units of Shotter and 3,000 units of Tross. 8,000 hours production of Alba and 4,000 hours of Tross must be sub-contracted. This will be the cheapest production policy available.

(e)

Component	*Machine hours*	*Number of units*	*Unit variable cost*	*Total variable cost*
Make			£	£
Shotter	12,000	4,000	20	80,000
Tross (balance)	12,000	3,000	24	72,000
	24,000			152,000
Buy	*Hours saved*			
Tross (balance)	4,000	1,000	34	34,000
Alba	8,000	4,000	40	160,000
		Total variable costs of components		346,000
		Assembly costs (4,000 × £20)		80,000
		Total variable costs		426,000

6 SHUTDOWN PROBLEMS

6.1 Shutdown problems involve the following type of decisions.

- **Whether or not to close down** a factory, department, product line or other activity, either because it is making losses or because it is too expensive to run
- If the decision is to shut down, **whether the closure should be permanent or temporary**

6.2 In practice, shutdown decisions will involve **longer-term considerations**, and capital expenditures and revenues.

- A **shutdown** should **result in savings in annual operating costs for a number of years** into the future.

- Closure will probably **release unwanted fixed assets for sale**. Some assets might have a small scrap value, but other assets, in particular property, might have a substantial sale value.
- **Employees** affected by the closure must be made redundant or relocated, perhaps after retraining, or else offered early retirement. There will be lump sum payments involved which must be taken into account in the financial arithmetic. For example, suppose that the closure of a regional office would result in annual savings of £100,000, fixed assets could be sold off to earn income of £2 million, but redundancy payments would be £3 million. The shutdown decision would involve an assessment of the net capital cost of closure (£1 million) against the annual benefits (£100,000 pa).

6.3 It is possible, however, for **shutdown problems to be simplified into short-run decisions,** by assuming that either fixed asset sales and redundancy costs would be negligible or that income from fixed asset sales would match redundancy costs and so these **capital items would be self-cancelling.** In such circumstances the financial aspect of shutdown decisions would be based on short-run relevant costs.

6.4 EXAMPLE: ADDING OR DELETING PRODUCTS (OR DEPARTMENTS)

A company manufactures three products, Pawns, Rooks and Bishops. The present net annual income from these is as follows.

	Pawns	*Rooks*	*Bishops*	*Total*
	£	£	£	£
Sales	50,000	40,000	60,000	150,000
Variable costs	30,000	25,000	35,000	90,000
Contribution	20,000	15,000	25,000	60,000
Fixed costs	17,000	18,000	20,000	55,000
Profit/loss	3,000	(3,000)	5,000	5,000

The company is concerned about its poor profit performance, and is considering whether or not to cease selling Rooks. It is felt that selling prices cannot be raised or lowered without adversely affecting net income. £5,000 of the fixed costs of Rooks are direct fixed costs which would be saved if production ceased (that is, there are some attributable fixed costs). All other fixed costs, it is considered, would remain the same.

By stopping production of Rooks, the consequences would be a £10,000 fall in profits.

	£
Loss of contribution	(15,000)
Savings in fixed costs	5,000
Incremental loss	(10,000)

Suppose, however, it were possible to use the resources realised by stopping production of Rooks and switch to producing a new item, Crowners, which would sell for £50,000 and incur variable costs of £30,000 and extra direct fixed costs of £6,000. A new decision is now required.

	Rooks	*Crowners*
	£	£
Sales	40,000	50,000
Less variable costs	25,000	30,000
	15,000	20,000
Less direct fixed costs	5,000	6,000
Contribution to shared fixed costs and profit	10,000	14,000

It would be more profitable to shut down production of Rooks and switch resources to making Crowners, in order to boost profits by £4,000 to £9,000.

Temporary closure

6.5 The decision whether to shut down temporarily should take into account the following factors.

- The **impact on the organisation's other products** and the product in question
- Problems of **recruitment** of skilled labour when production begins again
- Possibility of **plant obsolescence**
- Problems of closing down and **restarting production** in some industries
- **Additional expenditure** on the disconnection of services, protective covering for machinery, start up costs and so on

If contribution is only just covering fixed costs but improved trading conditions in the future seem likely it may be worth continuing the business.

Idle production capacity 6/96

6.6 If an organisation does decide to shut down a factory, department, product line or other activity, it may well be faced with a decision about what to do with the resulting idle production capacity.

- **Marketing strategies** could be used to increase demand for existing products.
- **Idle plant and machinery could be moved to another department** or factory, thereby reducing expenditure on new plant and machinery and/or interest charges.
- **Special orders could be accepted**, providing that the contribution generated is either greater than any reduction in fixed overheads which would occur if the idle capacity was not used or greater than any increase in fixed overheads if the idle capacity were to be used.
- **Space could be sub-let** to a third party.

Such considerations are particularly important if the closure is only temporary.

7 EXTRA SHIFT DECISIONS AND OVERTIME

7.1 Extra shift decisions are another type of decision problem. They are concerned with whether or not it is worth opening up an extra shift for operations, typically from eight hours a day to 16 hours a day, or from 12 hours a day to a 24 hour round-the-clock service, or from a weekday-only service to Saturday and Sunday services as well.

7.2 **Qualitative factors** in extra shift decisions include the following.

- **Would the work force be willing** to work the shift hours, and if so, what overtime or shift work premium over their basic pay might they expect to receive?
- **Do extra hours have to be worked just to remain competitive**? Banks might decide to open on Saturdays, or shops might decide to have a late opening day each week, just to match what competitors are doing and so keep customers.
- Would extra hours result in **more sales revenue, or would there merely be a change in the demand pattern**? For example, if a do-it-yourself supermarket were trying to decide whether to open on Sundays, one consideration would be whether

the customers it would get on Sunday would simply be customers who would otherwise have done their shopping at the supermarket on another day of the week instead, or whether they would be additional customers providing extra total revenue for the supermarket.

7.3 When a business expands, the management is often faced with the problems of whether to acquire larger premises and more plant and machinery and whether to persuade existing personnel to work longer hours (on an overtime basis) or to engage extra staff who would use the existing equipment but at a different time (on a shift basis).

7.4 If the management decide to **incur additional expenditure on premises** and plant, that expenditure is a **fixed cost**. It will therefore be necessary to determine how much additional contribution will be required from the anticipated increased production to cover the extra fixed cost.

If it is decided to use the existing fixed assets, but for a longer period each day, the choice of shift working or overtime will also involve a marginal costing consideration.

- If **overtime** is selected, the **direct wages cost per unit produced will be increased** because the wages paid to workers on overtime are a basic rate plus an overtime bonus.
- If the management opt for **shift working** the shift premium may not be as expensive as the overtime premium so the **direct wages cost may be relatively lower**. On the other hand, there may be **an increase in fixed (or semi-fixed) costs** such as lighting, heating and canteen facilities.

8 ACCEPTING OR REJECTING ORDERS 12/97

Exam focus point

Eleven marks were available in the 12/97 exam for the discussion of two independent business opportunities, supported by some calculations.

8.1 In general terms, an order will probably be accepted if it increases contribution and profit, and rejected if it reduces profit. Examination questions often set problems relating to the acceptance or rejection of a 'special' (one-off) order, at a price below the normal price for the product.

If an organisation has **spare capacity** (which means that it would *not* have to turn away existing business), the order should be **accepted if the price offered makes some contribution to fixed costs and profit**. In other words, the variable cost of the order needs to be less than the price offered. Fixed costs are irrelevant to such a decision since they will be incurred regardless of whether or not the order is accepted. Additional fixed costs incurred as a result of accepting the order must be taken into account, however.

If an organisation **does not have sufficient spare capacity, existing business should only be turned away if the contribution from the order is greater than the contribution from the business which must be sacrificed.**

8.2 EXAMPLE: ACCEPTING OR REJECTING ORDERS

Holdup Ltd makes a single product which sells for £20, and for which there is great demand. It has a variable cost of £12, made up as follows.

	£
Direct material	4
Direct labour (2 hrs)	6
Variable overhead	2
	12

The labour force is currently working at full capacity producing a product that earns a contribution of £4 per labour hour. A customer has approached the company with a request for the manufacture of a special order for which he is willing to pay £5,500. The costs of the order would be £2,000 for direct materials, and 500 labour hours will be required.

Required

Decide whether the order should be accepted.

8.3 SOLUTION

(a) Labour is a limiting factor. By accepting the order, work would have to be diverted away from the standard product, and contribution will be lost, that is, there is an opportunity cost of accepting the new order, which is the contribution forgone by being unable to make the standard product.

(b) Direct labour pay costs £3 per hour, but it is also usually assumed that variable production overhead varies with hours worked, and must therefore be spent in addition to the wages cost of the 500 hours.

(c)

	£	£
Value of order		5,500
Cost of order		
Direct materials	2,000	
Direct labour (500 hrs × £3)	1,500	
Variable overhead (500 hrs × £1)	500	
Opportunity cost (500 hrs × £4) (Contribution forgone)	2,000	
Relevant cost of the order		6,000
Loss incurred by accepting the order		(500)

The order should not be accepted. In other words, although accepting the order would earn a contribution of £1,500 (£5,500 – £4,000), the lost production of the standard product would reduce contribution earned elsewhere by £2,000.

Other considerations must also be taken into account, however.

- Will **relationships with existing customers**, or prices that can be commanded in the market, be affected if the order is accepted?
- As a loss leader, could it **create further business opportunities**?
- Should existing business be turned away in order to fulfil a one-off enquiry or could a **long-term contract** be established?

9 COST-VOLUME-PROFIT ANALYSIS 6/97

Knowledge brought forward from Paper 3

Cost-volume-profit (breakeven) analysis

- Contribution per unit = unit selling price – unit variable costs
- Profit = (sales volume × contribution per unit) – fixed costs
- Breakeven point = activity level at which there is neither profit nor loss

$$= \frac{\text{total fixed costs}}{\text{contribution per unit}} = \frac{\text{contribution required to breakeven}}{\text{contribution per unit}}$$

- Contribution/sales (C/S) ratio = profit/volume (P/V) ratio = (contribution/sales) × 100%
- Sales revenue at breakeven point = fixed costs ÷ C/S ratio
- Margin of safety (in units) = budgeted sales units – breakeven sales units
- Margin of safety (as %) $= \dfrac{\text{budgeted sales} - \text{breakeven sales}}{\text{budgeted sales}} \times 100\%$
- Sales volume to achieve a target profit $= \dfrac{\text{fixed cost} + \text{target profit}}{\text{contribution per unit}}$

- Breakeven chart

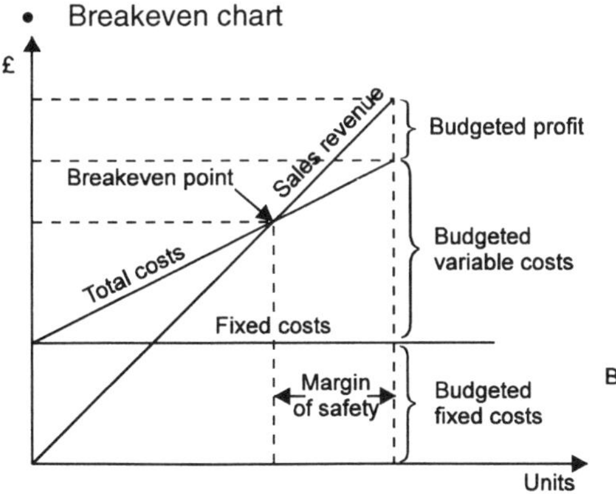

- Contribution (contribution breakeven) chart

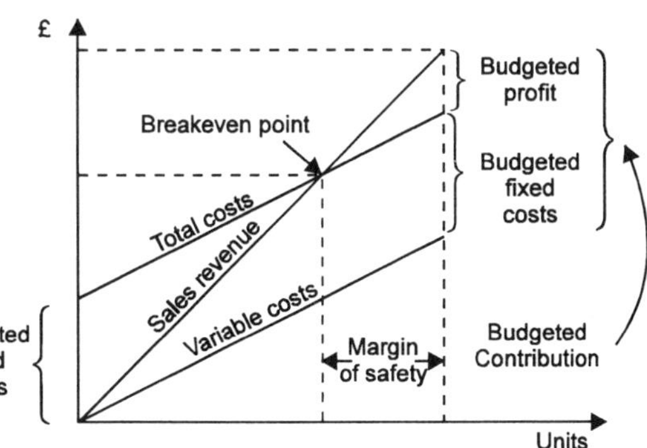

- Profit/volume (P/V) chart
- Multiproduct chart

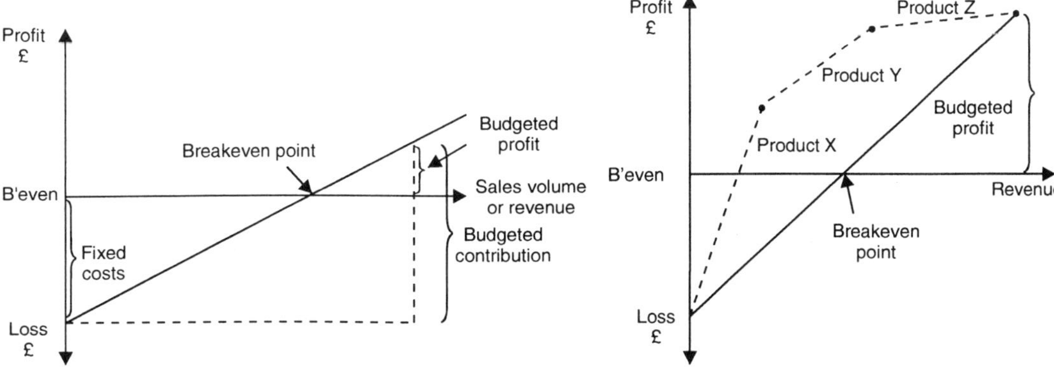

The gradient of the straight line is the contribution per unit (if the horizontal axis is measured in sales units) or the c/s ratio (if the horizontal axis is measured in sales value).

- Assume that the output and sales mix is 'fixed' in certain proportions.
- Calculate the C/S ratio for each product at the budgeted output level.
- Beginning with the product with the highest C/S ratio and working from left to right, plot cumulative profit against cumulative sales.

10 JOINT PRODUCT DECISIONS

10.1 When a manufacturing company carries out process operations in which two or more joint products are made from a common process, a number of decision problems can arise.

Joint products: the further processing decision

10.2 The contribution approach, or incremental approach, to joint product decisions concerns the decision as to **whether or not a joint product should be processed further after the point of separation, or whether it should be sold without further processing.** Note that **joint (pre-separation) costs** are incurred regardless of the decision and are therefore **irrelevant**.

10.3 EXAMPLE: FURTHER PROCESSING

The Poison Chemical Company produces two joint products, Alash and Pottum from the same process. Joint processing costs of £150,000 are incurred up to split-off point, when 100,000 units of Alash and 50,000 units of Pottum are produced. The selling prices at split-off point are £1.25 per unit for Alash and £2.00 per unit for Pottum.

The units of Alash could be processed further to produce 60,000 units of a new chemical, Alashplus, but at an extra fixed cost of £20,000 and variable cost of 30p per unit of input. The selling price of Alashplus would be £3.25 per unit.

Required

Ascertain whether the company should sell Alash or Alashplus.

10.4 SOLUTION

The only relevant costs/incomes are those which compare selling Alash against selling Alashplus. Every other cost is irrelevant: they will be incurred regardless of what the decision is.

	Alash			*Alashplus*
Selling price per unit	£1.25			£3.25
	£		£	£
Total sales	125,000			195,000
		Fixed	20,000	
		Variable	30,000	
Post-separation processing costs	-			50,000
Sales minus post-separation (further processing) costs	125,000			145,000

It is £20,000 more profitable to convert Alash into Alashplus.

Question

A company manufactures four products from an input of a raw material to Process 1. Following this process, product A is processed in Process 2, product B in Process 3, product C in Process 4 and product D in Process 5.

The normal loss in Process 1 is 10% of input, and there are no expected losses in the other processes. Scrap value in Process 1 is £0.50 per litre. The costs incurred in Process 1 are apportioned to each product according to the volume of output of each product. Production overhead is absorbed as a percentage of direct wages.

Data in respect of the month of October

	Process					
	1	*2*	*3*	*4*	*5*	*Total*
	£'000	£'000	£'000	£'000	£'000	£'000
Direct materials at £1.25 per litre	100					100
Direct wages	48	12	8	4	16	88
Production overhead						66

	Product			
	A	*B*	*C*	*D*
	Litres	Litres	Litres	Litres
Output	22,000	20,000	10,000	18,000
	£	£	£	£
Selling price	4.00	3.00	2.00	5.00
Estimated sales value at end of Process 1	2.50	2.80	1.20	3.00

Required

Suggest and evaluate an alternative production strategy which would optimise profit for the month. It should not be assumed that the output of Process 1 can be changed.

Answer

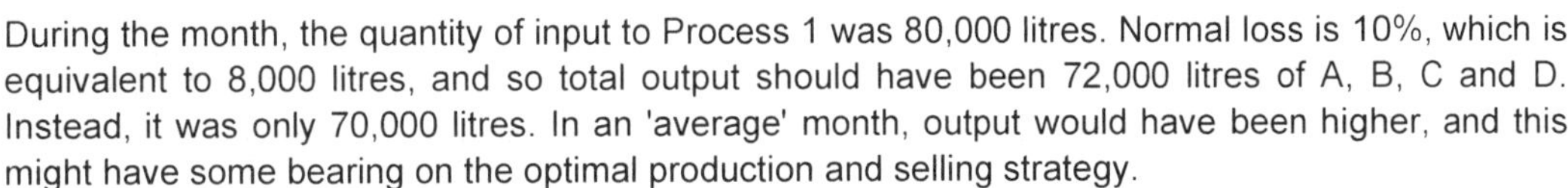

During the month, the quantity of input to Process 1 was 80,000 litres. Normal loss is 10%, which is equivalent to 8,000 litres, and so total output should have been 72,000 litres of A, B, C and D. Instead, it was only 70,000 litres. In an 'average' month, output would have been higher, and this might have some bearing on the optimal production and selling strategy.

The central question is whether or not the output from Process 1 should be processed further in processes 2, 3, 4 and 5, or whether it should be sold at the 'split-off' point, at the end of Process 1. Each joint product can be looked at individually.

A further question is whether the wages costs in process 2, 3, 4 and 5 would be avoided if the joint products were sold at the end of process 1 and not processed further. It will be assumed that all the wages costs would be avoidable, but none of the production overhead costs would be. This assumption can be challenged, and in practice would have to be investigated.

	A	*B*	*C*	*D*
	£	£	£	£
Selling price, per litre	4.00	3.00	2.00	5.00
Selling price at end of process 1	2.50	2.80	1.20	3.00
Incremental selling price, per litre	1.50	0.20	0.80	2.00
Litres output	22,000	20,000	10,000	18,000

	A	*B*	*C*	*D*
	£'000	£'000	£'000	£'000
Total incremental revenue from further processing	33	4	8	36
Avoidable costs from selling at split-off point (wages saved)	12	8	4	16
Incremental benefit/(cost) of further processing	21	(4)	4	20

This analysis would seem to indicate that products A, C and D should be further processed in processes 2, 4 and 5 respectively, but that product B should be sold at the end of process 1, without further processing in process 3. The saving would be at least £4,000 per month.

If some production overhead (which is 75% of direct wages) were also avoidable, this would mean that:

(a) selling product B at the end of process 1 would offer further savings of up to (75% of £8,000) £6,000 in overheads, and so £10,000 in total;

(b) the incremental benefit from further processing product C might fall by up to (75% of £4,000) £3,000 to £1,000, meaning that it is only just profitable to process C beyond the split-off point.

Joint products: breakeven point of extra output

10.5 Another type of problem is to estimate the costs and profit from making and selling additional units of one joint product, but not another. **If more output is required from one joint product** (we shall call it JP1) **it would also be necessary to produce more output (at least up to the split-off point) of the other joint products.**

(a) If the other joint products are only partly completed at split-off point, and would require further processing to put them in a condition for sale, the breakeven point of additional output of JP1 will depend on the decision about the other joint products.

(b) The incremental costs of the extra output of JP1 should be reduced to allow for the net revenue from by-products and other joint products.

10.6 EXAMPLE: BREAK-EVEN POINT OF EXTRA OUTPUT

Knott Ltd manufactures three products, A, BX and CX in a series of processes. Production during period 3 of 19X6 is illustrated by the following diagram.

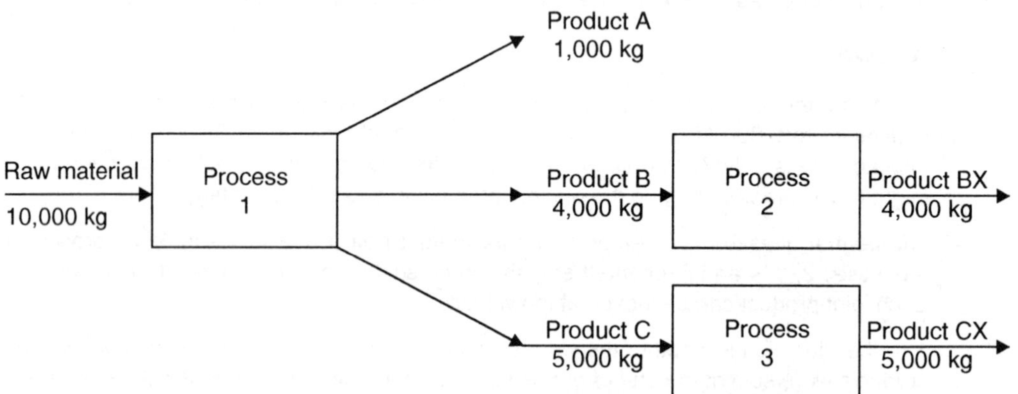

There was no opening or closing stock of work in progress in any process, nor any opening or closing stock of finished goods.

Cost and revenue details are as follows.

	Process 1	*Process 2*	*Process 3*
	£	£	£
Raw materials	40,000	-	-
Variable overhead costs	16,000	3,000	5,000
Fixed costs (including labour)	10,000	7,000	10,000
Selling price per kg	A	£3	
	BX	£12	
	CX	£10	

The output from process 1 is products B and C and these have a market price of £10 per kg and £6 per kg respectively, but Knott Ltd does not sell any of these products. Instead, all output of B and C is transferred to processes 2 and 3.

Required

(a) Determine whether the company is maximising its profits by further processing products B and C into BX and CX.

(b) Calculate the breakeven selling price for the extra output if the company received an order for a further 1,000 kg of product CX, which would incur an extra delivery cost of £1,800.

10.7 SOLUTION

(a) *The further processing decision*

	BX	*CX*
	£	£
Revenue from end product	48,000	50,000
Revenue from product B/C	40,000	30,000
Further revenue from further processing	8,000	20,000
Variable costs of further processing	3,000	5,000
Additional contribution from further processing	5,000	15,000
Fixed costs of further processing	7,000	10,000

It is clearly profitable to process CX further, since the additional contribution from further processing exceeds the fixed costs. In the case of BX, the profitability of further processing depends on how much of the £7,000 in fixed costs would be avoidable if process 2 were shut down. If avoidable fixed costs are less than £5,000, it is more profitable to produce BX and not to sell B.

(b) *Breakeven pricing*

Here, the problem is that to produce a further 1,000 kg of CX we must also produce 200 kg of A and 800 kg of B out of process 1.

Extra variable cost of producing 1,000 kg of C:

		£
In process 1:	raw material (× 20%)	8,000
	variable overhead (× 20%)	3,200
In process 3:	(20% × £5,000)	1,000
		12,200
Extra fixed costs of delivery		1,800
Total extra costs		14,000

Ignoring what could be done with the production of the extra products A and B, the breakeven price for the extra CX would be:

$$\frac{£14{,}000}{1{,}000 \text{ kg}} = £14 \text{ per kg}$$

If the extra A could be sold at its current market price, and the extra B were further processed into BX and sold at its current market price, the breakeven price of the extra CX would be much lower.

	£
Extra revenue from 800 kg of BX (× 12)	9,600
less variable costs of further processing in Process 2 (20% of 3,000)	600
	9,000
Extra revenue from 200 kg of A (× £3)	600
Extra contribution from extra A and BX	9,600
Extra costs, as shown above	14,000
Net extra costs of CX	4,400
Break-even price per kg of CX	£4.40

10.8 **Breakeven pricing for extra output decisions is therefore dependent on the assumptions that are made about what can be done with the extra output of the other joint products.**

Product mix decisions

10.9 A process manufacturing company might be faced with a decision about whether to **alter the product mix in its process**, so as to produce a greater proportion of one product and less of another. For example, if a process produces joint products X and Y in the ratio 2:1, an alteration to the process might be possible, whereby the output ratio is changed to, say, 3:2. Deciding whether or not to change a product mix should be based on the relevant costs and benefits of the change.

10.10 EXAMPLE: PRODUCT MIX DECISION

Marchmeat produces two joint products P and Q in the proportion 2:1. After the split-off point the products can be sold for industrial use or they can be taken to the mixing plant for blending and refining. The latter procedure is normally followed.

For a typical week, in which all the output is processed in the mixing plant, the following profit and loss account can be prepared:

	Product P	*Product Q*
Sales volume (litres)	2,000	1,000
Price per litre	£35	£60
	£	£
Sales revenue	70,000	60,000
Joint process cost (apportioned using output volume)	30,000	15,000
Blending and refining costs	25,000	25,000
Other separable costs	5,000	1,000
	60,000	41,000
Profit	10,000	19,000

The joint process costs are 75% fixed and 25% variable, whereas the mixing plant costs are 40% fixed and 60% variable and all the 'other separable costs' are variable.

There are only 40 hours available per week in the mixing plant. Typically 30 hours are taken up with the processing of product P and Q (15 hours for each product line) and 10 hours are used for other work that generates (on average) contribution of £2,000 per hour. The manager of the mixing plant considers that he could sell all the plant's processing time externally at a price that would provide this rate of profit.

It has been suggested that it might be possible to change the mix of products achieved in the mixing plant. It is possible to change the output proportions to 3:2 at a cost of £5 for each additional litre of Q produced by the distillation plant.

Required

Compare the costs and benefits of this proposal.

10.11 SOLUTION

Assuming that output remains 3,000 litres per week, the change in product mix would result in output of 1,800 litres of P and 1,200 litres of Q, compared with the current 2,000 litres of P and 1,000 litres of Q.

Since blending and refining costs are the same for P and Q at the moment, one litre of Q takes twice as much time to blend and refine as one litre of P. (This is an example of a key assumption in decision accounting problems which needs to be identified from data given in the question.)

Cost benefit analysis of proposal

	£	£
Additional sales revenue from extra 200 litres of Q (× £60)		12,000
Loss in revenue from 200 litres of P (× £35)		(7,000)
Extra joint processing costs (200 × £5)		(1,000)
Separable costs: all variable		
Extra cost of 200 litres of Q (× £1)	(200)	
Saving on 200 litres of P (× £2.5)	500	
Net saving		300
Blending and refining costs		
Extra cost of 200 litres of Q (200/1,000 × 60% of £25,000)	(3,000)	
Saving on 200 litres of P (200/2,000 × 60% of £25,000)	1,500	
		(1,500)
Extra blending and refining time needed for Q (200/1,000 × 15 hrs) = 3 hrs		
Less saving on time needed on P (200/2,000 × 15 hrs) = 1.5 hrs		
Net extra time = (3 – 1.5 hrs) = 1.5 hrs		
Opportunity cost of lost contribution from external work (1.5 × £2,000)		(3,000)
Net loss from change of product mix		(200)

The change in product mix would not be worthwhile, even though product Q seems more profitable per litre than product P!

11 PRICING DECISIONS 12/94, 12/95

Exam focus point

In 12/94, part of a longer question required candidates to explain the relevance of the concepts of 'price elasticity' and the 'cross elasticity' of demand to the product pricing decision.

11.1 Although, in general, the price charged for a product must exceed its cost, cost is only one of the **factors to bear in mind** when making a price-setting decision.

- **The organisation's objectives**. Although we generally assume that an organisation's objective is to maximise profit, it could be that increased market share, maximisation of sales revenue, to be known as a supplier of luxury goods or to provide a service to the community is the objective towards which an organisation is working and around it should base its pricing policy. The maximisation of sales revenue, for example, is most likely if either prices are very low so that volumes are high or if prices are exceptionally high (although volumes will, of course, be low).

- **The market in which the organisation operates**. If the organisation is operating under conditions of perfect competition (many buyers and many sellers all dealing in an identical product), neither producer nor user has any market power and both must accept the prevailing market price. If the organisation is in the position of a monopolist (one seller who dominates many buyers), it can use its market power to set a profit-maximising price. However, most of British industry can be described as an oligopoly (relatively few competitive companies dominate the market). Whilst each large firm has the ability to influence market prices, the unpredictable reaction from the other giants makes the final industry price difficult to determine.

- **Demand.** You should remember from your earlier studies that most organisations face a downward-sloping demand curve (the higher the price, the lower the demand). Economic theory suggests that the volume of demand for a good in the market as a whole is influenced by variables such as the following.
  - Price of the good
  - Price of other goods
  - Size and distribution of household income
  - Tastes and fashion
  - Expectations
  - Obsolescence
- The volume of demand for one organisation's goods rather than another's is influenced by three principal factors: product life cycle, quality and marketing.
  - **Product life cycle**. Most products pass through the following phases.
    - **Introduction.** The product is introduced to the market. Heavy capital expenditure will be incurred on product development and perhaps also on the purchase of new fixed assets and building up stocks for sale. The product will begin to earn some revenue, but initially demand is likely to be small. Potential customers will be unaware of the product or service, and the organisation may have to spend further on advertising to bring the product or service to the attention of the market.
    - **Growth.** The product gains a bigger market as demand builds up. Sales revenues increase and the product begins to make a profit. The initial costs of the investment in the new product are gradually recovered.
    - **Maturity**. Eventually, the growth in demand for the product will slow down and it will enter a period of relative maturity. It will continue to be profitable. The product may be modified or improved, as a means of sustaining its demand.
    - **Saturation and decline.** At some stage, the market will have bought enough of the product and it will therefore reach 'saturation point'. Demand will start to fall. For a while, the product will still be profitable in spite of declining sales, but eventually it will become a loss-maker and this is the time when the organisation should decide to stop selling the product or service, and so the product's life cycle should reach its end.

    Different versions of the same product may have different life cycles, and consumers are often aware of this. For example, the prospective buyer of a new car is more likely to purchase a recently introduced Ford than a Vauxhall that has been on the market for several years, even if there is nothing to choose in terms of quality and price.
  - **Quality**. One firm's product may be perceived to be better quality than another's, and may in some cases actually be so, if it uses sturdier materials, goes faster or does whatever it is meant to do in a 'better' way. Other things being equal, the better quality good will be more in demand than other versions.
  - **Marketing.** You may be familiar with the 'four Ps' of the marketing mix, all of which influence demand for a firm's goods.
    - Price
    - Product
    - Place
    - Promotion

- **Price elasticity of demand**. The price an organisation charges will be affected by whether demand for an item is *elastic* (a small change in the price produces a large change in the quantity demanded) or *inelastic* (a small change in the price produces only a small change in the quantity demanded).
- **Costs**. An organisation has to decide whether a price should be based on fully absorbed cost or marginal cost.
- **Competition**. When competitors sell exactly the same product in the same market, price differences are likely to have a significant effect on demand. For example, the price of petrol at filling stations in a local area will be much the same. If it was not, customers would go to the cheapest place. When organisations sell similar products which are not exactly identical, or where the geographical location of the sales point is of some significance, there is more scope for charging different prices.
- **Inflation**. An organisation should recognise the effects of inflation on its pricing decisions. When its costs are rising, it must try to ensure that its prices are increased sufficiently and regularly enough to make an adequate profit (in the case of a profit-making concern) or to cover its costs (in the case of non-profit-making organisations, where it is only necessary to break even).
- **Legislation**. Certain organisations have their prices controlled by legislation or regulatory bodies.
- **Availability of substitutes**. When an organisation is making a pricing decision it must take into account products/services that customers could switch to if they were not happy with the price set. For example, coach transport organisations have to consider the ability of customers to switch to travelling with British Rail.

There are, of course, other factors which organisations should consider when setting prices but those we have listed should make it clear that cost is only one of many factors which influence the pricing decision.

Approaches to pricing

Full cost plus pricing

11.2 A traditional approach to pricing products is full cost plus pricing, whereby the sales price is determined by **calculating the full cost of the product and adding a percentage mark-up for profit**.

11.3 A business might have an idea of the percentage profit margin it would like to earn and so might decide on an average profit mark-up as a general guideline for pricing decisions. This would be particularly useful for businesses that carry out a large amount of **contract work or jobbing work**, for which individual job or contract prices must be quoted regularly to prospective customers.

11.4 However, the **percentage profit mark-up** does not have to be fixed, but **can be varied** to suit the circumstances. In particular, the percentage mark-up can be varied to suit demand conditions in the market.

11.5 The full cost plus approach to pricing is commonly used in practice, but varying the size of the profit mark-up gives the pricing decisions much-needed flexibility so as to adapt to demand conditions.

11.6 There are a number of criticisms of this approach to pricing, perhaps the most important criticism being that it **fails to recognise that since demand may be determined by**

price, there will be a profit-maximising combination of price and demand. A cost plus based approach to pricing will be most unlikely to arrive at the profit-maximising price.

11.7 The **advantages** of full cost plus pricing are as follows.

- Since the size of the profit margin can be varied at management's discretion, a decision based on a price in excess of full cost should ensure that a company working at normal capacity will cover all its fixed costs and make a profit. Companies may benefit from cost plus pricing in the following circumstances.
  - When they carry out large contracts which must make a sufficient profit margin to cover a fair share of fixed costs
  - If they must justify their prices to potential customers (for example for government contracts)
  - If they find it difficult to estimate expected demand at different sales prices
- It is a simple, quick and cheap method of pricing which can be delegated to junior managers. This may be particularly important with jobbing work where many prices must be decided and quoted each day.

Marginal cost plus pricing

11.8 Instead of pricing products or services by adding a profit margin on to *full* cost, a business might **add a profit margin on to marginal cost** (either the marginal cost of production or else the marginal cost of sales). This is sometimes called **mark-up pricing**.

11.9 The **advantages** of a marginal cost plus approach to pricing are as follows.

- It is a simple and easy method to use.
- The mark-up can be varied, and so provided that a rigid mark-up is not used, mark-up pricing can be adjusted to reflect demand conditions.
- It draws management attention to contribution and the effects of higher or lower sales volumes on profit. In this way, it helps to create a better awareness of the concepts and implications of marginal costing and breakeven analysis. For example, if a product costs £10 a unit and a mark-up of 150% is added to reach a price of £25 a unit, management should be clearly aware that every additional £1 of sales revenue would add 60p to contribution and profit.
- Mark-up pricing is convenient where there is a readily identifiable basic variable cost. Retail industries are the most obvious example, and it is quite common for the prices of goods in shops to be fixed by adding a mark-up (20% or 33$^{1}/_{3}$%, say) to the purchase cost. For example, a department store might buy in items of pottery at £3 each, add a mark-up of one third and resell the items at £4.

11.10 There are, of course, **drawbacks** to marginal cost plus pricing.

- Although the size of the mark-up can be varied in accordance with demand conditions, it is not a method of pricing which ensures that sufficient attention is paid to demand conditions, competitors' prices and profit maximisation.
- It ignores fixed overheads in the pricing decision, but the price must be high enough to ensure that a profit is made after covering fixed costs. Pricing decisions cannot ignore fixed costs altogether.

Minimum pricing

11.11 A minimum price is the price that would have to be charged so that the **following costs are just covered.**

- **The incremental costs of producing and selling the item**
- **The opportunity costs of the resources consumed in making and selling the item**

A minimum price **would leave the business no better or worse off in financial terms than if it did not sell the item.**

11.12 Two essential points about a minimum price are as follows.

- It is based on relevant costs.
- It is **unlikely that a minimum price would actually be charged** because if it were, it would not provide the business with any incremental profit. However, the minimum price for an item **shows** the following.
    - **An absolute minimum below which the price should not be set.**
    - **The incremental profit that would be obtained from any price that is actually charged in excess of the minimum.** For example, if the minimum price is £200 and the actual price charged is £240, the incremental profit on the sale would be £40.

11.13 If there are **no scarce resources and a company has spare capacity, the minimum price of a product is the incremental cost of making it.** Any price in excess of this minimum would provide an incremental contribution towards profit.

11.14 **If there are scarce resources and a company makes more than one product,** minimum prices **must include an allowance for the opportunity cost** of using the scarce resources to make and sell the product (instead of using the resources on the next most profitable product).

12 QUALITATIVE FACTORS IN DECISION MAKING

12.1 Qualitative factors in decision making are factors which might influence the eventual decisions but which have not been quantified in terms of relevant income or costs. They may stem from two sources.

- Non-financial objectives
- Factors which might be quantifiable in money terms, but which have not been quantified, perhaps because there is insufficient information to make reliable estimates

12.2 Qualitative factors in decision making will vary with the circumstances and nature of the opportunity being considered. Here are some examples.

Qualitative factor	Detail
Availability of cash	There must be sufficient cash to finance any purchases of equipment and build-up of working capital. If cash is not available, new sources of funds (for example an overdraft or loan) must be sought.
Inflation	If the income from an opportunity is fixed by contract, but the costs might increase with inflation, the contract's profitability would be over-stated unless inflation is taken into account.
Employees	Any decision involving the shutdown of a plant, creation of a new work shift, or changes in work procedures or location will require acceptance by employees, and ought to have regard to employee welfare.
Customers	Decisions about new products or product closures, the quality of output or after-sales service will inevitably affect customer loyalty and customer demand. It is also important to remember that a decision involving one product may have repercussions on customer attitudes towards a range of products.
Competitors	In a competitive market, some decisions may stimulate a response from rival companies. For example, the decision to reduce selling prices in order to raise demand may not be successful if all competitors take similar action.
Timing factors	There might be a choice in deciding when to take up an opportunity. • Accept an opportunity now. • Do not accept the opportunity now, but wait before doing so. • Reject the opportunity. There might also be choice about the following. • If a department is shut down, will the closure be permanent, or temporary? Temporary closure may be a viable proposition during a period of slack demand. • If a decision is taken to sell goods at a low price where the contribution earned will be relatively small, it is important to consider the duration of the low price promotion. If it is a long-term feature of selling, and if demand for the product increases, the company's total contribution may sink to a level where it fails even to cover fixed costs.
Suppliers	Some decisions will affect suppliers, whose long-term goodwill maybe damaged by a decision to close a product line temporarily. Decisions to change the specifications for purchased components, or change stockholding policies so as to create patchy, uneven demand might also put a strain on suppliers.
Feasibility	A proposal may look good in outline, but technical experts or departmental managers may have some reservations about their ability to carry it out.
Flexibility and internal control	Decisions to subcontract work, or to enter into a long-term contract have the disadvantages of inflexibility and lack of controllability.

Qualitative factor	Detail
Unquantified opportunity costs	Even where no opportunity costs are specified, it is probable that other opportunities would be available for using the resources to earn profit, and it may be useful to qualify a recommendation by stating that a given project would appear to be viable on the assumption that there are no other more profitable opportunities available.
Political pressures	Some large companies may suffer political pressures applied by the government to influence their investment or disinvestment decisions.
Legal constraints	A decision might occasionally be rejected because of questions about the legality of the proposed action.

13 PRESENTATION OF INFORMATION

13.1 Once the decision analysis has been carried out by you, the accountant, **the results and conclusions must be clearly presented and communicated** to management so that they are in the best possible position to take a decision. As well as providing figures you must ensure that management are aware of and understand any assumptions underlying the figures. Management can then use their judgement on the course of action to take, whatever the figures show. Remember that management accounting is not governed by the stringent rules which cover financial accounting. It is therefore vital that management review figures with the same notions of how they were arrived at as those who prepared the figures.

Chapter roundup

- **Planning information** is gathered **internally** and **externally** from formal and informal sources.
- **Control information** provides a comparison between **actual** results and **planned** results.
- **Decision-making information** must be **relevant**.
- In making decisions, the only costs which are **relevant** are those which will be affected by the decision. Such costs will be **future**, **incremental** cash flows.
- Other terms used to describe relevant costs are **avoidable** costs, **differential** costs, and **out-of-pocket** costs.
- **Opportunity costs** are relevant costs. An opportunity cost is the benefit which could have been earned, but which has been given up by choosing one option instead of another.
- **Non-relevant costs** include sunk costs, committed costs, notional costs and historic costs.
- **Fixed costs** which are affected by a decision are called directly attributable fixed costs.
- A variety of assumptions are made in relevant costing.
- In a limiting factor situation, contribution will be maximised by earning the biggest possible contribution per unit of limiting factor.
- In a **make or buy situation with no limiting factors**, the relevant costs for the decision maker are the **differential costs** between the two options. With a limiting factor, total cost will be minimised where the extra marginal cost of buying from a subcontractor is least for each unit of limiting factor saved by buying in.
- If an organisation has to subcontract work to make up a shortfall in its own in-house capabilities, its total costs will be minimised if those products which have the least extra marginal cost of buying out per unit of scarce resource are subcontracted.
- The decision to work an extra shift should be taken on the basis of whether the costs of the shift are exceeded by the benefits to be obtained.
- If an organisation has **spare capacity** (which means that it would *not* have to turn away existing business), the order should be **accepted if the price offered makes some contribution to fixed costs and profit**. If an organisation **does not have sufficient spare capacity, existing business should only be turned away if the contribution from the order is greater than the contribution from the business which must be sacrificed.**
- Decisions about whether to process a joint product further or sell at the split-off point take no account of the joint costs, which are irrelevant to the decision. The decision is made on the basis of a **comparison between additional costs and additional revenues**.
- **Breakeven pricing** for extra output decisions is dependent on the assumptions that are made about what can be done with the extra output of the other joint products.
- Deciding whether or not to change a product mix should be based on the **relevant costs** and **benefits of the change**.
- Cost is only one of the factors to be considered in a pricing decision.
- Pricing approaches include **full cost plus**, **marginal cost plus** and **minimum pricing.**
- **Qualitative factors** can affect decisions and should therefore be taken into account.

Quick quiz

1. List six areas for which external planning information must be gathered. (see para 1.8)
2. What are relevant costs? (key terms)
3. Do accountants use profits or cash flows in decision accounting? (2.2)
4. What is an opportunity cost? (key terms)
5. Distinguish between an avoidable cost and a sunk cost. (key terms)
6. What is an attributable fixed cost? (2.7)
7. What is the relevant cost of materials that have already been purchased and will not be replaced? (2.10)
8. What are the assumptions on which relevant costing is based? (3.2)
9. What is the general rule for maximising contribution in a limiting factor decision? (4.3)
10. What matters other than cost should be considered in a make or buy situation? (5.5)
11. How can shutdown decisions be simplified into short-run decisions? (6.3)
12. Describe three types of decision problem that could arise if an organisation carries out process operations in which two or more joint products are made from a common process. (10.2, 10.5, 10.9)
13. What are the phases of a product life cycle? (11.1)

Question to try	Level	Marks	Time
14	Introductory	n/a	25 mins

Part E

The framework of financial management

Chapter 14

FINANCIAL MANAGEMENT AND FINANCIAL OBJECTIVES

Chapter topic list		Syllabus reference
1	The scope of financial management	4(a)
2	Objectives of private sector companies	4(c),(d),5(b)(viii)
3	Non-financial objectives	4(c),(d)
4	Stakeholders in a company	4(e)
5	Bodies which are not purely commercial	4(c),(d),(e)
6	Measuring performance	4(c),(d)
7	Performance measurement in the public sector	4(d)

Introduction

Starting with this chapter and in the remaining chapters of this Text, we examine the work of the financial manager and the framework within which the financial manager operates.

After introducing the **scope of financial management**, we consider the **objectives** of organisations. We go on to examine **performance indicators** for both business enterprises and non-commercial organisations.

In later chapters we will be studying the **resources** available for an organisation to meet objectives and the methods available for doing so.

Exam focus point

As we begin coverage of the FM part of the syllabus, bear in mind the format of the paper (as set out in the Introduction to this Study Text). The 60-mark allocation for FM and the compulsory 40-mark FM case study are there to make sure that you cannot pass Paper 8 without knowing the FM areas thoroughly. It is not possible to scrape through largely on MA knowledge without paying much attention to FM.

1 THE SCOPE OF FINANCIAL MANAGEMENT 6/94

What is financial management?

1.1 **Financial management** can be defined as the management of the finances of an organisation in order to achieve the financial objectives of the organisation. The usual assumption in financial management for the private sector is that the objective of the company is to **maximise shareholders' wealth**.

1.2 Broadly, there are two aspects of financial management.

- Financial planning
- Financial control

Financial planning

1.3 The financial manager will need to **plan** to ensure that enough funding is available at the right time to meet the needs of the organisation for short, medium and long-term capital. For example, in the short term, funds may be needed to pay for purchases of stocks, or to smooth out changes in debtors, creditors and cash: the financial manager is here ensuring that **working capital requirements** are met. In the medium or long term, the organisation may have planned purchases of fixed assets such as plant and equipment, for which the financial manager must ensure that funding is available. The financial manager contributes to decisions on the uses of funds raised by analysing financial data to determine uses which meet the organisation's financial objectives. Is project A to be preferred to Project B? Should a new asset be bought or leased?

Financial control

1.4 The **control** function of the financial manager becomes relevant for funding which has been raised. Are the various activities of the organisation meeting its objectives? Are assets being used efficiently? To answer these questions, the financial manager may compare data on actual performance with forecast performance. Forecast data will have been prepared in the light of past performance (historical data) modified to reflect expected future changes. Future changes may include the effects of economic development, for example an economic recovery leading to a forecast upturn in revenues.

Financial management decisions

1.5 The financial manager makes decisions relating to the following areas.

- Investment
- Financing
- Dividends

Investment decisions

1.6 Examples of different types of **investment decision** are as follows.

(a) Decisions internal to the business enterprise

(i) Whether to undertake new projects
(ii) Whether to invest in new plant and machinery
(iii) Research and development decisions
(iv) Investment in a marketing or advertising campaign

(b) Decisions involving external parties

(i) Whether to carry out a takeover or a merger involving another business
(ii) Whether to engage in a joint venture with another enterprise

(c) Disinvestment decisions

(i) Whether to sell off unprofitable segments of the business
(ii) Whether to sell old or surplus plant and machinery
(iii) The sale of subsidiary companies

Financing decisions

1.7 Investments in assets must be **financed** somehow. Financial management is also concerned with the management of short-term funds and with how funds can be raised over the long term, for example by the following methods.

(a) Taking more credit
(b) Retention of profits for reinvestment in the business
(c) The issue of new shares to raise capital
(d) Borrowing, from banks or other lenders
(e) Leasing of assets, as an alternative to outright purchase

Dividend decisions

1.8 Retention of profits was mentioned above as a financing decision. The other side of this decision is that if profits are retained, there is less to pay out to shareholders as dividends, which might deter investors. An appropriate balance needs to be struck in addressing the dividend decision: how much of its profits should the company pay out as dividends and how much should it retain for investment to provide for future growth and new investment opportunities?

1.9 We shall be looking at various aspects of the investment, financing and dividend decisions of financial management over the remaining chapters of this Study Text.

Question 1

'The financial manager should identify surplus assets and dispose of them'. Why?

Answer

A surplus asset earns no return for the business. The business is likely to be paying the 'cost of capital' in respect of the money tied up in the asset, ie the money which it can realise by selling it.

If surplus assets are sold, the business may be able to invest the cash released in more productive ways, or alternatively it may use the cash to cut its liabilities. Either way, it will enhance the return on capital employed for the business as a whole.

Although selling surplus assets yields short-term benefits, the business should not jeopardise its activities in the medium or long term by disposing of productive capacity until the likelihood of it being required in the future has been fully assessed.

2 OBJECTIVES OF PRIVATE SECTOR COMPANIES

Exam focus point

Financial objectives forms one of the topic areas which the Examiner treats as 'contextual material' on which *full* questions will not be set. However, the subject may be examined as context in a larger question, or could be the subject of subsections of questions.

2.1 In much of economic theory, it is assumed that the firm behaves in such a way as to maximise profits, where profit is viewed in an economist's sense. To the economist, profit is the difference between the total revenue received by the firm and the total costs which it incurs. Unlike the accountant's concept of cost, total costs by this economist's definition includes an element of reward for the risk-taking of the entrepreneur, called 'normal profit'.

2.2 This is because entrepreneurship is viewed by the economist as one of the factors of production which the firm makes use of. Like the other factors of production - land, labour, and capital - entrepreneurship requires the prospect of a reward if it is to be prevented from being used elsewhere (in another firm) instead.

Profit maximisation and other objectives of firms

2.3 Where the entrepreneur is in full managerial control of the firm, as in the case of a small owner-managed company or partnership, the **economist's assumption of profit maximisation** would seem to be very reasonable. Even in companies owned by shareholders but run by non-shareholding managers, if the manager is serving the company's (ie the shareholders') interests, we might expect that the profit maximisation assumption should be close to the truth.

2.4 However, some writers have suggested that objectives other than profit maximisation might be pursued by firms.

2.5 Managers are paid to make the decisions about prices and output, but it is the shareholders who expect to benefit from the profits. Managers, it is argued, will not necessarily make pricing decisions that will maximise profits, because:

(a) they have no personal interests at stake in the size of profits earned, except in so far as they are accountable to the shareholders for the profits they make; and

(b) there is no competitive pressure in the market to be efficient, minimise costs and maximise profits.

2.6 Given the **divorce of management from ownership**, it has been suggested that price and output decisions will be taken by managers with a managerial aim rather than the aim of profit maximisation, within the constraint that managers must take some account of shareholders' interests because they are formally responsible for them and so are accountable to shareholders for their decisions.

(a) One 'managerial model' of the firm, Baumol's **sales maximisation model,** assumes that the firm acts to maximise sales revenue rather than profits (subject to the constraint that the profit level must be satisfactory and so acceptable to shareholders and providing enough retained profits for future investment in growth). The management of a firm might opt for sales revenue maximisation in order to maintain or increase its market share, to ensure survival and to discourage competition. Managers benefit personally because of the prestige of running a large and successful company, and also because salaries and other perks are likely to be higher in bigger companies than smaller ones.

(b) Another managerial model, Williamson's **management discretion model,** assumes that managers act to further their own interests and so maximise their own utility, subject to a minimum profit requirement. Utility may be thought of in terms of prestige, influence and other personal satisfactions. The model states that utility, which a manager aims to maximise, is a function of the manager's own salary and also expenditure on his or her staff (prestige and influence depend on the numbers and pay levels of subordinate staff), the amount of perquisites (luxurious office, personal secretary, company car, expense account etc) and the authority to make 'discretionary investments' (ie new investments other than straightforward replacement decisions). The profit aimed for will not be maximum profit, because of management's wishes for expenditure on themselves, their staff and the perquisites of management.

2.7 Cyert and March's **consensus theory** suggested that a firm is an organisational coalition of shareholders, managers, employees and customers, with each group having different goals, and so there is a need for political compromise in establishing the goals of the firm. Each group must settle for less than it would ideally want to have - shareholders must settle for less than maximum profit, and managers for less than maximum utility, and so on.

2.8 The assumptions of economic theory and various theories of the firm all contain an element of truth. However, they do not provide the financial manager with an easy yardstick with which to work.

In the theory of company finance, such a yardstick is provided in the assumption that the financial manager's job is to maximise the market value of the company. Specifically, the main financial objective of a company should be to maximise the wealth of its ordinary shareholders. Within this context, the financial manager seeks to ensure that investments earn a **return**, for the benefit of shareholders.

2.9 A company is financed by ordinary shareholders, preference shareholders, loan stock holders and other long-term and short-term creditors. All surplus funds, however, belong to the legal owners of the company, its ordinary shareholders. Any retained profits are undistributed wealth of these equity shareholders.

How are the wealth of shareholders and the value of a company measured?

2.10 If the financial objective of a company is to maximise the value of the company, and in particular the value of its ordinary shares, we need to be able to put values on a company and its shares. How do we do it?

2.11 Three possible methods for the valuation of a company might occur to us.

(a) A **balance sheet valuation,** with assets valued on a going concern basis. Certainly, investors will look at a company's balance sheet. If retained profits rise every year, the company will be a profitable one. Balance sheet values are not a measure of 'market value', although retained profits might give some indication of what the company could pay as dividends to shareholders.

(b) The valuation of a company's assets on a **break-up basis**. This method of valuing a business is only of interest when the business is threatened with liquidation, or when its management is thinking about selling off individual assets (rather than a complete business) to raise cash.

(c) **Market values.** The market value is the price at which buyers and sellers will trade stocks and shares in a company. This is the method of valuation which is most relevant to the financial objectives of a company.

   (i) When shares are traded on a recognised stock market, such as the Stock Exchange, the market value of a company can be measured by the price at which shares are currently being traded.

   (ii) When shares are in a private company, and are not traded on any stock market, there is no easy way to measure their market value. Even so, the financial objective of these companies should be to maximise the wealth of their ordinary shareholders.

2.12 The wealth of the shareholders in a company comes from **dividends** received and the **market value of the shares**. A shareholder's return on investment is obtained in the form of dividends received and **capital gains** from increases in the market value of his or her shares.

2.13 Dividends are normally paid just twice a year by UK public companies (interim and final dividends), whereas a current market value is (for quoted shares) always known from share prices. There is also a theory, supported by much empirical evidence (and common sense), that market prices are influenced strongly by expectations of what future dividends will be. So we might conclude that the wealth of shareholders in quoted companies can be measured by the market value of the shares.

How is the value of a business increased?

2.14 If a company's shares are traded on a stock market, the wealth of shareholders is increased when the share price goes up. Ignoring day-to-day fluctuations in price caused by patterns of supply and demand, and ignoring fluctuations caused by **environmental factors** such as changes in interest rates, the price of a company's shares will go up when the company makes attractive profits, which it pays out as dividends or re-invests in the business to achieve future profit growth and dividend growth. However, to increase the share price the company should achieve its attractive profits without taking business risks and financial risks which worry shareholders.

2.15 If there is an increase in earnings and dividends, management can hope for an increase in the share price too, so that shareholders benefit from both higher revenue (dividends) and also capital gains (higher share prices).

Management should set targets for factors which they can influence directly, such as profits and dividend growth. And so a financial objective might be expressed as the aim of increasing profits, earnings per share and dividend per share by, say, 10% a year for each of the next five years.

2.16 **Earnings per share (EPS)** are the earnings (profits after tax and extraordinary items) attributable to each equity (ordinary) share.

2.17 Dividends are the direct reward to shareholders that a company pays out, and so dividends are evidence of a company's ability to provide a return for its shareholders. Companies might therefore set targets for growth in dividend per share.

Other financial targets

2.18 In addition to targets for earnings, EPS, and dividend per share, a company might set **other financial targets**, such as:

(a) a restriction on the company's level of **gearing**, or debt. For example, a company's management might decide that:

   (i) the ratio of long-term debt capital to equity capital should never exceed, say, 1:1;

   (ii) the cost of interest payments should never be higher than, say, 25% of total profits before interest and tax;

(b) a target for **profit retentions**. For example, management might set a target that dividend cover (the ratio of distributable profits to dividends actually distributed) should not be less than, say, 2.5 times;

(c) a target for **operating profitability**. For example, management might set a target for the profit/sales ratio (say, a minimum of 10%) or for a return on capital employed (say, a minimum ROCE of 20%).

2.19 These financial targets are not primary financial objectives, but they can act as subsidiary targets or constraints which should help a company to achieve its main financial objective without incurring excessive risks.

2.20 However, these targets are usually measured over a year rather than over the long term, and it is the maximisation of shareholder wealth in the long term that ought to be the corporate objective. Short-term measures of return can encourage a company to pursue **short-term** objectives at the expense of **long-term** ones, for example by deferring new capital investments, or spending only small amounts on research and development and on training.

2.21 A major problem with setting a number of different financial targets, either primary targets or supporting secondary targets, is that they might not all be consistent with each other, and so might not all be achievable at the same time. When this happens, some compromises will have to be accepted.

2.22 EXAMPLE: FINANCIAL TARGETS

Lion Grange Ltd has recently introduced a formal scheme of long range planning. At a meeting called to discuss the first draft plans, the following estimates emerged.

(a) Sales in the current year reached £10,000,000, and forecasts for the next five years are £10,600,000, £11,400,000, £12,400,000, £13,600,000 and £15,000,000.

(b) The ratio of net profit after tax to sales is 10%, and this is expected to continue throughout the planning period.

(c) Net asset turnover, currently 0.8 times, will remain more or less constant.

It was also suggested that:

(a) if profits rise, dividends should rise by at least the same percentage;

(b) an earnings retention rate of 50% should be maintained;

(c) the ratio of long-term borrowing to long-term funds (debt plus equity) is limited (by the market) to 30%, which happens also to be the current gearing level of the company.

Required

Prepare a financial analysis of the draft long range plan and suggested policies for dividends, retained earnings and gearing.

2.23 SOLUTION

The draft financial plan, for profits, dividends, assets required and funding, can be drawn up in a table, as follows.

	Current Year £m	*Year 1* £m	*Year 2* £m	*Year 3* £m	*Year 4* £m	*Year 5* £m
Sales	10.00	10.60	11.40	12.40	13.60	15.00
Net profit after tax	1.00	1.06	1.14	1.24	1.36	1.50
Dividends (50% of profit after tax)	0.50	0.53	0.57	0.62	0.68	0.75
Net assets (125% of sales)	12.50	13.25	14.25	15.50	17.00	18.75
Equity (increased by retained earnings)	8.75*	9.28	9.85	10.47	11.15	11.90
Maximum debt (30% of assets)	3.75	3.97	4.28	4.65	5.10	5.63
Funds available	12.50	13.25	14.13	15.12	16.25	17.53
(Shortfalls) in funds, given maximum gearing of 30% and no new issue of shares = funds available minus net assets required	0	0	(0.12)	(0.38)	(0.75)	(1.22)

* The current year equity figure is a balancing figure, equal to the difference between net assets and long-term debt, which is currently at the maximum level of 30% of net assets.

Question 2

Suggest policies on dividends, retained earnings and gearing for Lion Grange Limited, using the data in the example above.

Answer

These figures show that the financial objectives of the company are not compatible with each other, and adjustments will have to be made.

(a) Given the assumptions about sales, profits, dividends and net assets required, there will be an increasing shortfall of funds from year 2 onwards, unless new shares are issued or the gearing level rises above 30%.

(b) In years 2 and 3, the shortfall can be eliminated by retaining a greater percentage of profits, but this may have a serious adverse effect on the share price. In year 4 and year 5, the shortfall in funds cannot be removed even if dividend payments are reduced to nothing.

(c) The net asset turnover appears to be low. The situation would be eased if investments were able to generate a higher volume of sales, so that fewer fixed assets and less working capital would be required to support the projected level of sales.

(d) If asset turnover cannot be improved, it may be possible to increase the profit to sales ratio by reducing costs or increasing selling prices.

(e) If a new issue of shares is proposed to make up the shortfall in funds, the amount of funds required must be considered very carefully. Total dividends would have to be increased in order to pay dividends on the new shares. The company seems unable to offer prospects of suitable dividend payments, and so raising new equity might be difficult.

(f) It is conceivable that extra funds could be raised by issuing new debt capital, so that the level of gearing would be over 30%. It is uncertain whether investors would be prepared to lend money so as to increase gearing. If more funds were borrowed, profits after interest and tax would fall so that the share price might also be reduced.

3 NON-FINANCIAL OBJECTIVES

3.1 A company may have important **non-financial objectives,** which will limit the achievement of financial objectives.

Examples of non-financial objectives are as follows.

(a) **The welfare of employees**

A company might try to provide good wages and salaries, comfortable and safe working conditions, good training and career development, and good pensions. If redundancies are necessary, many companies will provide generous redundancy payments, or spend money trying to find alternative employment for redundant staff.

(b) **The welfare of management**

Managers will often take decisions to improve their own circumstances, even though their decisions will incur expenditure and so reduce profits. High salaries, company cars and other perks are all examples of managers promoting their own interests.

(c) **The welfare of society as a whole**

The management of some companies are aware of the role that their company has to play in providing for the well-being of society. As an example, many oil companies are aware of their role as providers of energy for society, faced with the problems of protecting the environment and preserving the Earth's dwindling energy resources. Companies may be aware of their responsibility to minimise pollution and other harmful 'externalities' (to use the economist's term) which their activities generate. In delivering 'green' environmental policies, a company may improve its corporate image as well as reducing harmful externality effects.

(d) **The provision of a service**

The major objectives of some companies will include fulfilment of a responsibility to provide a service to the public. Examples are the privatised British Telecom and British Gas.

(e) **The fulfilment of responsibilities towards customers and suppliers**

(i) Responsibilities towards customers include providing a product or service of a quality that customers expect, and dealing honestly and fairly with customers.

(ii) Responsibilities towards suppliers are expressed mainly in terms of trading relationships. A company's size could give it considerable power as a buyer. The company should not use its power unscrupulously. Suppliers might rely on getting prompt payment, in accordance with the agreed terms of trade.

Financial and non-financial objectives

3.2 Non-financial objectives do not negate financial objectives, but they do suggest that the simple theory of company finance, that the objective of a firm is to maximise the wealth of ordinary shareholders, is too simplistic. Financial objectives may have to be compromised in order to satisfy non-financial objectives.

4 STAKEHOLDERS IN A COMPANY

Stakeholders and constituents

KEY TERM

There is a variety of different groups or individuals whose interests are directly affected by the activities of a firm. These groups or individuals are referred to as **stakeholders** in the firms.

4.1 Sharplin (*Strategic management*) has listed the various stakeholder groups in a firm as follows.

Stakeholder groups	
• Common shareholders	• Competitors
• Preferred shareholders	• Neighbours
• Trade creditors	• The immediate community
• Holders of unsecured debt securities	• The national society
• Holders of secured debt securities	• The world society
• Intermediate (business) customers	• Corporate management
• Final (consumer) customers	• Organisational strategists
• Suppliers	• The chief executive
• Employees	• The board of directors
• Past employees	• Government
• Retirees	• Special interest groups

4.2 Stakeholder groups can exert influence on strategy. The greater the power of the stakeholder, the greater his influence will be. Johnson and Scholes separate power groups into **internal coalitions** and **external stakeholder groups**. Internal coalitions will include the marketing department, the finance department, the manufacturing department, the chairman and the board of directors.

4.3 Each internal coalition or external stakeholder will have different expectations about what it wants, and the expectations of the various groups will conflict. Each group, however, will influence strategic decision making.

4.4 As just one example, the Ferranti scandal in 1989 brought to the public attention the disagreement a few years earlier between the chairman of Ferranti and some of the company's major institutional shareholders, who opposed (unsuccessfully) the company's strategy to take over ISC, the secretive US defence equipment manufacturer. When details of a fraud within ISC eventually emerged, the institutional shareholders were accused in the press of having failed to use their influence more powerfully to prevent the takeover in the first place.

4.5 Many managers acknowledge that the interests of some stakeholder groups - eg themselves and employees - should be recognised and provided for, even if this means that the interests of shareholders might be adversely affected. Not all stakeholder group interests can be given specific attention in the decisions of management, but those stakeholders for whom management recognises and accepts a responsibility are referred to as **constituents** of the firm.

4.6 Sharplin commented as follows.

> There can be no debate about whether corporations should acknowledge and respond to the interest of every stakeholder to the extent that the interests are embodied in law or enforced by market forces ... The debate is ongoing, however, about whether the plural stakeholders should be served as legitimate claimants in their own right rather than simply as a way of serving the primary corporate constituency, the common shareholder.

Shareholders and management

4.7 Although ordinary shareholders (equity shareholders) are the owners of the company to whom the board of directors are accountable, the actual powers of shareholders tend to be restricted, except in companies where the shareholders are also the directors.

4.8 The day-to-day running of a company is the responsibility of the management, and although the company's results are submitted for shareholders' approval at the annual general meeting (AGM), there is often apathy and acquiescence in directors' recommendations. AGMs are often very poorly attended.

4.9 Shareholders are often ignorant about their company's current situation and future prospects. They have no right to inspect the books of account, and their forecasts of future prospects are gleaned from the annual report and accounts, stockbrokers, investment journals and daily newspapers.

4.10 The relationship between management and shareholders is sometimes referred to as an **agency relationship**, in which managers act as agents for the shareholders.

KEY TERM

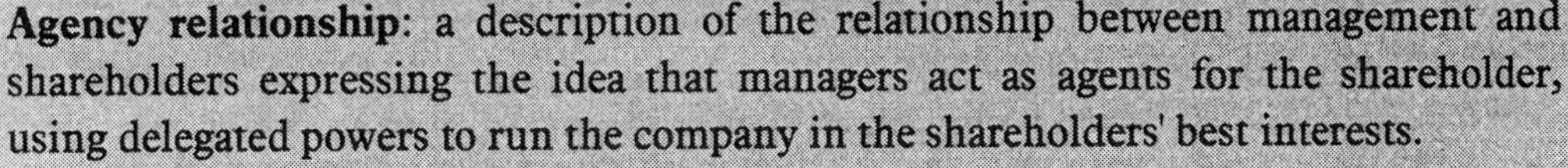

Agency relationship: a description of the relationship between management and shareholders expressing the idea that managers act as agents for the shareholder, using delegated powers to run the company in the shareholders' best interests.

4.11 However, if managers hold none or very few of the equity shares of the company they work for, what is to stop them from:

(a) working inefficiently?
(b) not bothering to look for profitable new investment opportunities?
(c) giving themselves high salaries and perks?

4.12 One power that shareholders possess is the right to remove the directors from office. But shareholders have to take the initiative to do this, and in many companies, the shareholders lack the energy and organisation to take such a step. Even so, directors will want the company's report and accounts, and the proposed final dividend, to meet with shareholders' approval at the AGM.

4.13 For management below director level, it is the responsibility of the directors to ensure that they perform well. Getting the best out of subordinates is one of the functions of management, and directors should be expected to do it as well as they can.

4.14 Another reason why managers might do their best to improve the financial performance of their company is that managers' pay is often related to the size or profitability of the company. Managers in very big companies, or in very profitable companies, will normally expect to earn higher salaries than managers in smaller or less successful companies. There is also an argument for giving managers some profit-related pay, or providing incentives which are related to profits or share price.

Why should managers bother to know who their shareholders are?

4.15 A company's senior management should remain aware of who its major shareholders are, and it will often help to retain shareholders' support if the chairman or the managing director meets occasionally with the major shareholders, to exchange views.

4.16 Advantages of knowing who the company's shareholders are as follows.

(a) The company's management might learn about shareholders' preferences for either high dividends or high retained earnings for profit growth and capital gain.

(b) For public companies, changes in shareholdings might help to explain recent share price movements.

(c) The company's management should be able to learn about shareholders' attitudes to both risk and gearing. If a company is planning a new investment, its management might have to consider the relative merits of seeking equity finance or debt finance, and shareholders' attitudes would be worth knowing about before the decision is taken.

(d) Management might need to know its shareholders in the event of an unwelcome takeover bid from another company, in order to identify key shareholders whose views on the takeover bid might be crucial to the final outcome.

4.17 The advantages of having a wide range of shareholders include the following.

(a) There is likely to be greater activity in the market in the firm's shares.

(b) There is less likelihood of one shareholder having a controlling interest.

(c) Since shareholdings are smaller on average, there is likely to be less effect on the share price if one shareholder sells his holding.

(d) There is a greater likelihood of a takeover bid being frustrated.

Disadvantages of a large number of shareholders include the following.

(a) Administrative costs will be high. These include the costs of sending out copies of the annual report and accounts, counting proxy votes, registering new shareholders and paying dividends.

(b) Shareholders will have differing tax positions and objectives in holding the firm's shares, which makes a dividend/retention policy more difficult for the management to decide upon.

Shareholders, managers and the company's long-term creditors

4.18 The relationship between long-term creditors of a company, the management and the shareholders of a company encompasses the following factors.

(a) Management may decide to raise finance for a company by taking out long-term or medium-term loans. They might well be taking risky investment decisions using outsiders' money to finance them.

(b) Investors who provide debt finance will rely on the company's management to generate enough net cash inflows to make interest payments on time, and eventually to repay loans.

However, long-term creditors will often take security for their loan, perhaps in the form of a fixed charge over an asset (such as a mortgage on a building). Debentures are also often subject to certain restrictive covenants, which restrict the company's rights to borrow more money until the debentures have been repaid.

If a company is unable to pay what it owes its creditors, the creditors may decide:

(i) to exercise their security; or
(ii) to apply for the company to be wound up.

(c) The money that is provided by long-term creditors will be invested to earn profits, and the profits (in excess of what is needed to pay interest on the borrowing) will provide extra dividends or retained profits for the shareholders of the company. In other words, shareholders will expect to increase their wealth using creditors' money.

Shareholders, managers and government

4.19 The government does not have a direct interest in companies (except for those in which it actually holds shares). However, the government does often have a strong indirect interest in companies' affairs.

(a) **Taxation.** The government raises taxes on sales and profits and on shareholders' dividends. It also expects companies to act as tax collectors for income tax and VAT. The tax structure might influence investors' preferences for either dividends or capital growth.

(b) Encouraging **new investments.** The government might provide funds towards the cost of some investment projects. It might also encourage private investment by offering tax incentives.

(c) Encouraging **a wider spread of share ownership.** In the UK, the government has made some attempts to encourage more private individuals to become company shareholders, by means of attractive privatisation issues (such as in the electricity, gas and telecommunications industries) and tax incentives, such as PEPs (personal equity plans) to encourage individuals to invest in shares.

(d) **Legislation.** The government also influences companies, and the relationships between shareholders, creditors, management, employees and the general public, through legislation, including the Companies Acts, legislation on employment, health and safety regulations, legislation on consumer protection and consumer rights and environmental legislation.

(e) **Economic policy.** A government's economic policy will affect business activity. For example, exchange rate policy will have implications for the revenues of exporting firms and for the purchase costs of importing firms. Policies on economic growth, inflation, employment, interest rates and so on are all relevant to business activities.

5 BODIES WHICH ARE NOT PURELY COMMERCIAL

Nationalised industries

5.1 The framework of financial management in **nationalised industries** consists of:

(a) strategic objectives;
(b) rules about investment plans and their appraisal;
(c) corporate plans, targets and aims;
(d) external financing limits.

Following the privatisation programme of the 1980s and early 1990s, the UK's nationalised industries are much fewer in number than they were. The largest nationalised industries remaining is the Post Office. London Transport is another.

Strategic objectives for the nationalised industries

5.2 Nationalised industries are financed by government loans, and some borrowing from the capital markets. They do not have equity capital, and there is no stock exchange to give a day-by-day valuation of the business.

5.3 The financial objective cannot be to maximise the wealth of its owners, the government or the general public, because this is not a concept which can be applied in practice. Nevertheless, there will be a financial objective, to contribute in a certain way to the national economy. This objective may be varied according to the political views of the government.

(a) There may be an objective to earn enough profits for the industry to provide for a certain proportion of its investment needs from its own resources.

(b) A very profitable industry may be expected to lend surplus funds to the government.

5.4 Even so, the principal objective of a nationalised industry will in most cases not be a financial one at all. The financial objectives will therefore be subordinated to a number of political and social considerations.

(a) A nationalised industry may be expected to provide a certain **standard of service** to all customers, regardless of the fact that some individuals will receive a service at a charge well below its cost. For example, the postal service must deliver letters to remote locations for the price of an ordinary first or second class stamp.

(b) The need to provide a service may be of such overriding social and political importance that the government is prepared to **subsidise** the industry. There is a strong body of opinion, for example, which argues that public transport is a social necessity and a certain level of service must be provided, with losses made up by government subsidies.

Investment plans and investment appraisal in nationalised industries

5.5 Nationalised industries in the UK have generally been expected to aim at a **rate of return** (before interest and tax) on their new investment programmes of 5% in real terms. This is required so that the industries do not divert resources away from those areas where they could be used to best effect.

Corporate plans, targets and aims for nationalised industries

5.6 Each nationalised industry has **financial targets** and a series of **performance aims**. These targets and performance aims are set for a period of three to five years ahead, and may be included within a broader corporate plan.

5.7 Financial targets vary from industry to industry, depending on how profitable or unprofitable it is expected to be. For profitable industries, the financial target has so far been set in terms of achieving a target rate of return. The return is measured as a current cost operating profit on the net replacement cost of assets employed.

5.8 Performance aims are intended to back up the financial targets, and may be expressed in terms of target cost reductions or efficiency improvements. Achieving cost reduction through efficiency improvements has been a prime target of nationalised industries in the UK in recent years. The Post Office, for example, has in the past had a target to reduce real unit costs in its mail business and in its counters business.

External financing limits (EFLs) for nationalised industries

5.9 **External financing limits (EFLs)** control the flow of finance to and from nationalised industries. They set a limit on the amount of finance the industry can obtain from the government, and in the case of very profitable industries, they set requirements for the net repayment of finance to the government.

Not-for-profit organisations

5.10 Some organisations, such as **charities,** are set up with a prime objective which is not related to making profits.

5.11 These organisations exist to pursue non-financial aims, such as providing a service to the community. However, there will be financial constraints which limit what any such organisation can do.

(a) A not-for-profit organisation needs finance to pay for its operations, and the major financial constraint is the amount of funds that it can obtain.

(b) Having obtained funds, a not-for-profit organisation should seek to use the funds:

(i) economically: not spending £2 when the same thing can be bought for £1;
(ii) efficiently: getting the best use out of what money is spent on;
(iii) effectively: spending funds so as to achieve the organisation's objectives.

5.12 The nature of financial objectives in a not-for-profit organisation can be explained in more detail, using **government departments** in the UK as an illustration.

Government departments

5.13 Financial management in government departments is different from financial management in an industrial or commercial company for some fairly obvious reasons.

(a) Government departments do not operate to make a profit, and the objectives of a department or of a programme of spending cannot be expressed in terms of maximising the return on capital employed.

(b) Government services are provided without the commercial pressure of competition. There are no competitive reasons for controlling costs, being efficient or, when services are charged for (such as medical prescriptions), keeping prices down.

(c) Government departments have full-time professional civil servants as their managers, but decisions are also taken by politicians.

(d) The government gets its money for spending from taxes, other sources of income and borrowing (such as issuing gilts) and the nature of its fund-raising differs substantially from fund-raising by companies.

(i) The financial markets regard the government as a totally secure borrower, and so the government can usually borrow whatever it likes, provided it is prepared to pay a suitable rate of interest.

(ii) Central government borrowing is co-ordinated centrally by the Treasury and the Bank of England. Individual departments of government do not have to borrow funds themselves.

(iii) Local governments raise some taxes locally and can do some borrowing in the financial markets, but they also rely for some of their funds on central government.

(iv) Companies rely heavily on retained profits as a source of funds. Government departments cannot rely on any such source, because they do not make profits. Some government services must be paid for by customers, for example medical prescriptions and school meals, although the price that is charged might not cover the costs in full.

5.14 Since managing government is different from managing a company, a different framework is needed for planning and control. This is achieved by:

(a) setting objectives for each department;
(b) careful planning of public expenditure proposals;
(c) emphasis on getting value for money.

5.15 A development in recent years has been the creation of agencies to carry out specific functions (such as vehicle licensing). These **executive agencies** are answerable to the government for providing a certain level of service, but are independently managed on business principles.

6 MEASURING PERFORMANCE 6/95, 6/96, 12/96, 6/97

Measuring financial performance

6.1 As part of the system of financial control in an organisation, it will be necessary to have ways of measuring the progress of the enterprise, so that managers know how well the company is doing. A common means of doing this is through ratio analysis, which is concerned with comparing and quantifying relationships between financial variables, such as those variables found in the balance sheet and profit and loss account of the enterprise.

Exam focus point

The examiner has said, more than once, that knowledge of how to calculate and interpret key ratios is a weak point for many candidates. Make sure that it is one of your strong points. In reviewing ratio analysis below, we are in part revising material included in Paper 1 *The Accounting Framework*.

The broad categories of ratios

6.2 Ratios can be grouped into the following four categories:

- profitability and return
- debt and gearing
- liquidity: control of cash and other working capital items
- shareholders' investment ratios ('stock market ratios')

6.3 The key to obtaining meaningful information from ratio analysis is comparison: comparing ratios over a number of periods within the same business to establish whether the business is improving or declining, and comparing ratios between similar businesses to see whether the company you are analysing is better or worse than average within its own business sector.

Ratio pyramids

6.4 The Du Pont system of ratio analysis involves constructing a pyramid of interrelated ratios like that below.

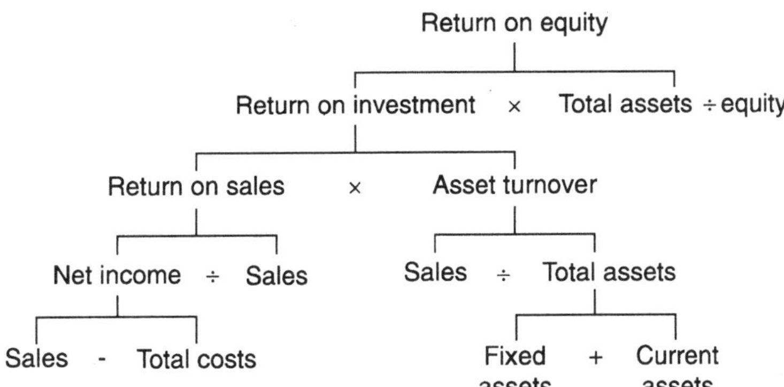

6.5 Such ratio pyramids help in providing for an overall management plan to achieve profitability, and allow the interrelationships between ratios to be checked.

Profitability

6.6 A company ought of course to be profitable if it is to maximise shareholder wealth, and obvious checks on profitability are:

(a) whether the company has made a profit or a loss on its ordinary activities;

(b) by how much this year's profit or loss is bigger or smaller than last year's profit or loss.

6.7 Profit **before** taxation is generally thought to be a better figure to use than profit after taxation, because there might be unusual variations in the tax charge from year to year which would not affect the underlying profitability of the company's operations.

6.8 Another profit figure that should be considered is **profit before interest and tax (PBIT)**. This is the amount of profit which the company earned before having to pay interest to the providers of loan capital. By providers of loan capital, we usually mean **longer term** loan capital, such as debentures and medium-term bank loans, which will be shown in the balance sheet as 'Creditors: amounts falling due after more than one year.' This figure is of particular importance to bankers and lenders.

6.9 Profit before interest and tax is therefore:

(a) the profit before taxation; *plus*
(b) interest charges on long-term loan capital.

6.10 To calculate PBIT, look at the **interest payments** in the relevant note to the accounts. Do not take the net interest figure in the profit and loss account itself, because this represents interest payments less interest received, and PBIT is profit including interest received but before interest payments.

6.11 The note to the accounts on interest charges, unfortunately, does not give us the exact figure we want, and we have to take the most suitable figure available. Company law requires companies to show the amount of interest in respect of:

(a) bank loans and bank overdrafts, and other loans which are repayable within five years;

(b) loans repayable by instalments (for example finance leases) beyond five years;

(c) all other loans (for example long term debentures).

6.12 The interest cost we want is (c) plus (b) and probably a part of (a) (for interest on loans repayable within one to five years which are 'Creditors: amounts falling due after more than one year.'). Unless a company gives clear details of its interest costs, it is probably simplest to approximate the interest for PBIT as the total of (a), (b) and (c).

Profitability and return: the return on investment (ROI)

6.13 It is impossible to assess profits or profit growth properly without relating them to the amount of funds (the capital) employed in making the profits. The most important profitability ratio is therefore **return on capital employed (ROCE),** also called **return on investment (ROI),** which states the profit as a percentage of the amount of capital employed.

6.14 Profit is usually taken as PBIT, and capital employed is shareholders' capital plus long-term liabilities and debt capital. This is the same as total assets less current liabilities. The underlying principle is that we must compare like with like, and so if capital means share capital and reserves plus long-term liabilities and debt capital, profit must mean the profit earned by all this capital together. This is PBIT, since interest is the return for loan capital.

$$\text{Thus ROCE} = \frac{\text{Profit on ordinary activities before interest and taxation (PBIT)}}{\text{Capital employed}}$$

Capital employed = Shareholders' funds *plus* 'creditors: amounts falling due after more than one year' *plus* any long-term provisions for liabilities and charges.

Evaluating the ROCE

6.15 What does a company's ROCE tell us? What should we be looking for? There are three comparisons that can be made.

(a) The change in ROCE from one year to the next.

(b) The ROCE being earned by other companies, if this information is available.

(c) A comparison of the ROCE with current market borrowing rates.

(i) What would be the cost of extra borrowing to the company if it needed more loans, and is it earning a ROCE that suggests it could make high enough profits to make such borrowing worthwhile?

(ii) Is the company making a ROCE which suggests that it is making profitable use of its current borrowing?

6.16 However, it is possible that a company's ROCE is artificially high. This is because a company's fixed assets, especially property, might be undervalued in its balance sheet, and if they are, the company would be undervaluing its capital employed. This in turn would make its ROCE higher. For example, a profit of £10,000 on capital employed of

£100,000 gives a ROCE of 10%, but if capital employed is valued lower, say at £80,000, the ROCE would be 12½% for the same profit figure. What this means is that if a company's ROCE is, say, 20% you cannot assume that this is a good performance without first deciding whether the result has been due to good profits or whether it has been due to an undervaluation of capital employed.

6.17 If a company had earned a ROCE not of 20% but of, say, only 6%, then its return would have been below current borrowing rates and so disappointingly low.

Secondary ratios

6.18 We may analyse the ROCE by looking at the kinds of interrelationships between ratios used in ratio pyramids, which we mentioned earlier. We can thus find out why the ROCE is high or low, or better or worse than last year.

Profit margin and asset turnover together explain the ROCE, and if the ROCE is the primary profitability ratio, these other two are the secondary ratios. The relationship between the three ratios is as follows.

Profit margin × asset turnover = ROCE

$$\frac{\text{PBIT}}{\text{Sales}} \times \frac{\text{Sales}}{\text{Capital employed}} = \frac{\text{PBIT}}{\text{Capital employed}}$$

Changes in turnover

6.19 It is also worth commenting on the change in turnover from one year to the next. Strong sales growth will usually indicate volume growth as well as turnover increases due to price rises, and volume growth is one sign of a prosperous company.

The gross profit margin, the net profit margin and profit analysis

6.20 Depending on the format of the profit and loss account, you may be able to calculate the gross profit margin as well as the net profit margin. Looking at the two together can be quite informative.

6.21 EXAMPLE: PROFIT MARGINS

A company has the following summarised profit and loss accounts for two consecutive years.

	Year 1	*Year 2*
	£	£
Turnover	70,000	100,000
Less cost of sales	42,000	55,000
Gross profit	28,000	45,000
Less expenses	21,000	35,000
Net profit	7,000	10,000

Although the net profit margin is the same for both years at 10%, the gross profit margin is not.

In year 1 it is: $\frac{28,000}{70,000} = 40\%$

and in year 2 it is: $\frac{45,000}{100,000} = 45\%$

6.22 Is this good or bad for the business? An increased profit margin must be good because this indicates a wider gap between selling price and cost of sales. However, given that the net profit ratio has stayed the same in the second year, expenses must be rising. In year 1 expenses were 30% of turnover, whereas in year 2 they were 35% of turnover. This indicates that administration or selling and distribution expenses require tight control.

6.23 A percentage analysis of profit between year 1 and year 2 is as follows.

	Year 1	*Year 2*
	%	%
Cost of sales as a % of sales	60	55
Gross profit as a % of sales	40	45
	100	100
Expenses as a % of sales	30	35
Net profit as a % of sales	10	10
Gross profit as a % of sales	40	45

Debt and gearing ratios

6.24 Debt ratios are concerned with how much the company owes in relation to its size and whether it is getting into heavier debt or improving its situation.

(a) When a company is heavily in debt, and seems to be getting even more heavily into debt, the thought that should occur to you is that this cannot continue. If the company carries on wanting to borrow more, banks and other would-be lenders are very soon likely to refuse further borrowing and the company might well find itself in trouble.

(b) When a company is earning only a modest profit before interest and tax, and has a heavy debt burden, there will be very little profit left over for shareholders after the interest charges have been paid. And so if interest rates were to go up or the company were to borrow even more, it might soon be incurring interest charges in excess of PBIT. This might eventually lead to the liquidation of the company.

6.25 These are the two main reasons why companies should keep their debt burden under control. Three ratios that are particularly worth looking at are the debt ratio, the gearing ratio and the interest cover.

The debt ratio

6.26 The **debt ratio** is the ratio of a company's total debts to its total assets.

(a) Assets consist of fixed assets at their balance sheet value, plus current assets.

(b) Debts consist of all creditors, whether amounts falling due within one year or after more than one year.

6.27 You can ignore long-term provisions and liabilities, such as deferred taxation.

6.28 Gearing measures the relationships between shareholders' capital plus reserves, and either prior charge capital or borrowings or both.

6.29 **Prior charge capital** is capital which has:

(a) a right to payment of interest or preference dividend before there can be any earnings for ordinary shareholders.

(b) a prior claim on the company's assets in the event of a winding up.

6.30 Although there is no single definition of prior charge capital, it is usual to regard it as consisting of:

(a) any preference share capital;

(b) interest-bearing long-term capital:

(c) interest-bearing short-term debt capital with less than 12 months to maturity, including any bank overdraft.

However, (c) might be excluded.

6.31 Commonly used measures of gearing are based on the balance sheet values of the fixed interest and equity capital. They include:

$$\frac{\text{Prior charge capital}}{\text{Equity capital (including reserves)}}$$

and

$$\frac{\text{Prior charge capital}}{\text{Total capital employed}\star}$$

⋆ This can either include or exclude minority interests, deferred tax and deferred income: balance sheet items which are neither equity nor prior charge capital.

The gearing ratio

6.32 Capital gearing is concerned with a company's *long-term* capital structure, and this is discussed further in Chapter 24.

6.33 As with the debt ratio, there is no absolute limit to what a **gearing ratio** ought to be. Many companies are highly geared, but if a highly geared company is increasing its gearing, it is likely to have difficulty in the future when it wants to borrow even more, unless it can also boost its shareholders' capital, either with retained profits or with a new share issue.

Interest cover

6.34 The **interest cover** ratio shows whether a company is earning enough profits before interest and tax to pay its interest costs comfortably, or whether its interest costs are high in relation to the size of its profits, so that a fall in PBIT would then have a significant effect on profits available for ordinary shareholders.

6.35 Interest cover equals $\frac{\text{Profit before interest and tax}}{\text{Interest charges}}$

6.36 Interest payments should be taken gross, from the note to the accounts, and not net of interest receipts, as shown in the profit and loss account.

6.37 An interest cover of 2 times or less would be low, and it should really exceed 3 times before the company's interest costs can be considered to be within acceptable limits.

Liquidity ratios: cash and working capital

6.38 Profitability is of course an important aspect of a company's performance, and debt or gearing is another. Neither, however, addresses directly the key issue of **liquidity**. A company needs liquid assets so that it can meet its debts when they fall due. The main liquidity ratios will be described in Chapter 20.

Shareholders' investment ratios

6.39 A further set of ratios of importance to the financial manager are the ratios which help equity shareholders and other investors to assess the value and quality of an investment in the ordinary shares of a company. These ratios will be described in Chapter 22.

The main stock market ratios are:

- the dividend yield;
- earnings per share;
- the price/earnings (P/E) ratio;
- the dividend cover;
- the earnings yield.

6.40 EXAMPLE: RATIO ANALYSIS

Your company is considering diversifying its activities by investing in a company engaged in computer services, notably software development and implementation. The United Kingdom market for such services is said to be growing at about 20% per annum. The business is seasonal, peaking between September and March.

Your attention has been drawn to two possible companies, X plc and Y plc, both of which have recently joined the Alternative Investment Market (AIM) by way of placings.

An analyst has prepared for you the comparative data shown in the Appendix to this question.

You are required, in the light of this information:

(a) to compare the performance of the two companies;
(b) to give your reasons for selecting one of them as the company in which to invest.

It may be assumed that the difference in size of the two companies does not invalidate a comparison of the ratios provided.

Appendix

Ratio analysis

		X plc			*Y plc*		
		19X9	*19X8*	*19X7*	*19X9*	*19X8*	*19X7*
Return on operating capital employed	%	134	142	47	38	40	52
Operating profit: Sales	%	17	16	6	10	8	5
Sales: Operating capital employed	×	8	9	8	4	5	10
Percentages to sales value:							
Cost of sales	%	65	67	71	49	49	51
Selling & distribution costs	%	12	11	15	15	16	19
Administration expenses	%	6	6	8	26	27	25
Number of employees		123	127	88	123	114	91
Sales per employee	£'000	40	37	31	58	52	47
Average remuneration per employee	£'000	13	13	12	16	14	13
Tangible fixed assets							
Turnover rate	×	20	21	14	9	11	14
Additions, at cost	%	57	47	58	303	9	124
Percentage depreciated	%	45	36	20	41	60	72
Product development costs carried forward as a percentage of turnover	%	-	-	-	10	8	6
Debtors : Sales	%	18	18	22	61	41	39
Stocks : Sales	%	0	1	0	2	2	1
Cash : Sales	%	7	9	2	1	1	0
Trade creditors : Sales	%	2	2	3	32	21	24
Trade creditors : Debtors	%	11	14	15	53	50	62
Current ratio (:1)		1.5	1.3	1.2	1.1	1.1	0.9
Liquid ratio (:1)		1.5	1.3	1.2	1.0	1.0	0.9
Liquid ratio excluding bank overdraft		-	-	-	1.4	1.5	1.2
Total debt : Total assets	%	61	71	109	75	72	84
Prior-charge capital:							
Equity	%	10	46	480	81	75	132
Interest cover	×	18	13	3	6	12	5
Earnings per share	pence	4.5	2.9	0.4	13.2	8.6	4.2
Dividend cover	×	13.3	10.2	56.0	15.1	7.3	4.5

	X plc	*Y plc*
Date of formation	5 years ago, as the result of a management buyout	10 years ago
Current market price of ordinary shares	£1.15	£1.45
Financial year-end	30 June	30 September
Turnover in most recent year (£'000)		
Home	2,856	6,080
Export	2,080	1,084
Total	4,936	7,164
Index of turnover 19X9 (19X6 = 100)		
Home	190%	235%
Export	220%	150%
Total	200%	220%
Operating profit 19X9 (£'000)	840	720
Operating capital employed 19X9 (£'000)	625	1,895

Data in this Appendix should be accepted as correct. Any apparent internal inconsistencies are due to rounding of the figures.

6.41 SOLUTION

(a) *Comparison of performance*

X plc is the more profitable company, both in absolute terms and in proportion to sales and to operating capital employed. This may indicate that X plc is much better managed than Y plc, but this is not the only possibility, and a study of the other data shows that Y plc's profitability, while at present lower, may be more sustainable.

A higher percentage of Y's sales are to the home market, while it has still achieved fairly substantial export sales. This suggests that Y could have done better in exploiting the export market, but also that Y is less exposed than X to exchange rate fluctuations and the possible imposition of trade barriers. The prospects for the home market appear good, and should give scope for adequate growth. Y has achieved higher growth in total turnover than X over the past three years.

While Y appears to be making worse use of its assets than X, with asset turnover ratios lower than X's and falling, this seems to be largely because Y has recently acquired substantial new assets. It may be that within the next few years X will have to undertake a major renewals programme, with consequent adverse effects on its asset turnover ratios. While X may be making better use of its assets (subject to the reservations set out above), Y is making sales per employee about 50% higher than X, and has consistently done so over the past three years. In favour of X, it could be pointed out that Y has been established twice as long as X; on the other hand, X shows no sign of catching up, despite the fact that its total number of employees has recently fallen slightly. The modest rises in sales per employee over the past three years in both X and Y may be due largely to inflation.

Y seems to be significantly better than X at controlling cost of sales (49% of sales in Y, and 65% in X), though X has made improvements over the past three years while there has been little change in Y. On the other hand, X's administration expenses have been only 6% of sales, while Y's have been 26% of sales. This contrast between the two types of cost suggests that different categorisations of costs may have been used. If we combine cost of sales and administration, then for X they total 71% of sales and for Y they total 75% of sales.

There is thus little difference between the companies, though X has shown improved cost control while Y has not. X has also had lower selling and distribution costs. One must however bear in mind that X will have had a lower depreciation element in its costs than Y, because Y has recently invested substantially in fixed assets. Y's costs will also be increased by its higher salaries, which may pay off in better employee motivation and hence higher sales per employee. On the other hand, Y's costs have been kept down by the carrying forward of an increasing amount of product development costs, an accounting policy which may well be regarded as imprudent.

In working capital management, X has the edge. Y has very high debtors, and these have recently risen sharply as a proportion of turnover. Y also carries rather more stock than X, and has very little cash. While both companies have tolerable current and liquid ratios, X's are certainly safer. Y achieves a liquid ratio of 1:1 almost entirely by relying on debtors. If it suffers substantial bad debts, or if the bank should become concerned and call in the overdraft, Y could suffer serious liquidity problems. It also depends heavily on trade credit to finance debtors. While it is sensible to take advantage of trade credit offered, Y may depend too much on the continued goodwill of its suppliers. This, and Y's deteriorating (though still adequate) interest cover may indicate the need for a fresh injection of equity.

X's interest cover has risen sharply, as its debt has fallen. Presumably the substantial borrowings needed for a management buyout are now being repaid. Returns to equity, measured by earnings per share, have increased significantly in both companies, though much faster in X than in Y. Dividend cover has shown good growth in Y, paralleling that in earnings per share and showing that dividends have hardly changed, perhaps because of liquidity problems. After paying virtually no dividend in 19X7, X seems to be settling down to a dividend policy appropriate to a company which is no longer new. The ample dividend cover leaves plenty of room to improve dividends when retention of most of the profits is no longer necessary.

(b) *The choice of company*

X is recommended, for the following reasons.

(i) Its liquidity position is far safer than Y's.

(ii) It appears to have greater potential for growth, so long as the high motivation of the management and staff following the management buyout can be sustained. However, substantial funds may need to be invested for little short term return, while the company develops.

(iii) Y's management appear to have lost interest in efficient working capital control and cost control, and the company may be losing its way.

(iv) X has come to the AIM after five years, while Y took ten years to reach that stage. This suggests that X has investors' confidence, so further capital should be readily obtainable if it is needed.

Environmental reporting

6.42 As well as tracking financial performance, managers of organisations need to understand the impact of the operations of the organisation on the environment. This is important not just because of external pressures, but also so that organisations can gain from opportunities and avoid necessary penalties or costs. It has been argued that environmental reports should become a part of the regular process of financial reporting. Norsk Hydro was a pioneer in this field when it produced an environmental report in 1990.

6.43 Environmental reporting has become fairly widespread, with the majority of large UK companies now mentioning the environment in their annual report and accounts. In other countries, Dow Chemicals, Danish Steelworks, Kunert and BSO Origin are among those that have experimented with green reporting. Many companies include statements of environmental policy in their annual reports. A smaller number include quantified indicators of environmental performance. For example, ICI plc includes statements reporting progress against targets, one of which relates to the reduction of hazardous wastes. However, environmental reporting is relatively rare among smaller companies. There has also been evidence since the mid-1990s that the amount of environmental reporting to shareholders has begun to show a downward trend.

6.44 The development of environmental reporting occurred in a period of increasing regulatory requirements in the UK and in the rest of the EU to report more specific data on environmental matters. Over the same period, many large companies sought ways of promoting their corporate image as well as their individual products: provided the data presents the company's efforts in a positive light, reporting of environmental data should help to enhance people's perception of a company's qualities.

7 PERFORMANCE MEASUREMENT IN THE PUBLIC SECTOR

7.1 In public sector organisations, an increasing volume of information on performance and 'value for money' is produced for internal and external use. The ways in which performance can be measured depends very much upon which organisation is involved.

(a) The first question which would need to be asked is 'what are the aims and objectives of the organisation?' For example, the objective of Companies House is to maintain and make available records of company reports.

(b) The next question to ask is 'How can we tell if the organisation is meeting the objectives?' Quantified information - ie information in the form of numbers - will be useful, and this will consist mainly of output and performance measures and indicators. For these, targets can be set. Any individual organisational unit should have no more than a handful of key targets.

7.2 Individual targets are likely to fall under the following broad headings.

- Financial performance targets
- Volume of output targets
- Quality of service targets
- Efficiency targets

Performance measurement in central government

7.3 Over recent years, much of the work of central government has been reorganised into semi-autonomous **executive agencies**, which we mentioned earlier in the Chapter.

7.4 The following are examples of targets related to **financial performance** in executive agencies.

(a) Full cost recovery (Civil Service College, Central Office of Information and others), plus unit cost targets.

(b) Commercial revenue to offset costs (Met Office).

(c) Non-Exchequer income as a percentage of total income (National Engineering Laboratory).

7.5 Targets related to **output** can be difficult to set. While the output of the Vehicle Inspectorate can be measured on the number of tests performed, and the output of the Hydrographic Office consists of charts for navigators, in many other cases the output of executive agencies is less tangible. For example, the Historic Royal Palaces Agency not only deals with visitors, whose numbers can be counted, but is also responsible for maintaining the fabric of royal palaces - an output which is more difficult to measure. In such cases, performance will be best measured by appraising the progress of the project as a whole.

7.6 Example of **quality** targets set for executive agencies include the following.

(a) **Timeliness**

(i) time to handle applications (Passport Agency, Vehicle Certification Agency and many others);

(ii) car driving tests to be reduced to 6 weeks nationally and 10 weeks in London (Driving Standards Agency);

(iii) all cheques to be banked within 35 hours (Accounts Services Agency).

(b) **Quality of product**

(i) number of print orders delivered without fault (HMSO);

(ii) error rate in the value of benefit payments (Employment Service);

(iii) 95% business complaints handled within 5 days (Radio Communications Agency);

(iv) 85% overall customer satisfaction rating (Recruitment and Assessment Services Agency);

(v) meetings of creditors held within 12 weeks in 90% of cases (Insolvency Service).

7.7 Efficiency improvements may come through reducing the cost of inputs without reducing the quality of outputs. Alternatively, areas of activity affecting total costs may be reduced. Targets related to **efficiency** include the following.

(a) Percentage reduction in price paid for purchases of stationery and paper (HMSO).

(b) Reduction in the ratio of cost of support services to total cost (Laboratory of the Government Chemist).

(c) 8.7% efficiency increase in the use of accommodation (Recruitment and Assessment Services Agency).

Performance measurement in local government

7.8 The performance measures chosen by local authorities usually consist of comparative statistics and unit costs. These measures do two things.

(a) They give details, statistics and unit costs of an authority's own activities.

(b) They show statistical and cost comparisons with other authorities or clusters of authorities.

7.9 Reporting on comparative statistics was recommended by the Department of the Environment in its code of practice *Local authority annual reports* (1982).

7.10 The following list illustrates the types of comparative statistics suggested in the code of practice.

Performance measures in local government	
For the authority's total expenditure and for each function	Net cost per 1,000 population Manpower per 1,000 population
Primary education, secondary education	Pupil/teacher ratio Cost per pupil
School meals	Revenue/cost ratio Pupils receiving free meals as a proportion of school roll
Children in care	As a proportion of total under-18 population Cost per child in care
Care of elderly	Residents of council homes as a proportion of total over-75 population Cost per resident week
Home helps	Contract hours per 1,000 population over 65

Police	Population per police officer Serious offences per 1,000 population
Fire	Proportion of area at high risk
Public transport	Passenger journeys per week per 1,000 population
Highways	Maintenance cost per kilometre
Housing	Rents as a proportion of total cost Management cost per dwelling per week Rent arrears as a percentage of year's rent income Construction cost per dwelling completed
Trading services	Revenue/gross cost ratio

Chapter roundup

- Financial management decisions cover the following aspects
  - **Investment** decisions
  - **Financing** decisions
  - **Dividend** decisions
- We have discussed the **objectives** of companies and other bodies, considering alternative models for such objectives and examining the importance of relationships between **stakeholders**.
- The usual assumption in financial management for the private sector is that the objective of the company is to **maximise shareholders' wealth**
- **Performance measurement** is a part of the system of financial control of an enterprise as well as being important to investors.

Quick quiz

1. What is financial management and with what types of decisions is it concerned? (see paras 1.1, 1.2, 1.5 - 1.9)
2. What is assumed to be the objective of a company in the theory of company finance? (2.8)
3. What are the main factors which contribute to an increase in a company's equity share price? (2.14, 2.15)
4. How are a company's financial objectives usually expressed? (2.15) What subsidiary financial targets might a company try to achieve? (2.18)
5. What non-financial objectives might a company have? (3.1)
6. What are the main problems in the relationship between shareholders and management? (4.11)
7. What are the main elements in the relationship between a company and its long-term creditors? (4.18)
8. What might be the principal objective of a nationalised industry? (5.3, 5.4)
9. In what ways does financial management in government differ from financial management in a large public company? (5.13)
10. Define return on capital employed. (6.14)
11. What is the debt ratio? (6.26)
12. Give examples of targets related to financial performance which might be used by an executive agency. (7.4)
13. What is a 'Z score'? (8.3)

Question to try	Level	Marks	Time
15	Introductory	n/a	20 mins

Chapter 15

THE MONEY AND CAPITAL MARKETS

Introduction

Having discussed the scope of financial management and the objectives of firms and other organisations in Chapter 14, we now introduce the **markets** and **institutions** through which the financing of a business takes place. We also look at some theoretical aspects of how this framework operates including the **efficient market hypothesis**, which tries to account for why share prices behave as they do.

1 FINANCIAL INTERMEDIATION AND CREDIT CREATION 6/95, 12/95

1.1 The term **financial intermediation** defines a key role in the financial system.

> 'The financial system is a complex network embracing payments mechanisms and the borrowing and lending of funds. Though they also have other important functions, the key role played by the financial institutions in the system .... is to act as financial intermediaries channelling funds from those with income in excess of their needs to those wishing to borrow' *(The Report of the Wilson Committee).*

1.2 An intermediary is a go-between, and as the above quotation implies, a **financial intermediary** is an institution which links lenders with borrowers, by obtaining deposits from lenders and then re-lending them to borrowers.

1.3 The basic process of financial intermediation can be shown by simple diagrams.

(a) If no financial intermediation takes place, lending and borrowing will be direct.

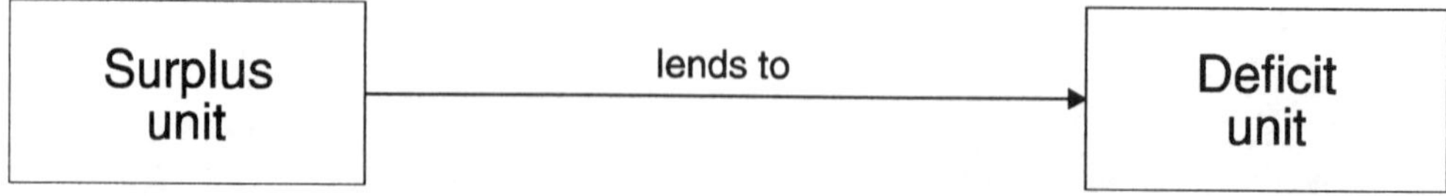

(b) If financial intermediation does take place, the situation will be as follows.

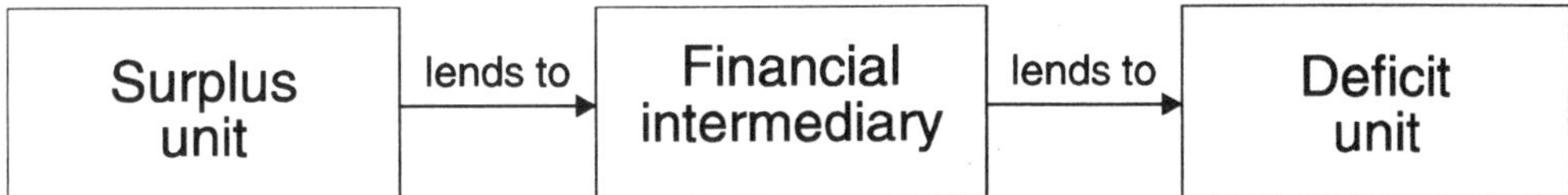

For example, a person (surplus unit) might deposit savings with a bank and the bank (as financial intermediary) might use its collective deposits of savings to provide a loan to a company (deficit unit).

KEY TERM

Financial intermediary: a party bringing together providers and users of finance, either as broker or as principal.

1.4 Not all intermediation takes place between savers and investors. Some institutions (such as the discount houses which intermediate between the Bank of England and the commercial banks) act mainly as intermediaries between other institutions. Almost all place part of their funds with other institutions, and a number (including finance houses, leasing companies and factoring companies) obtain most of their funds by borrowing from other institutions.

1.5 Financial intermediaries may also lend abroad or borrow from abroad. The resulting flows of funds within the economy can be illustrated as below.

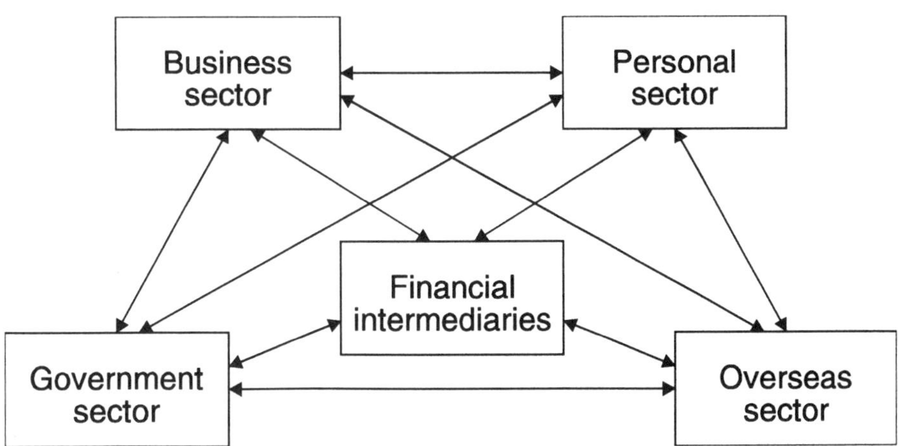

Flow of funds in an economy, including financial intermediation

Exam focus point

Bear in mind that *financial markets* and *institutions* are topic areas on which the examiner is not expected to set full question. These topics could, however, be examined in subsections of a question.

1.6 In the UK, financial intermediaries include the commercial banks, finance houses, building societies, the government's National Savings department and institutional investors such as pension funds and investment trusts.

The benefits of financial intermediation

1.7 If financial intermediation did not exist, a person or organisation with money to lend:

(a) would have to bear the risk that the borrower would fail to repay the money lent;

(b) would have to go to the considerable trouble of finding a borrower who appeared trustworthy, would be willing to pay a rate of interest the lender would expect to receive, and who would be prepared to borrow money in the quantities the lender had available;

(c) might want to retain some liquidity, (ie convert his investment back into money at short notice) whereas a borrower might be most reluctant to agree to a loan whose terms provided for its repayment at any time chosen by the lender!

(d) might not have enough to lend to satisfy the financing needs of the borrower.

1.8 Without financial intermediation, a borrower wanting money:

(a) might find it difficult to locate people or firms with money to lend. In other words, the money to borrow might not be readily available;

(b) might find that the lender wants to terminate the loan at an inconvenient time, before the borrower can really afford to repay the money.

1.9 Financial intermediaries overcome these problems for both the lender and the borrower.

(a) They provide obvious and **convenient** ways in which a lender can save money. Instead of having to find a suitable borrower for his money, the lender can deposit his money with a bank, building society, pension fund, investment trust company, National Savings scheme etc. All the lender has to do is decide for how long he might want to lend the money, and what sort of return he requires, and he can then choose a financial intermediary that offers a financial instrument to suit his requirements. They also provide a ready source of funds for borrowers. Even when money is in short supply, a borrower will usually find a financial intermediary prepared to lend some.

(b) They can aggregate or 'package' the amounts lent by savers and lend on to borrowers in different amounts. By aggregating the deposits of hundreds of small savers, a building society is able to package up the amounts and lend on to several borrowers in the form of larger mortgages. Or a bank might take in a large deposit from a corporate lender for six months, and repackage the deposit in the form of hundreds of short-term overdrafts. Through **aggregation**, institutions can use their size to exploit **economies of scale.**

(c) **Risk** for individual lenders is reduced by **pooling**. Since financial intermediaries lend to a large number of individuals and organisations, any losses suffered through default by borrowers or capital losses are effectively pooled and borne as costs by the intermediary. Such losses are shared among lenders in general. Provided that the financial intermediary is itself financially sound, the lender would not run the risk of losing his investment. Bad debts would be borne by the financial intermediary in its re-lending operations.

(d) By pooling the funds of large numbers of people, some financial institutions are able to give investors access to **diversified portfolios** covering a varied range of different securities, such as unit trusts and investment trusts.

(e) Financial intermediaries, most importantly, provide **maturity transformation**; ie they bridge the gap between the wish of most lenders for liquidity and the desire of most borrowers for loans over longer periods. They do this by providing investors with financial instruments which are liquid enough for the investors' needs and by providing funds to borrowers in a different longer term form.

Bank deposits and the creation of money ('credit creation')

1.10 An important aspect of financial intermediation affecting the workings of the economy as a whole is that of credit creation, which occurs as follows. Banks create money when they lend because when a bank lends money, most of the money will find its way back into the banking system as new customer deposits. This means that the amount lent by the bank adds to the money supply.

1.11 Suppose, for example, that in a country with a single bank, a customer C deposits £100,000. The bank, we will assume, re-lends all these deposits to another customer D. This customer D uses the money he has borrowed to buy goods and services from firm Y. If firm Y, after receiving payment, then puts the money into its own account with the bank, the bank's deposits will have doubled.

Liabilities of the bank		*Assets of the bank*	
	£		£
Deposit of customer C	100,000	Loan to customer D	100,000
Deposit of firm Y	100,000		
	200,000		

1.12 This will enable the bank to re-lend more money (another £100,000), to bring its assets up to £200,000 and this in turn will create even more bank deposits. This cycle could go on and on, with the bank making more and more loans, and the people who are paid for goods and services bought with the loans putting all their receipts back into the bank as extra deposits. In short, 'every loan creates a deposit'.

1.13 In the case of a building society, the situation is the same if we define money to include building society deposits. If a customer places a deposit with a building society, the building society can re-lend the money as a mortgage to a house-buyer. The seller (or 'vendor') of the house will then perhaps put his money into a building society deposit, so that the money supply will have increased.

1.14 With other non-bank financial institutions, the situation is different. It is the fact that most additions to lending end up as money in someone's bank account, adding to total customer deposits with the banks, that give banks this special ability to create money - an ability now shared by building societies.

1.15 Extra bank lending (and building society lending) therefore has a dual effect.

(a) It increases the money supply.

(b) It provides credit which borrowers use to increase their amount of spending. Lending adds to spending in the economy.

KEY TERM

Credit creation is the process whereby banks and other deposit-taking and lending institutions can, on the basis of an increase in reserve assets, expand the volume of lending and deposit liabilities by more than the initial increase in reserves.

2 COMMERCIAL BANKS AS PROVIDERS OF FUNDS

2.1 An important grouping of financial intermediaries is the **commercial banks**, which include both the retail banks, which include the well known 'High Street' banks, and the wholesale banks, which offer services mainly to larger customers, including large companies. The wholesale banks include merchant banks and overseas banks.

The functions of the commercial banks

2.2 The functions of the commercial banks include the following.

(a) They provide a payments mechanism - a way in which individuals, firms and government can make payments to each other. The 'clearing system' of the clearing banks is the major payments mechanism in the UK, and it enables individuals and firms to make payments by cheque. The banks are also a source from which individuals and firms can obtain notes and coin. (Other institutions such as building societies also act as a source of notes and coin for individuals, but most building societies in their turn obtain their notes and coin from their bank.)

(b) They provide a place for individuals, firms and government to store their wealth. Banks compete with other financial institutions to attract the funds of individuals and firms.

(c) They act as providers of funds by lending money in the form of loans or overdrafts.

Bank borrowing

2.3 Borrowings from banks are an important source of finance to companies as well as to unincorporated businesses. Bank lending is still mainly short-term (including provision of an overdraft facility) although medium-term lending has grown considerably in recent years.

2.4 Short-term borrowing may be in the form of:

(a) an **overdraft**, which a company should keep within a limit set by the bank. Interest is charged (at a variable rate) on the amount by which the company is overdrawn from day to day;

(b) a short-term loan, for up to three years.

Medium-term loans are loans for a period of from three to ten years.

2.5 The rate of interest charged on medium-term bank lending to large companies will typically be a set margin above the **London Inter-Bank Offered Rate (LIBOR)**, with the size of the margin depending on the credit standing and riskiness of the borrower. A loan may have a fixed rate of interest, or a variable interest rate with the rate of interest charged being adjusted every three, six, nine or 12 months in line with movements in the LIBOR.

2.6 Lending to smaller companies will typically be at a margin above the bank's base rate and at either a variable or a fixed rate of interest. Lending on overdraft is always at a variable rate. A loan at a variable rate of interest is sometimes referred to as a **floating rate loan.**

2.7 Longer term bank loans will sometimes be available, usually for the purchase of property, where the loan takes the form of a mortgage.

Overdraft finance 12/96

2.8 Overdraft finance may carry a higher rate of interest than a medium-term loan, but for the borrower it has the major advantage of flexibility: as cash flows into the business, the overdraft will reduce and the business will only be paying for the finance it needs from day to day. A medium-term loan is, on the other hand, likely to be for a fixed amount, and there are likely to be penalties for early repayment.

2.9 Small but rapidly growing companies often have a greater proportion of their debt in the form of overdraft than larger longer established firms due to the problems of providing sufficient security to lenders. However, a term loan will often be more attractive to the borrower than an overdraft for the following reasons.

(a) Overdraft finance is generally repayable on demand. It therefore carries a higher level of financial risk than does a term loan.

(b) The bank may be uncomfortable with a growing overdraft and may seek to secure scheduled repayment or other conditions from the company. This can present a growing firm with cash flow problems.

(c) Overdraft finance is generally at a floating rate, thus exposing the company to risk from interest rate changes. Term loans can be negotiated at a fixed rate, thus reducing this element of risk and assisting with cash flow forecasting.

(d) Term loans can be negotiated over a timescale that can be related to the company's forecast need for financing, and with a repayment schedule that can be tailored to the company's requirements. For example, capital may be repaid in stages or at the end of the period.

(e) If the company has a good trading record and/or a good asset base and can therefore offer reasonable security, it may be able to negotiate a lower interest rate than would be payable on an overdraft.

3 MONEY MARKETS AND CAPITAL MARKETS

3.1 The **capital markets**, being markets for long-term capital, are distinguished from the **money markets**, which are markets for (i) trading short-term financial instruments and (ii) short-term lending and borrowing.

(a) By short-term capital, we mean capital that is lent or borrowed for a period which might range from as short as overnight up to about one year, and sometimes longer.

(b) By long-term capital, we mean capital invested or lent and borrowed for a period of five years or more.

3.2 There is a 'grey area' between long-term and short-term capital, which is lending and borrowing for a period from about a year up to about five years, which is not surprisingly sometimes referred to as medium-term capital. In the UK, the bulk of medium-term borrowing by firms is done through banks.

The money markets

3.3 The money markets are operated by the banks and other financial institutions. Although the money markets largely involve borrowing and lending by banks, some large companies and nationalised industries, as well as the government, are involved in money market operations. The building societies have also become major participants in the money markets since liberalisation of the building societies has allowed them to raise wholesale funds.

3.4 The money markets consist of the following.

(a) The **primary market**. This is a market where approved institutions buy and sell bills of exchange and other short-term financial instruments in daily trading with the **Bank of England**. The Bank of England – the **central bank** of the UK - uses this trading, known as **open market operations**, to control or influence the level of short-term interest rates.

(b) The **interbank market.** This is the 'market' in which banks lend short-term funds to one another.

(c) The **eurocurrency market.** This is the market operated by banks for lending and borrowing in foreign currencies, which we discuss later in this chapter.

(d) The **certificate of deposit market.** This is a market for trading in Certificates of Deposit, which are negotiable documents issued by banks acknowledging a deposit of money with the bank.

(e) The **local authority market**. This is a market in which local authorities borrow short term funds from banks and other investors, by issuing and selling short term 'debt instruments'.

(f) The **finance house market**. This refers to the short-term loans raised from the money markets by the finance houses.

(g) The **inter-company market.** This refers to direct short-term lending between companies, without any financial intermediary. This market is very small, and restricted to the treasury departments of large companies.

3.5 A distinction is sometimes made between the official market - formerly called the discount market ((a) above) - and all the other money markets ((b) to (g)) which are referred to collectively as the parallel markets or wholesale markets.

The capital markets

3.6 Capital markets are markets for trading in long-term finance, in the form of long-term financial instruments such as equities and debentures.

In the UK, the principal capital markets are the Stock Exchange '**main market**' (for companies with a full Stock Exchange listing) and the more loosely regulated 'second tier' **Alternative Investment Market (AIM)** (launched in 1995 to replace the Unlisted Securities Market (USM)) which is also regulated by the Stock Exchange. Apart from regulating these two markets, the Stock Exchange is also the market for dealings in government securities (gilts).

Large companies might also borrow long-term funds in a foreign currency on the eurobond market, which we consider later in this chapter.

3.7 Firms obtain long-term or medium-term capital in one of the following ways.

(a) They may raise **share capital**. Most new issues of share capital are in the form of ordinary share capital (as distinct from preference share capital) and shareholders are the owners or members of the company. Firms that issue ordinary share capital are inviting investors to take an equity stake in the business, or to increase their existing equity stake.

(b) They may raise **loan capital**. Long-term loan capital might be raised in the form of a mortgage or debenture. The lender will usually want some security for the loan, and the mortgage deed or debenture deed will specify the security. Most loans have a fixed term to maturity. Debenture stock, like shares, can be issued on the stock market and then bought and sold in 'secondhand' trading. Interest is paid on the stock and the loan is repaid when the stock reaches its maturity date.

3.8 The stock markets serve two main purposes.

(a) As **primary markets** they enable organisations to raise new finance, by issuing new shares or new debentures. In the UK, a company must have public company status (be a plc) to be allowed to raise finance from the public on a capital market.

Capital markets make it easier for companies to raise new long-term finance than if they had to raise funds privately by contacting investors individually.

(b) As **secondary markets** they enable existing investors to sell their investments, should they wish to do so. A shareholder in a 'listed' company can sell his shares whenever he wants to on the Stock Exchange. The marketability of securities is a very important feature of the capital markets, because investors are more willing to buy stocks and shares if they know that they could sell them easily, should they wish to.

Most trading of stocks and shares on the capital markets is in existing securities, rather than new issues.

3.9 These are the main functions of a stock market, but we can add two more important ones.

(a) When a company comes to the stock market for the first time, and 'floats' its shares on the market, the owners of the company can realise some of the value of their shares in cash, because they will offer a proportion of their personally-held shares for sale to new investors.

(b) When one company wants to take over another, it is common to do so by issuing shares to finance the takeover. For example, if ABC plc wants to take over XYZ plc, it might offer XYZ plc shareholders three new shares in ABC plc for every two shares held in XYZ plc. Takeovers by means of a share exchange are only feasible if the shares that are offered can be readily traded on a stock market, and so have an identifiable market value.

Question 1

Get hold of a copy of the Companies and Markets section of the weekday Financial Times, and look out for points relevant to your studies. Note the various London Money Rates in the Money Markets section, the parts covering the London Stock Exchange, and the share prices quotations on the London Share Service pages.

This may help to put some of the topics covered here into context.

Over-the-counter markets

3.10 Shares and other financial instruments are bought and sold outside the supervised and regulated official exchanges in the **'over the counter' (OTC) markets**. Regulators are reported to be increasingly concerned about the growth of OTC markets. It is feared that dealers on the OTC markets could manipulate prices on the official markets, and that some may be using the secrecy of these markets to conceal illegal insider dealing and other illicit transactions. However, shares are traded 'off the market' to reduce costs as well as to maintain secrecy.

Institutional investors

3.11 **Institutional investors** are institutions which have large amounts of funds which they want to invest, and they will invest in stocks and shares or any other assets (such as gold or works of art) which offer satisfactory returns and security. The institutional investors are now the biggest investors on the stock market but they might also invest venture capital, or lend directly to companies.

3.12 The major institutional investors in the UK are:

- pension funds
- insurance companies
- investment trusts
- unit trusts
- venture capital organisations (discussed in Chapter 22 of this Study Text)

Of these, pension funds and insurance companies have the largest amounts of funds to invest.

Pension funds as institutional investors

3.13 **Pension funds** comprise funds set aside to provide for retirement pensions. They are financed from pension contributions paid into a fund by:

(a) a company and its employees;
(b) private individuals.

3.14 Pension funds are continually receiving large amounts of money from pension contributions and as dividends and interest. They are also continually paying out money for pensions, as:

(a) lump sums;
(b) regular pension payments to beneficiaries.

3.15 Money coming in can be diverted to meet payment obligations, but there will usually be an excess of contributions coming in over pensions going out, and this excess must be invested.

3.16 A **fund manager** is the person who makes the investment decisions, buying and selling securities. Fund managers must attempt to ensure that their investments will provide enough income to meet future pension commitments. Generally speaking, most holdings are considered to be long-term. Few fund managers would expect to make a substantial profit from short-term speculation as such dealing is highly risky. Often a portion of the fund is invested in high yield securities, such as gilts which will, hopefully, give enough income to meet current commitments, and the balance is invested in growth assets such as equities or property.

Insurance companies

3.17 **Insurance companies** sell insurance policies (life assurance policies, car insurance, house insurance, pension policies and so on). They need cash to pay out for claims or other entitlements under the terms of their policies, but they will have substantial cash income to invest.

3.18 The investment strategy of insurance companies is broadly similar to the investment strategy of pension fund managers.

(a) They invest in a portfolio of company stocks and shares, government securities (gilts), direct loans and mortgages and other investments.

(b) They limit investment risks, investing most of their funds in secure companies.

(c) They deal in large blocks of stocks and shares, because the potential return from small investments is often not worth the trouble.

Investment trusts

3.19 **Investment trusts** are companies whose business is to invest in the securities of a wide range of other companies. Their portfolios may change continually, as circumstances require.

(a) Having a capital structure, similarly to any other company they pay dividends to shareholders from profits which arise from their investment income. An investment trust company with a Stock Exchange listing must have a clause in its Memorandum or Articles prohibiting the distribution as dividend of any surpluses arising from the sale of investments it holds.

(b) Most of the funds of investment trusts are invested directly through the Stock Exchange, and little money goes into unquoted shares. Normally they are only interested in larger unquoted companies but some investment trusts might be prepared to take a block of shares in a smaller unquoted company.

Unit trusts

3.20 **Unit trusts** cater for small investors who wish to spread their investment risk over a wide range of securities, but have insufficient funds to create such a portfolio by themselves. A 'unit' is a portfolio of shares or other investments managed by a unit trust company in which individual investors are invited to take a stake (sub-unit).

3.21 The unit trust is based on a trust deed. Unit holders receive their income as a proportionate share of the investment income from the securities in the unit after deducting expenses of the management company. When a unit holder wants to realise his investment, he can sell his unit. Unit prices vary in market value according to the value of the shares or other securities which make up the unit's portfolio.

Capital market participants

3.22 The various participants in the capital markets are summarised in the diagram below.

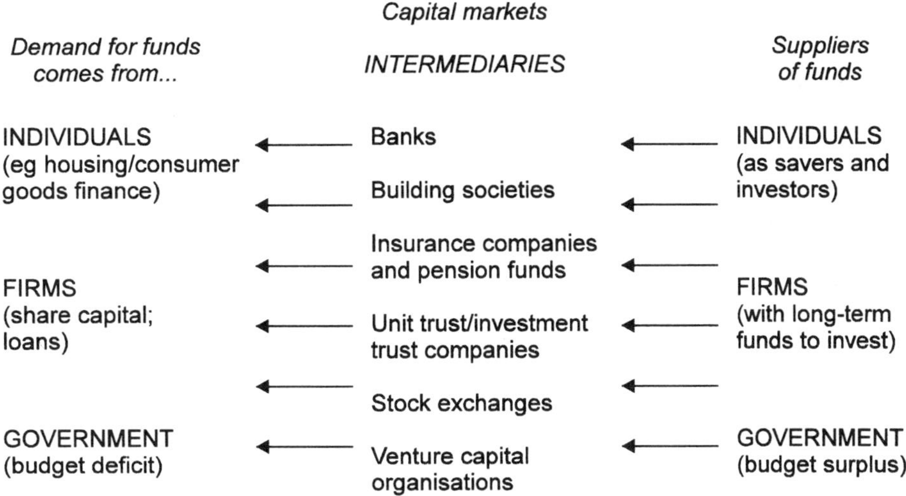

4 THE EFFICIENT MARKET HYPOTHESIS 6/94, 12/96

4.1 It has been argued that the UK and US stock markets are efficient capital markets. An 'efficient capital market' in this context is one in which:

(a) the prices of securities bought and sold reflect all the relevant information which is available to the buyers and sellers. In other words, share prices change quickly to reflect all new information about future prospects;

(b) no individual dominates the market;

(c) transaction costs of buying and selling are not so high as to discourage trading significantly.

4.2 If the stock market is efficient, share prices should vary in a rational way.

(a) If a company makes a profitable investment, shareholders will get to know about it, and the market price of its shares will rise in anticipation of future dividend increases.

(b) If a company makes a bad investment shareholders will find out and so the price of its shares will fall.

(c) If interest rates rise, shareholders will want a higher return from their investments, so market prices will fall.

4.3 An efficient market with regard to the **processing of information** is one in which the market prices of all the securities traded on it reflect all the available information. In such a market, there would be no possibility of 'speculative bubbles' in which share prices are pushed up or down by speculative pressure to unrealistically high or low levels.

Varying degrees of efficiency

4.4 Three degrees or 'forms' of 'information processing' efficiency have been proposed:

- weak form
- semi-strong form
- strong form

Weak form efficiency

4.5 The **weak form** hypothesis of market efficiency explains changes in share prices as the result of new information which becomes available to investors. In other words, share prices only change when new information about a company and its profits have become available. Share prices do not change in anticipation of new information being announced.

4.6 Research to prove that the stock market displays weak form efficiency has been based on the principle that:

(a) if share price changes are random, and

(b) if there is no connection between past price movements and new share price changes,

then it should be possible to prove statistically there is no correlation between successive changes in the price of a share, that is, that trends in prices cannot be detected. Proofs of the absence of trends have been claimed in the work of various writers.

Semi-strong form efficiency

4.7 **Semi-strong form** tests attempt to show that the stock market displays semi-strong efficiency, by which we mean that current share prices reflect both:

(a) all relevant information about past price movements and their implications; and
(b) all knowledge which is available publicly.

4.8 Research in both the UK and the USA has suggested that market prices anticipate mergers several months before they are formally announced, and the conclusion drawn is that the stock markets in these countries *do* exhibit semi-strong efficiency.

Strong form efficiency

4.9 **Strong form** efficiency means that share prices reflect all information available:

(a) from past price changes;

(b) from public knowledge or anticipation; and

(c) from insider knowledge available to specialists or experts (such as investment managers).

It would then follow that in order to maximise the wealth of shareholders, management should concentrate simply on maximising the net present value of its investments and it need not worry, for example, about the effect on share prices of financial results in the published accounts because investors will make allowances for low profits or dividends in the current year if higher profits or dividends are expected in the future.

4.10 In theory an expert, such as an investment manager, should be able to use his privileged access to additional information about companies to earn a higher rate of return than an ordinary investor. Unit trusts should in theory therefore perform better than the average investor. Research to date has suggested, however, that this expert skill does not exist (or at least, that any higher returns earned by experts are offset by management charges).

The implications of the efficient market hypothesis

4.11 If the strong form of the efficient market hypothesis is correct, a company's real financial position will be reflected in its share price. Its real financial position includes both its current position and its expected future profitability.

If the management of a company attempt to maximise the net present value of their investments and to make public any relevant information about those investments then current share prices will in turn be maximised.

4.12 The implication for an investor is that if the market shows strong form or semi-strong form efficiency, he can rarely spot shares at a bargain price that will soon rise sharply in value. This is because the market will already have anticipated future developments, and will have reflected these in the share price. All an investor can do, instead of looking for share bargains, is to concentrate on building up a good spread of shares (a portfolio) in order to achieve a satisfactory balance between risk and return.

Question 2

In the share price crash of October 1987, share prices on the world's stock markets fell suddenly by 20% to 40%. Why does this raise a question about the validity of the efficient market hypothesis?

Outline answer

The question is: if EMH is correct, how can shares that were valued at one level on one day suddenly be worth 40% less the next day, without any change in expectations of corporate profits and dividends? It would appear that speculation must have caused share prices to rise to levels which were unsustainable in the longer term.

5 RATES OF INTEREST AND RATES OF RETURN 12/96, 6/97

The money markets and rates of interest

5.1 As we have seen, the money markets are markets for short-term lending and borrowing. We outlined the difference between the money markets and capital markets at the beginning of Section 3 of this chapter.

5.2 **Interest rates** are effectively the 'prices' governing lending and borrowing. The borrower pays interest to the lender at a certain percentage of the capital sum, as the price for the use of the funds borrowed. As with other prices, supply and demand effects apply. For example, the higher the rates of interest that are charged, the lower will be the demand for funds from borrowers. To give another example, if lenders have an increased amount of funds to lend, then rates of interest may need to fall a little if borrowers are to take up all the funds now available.

The pattern of interest rates

5.3 The pattern of interest rates refers to the variety of interest rates on different financial assets, and the margin between interest rates on lending and deposits that are set by banks. Note that the **pattern of interest rates** is a different thing from the **general level of interest rates.**

5.4 Why are there such a large number of interest rates? In other words, how is the **pattern** of interest rates to be explained?

5.5 The answer to this question relates to several factors.

(a) **Risk.** There is a trade-off between risk and return. Higher-risk borrowers must pay higher yields on their borrowing, to compensate lenders for the greater risk involved.

For this reason, a bank will charge a higher rate of interest on loans to borrowers from a high-risk category than to a low-risk category borrower. Banks will assess the creditworthiness of the borrower, and set a rate of interest on its loan at a certain mark-up above its base rate or the LIBOR. In general, larger companies are charged at a lower rate of interest than smaller companies.

(b) The **need to make a profit on re-lending.** Financial intermediaries make their profits from re-lending at a higher rate of interest than the cost of their borrowing. Intermediaries must pay various costs out of the differences, including bad debts and administration charges. What is left will be profit.

For example:

(i) the interest rate charged on bank loans exceeds the rate paid on deposits;

(ii) the mortgage rate charged by building societies exceeds the interest rate paid on deposits.

The rates of interest paid on government borrowing (the Treasury bill rate for short-term borrowing and the gilt-edged rate for long-dated government stocks) provide benchmarks for other interest rates. For example:

(i) clearing banks might set the three months inter-bank rate (LIBOR) at about 1% above the Treasury bill rate;

(ii) banks in turn lend (wholesale) at a rate higher than LIBOR.

(c) The **duration of the lending.** The term of the loan or asset will affect the rate of interest charged on it. In general, longer-dated assets will earn a higher yield than similar short-dated assets but this is not always the case. The differences are referred to as the **term structure** of interest rates.

(d) The **size of the loan or deposit.** The yield on assets might vary with the size of the loan or deposit.

(i) Time deposits above a certain amount will probably attract higher rates of interest than smaller-sized time deposits. The intermediary might be prepared to pay extra for the benefit of holding the liability as a single deposit (greater convenience of administration).

(ii) The administrative convenience of handling wholesale loans rather than a large number of small retail loans partially explains the lower rates of interest charged by banks on larger loans. (The greater security in lending to a low-risk borrower could also be a factor.)

(e) **Different types of financial asset.** Different types of financial asset attract different rates of interest. This is partly because different types of asset attract different sorts of lender/investor. For example, bank deposits attract individuals and companies, whereas long-dated government securities are particularly attractive to various institutional investors.

The term structure of interest rates: the yield curve

5.6 Suppose that an investor decides to buy some government securities (gilts). Since the securities represent borrowing by the government, it might seem reasonable to expect that the nominal rate of interest paid would be the same, no matter what the type of security.

5.7 Obviously, this is not the case. One reason why this is so is that the government borrows by issuing new securities from time to time, and the rate of interest offered on a new issue of securities will depend on conditions in the market at the time. This will explain why the nominal interest rate on new gilt-edged securities might be 12% on one occasion, 10% on another and 8% on another.

5.8 There is another important reason why interest rates on the same type of financial asset might vary. This is that interest rates depend on the term to maturity of the asset. For example, Treasury Stock might be short-dated, medium-dated, or long-dated. The **term structure of interest rates** refers to the way in which the yield on a security varies according to the term of the borrowing, that is the length of time until the debt will be repaid as shown by the **yield curve**. Normally, the longer the term of an asset to maturity, the higher the rate of interest paid on the asset.

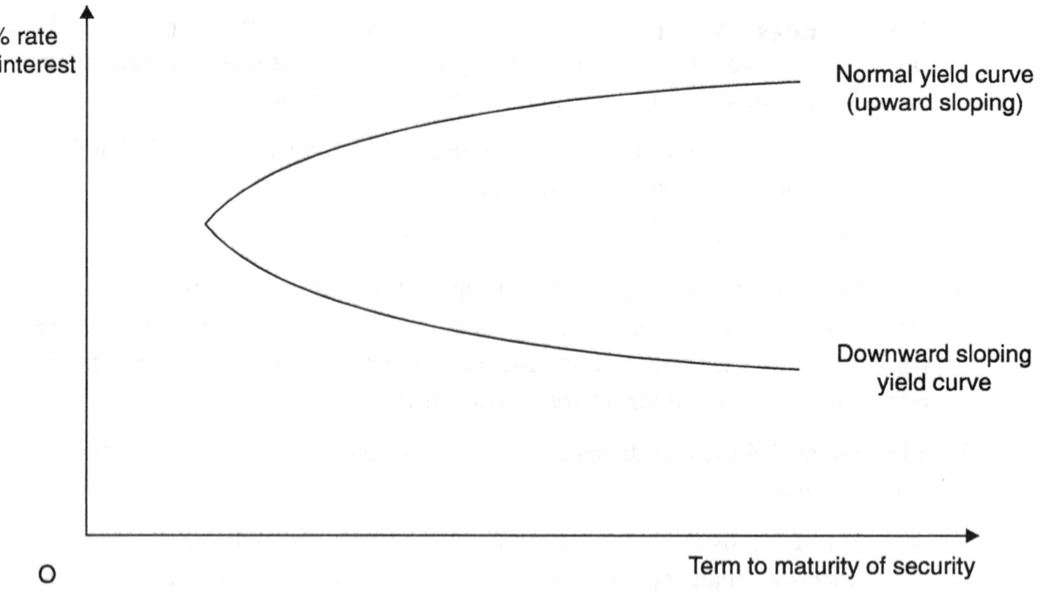

The general level of interest rates

5.9 Interest rates on any one type of financial asset will vary over time. In other words, the general level of interest rates might go up or down. The general level of interest rates is affected by several factors.

(a) The **need for a real return.** It is generally accepted that investors will want to earn a 'real' rate of return on their investment. The appropriate 'real' rate of return will depend on factors such as investment risk.

(b) **Inflation.** Nominal rates of interest should be sufficient to cover expected rates of inflation over the term of the investment and to provide a real return. Interest rates will generally be higher in countries with higher inflation because investors will expect to be compensated for the erosion in the value of the sum invested through inflation.

(c) **Uncertainty about future rates of inflation.** When investors are uncertain about inflation and therefore about what future nominal and real interest rates will be, they are likely to require higher interest yields to persuade them to take the risk of investing, especially in the longer term.

(d) **Liquidity preference of investors and the demand for borrowing.** Higher interest rates have to be offered to persuade savers to invest their surplus money. When the demand to borrow increases, interest rates will rise. An increased demand for borrowing on the part of the government may result in higher interest rates.

(e) The **balance of payments.** When a country has a continuing deficit on the current account of its balance of payments, and the authorities are unwilling to allow the exchange rate to depreciate by more than a certain amount, interest rates may have to be raised to attract capital into the country, so that the country can finance the deficit by borrowing from abroad.

(f) **Monetary policy**. The authorities may wish to influence the general level of interest rates, for example in order to control the volume of credit. From mid-1997, decisions over UK interest rate policy have been made by the Monetary Policy Committee of the Bank of England. The Bank of England influences very short-term money market rates by means of open market operations, which we mentioned earlier. Usually, but not always, longer term money market rates, and then banks' base rates, will respond to the authorities' wish for interest rate changes.

(g) **Interest rates abroad.** An appropriate rate of interest in one country will be influenced by external factors, such as interest rates in other countries and expectations about the exchange rate. When interest rates in overseas countries (and on foreign currency investments) are high, interest rates on domestic currency investments must be comparably high too, to avoid capital transfers abroad and a fall in the exchange rate of the domestic currency against other currencies.

The risk-return trade-off

5.10 We have explained how rates of interest, and therefore rates of return to lenders, will be affected by the risk involved in lending. The idea of a risk-return trade-off can, however, be extended beyond a consideration of interest rates.

5.11 An investor has the choice between different forms of investment. The investor may earn interest by depositing funds with a financial intermediary who will lend on to, say, a company, or it may invest in loan stock of a company. Alternatively, the investor may invest directly in a company by purchasing shares in it.

5.12 The current market price of a security is found by discounting the future expected earnings stream at a rate suitably adjusted for risk. This means that investments carrying a higher degree of risk will demand a higher rate of return. This rate of return or yield has two components:

(a) annual income ie dividend or interest
(b) expected capital gain

In general, the higher the risk of the security, the more important is the capital gain component of the expected yield.

5.13 Some of the main forms of investment are listed below in ascending order of risk

(a) **Government stock.** The risk of default is negligible and hence this tends to form the base level for returns in the market. The only uncertainty concerns the movement of interest rates over time, and hence longer dated stocks will tend to carry a higher rate of interest.

(b) **Company loan stock.** Although there is some risk of default on company loan stock (also called corporate bonds), the stock is usually secured against corporate assets.

(c) **Preference shares.** These are generally riskier than loan stock since they rank behind debt in the event of a liquidation, although they rank ahead of equity. The return takes the form of a fixed percentage dividend based on the par value of the share. Sometimes it is possible for investors to receive a higher rate of return if distributable profits exceed a given level. However, the dividend may be missed if results are particularly poor.

(d) **Ordinary shares.** Ordinary shares carry a high level of risk. Dividends are paid out of distributable profits after all other liabilities have been paid and can be subject to large fluctuations from year to year. However, there is the potential for significant capital appreciation in times of growth. In general, the level of risk will vary with the operational and financial gearing of the company and the nature of the markets in which it operates.

The reverse yield gap

5.14 Because debt involves lower risk than equity investment, we might expect yields on debt to be lower than yields on shares. More usually, however, the opposite applies and the yields on shares are lower than on low-risk debt: this situation is known as a **reverse yield gap**. A reverse yield gap can occur because shareholders may be willing to accept lower returns on their investment in the short term, in anticipation that they will make capital gains in the future.

Interest rates and shareholders' required rates of return

5.15 Given that equity shares and interest-earning investments stand as alternatives from the investor's point of view, changes in the general level of interest rates can be expected to have an effect on the rates of return which shareholders will expect.

5.16 If the return expected by an investor from an equity investment (ie an investment in shares) is 11% and the dividend paid on the shares is 15 pence, the market value of one share will be:

$$\frac{15 \text{ pence}}{11\%} = £1.36$$

5.17 Suppose that interest rates then fall. Because the option of putting the funds on deposit has become less attractive, the shareholders' required return will fall, to say, 9%. Then the market value of one share will increase to:

$$\frac{15 \text{ pence}}{9\%} = £1.67$$

5.18 You can see from this that an increase in the shareholders' required rate of return (perhaps resulting from an increase in the general level of interest rates) will lead to a fall in the market value of the share.

6 INTERNATIONAL MONEY AND CAPITAL MARKETS

6.1 In this section, we consider (in outline) foreign currency and international borrowing.

6.2 Larger companies are able to borrow funds on the **eurocurrency markets** (which are international money markets) and on the markets for **eurobonds** (international capital markets).

Exam focus point

Don't suggest these international markets as possible sources of finance for a *smaller* business in an exam answer.

Eurocurrency markets

6.3 A UK company might borrow money from a bank or from the investing public, in sterling. But it might also borrow in a foreign currency, especially if it trades abroad, or if it already has assets or liabilities abroad denominated in a foreign currency. When a company borrows in a foreign currency, the loan is known as a **eurocurrency loan.**

KEY TERM

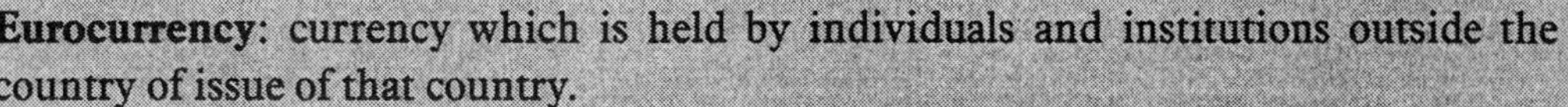

Eurocurrency: currency which is held by individuals and institutions outside the country of issue of that country.

6.4 For example, if a UK company borrows US $50,000 from its bank, the loan will be a 'eurodollar' loan. London is a major centre for eurocurrency lending and companies with foreign trade interests might choose to borrow from their bank in another currency.

6.5 The **eurocurrency markets** involve the depositing of funds with a bank outside the country of the currency in which the funds are denominated and re-lending these funds for a fairly short term, typically three months. Most eurocurrency transactions in fact takes place between banks of different countries and take the form of negotiable certificates of deposit.

International capital markets

6.6 Large companies may arrange borrowing facilities from their bank, in the form of bank loans or bank overdrafts. Instead, however, they might prefer to borrow from private investors. In other words, instead of obtaining a £10,000,000 bank loan, a company might issue 'bonds', or 'paper' in order to borrow directly from investors, with:

(a) the bank merely arranging the transaction, finding investors who will take up the bonds or paper that the borrowing company issues;

(b) interest being payable to the investors themselves, not to a bank.

6.7 In recent years, a strong international market has built up which allows very large companies to borrow in this way, long-term or short-term. As well as eurobonds, there is also a less highly developed market in international equity share issues ('**euro-equity**').

Eurobonds

KEY TERM

A **eurobond** is a bond denominated in a currency which often differs from that of the country of issue.

6.8 Eurobonds are long-term loans raised by international companies or other institutions and sold to investors in several countries at the same time. Such bonds can be sold by one holder to another.

The term of a eurobond issue is typically ten to 15 years.

6.9 Eurobonds may be the most suitable source of finance for a large organisation with an excellent credit rating, such as a large successful multinational company, which:

(a) requires a long-term loan to finance a big capital expansion programme (with a loan for at least five years and up to 20 years);

(b) requires borrowing which is not subject to the national exchange controls of any government (a company in country X could raise funds in the currency of country Y by means of a eurobond issue, and thereby avoid any exchange control restrictions which might exist in country X). In addition, domestic capital issues may be regulated by the government or central bank, with an orderly queue for issues. In contrast, eurobond issues can be made whenever market conditions seem favourable.

6.10 The interest rate on a bond issue may be fixed or variable. Many variable rate issues have a minimum interest rate which the bond holders are guaranteed, even if market rates fall even lower. These bonds convert to a fixed rate of interest when market rates do fall to this level. For this reason, they are called 'drop lock' floating rate bonds.

Eurobond issues and currency risk

6.11 A borrower who is contemplating a eurobond issue must consider the exchange risk of a long-term foreign currency loan.

(a) If the money is to be used to purchase assets which will earn revenue in a currency different to that of the bond issue, the borrower will run the risk of exchange losses. These losses would be due to adverse movements in exchange rates, if the currency of the loan strengthens against the currency of the revenues out of which the bond (and interest) must be repaid. Borrowers cannot obtain long-term forward cover in the forward exchange market, and would have to accept the risks of foreign exchange exposure.

(b) If the money is to be used to purchase assets which will earn revenue in the same currency, the borrower can match these revenues with payments on the bond, and so remove or reduce the exchange risk.

Eurobonds and the investor

6.12 An investor subscribing to a bond issue will be concerned about the following factors.

(a) **Security**. The borrower must be of high quality. A standard condition of a bond issue is a 'negative pledge clause' in which the borrower undertakes not to give any prior charge over its assets, during the life of the bond issue, that would rank ahead of the rights of the investors in the event of a liquidation.

(b) **Marketability.** Investors will wish to have a ready market in which bonds can be bought and sold. If the borrower is of high quality the bonds or notes will be readily negotiable.

(c) **Anonymity.** Investors in eurobonds tend to be attracted to the anonymity of this type of issue, as the bonds are generally issued to bearer.

(d) The **return on the investment.** This is paid tax-free.

International banks

6.13 The period since World War II has seen the development of international financial centres as well as growth in international trade and multinational business activities. The most important such centres are London, New York and Tokyo.

6.14 International banks, most of whom are themselves large multinational enterprises, are the most important financial intermediaries in these financial centres.

6.15 These banks assist larger enterprises in the following ways, with some specialising in particular areas:

(a) the financing of foreign trade;
(b) the financing of capital projects;

(c) international cash management services;
(d) providing full local banking services in different countries;
(e) trading in foreign exchange and currency options;
(f) lending and borrowing in the eurocurrency market;
(g) participating in syndicated loan facilities;
(h) underwriting of eurobonds;
(i) provision of advice and information.

Chapter roundup

- In this chapter, we have covered some important aspects of the **markets** and **institutions** which are relevant to the practice of financial management.
- A **financial intermediary** links those with surplus funds (eg **lenders**) to those with funds deficits (eg potential **borrowers**) thus providing:
  - aggregation and economies of scale
  - risk pooling
  - maturity transformation
- The **capital markets** and **money markets** are markets for long-term and short-term capital respectively.
- A **stock market** (in the UK: the **main market** plus the **AIM**) acts as a **primary market** for raising finance, and as a **secondary market** for the trading of existing securities (ie stocks and shares).
- The **efficient market hypothesis** suggests that share prices reflect the type of information which is available to investors.
- The pattern of **interest rates** on financial assets is influenced by the risk of the assets, the duration of the lending, and the size of the loan.
- There is a **trade-off between risk and return**. Investors in riskier assets expect to be compensated for the risk. In the case of ordinary shares, investors hope to achieve their return in the form of an increase in the share price (a **capital gain**) as well as from **dividends**.
- **International money and capital markets** are available for larger companies wishing to raise larger amounts of finance.

Quick quiz

1. Sketch a diagram illustrating the flow of funds in an economy, showing the position of financial intermediaries. (see para 1.5)
2. Distinguish money markets and capital markets. (3.1)
3. Identify the main types of institutional investor in the UK. (3.12)
4. What is the efficient market hypothesis? (4.2)
5. What factors affect the pattern of interest rates? (5.5)
6. What factors affect the general level of interest rates? (5.9)
7. Identify international money and capital markets on which companies are able to raise funds. (6.2)

Question to try	Level	Marks	Time
16	Introductory	n/a	30 mins

Part F
Economic influences

Chapter 16

OVERVIEW OF MACROECONOMIC POLICY

Chapter topic list		Syllabus reference
1	**Macroeconomic policy**	5(b)(i)
2	**The national and international economy**	5(b)(i)

Introduction

In Chapters 16 to 19 we shall be concerned with the wider **economic framework** and how it affects **individual businesses**.

No business is completely insulated from events in the economy as a whole. In turn, no national economy is completely insulated from the wider world. In this chapter, we will be emphasising the **constraints on economic policy-making** as well as examining **the record of the UK economy** compared with the other G7 ('Group of Seven') countries, now (in 1998) made into the G8 with the addition of Russia.

1 MACROECONOMIC POLICY

Exam focus point

The knowledge expected on the economic environment for Paper 8 - covered in this part of the Study Text - is quite extensive, particularly since the examiner has stated that a full question will not be set on it. Topics in economics will be tested in parts of longer FM questions only. But the economics in the paper should not be neglected - lack of economics knowledge has been highlighted by the examiner as one of the main reasons for poor performance.

Be prepared for part-questions on economics topics you have covered in earlier studies. For example, Paper 8 candidates were asked about price and cross elasticities of demand in 12/94 and about cartels in 12/96.

Microeconomics, macroeconomics and economic policy

1.1 As you will recall from your earlier studies, a distinction is drawn between two areas of study in economics.

KEY TERMS

Microeconomics is concerned with the behaviour of individual firms and consumers or households. **Macroeconomics** is concerned with the economy at large, and with the behaviour of large aggregates such as the national income, the money supply and the level of employment.

1.2 A government will of course be concerned with how the economy is behaving as a whole, and therefore with **macroeconomic variables**. Much government economic policy seeks to influence macroeconomic variables, including for example the rate of inflation, the level of government borrowing and the level of unemployment. As we shall see, there are various different kinds of policy tools or instruments which the government might use. Macroeconomic policy can affect planning and decision making in various ways, for example via interest rate changes, which affect borrowing costs and required rates of return, as we saw earlier.

1.3 Note also that a government might adopt policies which try to exert influence at the **microeconomic** level. Examples include policies to remove regulations which restrict competition in particular labour markets or goods markets and policies to bring state-owned businesses into private ownership. This microeconomic focus in economic policy is emphasised in the so-called **'supply side' policy approach** which we shall return to later in this Study Text.

Knowledge brought forward from Paper 4

Macroeconomics

From your previous studies, you should have an understanding of:

- National income and its measurement
- The determination of national income: Keynesian analysis
- The multiplier effect
- The business cycle or trade cycle
- Economic goals and economic growth

If you are unsure on any of these areas, now is the time to revise your economics notes on them.

Economic policies and objectives

1.4 Every government has a range of economic policies - for example on government spending, taxation, the exchange rate, the balance of payments, the level of interest rates and the money supply.

The policies pursued by a government may serve various objectives. Among the aims of a government's economic policy may be the following.

(a) To achieve **economic growth,** and national income per head of the population. 'Growth' implies an increase in national income in 'real' terms - ie increases caused by price inflation are not real increases at all.

(b) To control price inflation, ie to achieve **stable prices**. This has become a central objective of UK economic policy in recent years.

(c) To achieve **'full' employment.** Full employment does not mean that everyone who wants a job has one all the time, but it does mean that unemployment levels are low, and involuntary unemployment is short-term.

(d) To achieve a **balance between exports and imports** over a period of years. The wealth of a country relative to others, a country's creditworthiness as a borrower, and the goodwill between countries in international relations might all depend on the achievement of an external trade balance over time. Deficits in external trade, with imports exceeding exports, might also be damaging for the prospects of economic growth.

Policy instruments and policy targets

1.5 To try to achieve its intermediate and overall objectives, a government will use a number of different policy tools or policy instruments. These include the following.

(a) **Monetary policy.** Monetarist economists believe that control over the growth of the money supply is necessary to reduce inflation and that inflation is harmful to the economy because it creates economic uncertainty which deters growth.

(b) **Fiscal policy.** Keynesian economists believe that when an economy has spare production capacity and unemployment, investment and output can be stimulated (through government spending or tax cuts) so as to reduce unemployment without creating more inflation.

(c) **Prices and incomes policy**. Some economists argue that inflation must be tackled directly through government controls over prices and incomes.

(d) **Exchange rate policy**. Some economists argue that economic objectives can be achieved through management of the exchange rate by the government. The strength or weakness of sterling's value, for example, will influence the volume of UK imports and exports, the balance of payments and interest rates.

(e) **External trade policy.** A government might have a policy for promoting economic growth by stimulating exports. Another argument is that there should be import controls to provide some form of protection for domestic manufacturing industries by making the cost of imports higher and the volume of imports lower. Protection could encourage domestic output to rise, stimulating the domestic economy.

1.6 These policy tools are not mutually exclusive and a government might adopt a policy mix of monetary policy, fiscal policy and exchange rate policy in an attempt to achieve its intermediate and ultimate economic objectives.

1.7 A policy target is a quantified level or range which government policy is supposed to try to achieve. For example, the Government of the UK has set a target for the rate of general price inflation (excluding mortgage interest payments) of 2.5 per cent.

Conflicts in policy objectives and instruments

1.8 Macroeconomic policy aims cannot necessarily all be sustained together for a long period of time; attempts to achieve one objective will often have adverse effects on others, sooner or later.

(a) To some extent, there is a conflict between steady balanced growth in the economy and full employment. Although a growing economy should be able to provide more jobs, there is some concern that since an economy must be modernised to grow and modern technology is labour-saving, it might be possible to achieve growth without creating many more jobs, and so keeping unemployment at a high level.

(b) In the UK, problems with creating more employment and a steady growth in the economy have been the balance of payments, the foreign exchange value of sterling, inflation and the money supply. The objectives of lower unemployment and economic growth have been difficult to achieve because of the problems and conflicts with secondary objectives.

(i) To create jobs and growth, there must be an increase in aggregate demand (either at home and abroad). When demand picks up there will be a surge in imports, with foreign goods bought by UK manufacturers (eg raw materials) and consumers.

(ii) The high rate of imports creates a deficit in the balance of payments, which in turn will weaken sterling and raise the cost of imports, thus giving some impetus to price rises.

(iii) To maintain the value of sterling, interest rates in the UK might need to be kept high, and high interest rates appear to deter companies from investing.

(c) There is a possible connection between the unemployment level and the rate of inflation (discussed further in Chapter 18).

1.9 In practice, achieving the best mix of economic policies also involves a number of problems, such as the following.

- Inadequate **information**
- **Time lags** between use of policy and effects being noticeable
- **Political pressures** for short-term solutions
- Unpredictable **side-effects** of policies
- The influence of **other countries**
- **Conflict** between policy instruments

1.10 Conflicts between policy instruments include the following.

(a) A fiscal deficit necessitates government borrowing. This may force up interest rates and discourage investment (the **crowding out effect**).

(b) Tighter monetary policy to limit inflation will force up interest rates. This in turn will increase the Retail Prices Index (as mortgage costs are part of the RPI) and could discourage investment. Lower investment means lower efficiency and higher costs.

(c) Prices and incomes policy introduced to reduce inflation may lead to industrial disruption, in turn causing a fall in output and possible balance of payments deficits.

Effects of economic policy on business enterprises

1.11 Economic policy affects business enterprises in both service and manufacturing industries in various ways, for example as follows. (Other effects of policy on business will be discussed at various stages in the coming chapters of this Study Text.)

(a) Interest rate changes brought about by government policy affect the borrowing costs of business.

(b) Inflation, perhaps induced by policies to boost demand, can create uncertainty for business as well as consumers. Businesses will be affected variously, depending on the relative price inflation on its input prices and output prices. A manufacturing industry may indeed make gains from increasing selling prices on stocks it has built up when its purchase prices were lower.

(c) Membership of an exchange rate system may reduce uncertainties for businesses involved in international trade because exchange rate fluctuations will be reduced. A service industry is less likely to be affected because it is less likely to be involved in substantial international trade.

2 THE NATIONAL AND INTERNATIONAL ECONOMY

UK economic policy in the 1980s and early 1990s

2.1 From 1980 onwards, UK economic policy was based on the Conservative Government's Medium-Term Financial Strategy (MTFS), which was an annually-revised plan setting targets for the growth of the money supply for the following four-year period. The targets tightened progressively over the four-year period in order to 'put the squeeze' on inflation. The MTFS also included targets for the PSBR.

2.2 From the mid 1980s, it became apparent in the UK and other countries that keeping the money supply within target ranges was very difficult, and the UK government adopted a more pragmatic approach. Although the MTFS lived on in name, the main monetary targets were abandoned in 1987, to be replaced more recently by 'monitoring ranges' for M0 and M4 growth.

2.3 A major reason for the change of the mid-1980s was the need to curb fluctuations in the exchange rate of sterling. Interest rate policy needed to be used to influence the exchange rate, and this meant that it could not be used to achieve a money supply target as well. While the UK was a number of the European Exchange Rate Mechanism (ERM) between 1990 and 1992, the government's monetary policy was almost entirely restricted to maintaining the value of sterling within its permitted ERM bands.

2.4 Following withdrawal from the ERM in 1992, the government announced that it would place particular emphasis on factors affecting inflation.

(a) The government would judge inflationary trends according to a wide range of factors, including domestic monetary targets. There would be a general emphasis on reaching a judgement on inflationary trends and on whether the government's objectives are likely to be achieved.

(b) The Treasury would also monitor money market interest rates, and asset prices including house prices. Officials would pay particular attention to periods when house prices are falling or accelerating sharply.

(c) At the same time, it was recognised that events outside the government's control might take inflation temporarily outside the target range. That could arise, for example, if there were a sharp movement in world commodity prices.

Recent UK economic developments

2.5 **Economic growth and demand.** GDP growth was 3.1% in 1997 and is expected to fall back to 2.2% for 1998, which is viewed as approximately its 'trend rate'. The main factor driving the UK economy's resilient growth in output has been the level of consumer demand, which has been boosted by rising real incomes and a marked recovery in the housing market.

2.6 **Inflation.** Annual RPI inflation stood at 3.6% in 1997. RPIX underlying inflation is projected to remain close to the Government's target level of 2.5% for some time, except for a temporary rise to about 3% following Budget changes to the timing of excise duty increases.

2.7 **Unemployment.** Unemployment has continued to fall, standing at 1.40 million at the end of 1997, the lowest for over six years. The total is however affected by changes to the compilation of the official statistics and benefit entitlements from time to time.

2.8 **Current account.** The balance of payments current account was in surplus (£4.5 billion) for 1997. A recent forecast for 1998 was for a deficit of £5 billion. Export growth has all but come to a stop because the high value of sterling has made export prices less competitive.

Problems with a target for inflation

2.9 Both the previous Conservative Government and the 1997 Labour Government of the UK have had publicly announced inflation targets. A problem with treating the inflation rate as an economic policy target is to do with the time lag of one or two years after which interest rates affect economic activity, and the further one or two year time lag before the effect on inflation works through.

2.10 If governments over-react to current inflation figures, there is the risk of an inappropriate policy response. Indeed looking back over years in the recent past, many would argue that:

(a) if interest rates had been raised earlier during the low-inflation period of 1985-88, the ensuring cycle of inflationary boom (1988-89) and later recession (1990-92) need not have occurred; and

(b) if interest rates had not been maintained at 15% for so long while inflation was rising above 10% in 1990, the economic recession which followed would not have been so severe.

2. 11 With the new Labour government of 1997, the switching of interest rate policy decisions to the Bank of England does not necessarily mean that this risk is removed, since the Bank may still get it wrong. However, it does reduce the influence of **political pressures** on interest rate policy.

Exam focus point

The ACCA's Teaching Guide for Paper 8 indicates that you should examine the recent record of the UK in relation to other G7 (ie G8 excluding Russia) countries, as discussed below. Such knowledge is unlikely to be examined directly, but knowledge of world economic trends and events may be needed to underpin questions indirectly.

2.12 The **G7 (Group of Seven) countries** are Germany, France, Italy, Japan, the USA, Canada and the UK. Russia has recently joined the grouping, to form the G8. Key points on the recent economic performance of the G7 countries, with reference also to wider world issues, are as follows.

(a) In the five or six years up to 1997, **growth in economic output** in the USA has been consistently high. Canada has also enjoyed strong economic growth. The economies of Japan and Europe have been weaker and more volatile.

(b) Although economic recovery from the recession of the early 1990s is well established in the UK, GDP growth in Germany, France and Italy remains particularly weak relative to many smaller EU countries (for example, Ireland, the Netherlands, Finland, Greece and Portugal).

(c) A recent economic recovery in Japan has been uneven, with international trade offsetting falls in domestic demand.

(d) Inflation in Japan and the major European countries has remained low recently. This probably reflects the 'output gaps' (spare capacity) in these economies. This explanation does not, however, fit the recent experience in the USA, where inflation has been very low in spite of unemployment reaching what is thought to be its 'natural rate'.

(e) Worldwide trends in economic growth are also currently favourable. Growth appears to be stabilising at a sustainable level in dynamic Asian economies of Central and Eastern Europe.

(f) There has been a global trend toward **slower inflation** recently, with average consumer price inflation falling between 1995 and 1996 from 20% to 13% in developing countries and from 128% to 41% in transition countries. The IMF attributes a large part of this decline to the use of non-inflationary economic policies.

2.13 Looking back a little further, the record of the UK economy has in important respects under-performed in comparison with the G7 taken as a whole and other major industrialised countries.

(a) Although the recent recovery in UK output has been strong, the earlier economic recession of 1990 to 1992 was relatively severe, resulting in negative growth of around –2% to –3% at the 'trough' of the recession.

(b) UK consumer price inflation has been worse than the average for the G7. Only in Italy has inflation been higher during the 1990s.

(c) Since 1980, the UK has experienced rates of unemployment of up to around 11% and UK employment has been higher than the G7 average. Other G7 countries with relatively high unemployment rates are Canada, France and Italy.

2.14 Differences between the different sectors of the economy can be significant. The table below shows that the **service sector** has grown more quickly than the **manufacturing sector** in the UK in the 1990s.

Output growth by sector 1990 Quarter 1 - 1995 Quarter 3

	Service	*Industrial*
	%	%
United Kingdom	7.8	5.8
Germany	23.5	–16.9
France	7.5	2.4
Italy	8.6	9.4
United States	17.6	2.0

(*Source: Bank of England*)

2.15 How can this be explained? As pointed out in the *Bank of England Quarterly Bulletin*, sectoral growth has been closely linked with economic activity, but services are much less cyclical than the rest of the economy, for the following reasons.

(a) The counter-cyclical parts of government spending are centred in services.

(b) Manufacturing is much more accurately measured than services in the national accounts: if people trade down in services in times of recession it might not be reflected by the statistics.

2.16 As the *BEQB* points out, there are also long and short-term trends.

(a) 'Services have grown more quickly than industrial output on average throughout the post-war period in Western Europe and North America. This is partly because of growing incomes and wealth, which have led to a relative increase in demand for leisure services, and partly due to the comparative advantage in industrial production in Japan and more recently the NIEs (newly industrialised economies).

(b) The information technology revolution has recently led to fast growth in communications, which in the short run will favour services, but in the long term is likely to raise output throughout the economy.'

2.17 'An important influence on the relative performance of different countries' sectors is the real exchange rate. If a country's real exchange rate has appreciated, it will hit the manufacturing sector - which produces a higher proportion of tradables - harder than the service sector. This largely explains the relatively poor performance of manufacturing in Germany and its relatively good performance in Italy over the last few years, as illustrated in the table' (*BEQB*).

Question

Review the financial press for articles about the recent economic record of the UK in relation to other 'Group of Seven' economies (USA, Japan, Germany, France, Italy and Canada).

The interdependence of national economies

2.18 In the modern economy, production is based on a high degree of specialisation. Within a country, individuals specialise, factories specialise and whole regions specialise. Specialisation increases productivity and raises the standard of living. International trade extends the principle of the division of labour and specialisation to countries. International trade originated on the basis of nations exchanging their products for others which they could not produce for themselves. Britain, for example, imports tea and coffee and exports oil to non-oil producing countries (although there is also plenty of trade in different types of oil between oil-producing countries themselves).

2.19 As you may recall from your earlier studies, international trade arises for a number of reasons.

(a) Different goods require different proportions of factor inputs in their production.
(b) Economic resources are unevenly distributed throughout the world.
(c) The international mobility of resources is extremely limited.

2.20 Since it is difficult to move resources between nations, the goods which 'embody' the resources must move. Thus, nations which have an abundance of land relative to labour will concentrate on land-intensive commodities such as agricultural products. These will be exchanged for labour-intensive products such as manufactured goods made by countries which have an abundance of labour and capital relative to land. The main reason for trade therefore is that there are differences in the relative efficiency with which different countries can produce different goods and service.

2.21 As you will recall from your earlier studies in economics, the main economic justification for international trade derives from the principle of comparative advantage. Countries gain from trade by exporting goods in whose production they have a relative cost advantage. International trade in goods and services increases economic wealth, and also increases countries' dependence on each other.

2.22 Free trade exists when there are no restrictions imposed by countries or by larger trading blocs on imports from other countries. Protectionist measures, including tariffs, import quotas and also less obvious policies such as excessive bureaucracy and 'hidden' export subsidies are, however, fairly common in practice, and limit the scope for free trade. The World Trade Organisation has been set up to implement the General Agreement on Tariffs and Trade (GATT), which has reduced many tariffs and other restrictions from the even higher levels experienced around 40 years ago.

2.23 Trade in goods and services is one aspect of the interdependence of national economies. Another is the **globalisation of financial markets**.

- The **capital markets**, which we looked at in an earlier chapter, have become increasingly integrated on an international basis: securities issued in one country can now be traded in capital markets around the world.
- **Multinational enterprises** have grown in their influence, with the largest US multinational companies - such as Ford, General Motors and Exxon - each having a turnover larger than that of a medium-sized national economy.
- The size of **currency markets** also reflect the internationalisation of finance. London is by far the largest currency trading centre, with *daily* turnover of $464 *billion* reported in a 1995 survey, 60% up on three years earlier - an amount which makes most governments' foreign currency reserves seem like small change.

Chapter roundup

- We can distinguish:
  - Policy **objectives** - the ultimate aims of economic policy
  - Policy **targets** - quantified levels or ranges which policy is intended to achieve
  - Policy **instruments** - the tools used to achieve objectives
- Achievement of **economic growth**, **low inflation, full employment** and a **trade balance** are policy objectives.
- Policy targets might be set for **money supply growth** or the **rate of inflation,** for example.
- **Monetary policy** and **fiscal policy** are two important policy instruments.
- We have reviewed the UK economic record compared with that of the G7 countries.
- National economies are increasingly interdependent due to factors such as growth in **international trade** and the **globalisation** of financial markets.

Quick quiz

1 List the major objectives of governments' economic policies. (see para 1.4)

2 What are the main types of policy instrument used by governments to achieve economic policy objectives? (1.5)

3 What is meant by a macroeconomic policy target? (1.7)

4 Outline possible conflicts between economic policy instruments. (1.10)

5 How does the recent record of the UK economy compare with other 'G7' countries? (2.12 - 2.17)

Question to try	Level	Marks	Time
17	Introductory	n/a	30 mins

Chapter 17

FISCAL POLICY AND MONETARY POLICY

Chapter topic list		Syllabus reference
1	Fiscal policy	5(b)(ii)
2	Monetary policy	5(b)(iii),(iv)

Introduction

Having looked at the macroeconomy and at macroeconomic policy in overview in Chapter 16, in this chapter we explore in more detail **fiscal policy** and **monetary policy**.

1 FISCAL POLICY 6/95, 12/95, 12/96

Exam focus point

The topics relating to fiscal policy tested so far in the exam have been wide-ranging and include government spending limits, the effects of a government deficit on business, and problems with the use of fiscal policy.

Fiscal policy, national income and demand management

1.1 The word 'fisc' means the state treasury or the public purse. **Fiscal policy** relates to matters concerning the state treasury. More specifically, fiscal policy is action by the government to spend money, or to collect money in taxes, with the purpose of influencing the condition of the national economy. A government might intervene in the economy by:

(a) spending more money and financing this expenditure by borrowing;

(b) collecting more in taxes without increasing public spending;

(c) collecting more in taxes in order to increase public spending, thus diverting income from one part of the economy to another.

1.2 **Demand management** is a term used to describe the economic policy of a government when it attempts to influence the economy by changing aggregate demand. Government spending is an 'injection' into the economy, adding to aggregate demand and therefore national income, whereas taxes are a 'withdrawal' from the economy. Fiscal policy can thus be used as an instrument of demand management.

Three elements of public finance

1.3 Broadly, there are three elements in public finance.

(a) **Expenditure**

Expenditure by the government (public expenditure), at a national and local level, has several purposes, for example:

(i) to provide goods and services, such as a health service, public education, a police force, roads and public buildings, and to pay its administrative work force;

(ii) to provide payments to certain members of society, such as old age pensioners and the unemployed;

(iii) perhaps, to provide finance to encourage investment by private industry, eg by means of grants.

(iii) to ensure that total public expenditure is in line with its overall fiscal policy, the government may impose limits on the expenditure of local and regional authorities, which forms a part of total public spending.

(b) **Income**

Expenditure must be financed, and the government must have income.

(i) Most government income comes from taxation.

(ii) Some income is obtained from direct charges to users of government services (for example, charges to consumers by nationalised industries, and National Health Service charges).

(c) **Borrowing**

To the extent that a government's expenditure exceeds its income, it must borrow to make up the difference. The amount that the government must borrow each year is the public sector borrowing requirement or PSBR.

(i) The government may borrow from the non-bank sector by issuing relatively illiquid forms of debt (eg national savings certificates and long-term government debt). This is known as 'funding' the debt.

(ii) The government can issue relatively liquid debt such as Treasury bills to the bank sector. This is known as 'unfunded' debt.

1.4 **Funding policy** refers to the balance between funded and unfunded debt, which differ in the effects they have on the economy.

(a) In the case of 'funded' debt, the government is in competition with other borrowers and so the issuing of funded debt by government may 'crowd out' these other borrowers from the market.

(b) 'Unfunded' debt will have different effects. The liquid assets held by the banking system will be increased, enabling the banks to create more credit. The resulting increase in the money supply may be inflationary.

Taxation as a deterrent to economic growth

1.5 In most modern societies, some taxation is essential, because governments have to raise money somehow to carry on their own activities - running the country, providing defence forces, a police force, a fire service, a health service, education, roads and so on.

Governments can use tax revenues to invest in new enterprises, or to fund important research.

Excessive taxation might deter investment and risk-taking and might curb individuals' initiative and efforts, although the evidence to support this is not conclusive. In the case of taxation of individuals, a counter-argument is that the higher the level of tax on income, the harder an individual will work in order to maintain an adequate level of post-tax income.

1.6 Fiscal policy could be formulated within the guidelines that:

(a) taxes should be high enough to allow the government to carry on its functions; but
(b) they should not be set so as to deter private investment and initiative.

Fiscal policy and macroeconomic objectives

1.7 Fiscal policy is concerned with government spending (an injection into the circular flow of income) and taxation (a withdrawal).

(a) If government spending is increased, there will be an increase in the amount of injections in the economic system, expenditure in the economy will rise and so national income will rise (either in real terms, or in terms of price levels only; ie the increase in national income might be 'real' or 'inflationary').

(b) If government taxation is increased, there will be an increase in withdrawals from the economy, and expenditure and national income will fall. A government might deliberately raise taxation to take inflationary pressures out of the economy.

Achieving growth in national income without inflation has been a problem bedevilling governments for many years. Certainly, government spending and government taxation policies can affect economic growth (ie the national income level in real terms) but it can also stimulate further inflation.

1.8 Fiscal policy could be used to reduce unemployment and provide jobs. For example:

(a) more government spending on capital projects would create jobs in the construction industries;

(b) government-funded training schemes are a means of government spending to improve training, so as to make people more qualified for jobs in private industry;

(c) a government may tax companies on the basis of the numbers of people they employ or their level of pay (eg national insurance). Lower 'employment taxes' would possibly make employers more willing to take on extra numbers of employees.

Government spending could however create inflationary pressures, and inflation tends to create more unemployment. Fiscal policy must be used with care, even to create new jobs.

1.9 Since government spending or tax reductions can be inflationary, and higher domestic prices make imports relatively cheaper and exports less competitive in foreign markets, fiscal policy may have possible implications for the balance of trade (exports less imports).

If macroeconomic objectives are economic growth, full employment, low or no inflation and equilibrium in the balance between exports and imports, fiscal policy can certainly influence those objectives, and governments use fiscal policy to do so (as well as to carry out other non-economic objectives). However, the impact of changes in fiscal policy is not always certain, and fiscal policy to pursue one aim (eg lower inflation) might for a while create barriers to the pursuit of other aims (eg full employment).

Budget surplus; budget deficit; balanced budget

1.10 Suppose that the government wants to stimulate demand in the economy.

(a) It can increase demand directly by spending more itself - eg on the health service or education, and by employing more people itself.

(i) This extra spending could be financed by higher taxes, but this would reduce spending by the private sector of the economy because the private sector's after-tax income would be lower.

(ii) The extra government spending could also be financed by extra government borrowing. Just as individuals can borrow money for spending, so too can a government.

(b) It can increase demand indirectly by reducing taxation and so allowing firms and individuals more after-tax income to spend (or save).

(i) Cuts in taxation can be matched by cuts in government spending, in which case total demand in the economy will not be stimulated significantly, if at all.

(ii) Alternatively, tax cuts can be 'financed' by more government borrowing.

1.11 Just as aggregate demand in the economy can be boosted by either more government spending or by tax cuts, financed in either case by higher government spending, so too can demand in the economy be reduced by cutting government spending or by raising taxes, and using the savings or higher income to cut government borrowing.

1.12 Expenditure changes and tax changes are not mutually exclusive options, of course. A government has the choice of:

(a) both increasing expenditure and reducing taxes, with these changes financed by a higher PSBR;

(b) both reducing expenditure and increasing taxes, with these changes reducing the size of the PSBR;

(c) increasing expenditure and partly or wholly financing this extra spending with higher taxes;

(d) reducing expenditure and using these 'savings' to reduce taxes.

1.13 When a government's income exceeds its expenditure, and there is a negative PSBR - ie a public sector debt repayment or 'PSDR' - we say that the government is running a **budget surplus.**

When a government's expenditure exceeds its income, so that it must borrow to make up the difference, there is a PSBR and we say that the government is running a **budget deficit**.

When a government's expenditure and income are the same, so that the PSBR is nil, there is a **balanced budget**.

The balanced budget multiplier

1.14 To maintain a balanced budget, government expenditure changes need to be matched exactly by a change in government revenue to leave the net budgetary position unaltered. For example, an increase in government expenditure of £1 billion will be matched by an increase in taxation of £1 billion. The **balanced budget multiplier** shows the effect on national income of equal changes in government spending and taxation.

1.15 It might be expected that the net effect of any balanced budget change would be nil, so that national income would remain the same. However, when an extra £1 billion in taxes is taken away from households, they usually reduce their spending on domestically produced goods by less than £1 billion. If, for example, their 'marginal propensity to consume' out of disposable income is 0.8, then their spending will decline by £800 million. The other £200 million of the tax payment will be made by reducing their savings by that amount. If the government then spends the whole £1 billion on domestically produced goods, aggregate expenditure in the economy will rise by £200m, representing the decline in the leakage from the circular flow of income in the form of savings. This injection will now increase the national income by an amount that is equal to £200m multiplied by the national income multiplier.

1.16 What this implies is that if the government wishes to increase national output, employment and income by the maximum possible amount, then it should use the £1 billion to increase its expenditure (so that the multiplier can work on the £1 billion injection), rather than reduce taxes (in which case the multiplier can work only on £1 billion minus the savings from the extra disposable income).

Fiscal policy and the Budget

1.17 A government must plan what it wants to spend, and so how much it needs to raise in income or by borrowing. It needs to make a plan in order to establish how much taxation there should be, what form the taxes should take and so which sectors of society (firms or households, the rich or the poor etc) the money should come from. This formal planning of fiscal policy is usually done once a year. The taxation aspects are set out in the annual Budget, which for the UK takes place towards the end of the calendar year.

1.18 This annual review of taxation means that a full review of the government's fiscal policy can only be done once a year. In between Budgets, a government must resort to other non-fiscal policy instruments to control the economy, such as influencing interest rate levels and other monetary policy measures. (Monetary policy is discussed later in this chapter.) In 1997, an additional July Budget was introduced by the incoming Labour Government so that it could present new proposals soon after taking office.

The broad aims of fiscal policy

1.19 Fiscal policy appears to offer a method of managing aggregate demand in the economy.

(a) If the government spends more - for example, on public works such as hospitals, roads and sewers - without raising more money in taxation (ie by borrowing more) it will increase expenditure in the economy, and so raise demand. The economist John Maynard **Keynes** argued that an initial boost of extra government spending on public works would stimulate demand by a multiple of the initial spending increase.

(b) If the government kept its own spending at the same level, but reduced the levels of taxation, it would also stimulate demand in the economy because firms and households would have more of their own money after tax for consumption or saving/investing.

(c) In the same way, a government can reduce demand in the economy by raising taxes or reducing its expenditure.

Fine tuning

1.20 In the 1950s and 1960s in Britain, fiscal policies were thought to be the only real method of controlling the economy. Some economists thought that frequent small changes to the level of government spending and taxation would be sufficient to keep national income at a full employment level. The fiscal policy of frequent (perhaps annual) changes in government expenditure and taxation to control national income and employment is known as **fine tuning** the economy - the economy was considered to be in reasonably good shape, but minor adjustments made by means of fiscal policy would help the economy to settle at exactly the right level of income.

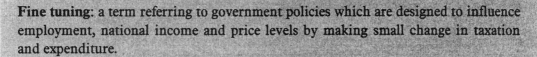

KEY TERM

Fine tuning: a term referring to government policies which are designed to influence employment, national income and price levels by making small change in taxation and expenditure.

1.21 In the 1970s and early 1980s it became clear that minor fiscal adjustments - ie fine tuning - were no longer adequate to influence the economy sufficiently to stimulate growth or reduce unemployment. A fine tuning approach is also hampered by the fact that there will inevitably be a considerable time lag between the time when reliable data on current economic indicators is available and the implementation of policies in response to this data.

1.22 Particularly in the United States and Britain, the success of fiscal policy as a means of influencing the economy sufficiently has been called into question. One of the assumptions built into the use of fiscal policy had been the **multiplier effect.** This is the assumption that a small change in fiscal policy, for example increasing public sector capital investment, will have a 'reverberating' effect through the rest of the economy. Jackson and Cook (1979) concluded from experiments with the UK Treasury's macroeconomic model that the multiplier effect of various fiscal policies is quite small (perhaps less than 1.0 after the first year). The implication of this conclusion is that any fiscal policy to increase government spending by borrowing more might have a disappointingly small effect on demand and employment in the UK.

KEY TERM

Demand management is an approach to economic policy asking which seeks to control the level of aggregate demand through fiscal policy and/or monetary policy.

1.23 The Keynesian (demand management) view is that a depressed economy can be revived by increases in public expenditure (ie through fiscal policy).

By increasing investment, an initial stimulus to expenditure, through the multiplier-accelerator effect, will result in an even bigger increase in national income. If this increased expenditure must be financed by borrowing there will be an increase in the PSBR. Keynesians consider this unimportant:

(a) because the size of the PSBR, they argue, has no effect on interest rates;

(b) because, although it is possible that the PSBR may be responsible for the growth of the money supply, it is not at all certain that an increase in the money supply will lead to higher inflation.

1.24 Monetarists disagree. They believe that a depressed economy cannot be successfully revived by an increase in public expenditure, since any increase in expenditure will normally have to be financed by increased borrowing which will:

(a) further depress the economy through a 'crowding out' effect, and higher interest rates;

(b) increase the money supply and thus cause more inflation.

The UK Labour government's fiscal policy approach

1.25 The UK Labour government elected in 1997 set out five principles which were to lie at the heart of its fixed policy framework.

- **transparency** in the setting of fiscal policy objectives, the implementation of fiscal policy and in the presentation of the public accounts
- **stability** in the fiscal policy-making process and in the way fiscal policy impacts on the economy
- **responsibility** in the management of the public finances
- **fairness,** including between generations
- **efficiency** in the design and implementation of fiscal policy and in managing both sides of the public sector balance sheet.

1.26 These approaches are intended to underlie what the government calls a commonsense approach to fiscal management. The government's new 'Code for Fiscal Stability' is intended to set out the requirements for an open, transparent and accountable approach to managing the public finances, with the declared aim of ensuring that fiscal policy is set in the UK's long-term interests.

1.27 Fiscal policy is based on the following two fiscal rules announced in the July 1997 Budget.

- The **golden rule**: over the economic cycle, the government will borrow only to invest and not to fund current spending; and
- **public debt** as a proportion of national income will be held over the economic cycle at a **stable and prudent level**

Crowding out

1.28 The concept of **crowding out** is an important one in **monetarist** analysis and has influenced the economic policy of the Conservative Governments of the UK from 1979 onwards. The idea has been applied not just in the context of the policy measures necessary to revive a depressed economy: more widely, 'crowding out' by the public sector has been blamed for causing the long-term decline of UK industry.

1.29 It was held that industry was being displaced by the growth of the non-market public sector, meaning that part of the public sector, including health and education, which did not market its output in the same way as a private sector company, since its output is generally provided free. Nationalised industries which sell this output are not part of the 'non-market' sector. The non-market private sector, however, uses resources which must be provided by the market sector but does not supply output to the market and must be supported by taxation.

1.30 The argument goes that if the market sector does not accommodate the requirements of a growing non-market sector by reducing its claims on its own output, then in an open international economy, the adjustment will be made by either more imports or less exports (or both). The crowding out effect of a growing non-market public sector was thus seen as causing higher taxes, higher interest rates to finance higher public spending, inflation pressures, low investment and balance of payments problems, creating the conditions for decline.

1.31 These ideas provided justification for the Conservative UK governments' public spending and taxation policies from 1979. However, the experience of the 1980s was that attempts to reduce public expenditure and taxation merely served to accelerate industrial decline, suggesting that the theory was too simplistic to be accepted as the central basis for fiscal policy. The 'crowding out' argument would suggest that industry was being denied labour by the growth of the non-market sector but the high employment of the 1980s showed that this cannot have been the case. The argument is also naive in its analysis of the role of the non-market public sector, since this sector clearly provides important input to the market sector. This is particularly so in the case of education, which is crucial to improving the skills of the workforce.

The Private Finance Initiative (PFI)

1.32 Under the UK's **Private Finance Initiative**, launched in 1992, no public expenditure is approved without private sector options being explored first.

1.33 The PFI is intended to promote the use of private sector finance for public projects, so as to:

(a) transfer some of the risks associated with the projects to the private sector;

(b) make use of the skills, experience and risk management expertise of the private sector.

1.34 The PFI applies to various types of public expenditure, from relatively simple catering or cleaning contracts to complex contracts such as a new train system or roadway involving design, construction and long-term operation and maintenance.

1.35 From its launch in 1992 up to October 1997, the total of PFI signed deals was £7.5 billion. Over this period, this total is not very large. The new Labour Government has reviewed the Initiative during 1997, and has introduced simplified procedures in an attempt to improve the level of take-up.

2 MONETARY POLICY

The functions of money

2.1 In modern economies, money is used as a means of paying for goods and services, and paying for labour, capital and other resources.

KEY TERM

Money: something which is generally acceptable in settling debts, or in exchanging for goods.

2.2 Money is important because:

(a) it 'oils the wheels' of economic activity, providing an easy method for exchanging goods and services (ie buying and selling);

(b) the total amount of money in a national economy may have a significant influence on economic activity and inflation.

2.3 Attempts to define money have traditionally started with identifying what money does - ie what are the **functions of money**? Money acts as:

- a means of exchange
- a unit of account
- a standard of deferred payment
- a store of value

Money as a means of exchange

2.4 This is arguably the most important function of money in an economy, because without money, the only way of exchanging goods and services would be by means of **barter**, ie by a **direct exchange** of goods or services. In other words, if a shoemaker wanted to buy a horse, he would have either:

(a) to find a horse-owner prepared to exchange a horse for a sufficient quantity of shoes of equal value to the horse; or else

(b) to find other people willing to exchange different goods (eg food, clothes etc) for shoes, and then trade these goods in exchange for a horse from the horse-owner.

2.5 A **monetary economy** is the only alternative to a barter economy, and it is a means of encouraging economic development and growth.

(a) People are prepared to organise and work for an employer, and in return receive money wages.

(b) A business will exchange its goods or services for money in return.

(c) People will pay out money in order to obtain goods or services.

Money as a unit of account

2.6 This function of money is associated with the use of money as a means of exchange. Money should be able to measure exactly what something is worth. It should provide an agreed standard measure by which the **value** of different goods and services can be compared.

2.7 For example, suppose that only four products are traded in a market. These are pigs, sheep, hens and corn. The relative value of these products must be agreed before exchange can take place in the market. It might be decided that:

(a) 1 pig has the same value as 0.75 sheep, 3 hens or 1.5 bags of corn;
(b) 1 sheep is the same value as 1.33 pigs, 4 hens or 2 bags of corn;

(c) 1 hen is worth 0.33 pigs, 0.25 sheep or 0.5 bags of corn;

(d) 1 bag of corn has the same value as 0.67 pigs, 0.5 sheep or 2 hens.

(In a market with more than four products, the relative values of each product compared with others could be worked out in the same way, although there would be many more value or price ratios to calculate.)

2.8 The function of money in the economy would be to establish a common unit of 'value measurement' or 'account' by which the relative exchange values or prices of goods can be established.

Question 1

In the above example of a four-product market, simplify the value relationship by expressing the worth of a pig, a sheep, a hen and a bag of corn in terms of a common unit of money.

Answer

You might have calculated as follows.

A pig	=	3 units
A sheep	=	4 units
A hen	=	1 unit
A bag of corn	=	2 units

Other results (such as 6, 8, 2 and 4 respectively) would work just as well.

Money as a standard of deferred payment

2.9 When a person buys a good or service, he might not want to pay for it straightaway, perhaps because he has not yet got the money. Instead, he might ask for credit. Selling goods on credit is not an essential feature of an economy, but it certainly helps to stimulate trade. The function of money in this respect is to establish, by agreement between buyer and seller, how much value will be given in return at some future date for goods provided/received now.

Similarly, when a buyer and seller agree now to make a contract for the supply of certain goods in the future, the function of money is to establish the value of the contract, ie how much the buyer will eventually pay the seller for the goods.

2.10 In order to provide an acceptable standard for deferred payments, it is important that money should maintain its value over a period of time. Suppose, for example, that a customer buys goods for an agreed sum of money, but on three months' credit. Now if the value of money falls in the three-month credit period, the sum of money which the seller eventually receives will be worth less than it was at the time of sale. The seller will have lost value by allowing the credit.

When the value of money falls (or rises) over time, sellers (or buyers) will be reluctant to arrange credit, or to agree the price for future contracts. Money would then be failing to fulfil its function as a standard for deferred payments.

2.11 One major reason why money might lose value is because of price inflation. When inflation is high:

(a) sellers will be reluctant to allow credit to buyers. For example, if a buyer asks for three months credit, and inflation is running at 20% per annum, the 'real' value of the debt that the buyer owes will fall by about 5% over the three month credit period;

(b) sellers will be reluctant to agree to a fixed price for long term contracts. For example, a house-builder might refuse to quote a price for building a house over a twelve month period, and instead insist on asking a price which is 'index-linked' and rises in step with the general rate of inflation.

Money as a store of value

2.12 Money acts as a **store of value**, or **wealth**. So too do many other assets (eg land, buildings, art treasures, motorcars, machinery) some of which maintain or increase their money value over time, and some of which depreciate in value. This means of course that money is not the only asset which acts as a store of wealth, and we need to extend our definition of this function of money.

2.13 Money is more properly described as acting as a liquid store of value. This definition has two parts to it.

(a) Money is a store of value or wealth. A person can hold money for an extended period, for the purpose of exchanging it for services or goods or other assets.

(b) Money is a liquid asset.

2.14 The potential erosion of the value of money due to inflation provides one good reason why someone with wealth to store should hold assets which are not money.

The role and aims of monetary policy

2.15 Monetary policy is perhaps best thought of as a means towards the achievement of an intermediate economic target, which in turn is a means towards the achievement of an ultimate economic objective.

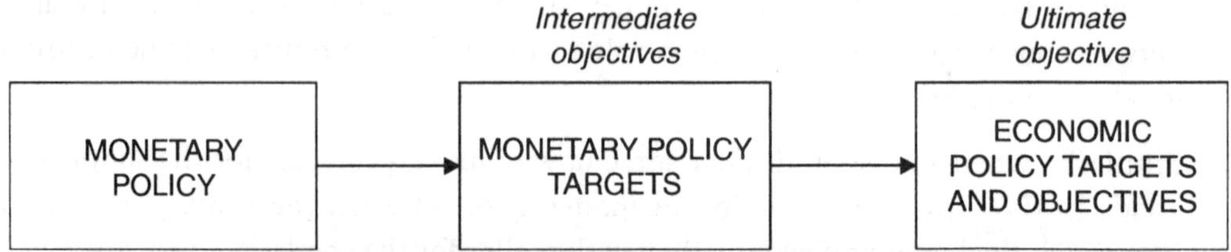

KEY TERM

Monetary policy is the regulation of the economy through control of the monetary system by operating on such variables as the money supply, the level of interest rates and the conditions for availability of credit.

2.16 The **effectiveness** of monetary policy will depend on:

(a) whether the targets of monetary policy are achieved successfully;

(b) whether the success of monetary policy leads on to the successful achievement of the intermediate target (eg lower inflation); and

(c) whether the successful achievement of the intermediate target (eg lower inflation) leads on to the successful achievement of the overall objective (eg strong economic growth).

2.17 Monetary policy in the UK has for some years been directed primarily at the intermediate objective of keeping the rate of inflation under control.

Targets of monetary policy

2.18 When a government chooses its monetary policy it will express its policy aims in terms of qualified targets for achievement. These **targets of monetary policy** must be selected and should relate to something:

(a) over which the government or central bank can exert influence; and

(b) which will contribute to the achievement of the government's overall economic objectives.

2.19 Targets of monetary policy are likely to relate to the volume of national income and expenditure. The targets of monetary policy which might have some influence on national income (ie 'national income', 'GNP' or 'GDP') are:

(a) growth in the size of the money stock (money supply);
(b) the level of interest rates;
(c) the volume of credit or growth in the volume of credit;
(d) the exchange rate;
(e) the volume of expenditure in the economy (ie national income or GNP itself).

Before looking at some of these possible targets of monetary policy in more detail, we need to explain different ways in which the stock of money can be measured, and outline different ideas about the demand for money.

The stock of money in an economy

2.20 The money supply is the total amount of money in the economy. It is also referred to as the money stock. A monetary aggregate is a total of the money stock or money supply. In the UK, there are four different monetary aggregates which are published by the Bank of England. These are:

M0, M2, M4 and M3H.

Various other aggregates, including M1, M3 and M5 have been published at various times in the past.

2.21 Note the following points about the monetary aggregates in current use.

(a) **M0** is the 'narrowest' definition of money, the great majority of which is made up of notes and coin in circulation outside the Bank of England.

(b) **M2** is effectively a measure of all sterling deposits used for **transaction** purposes (as distinct from 'investment' purposes).

(c) **M4** is a 'broad' definition of money, including deposits held for savings as well as spending purposes. The Bank of England also now publishes statistics for various 'liquid assets outside M4' for the benefit of those who are interested in a still broader definition of the money stock.

(d) **M3H** is a standardised European broad money measure which can normally be expected to move roughly in line with M4.

2.22 The main purpose of measuring a monetary aggregate is to discover by how much (and how rapidly) the money supply is rising in the economy, and

(a) to predict from this rise what future changes in economic activity might be;

(b) also to discover whether past changes in the money supply help to explain changes in economic activity which have already occurred.

2.23 There is also the view that by controlling the rate of increase in the money supply, inflation can be brought under control and economic conditions made more suitable for achieving economic growth and fuller employment.

Difficulties in defining monetary aggregates

2.24 The Bank of England has accepted that there is considerable difficulty in defining an acceptable aggregate for the money stock or for the liquid assets held by various sectors of the economy. There are several reasons for this difficulty.

(a) Money is both a means of payment and a store of wealth. To be a means of payment, money must be liquid. However, as a store of wealth, the requirement for liquidity is not so immediate. People are prepared to sacrifice some liquidity to obtain higher interest. A problem in defining a monetary aggregate can be stated as:

'When does a financial asset become so non-liquid that it cannot be classed as money?'

(b) There are so many different financial instruments in the UK that no matter where the line is drawn between money and non-money there will always be borderline cases where the difference between items included and excluded is small.

(c) The government has found from experience that there is no single monetary aggregate which is good enough on its own to show the relationship between changes in the money supply and other economic activity.

Monetary aggregates figures

2.25 To give you some idea of the relative 'sizes' of the main definitions of money, UK money stock figures for a particular month are shown below.

			£bn
M0	=	notes and coin in circulation outside the Bank of England	21.3
	+	banks' operational deposits with the Bank of England	0.1
			21.4
M2	=	non-bank sector holdings of notes and coin	18.1
	+	non bank private sector's retail sterling deposits with UK banks and building societies	384.6
			402.7
M4	=	non-bank private sector holdings of:	
		notes and coin	18.3
	+	banks' retail deposits	182.4
	+	building societies' shares and deposits	202.0
	+	other interest bearing deposits	158.0
			560.7

Different schools of thought in monetary theory

2.26 There are two broad schools of thought about monetary theory and economists are not in unanimous agreement. The two broadly differing views are:

(a) the **monetarist view**. The monetarist view of money supply and demand, and of the influence of money on interest rates and inflation, derives from the so-called quantity theory of money;

(b) the **Keynesian view**. Keynes developed a theory of the demand for money in the 1920s, known as liquidity preference theory, which challenged the quantity theory of money.

The quantity theory of money

2.27 Monetarist economists stress the significance of the role of money in the workings of the economy, and base their arguments on the old quantity theory of money.

2.28 The **classical quantity theory of money** was developed by Irving Fisher in 1911 at a time when the value of the pound was linked to the price of gold and the quantity of money therefore changed little. It was the generally accepted view until the 1930s about the relationship between the amount of money in the economy and the level of prices. It is a theory about how much money supply is needed to enable the economy to function.

2.29 The quantity theory took the view that money was used only as a medium of exchange, to settle transactions involving the demand and supply for goods and services.

This is quite important to remember. Whereas the quantity theory states that the demand for money is simply for spending on foreseeable transactions (and monetarist economists agree with this view) Keynesian economists argue that there are other reasons for wanting to hold money.

2.30 If the number of transactions in the economy is fixed, and independent of the amount of the money supply, then the total money value of transactions will be PT, where P is the price level of goods and services bought and sold and T is the number or quantity of transactions.

2.31 The amount of money needed to pay for these transactions will depend on the **velocity of circulation**. Money changes hands. A person receiving money can use it to make his own purchases. For example, if A pays B £2 for transaction X, B can use the £2 to pay C for transaction Y and C can use the same £2 to pay D for transaction Z. If the three transactions X, Y, and Z all occur within a given period of time then the money value of the transactions is:

$$PT = £2 \times 3 \text{ transactions} = £6.$$

The total amount of money is the same £2 in circulation for all three transactions but this money has exchanged hands three times. The velocity of circulation is 3 and MV = 6,

where M is the money supply; and
V is the velocity of circulation.

2.32 This brings us to the 'identity' of the quantity theory of money:

$$MV = PT$$

MV *must* equal PT because they are two different ways of measuring the same transactions. In practice, the velocity of circulation V is calculated as the balancing figure where:

$$V = \frac{PT}{M}$$

2.33 For example, if the total money value of transactions in Ruritania in 1988 was 50,000,000 Roubles and the money supply amounted to 10,000,000 Roubles, the velocity of circulation would be 5.

Equations in the quantity theory of money

(1) Demand for money $= M_d$

$M_dV = PT$

(2) Supply of money M_s is a certain amount M, ie:

$M_s = M$

(3) For an equilibrium condition, money supply must equal the demand for money:

$M_s = M_d$

(4) From (1) (2) and (3) we get:

$MV = PT$

Conclusion from the quantity theory of money

2.34 The identity (or 'equation') of the quantity theory of money does not really say very much. It is assumed that M is both the quantity of *demand* for money and also the money *supply*.

(a) An increase in M would reduce V or increase either P or T.
(b) An increase in V would reduce M or increase either P or T.
(c) An increase in P would reduce T or increase either M or V.
(d) An increase in T would reduce P or increase either M or V.

2.35 However, three further assumptions can be made.

(a) V has a roughly constant value. The velocity of circulation of money remains the same at all times, or at least only changes very slowly over time. There were reasons for making this assumption which we need not delve into here. Whether V is constant or not is discussed later.

(b) T is either given or it is independent of the amount of money, M. The reason why T should be a given total was that the supporters of the quantity theory argued that in the economy, full employment of resources is the norm and if all resources are fully utilised the volume of transactions T must be a constant value.

(c) The amount of M is determined by other factors and is independent of V, T or (most significantly) P. The money supply could be controlled by government authorities (eg the central bank).

2.36 Given these assumptions, the quantity theory of money becomes a theory of price levels because, since MV = PT:

then $P = \frac{MV}{T}$

If V and T are roughly constant values, P will vary directly with increases or decreases in the amount of M and it is changes in the money supply M that cause prices P to change, not changes in price that cause changes in the money supply. In other words, inflation would be directly related to the money supply, and a 10% increase in the money supply, say, would result in 10% inflation.

2.37 Monetarist economists have argued that in spite of short-term fluctuations, the velocity of circulation V is constant in the long term. Keynesians economists disagree, and argue that V is variable and so there is no direct connection between the money supply and inflation. In the UK, statistics show that the velocity of circulation increased during the

1970s but slowed down during the 1980s except for M0. Even so, it is probably reasonable to suppose that *over a longer period of time*, V should remain fairly stable.

The demand for money

2.38 We shall now look more closely at the **demand** for money, which will take us further into the conflicting theories of Keynesian and monetarist economists.

2.39 It helps to start by getting a clear idea of what we mean by money. When we consider the **theories** of demand for money, we take money to mean a **non-interest bearing store of wealth**.

(a) Bank notes and current (bank) accounts ('sight deposits') are money.
(b) Funds in a bank time deposit account are not money. Nor are building society deposits.

Our definition of money has now therefore switched from a **broad money** definition (M4) to a **narrow money** definition.

2.40 You might think this is a bit unrealistic, because depositors can go to a bank or building society nowadays and withdraw funds from many interest-bearing accounts on demand, and so these deposits are virtually money. Even so, this is not the view that economic theory takes. Interest-bearing deposits are categorised collectively as **bonds**. When an individual puts funds from a bank current account into a building society account, say, he or she is supplying money in exchange for 'bonds'.

2.41 Another basic distinction about money and 'non-money' bonds which we shall make, and which is not altogether valid in today's financial world, is that whereas money is a liquid store of wealth, interest-bearing bonds are not fully liquid. Someone with an interest-bearing deposit or investment must usually go to a bit of trouble, and give some notice, to cash in the investment. For example, it is usual to give 7 days' notice to transfer funds from a bank deposit account to a current account, without forgoing entitlement to interest. Holding bonds therefore means sacrificing some liquidity.

2.42 The distinction between 'money' and 'bonds' is really not so clear-cut, but to get the theory of demand for money sorted out, it will help if you can forget the blurred distinction, and think of money and bonds as they have been defined here.

Liquidity preference and reasons for holding money

2.43 'Liquidity' means assets in the form of cash or 'near-cash', in particular notes and coin and money in a current bank account. **Liquidity preference** refers to the preference of people to hold on to their savings as money (ie in liquid form) rather than investing it.

2.44 Keynes identified three reasons or motives why people hold wealth as money rather than as interest-bearing securities. These were:

(a) the **transactions motive**: households need money to pay for their day-to-day purchases. The level of transactions demand for money depends on household incomes;

(b) the **precautionary motive**: people choose to keep money on hand or in the bank as a precaution for a 'rainy day' when it might suddenly be needed;

(c) the **speculative motive**: some people choose to keep ready money to take advantage of a profitable opportunity to invest in bonds which may arise (or they may sell bonds for money when they fear a fall in bonds' market prices).

2.45 The **speculative motive** for holding money needs explaining a bit further.

(a) If individuals hold money for speculative purposes, this means that they are not using the money to invest in bonds.

(If individuals are saving, but not investing their savings in bonds, they will be holding on to their savings for speculative reasons. Hence, savings and investment might not be in equilibrium, with consequences for changes in national income which will be discussed in a later chapter).

(b) The reason for holding money instead of investing in bonds is that interest rates are expected to go up. If interest rates go up, bond prices will fall.

For example, if the current market price of bonds which pay 5% interest is £100, and interest rates doubled to 10%, the market value of the bonds would fall, perhaps to £50. So if interest rates are expected to go up, any bonds held now will be expected to lose value, and bond holders would make a capital loss. Thus, it makes sense to hold on to money, for investing in bonds later, *after* interest rates have gone up.

(c) What causes individuals to have expectations about interest rate changes in the future?

Keynes argued that each individual has some expectation of a normal rate of interest. This perception of a normal interest rate reflects past levels and movements in the interest rate, and expectations of the future rate level, obtained from available market information.

(i) For example, if someone believes that the normal rate of interest is above the current level, he will expect the interest rate to rise and will therefore expect bond prices to fall. To avoid a capital loss the individual will sell bonds and hold money.

(ii) Conversely, if an individual believes that the normal rate of interest is below the current market interest rate, he will expect the market interest rate to fall and bond prices to rise. Hence he will buy bonds, and run down speculative money holdings, in order to make a capital gain.

KEY TERM

Liquidity preference: the term used by Keynes for the desire to hold money rather than other forms of wealth, arising from the transactions motive, the speculative motive and the precautionary motive.

2.46 Keynes argued further that people will need money to satisfy the transactions motive and precautionary motive regardless of the level of interest. It is only the speculative motive which alters the demand for money as a result of interest rates.

(a) If interest rates are high, people will lend more money (eg by buying government stocks), hold little cash, and will have *low* liquidity preference.

(b) If interest rates are low and people expect them to rise, there is a danger that current bond prices will fall when interest rates go up. People will therefore hold money to satisfy the speculative motive, ie want to invest later in bonds, and their liquidity preference will be *high*.

2.47 The conclusion is that the demand for money will be high (ie liquidity preference will be high) when interest rates are low. This is because the speculative demand for money will be high when interest rates are low. Similarly, the demand for money will be low when interest rates are high, because the speculative demand for money will be low.

2.48 There is a minimum fixed demand for money (transactions and precautionary motives) and some demand for money that varies with interest rates (speculative motive). This can be shown as a liquidity preference schedule or curve (Figure 1).

In Figure 1, X is the minimum quantity of money needed, regardless of interest rate, to satisfy the minimum demand arising from the transactions and precautionary motives for holding money.

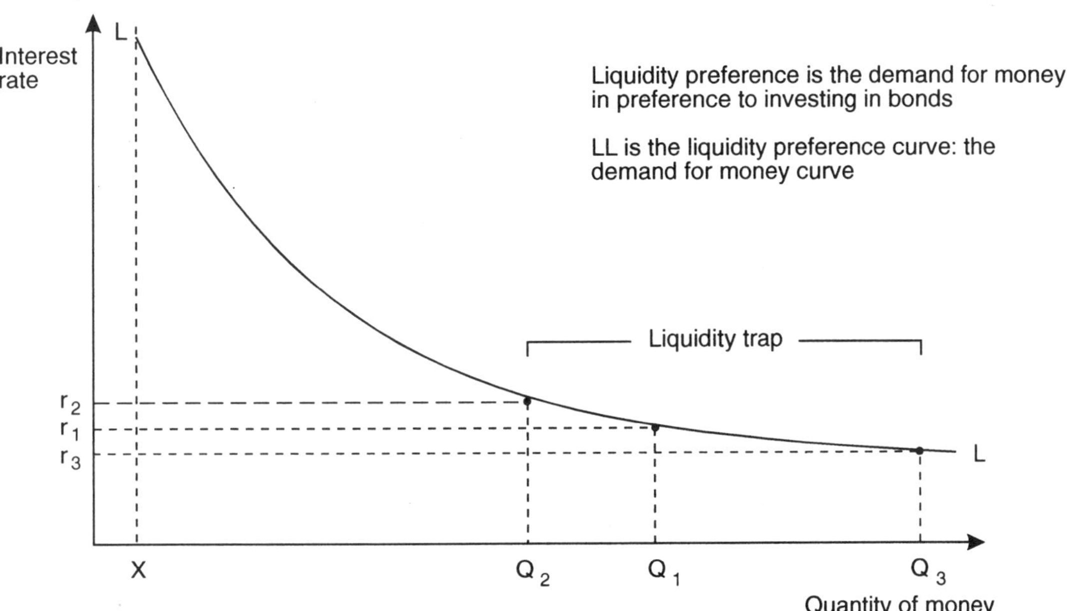

Figure 1 Liquidity preference schedule

2.49 Where the liquidity preference curve is elastic (ie has a shallow slope), the government will find it hard to change the rate of interest. If the rate is to be lowered from r_2 to r_1, an increase in the money supply is required (the amount $Q_1 - Q_2$ in Figure 1). An equal fall in the interest rate, from r_1 to r_3 requires the much larger increase of $(Q_3 - Q_1)$ in the money supply. Liquidity preference becomes increasingly elastic at lower interest rates (ie 'households' will wish to give up large quantities of 'bonds' for cash in response to a very small change in the interest rate). Liquidity preference could even become infinitely elastic at a particularly low interest rate.

The region of the liquidity preference curve which approaches infinite elasticity (ie approaches the horizontal) is called the **liquidity trap.**

Keynesian view on interest rates and money demand and supply

2.50 If the money supply is assumed to be fixed by government decision, the size of the money supply is perfectly inelastic with respect to changes in the rate of interest. Keynes argued that the level of interest rates in the economy would then be reached by the interaction of money supply (fixed) and money demand (liquidity preference).

If the money supply is 'fixed' it then follows that interest rates in the economy will be determined by the demand for money (Figure 2).

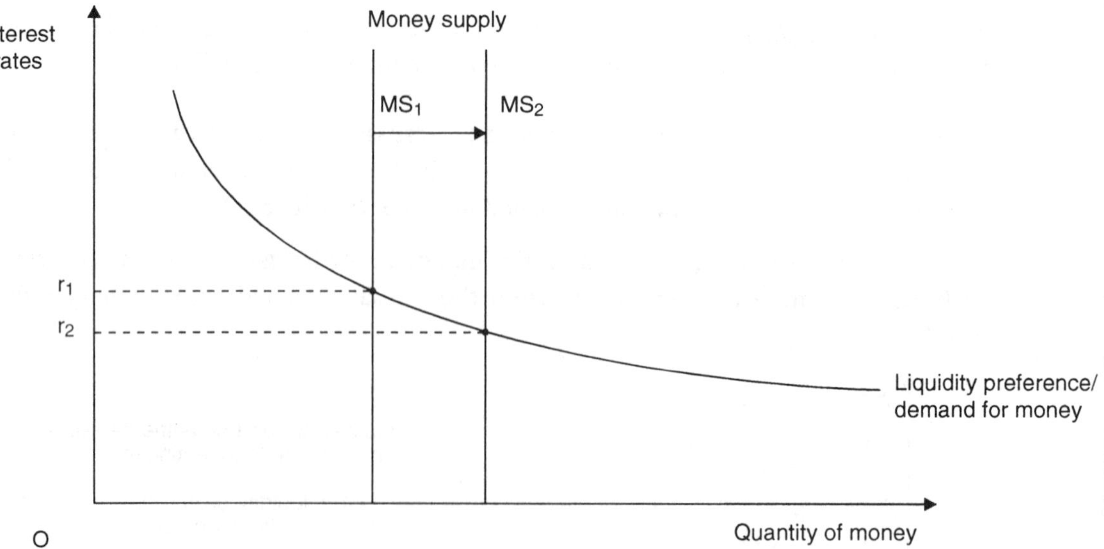

Figure 2 Consequences of an increase in the money supply: Keynesian views

2.51 If there is an increase in the money supply, from MS_1 to MS_2 in Figure 2, interest rates will fall from r_1 to r_2. There will be some increase in the level of investment spending, since it now becomes more profitable for firms to invest in new capital. The increase in investment, being an injection into the circular flow of income, causes some increase in the level of national income through the multiplier process.

2.52 According to the Keynesians, therefore, an increase (or decrease) in the money supply only affects the demand for goods and services - and hence the level of income - indirectly, via a change in the rate of interest.

2.53 The impact on the economy of the increase in the money supply therefore depends on the effect that the fall in interest rates produces. According to the Keynesian view, both investment demand and consumer spending are relatively insensitive to interest rate changes, that is, they are relatively interest inelastic. The volume of investment depends heavily, Keynes argued, on **technological changes** and **business confidence and expectations** too. It follows that the increase in the money supply will have only a limited effect on aggregate demand and consequently relatively little effect on output and employment.

2.54 If the rate of interest is at a point where the demand for money is in the so-called liquidity trap, an increase in the money supply would have a very small effect on interest rates. Investment would then be hardly affected at all. Keynes explained this by saying that the increases in the money supply would be offset by a reduction in the velocity of circulation, so that the increase in the money supply would have a neutral effect on the economy.

2.55 Keynesians therefore argue that monetary policy to control the money supply would possibly, though not always, have an effect on interest rates (an increase in the money supply without an increase in the demand for money would make individuals use the extra money available to buy more bonds, and the higher demand for bonds would push down interest rates) and changes in interest rates might in the longer term affect investment. In other respects, however, monetary policy would not really affect the economy and national income, because increases in the money supply would be neutralised by reductions in the velocity of circulation, leaving PT unaffected.

The monetarist viewpoint

2.56 Monetarist economists such as Professor Friedman revived the quantity theory of money and argued that there is a much more direct link between the money supply and national income.

In other words, whereas Keynes argued that an increase in the money supply would merely result in lower interest rates, with no immediate effect on national income, monetarists argue that an increase in the money supply will lead directly and quickly to changes in national income and PT, with the velocity of circulation V remaining fairly constant.

2.57 Monetarists argue that since money is a direct substitute for all other assets, an increase in the money supply, given a fairly stable velocity of circulation, will have a direct effect on demand for other assets because there will be more money to spend on those assets. If the total output of the economy is fixed, then an increase in the money supply will lead directly to higher prices.

2.58 The ideas of the monetarists might become more clear to you if we consider the effects of a fairly rapid **increase in the money supply**.

(a) Since there is more money held as an asset, the gain in convenience from the additional money holdings will fall.

(b) People will spend money on substitute assets. These are not just bonds, as Keynes argued, but also equities and physical assets (goods).

(c) If the economy is already at full employment, the extra money spent on the same quantity of goods purchased will result in a rise in prices. (This is significantly at odds with Keynes' analysis which was that the only effect of a bigger money supply would be lower interest rates.)

(d) Unlike Keynesians, monetarists also suggest that an increase in prices will probably lead to an increase in money incomes as well; for example, wages and salaries will be raised to keep pace with the rate of inflation.

(e) In the short run, interest rates will fall. In this respect they agree with the Keynesians. This is because the demand for financial assets will rise.

(f) If the economy is at less than full employment, in the short run an increase in the money supply might raise the volume of real transactions, ie output and 'real' incomes, as well as prices. However, this view does not have the same prominence in monetarist theory as (c) and (d) above because it only has a short run effect.

(g) If the increase in the money supply is quite rapid, the economy will be unable to produce extra output quickly enough, even if it has unemployed resources, and some inflation will be inevitable, even if there is some rise in output too.

(h) Higher prices will make workers demand higher wages to protect their real income.

(i) The end result is that prices will go up further and in the long run the increase in the money supply will affect prices only and not output.

(j) In the long run too, higher inflation will cause an increase in interest rates so that the short-term reduction in interest rates will not last.

(k) Once the rate of inflation has started to increase, inflationary expectations will be aroused. People will continue to demand higher and higher wages to protect their real income, and inflation will be perpetuated.

2.59 Monetarists therefore reach the same basic conclusion as the old quantity theory of money. A rise in the money supply will lead to a rise in prices and probably also to a rise in money incomes. (It is also assumed by monetarists that the velocity of circulation remains fairly constant - again, taking a view similar to the old quantity theory.)

The money stock as a target of monetary policy 6/96

2.60 To monetarist economists, the money stock is a possible intermediate target of economic policy. This is because they claim that an increase in the money supply will raise prices and money incomes, and this in turn will raise the demand for money to spend.

2.61 It is a crucial aspect of monetarist theory that the link between the money supply and prices, incomes and expenditure is reasonably predictable and stable. In other words, the velocity of circulation must remain fairly stable so that money expenditure and money income are directly influenced by changes in the money supply. If this link is not reliable, government policy to control the growth of the money stock will have unpredictable consequences for both inflation and 'real' expenditure in the economy and so would be a poor weapon of government policy.

Unpredictable variations in the money supply will be disliked by financial managers because stability is an aid to forward planning. If the rate of expansion of the money supply is known, decision makers can incorporate the expected rate of inflation in their pricing policies and investment appraisals, for example.

2.62 Controlling the growth of the money supply is only a medium-term policy, however, and it cannot work miracle cures for the economy in a short time. When such a policy is first introduced, the short-term effect would be unpredictable because:

(a) the effect on interest rates might be erratic;

(b) there might be a time lag before anything can be done. Gathering accurate economic data on which policy needs to be based takes time. It also takes time to cut government spending, for example, and cuts in the PSBR might be an instrument of monetary policy to control the growth in M0 or M4;

(c) there might be a time lag before control of the money supply alters expectations about inflation and thus wage demands.

2.63 The money stock, if it is a monetary policy target, should therefore be a **medium-term target**. When the UK government set targets for the growth of the money supply as a main feature of its economic policy strategy from 1980, it was prepared to wait for some years to see any benefits from its policies and therefore set out its policy targets in what was called a **medium-term financial strategy**.

2.64 During the late 1980s and the 1990s, monetary targeting fell out of fashion among academics and other commentators. There are signs now, however, that it could be making a comeback because of its likely use by the new **European Central Bank (ECB)** which will take charge of monetary policy in respect of the euro, the new **single European currency** soon to be adopted by some European Union states. At the time of writing (June 1998), it is considered probable that the ECB will follow the German Bundesbank in choosing an intermediate monetary measure such as **M3** for targeting purposes.

Interest rates as a target for monetary policy

2.65 The authorities may decide that interest rates themselves should be a target of monetary policy. This would be appropriate if it is considered that there is a direct relationship between interest rates and the level of expenditure in the economy.

Although it is generally accepted that there is likely to be a connection between interest rates and investment (by companies) and consumer expenditure, the connection is not a stable and predictable one, and interest rate changes are only likely to affect the level of expenditure after a considerable time lag.

2.66 In the UK, the government's main monetary policy weapon in the late 1980s was high interest rates. High interest rates, it was argued, will help reduce the rate of inflation which is seen to be caused mainly by a boom in consumer spending.

(a) High interest rates will deter consumer borrowing, it is believed. If consumer borrowing can be controlled, consumer spending will be controlled too, at least to the extent that consumer spending is financed by borrowing.

(b) High interest repayments on existing loans will leave borrowers with less money to spend on other things.

(c) High interest rates will tend to keep the value of sterling high. This will tend to keep down the cost of imports, which will include imports of raw materials. It is hoped that this will help to prevent 'import-cost-push' inflation.

2.67 An important reason for pursuing an interest rate policy is that the authorities are able to influence interest rates much more effectively than they can influence other policy targets, such as the money supply or the volume of credit.

2.68 As mentioned earlier, in 1997 the new Labour Government of the UK gave responsibility for setting short-term interest rates to the central bank, the Bank of England. The Bank now sets rates at a level which it considers appropriate, given the inflation rate target set by the Government. The purpose of having the central bank setting interest rates is to remove the risk of **political influence** over the decisions.

The growth in the volume of credit as a target for monetary policy

2.69 The government might decide to restrict credit lending (impose a 'credit squeeze') and so set targets for limited growth of credit in the economy. An increase in bank lending (ie in the volume of credit) is likely to lead to a rise in the level of expenditure in the economy because people borrow money in order to spend it. Higher bank lending is also likely to result in higher bank deposits and thus an increase in the money stock.

2.70 Control over the total volume of bank credit, and perhaps the total volume of credit of other non-bank financial institutions too, might be:

(a) a direct way of reducing the level of expenditure in the economy; and

(b) a way of affecting expenditure in the economy *indirectly* by containing the growth of the money supply.

However, a credit squeeze needs to be efficient and fair. It might be seen as unfair, for example, to restrict banks from giving more credit if similar restrictions are not also placed on non-bank financial institutions that also give credit.

Fiscal policy as an instrument of monetary policy

2.71 Fiscal policy, as we have seen, refers to the government's policy on public expenditure and taxation. Fiscal policy can work in co-operation with monetary policy. For example, a fiscal policy of reducing government expenditure and cutting the PSBR will have the effect of reducing the growth in M4. An important weakness of fiscal policy as an **instrument of**

monetary policy is that fiscal policy changes only once a year, at Budget time, and so for much of the year, the monetary authorities must take fiscal conditions as largely given.

2.72 More often than not, the government has expenditures in excess of revenues and so in most years, the government borrows.

- The additional borrowing each year is the **Public sector borrowing requirement (PSBR)**
- The total cumulative debt of the country is the **National Debt**

2.73 The government might wish to reduce the PSBR, as a monetary policy target. A reason for wanting to reduce the PSBR could be because the government wants to cut its spending and reduce the role of government in the economy, leaving the performance of the economy to 'free market forces'. The PSBR could be reduced either by cutting government expenditure or raising tax revenues.

Reserve requirements on banks as a means of controlling the money supply

2.74 As another technique for controlling money supply growth, the government might impose reserve requirements on banks.

(a) One type of reserve requirement is a compulsory **minimum cash reserve ratio** (ie the ratio of cash to total assets).

(b) Another form of reserve requirement is that banks should have a minimum ratio of **reserve assets** to total deposits. Reserve assets are types of short-term liquid assets, and by insisting that banks hold a certain proportion of these assets in their asset portfolios, the authorities would hope to reduce the volume of bank loans and therefore the volume of bank deposits.

Direct controls as a technique of monetary control

2.75 Yet another way of controlling the growth of the money supply is to impose direct controls on bank lending. Direct controls may be either quantitative or qualitative.

(a) **Quantitative controls** might be imposed on either bank lending (assets) or bank deposits (liabilities). For example, the government might put 'lending ceilings' on the clearing banks which restrict the growth of the banks' lending (assets). For example, banks might be forbidden to increase their lending by more than, say, 5% per annum.

(b) **Qualitative controls** might be used to alter the type of lending by banks. For example, the government (via the Bank) can ask the banks to limit their lending to the personal sector, and lend more to industry, or to lend less to a particular type of firm (such as, for example, property companies) and more to manufacturing businesses.

Prudential controls

2.76 Prudential control refers to the monitoring of banks and other financial institutions by the authorities to ensure that they have an adequate capital structure, liquidity (asset portfolio) and/or foreign exchange exposure.

2.77 The prudential control by a country's central bank as a supervisor of the banking system belongs to a grey area between quantitative and qualitative controls. Prudential controls are not used directly to control the money supply but they might have some indirect influence and so it is useful to mention them here.

Under proposals announced in 1997, supervision of the UK banking system is to be transferred from the Bank of England to an expanded Securities and Investments Board (SIB) in the future.

Exchange rate control as an instrument or target of monetary policy

2.78 The **exchange rates** between the domestic currencies and other currencies and changes in exchange rates, have implications for:

(a) the balance of payments;
(b) inflation;
(c) economic growth.

The government might seek to achieve a target exchange rate for its currency.

Question 2

Outline the effects on the economy of a policy of high interest rates to dampen demand and inflation.

Answer

An increase in interest rates is thought to reduce the money supply in the economy and thereby to reduce the level of effective demand which will, in turn, decrease inflation and improve the balance of payments (the latter by decreasing the demand for imports, and freeing more domestic output for sale abroad).

Aggregate expenditure in the economy will decrease, for various reasons.

(a) A higher interest rate encourages savings at the expense of consumer expenditure.

(b) Higher interest rates will increase mortgage payments and will thus reduce the amount of disposable income in the hands of home buyers for discretionary spending.

(c) The higher cost of consumer credit will deter borrowing and spending on consumer durables.

(d) Higher prices of goods due to higher borrowing costs for industry will also reduce some consumer expenditure in the economy.

Investment expenditure may also decline for two reasons.

(a) Higher interest rates deter some investment due to increased borrowing costs.

(b) Higher interest rates may make the corporate sector pessimistic about future business prospects and confidence in the economy. This may further reduce investment in the economy.

To the extent that higher domestic interest rates lead to an appreciation of the exchange rate, this should reduce inflation by lowering the cost of imported items. Exporters will experience pressure on their costs as the result of the more competitive price conditions they face, and may be less willing to concede high wage demands, and thus wage inflation may be constrained.

The desired outcomes of the authorities' interest rate policy which we have noted above may be negated by the following effects of higher interest rates.

(a) Higher interest results in greater interest income for savers, who may increase their spending due to this interest windfall.

(b) Since mortgage payments are the single largest constituent of the Retail Prices Index (RPI), any increase in them will be reflected immediately in RPI increases. This could lead to higher wage demands in the economy, and may result in a wage-price spiral.

(c) By encouraging capital inflows, higher interest rates will tend to lead to an appreciation of the currency's exchange rate. This makes exports less competitive and imports more attractive.

(d) A reduction in investment may decrease the pressure of demand in the economy but at the same time it will set in motion a process which in the future could reduce the economy's potential for production.

(e) To the extent that higher interest rates do squeeze demand in the economy, they will reduce employment, decreasing the proceeds of taxation and increasing the government expenditure on the unemployed.

The effects of higher interest rates may be perverse and in the longer run, rather ambiguous. This conclusion is firmly borne out by the experience of the British economy over the period from 1988 to

1990. The policy of high interest rates which was begun in 1988 took much longer to take effect than policy makers had anticipated, with increases in the annual inflation rate continuing until late 1990. The effects of the policy were most keenly felt in 1991, when it may have precipitated a deeper recession than might otherwise have occurred.

Chapter roundup

- **Fiscal policy** seeks to influence the economy by managing the amounts which the government spends and the amounts it collects through taxation. Fiscal policy can be used as an instrument of **demand management**.
- A government may use **monetary policies** to pursue its economic aims. It may do so by setting 'intermediate' targets, for interest rate levels, growth in the money supply, the exchange rate or growth in bank lending.
- **Tools** for implementing monetary policy include influence over interest rates, fiscal policy, exchange rate policy, or the regulation of banks and other financial institutions.

Quick quiz

1 Why might taxation be considered a deterrent to economic growth? (see paras 1.5, 1.6)
2 How might fiscal policy be used by a government to affect national income? (1.7)
3 Define a budget surplus and a budget deficit. (1.13)
4 What is meant by 'fine tuning?' (1.20)
5 What is meant by 'crowding out'? (1.28 - 1.31)
6 What are the possible targets of monetary policy? (2.19)
7 Which three motives for holding money did Keynes identify? (2.44)

Question to try	Level	Marks	Time
18	Introductory	n/a	35 mins

Chapter 18

INFLATION

Chapter topic list		Syllabus reference
1	Defining and measuring inflation	5(a)
2	Consequences of inflation	5(a)
3	The causes of inflation	5(a)

Introduction

Many of the macroeconomic policy measures discussed in Chapters 16 and 17 are directed at finding a balance in which there is **steady economic growth** with low (or no) general **price inflation**.

The emphasis placed by policy-makers on low inflation has increased in recent years. So what is so bad about rising prices? In this chapter, we look at the consequences of **inflation** and at measures which can be taken by individuals and firms to mitigate its negative consequences.

We will be examining the effect of inflation on **capital investment appraisal** later in the text.

1 DEFINING AND MEASURING INFLATION

What is inflation?

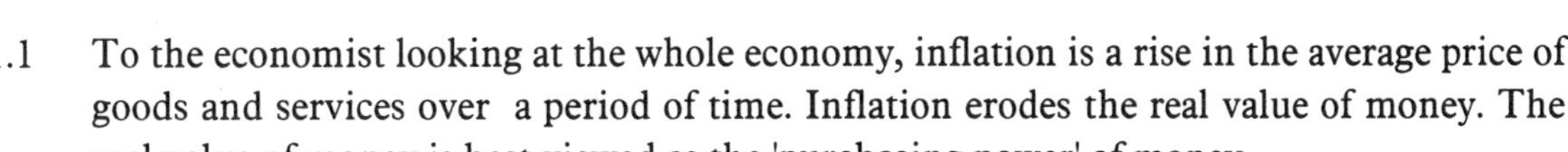

KEY TERM

Inflation refers to a substantial increase in the general level of prices over time.

1.1 To the economist looking at the whole economy, inflation is a rise in the average price of goods and services over a period of time. Inflation erodes the real value of money. The real value of money is best viewed as the 'purchasing power' of money.

Measuring inflation

1.2 In order to measure changes in the real value of money as a single figure, we need to group all goods and services into a single price index. This process is subject to statistical error and misrepresentation, which we will not discuss further here; however, the government measures changes in the prices of a number of groups of goods and services and publishes a number of different price indices.

1.3 The most important measure of the general rate of inflation in the UK is the **Retail Prices Index (RPI)**. (There are also other government-produced price indices for the prices of more specific items and commodities, such as wholesale prices indices.)

The Retail Prices Index

1.4 The RPI measures the percentage changes month by month in the average level of prices of the commodities and services including housing costs purchased by the great majority of households in the UK, including practically all wage earners and most small and medium salary earners.

1.5 The weights used for combining the indices for the various groups (of commodities) are revised annually on the basis of information from the Family Expenditure Survey for the year ended in the previous June. The items of expenditure within the RPI are intended to be a representative list of items, current prices for which are collected at regular intervals.

The 'underlying' rate of inflation

1.6 There are nevertheless problems in using the RPI as an indicator of inflationary pressures in the economy. The RPI includes households' mortgage costs and the local tax known as the council tax (previously the community charge). This makes it difficult to make comparisons with inflation statistics of other countries which exclude these elements.

1.7 The term **underlying rate of inflation** is usually used to refer to the RPI adjusted to exclude mortgage costs and sometimes other elements as well (such as the council tax). The effects of interest rate changes noted above help to make the RPI fluctuate more widely than the underlying rate of inflation. Because of the distorting effects of mortgage interest rates on the RPI, the underlying rate of inflation is arguably a better 'barometer' than the RPI of the inflationary pressures present in the economy.

1.8 The UK government's target range for inflation, which was introduced in 1992, is defined in terms of 'RPIX', which is the underlying rate of inflation measured as the increase in the RPI excluding mortgage interest payments.

'RPIY' is a further measure of underlining inflation which excludes indirect taxes as well as mortgage interest payments.

1.9 EXAMPLE: RPI AS A MEASURE OF INFLATION

Quoted rates of inflation are usually annual rates, calculated as the percentage change in the index concerned during the twelve months up to the date quoted. Suppose that the RPI on 1 January was 330 and on 31 December was 348.

(a) The decline in real terms of £100 in banknotes during the year would be:

$$\frac{(348 - 330)}{330} \times 100\% = 5.45\%$$

In other words, the decline in the buying power or 'purchasing power' of money would be 5.45% over the course of the year.

(b) The amount of money the person would need on 31 December to maintain his spending power as at 1 January would be:

$$\frac{348}{330} \times £100 = £105.45$$

The general rate of inflation during the year was about $5^1/_2$% (ie 5.45%).

Knowledge brought forward from Paper 4

Inflation

- Understanding of inflation and its consequences
- Inflation and unemployment: the Phillips curve

These topics are revised below. If you know these topics well, you may wish to skim-read some of what follows.

2 CONSEQUENCES OF INFLATION

Why is inflation a problem?

2.1 The economic policy objective of stable prices now has a central place in the policy approaches of the governments of many developed countries. Why is a high rate of price inflation harmful and undesirable?

2.2 It is useful first to draw a distinction between inflation which can be perfectly anticipated by everyone and inflation which is unexpected. If inflation is perfectly predicted in advance by everyone, it need not in theory have any significant effects. All transactions would effectively be 'indexed' by the perfectly known rate of inflation and nothing 'real' need be affected. However, perfect knowledge is not in practice available, and inflation has a number of undesirable consequences, as identified below.

Redistribution of income and wealth

2.3 Inflation leads to a redistribution of income and wealth in ways which may be undesirable. Redistribution of wealth might take place from creditors to debtors. This is because debts lose real value with inflation. For example, if you owed £1,000, and prices then doubled, you would still owe £1,000, but the real value of your debt would have been halved.

In general, in times of inflation those with economic power tend to gain at the expense of others, particularly those on fixed incomes.

Balance of payments effects

2.4 If a country has a higher rate of inflation than its major trading partners, its exports will become relatively expensive and imports relatively cheap. As a result, the balance of trade will suffer, affecting employment in exporting industries and in industries producing import-substitutes.

Uncertainty of the value of money and prices

2.5 If the rate of inflation is imperfectly anticipated, no one has certain knowledge of the true rate of inflation. As a result, no one has certain knowledge of the value of money or of the real meaning of prices. If the rate of inflation becomes excessive, and there is 'hyperinflation', this problem becomes so exaggerated that money becomes worthless, so that people are unwilling to use it and are forced to resort to barter. In less extreme circumstances, the results are less dramatic, but the same problem exists. As prices convey less information, the process of resource allocation is less efficient and rational decision-making is almost impossible.

Resource costs of changing prices

2.6 A fourth reason to aim for stable prices is the resource cost of frequently changing prices. In times of high inflation substantial labour time is spent on planning and implementing price changes. Customers may also have to spend more time making price comparisons if they seek to buy from the lowest cost source.

Economic growth and investment

2.7 It is sometimes claimed that inflation is harmful to a country's economic growth and level of investment. A study by Robert Barro (*Bank of England Quarterly Bulletin*, May 1995) examined whether the evidence available supports this view. Barro found from data covering over 100 countries from 1960 to 1990 that, on average, an increase in inflation of ten percentage points per year reduced the growth rate of real GDP per capita by 0.2 to 0.3 percentage points per year, and lowered the ratio of investment to GDP by 0.4 to 0.6 percentage points. Although the adverse influence of inflation on economic growth and investment appears small, some causal effect would appear to exist, which could affect a country's standard of living fairly significantly over the long term.

Question

Outline the impact of price inflation on your organisation.

If the prices of imports (raw materials, labour and so on) rise, would the organisation be able to 'pass on' these increases in higher prices for its outputs?

Overcoming inflation for the person or firm

2.8 A person or firm having surplus money in a period of inflation can do either of the following two things to try to protect the real value of their wealth.

(a) They can deposit their money with a financial institution which pays **interest** on the deposit (or invest in securities which pay interest or dividends).

(b) Alternatively, they can invest in index-linked savings or securities, which protect the **capital value** of the investment against inflation.

2.9 There is another option - to spend the money at once to buy goods and services, and not to invest it at all. Some people or firms might decide to do this, but on the whole, people with a lot of money to spare will not spend all of it, despite inflation.

Interest-bearing investments

2.10 When an investor puts money into an interest-bearing deposit account or into interest-bearing securities, he might expect to sacrifice some liquidity in exchange for earning interest. The extent to which interest protects the real value of an investment in a period of inflation will depend on the interest rate paid and on the rate of inflation.

(a) If the rate of inflation is, say 10% per annum and interest payable on an investment is also 10%, the investor would exactly maintain his wealth in real terms.

(b) If the rate of inflation is, say, 8% per annum and the rate of interest is, say 10% per annum, the investor's real wealth would increase at the rate of about 2% per annum. More exactly, the increase rate in real wealth would be:

$$(\frac{110}{108} \times 100\%) - 100\% = 1.85\% \text{ pa}$$

(c) If the rate of inflation is, say, 17% and the rate of interest only 14%, the investor's real wealth would decline at the rate of about 3% per annum. More exactly, the rate of decline in real wealth would be:

$$100\% - (\frac{114}{117} \times 100)\% = 2.56\% \text{ pa}$$

Even so, it is better to earn interest at 14% than to hold money which earns no interest at all.

Index-linked investments

2.11 Index-linked investments are investments whose value is increased in line with increases in the general rate of inflation. For example, if an investor puts £1,000 into index-linked savings for five years, and during this time the retail price index rises from 195 to 340, at the end of five years when the investment matures he will receive.

$$\frac{340}{195} \times £1,000 = £1,743.59$$

2.12 The purpose of index-linking is to offer investors a means of holding their wealth in the form of an asset that will maintain its value over time. However, since index-linked financial assets are usually long-term investments, they are not 'money'.

2.13 In the UK, index-linked financial assets include some National Savings investments, including index-linked National Savings Certificates. There are also some index-linked British government stocks (gilts).

Other cases of index-linking

2.14 Index-linking has also been extended to other aspects of economic activity and financial reporting in the UK.

(a) Personal tax allowances, various social security benefits and state pensions are often index-linked.

(b) Capital gains are index-linked, so that capital gains tax is payable on the 'real' gain from re-selling an asset or investment and not on the nominal value of the gain.

(c) In financial accounting, the need to recognise the effects of inflation on 'real' asset values and profits led to the introduction of a system of current cost accounting in 1980, which applied cost or price indices to asset values. The system proved very unsatisfactory and unpopular and is rarely used. A more effective system of inflation accounting has not yet been devised, in spite of the efforts of the accountancy profession.

Inflation and the required rate of return

2.15 Inflation has an effect on the returns an investor will require, and therefore on the appraisal of capital investment decisions by companies. As the inflation rate increases, so will the minimum return required by an investor. For example, you might be happy with a return of 5% in an inflation-free world, but if inflation was running at 15% you would expect a considerably greater yield. You should also be able to appreciate that the required rate of return, and therefore the general level of interest rates, will tend to be higher in countries where higher inflation is expected.

2.16 A return of 5% will provide £105 back in one years' time for an investment of £100 now. If inflation of 15% is expected, then £105 in one year's time will buy only 105/1.15 = £91.30 worth of goods at today's prices. In order to be able to purchase £105 worth of goods at today's prices, the investor will need a nominal return of 1.05 × 1.15 = 1.2075, ie a return of 20.75%. Thus, a nominal rates of interest of 20.75% is required to give the investor a real rate of return of 5%. This is sometimes called the **Fisher effect**.

The rate of inflation and exchange rates: purchasing power parity theory

2.17 The **law of one price** holds that, assuming no transaction and transport costs, the prices of identical tradable goods should be the same in different countries of the world based on the exchange rates between currencies. If they are not, then arbitrage should be possible: people would be able to make a profit buying goods in one market and selling them in another market in which the price is higher.

2.18 In reality, markets are less than perfect and transaction and transport costs are not zero. A case in point is the retail motor industry in Europe. Car dealers are able to charge higher prices in the UK than in other European countries while purchasers face considerable additional cost if they buy a car in another country for use in the UK.

2.19 **Purchasing power parity theory**, which developed in the 1920s, applied the law of one price, attempting to explain changes in the exchange rate exclusively by the rate of inflation in different countries. The theory predicted that the exchange value of a foreign currency depends on the relative purchasing power of each currency in its own country. As a simple example, suppose that there is only one commodity, which costs £110 in the UK and 880 francs in France. The exchange rate would be £1 = 8 francs. If, as a result of inflation, the cost of the commodity in the UK rises to £120, the exchange rate would adjust to:

$$[8 \times \frac{110}{120}] \times £1 = 7.33\text{francs}$$

2.20 If the exchange rate remained at £1 = 8 francs, it would be cheaper to import more of the commodity from France for £110 and the UK would have a balance of trade deficit. This would only be corrected by an alteration in the exchange rate, with the pound weakening against the franc.

2.21 Purchasing power parity theory states that a foreign exchange rate is set as:

$$\frac{\text{Price level in country A}}{\text{Price level in country B}}$$

2.22 This theory has been found to be inadequate to explain movements in exchange rates in the **short term**, mainly because it ignores payments between countries (ie demand and supply transactions) and the influence of supply and demand for currency on exchange rates.

KEY TERM

Purchasing power parity theory: the theory that, in the long run at least, exchange rates between currencies will tend to reflect the relative purchasing powers of each currency.

2.23 Purchasing power parity theory is more likely to have some validity in the long run, and it is certainly true that the currency of a country which has a much higher rate of inflation than other countries will weaken on the foreign exchange market. In other words, the rate of inflation relative to other countries is certainly a factor which influences the exchange rate.

The impact of inflation on the assessment of company profits

2.24 Profit can be measured as the difference between how wealthy a company is at the beginning and at the end of an accounting period. This wealth can be expressed in terms of the capital of a company as shown in its opening and closing balance sheets. A business which maintains its capital unchanged during an accounting period can be said to have broken even. Once capital has been maintained, anything achieved in excess represents profit.

2.25 For this analysis to be of any use, we must be able to draw up a company's balance sheet at the beginning and at the end of a period, so as to place a value on the opening and closing capital. There are particular difficulties in doing this during a period of rising prices.

2.26 In conventional historical cost accounts, assets are stated in the balance sheet at the amount it cost to acquire them (less any amounts written off in respect of depreciation or diminution in value). Capital is simply the difference between assets and liabilities. If prices are rising, it is possible for a company to show a profit in its historical cost accounts despite having identical physical assets and owing identical liabilities at the beginning and end of its accounting period.

2.27 For example, consider the following opening and closing balance sheets of a company:

	Opening	*Closing*
	£	£
Stock (100 items at cost)	500	600
Other net assets	1,000	1,000
Capital	1,500	1,600

2.28 Assuming that no new capital has been introduced during the year, and no capital has been distributed as dividends, the profits shown in historical cost accounts would be £100, being the excess of closing capital over opening capital. And yet in physical terms the company is not better off: it still has 100 units of stock (which cost £5 each at the beginning of the period, but £6 each at the end) and its other net assets are identical. The 'profit' earned has barely enabled the company to keep pace with inflation.

2.29 An alternative to the concept of capital maintenance based on historical costs is to express capital **in physical terms**. On this basis, no profit would be recognised in the example above because the physical substance of the company is unchanged over the accounting period. In the UK, a system of accounting (called **current cost accounting** or CCA) was introduced in 1980 by SSAP 16 and had as its conceptual basis a concept of capital maintenance based on 'operating capability'. Capital is maintained if at the end of the period the company is in a position to achieve the same physical output as it was at the beginning of the period. In practice, CCA aroused little enthusiasm and SSAP 16 was finally withdrawn in April 1988.

The unit of measurement

2.30 Another way to tackle the problems of capital maintenance in times of rising prices is to look at the **unit of measurement** in which accounting values are expressed. For example, the system of accounting called **current purchasing power (CPP) accounting** is based on the idea of re-stating all accounts items in terms of a stable monetary unit (for example, pounds of current purchasing power).

2.31 Section summary

Inflation has various effects.

- It can be a problem for both households and firms, including when they are lenders and borrowers.
- Different rates of inflation in different countries can have an impact on the international competitiveness of firms, although changes in exchange rates must also be borne in mind.
- Inflation also has a distorting effect on information about company performance, making comparisons across different time periods more difficult.

3 THE CAUSES OF INFLATION

3.1 The causes of inflation are complex, because there will be several factors operating simultaneously, each having some effect on price levels. The relative strength of influence of each of these factors at any given time may be difficult to assess. It is debatable whether inflation can ever be fully cured, although a reduction in the rate of inflation to a low level over a long period of time would presumably be considered a cure.

3.2 The causes of inflation might be:

- demand-pull factors
- cost-push factors
- import-cost factors
- expectations
- growth in the money supply

3.3 **Demand-pull inflation** occurs when the economy is buoyant and there is a high aggregate demand which is in excess of the economy's ability to supply.

(a) Because aggregate demand exceeds supply, prices rise.

(b) Since supply needs to be raised to meet the higher demand, there will be an increase in demand for factors of production, and so factor rewards (wages, interest rates, and so on) will also rise.

(c) Since aggregate demand exceeds the output capability of the economy, it should follow that demand-pull inflation can only exist when unemployment is low. A feature of inflation in the UK in the 1970s and early 1980s, however, was high inflation coupled with high unemployment.

Traditionally Keynesian economists saw inflation as being caused by demand-pull factors. However, they now accept that cost-push factors are involved as well.

3.4 **Cost-push inflation** occurs where the costs of factors of production rise regardless of whether or not they are in short supply. This appears to be particularly the case with wages: workers anticipate inflation rates and demand wage increases to compensate, thus initiating a wage-price spiral. Interest rate rises can also add to the rate of inflation, because mortgage cost will rise.

3.5 **Import cost-push inflation** occurs when the costs of essential imports rise regardless of whether or not they are in short supply. This has occurred in the past with the oil price rises of the 1970s. Additionally, a fall in the value of a country's currency will have import cost-push effects since a weakening currency increases the price of imports.

3.6 A further problem is that once the rate of inflation has begun to increase, a serious danger of **expectational inflation** will occur. This means, regardless of whether the factors that have caused inflation are still persistent or not, there will arise a generally held view of what inflation is likely to be, and so to protect future income, wages and prices will be raised by the expected amount of future inflation. This can lead to the vicious circle known as the **wage-price spiral**, in which inflation becomes a relatively permanent feature because of people's expectation that it will occur.

3.7 The monetarists argue that inflation is caused by **increase in the supply of money**. There is a considerable debate as to whether increases in the money supply are a **cause** of inflation or whether increases in the money supply are a **symptom** of inflation. The monetarists argue that since inflation is caused by an increase in the money supply, inflation can be brought under control by reducing the rate of growth of the money supply.

Relationship between unemployment and inflation: the Phillips curve

3.8 A W Phillips discovered (1958) a statistical relationship between unemployment and the rate of money wage inflation which implied that, in general, the rate of inflation fell as unemployment rose and vice versa. A curve, known as a **Phillips curve**, can be drawn linking inflation and unemployment (Figure 1).

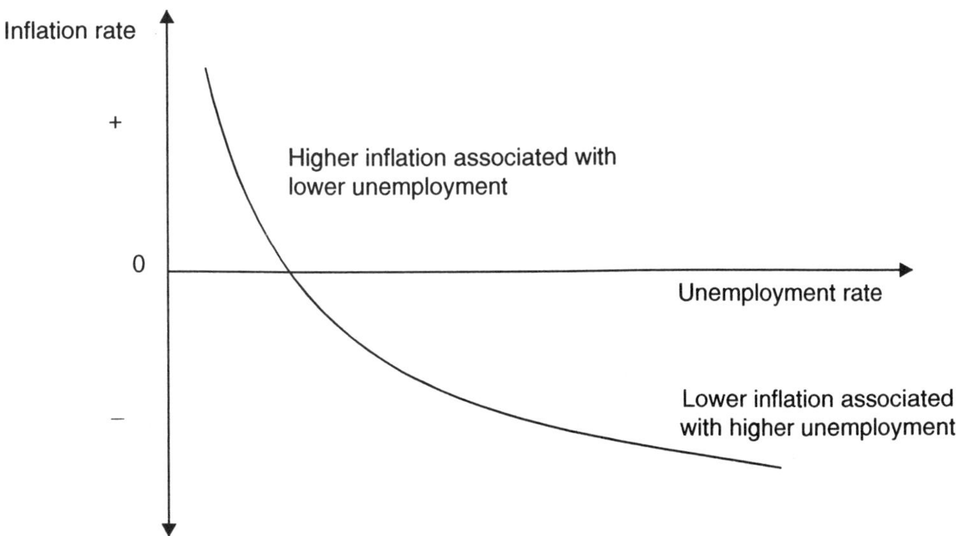

Figure 1 Phillips curve

3.9 Two points should be noticed about the Phillips curve.

(a) The curve crosses the horizontal axis at a positive value for the unemployment rate. This means that zero inflation will be associated with some unemployment; it is not possible to achieve zero inflation and zero unemployment at the same time.

(b) The shape of the curve (concave) means that the lower level of unemployment, the higher the rate of increase in inflation.

3.10 The existence of a relationship between inflation and unemployment of the type indicated by the Phillips curve suggests that the government should be able to choose some point on the curve, according to its preference, and use demand management policies to take the economy to that point - ie to 'strike a balance' between acceptable levels of inflation and unemployment.

This re-emphasises the argument of Keynesian economists that in order to achieve full employment, some inflation is unavoidable. If achieving full employment is an economic policy objective, a government must therefore be prepared to accept a certain level of inflation as a 'necessary evil'.

3.11 However, the Phillips curve relationship between inflation and unemployment broke down at the end of the 1960s when Britain began to experience rising inflation at the same time as rising unemployment. In other words, the new curve seemed to be *upward* sloping.

Inflationary expectations: refinements to the Phillips curve

3.12 An explanation of rising inflation rates combined with rising unemployment was put forward, based on inflationary expectations. This 'natural rate hypothesis' is supported by monetarist economists.

3.13 'Inflationary expectations' are the rates of inflation that are expected in the future. The inflationary expectations of the work force will be reflected in the level of wage rises that is demanded in the annual round of pay negotiations between employers and workers.

(a) If the work force expects inflation next year to be 3%, they will demand a 3% wage increase in order to maintain the real value of their wages.

(b) If we now accept that any increase in wages will result in price inflation (which is the monetarist argument), then a 3% pay rise to cover expected inflation will result in an actual rate of inflation of 3%.

(c) The work force might also try to achieve some increase in the real value of wages. If inflation next year is expected to be 3%, the work force might demand a pay rise of say, 4%. According to monetarist economists, a pay rise of 4% would simply mean inflation of 4%. If workers wish to achieve a 1% increase in real wages each year, then during each successive period the rate of inflation will begin to accelerate from 5% to 6% to 7% etc, and the real increases in wages will not happen.

(d) To compound the problem of inflation still further, it is argued that if mistakes are made over expectations, then money wages will be adjusted upwards next period in order to rectify the mistake made last period.

    (i) For example, in one year the work force might expect inflation to be 3%, and so demand a 3% increase in wages. If this is achieved, but the actual rate of inflation during the year is 5%, the work force will try to put things right. They will demand a 2% pay increase, just to cover the 'lost ground' last year, as well as an increase to cover expected inflation next year.

    (ii) It follows that if expected inflation next year is 5%, the pay demand will be 7% (plus any demand for an increase in the value of wages). If a 7% pay rise is granted, inflation will go up to 7% pa.

(e) Any 'external' factor (such as increases in the prices of imported goods, or higher indirect taxes) which may lead wage earners to expect higher prices in the near future will of course result in even higher wage claims.

3.14 Monetarist economists argue that:

(a) the only way to reduce the rate of inflation is to get inflationary expectation out of the system. In doing so, excessive demands for wage rises should be resisted by employers;

(b) a firm approach to reducing the rate of inflation could mean having to accept high levels of unemployment for a while;

(c) attempts to get the unemployment level below its natural rate (whatever this is) will only result in the long run in higher inflation. The choice for government is therefore *not* between inflation or unemployment; instead, a balance or choice must be made between the *level* of unemployment and the *rate* of inflation.

Chapter roundup

- **Inflation** is a sustained increase in the general level of prices over time.
- **Stability in prices** is seen as a key objective of macroeconomic policy.
- The main measure of inflation in the UK is the **Retail Prices Index**. The RPI with mortgage interest payments removed gives **RPIX**, the **underlying rate of inflation**, a more important measure for the purposes of economic policy.
- Inflation is a problem for individuals and firms, for example **lenders** and those on **fixed incomes.**
- It could also affect economic growth, **investment, international competitiveness**, and the **evaluation of companies' performance**.
- Individuals and firms may seek to protest the purchasing power of surplus money by making interest-bearing or index-linked **investments**.
- The **law of one price** holds that the prices of goods should not vary between countries (**purchasing power parity**). In reality, this law only seems to apply over the long term.
- Causes of inflation may include **demand-pull, cost-push** (including **import** costs), **expectations** and **money supply growth.**
- The **Phillips curve** suggests that there is an inverse relationship between rates of **inflation** and **unemployment.**

Quick quiz

1 What main alternative ways are there of measuring inflation? (see paras 1.2, 1.3)

2 Why is inflation a problem for firms? (2.2 - 2.6)

3 What is purchasing power parity theory? (2.17 - 2.19)

4 Outline how inflation can distort the assessment of company performance. (2.24 - 2.30)

5 What are the main causes of inflation? (3.2)

Question to try	Level	Marks	Time
19	Introductory	n/a	30 mins

Chapter 19

GOVERNMENT INTERVENTION IN INDUSTRIES AND MARKETS

Chapter topic list		Syllabus reference
1	Competition policy	5(b)(vi)
2	Official aid schemes	5(b)(vi)
3	Supply side policies	5(b)(v)
4	Externalities and government intervention	5(b)(vii)
5	Environmental ('green') policies	5(b)(vii)

Introduction

This chapter is the last in the book to deal with the broader economic environment within which organisations operate. Here we look at the role of **government** in ensuring that there is fair **competition** in markets.

We also cover **government assistance**, **'supply side' policies** and **environmental ('green') policies**.

Exam focus point

This part of the syllabus contains a number of topics which could appear as short parts of questions, eg monopolies regulation, privatisation, supply side economics and policies on pollution. You may be asked to discuss effects upon *businesses* specifically: whatever exact form the question takes, make sure that your answer is to the point.

1 COMPETITION POLICY

Regulation and market failure

KEY TERM

Market failure is said to occur when the market mechanism fails to result in economic efficiency, and therefore the outcome is sub-optimal.

1.1 An important role of the government is the regulation of private markets where these fail to bring about an efficient use of resources. In response to the existence of market failure, and as an alternative to taxation and public provision of production, the state often resorts to regulating economic activity in a variety of ways. Of the various forms of market failure, the following are the cases where regulation of markets can often be the most appropriate policy response.

(a) **Imperfect competition.** Where monopoly power is leading to inefficiency or excessive monopoly profits, the state may intervene, for example through controls on prices or profits, in order to try to reduce the effects of monopoly.

(b) **Externalities.** A possible means of dealing with the problem of external costs and benefits is *via* some form of regulation. Regulations might include, for example, controls on emissions of pollutants, restrictions on car use in urban areas, the banning of smoking in public buildings, compulsory car insurance and compulsory education.

(c) **Imperfect information.** Regulation is often the best form of government action whenever informational inadequacies are undermining the efficient operation of private markets. This is particularly so when consumer choice is being distorted. Examples here would include legally enforced product quality/safety standards, consumer protection legislation, the provision of job centres and other means of improving information flows in the labour market and so on.

(d) **Equity**. The government may also resort to regulation to improve social justice. For example, legislation to prevent racial and/or sexual discrimination in the labour market; regulation to ensure equal access to goods such as health care, education and housing; minimum wage regulations and equal pay legislation.

Knowledge brought forward from Paper 4

You should have from your earlier studies an understanding of the following.

- The **assumptions of perfect competition**:
  - A large number of buyers and sellers
  - Producers and consumers acting rationally and possessing the same information
  - Homogeneous product
  - Free entry of firms into and exit out of the market
  - No transport costs or information-gathering costs
- **Imperfect competition**, the main market types being **monopoly, monopolistic competition** and **oligopoly**

Types of regulation

1.2 **Regulation** can be defined as any form of state interference with the operation of the free market. This could involve regulating demand, supply, price, profit, quantity, quality, entry, exit, information, technology, or any other aspect of production and consumption in the market.

1.3 Bear in mind that in many markets the participants (especially the firms) may decide to maintain a system of voluntary **self-regulation**, possibly in order to try to avert the imposition of government controls. Areas where self-regulation often exists are the professions (eg the Law Society, the British Medical Association and other professional bodies), and financial markets (eg the Council of the Stock Exchange, the Take-over Panel and the Securities and Investments Board).

Competition policy in the UK

1.4 State legislation in the UK on monopoly and other anti-competitive practices came with the enactment of the Monopolies and Restrictive Practices Act in 1948. This was followed by the Restrictive Practices Acts of 1956 and 1976, the Monopolies and Mergers Act 1965, and later the Fair Trading Act 1973 and the Competition Act 1980. These

pieces of legislation, especially the Fair Trading Act in 1973, established the framework under which UK competition policy currently operates. This is illustrated in the following diagram.

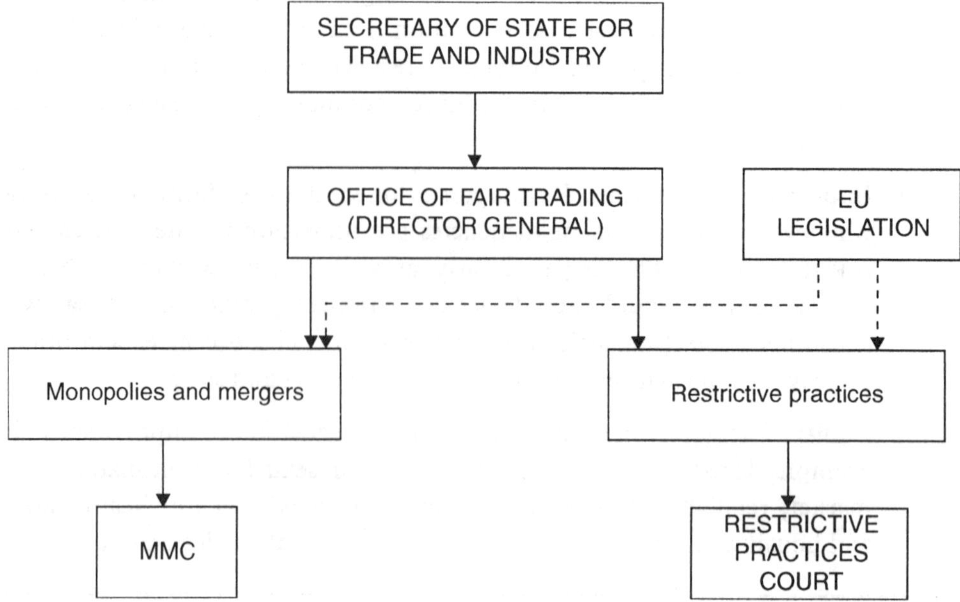

1.5 Overall responsibility for the conduct of policy lies with the Secretary of State for Trade and Industry. However, day to day supervision is carried out by the Office of Fair Trading (OFT), headed by its Director General (DG). The OFT monitors the performance of businesses and markets in order to try to ensure that the law relating to competition and consumer protection is enforced. It is the OFT which will, if necessary, and subject to ministerial veto, refer companies to the Monopolies and Mergers Commission (MMC) or the Restrictive Practices Court for investigation.

1.6 Competition policy falls into two broad areas.

(a) **Monopolies and mergers**. This is concerned with the investigation of (a) firms having a monopoly situation in their market, and (b) mergers between two or more companies which may result in a monopoly or other threat to competition. Any existing or potential monopoly situation may (it is not automatic) be investigated by the MMC.

(b) **Restrictive practices**. These are any explicit or implicit agreement between firms aimed at restricting competition. Generally, these are deemed illegal, and may be investigated by the Restrictive Practices Court.

Monopolies and mergers

1.7 There are two types of monopoly situation defined by the Fair Trading Act.

(a) **Scale monopoly** - where one firm controls 25% or more of the UK sales of a particular industry.

(b) **Complex monopoly** - where several firms collude, intentionally or not, to restrict competition, and collectively supply 25% or more of the market.

1.8 Under the legislation, then, a monopoly does not mean a pure monopoly of the whole of the market. The MMC can also be asked to investigate what could be called 'oligopoly situations' involving explicit or implicit collusion between firms.

1.9 As mentioned above, the investigation is not automatic. The DG, in agreement with the Secretary of State, must decide that a referral to the MMC is warranted. Once referred, the MMC must decide whether or not the monopoly is acting 'against the public interest'. This key criterion is not precisely defined in the legislation and hence is open to interpretation. In practice the MMC adopts a pragmatic approach, weighing up the costs and benefits of each situation.

1.10 In its report, the MMC will say if a monopoly situation has been found to exist and, if so, will make recommendations to deal with it. These may involve measures such as price cuts, price and profit controls or removal of entry barriers. In some (rare) cases the Commission may recommend the breaking up of the firm in order to eliminate the monopoly. It is up to the Secretary of State to decide which, if any, of the MMC's recommendations will be acted upon. Critics of the UK's anti-monopoly machinery have argued that the machinery is insufficiently powerful to deal adequately with the preservation of competitive forces. They contend that the MMC lacks teeth, and that the Secretary of State will often water down, or worse, ignore the Commission's recommendations altogether.

Case example

In the MMC's investigation into the UK brewing industry, the Commission concluded, after a lengthy and detailed scrutiny, that a complex monopoly did exist in favour of the big six national brewers. This oligopoly restricted effective competition at the expense of the smaller regional brewers and, in particular, the vertical integration engendered by the system of tied public houses created a serious barrier to entry into the market.

The MMC made several wide-ranging recommendations, the most radical of which was the requirement for the six nationals to sell off all of their public houses and other retail outlets above a limit of 2,000. Following sustained lobbying by the brewing industry (although whether this really influenced the final decision is an open question), the Secretary of State for Trade and Industry at the time (Lord Young) decided not to implement this crucial proposal. Instead, the nationals were required to operate their pubs (above the 2,000 ceiling) as 'free houses', so that the publican could, if he wished, sell beers from other brewers. Critics of the government's decision maintain that this watering down of the MMC's key proposal to reduce the vertical integration of the industry, means that the monopoly power of the big six national brewers will not be substantially undermined.

1.11 A prospective merger between two or more companies may be referred to the MMC for investigation if either of two criteria are satisfied:

(a) the merger will create a firm with monopoly power, ie one that has 25% or more market share;

(b) the merger involves the transfer of at least £30 million of assets.

1.12 Again, referral to the MMC is not automatic, and since the legislation was first introduced, only a small proportion of all merger proposals have been referred. It has been suggested that this reflects a desire by all past governments to encourage mergers, in the main because they believed that the advantages of greater economies of scale and the ability of larger UK firms to compete more effectively in international markets, would outweigh the costs of increased monopoly power. However, research by economists into the post-merger performance of companies has tended to reveal little evidence of improvements. One study concluded, for example, that the increases in productivity of merged firms were no better than the industry average.

1.13 If a potential merger is investigated, the MMC has again to determine whether or not the merger would be against the public interest. As with monopolies, it will assess the relative benefits and costs in order to arrive at a decision.

Question 1

Look through newspapers for a report on the activities of the MMC. Why is the investigation being carried out and how was it initiated?

Answer

One example of MMC activity is as follows (reported in the *Financial Times* on 9 September 1992).

'Private medical fees in the UK are to come under official scrutiny for the first time in a widespread investigation by the Monopolies and Mergers Commission.

Sir Bryan Carsberg, Director General of Fair Trading, yesterday asked the MMC to investigate the way in which private medical fees are set by consultants.

The inquiry has been prompted by concerns over guideline charges first published by the British Medical Association in 1989. The OFT says these "set recommended fee rates" for medical and surgical procedures, with separate amounts for the contribution made by anaesthetists.

The BMA strongly rejected the OFT's assertion that it had laid down recommended rates and said the guidelines reflected the average rate charged by consultants for private work around the country. "We have always acted in the spirit of competition in producing these guidelines and our publication serves the public interest," it said.

The MMC will investigate whether a monopoly exists and, if so, whether any aspects of the supply of these services operates against the public interest. It now has 12 months to report to Mr Michael Heseltine, the Trade and Industry Secretary.'

Restrictive practices

1.14 The other strand of competition policy is concerned with preventing the development of anti-competitive practices such as price-fixing agreements (cartels). Under the legislation, all agreements between firms must be notified to the OFT and the DG will then decide if the agreement should be examined by the Restrictive Practices Court. The presumption of the Court is that the agreement will be declared illegal, unless it can be shown to satisfy one or more of eight so-called 'gateways' as defined in the Restrictive Practices Act 1976.

1.15 These gateways (ie reasons for allowing the agreement) include the following.

The agreement is necessary:

(a) to protect employment in a particular area;
(b) to protect the public against injury;
(c) because its removal would jeopardise exports;
(d) to counter measures taken by other firms which restrict competition.

1.16 If an agreement satisfies one of the gateways, there is a final hurdle, known as the 'tailpiece'. This is that the court must believe that the benefits of the practice outweigh the costs.

1.17 Over the last thirty years or so, over 5,000 agreements have been registered with the OFT, the majority of which were either abandoned voluntarily by the firms involved (the most common outcome) or after the court found against them. At first sight, then, it would appear that the policy towards restrictive practices has been largely successful. But this conclusion ignores the possibility that many collusive activities still exist in a covert fashion. Indeed, one of the consequences of the legislation might have to drive many agreements 'underground'.

European Union competition policy

1.18 As a member of the European Union (EU), the UK is also now subject to EU competition policy. This is enshrined in Articles 85 (dealing with restrictive practices) and 86 (concerned with monopoly) of the Treaty of Rome. The provisions of Article 85 are similar to UK legislation, whilst Article 86 prohibits the abuse by any firm of its 'dominant position'. Unfortunately, this term is not clearly defined here, hence it is less clear cut than the 25% market share criterion employed in the UK.

1.19 The European Commission, rather than the Monopolies and Mergers Commission, must approve mergers where the worldwide turnovers of all the companies concerned total more than a certain threshold. However, the European Commission does not regulate mergers where each company derives at least two thirds of its European Union-wide turnover from one and the same member state: such mergers remain within the remit of the Monopolies and Mergers Commission (or similar bodies in other states).

1.20 The European Commission is the body responsible for implementing the policy and for carrying out any necessary investigations. A relatively recent case involving the UK was that of the so-called 'sweeteners' to British Aerospace to encourage its takeover of the Rover group.

Current prospects for UK competition policy

1.21 The UK Labour Party forming the new 1997 Government has proposed replacing the MMC and the OFT with a single competition authority.

1.22 The employers' organisation, the Confederation of British Industry (CBI), shares Labour's desire for a much more powerful competition authority based on the OFT which would take over the investigative powers of the MMC. The MMC might then be turned into a body that hears appeals.

1.23 Both the Labour Party and the CBI also seem to favour a shift towards the European 'prohibition approach' to the control of monopolies and abuse of market power, as used by the European Commission under Article 86 of the Treaty of Rome. Although the Conservative Party did not favour such a shift, it is in agreement with the Labour Party and the CBI over the need for a reform of the law on restrictive trade practices and cartels. Currently, stopping abuses in these areas usually involves lengthy inquiries and Court proceedings. Before it left office in 1997, the Conservative Government was consulting on laws which would give the OFT powers to raid and search, to block illegal practices as soon as they come to light and to levy substantial fines, backed by an appeals procedure.

Deregulation

1.24 Deregulation or 'liberalisation' is, in general, the opposite of regulation. Deregulation can be defined as the removal or weakening of any form of statutory (or voluntary) regulation of free market activity. Deregulation allows free market forces more scope to determine the outcome.

1.25 There was a shift in policy in the 1980s in the UK and in the USA towards greater deregulation of markets, in the belief that this would improve efficiency. Indeed, many politicians and commentators believed that it was state over-regulation of British industry that was largely responsible for Britain's comparatively uncompetitive and inefficient performance. Whether or not this was, or remains, true is an open question.

Case examples

Here are some examples of deregulation in the UK over recent years.

(a) Deregulation of road passenger transport - both buses (stage services) and coaches (express services) - was brought about by the Transport Acts of 1980 and 1985. There is now effective free entry into both markets (except in London).

(b) The monopoly position enjoyed by some professions has been removed, for example in opticians' supply of spectacles and solicitors' monopoly over house conveyancing. In addition, the controls on advertising by professionals have been loosened.

1.26 As with the appraisal of regulation, a rational assessment of a deregulatory measure or a programme of such measures should weigh up the potential *social* benefits against the *social* costs. If there will be a net gain to society, we can say that the deregulation should proceed. It would be simplistic to contend that *all* regulation is detrimental to the economy. Where there is a clear case of market failure, then state regulation may be the most appropriate way of achieving a more socially efficient or equitable outcome.

1.27 Deregulation, whose main aim is to introduce more competition into an industry by removing statutory or other entry barriers, has the following potential benefits.

(a) **Improved incentives for internal/cost efficiency.** Greater competition compels managers to try harder to keep down costs.

(b) **Improved allocative efficiency.** Competition keeps down prices closer to marginal cost, and firms therefore produce closer to the socially optimal output level.

1.28 In some industries it could have certain disadvantages, including the following.

(a) **Loss of economies of scale.** If increased competition means that each firm produces less output on a smaller scale, unit costs will be higher.

(b) **Lower quality or quantity of service.** The need to reduce costs may lead firms to reduce quality or eliminate unprofitable but socially valuable services.

(c) **Need to protect competition.** It may be necessary to implement a regulatory regime to protect competition where inherent forces have a tendency to eliminate it, for example if there is a dominant firm already in the industry, as in the case of British Telecom. In this type of situation, effective 'regulation for competition' will be required, ie regulatory measures aimed at maintaining competitive pressures, whether existing or potential.

Privatisation and denationalisation **12/94, 12/95**

1.29 **Privatisation** takes three broad forms.

(a) The deregulation of industries, to allow private firms to compete against state-owned businesses where they were not allowed to compete before (for example, deregulation of bus and coach services; deregulation of postal services).

(b) Contracting out work to private firms, where the work was previously done by government employees - for example, refuse collection or hospital laundry work.

(c) Transferring the ownership of assets from the state to private shareholders - for example, the denationalisation of British Gas and British Telecom (now called BT).

1.30 The UK government has carried out a policy of denationalisation in recent years. British Gas, BT, the regional water companies and much of the electricity industry have been among the enterprises which have been privatised. Most of the utility industries which have been privatised are still subject to regulations, for example limiting price increases to the rate of RPI inflation less a certain percentage.

1.31 Privatisation can improve efficiency, in one of two ways.

(a) If the effect of privatisation is to increase competition, the effect might be to reduce or eliminate allocative inefficiency.

(b) If nationalised industries are X-inefficient the effect of denationalisation might be to make the industries more cost-conscious, because they will be directly answerable to shareholders, and under scrutiny from stock market investors. X-inefficiencies might therefore be reduced or eliminated.

1.32 There are other possible advantages of privatisation.

(a) Denationalisation provides an immediate source of money for the government.

(b) Privatisation reduces bureaucratic and political meddling in the industries concerned.

(c) There is a view that wider share ownership should be encouraged. Denationalisation is one method of creating wider share ownership, as the sale of BT, British Gas and some other nationalised industries have shown in the UK.

1.33 There are arguments against privatisation too.

(a) State-owned industries are more likely to respond to the public interest, ahead of the profit motive. For example, state-owned industries are more likely to cross-subsidise unprofitable operations from profitable ones; for example the Post Office will continue to deliver letters to the isles of Scotland even though the service might be very unprofitable.

(b) Encouraging private competition to state-run industries might be inadvisable where significant economies of scale can be achieved by monopoly operations.

1.34 The advantages of having a controlled economy, rather than a free enterprise economy, can also be advanced as a possible reason in favour of having nationalised industries.

2 OFFICIAL AID SCHEMES

2.1 The government provides finance to companies in cash grants and other forms of official direct assistance, as part of its policy of helping to develop the national economy, especially in high technology industries and in areas of high unemployment.

2.2 Government incentives might be offered on:

(a) a **regional basis**, giving help to firms that invest in an economically depressed area of the country;

(b) a **selective national basis**, giving help to firms that invest in an industry that the government would like to see developing more quickly, for example robotics or fibre optics.

2.3 In Europe, such assistance is increasingly limited by European Union policies designed to prevent the distortion of free market competition. The UK government's powers to grant aid for modernisation and development are now severely restricted.

The Enterprise Initiative

2.4 The Enterprise Initiative is a package of measures offered by the Department of Trade and Industry (DTI) to businesses in the UK. It includes regional selective grant assistance. A network of 'Business Links', which are local business advice centres, is also provided.

2.6 **Regional selective assistance** is available for investment projects undertaken by firms in **Assisted Areas.**

The project must be commercially viable, create or safeguard employment, demonstrate a need for assistance and offer a distinct regional and national benefit.

The amount of grant will be negotiated as the minimum necessary to ensure the project goes ahead.

2.7 The **Regional Enterprise Grants** scheme is specially geared to help small firms employing fewer than 25 in one of the **Development Areas** to expand and diversify. Regional enterprise grants can help finance viable projects for:

(a) investment - grants of 15% of the cost of fixed assets up to a maximum of £15,000 are available;

(b) innovation - grants of 50% of the agreed project cost up to a maximum grant of £25,000 are available.

European Regional Development Fund

2.8 The European Regional Development Fund (ERDF) is financed from the general budget of the European Union (EU). The funds are given directly to EU member governments. In the ERDF's first 15 years of operation, the UK received £3.6 billion from the fund. Approximately 80% of the funds available are allocated to the four poorest countries in the EU.

2.9 Although ERDF assistance is intended to supplement the regional aid programme of the EU countries, there has been criticism that, under the quota system used to allocate the funds, the money has been used to replace governments' own aid rather than to supplement it. In an effort to meet this criticism, 5% of ERDF payments are linked to specific projects put forward by member governments rather than being allocated on a quota basis.

The Small Firms Loan Guarantee Scheme

2.10 The **Loan Guarantee Scheme** for small firms was introduced by the government in 1981. It is intended to help small businesses to get a loan from the bank, when a bank would otherwise be unwilling to lend because the business cannot offer the security that the bank would want. The borrower's annual turnover must not exceed a limit which depends on the type of business.

2.11 Under the scheme, which was revised in 1993, the bank can lend up to £250,000 without security over *personal* assets or a personal guarantee being required of the borrower. However, all available business assets must be used as security if required. The government will guarantee the bulk of the loan, while the borrower must pay an annual premium on the guaranteed part of the loan.

2.12 Most types of business can apply for such a loan through their bank. This includes sole traders and partnerships as well as limited companies. Some business activities, however, are excluded (for example retailing, catering, agriculture, fisheries, banking, education, forestry, estate agents, insurance companies, medical services, night clubs, postal services, coal, shipbuilding, steel and transport).

The Enterprise Investment Scheme

2.13 The **Enterprise Investment Scheme (EIS)** replaces the Business Expansion Scheme which ended on 31 December 1993. The EIS is intended to encourage investment in the ordinary shares of unquoted companies. When a qualifying individual subscribes for eligible shares in a qualifying company, the individual saves tax at 20% on the amount subscribed (including any share premium) up to a limit of £1,000,000 per company (or £5,000,000 if the company's trade is ship chartering). A **qualifying individual** is one who is not connected with the company at any time in the period from two years before the issue (or from incorporation if later) to five years after the issue. The maximum total investment that can qualify in a tax year is £100,000 per individual. Investments in private rented housing are excluded. Capital gains generated by individual investments in the EIS are tax-free provided the investment is held for five years.

2.14 The scheme includes a measure to encourage **business angels** who introduce finance to small companies which allows them to become paid directors of the companies they invest in without loss of tax relief.

2.15 There has been a rather low level of take-up for the EIS. This is probably partly due to the lower tax relief that is available under the EIS compared with the more generous Business Expansion Scheme which it replaced.

As the scheme attracts more attention, it is likely that EIS funds will be formed as collective investment vehicles through which a fund manager can reduce the risk for investors by spreading the money which investors have provided across a range of EIS companies.

Venture capital trusts

2.16 Venture capital providers have been around for many years, but in the November 1993 Budget, the Chancellor of the Exchequer Mr Kenneth Clarke also announced a second measure to encourage equity investment in the form of a new kind of investment trust called a venture capital trust (VCT). This followed criticism from banks and small business groups that small companies were too dependent on short-term finance.

2.17 The new type of investment trust is to invest a large proportion of assets in unquoted companies, with investors gaining 20% income tax relief on dividends provided shares are held in the VCT for five years, and capital gains rollover relief if the gain is invested in a VCT. There is an investment ceiling per person of £100,000. The maximum investment that VCTs are permitted to make in each unquoted company is £1 million.

2.18 The venture capital trust limits the risk investors take by diversifying their risk across a portfolio of small companies. However, some have criticised this investment vehicle, warning that it is likely to result in funding going toward management buyouts rather than start-ups, early-stage ventures and rescues, which are the areas most in need of capital.

3 SUPPLY SIDE POLICIES 6/94

3.1 A set of policies formulated by monetarists which has gained favour in the USA and UK is that based upon **supply side economics**.

3.2 The use of fiscal and monetary policies by government to reach their macroeconomic policy objectives - demand management - relies upon the proposition that the level of aggregate demand determines the level of national income and prices, ie that demand creates supply.

3.3 Supply side economists, in contrast, would focus policy upon the conditions of aggregate supply, taking the view that the availability, quality, and cost of resources are the long-term determinants of national income and prices. They argue that by putting resources to work an economy will automatically generate the additional income necessary to purchase the higher outputs, ie **supply creates its own demand.**

3.4 Supply side economics is characterised by the following propositions.

(a) The predominant long-term influence upon output, prices, and employment is the conditions of aggregate supply.

(b) Left to itself, the free market will automatically generate the highest level of national income and employment available to the economy.

(c) Inflexibility in the labour market through the existence of trade unions and other restrictive practices keep wages at uncompetitively high levels. This creates unemployment and restricts aggregate supply.

(d) The rates of direct taxation exert a major influence upon aggregate supply through their effects upon the incentive to work.

(e) There is only a limited role for government in the economic system. Demand management can only influence output and employment 'artificially' in the short run, whilst in the long run creating inflation and hampering growth. Similarly state-owned industries are likely to be uncompetitive and thus restrict aggregate supply.

3.5 The economy will self-regulate through the actions of the price mechanism in each market. Flexible prices in goods and factor markets will ensure that at the microeconomics level each market tends towards a market-clearing equilibrium. At the macroeconomic level the maximum attainable level of national income is at the level of maximum employment. The exponents of supply side economics argue that flexible wages will ensure that the economy reaches this point. The importance of flexible wages is illustrated by Figure 1.

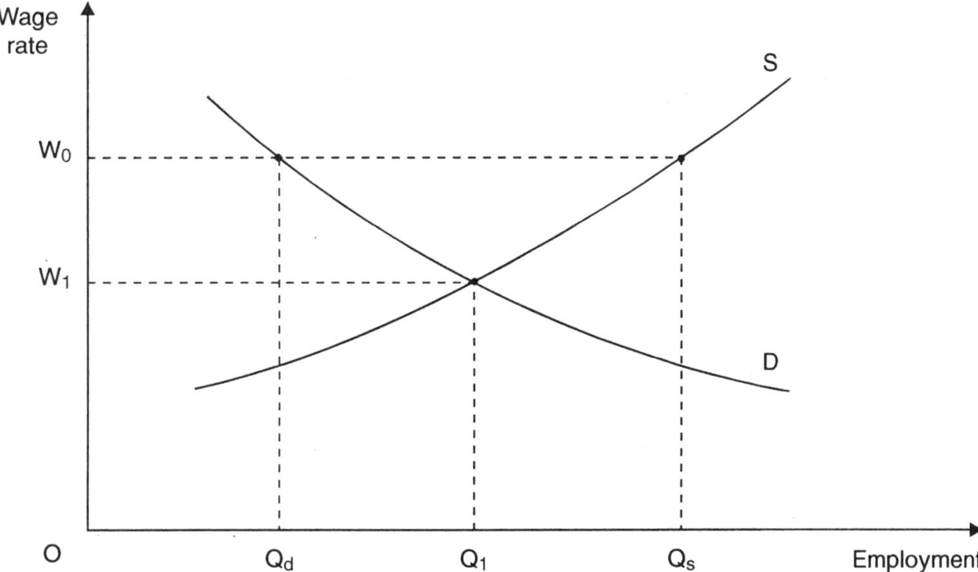

Figure 1 Flexible wages

When the wage rate is at W_0, the demand for labour is Q_d while the total supply of labour stands at Q_s. This creates involuntary unemployment of $(Q_s - Q_d)$ at the prevailing wage rate. By accepting lower wages, workers can 'price themselves back into jobs' and consequently unemployment falls. If wages were perfectly flexible downwards then the market would restore full employment at wage rate W_1. This would leave unemployment at its 'natural rate'.

3.6 High taxation acts as a disincentive to work because if marginal tax rates (ie the proportion of additional income taken as tax) are high, the individual is likely to behave in one of two ways:

(a) forgo opportunities to increase income through additional effort on the basis that the increase in net income does not adequately reward the effort or risk;

(b) resort to working in the parallel ('black') economy to avoid paying the tax.

3.7 The **Laffer curve** (named after Professor Arthur Laffer) illustrates the effect of tax rates upon government revenue and national income.

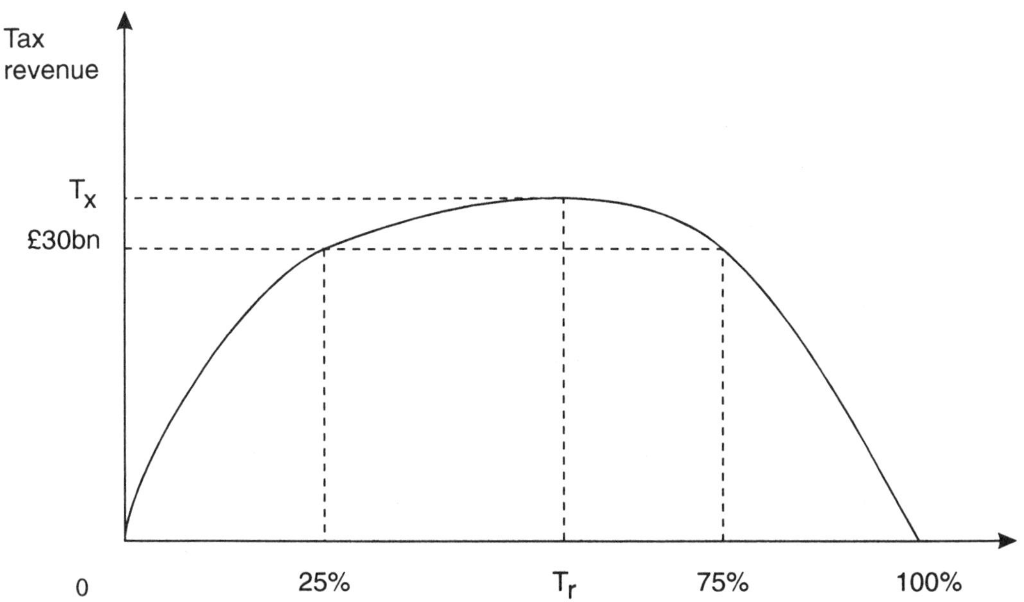

Figure 2 Laffer curve for a hypothetical economy

In the hypothetical economy depicted in Figure 2, a tax rate of 0% results in the government receiving no tax revenue irrespective of the level of national income. If the rate is 100% then nobody will work because they keep none of their earnings and so once again total tax revenue is zero. At 25% tax rates the government will achieve a total tax take of £30bn; the same as the revenue they enjoy at rates of 75%. By deduction, the level of national income when taxes are 25% must be £120bn compared with only £40bn if taxes are 75%. High taxation appears to operate as a disincentive.

3.8 Three consequences flow from this Laffer curve analysis.

(a) High rates of taxation act as a disincentive to work and accordingly reduce output and employment.

(b) Governments cannot always expect to increase tax revenue by increasing tax rates. There appears to be a crucial tax rate beyond which the fall in national income resulting from the erosion of incentives and effort outweighs the increased tax rate. In Figure 5 the maximum tax revenue is at T_x at average tax rate T_r. If tax rates are above T_r, the government can increase tax revenues by cutting tax rates.

(c) There will always be two tax rates available which can yield the same total tax revenue; one associated with a high level of national income and another associated with a lower level. In consequence governments committed to high government expenditure need not always be associated with high rates of tax.

KEY TERM

Laffer curve: a curve depicting the relationship between tax revenue and the average tax rate, designed to illustrate the thesis that there is an optimal tax rate at which tax revenues are maximised.

3.9 Supply side economists advise against state involvement in the economy at both the microeconomic and macroeconomic levels.

Microeconomic involvement is disliked for the following reasons.

(a) Price regulation distorts the signalling function essential for markets to reach optimal equilibrium.

(b) Wage regulation distorts the labour market's ability to ensure full employment.

(c) Public ownership blunts the incentive effects of the profit motive and leads to inefficiency.

(d) Government grants and subsidies encourage inefficient and lame-duck industries.

(e) Public provision of services may not encourage efficiency and can limit the discipline of consumer choice.

(f) Employment legislation, such as employment protection, limits market flexibility by discouraging recruitment and encouraging over-manning.

Macroeconomic intervention by government is regarded as harmful for several reasons.

(a) Demand management will be inflationary in the long run.

(b) High taxes will act as a disincentive.

(c) The possibility of politically motivated policy changes will create damaging uncertainty in the economy. This will discourage long-term investment.

3.10 Although most would accept the need for expansion of the money stock by government to accommodate increases in aggregate demand, some supply-siders have denied even this role to the government.

4 EXTERNALITIES AND GOVERNMENT INTERVENTION

Social costs and private costs

4.1 In a free market, suppliers and households make their output and buying decisions for their own private benefit, and these decisions determine how the economy's scarce resources will be allocated to production and consumption. Private costs and private benefits therefore determine what goods are made and bought in a free market.

(a) **Private cost** measures the cost *to the firm* of the resources it uses to produce a good.

(b) **Social cost** measures the cost *to society as a whole* of the resources that a firm uses.

(c) **Private benefit** measures the benefit obtained directly by a supplier or by a consumer.

(d) **Social benefit** measures the total benefit obtained, both directly by a supplier or a consumer, and indirectly (at no extra cost), to other suppliers or consumers.

4.2 It can be argued that a free market system would result in a satisfactory allocation of resources, *provided that* private costs are the same as social costs, and private benefits are the same as social benefits. In this situation, suppliers will maximise profits by supplying goods and services that benefit customers, and that customers want to buy. By producing their goods and services, suppliers are giving benefit to both themselves and also the community.

4.3 However, there are instances when either:

(a) members of the economy (suppliers or households) do things which give benefit to others, but no reward to themselves; or

(b) members of the economy do things which are harmful to others, but at no cost to themselves.

4.4 When private benefit is not the same as social benefit, or when private cost is not the same as social cost, an allocation of resources which reflects private costs and benefits only may not be socially acceptable.

4.5 Here are some examples of situations where private cost and social cost differ.

(a) A firm produces a good, and during the production process, pollution is discharged into the air. The private cost to the firm is the cost of the resources needed to make the good. The social cost consists of the private cost plus the additional 'costs' incurred by other members of society, who suffer from the pollution.

(b) The private cost of transporting goods by road is the cost to the haulage firm of the resources to provide the transport. The social cost of road haulage would consist of the private cost plus the social cost of environmental damage, including the extra cost of repairs and maintenance of the road system, which sustains serious damage from heavy goods vehicles.

Private benefit and social benefit

4.6 Here are some examples of situations where private benefit and social benefit differ.

(a) Customers at a café in a piazza benefit from the entertainment provided by professional musicians, who are hired by the café. The customers of the café are paying for the service, in the prices they pay, and they obtain a private benefit from it. At the same time, other people in the piazza, who are not customers of the café, might stop and listen to the music. They will obtain a benefit, but at no extra cost to themselves. They are **free riders,** taking advantage of the service without contributing to its cost. The social benefit from the musicians' service is greater than the private benefit to the café's customers.

(b) Suppose that a large firm pays for the training of employees as accountants, expecting a certain proportion of these employees to leave the firm in search of a better job once they have qualified. The private benefits to the firm are the benefits of the training of those employees who continue to work for it. The total social benefit includes the benefit of the training of those employees who go to work for other firms. These other firms benefit, but at no extra cost to themselves.

Question 2

Think of some situations other than those mentioned above in which private costs differ from social costs and private benefits differ from social benefits. How might these differences be prevented or compensated for in each situation?

Externalities

4.7 **Externality** is the name given to a difference between the private and the social costs, or benefits, arising from an activity. Less formally, an 'externality' is a cost or benefit affecting people who are not involved in the transaction involved and which the market mechanism therefore fails to take into account. One activity might produce both harmful and beneficial externalities.

KEY TERM

Externalities: positive or negative effects on third parties resulting from production and consumption activities.

Question 3

Much Wapping is a small town where a municipal swimming pool and sports centre has just been built by a private firm. Which of the following is an external benefit of the project?

(a) The increased trade for local shops
(b) The increased traffic in the neighbourhood
(c) The increased profits for the sports firm
(d) The increased building on previously open land

Answer

Item (b) is an external cost of the project, since increased volumes of traffic are harmful to the environment. Item (c) is a private benefit for the firm. Item (d) would only be an external benefit if a building is better for society than the use of open land, which is unlikely. Item (a) is correct because the benefits to local shops are additional to the private benefits of the sports firm and as such are external benefits.

4.8 We can use demand and supply analysis to illustrate the consequences of externalities. If an adverse externality exists, so that the social cost of supplying a good is greater than the private cost to the supplier firm, then a supply curve which reflects total social costs will be to the left of the (private cost) market supply curve.

4.9 In Figure 3:

(a) if a free market exists, the amount of the good produced will be determined by the interaction of demand (curve D) and supply curve S. Here, output would be Y, at price P_y;

(b) if social costs were taken into account, and the market operated successfully, the amount of the good produced should be X, at price P_x.

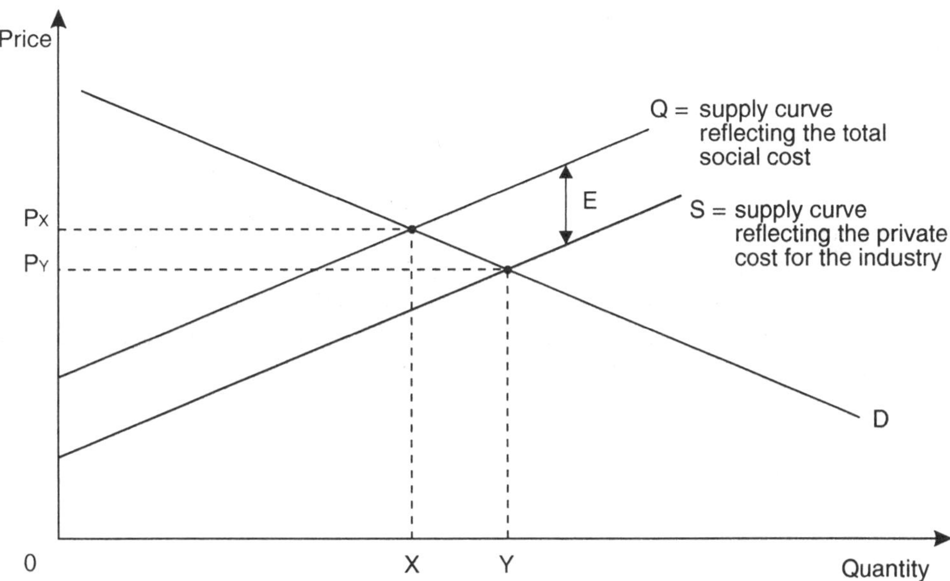

Figure 3 Externalities

4.10 Given a free market, output of the good will exceed what it ideally should be, and so resources will have been over-allocated to production of this particular good.

Public goods

4.11 Some goods, by their very nature, involve so much 'spillover' of externalities that they are difficult to provide except as **public goods** whose production is organised by the government.

KEY TERM

A public good is a good whose benefits cannot be restricted to a particular consumer. Consumption of a public good is non-rivalrous, meaning that consumption by one person does not deprive others of the good.

4.12 In the case of public goods, the consumption of the good by one individual or group does not significantly reduce the amount available for others. And if one individual makes use of the good, it does not reduce the availability of the good and its benefits to other individuals. Furthermore, it is often difficult or impossible to exclude anyone from its benefits, once the good has been provided. As a result, in a free market individuals benefiting from the good would have no economic incentive to pay for them, since they might as well be 'free riders' if they can, enjoying the good while others pay for it.

4.13 Defence and policing are perhaps the most obvious examples of public goods. It is not practicable for individuals to buy their own defence systems or policing arrangements.

Merit goods

4.14 The existence of market failure and of externalities suggests the need for intervention in markets by the government, in order to improve the allocation of resources. Another possible reason for intervention is to increase the consumption of what are termed **merit goods**. Such goods are considered to be worth providing in greater volume than would be purchased in a free market, because higher consumption is in the long-term public interest. Education is one of the chief examples of a merit good.

On the other hand, many governments want to see *less* consumption of certain **demerit goods**, such as tobacco.

KEY TERM

A **merit good** is a good which is considered to be desirable in itself. A government may supply merit goods such as health and education, which free markets alone may provide in insufficient quantities for the public good.

4.15 Apart from providing public goods and merit goods, a government might choose to intervene in the workings of markets are by:

(a) controlling the means of production (for example, through state ownership of industries);

(b) influencing markets through legislation and regulation (regulation of monopolies, bans on dangerous drugs, enforcement of the use of some goods such as car seat belts, laws on pollution control and so on) or by persuasion (for example, using anti-tobacco advertising);

(c) re-distribution of wealth, perhaps by taxing relatively wealthy members of society and re-distributing this tax income so as to benefit the poorer members;

(d) influencing market supply and demand through:

   (i) price legislation;

   (ii) indirect taxation - for example, the lower tax on lead-free petrol in the UK compared with leaded petrol is aimed at encouraging greater demand for unleaded petrol so as to reduce environmental pollution;

   (iii) subsidies;

(e) creating a demand for output that is labour-creating. A free price mechanism will result in a total demand for goods and services that would be met by a matching total supply, but this total supply quantity might be insufficient to create full employment within the economy. Government might therefore wish to intervene to create a demand for output in order to create more jobs.

5 ENVIRONMENTAL ('GREEN') POLICIES 12/97

5.1 Some externalities, particularly the problems of pollution and the environment, appear to call for international co-operation between governments. Pollutants expelled into the atmosphere in the UK are said to cause 'acid rain' to fall in Scandinavia, for example.

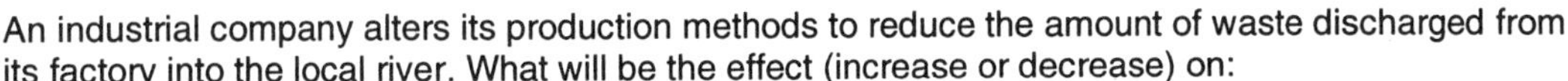

Question 4

An industrial company alters its production methods to reduce the amount of waste discharged from its factory into the local river. What will be the effect (increase or decrease) on:

(a) private costs;
(b) external benefits;
(c) social costs?

Answer

(a) Private costs of the company will presumably increase: the anti-pollution measures will have involved a financial outlay.

(b) External benefits will presumably increase: the public will benefit from a cleaner river.

(c) Social costs may stay the same: the increase in private costs may be balanced by the reduction the external costs to society.

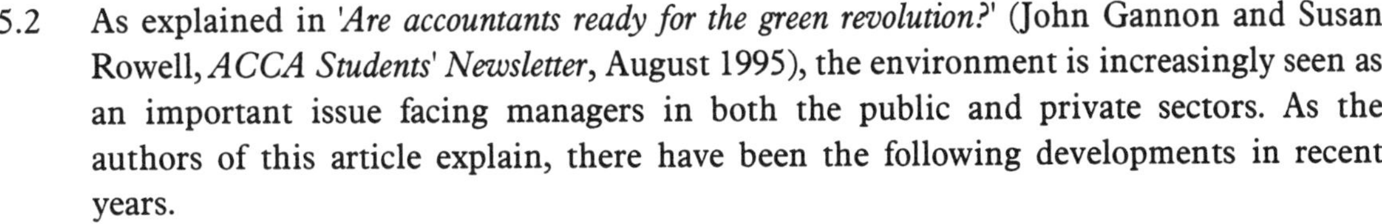

5.2 As explained in '*Are accountants ready for the green revolution?*' (John Gannon and Susan Rowell, *ACCA Students' Newsletter*, August 1995), the environment is increasingly seen as an important issue facing managers in both the public and private sectors. As the authors of this article explain, there have been the following developments in recent years.

(a) The 1989 'Pearce Report', *Blueprint for a green economy,* commissioned by the Government, received a favourable reaction from the Secretary of State for the Environment. Sustainability, it was argued, could be achieved by market interventions which adjusted the price mechanism and made organisations aware of the full cost of their actions, including environmental costs. An effective form of intervention, according to Pearce, was the Polluter Pays Principle, which requires those who produce products or provide services to bear the cost of achieving agreed standards of environmental quality.

(b) The 1990 Environmental Protection Act sought to implement the PPP through a system of integrated pollution control. The Act provided for levies on certain categories of companies to fund the regulatory and control bodies which were to enforce it. The Act also established the principle of **BATNEEC** - an acronym for **best available technology not entailing excessive cost**. If a company operates an authorised process, the methods it uses must conform to BATNEEC.

(c) A focus of media attention was provided by the June 1992 Rio Earth Summit, the first time that governments and non-government organisations (NGOs) had considered the environment on a worldwide basis. An ambitious action plan for the twenty first century called 'Agenda 21' was drawn up.

(d) Recognising that sustainability is the only realistic choice facing the world as a whole, Agenda 21 calls for a substantial change in priorities by governments, companies, funding agencies and individuals. Environmental considerations must, it argues, figure in economic policy and decision making at all levels. Shifts must also occur in financial resources at both national and international levels.

Pollution policy

5.3 **Pollution**, for example from exhaust gas emissions or the dumping of waste, is often discussed in relation to environmental policy. If polluters take little or no account of their actions on others, this generally results in the output of polluting industries being greater than is optimal. If polluters were forced to pay for any externalities they impose on society, producers would almost certainly change their production techniques so as to minimise pollution and consumers would choose to consume less of those goods which cause pollution. One solution is to levy a tax on polluters equal to the cost of removing the effect of the externality they generate: the **polluter pays principle**. This will encourage firms to cut emissions and provides an incentive for them to research ways of permanently reducing pollution. This approach is generally held to be preferable to limiting the amount of pollution firms can impose on the environment by regulation, as this can be difficult to enforce and provides less incentive to reduce pollution levels permanently.

5.4 To derive the full social cost of production where there are externalities, we need to add the costs (or benefits) of the externalities borne by society as a whole to the private costs of production incurred by the individuals or firms responsible for them. Clearly the existence of externalities means that social costs and private costs will diverge, which has an important bearing on the allocation of resources in the economy.

5.5 The polluter pays principle can be analysed using Figure 3 above. In a competitive market the firm will produce output Y at a price of P_Y considering only the costs it experiences directly, as shown by the marginal private cost (MPC) curves. The pollution created, however, must be taken into account in determining the social costs of production and hence the marginal social cost (MSC) curve Q lies above the MPC, the distance between them being determined by the extent of the externality.

5.6 The firm should be operating on the Q curve, producing output of X at price of P_X for allocative efficiency to be achieved. This can be achieved by imposing a tax on the firm equal to the external costs generated by production (E). This represents an optimal allocation of resources, maximising economic welfare as all costs will have been taken into account and hence this is regarded as beneficial to society as a whole.

5.7 'Polluter pays' taxes have the advantage that they provide an incentive to introduce measures to prevent pollution. The firm above will lose profits because of the tax and so, if it can reduce the amount of pollution generated, it can reduce the tax it pays, while MSC falls towards MPC, allowing the firm to increase both output and profits.

5.8 Apart from the imposition of a tax, there are a number of other measures open to the government in attempting to reduce pollution. One of the main measures available is the application of subsidies which may be used either to persuade polluters to reduce output and hence pollution, or to assist with expenditure on production processes, such as new machinery and air cleaning equipment, which reduce levels of pollution.

Problems with subsidies

5.9 A problem with using **subsidies** is that, unlike taxes, they do not provide an incentive to reduce pollution any further: indeed, profits are increased under subsidies which may have the perverse effect of encouraging more pollution to be generated in order to qualify for a subsidy. In addition, this is likely to be an expensive option for the government whereas imposing a tax actually provides the government with additional revenue.

5.10 One subsidy in the UK is that given to householders for loft insulation: this reduces energy consumption, in turn reducing emissions of pollutants. Another example of a subsidy to encourage a specific environmental alternative is that provided to a garbage burning power station opened in Lewisham, South London in 1994. The station receives a guaranteed high price for its power, which is effectively subsidised by electricity consumers. The subsidy actually encourages the plant to burn garbage wastefully.

Legislation

5.11 An alternative approach used in the UK is to impose **legislation** laying down regulations governing waste disposal and atmospheric emissions. Waste may only be disposed of with prior consent and if none is given, or it is exceeded, the polluter is fined. Examples of legislation in this area include the Control of Pollution Act 1974 and the Environmental Protection Act 1990. There may also be attempts with this type of approach to specify standards of, for example, air and water quality with appropriate penalties for not conforming to the required standards. Problems with this approach are the administrative burden it creates and the costs involved in monitoring and enforcement.

European 'agri-environmental' policies

5.12 One aspect of a 1992 reform of the European Union's Common Agricultural Policy (CAP) has been the introduction of environmental objectives into the CAP.

5.13 The main overall aim of the reform of the CAP has been to reduce overproduction by limiting support payments to fixed quotas and by bringing prices, particularly of cereals, down to world market prices.

5.14 The reformed EU scheme can give aid to farmers who substantially reduce the use of fertilisers or introduce or continue organic production; who extensify their production; who use farming practices compatible with the environment and natural resources; who set aside farmland for purposes connected with the environment and who manage land for public access.

5.15 Initially, funds are limited but by the end of the 1990s a substantial part of those deriving from the CAP is likely to be devoted to agri-environmental purposes.

Other environmental grants schemes

5.16 Other environmental grants schemes outside the CAP package include the Countryside Stewardship Scheme and the Environmentally Sensitive Areas Scheme.

Exam focus point

The new UK Chancellor of the Exchequer Gordon Brown has asserted that the environment would be put 'at the core of the government's objectives for the tax system'. This statement makes green taxes a topical issue, and therefore perhaps more likely to be examined.

Advantages of 'environmentally friendly policies' for a firm

5.17 There may be various reasons why a firm may gain from adopting a policy of strict compliance with environmental regulations, or of going further and taking voluntary initiatives to protect aspects of the environment.

(a) If potential customers perceive the firm to be environmentally friendly, some may be more inclined to buy its products.

(b) A corporate image which embraces environmentally friendly policies may enhance relationships with the public in general or with local communities.

(c) People may prefer to work for an environmentally friendly firm.

(d) 'Ethical' investment funds may be more likely to buy the firm's shares.

Chapter roundup

- The government influences markets in various ways, one of which is through direct **regulation** (eg the **MMC).**
- **Privatisation** is a policy of introducing private enterprise into industries which were previously stated-owned or state-operated.
- The freedom of European governments to offer cash **grants** and other forms of direct assistance to business is limited by European Union policies designed to prevent the distortion of free market competition.
- The **supply side economics** of the monetarists is directed at deregulation of markets and is commonly associated with a number of policy propositions.
    - Reduction in the role of government through elimination of budget deficits and reduction in the proportion of total expenditure attributable to government.
    - Elimination of restrictive trade practices in the goods market through de-regulation and liberalisation.
    - Reduction of labour market imperfections through legislation to weaken collective bargaining. This is often accompanied by the adoption of a tougher line by government towards unions in the public sector.
    - Reduction in the size of the public sector through privatisation of nationalised industries and disposal of public assets. This can also include greater reliance upon the private sector for the provision of public services.
    - Reduction in the rates of direct taxation through constraints on government expenditure and a shift towards indirect taxation.
- There are a number of policy approaches to **pollution** and other negative **externalities**, such as **polluter pays policies, subsidies** and direct **legislation**.

Quick quiz

1. Under what conditions might regulation be the appropriate policy response to market failure? (see para 1.1)
2. Outline the arguments for and against privatisation. (1.31 - 1.34)
3. How might direct government assistance be offered to firms? (2.1 - 2.3)
4. What is the ERDF? (2.8, 2.9)
5. What are the main propositions on which 'supply side economics' is based? (3.4)
6. What is the Laffer curve used to demonstrate? (3.7)
7. What is an externality? (4.7)
8. Define the polluter pays principle and BATNEEC. (5.2)

Question to try	Level	Marks	Time
20	Examination	20	36 mins

Part G

Working capital management

Chapter 20

INTRODUCTION TO WORKING CAPITAL MANAGEMENT

Chapter topic list		Syllabus reference
1	Working capital and its management	6(a), (b)
2	Working capital and cash flow	6(c)
3	Treasury management	6(c)

Introduction

The framework of **financial management** was described in Chapters 14 and 15. In Chapters 16 to 19, we have studied the **macroeconomic environment** within which all organisations and their financial managers must work.

In this chapter, we return to consider functions of the financial manager relating to the **management of working capital** in general terms.

In Chapter 21, we shall be looking at specific aspects of the management of **cash**, **stocks** (inventories), **debtors** and **creditors**.

1 WORKING CAPITAL AND ITS MANAGEMENT 6/94, 6/97

What is working capital?

1.1 The net working capital of a business can be defined as its current assets less its current liabilities. Current assets comprise cash, stocks of raw materials, work in progress and finished goods, marketable securities such as Treasury bills, and amounts receivable from debtors. Current liabilities comprise creditors falling due within one year, and may include amounts owed to trade creditors, taxation payable, dividend payments due, short-term loans, long-term debts maturing within one year, and so on.

1.2 Every business needs adequate **liquid resources** to maintain day-to-day cash flow. It needs enough to pay wages and salaries as they fall due and enough to pay creditors if it is to keep its workforce and ensure its supplies. Maintaining adequate working capital is not just important in the short term. Sufficient liquidity must be maintained in order to ensure the survival of the business in the long term as well. Even a profitable company may fail if it does not have adequate cash flow to meet its liabilities as they fall due.

What is working capital management?

1.3 Ensuring that sufficient liquid resources are maintained is a matter of working capital management. This involves achieving a balance between the requirement to minimise the risk of insolvency and the requirement to maximise the return on assets. An excessively conservative approach to working capital management resulting in high levels of cash holdings will harm profits because the opportunity to make a return on the assets tied up as cash will have been missed.

Exam focus point

The Examiner treats working capital management as a 'major' FM topic, and therefore tries to include some aspect of it in each exam paper.

Working capital (liquidity) ratios

The current ratio and the quick ratio

1.4 The standard test of liquidity is the **current ratio**. It can be obtained from the balance sheet, and is:

$$\frac{\text{Current assets}}{\text{Current liabilities}}$$

1.5 A company should have enough current assets that give a promise of 'cash to come' to meet its commitments to pay its current liabilities. Obviously, a ratio in excess of 1 should be expected. Otherwise, there would be the prospect that the company might be unable to pay its debts on time. In practice, a ratio comfortably in excess of 1 should be expected, but what is 'comfortable' varies between different types of businesses.

1.6 Companies are not able to convert all their current assets into cash very quickly. In particular, some manufacturing companies might hold large quantities of raw material stocks, which must be used in production to create finished goods. Finished goods might be warehoused for a long time, or sold on lengthy credit. In such businesses, where stock turnover is slow, most stocks are not very liquid assets, because the cash cycle is so long. For these reasons, we calculate an additional liquidity ratio, known as the quick ratio or acid test ratio.

1.7 The **quick ratio**, or **acid test ratio**, is $\frac{\text{Current assets less stocks}}{\text{Current liabilities}}$

1.8 This ratio should ideally be at least 1 for companies with a slow stock turnover. For companies with a fast stock turnover, a quick ratio can be less than 1 without suggesting that the company is in cash flow difficulties.

The debtors' payment period

1.9 A rough measure of the average length of time it takes for a company's debtors to pay what they owe is the '**debtor days**' ratio, or **average debtors' payment period**, which is:

$$\frac{\text{Average debtors}}{\text{Sales}} \times 365 \text{ days}$$

1.10 The figure for sales should be the turnover figure in the profit and loss account. The trade debtors are not the *total* figure for debtors in the balance sheet, which includes prepayments and non-trade debtors. The trade debtors figure will be itemised in an analysis of the total debtors, in a note to the accounts.

1.11 The estimate of debtor days is only approximate.

(a) The balance sheet value of debtors might be abnormally high or low compared with the 'normal' level the company usually has.

(b) Turnover in the profit and loss account excludes VAT, but the debtors' figure in the balance sheet includes VAT. We are not strictly comparing like with like.

The stock turnover period

1.12 Another ratio worth calculating is the stock turnover period, or stockholding period days. This is another estimated figure, obtainable from published accounts, which indicates the average number of days that items of stock are held for. As with the average debt collection period, it is only an approximate figure, but one which should be reliable enough for finding changes over time.

1.13 The number of stock days is $\frac{\text{Average stock}}{\text{Cost of sales}} \times 365$ days

1.14 The ratio $\frac{\text{Cost of sales}}{\text{Stock}}$ is called the stock turnover, and is another measure of how vigorously a business is trading. A lengthening stock turnover period indicates:

(a) a slowdown in trading; or

(b) a build-up in stock levels, perhaps suggesting that the investment in stocks is becoming excessive.

1.15 If we add together the stock days and the debtor days, this should give us an indication of how soon stock is convertible into cash, thereby giving a further indication of the company's liquidity.

The need for funds for investment in current assets

1.16 As we have seen, current assets may be financed either by long-term funds or by current liabilities. An 'ideal' current ratio (current assets: current liabilities) is generally accepted to be 2:1 (half of current assets should be financed by long-term funds), but this proportion can obviously be varied in practice, depending on the circumstances of an individual company. Similarly, the 'ideal' quick ratio or acid test ratio (current assets minus stocks: current liabilities) is 1:1, although in practice, companies often have much lower quick ratios than this.

1.17 These liquidity ratios are a guide to the risk of cash flow problems and insolvency. If a company suddenly finds that it is unable to renew its short-term liabilities (for example, if the bank suspends its overdraft facilities, or creditors start to demand earlier payment), there will be a danger of insolvency unless the company is able to turn enough of its current assets into cash quickly. A current ratio of 2:1 and a quick ratio of 1:1 are thought to indicate that a company is reasonably well protected against the danger of insolvency.

1.18 Current liabilities are often a cheap method of finance (trade creditors do not usually carry an interest cost) and companies may therefore consider that, in the interest of higher profits, it is worth accepting some risk of insolvency by increasing current liabilities, taking the maximum credit possible from suppliers.

The volume of current assets required

1.19 The volume of current assets required will depend on the nature of the company's business. For example, a manufacturing company may require more stocks than a company in a service industry. As the volume of output by a company increases, the volume of current assets required will also increase.

1.20 Even assuming efficient stock holding, debt collection procedures and cash management, there is still a certain degree of choice in the total volume of current assets required to meet output requirements. Policies of low stock-holding levels, tight credit and minimum cash holdings may be contrasted with policies of high stocks (to allow for safety or buffer stocks) easier credit and sizeable cash holdings (for precautionary reasons).

Over-capitalisation and working capital

1.21 If there are excessive stocks, debtors and cash, and very few creditors, there will be an over-investment by the company in current assets. Working capital will be excessive and the company will be in this respect over-capitalised. The return on investment will be lower than it should be, and long-term funds will be unnecessarily tied up when they could be invested elsewhere to earn profits.

1.22 **Over-capitalisation** with respect to working capital should not exist if there is good management, but the warning signs of excessive working capital would be poor accounting ratios. The ratios which can assist in judging whether the investment in working capital is reasonable include the following.

(a) **Sales/working capital.** The volume of sales as a multiple of the working capital investment should indicate whether, in comparison with previous years or with similar companies, the total volume of working capital is too high.

(b) **Liquidity ratios.** A current ratio in excess of 2:1 or a quick ratio in excess of 1:1 may indicate over-investment in working capital.

(c) **Turnover periods**. Excessive turnover periods for stocks and debtors, or a short period of credit taken from suppliers, might indicate that the volume of stocks or debtors is unnecessarily high, or the volume of creditors too low.

1.23 EXAMPLE: WORKING CAPITAL RATIOS

Calculate liquidity and working capital ratios from the following accounts of a manufacturer of products for the construction industry, and comment on the ratios.

	19X8	*19X7*
	£m	£m
Turnover	2,065.0	1,788.7
Cost of sales	1,478.6	1,304.0
Gross profit	586.4	484.7
Current assets		
Stocks	119.0	109.0
Debtors (note 1)	400.9	347.4
Short-term investments	4.2	18.8
Cash at bank and in hand	48.2	48.0
	572.3	523.2

	19X8	19X7
	£m	£m
Creditors: amounts falling due within one year		
Loans and overdrafts	49.1	35.3
Corporation taxes	62.0	46.7
Dividend	19.2	14.3
Creditors (note 2)	370.7	324.0
	501.0	420.3
Net current assets	71.3	102.9

Notes

		19X8	19X7
		£m	£m
1	Trade debtors	329.8	285.4
2	Trade creditors	236.2	210.8

1.24 SOLUTION

	19X8	19X7
Current ratio	$\frac{572.3}{501.0} = 1.14$	$\frac{523.2}{420.3} = 1.24$
Quick ratio	$\frac{453.3}{501.0} = 0.90$	$\frac{414.2}{420.3} = 0.99$
Debtors' payment period	$\frac{329.8}{2,065.0} \times 365 = 58$ days	$\frac{285.4}{1,788.7} \times 365 = 58$ days
Stock turnover period	$\frac{119.0}{1,478.6} \times 365 = 29$ days	$\frac{109.0}{1,304.0} \times 365 = 31$ days
Creditors' turnover period	$\frac{236.2}{1,478.6} \times 365 = 58$ days	$\frac{210.8}{1,304.0} \times 365 = 59$ days

The company is a manufacturing group serving the construction industry, and so would be expected to have a comparatively lengthy debtors' turnover period, because of the relatively poor cash flow in the construction industry. It is clear that the company compensates for this by ensuring that they do not pay for raw materials and other costs before they have sold their stocks of finished goods (hence the similarity of debtors' and creditors' turnover periods).

The company's current ratio is a little lower than average but its quick ratio is better than average and very little less than the current ratio. This suggests that stock levels are strictly controlled, which is reinforced by the low stock turnover period. It would seem that working capital is tightly managed, to avoid the poor liquidity which could be caused by a high debtors' turnover period and comparatively high creditors.

Creditors' turnover is ideally calculated by the formula:

$$\frac{\text{Average stock}}{\text{Purchases}} \times 365$$

However, it is rare to find purchases disclosed in published accounts and so cost of sales serves as an approximation. The creditors' turnover ratio often helps to assess a company's liquidity; an increase in creditor days is often a sign of lack of long-term finance or poor management of current assets, resulting in the use of extended credit from suppliers, increased bank overdraft and so on.

Overtrading

Exam focus point

You may, as in 6/94, be expected to diagnose overtrading from given information about a company.

1.25 In contrast with over-capitalisation, overtrading happens when a business tries to do too much too quickly with too little long-term capital, so that it is trying to support too large a volume of trade with the capital resources at its disposal.

Even if an overtrading business operates at a profit, it could easily run into serious trouble because it is short of money. Such liquidity troubles stem from the fact that it does not have enough capital to provide the cash to pay its debts as they fall due.

KEY TERM

Overtrading: excessive trading by a business with insufficient long-term capital at its disposal, raising the risks of liquidity problems.

1.26 EXAMPLE: OVERTRADING

Great Ambition Ltd appoints a new managing director who has great plans to expand the company. He wants to increase turnover by 100% within two years, and to do this he employs extra sales staff. He recognises that customers do not want to have to wait for deliveries, and so he decides that the company must build up its stock levels. There is a substantial increase in the company's stocks. These are held in additional warehouse space which is now rented. The company also buys new cars for its extra sales representatives.

The managing director's policies are immediately successful in boosting sales, which double in just over one year. Stock levels are now much higher, but the company takes longer credit from its suppliers, even though some suppliers have expressed their annoyance at the length of time they must wait for payment. Credit terms for debtors are unchanged, and so the volume of debtors, like the volume of sales, rises by 100%.

In spite of taking longer credit, the company still needs to increase its overdraft facilities with the bank, which are raised from a limit of £40,000 to one of £80,000. The company is profitable, and retains some profits in the business, but profit margins have fallen.

(a) Gross profit margins are lower because some prices have been reduced to obtain extra sales.

(b) Net profit margins are lower because overhead costs are higher. These include sales representatives' wages, car expenses and depreciation on cars, warehouse rent and additional losses from having to write off out-of-date and slow-moving stock items.

1.27 The balance sheet of the company might change over time from (A) to (B).

	Balance sheet (A)			Balance sheet (B)		
	£	£	£	£	£	£
Fixed assets			160,000			210,000
Current assets						
Stock		60,000			150,000	
Debtors		64,000			135,000	
Cash		1,000			-	
		125,000			285,000	
Current liabilities						
Bank	25,000			80,000		
Creditors	50,000			200,000		
		75,000			280,000	
			50,000			5,000
			210,000			215,000
Share capital			10,000			10,000
Profit and loss account			200,000			205,000
			210,000			215,000
Sales			£1,000,000			£2,000,000
Gross profit			£200,000			£300,000
Net profit			£50,000			£20,000

In situation (B), the company has reached its overdraft limit and has four times as many creditors as in situation (A) but with only twice the sales turnover. Stock levels are much higher, and stock turnover is lower.

The company is overtrading. If it had to pay its next trade creditor, or salaries and wages, before it received any income, it could not do so without the bank allowing it to exceed its overdraft limit. The company is profitable, although profit margins have fallen, and it ought to expect a prosperous future. But if it does not sort out its cash flow and liquidity, it will not survive to enjoy future profits.

1.28 Suitable solutions to the problem would be measures to reduce the degree of overtrading.

(a) New capital from the shareholders could be injected.

(b) Better control could be applied to stocks and debtors.

(c) The company could abandon ambitious plans for increased sales and more fixed asset purchases until the business has had time to consolidate its position, and build up its capital base with retained profits.

The causes of overtrading

1.29 Emphasis has been given so far to the danger of overtrading when a business seeks to increase its turnover too rapidly without an adequate capital base. In other words, overtrading is brought upon the business by the ambition of management. This is not the only cause of overtrading, however. Other causes are as follows.

(a) When a business repays a loan, it often replaces the old loan with a new one. However a business might repay a loan without replacing it, with the consequence that it has less long-term capital to finance its current level of operations.

(b) A business might be profitable, but in a period of inflation, its retained profits might be insufficient to pay for replacement fixed assets and stocks, which now cost more because of inflation. The business would then rely increasingly on credit, and find itself eventually unable to support its current volume of trading with a capital base that has fallen in real terms.

1.30 Symptoms of overtrading are as follows.

(a) There is a rapid increase in turnover.

(b) There is a rapid increase in the volume of current assets and possibly also fixed assets. Stock turnover and debtors turnover might slow down, in which case the rate of increase in stocks and debtors would be even greater than the rate of increase in sales.

(c) There is only a small increase in proprietors' capital (perhaps through retained profits). Most of the increase in assets is financed by credit, especially:

   (i) trade creditors. The payment period to creditors is likely to lengthen;

   (ii) a bank overdraft, which often reaches or even exceeds the limit of the facilities agreed by the bank.

(d) Some debt ratios and liquidity ratios alter dramatically.

   (i) The proportion of total assets financed by proprietors' capital falls, and the proportion financed by credit rises.

   (ii) The current ratio and the quick ratio fall.

   (iii) The business might have a liquid deficit, that is, an excess of current liabilities over current assets.

The working capital requirement

1.31 Computing the working capital requirement is a matter of calculating the value of current assets less current liabilities, perhaps by taking averages over a one year period.

1.32 EXAMPLE: WORKING CAPITAL REQUIREMENTS

The following data relate to Corn Ltd, a manufacturing company.

Turnover for the year	£1,500,000
Costs as percentages of sales	%
Direct materials	30
Direct labour	25
Variable overheads	10
Fixed overheads	15
Selling and distribution	5

On average:

(a) debtors take 2.5 months before payment;
(b) raw materials are in stock for three months;
(c) work-in-progress represents two months worth of half produced goods;
(d) finished goods represents one month's production;
(e) credit is taken as follows.

(i)	Direct materials	2 months
(ii)	Direct labour	1 week
(iii)	Variable overheads	1 month
(iv)	Fixed overheads	1 month
(v)	Selling and distribution	0.5 months

Work-in-progress and finished goods are valued at material, labour and variable expense cost.

Compute the working capital requirement of Corn Ltd assuming the labour force is paid for 50 working weeks a year.

1.33 SOLUTION

(a) The annual costs incurred will be as follows.

		£
Direct materials	30% of £1,500,000	450,000
Direct labour	25% of £1,500,000	375,000
Variable overheads	10% of £1,500,000	150,000
Fixed overheads	15% of £1,500,000	225,000
Selling and distribution	5% of £1,500,000	75,000

(b) The average value of current assets will be as follows.

		£	£
Raw materials	3/12 × 450,000		112,500
Work-in-progress			
Materials (50% complete)	1/12 × 450,000	37,500	
Labour (50% complete)	1/12 × 375,000	31,250	
Variable overheads (50% complete)	1/12 × 150,000	12,500	
			81,250
Finished goods			
Materials	1/12 × 450,000	37,500	
Labour	1/12 × 375,000	31,250	
Variable overheads	1/12 × 150,000	12,500	
			81,250
Debtors	2.5/12 × 1,500,000		312,500
			587,500

(c) Average value of current liabilities will be as follows.

Materials	2/12 × 450,000	75,000	
Labour	1/50 × 375,000	7,500	
Variable overheads	1/12 × 150,000	12,500	
Fixed overheads	1/12 × 225,000	18,750	
Selling and distribution	0.5/12 × 75,000	3,125	
			116,875

(d) Working capital required is (£(587,500 – 116,875)) = 470,625

It has been assumed that all the direct materials are allocated to work-in-progress when production starts.

Predicting business failure

1.34 The analysis of financial ratios in a commercial company is largely concerned with the efficiency and effectiveness of the use of resources by a company's management, and also with the financial stability of the company. Investors will wish to know:

(a) whether additional funds could be lent to the company with reasonable safety;
(b) whether the company would fail without additional funds.

1.35 One method of predicting business failure is the use of liquidity ratios (the current ratio and the quick ratio). A company with a current ratio well below 2:1 or a quick ratio well below 1:1 might be considered illiquid and in danger of failure. Research seems to indicate, however, that the current ratio and the quick ratio and trends in the variations of these ratios for a company, are poor indicators of eventual business failure.

Z scores

1.36 E I Altman researched into the simultaneous analysis of several financial ratios as a combined predictor of business failure. Altman analysed 22 accounting and non-accounting variables for a selection of failed and non-failed firms in the USA and from these, five key indicators emerged. These five indicators were then used to derive a **Z score**. Firms with a Z score above a certain level would be predicted to be financially sound, and firms with a Z score below a certain level would be categorised as probable failures. Altman also identified a range of Z scores in between the non-failure and failure categories in which eventual failure or non-failure was uncertain.

1.37 Altman's Z score model (derived in 1968) emerged as:

$$Z = 1.2X_1 + 1.4X_2 + 3.3X_3 + 0.6X_4 + 1.0X_5$$

where

X_1 = working capital/total assets
X_2 = retained earnings/total assets
X_3 = earnings before interest and tax/total assets
X_4 = market value of equity/book value of total debt (a form of gearing ratio)
X_5 = sales/total assets

2 WORKING CAPITAL AND CASH FLOW 6/96, 6/97

The operating cycle

2.1 The connection between investment in working capital and cash flow may be illustrated by means of the **cash cycle** (also called the **working capital cycle, operating cycle** or **trading cycle**).

2.2 The operating cycle may be expressed as the average number of days between the outlay on raw materials, wages and other expenses and the inflow of cash from the sale of the company's product.

In a manufacturing business, this equals:

The average time that raw materials remain in stock
less the period of credit taken from suppliers
plus the time taken to produce the goods
plus the time taken by customers to pay for the goods

2.3 If the turnover periods for stocks and debtors lengthen, or the payment period to creditors shortens:

(a) the operating cycle will lengthen;
(b) the investment in working capital will increase.

Cash flow planning

2.4 Since a company must have adequate cash inflows to survive, management should plan and control cash flows as well as profitability. Cash budgeting is an important element in short-term cash flow planning. Cash budget periods might be for one year, or less (for example monthly budgets).

2.5 The purpose of cash budgets is to make sure that the organisation will have enough cash inflows to meet its cash outflows. If a budget reveals that a short-term cash shortage can be expected, steps will be taken to meet the problem and avoid the cash crisis (perhaps by arranging a bigger bank overdraft facility).

2.6 Cash budgets and cash flow forecasts on their own do not give full protection against a cash shortage and enforced liquidation of the business by creditors. There may be unexpected changes in cash flow patterns.

Question

Give examples of unforeseen changes which may affect cash flow patterns.

Answer

Your list probably included some of the following:

(a) a change in the general economic environment. An economic recession will cause a slump in trade;

(b) a new product, launched by a competitor, which takes business away from a company's traditional and established product lines;

(c) new cost-saving product technology, which forces the company to invest in the new technology to remain competitive;

(d) moves by competitors which have to be countered (for example a price reduction or a sales promotion);

(e) changes in consumer preferences, resulting in a fall in demand;

(f) government action against certain trade practices or against trade with a country that a company has dealings with;

(g) strikes or other industrial action;

(h) natural disasters, such as floods or fire damage, which curtail an organisation's activities.

2.7 When unforeseen events have an adverse effect on cash inflows, a company will only survive if it can maintain adequate cash inflows despite the setbacks.

Strategic fund management

2.8 **Strategic fund management** is an extension of cash flow planning, which takes into consideration the ability of a business to overcome unforeseen problems with cash flows.

2.9 Strategic fund management recognises that the assets of a business can be divided into three categories.

(a) Assets which are needed to carry out the 'core' activities of the business. A group of companies will often have one or several main activities, and in addition will carry on several peripheral activities. The group's strategy should be primarily to develop its main activities, and so there has to be enough cash to maintain those activities and to finance their growth.

(b) Assets which are not essential for carrying out the main activities of the business, and which could be sold off at fairly short notice. These assets will consist mainly of short- term marketable investments.

(c) Assets which are not essential for carrying out the main activities of the business, and which could be sold off to raise cash, although it would probably take time to arrange the sale, and the amount of cash obtainable from the sale might be uncertain. These assets would include:

   (i) long-term investments (for example, substantial shareholdings in other companies);

   (ii) subsidiary companies engaged in 'peripheral' activities, which might be sold off to another company or in a management buyout;

   (iii) land and buildings.

2.10 If an unexpected event takes place which threatens a company's cash position, the company could meet the threat by:

(a) working capital management to improve cash flows by reducing stocks and debtors, taking more credit, or negotiating a higher bank overdraft facility;

(b) changes to dividend policy;

(c) arranging to sell off non-essential assets. The assets in category (b) above would be saleable at short notice, and arrangements could also be made to dispose of the assets in category (c), should the need arise and provided that there is enough time to arrange the sale.

3 TREASURY MANAGEMENT

KEY TERM

Treasury management can be defined as: 'The corporate handing of all financial matters, the generation of external and internal funds for business, the management of currencies and cash flows, and the complex strategies, policies and procedures of corporate finance.' (Association of Corporate Treasurers)

3.1 Large companies rely heavily on the financial and currency markets. These markets are volatile, with interest rates and foreign exchange rates changing continually and by significant amounts. To manage cash (funds) and currency efficiently, many large companies have set up a separate treasury department.

3.2 A treasury department, even in a large organisation, is likely to be quite small, with perhaps a staff of three to six qualified accountants, bankers or corporate treasurers working under the treasurer. In some cases, where the company or organisation handles very large amounts of cash or foreign currency dealings, and often has large cash surpluses, the treasury department might be a little bigger.

The role of the treasurer

3.3 The Association of Corporate Treasurers has listed the experience it will require from its student members before they are eligible for full membership of the Association. This list of required experience gives a good indication of the core roles of treasurership.

(a) **Corporate financial objectives**

(i) financial aims and strategies;
(ii) financial and treasury policies;
(iii) financial and treasury systems.

(b) **Liquidity management**

(i) working capital and money transmission management;
(ii) banking relationships and arrangements;
(iii) money management.

Cash management and liquidity management involve making sure that the organisation has the liquid funds it needs and invests any surplus funds, even for very short terms. In some organisations, the task is largely one of controlling stocks, debtors, creditors and bank overdrafts. In cash-rich companies, the treasurer will be heavily involved in the investment of surplus funds to earn a good yield until they are required again for another purpose.

A good relationship with one or more banks is desirable, so that the treasurer can negotiate overdraft facilities, money market loans or longer term loans at reasonable interest rates.

(c) **Funding management**

(i) funding policies and procedures;
(ii) sources of funds;
(iii) types of funds.

Funding management is concerned with all forms of borrowing, and alternative sources of funds, such as leasing and factoring.

The treasurer needs to know:

(i) where funds are obtainable;
(ii) for how long;
(iii) at what interest rate;
(iv) whether security would be required or not;
(v) whether interest rates would be fixed or variable.

If a company borrows, say, £10,000,000, even a difference of 0.25% in the interest cost of the loan obtained would be worth £25,000 in interest charges each year.

(d) **Currency management**

(i) exposure policies and procedures;
(ii) exchange dealing, including futures and options;
(iii) international monetary economics and exchange regulations.

Currency dealings can save or cost a company considerable amounts of money, and the success or shortcomings of the corporate treasurer can have a significant impact on the profit and loss account of a company which is heavily involved in foreign trade. A company (such as a multinational) which is involved in international transactions faces the possibility of exposure to foreign exchange risk: the values of assets and liabilities demoninated in one currency will change with fluctuations in the exchange rate against another.

(e) **Corporate finance**

(i) equity capital management;
(ii) business acquisitions and sales;
(iii) project finance and joint ventures.

Corporate finance is concerned with matters such as raising share capital, its form (ordinary or preference, or different classes of ordinary shares), obtaining a stock exchange listing, dividend policy, financial information for management, mergers, acquisitions and business sales.

(f) **Related subjects**

(i) corporate taxation (domestic and foreign tax);
(ii) risk management and insurance;
(iii) pension fund investment management.

As well as exposure to foreign exchange risk, an organisation may be subject to interest rate risk. For example, if a business takes out a variable rate loan, it faces the risk that interest rates will rise and it will have to pay more in interest than before. There are various financial investments, such as swaps and options, which can help to 'hedge' or reduce such risks.

Centralisation of the treasury department

3.4 The following are advantages of having a specialist **centralised treasury department**.

(a) **Centralised liquidity management:**

(i) avoids having a mix of cash surpluses and overdrafts in different localised bank accounts;

(ii) facilitates bulk cash flows, so that lower bank charges can be negotiated.

(b) Larger volumes of cash are available to invest, giving better **short-term investment opportunities** (for example money markets, high-interest accounts and CDs).

(c) Any borrowing can be arranged in bulk, at lower interest rates than for smaller borrowings, and perhaps on the eurocurrency or eurobond markets.

(d) **Foreign exchange risk management** is likely to be improved in a group of companies. A central treasury department can match foreign currency income earned by one subsidiary with expenditure in the same currency by another subsidiary. In this way, the risk of losses on adverse exchange rate movements can be avoided with out the expense of forward exchange contracts or other hedging methods.

(e) A specialist treasury department can employ **experts** with knowledge of dealing in forward contracts, futures, options, eurocurrency markets, swaps and so on. Localised departments could not have such expertise.

(f) The centralised pool of **funds required for precautionary purposes** will be smaller than the sum of separate precautionary balances which would need to be held under decentralised treasury arrangements.

(g) Through having a separate **profit centre**, attention will be focused on the contribution to group profit performance that can be achieved by good cash, funding, investment and foreign currency management.

3.5 Possible advantages of **decentralised** cash management are as follows.

(a) Sources of finance can be diversified and can match local assets.

(b) Greater autonomy can be given to subsidiaries and divisions because of the closer relationships they will have with the decentralised cash management function.

(c) A decentralised treasury function may be more responsive to the needs of individual operating units.

(d) Since cash balances will not be aggregated at group level, there will be more limited opportunities to invest such balances on a short-term basis.

Chapter roundup

- The amount tied up in **working capital** is equal to the value of raw materials, work-in-progress, finished stocks and debtors less creditors. The size of this net figure has a direct effect on the **liquidity** of an organisation.
- **Liquidity ratios** may help to indicate whether a company is **over-capitalised**, with excessive working capital, or if a business is likely to fail.
- A business which is trying to do too much too quickly with too little long-term capital is **overtrading**.
- **Treasury management** in a modern enterprise covers various areas, and in a large business may be a **centralised** function.

Quick quiz

1. Define the quick ratio. (see para 1.7)
2. What is over-capitalisation? (1.21)
3. What are the causes of overtrading? (1.27)
4. What is the operating cycle? (2.2)
5. What are the functions of a treasurer? (3.3)
6. What are the advantages of an organisation having a specialist treasury department? (3.5)

Question to try	Level	Marks	Time
21	Introductory	n/a	15 mins

Chapter 21

THE MANAGEMENT OF DEBTORS, CREDITORS, STOCKS AND CASH

	Chapter topic list	Syllabus reference
1	The management of debtors	6(d), 7(a)(viii)
2	The management of creditors and short-term finance	6(e), 7(a)(iv), (v)
3	The management of stocks	6(f)
4	The management of cash	6(c)
5	Foreign exchange risk	6(d), (e)

Introduction

This chapter, which deals with **specific techniques** in working capital management, should be studied after studying Chapter 20.

We also cover in outline here some techniques by which companies (eg in exporting or importing) can reduce **risks from fluctuating exchange rates**, a topic which becomes very important in Paper 14.

1 THE MANAGEMENT OF DEBTORS 6/94, 12/94, 6/95

Exam focus point

Debtors is an important area to cover thoroughly, as some aspect of it is frequently examined. In 1994 and 1995 exams, calculations on debtors policy came up twice, and there were two part-questions requiring discussion of credit control and factoring/invoice discounting respectively.

1.1 Several factors should be considered by management when a policy for **credit control** is formulated. These include:

(a) the administrative costs of debt collection;

(b) the procedures for controlling credit to individual customers and for debt collection;

(c) the amount of extra capital required to finance an extension of total credit. There might be an increase in debtors, stocks and creditors, and the net increase in working capital must be financed;

(d) the cost of the additional finance required for any increase in the volume of debtors (or the savings from a reduction in debtors). This cost might be bank overdraft interest, or the cost of long-term funds (such as loan stock or equity);

(e) any savings or additional expenses in operating the credit policy (for example the extra work involved in pursuing slow payers);

(f) the ways in which the credit policy could be implemented. For example:

  (i) credit could be eased by giving debtors a longer period in which to settle their accounts. The cost would be the resulting increase in debtors;

  (ii) a discount could be offered for early payment. The cost would be the amount of the discounts taken;

(g) the effects of easing credit, which might be:

  (i) to encourage a higher proportion of bad debts;
  (ii) an increase in sales volume.

  Provided that the extra gross contribution from the increase in sales exceeds the increase in fixed cost expenses, bad debts, discounts and the finance cost of an increase in working capital, a policy to relax credit terms would be profitable.

Some of the factors involved in credit policy decisions will now be considered in more detail.

The debt collection policy

1.2 The overall **debt collection policy** of the firm should be such that the administrative costs and other costs incurred in debt collection do not exceed the benefits from incurring those costs.

Some extra spending on debt collection procedures might:

(a) reduce bad debt losses;

(b) reduce the average collection period, and therefore the cost of the investment in debtors.

Beyond a certain level of spending, however, additional expenditure on debt collection would not have enough effect on bad debts or on the average collection period to justify the extra administrative costs.

1.3 EXAMPLE: DEBTOR MANAGEMENT (1)

Couttes Purse Ltd requires advice on its debt collection policy. Should the current policy be discarded in favour of Option 1 or Option 2?

	Current policy	*Option 1*	*Option 2*
Annual expenditure on debt collection procedures	£240,000	£300,000	£400,000
Bad debt losses (% of sales)	3%	2%	1%
Average collection period	2 months	1 1/2 months	1 month

Current sales are £4,800,000 a year, and the company requires a 15% return on its investments.

1.4 SOLUTION

	Current policy	Option 1	Option 2
	£	£	£
Average debtors	800,000	600,000	400,000
Reduction in working capital	-	200,000	400,000
(a) Interest saving (15% of reduction)		30,000	60,000
Bad debt losses (sales value)	144,000	96,000	48,000
(b) Reduction in losses	-	48,000	96,000
Benefits of each option (a) + (b)	-	78,000	156,000
Extra costs of debt collection	-	60,000	160,000
Benefit/(loss) from option		18,000	(4,000)

Option 1 is preferable to the current policy, but Option 2 is worse than the current policy.

Assessing creditworthiness

1.5 Credit control involves the initial investigation of potential credit customers and the continuing control of outstanding accounts.

The main points to note are as follows.

(a) New customers should give two good references, including one from a bank, before being granted credit.

(b) Credit ratings might be checked through a credit rating agency.

(c) A new customer's credit limit should be fixed at a low level and only increased if his payment record subsequently warrants it.

(d) For large value customers, a file should be maintained of any available financial information about the customer. This file should be reviewed regularly. Information is available from:

   (i) an analysis of the company's annual report and accounts;

   (ii) Extel cards (sheets of accounting information about public companies in the UK, and also major overseas companies, produced by Extel).

(e) The Department of Trade and Industry and the Export Credit Guarantee Department will both be able to advise on overseas companies.

(f) Press comments may give information about what a company is currently doing (as opposed to the historical results in Extel cards or published accounts which only show what the company has done in the past).

(g) The company could send a member of staff to visit the company concerned, to get a first-hand impression of the company and its prospects. This would be advisable in the case of a prospective major customer.

(h) Aged lists of debts should be produced and reviewed at regular intervals.

(i) The credit limit for an existing customer should be periodically reviewed, but it should only be raised if the customer's credit standing is good.

(j) It is essential to have procedures which ensure that further orders are not accepted from nor goods sent to a customer who is in difficulties. If a customer has exceeded his credit limit, or has not paid debts despite several reminders, or is otherwise known to be in difficulties, sales staff and warehouse staff must be notified immediately (and not, for example, at the end of the week, by which time more goods might have been supplied).

1.6 An organisation might devise a credit-rating system for new individual customers that is based on characteristics of the customer (such as whether the customer is a home owner, and the customer's age and occupation). Points would be awarded according to the characteristics of the customer, and the amount of credit that is offered would depend on his or her credit score.

Debt collection procedures

1.7 The three main areas which ought to be considered in connection with the control of debtors are:

- paperwork
- debt collection
- credit control

1.8 Sales **paperwork** should be dealt with promptly and accurately.

(a) Invoices should be sent out immediately after delivery.

(b) Checks should be carried out to ensure that invoices are accurate.

(c) The investigation of queries and complaints and, if appropriate, the issue of credit notes should be carried out promptly.

(d) If practical, monthly statements should be issued early so that all items on the statement might then be included in customers' monthly settlements of bills.

Total credit

1.9 To determine whether it would be profitable to extend the level of total credit, it is necessary to assess:

(a) the extra sales that a more generous credit policy would stimulate;
(b) the profitability of the extra sales;
(c) the extra length of the average debt collection period;
(d) the required rate of return on the investment in additional debtors.

1.10 EXAMPLE: DEBTOR MANAGEMENT (2)

Russian Beard Ltd is considering a change of credit policy which will result in an increase in the average collection period from one to two months. The relaxation in credit is expected to produce an increase in sales in each year amounting to 25% of the current sales volume.

Selling price per unit	£10
Variable cost per unit	£8.50
Current annual sales	£2,400,000

The required rate of return on investments is 20%.

Assume that the 25% increase in sales would result in additional stocks of £100,000 and additional creditors of £20,000.

Advise the company on whether or not to extend the credit period offered to customers, if:

(a) all customers take the longer credit of two months;

(b) existing customers do not change their payment habits, and only the new customers take a full two months credit.

1.11 SOLUTION

The change in credit policy is justifiable if the rate of return on the additional investment in working capital would exceed 20%.

Extra profit	
Contribution/sales ratio	15%
Increase in sales revenue	£600,000
Increase in contribution and profit	£90,000

(a) *Extra investment, if all debtors take two months credit*

	£
Average debtors after the sales increase (2/12 × £3,000,000)	500,000
Less current average debtors (1/12 × £2,400,000)	200,000
Increase in debtors	300,000
Increase in stocks	100,000
	400,000
Less increase in creditors	20,000
Net increase in working capital investment	380,000

Return on extra investment $\frac{£90,000}{£380,000} = 23.7\%$

(b) *Extra investment, if only the new debtors take two months credit*

	£
Increase in debtors (2/12 of £600,000)	100,000
Increase in stocks	100,000
	200,000
Less increase in creditors	20,000
Net increase in working capital investment	180,000

Return on extra investment $\frac{£90,000}{£180,000} = 50\%$

In both case (a) and case (b) the new credit policy appears to be worthwhile.

Settlement discounts 12/97

1.12 To see whether the offer of a **settlement discount** (for early payment) is financially worthwhile we must compare the cost of the discount with the benefit of a reduced investment in debtors.

1.13 Varying the discount allowed for early payment of debts:

(a) affects the average collection period;

(b) affects the volume of demand (and possibly, therefore, indirectly affects bad debt losses).

We shall begin with examples where the offer of a discount for early payment does not affect the volume of demand.

1.14 EXAMPLE: DEBTOR MANAGEMENT (3)

Lowe and Price Ltd has annual credit sales of £12,000,000, and three months are allowed for payment. The company decides to offer a 2% discount for payments made within ten days of the invoice being sent, and to reduce the maximum time allowed for payment to two months. It is estimated that 50% of customers will take the discount. If the company requires a 20% return on investments, what will be the effect of the discount? Assume that the volume of sales will be unaffected by the discount.

1.15 SOLUTION

Our approach is to calculate:

(a) the profits forgone by offering the discount;

(b) the interest charges saved or incurred as a result of the changes in the cash flows of the company.

Thus:

(a) The volume of debtors, if the company policy remains unchanged, would be:

3/12 × £12,000,000 = £3,000,000.

(b) If the policy is changed the volume of debtors would be:

$$(\frac{10}{365} \times 50\% \times £12{,}000{,}000) + (\frac{2}{12} \times 50\% \times £12{,}000{,}000)$$

= £164,384 + £1,000,000 = £1,164,384.

(c) There will be a reduction in debtors of £1,835,616.

(d) Since the company can invest at 20% a year, the value of a reduction in debtors (a source of funds) is 20% of £1,835,616 each year in perpetuity, that is, £367,123 a year.

(e) *Summary*

	£
Value of reduction in debtors each year	367,123
Less discounts allowed each year (2% × 50% × £12,000,000)	120,000
Net benefit of new discount policy each year	247,123

1.16 An extension of the payment period allowed to debtors may be introduced in order to increase sales volume.

Question 1

Enticement Ltd currently expects sales of £50,000 a month. Variable costs of sales are £40,000 a month (all payable in the month of sale). It is estimated that if the credit period allowed to debtors were to be increased from 30 days to 60 days, sales volume would increase by 20%. All customers would be expected to take advantage of the extended credit. If the cost of capital is 12½% a year (or approximately 1% a month), is the extension of the credit period justifiable in financial terms?

Answer

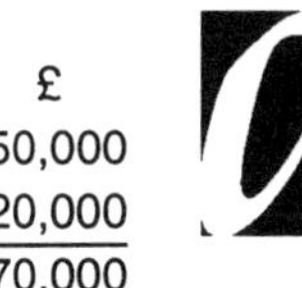

	£
Current debtors (1 month)	50,000
Debtors after implementing the proposal (2 months)	120,000
Increase in debtors	70,000

	£
Financing cost (× 12½%)	8,750
Annual contribution from additional sales (12 months x 20% x £10,000)	24,000
Annual net benefit from extending credit period	15,250

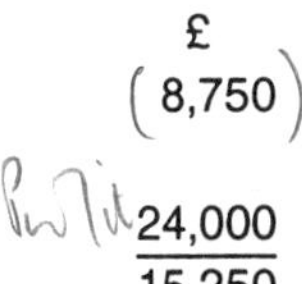

Bad debt risk

1.17 Different credit policies are likely to have differing levels of bad debt risk. The higher turnover resulting from easier credit terms should be sufficiently profitable to exceed the cost of:

(a) bad debts; and
(b) the additional investment necessary to achieve the higher sales.

1.18 EXAMPLE: DEBTOR MANAGEMENT (4)

Grabbit Quick Ltd achieves current annual sales of £1,800,000. The cost of sales is 80% of this amount, but bad debts average 1% of total sales, and the annual profit is as follows.

	£
Sales	1,800,000
Less cost of sales	1,440,000
	360,000
Less bad debts	18,000
Profit	342,000

The current debt collection period is one month, and the management consider that if credit terms were eased (option A), the effects would be as follows.

	Present policy	*Option A*
Additional sales (%)	–	25%
Average collection period	1 month	2 months
Bad debts (% of sales)	1%	3%

The company requires a 20% return on its investments. If the costs of sales are 75% variable and 25% fixed, and on the assumptions that:

(a) there would be no increase in fixed costs from the extra turnover;
(b) there would be no increase in average stocks or creditors;

what is the preferable policy, Option A or the present one?

1.19 SOLUTION

The increase in profit before the cost of additional finance for Option A can be found as follows.

(a)

	£
Increase in contribution from additional sales 25% × £1,800,000 × 40%*	180,000
Less increase in bad debts (3% × £2,250,000) – £18,000	49,500
Increase in annual profit	130,500

* The C/S ratio is (100% – 75%) × 80% = 40%

(b)

	£
Proposed investment in debtors £2,250,000 × 1/6	375,000
Less current investment in debtors £1,800,000 × 1/12	150,000
Additional investment required	225,000
Cost of additional finance at 20%	£45,000

(c) As the increase in profit exceeds the cost of additional finance, Option A should be adopted.

Credit insurance

1.20 Companies might be able to obtain credit insurance against certain approved debts going bad through a specialist credit insurance firm. A company cannot insure against all its bad debt losses, but may be able to insure against losses above the normal level.

1.21 When a company arranges **credit insurance**, it must submit specific proposals for credit to the insurance company, stating the name of each customer to which it wants to give credit and the amount of credit it wants to give. The insurance company will accept, amend or refuse these proposals, depending on its assessment of each of these customers.

1.22 Credit insurance is normally available for only up to about 75% of a company's potential bad debt loss. The remaining 25% of any bad debt costs are borne by the company itself. This is to ensure that the company does not become slack with its credit control and debt collection procedures, for example by indulging in overtrading and not chasing slow payers hard enough.

Factoring 12/97

1.23 A **factor** is defined as 'a doer or transactor of business for another', but a factoring organisation specialises in trade debts, and manages the debts owed to a client (a business customer) on the client's behalf.

KEY TERM

Factoring: an arrangement to have debts collected by a factor company, which advances a proportion of the money it is due to collect.

1.24 The main aspects of **factoring** are:

(a) administration of the client's invoicing, sales accounting and debt collection service;

(b) credit protection for the client's debts, whereby the factor takes over the risk of loss from bad debts and so 'insures' the client against such losses. This service is also referred to as 'debt underwriting' or the 'purchase of a client's debts'. The factor usually purchases these debts 'without recourse' to the client, which means that if the client's debtors do not pay what they owe, the factor will not ask for his money back from the client.

(c) making payments to the client in advance of collecting the debts. This is sometimes referred to as 'factor finance' because the factor is providing cash to the client against outstanding debts.

The debts administration service of factoring companies

1.25 A company might be struggling just to do the administrative tasks of recording credit sales, sending out invoices, sending out monthly statements and reminders, and collecting and recording payments from customers. If the company's turnover is growing rapidly, or if its sales are changing from largely cash sales to largely credit sales, the accounting administration might be unable to cope with the extra work. A factoring organisation can help.

1.26 The administration of a client's debts by the factor covers:

(a) keeping the books of account for sales;
(b) sending out invoices to customers;
(c) collecting the debts;
(d) credit control (ensuring that customers pay on time) and chasing late payers.

1.27 For the client the advantages are that:

(a) the factor takes on a job of administration which saves staff costs for the client;

(b) the factor performs the service economically, by taking advantage of economies of scale for a large debts administration organisation. This enables the factor to price his services reasonably.

1.28 The factor's service fee for debt administration varies according to the size of the client's operation, but it is typically between 0.75% and 2% of the book value of the client's debts. A business might be considered too small for factoring if its annual turnover were less than £250,000.

1.29 A factor is unlikely to agree to provide a service to small firms, firms which have only recently been established, firms in a high-risk market or with a history of bad debts, or businesses selling small value items to the general public (such as mail order firms).

Credit protection (debt underwriting) and factoring

1.30 Another problem that a company might have with its debtors is credit control and bad debts. If a company grants credit, how should it decide how much credit to give to each customer, and which customers should not be given any credit at all? The problem of bad debts can be controlled by exercising careful management over granting credit in the first place.

1.31 Many companies do not have the information or the capability to assess credit risks properly. Factors, however, do have this capability, and can therefore carry out the credit control function for a client, vetting individual customers and deciding whether to grant credit and how much credit to allow. Because they control credit in this way, they will also underwrite their client's debts.

1.32 Most factors provide a debts administration service in which **credit protection** is an integral part. This is because the service is usually without recourse to the client in the event of non-payment by the customer. Without recourse factoring or non-recourse factoring effectively means that the factor buys the client's debts from him and so the client is guaranteed protection against bad debts.

1.33 It is important to realise, however, that a factor is not a debt collection agency in the sense that he can be relied on to get money out of customers when no one else can. Factors are involved in normal debtors administration (bookkeeping, invoicing and credit management as well as collecting money) and do not want to get involved with problem customers.

1.34 Under a **without recourse** arrangement, the factor assumes full responsibility for credit control, because he now bears the credit risk.

(a) The factors will approve the amount of credit to be allowed to individual customers by the client.

(b) The factor will keep a continuous watch over customers' accounts.

(c) If a payment becomes overdue, the factor will consult the client. The client may decide to take over the bad debt risk from the factor, rather than incur badwill from the customer if the factor were to take legal action to recover the debt. Otherwise the factor is free to take non-payers to court to obtain payment.

1.35 Not every factoring organisation will purchase approved debts without recourse and '**with recourse**' factoring might be provided, for example for very large debts.

Making advances on debts (factor finance)

1.36 Some companies have difficulty in financing their debtors. There are two main reasons for this.

(a) If a company's turnover is rising rapidly, its total debtors will rise quickly too. Selling more on credit will put a strain on the company's cash flow. The company, although making profits, might find itself in difficulties because it has too many debtors and not enough cash.

(b) If a company grants long credit to its customers, it might run into cash flow difficulties for much the same reason. Exporting companies must often allow long periods of credit to foreign buyers.

1.37 Factors offer their clients a debt financing service to overcome these problems, and will be prepared to advance cash to the client against the security of the client's debtors. The client will assign his debtors to the factor.

1.38 A factoring organisation might be asked by a client to advance funds to the client against the debts which the factor has purchased, up to 80% of the value of the debts. For example, if a client makes credit sales of £100,000 a month, the factor might be willing to advance up to 80% of the invoice value (here £80,000) in return for a commission charge, and interest will be charged on the amount of funds advanced.

The rate of interest will be tied to bank base rate, and may be a little higher than the client would pay a bank for an overdraft. The balance of the money will be paid to the client when the customers have paid the factor, or after an agreed period.

1.39 Advances from factors should be used in order to finance the extra stock and debtors required for growth. The funds should not be used to finance fixed assets, and should not be a long-term source of funds. Factor financing might help a company to adjust to growth, but growth does not continue indefinitely, and when business settles down at a steady level, the need for money in advance ought to disappear.

The advantages of factoring

1.40 The benefits of factoring for a business customer include the following.

(a) The business can pay its suppliers promptly, and so be able to take advantage of any early payment discounts that are available.

(b) Optimum stock levels can be maintained, because the business will have enough cash to pay for the stocks it needs.

(c) Growth can be financed through sales rather than by injecting fresh external capital.

(d) The business gets finance linked to its volume of sales. In contrast, overdraft limits tend to be determined by historical balance sheets.

(e) The managers of the business do not have to spend their time on the problems of slow paying debtors.

(f) The business does not incur the costs of running its own sales ledger department.

1.41 An important disadvantage is that debtors will be making payments direct to the factor, which is likely to present a negative picture of the firm.

Factoring and bank finance

1.42 If a company arranges with a factor for advances to be made against its debts, the debts will become the security for the advance. This may require the consent of any bank which has a charge over the company. If the same company already has a bank overdraft facility, the bank may be relying on the debts as a form of security (perhaps not legal security, in the form of a floating charge over stocks and debtors, but as an element in the decision about how much overdraft to allow the company). The bank may therefore wish to reduce the company's overdraft limit. Certainly, a company should inform its bank when it makes an agreement with a factor for advances against debts.

1.43 EXAMPLE: FACTORING

A company makes annual credit sales of £1,500,000. Credit terms are 30 days, but its debt administration has been poor and the average collection period has been 45 days with 0.5% of sales resulting in bad debts which are written off.

A factor would take on the task of debt administration and credit checking, at an annual fee of 2.5% of credit sales. The company would save £30,000 a year in administration costs. The payment period would be 30 days.

The factor would also provide an advance of 80% of invoiced debts at an interest rate of 14% (3% over the current base rate). The company can obtain an overdraft facility to finance its debtors at a rate of 2.5% over base rate.

Should the factor's services be accepted? Assume a constant monthly turnover.

1.44 SOLUTION

It is assumed that the factor would advance an amount equal to 80% of the invoiced debts, and the balance 30 days later.

(a) The current situation is as follows, using the company's debt collection staff and a bank overdraft to finance all debts.

Credit sales	£1,500,000 pa
Average credit period	45 days

The annual cost is as follows:

	£
$\frac{45}{365} \times £1{,}500{,}000 \times 13.5\%$	24,966
Bad debts: 0.5% × £1,500,000	7,500
Total cost	32,466

(b) *The cost of the factor*

80% of credit sales financed by the factor would be 80% of £1,500,000 = £1,200,000. For a consistent comparison, we must assume that 20% of credit sales would be financed by a bank overdraft.

The average credit period would be only 30 days.

The annual cost would be as follows.

			£
Factor's finance:	$\frac{30}{365}$	× £1,200,000 × 14%	13,808
Overdraft:	$\frac{30}{365}$	× £300,000 × 13.5%	3,329
			17,137
Cost of factor's services: 2.5% × £1,500,000			37,500
Less savings in company's administration costs			(30,000)
Net cost of the factor			24,637

(c) *Conclusion*

The factor is cheaper. In this case, the factor's fees exactly equal the savings in bad debts (£7,500) and administration costs (£30,000). The factor is then cheaper overall because it will be more efficient at collecting debts. The advance of 80% of debts is not needed, however, if the company has sufficient overdraft facility because the factor's finance charge of 14% is higher than the company's overdraft rate of 13.5%.

Invoice discounting

1.45 **Invoice discounting** is related to factoring and many factors will provide an invoice discounting service. It is the purchase of a selection of invoices, at a discount. The invoice discounter does not take over the administration of the client's sales ledger, and the arrangement is purely for the advance of cash. A client should only want to have some invoices discounted when he has a temporary cash shortage, and so invoice discounting tends to consist of one-off deals.

KEY TERM

Invoice discounting: the purchase (by the provider of the discounting service) of trade debts at a discount. Invoice discounting enables the company from which the debts are purchased to raise working capital.

1.46 **Confidential invoice discounting** is an arrangement whereby a debt is confidentially assigned to the factor, and the client's customer will only become aware of the arrangement if he does not pay his debt to the client.

1.47 If a client needs to generate cash, he can approach a factor or invoice discounter, who will offer to purchase selected invoices and advance up to 75% of their value. At the end of each month, the factor will pay over the balance of the purchase price, less charges, on the invoices that have been settled in the month. (Receipts from the paid invoices belong to the invoice discounter or factor).

1.48 There is an element of credit protection in the invoice discounting service, but its real purpose is to improve the client's cash flow. Since the invoice discounter does not control debt administration, and relies on the client to collect the debts for him, it is a more risky operation than normal factoring and so a factor might only agree to offer an invoice discounting service to reliable, well-established companies.

Foreign trade and debt management 12/97

1.49 **Foreign debts** raise the following special problems.

(a) When goods are sold abroad, the customer might ask for credit. The period of credit might be 30 days or 60 days, say, after receipt of the goods; or perhaps 90 days after shipment.

Exports take time to arrange, and there might be complex paperwork. Transporting the goods can be slow, if they are sent by sea.

These delays in foreign trade mean that exporters often build up large investments in stocks and debtors. These working capital investments have to be financed somehow.

(b) The risk of bad debts can be greater with foreign trade than with domestic trade. If a foreign debtor refuses to pay a debt, the exporter must pursue the debt in the debtor's own country, where procedures will be subject to the laws of that country.

There are several measures available to exporters to overcome these problems.

Reducing the investment in foreign debtors

1.50 A company can reduce its investment in foreign debtors by insisting on earlier payment for goods.

1.51 Another approach is for an exporter to arrange for a bank to give cash for a foreign debt, sooner than the exporter would receive payment in the normal course of events. There are several ways in which this might be done.

(a) **Advances against collections**. Where the exporter asks his bank to handle the collection of payment (of a bill of exchange or a cheque) on his behalf, the bank may be prepared to make an advance to the exporter against the collection. The amount of the advance might be 80% to 90% of the value of the collection. The bank will expect repayment of the advance from the proceeds of the bill or the cheque.

Advances against collections would be arranged where the bill or cheque is payable in the exporter's own country.

(b) **Negotiation of bills or cheques**. This is similar to an advance against collection, but would be used where the bill or cheque is payable outside the exporter's country (for example in the foreign buyer's country).

(c) **Documentary credits**. These are described below.

Reducing the bad debt risk

1.52 Methods of minimising bad debt risks are broadly similar to those for domestic trade. An exporting company should vet the creditworthiness of each customer, and grant credit terms accordingly.

1.53 Three important methods of reducing the risks of bad debts in foreign trade are:

- export factoring
- export credit insurance
- documentary credits

Export factoring

1.54 The functions performed by an **overseas factor** or **export factor** are essentially the same as with the factoring of domestic trade debts, which was described earlier in this chapter. Many overseas factors are subsidiaries of UK banks or their agents, normally offering facilities to companies with annual export credit sales in excess of £250,000.

1.55 Small firms without a major overseas presence may gain from the provision of advice on the creditworthiness of overseas customers. Agents acting on their behalf in pursuing overseas debts may have useful expertise which can be tapped.

1.56 The charges levied by an overseas factor may turn out to be cheaper than using alternative methods such as letters of credit, which are discussed below.

Export credit insurance

1.57 **Export credit insurance** is insurance against the risk of non-payment by foreign customers for export debts.

Not all exporters take out export credit insurance because premiums are high and the benefits are sometimes not fully appreciated; but, if they do, they will obtain an insurance policy from a private insurance company that deals in export credit insurance.

1.58 Although a number of private sector companies in the UK (such as Trade Indemnity) offer export credit insurance, the largest provider is NCM UK, which insures more than 6,000 British companies in trade with 200 countries.

1.59 The government's Export Credit Guarantee Department (ECGD) also exists, providing guarantees to banks on behalf of exporters.

Documentary credits

1.60 **Documentary credits** provide a method of payment in international trade, which gives the exporter a secure risk-free method of obtaining payment. At the same time, documentary credits are a method of obtaining short-term finance from a bank, for working capital. This is because a bank might agree to discount or negotiate a bill of exchange, and so:

(a) the exporter receives immediate payment of the amount due to him, less the discount, instead of having to wait for payment until the end of the credit period allowed to the buyer;

(b) the buyer is able to get a period of credit before having to pay for the imports.

1.61 The buyer (a foreign buyer, or a UK importer) and the seller (a UK exporter or a foreign supplier) first of all agree a contract for the sale of the goods, which provides for payment through a documentary credit.

The *buyer* then requests a bank in his country to issue a **letter of credit** in favour of the exporter. The issuing bank, by issuing its letter of credit, guarantees payment to the beneficiary.

1.62 A documentary credit arrangement must be made between the exporter, the buyer and participating banks *before the export sale takes place*. Documentary credits are slow to arrange, and administratively cumbersome; however, they might be considered essential where the risk of non-payment is high.

Countertrade

1.63 Countertrade is a means of financing trade in which goods are exchanged for other goods. Three parties might be involved in a 'triangular' deal. Countertrade is thus a form of barter. It accounts for around 10% - 15% of total international trade according to one estimate.

Countertrade involving exchange of petroleum and manufacturing goods became popular in the early 1980s as such deals provided a way of avoiding OPEC export quotas for oil-producing countries. It is also common in deals with East European countries which are short of foreign exchange.

2 THE MANAGEMENT OF CREDITORS AND SHORT-TERM FINANCE

6/96

Exam focus point

It may seem an obvious point, but take care not to confuse debtors and creditors, as many students do under exam pressure.

Management of trade creditors

2.1 The management of trade creditors involves:

(a) attempting to obtain satisfactory credit from suppliers;
(b) attempting to extend credit during periods of cash shortage;
(c) maintaining good relations with regular and important suppliers.

If a supplier offers a discount for the early payment of debts, the evaluation of the decision whether or not to accept the discount is similar to the evaluation of the decision whether or not to *offer* a discount. One problem is the mirror image of the other. The methods of evaluating the offer of a discount to customers were described earlier.

Sources of short-term finance

2.2 Taking trade credit from suppliers is one way in which a company can obtain some *short-term* finance, in addition to its longer term sources. Short-term finance can also be obtained:

(a) with a bank overdraft;

(b) by raising finance from a bank or other organisation against the security of trade debtors, for example through factoring or invoice discounting (both described earlier in this chapter);

(c) for larger companies, by issuing short-term debt instruments, such as 'commercial paper'.

Trade credit

2.3 **Taking credit** from suppliers is a normal feature of business. Nearly every company has some trade creditors waiting for payment.

Trade credit is a source of short-term finance because it helps to keep working capital down. It is usually a cheap source of finance, since suppliers rarely charge interest. However, trade credit *will* have a cost, whenever a company is offered a discount for early payment, but opts instead to take longer credit.

Trade credit and the cost of lost early payment discounts

2.4 Trade credit from suppliers is a major source of finance. It is particularly important to small and fast growing firms. The costs of making maximum use of trade credit include:

(a) the loss of suppliers' goodwill;
(b) the loss of any available cash discounts for the early payment of debts.

2.5 The cost of lost cash discounts can be estimated by the formula:

$$\frac{d}{100-d} \times \frac{365}{t}$$

where d is the size of the discount. For a 5% discount, d = 5.
t is the reduction in the payment period in days which would be necessary to obtain the early payment discount

2.6 EXAMPLE: TRADE CREDIT

X Ltd has been offered credit terms from its major supplier of 2/10, net 45. That is, a cash discount of 2% will be given if payment is made within ten days of the invoice, and payments must be made within 45 days of the invoice.

The company has the choice of paying 98p per £1 on day 10 (to pay before day 10 would be unnecessary), or to invest the 98p for an additional 35 days and eventually pay the supplier £1 per £1. The decision as to whether the discount should be accepted depends on the opportunity cost of investing 98p for 35 days. What should the company do?

2.7 SOLUTION

If the company refuses the cash discount, and pays in full after 45 days, the implied cost in interest per annum would be approximately:

$$\frac{2}{100-2} \times \frac{365}{35} = 21.3\%$$

Suppose that X Ltd can invest cash to obtain an annual return of 25%, and that there is an invoice from the supplier for £1,000. The two alternatives are as follows.

	Refuse discount	*Accept discount*
	£	£
Payment to supplier	1,000.0	980
Return from investing £980 between day 10 and day 45:		
$£980 \times \frac{35}{365} \times 25\%$	23.5	—
Net cost	976.5	980

It is cheaper to refuse the discount because the investment rate of return on cash retained, in this example, exceeds the saving from the discount.

2.8 Although a company may delay payment beyond the final due date, thereby obtaining even longer credit from its suppliers, such a policy would be inadvisable (except where an unexpected short-term cash shortage has arisen). Unacceptable delays in payment will worsen the company's credit rating, and additional credit may become difficult to obtain.

Bills of exchange

2.9 **Bills of exchange** are a form of IOU. When A sells goods to B, the settlement of the debt might be arranged by means of a bill of exchange (called a **trade bill** as B is a trader). A will draw a bill on B (asking B to pay a certain sum of money on a certain date in the future, such as 90 days after the date of the bill). B then accepts the bill, by signing it, and returns it to A. By accepting the bill, B is acknowledging its debt to A and is giving a promise to pay. After the credit period (the term of the bill) has expired, B will pay A the money owed. A trade bill is therefore a form of trade credit.

Trade bills and obtaining finance against the security of debtors

2.10 When a company obtains payment from its customers through **trade bills**, it can arrange to obtain finance from its bank against the security of the bill.

2.11 For example, if A Ltd sells goods to B Ltd for £50,000, the terms of payment might be agreed so that A Ltd draws a 90 day bill of exchange on B Ltd for £50,000, which B Ltd 'accepts'. A Ltd can then ask its bank to discount the bill, and A Ltd will receive payment (less discount) now from the bank instead of in 90 days from B Ltd. After 90 days, B Ltd must pay the holder of the bill which might still be the bank.

2.12 The rate of discount on the bill, which is the cost to A Ltd of discounting, will depend on the 'quality' of the bill. A higher discount applies to trade bills (bills drawn on and accepted by companies such as B Ltd) than to bank bills (bills drawn on and accepted by a bank). A lower discount is called a 'finer' discount.

Bank bills, trade debts and obtaining short-term finance

2.13 Banks might agree to accept bills on a customer's behalf, provided that arrangements are made for the customer to reimburse the bank. Both trade bills and **bank bills** are used quite commonly in international trade.

For example, suppose that Bulldog Ltd in the UK sells goods to a company in Singapore. The terms of payment might be for Bulldog Ltd to draw a bill of exchange on the Singapore company's bank (in the UK or Singapore). The bank bill could then be used by Bulldog Ltd to raise finance, with the bill attracting a finer rate of discount because it has been accepted by a reputable bank.

Acceptance credits

2.14 **Acceptance credits** are a source of finance from banks for large companies, which are an alternative to bank overdrafts.

2.15 Acceptance credits have much in common with bills of exchange, but they are different. They are not the acceptance of bills of exchange by a bank on a customer's behalf, but are a development from this service. An acceptance credit facility, which is offered by clearing banks as well as merchant banks, operates as follows.

(a) A bank and a large corporate customer agree a facility which allows the customer to draw bills of exchange on the bank, which the bank will accept. The bills are normally payable after 60 or 90 days, but might have a term as long as 180 days. They can be denominated in sterling or in a foreign currency.

(b) The accepted bills are then sold (discounted) by the bank in the discount market on behalf of the customer, and the money obtained from the sale, minus the bank's acceptance commission, is made available to the customer. Because of the bank's standing and reputation, bills accepted by it can be sold in the market at a low rate of discount.

(c) When a bill matures, the company will pay the bank the value of the bill and the bank will use the money in turn to pay the bill holder.

2.16 A bank will only agree to provide an acceptance credit facility to a corporate customer of good standing, because the bank must be confident that its money is safe.

The length of time over which the acceptance credit facility is available will be subject to agreement between the bank and the customer, but may be as long as five years. The customer can draw bills on the bank throughout this period, up to the credit limit.

2.17 Acceptance credits are attractive to customers for the following reasons.

(a) They provide companies with alternative finance to a bank overdraft, with the money being obtained from a source outside the bank (the purchaser of the discounted bills).

(b) The amount of credit is promised to the customer for a stated period of time.

(c) There may be a cost advantage to the customer, because the rate of discount on bank bills in the discount market might be lower than the interest rate on a bank loan, or overdraft, which is related to the bank base rate or LIBOR. The reason for this is mainly that the interest rate on a discounted bill is fixed for the life of the bill (typically 90 days) because this rate is inherent in the discounted sale price of the bill. If market interest rates are rising during this period, and overdraft rates are going up, it would be more costly to maintain an overdraft than to have an acceptance credit facility.

(d) The company can assess the cost of its credit facility with more certainty, because costs are fixed over the life of a bill.

3 THE MANAGEMENT OF STOCKS 12/95, 6/97

3.1 Almost every company carries stocks of some sort, even if they are only stocks of consumables such as stationery. For a manufacturing business, stocks (sometimes called inventories), in the form of raw materials, work in progress and finished goods, may amount to a substantial proportion of the total assets of the business.

3.2 Some businesses attempt to control stocks on a scientific basis by balancing the costs of stock shortages against those of stock holding.

The 'scientific' control of stocks may be analysed into three parts.

(a) The **economic order quantity (EOQ) model** can be used to decide the optimum order size for stocks which will minimise the costs of ordering stocks plus stockholding costs.

(b) If discounts for bulk purchases are available, it may be cheaper to buy stocks in large order sizes so as to obtain the discounts.

(c) Uncertainty in the demand for stocks and/or the supply lead time may lead a company to decide to hold buffer stocks (thereby increasing its investment in working capital) in order to reduce or eliminate the risk of 'stock-outs' (running out of stock).

Stock costs

3.3 Stock costs can be conveniently classified into four groups.

(a) **Holding costs** comprise the cost of capital tied up, warehousing and handling costs, deterioration, obsolescence, insurance and pilferage.

(b) **Procuring costs** depend on how the stock is obtained but will consist of **ordering costs** for goods purchased externally, such as clerical costs, telephone charges and delivery costs.

(c) **Shortage costs** may be:

(i) the loss of a sale and the contribution which could have been earned from the sale;

(ii) the extra cost of having to buy an emergency supply of stocks at a high price;

(iii) the cost of lost production and sales, where the stock-out brings an entire process to a halt.

(d) The **cost of the stock** itself, the supplier's price or the direct cost per unit of production, will also need to be considered when the supplier offers a discount on orders for purchases in bulk.

Stock models

3.4 There are several different types of stock model, and these can be classified under the following headings.

(a) **Deterministic stock models**

A deterministic model is one in which all the 'parameters' are known with certainty. In particular, the rate of demand and the supply lead time are known.

(b) **Stochastic stock models**

A stochastic model is one in which the supply lead time or the rate of demand for an item is not known with certainty. However, the demand or the lead time follows a known probability distribution (probably constructed from a historical analysis of demand or lead time in the past).

In a deterministic system, since the demand and the lead time are known with certainty, there is no need for a safety stock. However, in a stochastic model, it may be necessary to have a buffer stock to limit the number of stock-outs or to avoid stock-outs completely.

3.5 Stochastic models are sometimes classified as follows.

(a) A **P system** is a **periodic review system** in which the requirement for stock is reviewed at fixed time intervals, and varying quantities are ordered on each occasion, according to the current level of stocks remaining.

(b) A **Q system** is a **re-order level system** in which a fixed quantity is ordered at irregular intervals, when stock levels have fallen to a re-order level specified on the store-keeper's records or 'bin card'.

A deterministic model: the basic EOQ formula

3.6 The economic order quantity (EOQ) is the optimal ordering quantity for an item of stock which will minimise costs.

Let D = usage in units for one year (the demand)
P = purchase price per item
O = cost of making one order
I = holding cost per unit of stock for one year, as a percentage of the purchase price
Q = as a reorder quantity

(O and I: relevant costs only)

Assume that:

(a) demand is constant;
(b) the lead time is constant or zero;
(c) purchase costs per unit are constant (ie no bulk discounts).

The total annual cost of having stock is:

Holding costs + ordering costs

$$\frac{Q \times I \times P}{2} + \frac{D \times O}{Q}$$

The objective is to minimise $T = \frac{Q \times I \times P}{2} + \frac{D \times O}{Q}$

3.7 The order quantity, Q, which will minimise these total costs is:

$$Q = \sqrt{\frac{2 \times D \times O}{I \times P}}$$

Exam focus point

When examined in 6/97, the EOQ formula was given in the exam question. But as it is quite simple, it will do you no harm to learn it.

3.8 EXAMPLE: ECONOMIC ORDER QUANTITY

The demand for a commodity is 40,000 units a year, at a steady rate. It costs £20 to place an order, and 40p to hold a unit for a year. Find the order size to minimise stock costs, the number of orders placed each year, and the length of the stock cycle.

3.9 SOLUTION

$Q = \sqrt{\frac{2 \times D \times O}{I \times P}} = \sqrt{\frac{2 \times 20 \times 40{,}000}{0.4}}$ = 2,000 units. This means that there will be $\frac{40{,}000}{2{,}000}$ = 20 orders placed each year, so that the stock cycle is once every 52 ÷ 20 = 2.6 weeks. Total costs will be (20 × £20) + ($\frac{2{,}000}{2}$ × 40p) = £800 a year.

Uncertainties in demand and lead times: a re-order level system

3.10 When the volume of demand is uncertain, or the supply lead time is variable, there are problems in deciding what the re-order level should be. By holding a 'safety stock', a company can reduce the likelihood that stocks run out during the re-order period (due to high demand or a long lead time before the new supply is delivered). The average annual cost of such a safety stock would be:

Quantity of safety stock (in units)	×	Stock holding cost per unit per annum

3.11 The behaviour of the system would appear as in Figure 1.

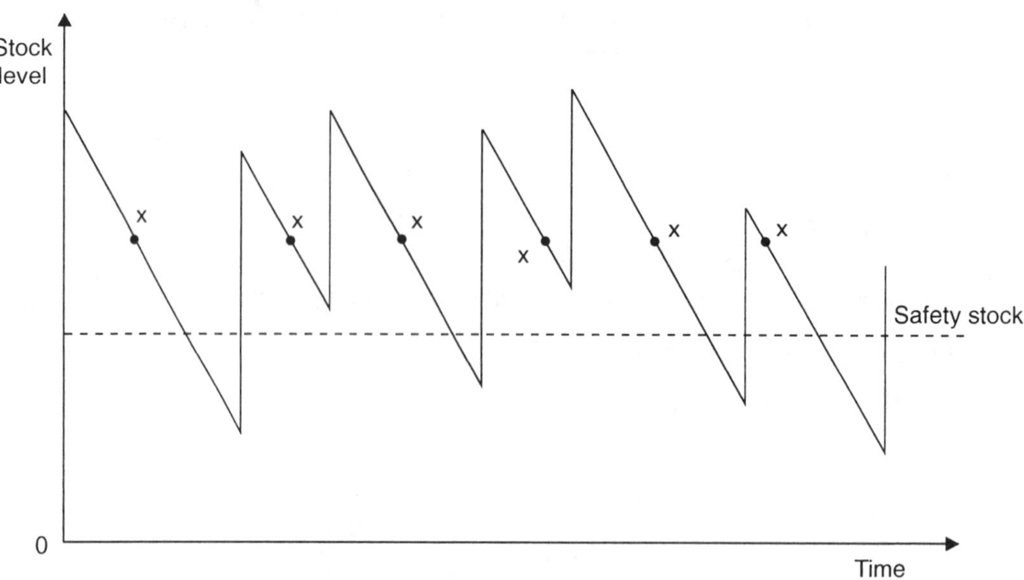

Figure 1

Points marked 'X' show the re-order level at which a new order is placed. The number of units ordered each time is the EOQ. Actual stock levels sometimes fall below the safety stock level, and sometimes the re-supply arrives before stocks have fallen to the safety level, but on average, extra stock holding amounts to the volume of safety stock.

The size of the safety stock will depend on whether stock-outs (running out of stock) are allowed.

The effect of discounts

3.12 The solution obtained from using the simple EOQ formula may need to be modified if bulk discounts (also called quantity discounts) are available.

3.13 To decide mathematically whether it would be worthwhile taking a discount and ordering larger quantities, it is necessary to minimise the total of:

(a) total material costs;
(b) ordering costs;
(c) stock holding costs.

3.14 The total cost will be minimised:

(a) at the pre-discount EOQ level, so that a discount is not worthwhile; or
(b) at the minimum order size necessary to earn the discount.

3.15 EXAMPLE: BULK DISCOUNTS

The annual demand for an item of stock is 45 units. The item costs £200 a unit to purchase, the holding cost for one unit for one year is 15% of the unit cost and ordering costs are £300 an order.

The supplier offers a 3% discount for orders of 60 units or more, and a discount of 5% for orders of 90 units or more.

What is the cost-minimising order size?

3.16 SOLUTION

(a) The EOQ ignoring discounts is:

$$\sqrt{\frac{2 \times 300 \times 45}{15\% \text{ of } 200}} = 30 \text{ units}$$

	£
Purchases (no discount) 45 × £200	9,000
Holding costs 15 units × £30	450
Ordering costs 1.5 orders × £300	450
Total annual costs	9,900

(b) With a discount of 3% and an order quantity of 60 units costs are as follows.

	£
Purchases £9,000 × 97%	8,730
Holding costs 30 units × 15% of 97% of £200	873
Ordering costs 0.75 orders × £300	225
Total annual costs	9,828

(c) With a discount of 5% and an order quantity of 90 units costs are as follows.

	£
Purchases £9,000 × 95%	8,550.0
Holding costs 45 units × 15% of 95% of £200	1,282.5
Ordering costs 0.5 orders × £300	150.0
Total annual costs	9,982.5

The cheapest option is to order 60 units at a time.

3.17 Note that the value of h varied according to the size of the discount, because h was a percentage of the purchase cost. This means that total holding costs are reduced because of a discount. This could easily happen if, for example, most of h was the cost of insurance, based on the cost of stock held.

Question 2

A company uses an item of stock as follows.

Purchase price:	£96 per unit
Annual demand:	4,000 units
Ordering cost:	£300
Annual holding cost:	10% of purchase price
Economic order quantity:	500 units

Should the company order 1,000 units at a time in order to secure an 8% discount?

Answer

The total annual cost at the economic order quantity of 500 units is as follows.

	£
Purchases 4,000 × £96	384,000
Ordering costs £300 × (4,000/500)	2,400
Holding costs £96 × 10% × (500/2)	2,400
	388,800

The total annual cost at an order quantity of 1,000 units would be as follows.

	£
Purchases £384,000 × 92%	353,280
Ordering costs £300 × (4,000/1,000)	1,200
Holding costs £96 × 92% × 10% × (1,000/2)	4,416
	358,896

The company should order the item 1,000 units at a time, saving £(388,800 - 358,896) = £29,904 a year.

Just-in-time (JIT) procurement 12/97

3.18 In recent years, there have been developments in the inventory policy of some manufacturing companies which have sought to reduce their inventories of raw materials and components to as low a level as possible. This approach differs from other models, such as the EOQ model, which seek to minimise **costs** rather than inventory levels.

3.19 **Just-in-time procurement** and **stockless production** are terms which describe a policy of obtaining goods from suppliers at the latest possible time (ie when they are needed) and so avoiding the need to carry any materials or components stock.

3.20 Introducing JIT might bring the following potential benefits.

(a) Reduction in stock holding costs
(b) Reduced manufacturing lead times
(c) Improved labour productivity
(d) Reduced scrap/rework/warranty cost
(e) Price reductions on purchased materials
(f) Reduction in the number of accounting transactions

Reduced stock levels mean that a lower level of investment in working capital will be required.

3.21 JIT will not be appropriate in some cases. For example, a restaurant might find it preferable to use the traditional economic order quantity approach for staple non-perishable food stocks but adopt JIT for perishable and 'exotic' items. In a hospital, a stock-out could quite literally be fatal and JIT would be quite unsuitable.

Exam focus point
In the 12/97 paper, you were required to evaluate the benefits of introducing a JIT arrangement, given certain assumptions about the costs and benefits.

Total quality management

3.22 A system of just-in-time procurement depends for its success on a smooth and predictable production flow, and so a JIT policy must also be aimed at improving production systems, eliminating waste (rejects and reworked items), avoiding production bottlenecks and so on. Many now argue that such improvements are necessary for the introduction of **advanced manufacturing technology (AMT)** and **total quality management (TQM)**.

3.23 TQM is a management technique, derived from Japanese companies, which focuses on the belief that 'total quality is essential to survival in a global market'.

3.24 The basic principle of TQM is that the cost of preventing mistakes is less than the cost of correcting them once they occur plus the cost of lost potential for future sales. The aim should therefore be to get things right first time consistently.

3.25 Two approaches to controlling quality and quality costs are as follows.

(a) **Approach 1**: minimise total quality costs by budgeting for a level of quality which minimises prevention costs plus inspection costs on the one hand and internal and external failure costs on the other.

(b) **Approach 2**: aim for zero rejects and 100% quality. The desired standard of production is contained within the product specification and every unit produced ought to achieve this standard; in other words, there ought to be no defects. Zero-defect targets are one aspect of Japanese management philosophy. However, the actual level of defects must be recorded and reported, even if the quality costs are not measured.

3.26 There is a fundamental difference of view in the sense that Approach 1 accepts some level of defects while Approach 2 takes the view that *all* defects are undesirable. Eventually, as modern manufacturing systems are introduced and JIT systems are employed, Approach 1 is likely to result in the conclusion that the cost of failure are so high (because they hold up production) that the only acceptable quality standard is a zero defect limit (Approach 2).

4 THE MANAGEMENT OF CASH 12/95, 12/96

4.1 How much cash should a company keep on hand or 'on short call' at a bank? The more cash which is on hand, the easier it will be for the company to meet its bills as they fall due and to take advantage of discounts. However, holding cash or near equivalents to cash has a cost - the loss of earning which would otherwise have been obtained by using the funds in another way. The financial manager must try to balance liquidity with profitability.

4.2 In the previous chapter, we introduced the operating cycle, which connects investment in working capital with cash flows. **Cash flow problems** can arise in various ways.

(a) **Making losses**. If a business is continually making losses, it will eventually have cash flow problems. Just how long it will take before a loss-making business runs into cash flow trouble will depend on:

(i) how big the losses are; and

(ii) whether the depreciation charge is big enough to create a loss despite a cash flow surplus. In such a situation, the cash flow troubles might only begin when the business needs to replace fixed assets.

(b) **Inflation**. In a period of inflation, a business needs ever-increasing amounts of cash just to replace used-up and worn-out assets. A business can be making a profit in historical cost accounting terms, but still not be receiving enough cash to buy the replacement assets it needs.

(c) **Growth**. When a business is growing, it needs to acquire more fixed assets, and to support higher amounts of stocks and debtors. These additional assets must be paid for somehow (or financed by creditors).

(d) **Seasonal business**. When a business has seasonal or cyclical sales, it may have cash flow difficulties at certain times of the year, when (i) cash inflows are low, but (ii) cash outflows are high, perhaps because the business is building up its stocks for the next period of high sales.

(e) **One-off items of expenditure**. There might occasionally be a single non-recurring item of expenditure that creates a cash flow problem, such as:

(i) the repayment of loan capital on maturity of the debt. Businesses often try to finance such loan repayments by borrowing again;

(ii) the purchase of an exceptionally expensive item. For example, a small or medium-sized business might decide to buy a freehold property which then stretches its cash resources for several months or even years.

Methods of easing cash shortages

4.3 The steps that are usually taken by a company when a need for cash arises, and when it cannot obtain resources from any other source such as a loan or an increased overdraft, are as follows.

(a) **Postponing capital expenditure**

Some capital expenditure items are more important and urgent than others.

(i) It might be imprudent to postpone expenditure on fixed assets which are needed for the development and growth of the business.

(ii) On the other hand, some capital expenditures are routine and might be postponable without serious consequences. The routine replacement of motor vehicles is an example. If a company's policy is to replace company cars every two years, but the company is facing a cash shortage, it might decide to replace cars every three years.

(b) **Accelerating cash inflows which would otherwise be expected in a later period**

The most obvious way of bringing forward cash inflows would be to press debtors for earlier payment. Often, this policy will result in a loss of goodwill and problems with customers. There will also be very little scope for speeding up payments when the credit period currently allowed to debtors is no more than the norm for the industry. It might be possible to encourage debtors to pay more quickly by offering discounts for earlier payment.

(c) **Reversing past investment decisions by selling assets previously acquired**

Some assets are less crucial to a business than others and so if cash flow problems are severe, the option of selling investments or property might have to be considered.

(d) **Negotiating a reduction in cash outflows, so as to postpone or even reduce payments**

There are several ways in which this could be done.

(i) Longer credit might be taken from suppliers. However, if the credit period allowed is already generous, creditors might be very reluctant to extend credit even further and any such extension of credit would have to be negotiated carefully. There would be a serious risk of having further supplies refused.

(ii) Loan repayments could be rescheduled by agreement with a bank.

(iii) A deferral of the payment of corporation tax could be agreed with the Inland Revenue. Corporation tax is payable nine months after a company's year end, but it might be possible to arrange a postponement by a few months. When this happens, the Inland Revenue will charge interest on the outstanding amount of tax.

(iv) Dividend payments could be reduced. Dividend payments are discretionary cash outflows, although a company's directors might be constrained by shareholders' expectations, so that they feel obliged to pay dividends even when there is a cash shortage.

Deviations from expected cash flows

4.4 **Cash budgets**, whether prepared on an annual, monthly, weekly or even a daily basis, can only be estimates of cash flows. Even the best estimates will not be exactly correct, so deviations from the cash budget are inevitable. This uncertainty about actual cash flows ought to be considered when the cash budget is prepared. It is desirable to prepare additional cash budgets based on different assumptions about sales levels, costs, collection periods, bad debts and so on.

4.5 A cash budget model could be constructed, using a microcomputer and a spreadsheet package, and the sensitivity of cash flow forecasts to changes in estimates of sales, costs and so on could be analysed. By planning for different eventualities, management should be able to prepare contingency measures in advance and also appreciate the key factors in the cash budget.

4.6 A knowledge of the probability distribution of possible outcomes for the cash position will allow a more accurate estimate to be made of the minimum cash balances, or the borrowing power necessary, to provide a satisfactory margin of safety. Unforeseen deficits can be hard to finance at short notice, and advance planning is desirable.

Float

4.7 The term **float** is sometimes used to describe the amount of money tied up between:

(a) the time when a payment is initiated (for example when a debtor sends a cheque in payment, probably by post); and

(b) the time when the funds become available for use in the recipient's bank account.

4.8 There are three reasons why there might be a lengthy float.

(a) **Transmission delay**. When payment is sent through the post, it will take a day or longer for the payment to reach the payee.

(b) **Delay in banking the payments received (lodgement delay).** The payee, on receipt of a cheque or cash, might delay presenting the cheque or the cash to his bank. The length of this delay will depend on administrative procedures in the payee's organisation.

(c) **The time needed for a bank to clear a cheque (clearance delay).** A payment is not available for use in the payee's bank account until the cheque has been cleared. This will usually take two or three days for cheques payable in the UK. For cheques payable abroad, the delay is much longer.

4.9 There are several measures that could be taken to reduce the float.

(a) The payee should ensure that the lodgement delay is kept to a minimum. **Cheques** received should be presented to the bank on the day of receipt.

(b) The payee might, in some cases, arrange to **collect cheques** from the payer's premises. This would only be practicable, however, if the payer is local. The payment would have to be large to make the extra effort worthwhile.

(c) The payer might be asked to pay through his own branch of a bank, using the **bank giro system.**

(d) **BACS** (Bankers' Automated Clearing Services Ltd) is a banking system which provides for the computerised transfer of funds between banks. In addition, BACS is available to corporate customers of banks for making payments. The customer must supply a magnetic tape or disk to BACS, which contains details of payments, and payment will be made in two days. BACS is now commonly used by companies for salary payments.

(e) For regular payments, **standing orders** or **direct debits** might be used.

(f) **CHAPS** (Clearing House Automated Payments System) is a computerised system for banks to make same-day clearances (that is, immediate payment) between each other. Each member bank of CHAPS can allow its own corporate customers to make immediate transfers of funds through CHAPS. However, there is a large minimum size for payments using CHAPS.

Inefficient cash management

4.10 A lengthy float suggests inefficient cash management. But there are other types of delay in receiving payment from debtors, which might also suggest inefficient cash management.

(a) There is the delay created by the length of credit given to customers. There is often a 'normal' credit period for an industry, and companies might be unable to grant less time for payment than this.

(b) There are avoidable delays caused by poor administration (in addition to lodgement delay), such as:

(i) failure to notify the invoicing department that goods have been despatched, so that invoices are not sent promptly;

(ii) cheques from debtors being made out incorrectly, to the wrong company perhaps, because invoices do not contain clear instructions.

4.11 EXAMPLE: CASH MANAGEMENT

Ryan Coates owns a chain of seven clothes shops in the London area. Takings at each shop are remitted once a week on Thursday evening to the head office, and are then banked at the start of business on Friday morning. As business is expanding, Ryan Coates has hired an accountant to help him. The accountant gave him the following advice.

'Turnover at the seven shops totalled £1,950,000 last year, at a constant daily rate, but you were paying bank overdraft charges at a rate of 11%. You could have reduced your overdraft costs by banking the shop takings each day, except for Saturday's takings. Saturday takings could have been banked on Mondays.'

Comment on the significance of this statement, stating your assumptions. The shops are closed on Sundays.

4.12 SOLUTION

(a) A bank overdraft rate of 11% a year is approximately 11/365 = 0.03% a day.

(b) Annual takings of £1,950,000 would be an average of £1,950,000/312 = £6,250 a day for the seven shops in total, on the assumption that they opened for a 52 week year of six days a week (312 days).

(c) Using the approximate overdraft cost of 0.03% a day, the cost of holding £6,250 for one day instead of banking it is 0.03% × £6,250 = £1.875.

(d) Banking all takings up to Thursday evening of each week on Friday morning involves an unnecessary delay in paying cash into the bank. The cost of this delay would be either:

(i) the opportunity cost of investment capital for the business; or
(ii) the cost of avoidable bank overdraft charges.

It is assumed here that the overdraft cost is higher and is therefore more appropriate to use. It is also assumed that, for interest purposes, funds are credited when banked.

Takings on	*Could be banked on*	*Number of days delay incurred by Friday banking*
Monday	Tuesday	3
Tuesday	Wednesday	2
Wednesday	Thursday	1
Thursday	Friday	0
Friday	Saturday	6
Saturday	Monday	4
		16

In one week, the total number of days delay incurred by Friday banking is 16. At a cost of £1.875 a day, the weekly cost of Friday banking was £1.875 × 16 = £30.00, and the annual cost of Friday banking was £30.00 × 52 = £1,560.

(e) *Conclusion.* The company could have saved about £1,560 a year in bank overdraft charges last year. If the overdraft rate remains at 11% and turnover continues to increase, the saving from daily banking would be even higher next year.

Inventory approach to cash management

4.13 There a number of different formal cash management models designed to indicate the optimum amount of cash that a company should hold. One such model is based on the idea that deciding on optimum cash balances is a similar question to deciding on optimum stock levels.

4.14 We can distinguish two types of cost which are involved in obtaining cash:

(a) the **fixed cost** represented for example, by the issue cost of equity finance or the cost of negotiating an overdraft;

(b) the **variable cost** (opportunity cost) of keeping the money in the form of cash.

4.15 The inventory approach uses an equation of the same form as the EOQ formula for stock management which we looked at earlier.

The average total cost incurred for period in holding a certain average level of cash (C) is:

$$\frac{Qi}{2} + \frac{FS}{Q}$$

Where S = the amount of cash to be used in each time period
F = the fixed cost of obtaining new funds
i = the interest cost of holding cash or near cash equivalents
Q = the total amount to be raised to provide for S

Similarly to the EOQ, C is minimised when:

$$Q = \sqrt{\frac{2FS}{i}}$$

4.16 EXAMPLE: INVENTORY APPROACH TO CASH MANAGEMENT

Finder Limited faces a fixed cost of £4,000 to obtain new funds. There is a requirement for £24,000 of cash over each period of one year for the foreseeable future. The interest cost of new funds is 12% per annum; the interest rate earned on short-term securities is 9% per annum. How much finance should Finder Limited raise at a time?

4.17 SOLUTION

The cost of holding cash is 12% – 9% = 3%

The optimum level of Q (the 'reorder quantity') is:

$$\sqrt{\frac{2 \times 4{,}000 \times 24{,}000}{0.03}} = £80{,}000$$

The optimum amount of new funds to raise is £80,000.

This amount is raised every 80,000 ÷ 24,000 = $3^1/_3$ years.

Drawbacks of the inventory approach

4.18 The inventory approach illustrated above has the following drawbacks.

(a) In reality, it is unlikely to be possible to predict amounts required over future periods with much certainty.

(b) No buffer stock of cash is allowed for. There may be costs associated with running out of cash.

(c) There may be other normal costs of holding cash which increase with the average amount held.

The Miller-Orr model

4.19 In an attempt to produce a more realistic approach to cash management, various models more complicated than the inventory approach have been developed. One of these, the **Miller-Orr model**, manages to achieve a reasonable degree of realism while not being too elaborate.

4.20 We can begin looking at the Miller-Orr model by asking what will happen if there is no attempt to manage cash balances. Clearly, the cash balance is likely to 'meander' upwards or downwards. The Miller-Orr model imposes limits to this meandering. If the cash balance reaches an upper limit (point A in the diagram below) the firm buys sufficient securities to return the cash balance to a normal level (called the 'return point'). When the cash balance reaches a lower limit (point B in the diagram), the firm sells securities to bring the balance back to the return point.

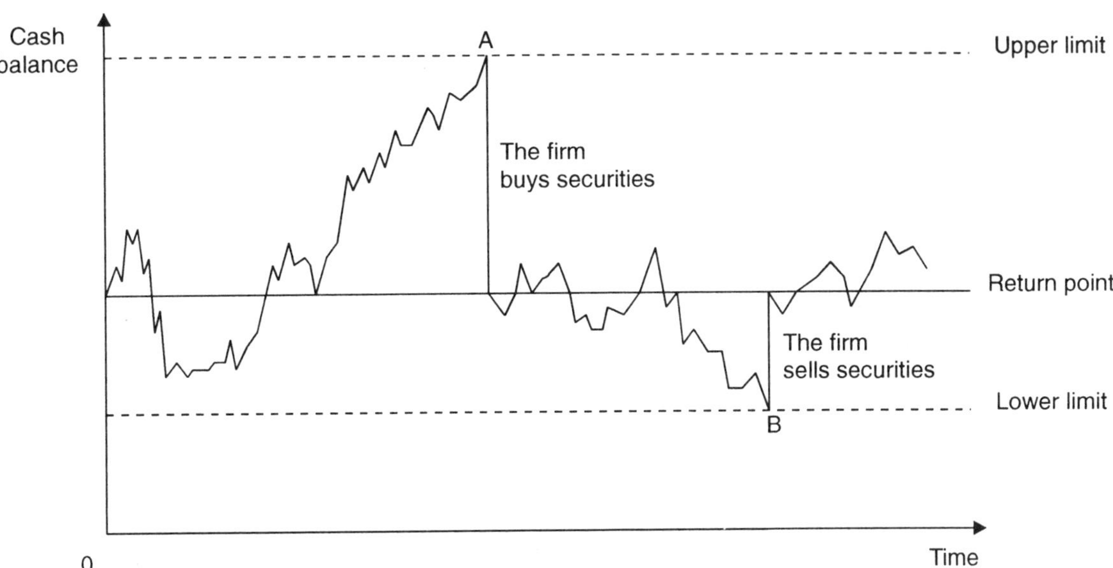

Figure 2 Miller-Orr model

4.21 How are the upper and lower limits and the return point set? Miller and Orr showed that the answer to this question depends on three factors:

(a) the variance of cash flows
(b) transaction costs
(c) interest rates

If the day-to-day variability of cash flows is high or the transaction cost in buying or selling securities is high, then wider limits should be set. If interest rates are high, the limits should be closer together.

4.22 To keep the interest costs of holding cash down, the return point is set at one-third of the distance (or 'spread') between the lower and the upper limit.

$$\text{Return point} = \text{Lower limit} + {}^{1}\!/_{3} \times \text{spread}$$

4.23 The formula for the spread is:

$$\text{Spread} = 3\left(\frac{3}{4} \times \frac{\text{transaction cost} \times \text{variance of cash flows}}{\text{interest rate}}\right)^{\frac{1}{3}}$$

4.24 To use the Miller-Orr model, it is necessary to follow the steps below.

(a) Set the lower limit for the cash balance. This may be zero, or it may be set at some minimum safety margin above zero.

(b) Estimate the variance of cash flows, for example from sample observations over a 100-day period.

(c) Note the interest rate and the transaction cost for each sale or purchase of securities (the latter is assumed to be fixed).

(d) Compute the upper limit and the return point from the model and instruct a clerk to implement the limits strategy.

4.25 Now try applying the Miller-Orr equations yourself in the following question.

Question 3

The following data applies to a company.

(a) The minimum cash balance is £8,000.

(b) The variance of daily cash flows is 4,000,000, equivalent to a standard deviation of £2,000 per day.

(c) The transaction cost for buying or selling securities is £50.

(d) The interest rate is 0.025 per cent per day.

Required

Formulate a decision rule using the Miller-Orr model.

Answer

The spread between the upper and the lower cash balance limits is calculated as follows.

$$\text{Spread} = 3\left(\frac{3}{4} \times \frac{\text{transaction cost} \times \text{variance of cash flows}}{\text{interest rate}}\right)^{\frac{1}{3}}$$

$$= 3\left(\frac{3}{4} \times \frac{50 \times 4{,}000{,}000}{0.00025}\right)^{\frac{1}{3}}$$

$$= £25{,}303, \text{ say } £25{,}300$$

The upper limit and return point are now calculated.

Upper limit = Lower limit + £25,300

= £8,000 + £25,300 = £33,300

Return point = lower limit + $^1/_3$ × spread

= £8,000 + $^1/_3$ × £25,300 = £16,433, say £16,400

The decision rule is as follows. If the cash balance reaches £33,300, buy £16,900 (= 33,300 – 16,400) in marketable securities. If the cash balance falls to £8,000, sell £8,400 of marketable securities for cash.

Advantages and disadvantages of the Miller-Orr model

4.26 The usefulness of the Miller-Orr model is limited by the assumptions on which it is based. In practice, cash inflows and outflows are unlikely to be entirely unpredictable as the model assumes: for example, for a retailer, seasonal factors are likely to affect cash inflows; for any company, dividend and tax payments will be known well in advance. However, the Miller-Orr model may save management time which might otherwise be spent in responding to those cash inflows and outflows which cannot be predicted.

Use of cash management models in practice

4.27 Some banks in the USA make cash management models available to their customers. These models vary from relatively simple spreadsheet-based models to more sophisticated systems such as those provided for multinational companies by the Chemical Bank. Like the basic Miller-Orr model, such models are designed to indicate minimum and maximum levels of cash holding in order to minimise the costs of holding idle cash balances and maximise interest earned on surplus funds.

4.28 As you might expect, such models require accurate inputs if they are to be effective. Sophisticated models, such as that used by the Chemical Bank, can take account of user's risk preferences by allowing limits to be set on the amount of funds allocated to any single investment. Users can manipulate variables to trace the effect on the short-term plan, which can help them to increase their awareness of the factors affecting day-to-day management decisions and the liquidity/profitability trade-off.

Applying probabilities in cash management problems

4.29 Probabilities can be applied to cash management problems. The following example illustrates this approach.

4.30 EXAMPLE: PROBABILITIES IN CASH MANAGEMENT

Sinkos Wim Ltd has an overdraft facility of £100,000, and currently has an overdraft balance at the bank of £34,000. The company maintains a cash float of £10,000 for transactions and precautionary purposes. It is unclear whether a long awaited economic recovery will take place, and the company has prepared cash budgets as set out below for the next three months using two different assumptions about economic events. The cash flow in months 2 and 3 depend on the cash flows in the previous month.

Estimated net cash flows

Month 1		*Month 2*		*Month 3*	
Probability	*Cash flow* £'000	*Probability*	*Cash flow* £'000	*Probability*	*Cash flow* £'000
		0.8	25	0.5	30
0.7	(40)			0.5	20
		0.2	10	0.5	10
				0.5	0
		0.8	0	0.5	(10)
0.3	(60)			0.5	(20)
		0.2	(10)	0.5	(40)
				0.5	(50)

Required

If the company intends to maintain a cash float of £10,000 at the end of each month, what is the probability that this will be possible at the end of each of months 1, 2 and 3 given the current overdraft limit?

4.31 SOLUTION

The opening balance at the beginning of month 1 is £10,000.

Month 1				*Month 2*				*Month 3*			
Prob.	*Cash flow* £'000	*Clos. bal.* £'000	*Over-draft* £'000	*Prob.*	*Cash flow* £'000	*Clos. bal.* £'000	*Over-draft* £'000	*Prob.*	*Cash flow* £'000	*Clos. bal.* £'000	*Over-draft* £'000
								0.28	30	10	19
				0.56	25	10	49	0.28	20	10	29
0.7	(40)	10	74								
								0.07	10	10	54
				0.14	10	10	64	0.07	0	10	64
								0.12	(10)	6	100
				0.24	0	10	94	0.12	(20)	(4)	100
0.3	(60)	10	94								
								0.03	(40)	(34)	100
				0.06	(10)	6	100	0.03	(50)	(44)	100

The probabilities that the cash float of £10,000 can be maintained at the end of each month are as follows.

Month 1: $0.7 + 0.3 = 1.0$

Month 2: $0.56 + 0.14 + 0.24 = 0.94$

Month 3: $0.28 + 0.28 + 0.07 + 0.07 = 0.7$

Question 4

Using the figures in the above example, state the probabilities that the company completely runs out of cash at the end of each month.

Answer

Under none of the projected outcomes for months 1 and 2 does the company run out of cash.

For month 3, the probability of the company running out of cash is:

$0.12 + 0.03 + 0.03 = 0.18$

Investing surplus cash 6/97

4.32 Companies and other organisations sometimes have a surplus of cash and become 'cash rich'. A cash surplus is likely to be temporary, but while it exists the company should seek to obtain a good return by investing or depositing the cash, without the risk of a capital loss (or at least, without the risk of an excessive capital loss).

4.33 Three possible reasons for a cash surplus are:

(a) profitability from trading operations;

(b) low capital expenditure, perhaps because of an absence of profitable new investment opportunities;

(c) receipts from selling parts of the business.

4.34 A company might keep surplus cash in liquid form:

(a) to **benefit from high interest rates** that might be available from bank deposits, when returns on re-investment in the company appear to be lower;

(b) to have cash available should a **strategic opportunity** arise, perhaps for the takeover of another company for which a cash consideration might be needed.

4.35 If a company has no plans to grow or to invest, then surplus cash not required for transactions or precautionary purposes should normally be returned to shareholders. Many businesses will be able to cover their precautionary cash needs by means of its overdraft facility, and so a small cash surplus for transaction purposes may be all that is needed.

4.36 Surplus cash may be returned to shareholders by:

(a) Increasing the usual level of the annual **dividends** which are paid;

(b) making a one-off **special dividend payment**. For example, National Power plc made such a payment to its shareholders in 1996, and BT plc has proposed making one during 1997;

(c) using the money to **buy back its own shares** from some of its shareholders. This will reduce the total number of shares in issue, and should therefore raise the level of **earnings per share**, assuming that the company can earn more on its ordinary activities than it would from investing its cash. Repurchase of a company's own shares, sometimes called a **share buy-back**, has become increasingly common, with for example many of the privatised regional electricity companies returning funds to their shareholders in this way in recent years.

Short-term investments

4.37 Temporary cash surpluses are likely to be:

(a) deposited with a bank or similar financial institution;

(b) invested in short-term debt instruments. Debt instruments are debt securities which can be traded;

(c) invested in longer term debt instruments, which can be sold on the stock market when the company eventually needs the cash;

(d) invested in shares of listed companies, which can be sold on the stock market when the company eventually needs the cash.

4.38 The problem with (c) and (d) is the risk of capital losses due to a fall in the market value of the securities. With short-term debt instruments (item (b)) any capital losses should not be large, because of the short term to maturity. With bank deposits (item (a)) the risk of capital losses is minimal.

Short-term deposits

4.39 Cash can of course be put into a bank deposit to earn interest. The rate of interest obtainable depends on the size of the deposit, and varies from bank to bank.

4.40 There are other types of deposit.

(a) **Money market lending.** There is a very large money market in the UK for inter-bank lending, with banks lending to each other and borrowing from each other for short terms ranging from as little as overnight up to terms of a year or more.

The interest rates in the market are related to the London Interbank Offer Rate (LIBOR) and the London Interbank Bid Rate (LIBID).

(i) A large company will be able to lend surplus cash directly to a borrowing bank in the market.

(ii) A smaller company with a fairly large cash surplus will usually be able to arrange to lend money on the interbank market, but through its bank, and possibly on condition that the money can only be withdrawn at three months notice.

(b) **Local authority deposits**. Local authorities often need short-term cash, and investors can deposit funds with them for periods ranging from overnight up to one year or more.

(c) **Finance house deposits**. These are time deposits with finance houses (usually subsidiaries of banks).

4.41 Deposits with banks, local authorities and finance houses are non-negotiable, which means that the investor who deposits funds cannot sell the deposit to another investor, should an unexpected need for cash arise. The deposit will only be released back to the investor when its term ends.

Short-term debt instruments

4.42 There are a number of **short-term debt instruments** which an investor can re-sell before the debt matures and is repaid. These debt instruments include **certificates of deposit** (CDs) and **Treasury bills**.

Certificates of deposit (CDs)

4.43 A **CD** is a security that is issued by a bank, acknowledging that a certain amount of money has been deposited with it for a certain period of time (usually, a short term). The CD is issued to the depositor, and attracts a stated amount of interest. The depositor will be another bank or a large commercial organisation. CDs are negotiable and traded on the CD market (a money market), so if a CD holder wishes to obtain immediate cash, he can sell the CD on the market at any time. This second-hand market in CDs makes them attractive, flexible investments for organisations with excess cash.

4.44 A company with surplus cash can:

(a) deposit a certain amount of cash with a bank for a fixed period, and receive a certificate of deposit from the bank; or

(b) buy an existing CD, which may have a much shorter period to maturity, on the CD market.

4.45 CDs are mainly denominated in sterling, but there is a growing market in US dollar CDs, and also in deposits linked to the value of the European Currency Unit (ecu).

Treasury bills

4.46 **Treasury bills** are issued weekly by the government to finance short-term cash deficiencies in the government's expenditure programme. They are IOUs issued by the government, giving a promise to pay a certain amount to their holder on maturity. Treasury bills have a term of 91 days to maturity, after which the holder is paid the full value of the bill. Most Treasury bills are denominated in sterling, but some are in ecus.

4.47 Treasury bills do not pay interest, but the purchase price of a Treasury bill is less than its face value, the amount that the government will eventually pay on maturity. There is thus an implied rate of interest in the price at which the bills are traded. The second-hand value of Treasury bills in the discount market (the money market in which they are traded) varies with current interest rates but will never exceed their face value.

4.48 A company can arrange through its bank to invest in Treasury bills. Since they are negotiable, they can be re-sold, if required, on the discount market before their maturity date.

5 FOREIGN EXCHANGE RISK 12/95, 12/97

Exam focus point

If any calculations are required relating to exchange rate risk in Paper 8, they will only be simple calculations.

5.1 A company may become exposed to risk from movements in exchange rates in a number of ways, including the following:

(a) as an exporter of goods or services;
(b) as an importer of goods or services;
(c) through having an overseas subsidiary;
(d) through being the subsidiary of an overseas company;
(e) through transactions in overseas capital markets.

Perhaps the most important aspect of **managing overseas debtors** is the problem that exchange rates may change before payment is received. Hedging involves measures to reduce exposure to such **foreign exchange risk**.

Currency of invoice

5.2 One way of avoiding exchange rate risk is for an exporter to invoice his foreign customer in his domestic currency, or for an importer to arrange with his foreign supplier to be invoiced in his domestic currency. However, although either the exporter or the importer can avoid any exchange risk in this way, only one of them can deal in his domestic currency. The other must accept the exchange risk, since there will be a period of time elapsing between agreeing a contract and paying for the goods (unless payment is made with the order).

Forward exchange contracts

5.3 Another method of overcoming foreign exchange transaction exposure is by means of a **forward exchange contract**, whereby the importer or exporter arranges for a bank to sell or buy a quantity of foreign currency at a future date, at a rate of exchange that is determined when the forward contract is made.

5.4 Forward exchange contracts allow a trader who knows that he will have to buy or sell foreign currency at a date in the future, to make the purchase or sale at a predetermined rate of exchange. The trader will therefore know in advance either how much local currency he will receive (if he is selling foreign currency to the bank) or how much local currency he must pay (if he is buying foreign currency from the bank).

KEY TERM

A **forward exchange contract** is:

(a) an immediately firm and binding contract between a bank and its customer;

(b) for the purchase or sale of a specified quantity of a stated foreign currency;

(c) at a rate of exchange fixed at the time the contract is made;

(d) for performance (delivery of the currency and payment for it) at a future time which is agreed upon when making the contract. This future time will be either a specified date, or any time between two specified dates.

Forward rates and future exchange rate movements

5.5 A forward price is the spot price ruling on the day a forward exchange contract is made plus or minus the interest differential for the period of the contract. It is wrong to think of a forward rate as a forecast of what the spot rate will be on a given date in the future, and it will be a coincidence if the forward rate turns out to be the same as the spot rate on that future date.

5.6 It is however likely that the spot rate will move in the direction indicated by the forward rate. Currencies with high interest rates are likely to depreciate in value against currencies with lower interest rates: the attraction of higher interest persuades investors to hold amounts of a currency that is expected to depreciate.

For example, suppose that a spot rate on 1 June is US$1.7430 - 1.7440 to £1, and the three months forward rate (for 1 September) is US$1.7380 - 1.7395 to £1. It is likely that between 1 June and 1 September, sterling will weaken slightly against the dollar. In this example, interest rates in the UK on 1 June would be higher than interest rates in the USA, which accounts for the forward rates for dollars against sterling being lower than the spot rates on 1 June.

Fixed and option contracts

5.7 A forward exchange contract may be either **fixed** or **option**.

(a) 'Fixed' means that performance of the contract will take place on a specified date in the future. For example, a two months forward fixed contract taken out on 1 September will require performance on 1 November.

(b) 'Option' means that performance of the contract may take place, at the option of the customer, either

(i) at any date from the contract being made up to and including a specified final date for performance; or

(ii) at any date between two specified dates.

(Option forward exchange contracts are different from **currency options**, which are not part of the Paper 8 syllabus.)

Premiums and discounts: quoting a forward rate

5.8 A forward exchange rate might be higher or lower than the spot rate. If it is higher, the quoted currency will be cheaper forward than spot. For example, if in the case of Italian lire against sterling (i) the spot rate is 2,156 - 2,166 and (ii) the three months forward rate is 2,207 - 2,222:

(a) a bank would sell 2,000,000 lire:

(i) at the spot rate, now, for £927.64 $\left(\frac{2,000,000}{2,156}\right)$

(ii) in three months time, under a forward contract, for £906.21 $\left(\frac{2,000,000}{2,207}\right)$

(b) a bank would buy 2,000,000 lire:

(i) at the spot rate, now, for £923.36 $\left(\frac{2,000,000}{2,166}\right)$

(ii) in three months time, under a forward contract, for £900.09 $\left(\frac{2,000,000}{2,222}\right)$

5.9 In both cases, the quoted currency (lire) would be worth less against sterling in a forward contract than at the current spot rate. This is because it is quoted forward cheaper, or 'at a discount', against sterling.

5.10 If the forward exchange rate is lower than the spot rate, the quoted currency will be more expensive forward than spot. For example,

(a) if the spot rate for DM against sterling is 3.05 - 3.06, and
(b) the one month forward rate is 3.03 - 3.04½,

then DM are more expensive (quoted 'at a premium') forward than spot.

5.11 If the forward rate for a currency is cheaper than the spot rate, it is at a forward **discount** to the spot rate. The forward rate will be higher than the spot rate by the amount of the discount.

If the forward rate for a currency is more expensive than the spot rate, it is at a forward **premium** to the spot rate. The forward rate will be lower than the spot rate by the amount of the premium.

The rule for adding or subtracting discounts and premiums

5.12 A **discount** is therefore *added* to the spot rate, and a **premium** is therefore *subtracted* from the spot rate.

It might help you to think of the mnemonic 'ADDIS'. This may help you to remember that we ADD DIScounts and so subtract premiums.

5.13 EXAMPLE: FORWARD EXCHANGE CONTRACTS

A UK importer knows on 1 April that he must pay a foreign seller 26,500 Swiss francs in one month's time, on 1 May. He can arrange a forward exchange contract with his bank on 1 April, whereby the bank undertakes to sell the importer 26,500 Swiss francs on 1 May, at a fixed rate of say 2.64.

The UK importer can be certain that whatever the spot rate is between Swiss francs and sterling on 1 May, he will have to pay on that date, at this forward rate:

$$\frac{26{,}500}{2.64} = £10{,}037.88.$$

(a) If the spot rate is lower than 2.64, the importer would have successfully protected himself against a weakening of sterling, and would have avoided paying more sterling to obtain the Swiss francs.

(b) If the spot rate is higher than 2.64, sterling's value against the Swiss franc would mean that the importer would pay more under the forward exchange contract than he would have had to pay if he had obtained the francs at the spot rate on 1 May. He cannot avoid this extra cost, because a forward contract is binding.

Option forward exchange contracts

5.14 As we saw above, option forward exchange contracts are forward exchange contracts where the customer has the option to call for performance of the contract:

(a) at any date from the contract being made up to a specified date in the future; or
(b) at any date between two dates both in the future.

The contract must be performed at some time: the customer cannot avoid performance altogether.

5.15 Option contracts are normally used to cover whole months straddling the likely payment date, where the customer is not sure of the exact date on which he will want to buy or sell currency. (The purpose of an option contract is to avoid having to renew a forward exchange contract and extend it by a few days, because extending a forward contract can be expensive.)

5.16 Option contracts can also be used bit by bit. For example, if a customer makes an option forward contract to sell DM 100,000 at any time between 3 July and 3 August, he might sell DM 20,000 on 5 July, DM 50,000 on 15 July and DM 30,000 on 1 August.

5.17 When a customer makes an option forward exchange contract with his bank, the bank will quote the rate which is most favourable to itself out of the forward rates for all dates within the option period. This is because the customer has the option to call for performance of the contract on any date within the period, and the bank will try to ensure that the customer does not obtain a favourable rate at the bank's expense.

Money market hedges

5.18 An exporter who invoices foreign customers in a foreign currency can hedge against the exchange risk by:

(a) borrowing an amount in the foreign currency immediately;
(b) converting the foreign currency into domestic currency at the spot rate;
(c) repaying the loan with interest out of the eventual foreign currency receipts.

5.19 Similarly, if a company has to make a foreign currency payment in the future, it can buy the currency now at the spot rate and put it on deposit, using the principal and the interest earned to make the foreign currency payment when it falls due.

Choosing between the forward exchange market and the money market

5.20 When a company expects to receive or pay a sum of foreign currency in the next few months, it can choose between using the forward exchange market and the money market to hedge against the foreign exchange risk. The cheaper option available is the one that ought to be chosen.

5.21 EXAMPLE: CHOOSING THE CHEAPEST METHOD

Trumpton plc has bought goods from a US supplier, and must pay $4,000,000 for them in three months time. The company's finance director wishes to hedge against the foreign exchange risk, and the methods which the company wishes to consider are:

(a) using forward exchange contracts;
(b) using money market borrowing or lending.

The following annual interest rates and exchange rates are currently available.

	US dollar		*Sterling*	
	Deposit rate	*Borrowing rate*	*Deposit rate*	*Borrowing rate*
	%	%	%	%
1 month	7	10.25	10.75	14.00
3 months	7	10.75	11.00	14.25

	$/£ exchange rate ($ = £1)
Spot	1.8625 - 1.8635
1 month forward	0.60c - 0.58c pm
3 months forward	1.80c - 1.75c pm

Which is the cheapest method for Trumpton plc? Ignore commission costs (the bank charges for arranging a forward contract or a loan).

5.22 SOLUTION

The two methods must be compared on a similar basis, which means working out the cost of each to Trumpton either now or in three months time. Here the cost to Trumpton now will be determined.

Choice 1: the forward exchange market

Trumpton must buy dollars in order to pay the US supplier. The exchange rate in a forward exchange contract to buy $4,000,000 in three months time (bank sells) is:

	$
Spot rate	1.8625
Less 3 months premium	0.0180
Forward rate	1.8445

The cost of the $4,000,000 to Trumpton in three months time will be:

$$\frac{\$4{,}000{,}000}{\$1.8445} = £2{,}168{,}609.38$$

This is the cost in three months. To work out the cost now, we could say that by deferring payment for three months, the company is:

(a) saving having to borrow money now at 14.25% a year to make the payment now; or
(b) avoiding the loss of interest on cash on deposit, earning 11% a year.

The choice between (a) and (b) depends on whether Trumpton plc needs to borrow to make any current payment (a) or is cash rich (b). Here, assumption (a) is selected, but (b) might in fact apply.

At an annual interest rate of 14.25% the rate for three months is approximately 14.25/4 = 3.5625%. The 'present cost' of £2,168,609.38 in three months time is:

$$\frac{£2{,}168{,}609.38}{1.035625} = £2{,}094{,}010.27$$

74,577·11 saving

Choice 2: the money markets

Using the money markets involves:

(a) borrowing in the foreign currency, if the company will eventually receive the currency;

(b) lending in the foreign currency, if the company will eventually pay the currency.

Here, Trumpton will pay $4,000,000 and so it would lend US dollars.

It would lend enough US dollars for three months, so that the principal repaid in three months time plus interest will amount to the payment due of $4,000,000.

(a) Since the US dollar deposit rate is 7%, the rate for three months is approximately 7/4 = 1.75%.

(b) To earn $4,000,000 in three months time at 1.75% interest, Trumpton would have to lend now:

$$\frac{\$4,000,000}{1.0175} = \$3,931,203.93$$

These dollars would have to be purchased now at the spot rate of (bank sells) $1.8625. The cost would be:

$$\frac{\$3,931,203.93}{\$1.8625} = £2,110,713.52$$

By lending US dollars for three months, Trumpton is matching eventual receipts and payments in US dollars, and so has hedged against foreign exchange risk.

Exam focus point

The management of working capital gets right down to the day-to-day practicalities of running a business. In answering questions on working capital management, you should always consider whether any proposed course of action really makes business sense.

Chapter roundup

- In managing **debtors,** the **creditworthiness** of customers needs to be assessed. The risks and costs of a customer defaulting will need to be balanced against the profitability of the business provided by that customer.
- **Settlement discounts** may be employed to shorten average credit periods, and to reduce the investment in debtors and therefore **interest costs**. The benefit in interest cost saved should exceed the cost of the discounts allowed.
- Some companies use **factoring** and **invoice discounting** to help short-term liquidity or to reduce administration costs.
- Effective management of **trade creditors** involves seeking satisfactory credit terms from supplier, getting credit extended during periods of cash shortage, and maintaining good relations with suppliers.
- An **economic order quantity** can be calculated as a guide to minimising costs in managing **stock** levels.
- Optimal **cash** holding levels can be calculated from formal models, such as the **inventory approach** and the **Miller-Orr model**.
- The use of **forward exchange contracts** in which a future rate of exchange is fixed in advance, is one of the most important ways of reducing **foreign exchange risk**.

Quick quiz

1 What factors should be considered by management in the formulation of a policy for credit control? (see para 1.1)

2 How might the creditworthiness of a potential new customer be checked? (1.5, 1.6)

3 What is credit insurance? (1.20 - 1.22)

4 What services do factors provide? (1.23)

5 What is invoice discounting? (1.45)

6 What are acceptance credits? (2.14, 2.15)

7 What is meant by JIT procurement? (3.19)

8 What is meant by total quality management? (3.23)

9 How do cash flow problems arise? (4.2)

10 How are cash management models used in practice? (4.27, 4.28)

11 Give examples of short-term debt instruments for the investment of surplus cash. (4.42)

12 What is a forward exchange contract? (5.3, 5.4)

Question to try	Level	Marks	Time
22	Introductory	n/a	30 mins

Part H

Long-term finance and capital structure

Chapter 22

LONG-TERM FINANCE I

Chapter topic list		Syllabus reference
1	Obtaining equity funds	7(a)(ii)
2	Scrip dividends, scrip issues and stock splits	7(a)(ii)
3	Venture capital	7(a)(vii)
4	Stock market ratios	7(a)(ii)
5	Dividend policy	7(a)(i),(iii)

Introduction

The most important source of finance for companies is **retained profits**. In the short term, as we saw earlier, an **overdraft** is a flexible source of finance. In the case of long-term finance (covered in this chapter and Chapter 23), the main choice is between **equity** and **debt** finance.

1 OBTAINING EQUITY FUNDS 6/94, 12/94, 6/95, 12/95, 12/96

Different sources of funds

1.1 A company might raise new funds from the following sources.

(a) Retained earnings - the most important form of finance in practice

(b) The capital markets:

(i) new share issues (for example by companies acquiring a stock market listing for the first time)

(ii) rights issues

(iii) issues of loan capital

(c) Bank borrowings

(d) Government sources

(e) Business expansion scheme funds

(f) Venture capital

(g) The international money and capital markets (eurocommercial paper, eurobonds and eurocurrency borrowing).

In this chapter, we first concentrate on the capital markets.

Exam focus point

Along with working capital management and investment appraisal, the Examiner treats **sources of finance** as one of the 'major' FM topics in the paper and therefore tries to include it, in some form, in each exam paper.

Ordinary (equity) shares

1.2 **Ordinary shares** are issued to the owners of a company. The ordinary shares of UK companies have a nominal or 'face' value, typically £1 or 50p, but shares with a nominal value of 1p, 2p or 25p are not uncommon. You should understand that the market value of a quoted company's shares bears *no* relationship to their nominal value, except that when ordinary shares are issued for cash, the issue price must be equal to or (more usually) *more than* the nominal value of the shares. Outside the UK it is not uncommon for a company's shares to have no nominal value.

1.3 **Deferred ordinary shares** are a form of ordinary shares, which are entitled to a dividend only after a certain date or only if profits rise above a certain amount. Voting rights might also differ from those attached to other ordinary shares.

1.4 Ordinary shareholders put funds into their company:

(a) by paying for a new issue of shares;
(b) through retained profits.

Simply, retaining profits, instead of paying them out in the form of dividends, offers an important, simple low-cost source of finance, although this method may not provide enough funds, for example if the firm is seeking to grow.

1.5 A new issue of shares might be made in a variety of different circumstances.

(a) The company might want to raise more cash, for example for expansion of its operations. If it issues ordinary shares for cash, should the shares be issued *pro rata* to existing shareholders, so that control or ownership of the company is not affected? If, for example, a company with 200,000 ordinary shares in issue decides to issue 50,000 new shares to raise cash, should it offer the new shares to existing shareholders, or should it sell them to new shareholders instead?

(i) If a company sells the new shares to existing shareholders in proportion to their existing shareholding in the company, we have a rights issue. In the example above, the 50,000 shares would be issued as a one for four rights issue, by offering shareholders one new share for every four shares they currently hold. This is the method preferred by the London Stock Exchange as it avoids dilution of existing interests.

(ii) If the number of new shares being issued is small compared to the number of shares already in issue, it might be decided instead to sell them to new shareholders, since ownership of the company would only be minimally affected.

(b) The company might want to issue new shares partly to raise cash but more importantly to 'float' its shares on a stock market. When a UK company is floated, for example on the main stock market, it is a requirement of the Stock Exchange that at least a minimum proportion of its shares should be made available to the general investing public if the shares are not already widely held.

(c) The company might issue new shares to the shareholders of another company, in order to take it over.

1.6 A company seeking to obtain additional equity funds may be:

(a) an unquoted company wishing to obtain a Stock Exchange main market or 'second tier' (**Alternative Investment Market** or **AIM**) listing;

(b) an unquoted company wishing to issue new shares, but without obtaining a main market or second tier quotation;

(c) a company which is already listed on the Stock Exchange main market or the AIM wishing to issue additional new shares.

The Alternative Investment Market

1.7 The London Stock Exchange launched the AIM in 1995 as a market for smaller, growing, companies that cannot qualify for or do not wish to join the Official List (or 'main market'). The AIM is not a direct replacement for the earlier Unlisted Securities Market (USM), as it has more lax entry requirements and regulations than either the USM or the Official List. Key characteristics of the AIM are as follows.

(a) There are no eligibility criteria for new entrants, whether in size, profitability or length of track record.

(b) Any type of security can be offered, provided there are no restrictions on transferability.

(c) There are no Stock Exchange requirements for the percentage of shares in public hands or the number of shareholders, although if too few shares are freely available, then there will be no realistic market price.

(d) There are fewer obligations to issue shareholder circulars; public announcements will generally be sufficient.

(e) Documents produced for admission to the AIM are the responsibility of the directors and are not reviewed by the Exchange.

(f) Every company whose securities trade on the AIM must have (at all times) a Nominated Adviser chosen from an official list and a Nominated Broker which must be a member firm of the Exchange. The Adviser's role is to advise the directors of the issuer on their obligations under AIM rules. The Broker's role is to support trading if there is no market maker and to act as a point of contact for investors.

(g) AIM shares are treated as unquoted for tax purposes, meaning that a number of reliefs are available to investors.

1.8 AIM companies might be new business 'start-ups' or well established family businesses, from high technology firms to traditional manufacturers. The AIM is expected to attract companies which wish to cut the cost of a stock market quotation. The Stock Exchange hopes that the failure rate among AIM companies will be minimised as a result of its careful vetting of Nominated Advisers.

1.9 In conclusion, the AIM would appear to offer the advantages of wider access to capital, enhanced credibility among financial institutions and a higher public profile, at a much lower cost than a full listing.

By May 1997, almost two years after its launch, the AIM had attracted 280 entrants which have a combined capitalisation of almost £6 billion and have raised £1.2 billion in new money.

Reason for seeking a stock market listing

1.10 The following are reasons why a company may seek a stock market listing.

(a) **Access to a wider pool of finance.** A company that is growing fast may need to raise larger sums than is possible as a private unlisted company. A stock market listing widens the number of potential investors. It may also improve the company's credit rating, making debt finance easier and cheaper to obtain.

(b) **Improved marketability of shares.** Shares that are traded on the stock market can be bought and sold in relatively small quantities at any time. This means that it is easier for exiting investors to realise a part of their holding.

(c) **Transfer of capital to other uses.** Founder owners may wish to liquidate the major part of their holding either for personal reasons or for investment in other new business opportunities.

(d) **Enhancement of the company image.** Quoted companies are commonly believed to be more financially stable, and listing may improve the image of the company with its customers and suppliers, allowing it to gain additional business and to improve its buying power.

(e) **Facilitation of growth by acquisition.** A listed company is in a better position to make a paper offer for a target company than an unlisted one.

1.11 However, the owners of a private company which becomes a listed 'plc' (public company) must accept that the change is likely to involve a significant loss of control to a wider circle of investors. The implications of this will need to be taken into account.

Obtaining a listing

1.12 The methods by which an unquoted company can obtain a listing on the stock market are:

(a) an offer for sale:
(b) a prospectus issue;
(c) a placing;
(d) an introduction.

Of these, (a) and (c) are the most common.

Offers for sale

1.13 An **offer for sale** is a means of selling the shares of a company to the public at large.

(a) An unquoted company may issue new shares, and sell them on the Stock Exchange, to raise cash for the company. All the shares in the company, not just the new ones, would then become marketable.

(b) Shareholders in an unquoted company may sell some of their existing shares to the general public. When this occurs, the company is not raising any new funds, but is merely providing a wider market for its existing shares (all of which would become marketable), and giving existing shareholders the chance to cash in some or all of their investment in their company.

1.14 When companies 'go public' for the first time, a *large* issue will probably take the form of an offer for sale (or occasionally an offer for sale by tender). A smaller issue is more likely to be a placing, since the amount to be raised can be obtained more cheaply if the issuing house or other sponsoring firm approaches selected institutional investors privately.

1.15 A company whose shares are already listed might issue new shares to the general public. It is likely, however, that a new issue by a quoted company will be either a placing or a rights issue, which are described later.

Issuing houses and sponsoring member firms

1.16 When an unquoted company applies for a Stock Exchange listing, it must be sponsored by a firm that is a member of the Stock Exchange. This sponsoring member firm has the responsibility of ensuring that the company meets the requirements for listing, and carries out the necessary procedures. The company will also employ the services of an issuing house, which might well be the sponsoring member firm itself. An issuing house has the job of trying to ensure a successful issue for the company's shares, by advising on an issue price for the shares, and trying to interest institutional investors in buying some of the shares.

The issue price and offers for sale

1.17 The offer price must be advertised a short time in advance, so it is fixed without certain knowledge of the condition of the market at the time applications are invited. In order to ensure the success of an issue, share prices are often set lower than they might otherwise be.

It is normal practice for an issuing house to try to ensure that a share price rises to a premium above its issue price soon after trading begins. A target premium of 20% above the issue price would be fairly typical.

1.18 Companies will be keen to avoid over-pricing an issue, so that the issue is under-subscribed, leaving underwriters with the unwelcome task of having to buy up the unsold shares.

On the other hand, if the issue price is too low then the issue will be oversubscribed and the company would have been able to raise the required capital by issuing fewer shares.

1.19 The share price of an issue is usually advertised as being based on a certain P/E ratio, the ratio of the price to the company's most recent earnings per share figure in its audited accounts. The issue's P/E ratio can then be compared by investors with the P/E ratios of similar quoted companies.

Offers for sale by tender

1.20 It is often very difficult to decide upon the price at which the shares should be offered to the general public. One way of trying to ensure that the issue price reflects the value of the shares as perceived by the market is to make an **offer for sale by tender.**

(a) A minimum price will be fixed and subscribers will be invited to tender for shares at prices equal to or above the minimum.

(b) The shares will be allotted at the highest price at which they will all be taken up. This is known as the striking price.

1.21 Offers by tender are less common than offers for sale.

The reasons why offers for sale by tender might not be preferred are as follows.

(a) It is sometimes felt that the decision to make an offer by tender reflects badly on the issuing house's ability to determine the issue price.

(b) It is claimed that the use of tenders leaves the determination of prices to the 'uninformed public' rather than the City 'experts'. However, in practice the major influence on the striking price will be the tenders of the institutional investors.

(c) An offer for sale is more certain in the amount of finance that will be raised.

(d) Some potential investors may be deterred from applying for shares as they do not wish to have to decide on a price.

1.22 An increase in the use of offers for sale by tender might follow a general increase in share values. When share prices are generally rising, the striking price in an offer for sale by tender is likely to be higher than the issue price that would have been set if the issuing company were to select the issue price itself, since the issue price would have to be sufficiently low to be reasonably sure that the issue would be fully subscribed by investors.

1.23 EXAMPLE: OFFER FOR SALE BY TENDER

Byte Henderson plc is a new company that is making its first public issue of shares. It has decided to make the issue by means of an offer for sale by tender. The intention is to issue up to 4,000,000 shares (the full amount of authorised share capital) at a minimum price of 300 pence. The money raised, net of issue costs of £1,000,000, would be invested in projects which would earn benefits with a present value equal to 130% of the net amount invested.

The following tenders have been received. (Each applicant has made only one offer.)

Price tendered per share	*Number of shares applied for at this price*
£	
6.00	50,000
5.50	100,000
5.00	300,000
4.50	450,000
4.00	1,100,000
3.50	1,500,000
3.00	2,500,000

(a) How many shares would be issued, and how much in total would be raised, if Byte Henderson plc chooses:

(i) to maximise the total amount raised?
(ii) to issue exactly 4,000,000 shares?

(b) Harvey Goldfinger, a private investor, has applied for 12,000 shares at a price of £5.50 and has sent a cheque for £66,000 to the issuing house that is handling the issue. In both cases (a)(i) and (ii), how many shares would be issued to Mr Goldfinger, assuming that any partial acceptance of offers would mean allotting shares to each accepted applicant in proportion to the number of shares applied for? How much will Mr Goldfinger receive back out of the £66,000 he has paid?

(c) Estimate the likely market value of shares in the company after the issue, assuming that the market price fully reflects the investment information given above and that exactly 4,000,000 shares are issued.

1.24 SOLUTION

(a) We begin by looking at the cumulative tenders.

Price	*Cumulative number of shares applied for*	*Amount raised if price is selected, before deducting issue costs*
£		£
6.00	50,000	300,000
5.50	150,000	825,000
5.00	450,000	2,250,000
4.50	900,000	4,050,000
4.00	2,000,000	8,000,000
3.50	3,500,000	12,250,000
3.00	6,000,000	12,000,000

(i) To maximise the total amount raised, the issue price should be £3.50. The total raised before deducting issue costs would be £12,250,000.

(ii) To issue exactly 4,000,000 shares, the issue price must be £3.00. The total raised would be £12,000,000, before deducting issue costs.

(b) (i) Harvey Goldfinger would be allotted 12,000 shares at £3.50 per share. He would receive a refund of 12,000 × £2 = £24,000 out of the £66,000 he has paid.

(ii) If 4,000,000 shares are issued, applicants would receive two thirds of the shares they tendered for. Harvey Goldfinger would be allotted 8,000 shares at £3 per share and would receive a refund of £42,000 out of the £66,000 he has paid.

(c) The net amount raised would be £12,000,000 minus issue costs of £1,000,000, £11,000,000.

The present value of the benefits from investment would be 130% of £11,000,000, £14,300,000. If the market price reflects this information, the price per share would rise to $\frac{£14,300,000}{4,000,000}$ = £3.575 per share.

A prospectus issue

1.25 In a **prospectus issue**, or public issue, a company offers its own shares to the general public. An issuing house or merchant bank may act as an agent, but not as an underwriter. This type of issue is therefore risky, and is very rare. Well known companies making a large new issue may use this method, and the company would almost certainly already have a quotation on the Stock Exchange.

A placing

1.26 A **placing** is an arrangement whereby the shares are not all offered to the public, but instead, the sponsoring market maker arranges for most of the issue to be bought by a small number of investors, usually institutional investors such as pension funds and insurance companies.

The choice between an offer for sale and a placing

1.27 When a company is planning a flotation on to the AIM, or a full Stock Exchange listing, is it likely to prefer an offer for sale of its shares, or a placing?

Placings are much cheaper, although most of the shares will be placed with a relatively small number of (institutional) shareholders, which means that most of the shares are unlikely to be available for trading after the flotation. This is a particular problem for smaller companies.

A Stock Exchange introduction

1.28 By this method of obtaining a quotation, no shares are made available to the market, neither existing nor newly created shares; nevertheless, the Stock Exchange grants a quotation. This will only happen where shares in a large company are already widely held, so that a market can be seen to exist. A company might want an **introduction** to obtain greater marketability for the shares, a known share valuation for inheritance tax purposes and easier access in the future to additional capital.

Underwriting

1.29 A company about to issue new securities in order to raise finance might decide to have the issue underwritten. **Underwriters** are financial institutions which agree (in exchange for a fixed fee, perhaps 2.25% of the finance to be raised) to buy at the issue price any securities which are not subscribed for by the investing public.

1.30 Underwriters remove the risk of a share issue's being under-subscribed, but at a cost to the company issuing the shares. It is not compulsory to have an issue underwritten.

(a) It is unnecessary to underwrite a placing since a purchaser for the shares is arranged in the issue process.

(b) An offer for sale by tender would only need underwriting if there is a risk that there will be under-subscription even at the minimum price.

(c) A rights issue should in theory not require underwriting, since new shares are being offered to existing shareholders. However, the underwriting of rights issues is common practice.

With underwriting, the company making the issue is sure of receiving the funds it wants to raise, net of expenses.

1.31 As an alternative to underwriting an issue, a company could choose to issue its share at a deep discount, that is, at a price well below the current market price, to ensure the success of the issue. This is less common. A major disadvantage of issuing shares at a deep discount is that, since companies try to avoid reducing the dividends paid out per share, the total amount required for dividends in future years will be that much higher, since more shares would have to be issued at the low price to raise the amount of finance required. If the company expects only moderate growth in total earnings and dividends, the company's shareholders might even suffer a fall in earnings per share.

Because of the costs of underwriting, there has been a trend in recent years for companies who securities are marketable to adopt the practice known as the '**bought deal**', whereby an investment bank buys the whole of a new issue at a small discount to the market.

Pricing shares for a stock market launch

1.32 Pricing shares for a stock market launch is a task for the company's sponsor.

Factors that the sponsor will take into account are as follows.

(a) Are there similar companies already quoted, whose P/E ratios can be used for comparison? The chosen P/E ratio can be multiplied by the company's most recent

EPS, as shown in the prospectus, to arrive at a draft share price. This price can be negotiated with the company's current owners.

A company which is coming to the AIM will obtain a lower P/E ratio than a similar company on the main market.

(b) What are current market conditions?

(c) With what accuracy can the company's future trading prospects be forecast?

(d) It is usual to set a price which gives an immediate premium when the launch takes place. A sponsor will usually try to ensure that the market price rises to a premium of about 20% over the launch price on the day that the launch takes place.

(e) A steady growth in the share price year by year should be achievable.

1.33 EXAMPLE: PRICING SHARES FOR A STOCK MARKET LAUNCH

Launchpad plc is proposing to obtain a Stock Exchange listing, to raise £10,000,000 from a placing of new shares. Issue costs will be 8% of the gross receipts.

The company already has 4,000,000 shares in issue. The company expects to earn a post-tax profit of £4,000,000 in its next year of operations, plus a 15% post-tax return on the newly raised funds, and to pay out 50% of its profits as dividends. Dividend growth would be 3% a year.

For the issue to be successful, Launchpad plc would have to issue shares at a 20% discount to what it considers the market value of the shares ought to be.

Shareholders will expect a net dividend yield (that is, net of the tax credit) of 12%.

Calculate a suitable issue price for the shares, and the number of shares that would have to be issued.

1.34 SOLUTION

(a) Receipts net of issue costs from the new issue = 92% of £10,000,000
= £ 9,200,000

(b) Post-tax profits on the newly raised funds in year 1 = 15% of £9,200,000
= £1,380,000

(c) Total post-tax profits in year 1 = £4,000,000 + £1,380,000
= £5,380,000

(d) Dividends in year 1 = 50% of £5,380,000
= £2,690,000

(e) Market value (P_0), based on a dividend growth model, expected dividend growth (g) of 3% a year from year 1 and a required return (r) of 12% is given by:

$$P_0 = \frac{D_1}{(r-g)} = \frac{£2,690,000}{(0.12-0.03)}$$

(The dividend growth model is explained later.) $= \frac{£2,690,000}{0.09}$
= £29,888,889

(f) Let the number of shares issued be X.

Total number of shares = 4,000,000 + X

Let the share price after the issue be P.

Total market value $= £29,888,889$

$(4,000,000 + X)P = £29,888,889$

(g) Let P_d be the discount price at which the new shares must be issued, which is 20% below what the share price P ought to be.

$P_d = 0.8P$

From (f) it follows that:

$$\frac{(4,000,000 + X)P_d}{0.8} = £29,888,889$$

$$4,000,000P_d + XP_d = £29,888,889 \times 0.8$$

$$= £23,911,111$$

(h) XP_d = number of new shares issued × issue price $= £10,000,000$

(i) Taking (g) and (h) together:

$$4,000,000P_d + 10,000,000 = £23,911,111$$

$$4,000,000\,P_d = £13,911,111$$

$$P_d = \frac{£13,911,111}{4,000,000} = £3.48$$

(j) Since $XP_d = £10,000,000$

$$X = \frac{£10,000,000}{£3.48}$$

$$= 2,873,563$$

Conclusions

(a) 2,873,563 shares should be issued at a price of £3.48 to raise £10,000,000.

(b) The price of £3.48 is at a 20% discount to the market value after the issue. The market value will be £3.48 ÷ 0.8 = £4.35 per share.

(c) After the issue, there will be 6,873,563 shares valued at £4.35 each or £29,899,999 in total. Allowing for rounding differences, this is the total valuation of £29,888,889 given in (g) above.

New issues of shares by quoted companies

1.35 When a quoted company makes an issue of new shares to raise capital, it could make an offer for sale, but it is more likely to issue the shares by means of:

- a rights issue, or
- a placing

Rights issues 6/96

KEY TERM

A **rights issue** is an offer to existing shareholders enabling them to buy more shares, usually at a price lower than the current market price.

1.36 Existing shareholders have **pre-emption rights** when new shares are issued. So that existing shareholders' rights are not diluted by the issue of new shares, section 89 of Companies Act 1985 requires that before any equity shares are allotted for cash they must first be offered to existing shareholders.

1.37 A **rights issue** provides a way of raising new share capital by means of an offer to existing shareholders, inviting them to subscribe cash for new shares in proportion to their existing holdings.

For example, a rights issue on a one for four basis at 280p per share would mean that a company is inviting its existing shareholders to subscribe for one new share for every four shares they hold, at a price of 280p per new share. A rights issue may be made by any type of company, private or public, listed or unlisted. The analysis below, however, applies primarily to listed companies.

1.38 The major advantages of a rights issue are as follows.

(a) Rights issues are cheaper than offers for sale to the general public. This is partly because no prospectus is required (provided that the issue is for less than 10% of the class of shares concerned), partly because the administration is simpler and partly because the cost of underwriting will be less.

(b) Rights issues are more beneficial to existing shareholders than issues to the general public. New shares are issued at a discount to the current market price, to make them attractive to investors. If the shares are issued to the general public, the benefit of the discount will be enjoyed by whoever buys the shares. A rights issue secures the discount on the market price for existing shareholders, who may either keep the shares or sell them if they wish.

(c) Relative voting rights are unaffected if shareholders all take up their rights.

(d) The finance raised may be used to reduce gearing in book value terms by increasing share capital and/or to pay off long-term debt which will reduce gearing in market value terms.

Deciding the issue price for a rights issue

1.39 The offer price in a rights issue will be lower than the current market price of existing shares. The size of the discount will vary, and will be larger for difficult issues.

The offer price must also be at or above the nominal value of the shares, so as not to contravene company law. Where the current market price of shares is below the nominal value, or only very slightly above it, a rights issue would therefore be impracticable.

1.40 A company making a rights issue must set a price which is:

(a) low enough to secure the acceptance of shareholders, who are being asked to provide extra funds;

(b) not too low, so as to avoid excessive dilution of the earnings per share.

Exam focus point

As in 6/94, a question could ask for discussion on the effect of a rights issue, as well as calculations, eg of the effect on EPS.

1.41 EXAMPLE: RIGHTS ISSUE (1)

Seagull plc can achieve a profit after tax of 20% on the capital employed. At present its capital structure is as follows.

	£
200,000 ordinary shares of £1 each	200,000
Retained earnings	100,000
	300,000

The directors propose to raise an additional £126,000 from a rights issue. The current market price is £1.80.

Required

(a) Calculate the number of shares that must be issued if the rights price is: £1.60; £1.50; £1.40; £1.20.

(b) Calculate the dilution in earnings per share in each case.

1.42 SOLUTION

The earnings at present are 20% of £300,000 = £60,000. This gives earnings per share of 30p. The earnings after the rights issue will be 20% of £426,000 = £85,200.

Rights price	*No of new share (£126,000 ÷ rights price)*	*EPS (£85,200 ÷ total no of shares)*	*Dilution*
£		Pence	Pence
1.60	78,750	30.6	+ 0.6
1.50	84,000	30.0	–
1.40	90,000	29.4	– 0.6
1.20	105,000	27.9	– 2.1

1.43 Note that at a high rights price the earnings per share are increased, not diluted. The breakeven point (zero dilution) occurs when the rights price is equal to the capital employed per share: £300,000 ÷ 200,000 = £1.50.

The market price of shares after a rights issue: the theoretical ex rights price

1.44 After the announcement of a rights issue, there is a tendency for share prices to fall, although the extent and duration of the fall may depend on the number of shareholders and the size of their holdings. This temporary fall is due to uncertainty in the market about the consequences of the issue, with respect to future profits, earnings and dividends.

1.45 After the issue has actually been made, the market price per share will normally fall, because there are more shares in issue and the new shares were issued at a discount price.

1.46 When a rights issue is announced, all existing shareholders have the right to subscribe for new shares, and so there are rights attached to the existing shares. The shares are therefore described as being 'cum rights' (with rights attached) and are traded cum rights.

On the first day of dealings in the newly issued shares, the rights no longer exist and the old shares are now 'ex rights' (without rights attached).

1.47 In theory, the new market price will be the consequence of an adjustment to allow for the discount price of the new issue, and a theoretical ex rights price can be calculated.

1.48 EXAMPLE: RIGHTS ISSUE (2)

Fundraiser plc has 1,000,000 ordinary shares of £1 in issue, which have a market price on 1 September of £2.10 per share. The company decides to make a rights issue, and offers its shareholders the right to subscribe for one new share at £1.50 each for every four shares already held. After the announcement of the issue, the share price fell to £1.95, but by the time just prior to the issue being made, it had recovered to £2 per share. This market value just before the issue is known as the cum rights price.

What is the theoretical ex rights price?

1.49 SOLUTION

In theory, the market price will fall after the issue, as follows.

	£
1,000,000 shares have a 'cum rights' value of (× £2)	2,000,000
250,000 shares will be issued to raise (× £1.50)	375,000
The theoretical value of 1,250,000 shares is	2,375,000

The theoretical ex rights price is $\frac{£2,375,000}{1,250,000}$ = £1.90 per share.

1.50 The same calculation is often shown as follows.

	£
Four shares have a cum rights value of (× £2)	8.00
One new share is issued for	1.50
The value of five shares is theoretically	9.50

The theoretical ex rights price is £9.50/5 = £1.90 per share.

The value of rights

1.51 The value of rights is the theoretical gain a shareholder would make by exercising his rights.

(a) Using the above example, if the price offered in the rights issue is £1.50 per share, and the market price after the issue is expected to be £1.90, the value attaching to a right is £1.90 – £1.50 = £0.40. A shareholder would therefore be expected to gain 40 pence for each new share he buys. If he does not have enough money to buy the share himself, he could sell the right to subscribe for a new share to another investor, and receive 40 pence from the sale. This other investor would then buy the new share for £1.50, so that his total outlay to acquire the share would be £0.40 + £1.50 = £1.90, the theoretical ex rights price.

(b) The value of rights attaching to existing shares is calculated in the same way. If the value of rights on a new share is 40 pence, and there is a one for four rights issue, the value of the rights attaching to each existing share is 40 ÷ 4 = 10 pence.

The theoretical gain or loss to shareholders

1.52 The possible courses of action open to shareholders are:

(a) to 'take up' or 'exercise' the rights, that is, to buy the new shares at the rights price. Shareholders who do this will maintain their percentage holdings in the company by subscribing for the new shares;

(b) to 'renounce' the rights and sell them on the market. Shareholders who do this will have lower percentage holdings of the company's equity after the issue than before the issue, and the total value of their shares will be less (on the assumption that the actual market price after the issue is close to the theoretical ex rights price);

(c) to renounce part of the rights and take up the remainder. For example, a shareholder may sell enough of his rights to enable him to buy the remaining rights shares he is entitled to with the sale proceeds, and so keep the total market value of his shareholding in the company unchanged;

(d) to do nothing at all. Shareholders may be protected from the consequences of their inaction because rights not taken up are sold on a shareholder's behalf by the company. The Stock Exchange rules state that if new securities are not taken up, they should be sold by the company to new subscribers for the benefit of the shareholders who were entitled to the rights. However, if the amount involved is small the shares can be sold or the benefit of the company. The shareholder (or the company) gets the difference between the issue price and the market price after the issue.

Unless a shareholder exercises all his rights, his proportion of the total equity of the company will decline.

Question 1

Gopher plc has issued 3,000,000 ordinary shares of £1 each, which are at present selling for £4 per share. The company plans to issue rights to purchase one new equity share at a price of £3.20 per share for every three shares held. A shareholder who owns 900 shares thinks that he will suffer a loss in his personal wealth because the new shares are being offered at a price lower than market value. On the assumption that the actual market value of shares will be equal to the theoretical ex rights price, what would be the effect on the shareholder's wealth if:

(a) he sells all the rights;
(b) he exercises half of the rights and sells the other half;
(c) he does nothing at all?

Answer

	£
Three shares 'cum rights' are worth (× £4)	12.00
One new share will raise	3.20
Four new shares will have a theoretical value of	15.20

The theoretical ex rights price is $\frac{£15.20}{4}$ = £3.80 per share

	£
Theoretical ex rights price	3.80
Price per new share	3.20
Value of rights per new share	0.60

The value of the rights attached to each existing share is $\frac{£0.60}{3}$ = £0.20.

We will assume that a shareholder is able to sell his rights for £0.20 per existing share held.

(a) If the shareholder sells all his rights:

	£
Sale value of rights (900 x £0.20)	180
Market value of his 900 shares, ex rights (x £3.80)	3,420
Total wealth	3,600
Total value of 900 shares cum rights (x £4)	£3,600

The shareholder would neither gain nor lose wealth. He would not be required to provide any additional funds to the company, but his shareholding as a proportion of the total equity of the company will be lower.

(b) If the shareholder exercises half of the rights (buys 450/3 = 150 shares at £3.20) and sells the other half:

	£
Sale value of rights (450 x £0.20)	90
Market value of his 1,050 shares, ex rights (x £3.80)	3,990
	4,080
Total value of 900 shares cum rights (x £4)	3,600
Additional investment (150 x £3.20)	480
	4,080

The shareholder would neither gain nor lose wealth, although he will have increased his investment in the company by £480.

(c) If the shareholder does nothing, but all other shareholders either exercise their rights or sell them, he would lose wealth as follows.

	£
Market value of 900 shares cum rights (x £4)	3,600
Market value of 900 shares ex rights (x £3.80)	3,420
Loss in wealth	180

It follows that the shareholder, to protect his existing investment, should either exercise his rights or sell them to another investor. If he does not exercise his rights, the new securities he was entitled to subscribe for might be sold for his benefit by the company, and this would protect him from losing wealth.

The actual market price after a rights issue

1.53 The actual market price of a share after a rights issue may differ from the theoretical ex rights price.

This will occur when the expected earnings yield from the new funds raised is different from the earnings yield from existing funds in the business. The market will take a view of how profitably the new funds will be invested, and will value the shares accordingly. An example will illustrate this point.

1.54 EXAMPLE: RIGHTS ISSUE (3)

Musk plc currently has 4,000,000 ordinary shares in issue, valued at £2 each, and the company has annual earnings equal to 20% of the market value of the shares. A one for four rights issue is proposed, at an issue price of £1.50. If the market continues to value the shares on a price/earnings ratio of 5, what would be the value per share if the new funds are expected to earn, as a percentage of the money raised:

(a) 15%?
(b) 20%?
(c) 25%?

How do these values in (a), (b) and (c) compare with the theoretical ex rights price? Ignore issue costs.

1.55 SOLUTION

The theoretical ex rights price will be calculated first.

	£
Four shares have a current value (× £2) of	8.00
One new share will be issued for	1.50
Five shares would have a theoretical value of	9.50

The theoretical ex rights price is $\frac{£9.50}{5} = £1.90$.

1.56 The new funds will raise 1,000,000 × £1.50 = £1,500,000.

Earnings as a % of money raised	*Additional earnings*	*Current earnings*	*Total earnings after the issue*
	£	£	£
15%	225,000	1,600,000	1,825,000
20%	300,000	1,600,000	1,900,000
25%	375,000	1,600,000	1,975,000

1.57 If the market values shares on a P/E ratio of 5, the total market value of equity and the market price per share would be as follows.

Total earnings	*Market value*	*Price per share (5,000,000 shares)*
£	£	£
1,825,000	9,125,000	1.825
1,900,000	9,500,000	1.900
1,975,000	9,875,000	1.975

1.58 (a) If the additional funds raised are expected to generate earnings at the same rate as existing funds, the actual market value will probably be the same as the theoretical ex rights price.

(b) If the new funds are expected to generate earnings at a lower rate, the market value will fall below the theoretical ex rights price. If this happens, shareholders will lose.

(c) If the new funds are expected to earn at a higher rate than current funds, the market value should be above the theoretical ex rights price. If this happens, shareholders will profit by taking up their rights.

1.59 The decision by individual shareholders as to whether they take up the offer will therefore depend on:

(a) the expected rate of return on the investment (and the risk associated with it);
(b) the return obtainable from other investments (allowing for the associated risk).

Rights issues or issuing shares for cash to new investors?

1.60 When shares are issued for cash to outside buyers, existing shareholders forfeit their **pre-emption rights** to shares.

1.61 Companies can issue shares for cash without obtaining prior approval from shareholders for each such share issue, provided that they have obtained approval from shareholders within the past 12 months to make new issues of shares for cash which are not rights issues. (This shareholder approval could be obtained at the company's AGM.)

1.62 Companies can thus issue shares for cash without having to bear the high costs of a rights issue, for example by placing shares for cash at a higher price than they might have been able to obtain from a rights issue.

Vendor placings

1.63 A vendor placing occurs when there is an issue of shares by one company to take over another, and these shares are then sold in a placing to raise cash for the shareholders in the target company, who are selling their shares in the takeover.

1.64 EXAMPLE: VENDOR PLACING

AB plc wants to take over Z Ltd. AB plc wants to finance the purchase by issuing more equity shares, and the shareholders of Z Ltd want to sell their shares for cash. AB plc can arrange a vendor placing whereby:

(a) AB plc issues new shares to finance the takeover;

(b) these shares are placed by AB plc's stockbrokers (market makers) with institutional investors, to raise cash;

(c) the cash that is raised is used to pay the shareholders in Z Ltd for their shares.

Other instances of issuing shares

1.65 There are some other methods of issuing shares on the Stock Exchange. These are as follows.

(a) An **open offer** is an offer to existing shareholders to subscribe for new shares in the company but, unlike a rights issue:

 (i) the offer is not necessarily *pro rata* to existing shareholdings;

 (ii) the offer is not allotted on renounceable documents. (With rights issues the offer to subscribe for new shares must be given on a renounceable letter, so that the shareholder can sell his rights if he so wishes).

(b) A **capitalisation issue** is a 'scrip issue' of shares which does not raise any new funds (see later in this chapter). It is made to 'capitalise' reserves of the company: in effect, to change some reserves into share capital. Shareholders receive new shares *pro rata* to their existing shareholdings.

(c) A **vendor consideration issue** is an issue of shares whereby one company acquires the shares of another in a takeover or merger. For example, if A plc wishes to take over B plc, A might make a 'paper' offer to B's shareholders, try to buy the shares of B by offering B's shareholders newly issued shares of A. This is now a common form of share issue, because mergers and takeovers are fairly frequent events.

(d) **Employee share option schemes** are schemes for awarding shares to employees. For example, in an employee share option scheme, a company awards its employees share options, which are rights to subscribe for new shares at a later date at a predetermined price (commonly, the market price of the shares when the options are awarded, or the market price less a discount). When and if the options are eventually exercised, the employees will receive the newly issued shares at a price that ought by then to be below the market price.

The timing and costs of new equity issues

1.66 New equity issues in general (offers for sale and placings as well as rights issues) will be more common when share prices are high than when share prices are low.

(a) When share price are high, investors' confidence will probably be high, and investors will be more willing to put money into companies with the potential for growth.

(b) By issuing shares at a high price, a company will reduce the number of shares it must issue to raise the amount of capital it wants. This will reduce the dilution of earnings for existing shareholders.

(c) Following on from (b), the company's total dividend commitment on the new shares, to meet shareholders' expectations, will be lower.

(d) If share prices are low, business confidence is likely to be low too. Companies may not want to raise capital for new investments until expectations begin to improve.

1.67 Typical **costs** of a share issue include:

(a) underwriting costs;

(b) the Stock Exchange listing fee (the initial charge) for the new securities;

(c) fees of the issuing house, solicitors' fees, auditors' fees, and fees of public relations consultants;

(d) charges for printing and distributing the prospectus;

(e) advertising, which must be done in national newspapers.

1.68 Costs vary according to whether equity or debt capital is being issued and whether the issue is a rights issue, an offer for sale or placing. With a placing, a full prospectus is not needed, advertising is cheaper and underwriting is not needed.

Some costs of flotation are variable (for example commission payable to an issuing house) but many costs are fixed (for example the costs of a prospectus, including professional fees, printing and advertising). The greater the amount of capital raised, the lower will be the costs of flotation as a percentage of the funds raised, because fixed costs are spread more thinly. High fixed costs help to explain why small companies have found it difficult and often undesirable to raise new funds through the Stock Exchange.

2 SCRIP DIVIDENDS, SCRIP ISSUES AND STOCK SPLITS 12/94

2.1 Scrip dividends, scrip issues and stock splits are not methods of raising new equity funds, but they *are* methods of:

(a) altering the share capital structure of a company;

(b) in the case of scrip dividends and scrip issues, increasing the issued share capital of the company.

Scrip dividends

2.2 A **scrip dividend** is a dividend payment which takes the form of new shares instead of cash. Effectively, it converts profit and loss reserves into issued share capital. When the directors of a company would prefer to retain funds within the business but consider that they must pay at least a certain amount of dividend, they might offer equity shareholders the choice of:

(a) a cash dividend;
(b) a scrip dividend.

Each shareholder would decide separately which to take. There is no need for all shareholders to agree on whether to have a cash dividend or a scrip dividend.

2.3 Scrip dividends have the advantage that no advance corporate tax (ACT) is payable on dividends issued in shares as there is for cash dividends.

2.4 Recently (particularly since 1993) **enhanced scrip dividends** have been offered by a number of companies. With enhanced scrip dividends, the value of the shares offered is much greater than the cash alternative, giving investors an incentive to choose the shares.

Case example

BAT Industries plc (BAT) was the first company to offer an enhanced scrip dividend, offering a share alternative worth 50 per cent more than the cash dividend. The reduced cash dividend enabled BAT to retain funds within the business for the future benefit of shareholders and reduced payments of ACT to the government. Companies such as BAT, which earn most of their profits overseas, typically have a mainstream corporation tax liability which is insufficient to offset all of their ACT payment on cash dividends.

Scrip issues

2.5 A **scrip issue** (or **bonus issue**) is an issue of new shares to existing shareholders, by converting equity reserves into issued share capital. For example, if a company with issued share capital of 100,000 ordinary shares of £1 each made a one for five scrip issue, 20,000 new shares would be issued to existing shareholders, one new share for every five old shares held. Issued share capital would be increased by £20,000, and reserves (probably share premium account, if there is one) reduced by this amount.

2.6 By creating more shares in this way, a scrip issue does not raise new funds, but does have the advantage of making shares cheaper and therefore (perhaps) more easily marketable on the Stock Exchange. For example, if a company's shares are priced at £6 on the Stock Exchange, and the company makes a one for two scrip issue, we should expect the share price after the issue to fall to £4 each. Shares at £4 each might be more easily marketable than shares at £6 each.

Stock splits

2.7 This advantage of a scrip issue is also the reason for a **stock split**. A stock split occurs where, for example, each ordinary share of £1 each is split into two shares of 50p each, thus creating cheaper shares with greater marketability. There is possibly an added psychological advantage, in that investors should expect a company which splits its shares in this way to be planning for substantial earnings growth and dividend growth in the future. As a consequence, the market price of shares may benefit. For example, if one existing share of £1 has a market value of £6, and is then split into two shares of 50p each, the market value of the new shares might settle at, say, £3.10 instead of the expected £3, in anticipation of strong future growth in earnings and dividends.

2.8 The difference between a stock split and a scrip issue is that a scrip issue converts equity reserves into share capital, whereas a stock split leaves reserves unaffected. Both are popular with investors as they are seen as likely to lead to increased dividends. Scrip dividends can, however, lead to tax complications for individual investors.

3 VENTURE CAPITAL 12/95

Sources of capital for smaller companies

Exam focus point

The new FM examiner for Paper 8 has stressed that issues of funding for small and growing firms will be given equal importance to those facing larger concerns.

3.1 Compared to large companies, small companies have much more difficulty in obtaining funds. Smaller companies are perceived as being more risky, and investors either refuse to invest or expect a higher return on their investment, which the borrowing firm must then be able to pay.

3.2 Small and unquoted companies do not have ready access to new long-term funds, except for:

(a) retained earnings;
(b) perhaps, extra finance obtained by issuing more shares to private shareholders;
(c) some bank borrowing.

So how are small companies to overcome financial restrictions and achieve a good rate of growth?

3.3 The problems of finance for small businesses have received much publicity in recent years, and some efforts have been made to provide them with access to sources of funds. Most of these sources are referred to as 'venture capital'.

What is venture capital?

3.4 A businessperson starting up a new business will invest **venture capital** of his own, but he will probably need additional funding from a source other than his own pocket. The term 'venture capital' is generally more specifically associated with putting money, usually in return for an equity stake, into a new business, a management buy-out or a major expansion scheme.

KEY TERM

Venture capital: risk capital, normally lent in return for an equity stake.

3.5 The institution that puts in the money recognises the gamble inherent in the funding. There is a serious risk of losing the entire investment, and it might take a long time before any profits and returns materialise. But there is also the prospect of very high profits and a substantial return on the investment. A venture capitalist will require a high expected rate of return on investments, to compensate for the high risk.

3.6 A venture capital organisation will not want to retain its investment in a business indefinitely, and when it considers putting money into a business venture, it will also consider its 'exit', that is how it will be able to pull out of the business eventually (after five to seven years, say) and realise its profits.

With the development of the Unlisted Securities Market and more recently its replacement the Alternative Investment Market as 'second-tier' share markets, obtaining a second-tier quotation for the company's shares has become an attractive exit because the venture capitalists can sell their shares at the market price and so pull out of the company.

Venture capital organisations

3.7 Venture capital organisations have been operating for many years. There are now quite a large number of such organisations. The British Venture Capital Association is a regulatory body for all the institutions that have joined it as members.

3.8 Examples of venture capital organisations are:

(a) Investors in Industry plc (the 3i group);
(b) Equity Capital for Industry;
(c) venture capital subsidiaries of the clearing banks.

The 3i group

3.9 Investors in Industry plc, or the 3i group as it is more commonly known, is the biggest and oldest of the venture capital organisations. It is involved in many venture capital schemes. The 3i group was owned by the clearing banks and the Bank of England until its flotation on the stock market during 1994.

3.10 Like other venture capitalists, the 3i group will only invest in a company if there is a reasonable chance that the company will be successful. The group's publicity material states that successful investments have three common characteristics.

(a) There is a good basic idea, a product or service which meets real customer needs.

(b) There is finance, in the right form to turn the idea into a solid business.

(c) There is the commitment and drive of an individual or group, the determination to succeed.

3.11 The types of venture that the 3i group might invest in include the following.

(a) **Business start-ups**. When a business has been set up by someone who has already put time and money into getting it started, the group may be willing to provide finance to enable it to get off the ground. With start-ups, the 3i group often prefers to be one of several financial institutions putting in venture capital.

(b) **Business development**. The group may be willing to provide development capital for a company which wants to invest in new products or new markets or to make a business acquisition, and so which needs a major capital injection.

(c) **Management buyouts**. A management buyout is the purchase of all or parts of a business from its owners by its managers.

(d) Helping a company where one of its owners wants to **realise all or part of his investment**. The 3i group may be prepared to buy some of the company's equity.

Venture capital funds

3.12 Some other organisations are engaged in the creation of **venture capital funds**, whereby the organisation:

(a) raises venture capital funds from investors;
(b) invests in management buyouts or expanding companies.

3.13 The venture capital fund managers usually reward themselves by taking a percentage of the portfolio of the fund's investments.

3.14 As mentioned earlier, in 1993, a new form of venture capital investment trust whose investors would enjoy special tax reliefs (venture capital trusts or VCTs) was introduced.

The clearing banks and venture capital

3.15 In one sense, the clearing banks have been venture capitalists for many years, providing loans and overdrafts to small companies, often without security. However, an overdraft or loan is not venture capital, in the sense that the bank does not take an equity stake in the business. Even so, virtually all businesses, old, new, small and large, rely to some extent on financial assistance from their bank. The banks also provide venture capital in return for an equity stake through their venture capital subsidiaries.

Finding venture capital

3.16 When a company's directors look for help from a venture capital institution, they must recognise that:

(a) the institution will want an equity stake in the company;

(b) it will need convincing that the company can be successful (management buyouts of companies which already have a record of successful trading have been increasingly favoured by venture capitalists in recent years);

(c) it may want to have a representative appointed to the company's board, to look after its interests.

3.17 The directors of the company must then contact venture capital organisations, to try to find one or more which would be willing to offer finance. A venture capital organisation will only give funds to a company that it believes can succeed, and before it will make any definite offer, it will want from the company's management:

(a) a business plan;

(b) details of how much finance is needed and how it would be used;

(c) the most recent trading figures of the company, a balance sheet, a cash flow forecast and a profit forecast;

(d) details of the management team, with evidence of a wide range of management skills;

(e) details of major shareholders;

(f) details of the company's current banking arrangements and any other sources of finance;

(g) any sales literature or publicity material that the company has issued.

A survey has indicated that around 75% of requests for venture capital are rejected on an initial screening, and only about 3% of all requests survive both this screening and further investigation and result in actual investments.

4 STOCK MARKET RATIOS 6/95

4.1 A company will only be able to raise finance if investors think that the returns they can expect are satisfactory in view of the risks they are taking. We must therefore consider how investors appraise companies. We will concentrate on quoted companies.

4.2 Information that is relevant to market prices and returns is available from published stock market information, and in particular from certain **stock market ratios**. The main stock market ratios are:

- the dividend yield / Interest yield
- earnings per share
- the price/earnings ratio
- the dividend cover
- the earnings yield

The dividend yield

4.3 The **dividend yield** is given by $\frac{\text{Gross dividend per share}}{\text{Market price per share}} \times 100\%$

The gross dividend is the dividend paid plus the appropriate tax credit. The gross dividend yield is used in preference to a net dividend yield, so that investors can make a direct comparison with (gross) interest yields from loan stock and gilts.

4.4 EXAMPLE: DIVIDEND YIELD

A company pays a dividend of 15p (net) per share. The market price is 240p. What is the dividend yield if the rate of tax credit and ACT is 20%?

Gross dividend per share $= 15\text{p} \times \frac{100}{(100-20)} = 18.75\text{p}$

Dividend yield $= \frac{18.75\text{p}}{240\text{p}} \times 100\% = 7.8125\%$

Interest yield

4.5 Interest yield $= \frac{\text{Gross interest}}{\text{Market value of loan stock}} \times 100\%$

4.6 EXAMPLE: INTEREST YIELD

An investment buys £1,000 (nominal value) of a bond with a coupon of 8% for the current market value of £750.

Interest yield $= \frac{1{,}000 \times 8\%}{750} \times 100\%$

$= 10.67\%$

Exam focus point

Note carefully that the interest yield, which is the investor's rate of return, is different from the coupon rate of 8%. Many students confuse these in their exam answers.

Dividend yield and interest yield

4.7 In practice, we usually find with quoted companies that:

(a) the dividend yield on shares is less than the interest yield on debentures and loan stock (and also less than the yield paid on gilt-edged securities);

(b) the share price often rises each year, giving shareholders capital gains.

In the long run, shareholders will want the return on their shares, in terms of dividends received plus capital gains, to exceed the return that investors get from fixed interest securities.

Earnings per share (EPS) 6/96, 12/96

4.8 **Earnings per share (EPS)** is widely used as a measure of a company's performance and is of particular importance in comparing results over a period of several years. A company must be able to sustain its earnings in order to pay dividends and re-invest in the business so as to achieve future growth. Investors also look for *growth* in the EPS from one year to the next.

4.9 EPS is defined (in Financial Reporting Standard 3) as the profit in pence attributable to each equity (ordinary) share, based on:

(a) the profit (or in the case of a group the consolidated profit) of the period after tax, minority interests and extraordinary items*, and after deducting preference dividends;

(b) divided by the number of equity shares in issue and ranking for dividend.

* Extraordinary items have effectively been outlawed by FRS3.

Question 2

Walter Wall Carpets plc made profits before tax in 19X8 of £9,320,000. Tax amounted to £2,800,000.

The company's share capital is as follows.

	£
Ordinary shares (10,000,000 shares of £1)	10,000,000
8% preference shares	2,000,000
	12,000,000

Calculate the EPS for 19X8.

Answer

	£
Profits before tax	9,320,000
Less tax	2,800,000
Profits after tax	6,520,000
Less preference dividend (8% of £2,000,000)	160,000
Earnings	6,360,000
Number of ordinary shares	10,000,000
EPS	63.6p

4.10 EPS on its own does not tell us anything. It must be seen in the context of several other matters.

(a) EPS is used for the comparing results of a company over time. Is its EPS growing? What is the rate of growth? Is the rate of growth increasing or decreasing?

(b) Is there likely to be a significant dilution of EPS in the future, perhaps due to the exercise of share options or warrants, or the conversion of convertible loan stock into equity?

(c) EPS should not be used blindly to compare the earnings of one company with another. For example, if A plc has an EPS of 12p for its 10,000,000 10p shares and B plc has an EPS of 24p for its 50,000,000 25p shares, we must take account of the numbers of shares. When earnings are used to compare one company's shares with another, this is done using the P/E ratio or perhaps the earnings yield.

(d) If EPS is to be a reliable basis for comparing results, it must be calculated consistently. The EPS of one company must be directly comparable with the EPS of others, and the EPS of a company in one year must be directly comparable with its published EPS figures for previous years. Changes in the share capital of a company during the course of a year cause problems of comparability.

4.11 Note that:

(a) EPS is a figure based on past data; and

(b) it is easily manipulated by changes in accounting policies and by mergers or acquisitions.

The use of the measure in calculating management bonuses makes it particularly liable to manipulation. The attention given to EPS as a performance measure by City analysts is arguably disproportionate to its true worth. Investors should be more concerned with future earnings, but of course estimates of these are more difficult to reach than the readily available figure.

4.12 A **fully diluted EPS** (FDEPS) can be measured where the company has issued securities that might be converted into ordinary shares at some future date, such as convertible loan stock, share warrants or share options.

4.13 The FDEPS measures a hypothetical EPS, based on earnings in the period under review, if the company's ordinary shares were increased to their maximum number by the exercise of all existing share options and warrants, and the conversion of existing convertible loan stock etc. The FDEPS gives investors an appreciation of by how much EPS might be affected if and when the options, warrants or conversion rights are exercised.

4.14 Total earnings are increased by:

(a) the savings in interest (net of tax) from the conversion of loan stock into shares;

(b) in the case of share options or warrants, the addition to profits (net of tax) from investing the cash obtained from their exercise (estimated on the assumption that the cash is invested in $2^1/_2$% Consolidated Stock at their market price on the first) day of the period).

$$\text{FDEPS} = \frac{\text{Adjusted earnings}}{\text{Maximum number of ordinary shares}}$$

4.15 EXAMPLE: FULLY DILUTED EARNING PER SHARE

Suppose that Walter Wall Carpets plc (see Question 2 above) has in issue £4,000,000 8% convertible unsecured loan stock, convertible in three years' time, with a conversion ratio of 5 shares per £100 of loan stock. The company pays tax at 33%. What is the fully diluted EPS?

4.16 SOLUTION

Undiluted EPS is 63.6 pence, as shown in Question 2.

If all holders of the convertible stock convert their holding to ordinary shares, an additional 200,000 (= 4,000,000/100 × 5) shares will be issued in three years' time.

The interest saving on conversion is:

£4,000,000 × 8% × 0.67 = £214,400.

Therefore:

$$\text{FDEPS} = \frac{6{,}360{,}000 + 214{,}400}{10{,}000{,}000 + 200{,}000}$$

$$= \frac{6{,}574{,}400}{10{,}200{,}000} = 64.5 \text{ pence}$$

The price earnings ratio

4.17 The **price earnings (P/E) ratio** is the most important yardstick for assessing the relative worth of a share. It is:

$$\frac{\text{Market price of share in pence}}{\text{EPS in pence on the net basis}}$$

This is the same as:

$$\frac{\text{Total market value of equity}}{\text{Total earnings on the net basis}}$$

The 'net basis' means that account is taken of the ACT effects of any dividend payments.

4.18 The value of the P/E ratio reflects the market's appraisal of the share's future prospects. In other words, if one company has a higher P/E ratio than another it is because investors either expect its earnings to increase faster than the other's or consider that it is a less risky company or in a more secure industry.

4.19 The P/E ratio is, simply, a measure of the relationship between the market value of a company's shares and the earnings from those shares. It is an important ratio because it relates two key considerations for investors, the market price of a share and its earnings capacity. It is significant only as a measure of this relationship between earnings and value.

4.20 EXAMPLE: PRICE EARNINGS RATIO

A company has recently declared a dividend of 12p per share. The share price is £3.72 cum div and earnings for the most recent year were 30p per share. Calculate the P/E ratio.

4.21 SOLUTION

$$\text{P/E ratio} = \frac{\text{MV ex div}}{\text{EPS}} = \frac{£3.60}{30\text{p}} = 12$$

Changes in EPS: the P/E ratio and the share price

4.22 The dividend valuation model or fundamental theory of share values is the theory that share prices are related to expected future dividends on the shares.

4.23 Another approach to assessing what share prices ought to be, which is often used in practice, is a P/E ratio approach. It is a commonsense approach to share price assessment (although not as well founded in theory as the dividend valuation model), which is that:

(a) the relationship between the EPS and the share price is measured by the P/E ratio;

(b) there is no reason to suppose, in normal circumstances, that the P/E ratio will vary much over time;

(c) so if the EPS goes up or down, the share price should be expected to move up or down too, and the new share price will be the new EPS multiplied by the constant P/E ratio.

4.24 For example, if a company had an EPS last year of 30p and a share price of £3.60, its P/E ratio would have been 12. If the current year's EPS is 33p, we might expect that the P/E ratio would remain the same, 12, and so the share price ought to go up to 12 × 33p = £3.96.

4.25 EXAMPLE: EFFECTS OF A RIGHTS ISSUE

Annette Cord Sports Goods plc has 6,000,000 ordinary shares in issue, and the company has been making regular annual profits after tax of £3,000,000 for some years. The share price is £5.

A proposal has been made to issue 2,000,000 new shares in a rights issue, at an issue price of £4.50 per share. The funds would be used to redeem £9,000,000 of 12% debenture stock.

The rate of corporation tax is 31%.

What would be the predicted effect of the rights issue on the share price, and would you recommend that the issue should take place?

4.26 SOLUTION

If the stock market shows semi-strong form efficiency, the share price will change on announcement of the rights issue, in anticipation of the change in EPS. The current EPS is 50p per share, and so the current P/E ratio is 10.

	£	£
Current annual earnings		3,000,000
Increase in earnings after rights issue		
Interest saved (12% × £9,000,000)	1,080,000	
Less tax on extra profits (31%)	334,800	
		745,200
Anticipated annual earnings		3,745,200
Number of shares (6,000,000 + 2,000,000)		8,000,000
EPS		46.8 pence
Current P/E ratio		10

The anticipated P/E ratio is assumed to be the same.

Anticipated share price	468 pence

The proposed share issue is a one for three rights issue, and we can estimate the theoretical ex rights price.

	£
Current value of three shares (× £5)	15.00
Rights issue price of one share	4.50
Theoretical value of four shares	19.50

Theoretical ex rights price $\frac{£19.50}{4} = £4.875$

4.27 The anticipated share price after redeeming the debentures would be 468 pence per share, which is less than the theoretical ex rights price. If the rights issue goes ahead and the P/E ratio remains at 10, shareholders should expect a fall in share price below the theoretical ex rights price, which indicates that there would be a capital loss on their investment. The rights issue is for this reason not recommended.

Changes in the P/E ratio over time

4.28 Changes in the P/E ratios of companies over time will depend on several factors.

(a) If interest rates go up, investors will be attracted away from shares and into debt capital. Share prices will fall, and so P/E ratios will fall. Similarly, if interest rates go down, shares will become relatively more attractive to invest in, so share prices and P/E ratios will go up.

(b) If prospects for company profits improve, share prices will go up, and P/E ratios will rise. Share prices depend on expectations of future earnings, not historical earnings, and so a change in prospects, perhaps caused by a substantial rise in international trade, or an economic recession, will affect prices and P/E ratios.

(c) Investors' confidence might be changed by a variety of circumstances, such as:

(i) the prospect of a change in government;
(ii) the prospects for greater exchange rate stability between currencies.

Dividend cover 12/97

4.29 The **dividend cover** is the number of times the actual dividend could be paid out of current profits. The dividend cover is equal to:

$$\frac{\text{Maximum possible equity dividend that could be paid out of current profits}}{\text{Actual dividend for ordinary shareholders}}$$

The figures for the maximum dividend and the actual dividend may be either:

(a) both gross; or
(b) both net.

4.30 The dividend cover indicates:

(a) the proportion of distributable profits for the year that is being retained by the company; and

(b) the level of risk that the company will not be able to maintain the same dividend payments in future years, should earnings fall.

A high dividend cover means that a high proportion of profits are being retained, which might indicate that the company is investing to achieve earnings growth in the future.

Dividend payout ratio

4.31 The **dividend payout ratio** is closely related to the dividend cover, as it calculates the percentage of post-tax earnings that are distributed as dividends.

4.32 EXAMPLE: DIVIDEND COVER AND DIVIDEND PAYOUT RATIO

The EPS of York plc is 20p. The dividend was 20% on the 25p ordinary shares. Calculate the dividend cover.

4.33 SOLUTION

$$\text{Dividend cover} = \frac{20\text{p}}{20\% \text{ of } 25\text{p}} = 4$$

A dividend cover of 4 means that the company is retaining 75% of its earnings for reinvestment.

The dividend payout ratio is 25%.

The earnings yield

4.34 The most common definition of the **earnings yield** currently used is:

$$\frac{\text{Grossed up equivalent of EPS calculated on the net basis}}{\text{Market price per share}} \times 100\%$$

The earnings are grossed up to put the earnings yield on the same basis as the dividend yield. 'Net basis' means that earnings are calculated by deducting the **actual** taxation charge, as required by SSAP 3.

4.35 EXAMPLE: EARNINGS YIELD

The EPS of Cumbria plc calculated on the net basis is 25p and the market price per ordinary share is 200p. Calculate the earnings yield assuming that the lower rate of income tax is 20%.

4.36 SOLUTION

$$\text{Earnings yield} = \frac{25 \times 100/80}{200} \times 100\% = 15.625\%$$

5 DIVIDEND POLICY 12/97

5.1 For any company, the amount of earnings retained within the business has a direct impact on the amount of dividends. Profit re-invested as retained earnings is profit that could have been paid as a **dividend**.

5.2 The major **reasons for using retained earnings** to finance new investments, rather than to pay higher dividends and then raise new equity funds for the new investments, are as follows.

(a) The management of many companies believe that retained earnings are funds which do not cost anything, although this is not true. However, it is true that the use of retained earnings as a source of funds does not lead to a payment of cash.

(b) The dividend policy of a company is in practice determined by the directors. From their standpoint, retained earnings are an attractive source of finance because investment projects can be undertaken without involving either the shareholders or any outsiders.

(c) The use of retained earnings as opposed to new shares or debentures avoids issue costs.

(d) The use of retained earnings avoids the possibility of a change in control resulting from an issue of new shares.

5.3 Another factor that may be of importance is the financial and taxation position of the company's shareholders. If, for example, because of taxation considerations, they would rather make a capital profit (which will only be taxed when the shares are sold) than receive current income, then finance through retained earnings would be preferred to other methods.

5.4 A company must restrict its self-financing through retained profits because shareholders should be paid a reasonable dividend, in line with realistic expectations, even if the directors would rather keep the funds for re-investing. At the same time, a company that is looking for extra funds will not be expected by investors (such as banks) to pay generous dividends, nor over-generous salaries to owner-directors.

Signalling effects

5.5 The signalling effect of a company's dividend policy may be used by the management of a company which faces a possible takeover. The dividend level might be increased as a defence against the takeover: investors may take the increased dividend as a signal of improved future prospects, thus driving the share price higher and making the company more expensive for a potential bidder to take over.

5.6 Investors usually expect a consistent dividend policy from the company, with stable dividends each year or, even better, steady dividend growth. A large rise or fall in dividends in any year can have a marked effect on the company's share price. Stable dividends or steady dividend growth are usually needed for share price stability. A cut in dividends may be treated by investors as signalling that the future prospects of the company are weak.

5.7 Thus, the dividend which is paid acts, possibly without justification, as a signal of the future prospects of the company and such a signal can influence the share price.

Dividends and market values

5.8 What affects the market value of a company's shares? It seems reasonable to suppose that share values will depend upon:

(a) the amount in dividends that a company pays;
(b) the rate of growth of dividends;
(c) the rate of return which shareholders require.

5.9 The purpose of a company's dividend policy should be to maximise shareholders' wealth, which depends on both current dividends and capital gains. Capital gains can be achieved by retaining some earnings for reinvestment and dividend growth in the future.

5.10 The rate of growth in dividends is sometimes expressed, theoretically, as:

$$g = bR$$

where g is the annual growth rate in dividends
R is the proportion of profits that are retained
b is the rate of return on new investments.

5.11 EXAMPLE: DIVIDEND GROWTH

(a) If a company has a payout ratio of 40%, and retains the rest for investing in projects which yield 15%, the annual rate of growth in dividends could be estimated as 15% × 60% = 9%.

(b) If a company pays out 80% of its profits as dividends, and retains the rest for reinvestment at 15%, the current dividend would be twice as big as in (a), but annual dividend growth would be only 15% × 20% = 3%.

An approach to dividend and retentions policy

5.12 A well established theory of share values is that an equilibrium price for any share (or bond) on a stock market is:

(a) the future expected stream of income from the security
(b) discounted at a suitable cost of capital.

Equilibrium market price is thus a present value of a future expected income stream.

5.13 The annual income stream for a share is the expected dividend every year in perpetuity. Even if an investor expects to *sell* his shares at some time in the future, the price he will get is the present value of the expected future dividend stream in perpetuity, and so (assuming insignificant transaction costs) we can ignore expected capital gains on share sales, and use dividend streams to value shares.

5.14 The basic dividend-based formula for the market value of shares is expressed in the dividend valuation model as follows:

$$\text{MV (ex div)} = \frac{D}{1+r} + \frac{D}{(1+r)^2} + \frac{D}{(1+r)^3} + \ldots = \frac{D}{r}$$

where P_0 is the ex dividend market value of the shares, D is a constant annual dividend, and r is the shareholders' required rate of return. This formula assumes a constant dividend, and no dividend growth at all, so an assumption on which this formula is based is that all earnings are paid out as dividends.

5.15 Using the dividend growth model, we have:

$$P_0 = \frac{D_0(1+g)}{(1+r)} + \frac{D_0(1+g)^2}{(1+r)} + \ldots = \frac{D_0(1+g)}{(r-g)}$$

where D_0 is the current year's dividend (year 0) and g is the growth rate in earnings and dividends, so $D_0(1 + g)$ is the expected dividend in one year's time; and P_0 is the market value excluding any dividend currently payable.

5.16 EXAMPLE: DIVIDEND GROWTH MODEL

Tantrum plc has achieved earnings of £800,000 this year. The company intends to pursue a policy of financing all its investment opportunities out of retained earnings. There are considerable investment opportunities, which are expected to be available indefinitely. However, if Tantrum plc does not exploit any of the available opportunities, its annual earnings will remain at £800,000 in perpetuity. The following figures are available.

Proportion of earnings retained	*Growth rate in earnings*	*Required return on all investments by shareholders*
%	%	%
0	0	14
25	5	15
40	7	16

The rate of return required by shareholders would rise if earnings are retained, because of the risk associated with the new investments.

What is the optimum retentions policy for Tantrum plc? The full dividend payment for this year will be paid in the near future in any case.

5.17 SOLUTION

Since $P_0 \text{ (MV ex div)} = \dfrac{D(1+g)}{(r-g)}$

$$\text{MV cum div} = \frac{D(1+g)}{(r-g)} + D$$

We are trying to maximise the value of shareholder wealth, which is currently represented by the cum div market value, since a dividend will soon be paid.

(a) If retentions are 0%:

$$\text{MV cum div} = \frac{800{,}000}{0.14} + 800{,}000$$

$$= £6{,}514{,}286$$

(b) If retentions are 25%, the current dividend will be £600,000 and:

$$\text{MV cum div} = \frac{600{,}000(1.05)}{(0.15-0.05)} + 600{,}000$$

$$= £6{,}900{,}000$$

(c) If retentions are 40%, the current dividend will be £480,000 and:

$$\text{MV cum div} = \frac{480{,}000(1.07)}{(0.16-0.07)} + 480{,}000$$

$$= £6{,}186{,}667$$

The best policy (out of the three for which figures are provided) would be to retain 25% of earnings.

Dividend policy and shareholders' personal taxation

5.18 The market value of a share has been defined as the sum of all future dividends, discounted at the shareholder's marginal cost of capital. When constant dividends are expected, we have:

$$P_0 = \frac{D}{r}$$

5.19 The cost of capital is generally taken to be a tax-free rate, ignoring the actual rates of personal taxation paid on dividends by different shareholders. To each individual shareholder, however, the dividends are subject to income tax at a rate which depends on his own tax position, and it is possible to re-define his valuation of a share as:

$$P_0 = \frac{D_g(1-t)}{r_t}$$

where D_g = gross dividend (assumed to be constant each year)
t = rate of personal tax on the dividend
r_t = the shareholder's after tax marginal cost of capital

5.20 Presumably, a company should choose between dividend payout and earnings retention so as to maximise the wealth of its shareholders; however, if not all shareholders have the same tax rates and after tax cost of capital, there might not be an optimum policy which satisfies all shareholders.

5.21 A further problem occurs when income from dividends might be taxed either more or less heavily than capital gains. In the UK, individuals have an annual capital gains exemption which is not available against income, and companies are taxed on capital gains but not on dividend income.

Since the purpose of a dividend policy should be to maximise the wealth of shareholders, it is important to consider whether it would be better to pay a dividend now, subject to tax on income, or to retain earnings so as to increase the shareholders' capital gains (which will be subject to capital gains tax when the shareholders eventually sell their shares).

A practical approach to dividends

5.22 So far, we have concentrated on a theoretical approach to establishing an optimal dividend and retentions policy. A practical approach to dividends and retentions should take the following extra factors into consideration.

(a) The need to remain profitable. Dividends are paid out of profits, and an unprofitable company cannot for ever go on paying dividends out of retained profits made in the past.

(b) The law on distributable profits.

(c) Any dividend restraints which might be imposed by loan agreements.

(d) The effect of inflation, and the need to retain some profit within the business just to maintain its operating capability unchanged.

(e) The company's gearing level. If the company wants extra finance, the sources of funds used should strike a balance between equity and debt finance. Cash from retained earnings is the most readily available source of growth in equity finance.

(f) The company's liquidity position. Dividends are a cash payment, and a company must have enough cash to pay the dividends it declares.

(g) Investors usually expect a consistent dividend policy from the company, with stable dividends each year or, even better, steady dividend growth.

(h) A large rise or fall in dividends in any year will have a marked effect on the company's share price. Stable dividends or steady dividend growth are usually needed for share price stability.

(i) The ease with which the company could raise extra finance from sources other than cash from retained earnings. Small companies which find it hard to raise finance might have to rely more heavily on cash generated from retained earnings than large companies.

(j) If a company wants extra finance to invest, cash might be generated through retention of earnings can be obtained without incurring transaction costs. Costs of raising new share capital can be high, and even bank borrowings can be quite expensive.

5.23 In practical terms, it is unclear how far dividends play a predominant role in determining share values. At some times, dividends seem to be more important to the market, while at other times, earning figures seem to become predominant. The subject remains controversial. A proposition put forward by Modigliani and Miller, whose work is studied in ACCA Paper 14 *Financial Strategy*, is that under certain assumptions, the policy on dividends is irrelevant in determining the share price.

Question 3

Ochre plc is a company that is still managed by the two individuals who set it up 12 years ago. In the current year, the company acquired plc status and was launched on the Alternative Investment Market (AIM). Previously, all of the shares had been owned by its two founders and certain employees. Now, 40% of the shares are in the hands of the investing public.

The company's profit growth and dividend policy are set out below. Will a continuation of the same dividend policy as in the past be suitable now that the company is quoted on the AIM?

	Profits	*Dividend*	*Shares in issue*
	£'000	£'000	
4 years ago	176	88	800,000
3 years ago	200	104	800,000
2 years ago	240	120	1,000,000
1 year ago	290	150	1,000,000
Current year	444	222 (proposed)	1,500,000

Answer

	Dividend per share	*Dividend as % of profit*
	p	
4 years ago	11.0	50%
3 years ago	13.0	52%
2 years ago	12.0	50%
1 year ago	15.0	52%
Current year	14.8	50%

The company appears to have pursued a dividend policy of paying out half of after-tax profits in dividend.

This policy is only suitable when a company achieves a stable EPS or steady EPS growth. Investors do not like a fall in dividend from one year to the next, and the fall in dividend per share in the current year is likely to be unpopular, and to result in a fall in the share price.

The company would probably serve its shareholders better by paying a dividend of at least 15p per share, possibly more, in the current year, even though the dividend as a percentage of profit would then be higher.

Exam focus point

Take care not to write in the exam that new investment can be financed by reserves or retained earnings. It is the cash generated from retention of earnings which can be used for financing purposes.

Chapter roundup

- A company can obtain a **stock market listing** for its shares through an offer for sale, a prospectus issue, a placing or an introduction.
- **Venture capital** is available to risky enterprises, usually in return for an equity stake. The venture capital company will often put a director on the board.
- A **rights issue** is an offer to existing shareholders for them to buy more shares, usually at lower than the current share price.
- **Scrip dividend schemes** involve shareholders being issued with new shares in lieu of a cash dividend.
- **Bonus** or **scrip issues**, and **stock splits**, are ways of increasing the *number* of shares without raising any extra capital.
- Indicator such as **dividend yield**, **EPS**, **PE ratio** and **dividend cover** can be used to assess investor returns.
- The **dividend valuation model** can be applied with or without dividend growth. The model assumes that a stock market value depends upon the future flow of dividends which can be expected.
- Practical considerations of **dividend policy** suggest that both **dividends** and **earnings** may be important in determining share price.

Quick quiz

1 What is an offer for sale? (see para 1.13)
2 What is a placing? (1.26)
3 What factors should be taken into account when setting the price of shares for launching a company on to the stock market? (1.32)
4 What courses of action are open to a shareholder when there is a rights issue of shares? (1.52)
5 What are the costs of an issue of shares on the stock market? (1.67)
6 How does a stock split differ from a scrip issue? (2.8)
7 What is venture capital? (3.4)
8 How is dividend yield calculated? (4.3)
9 How might EPS be used to judge the returns that a company is making for its equity investors? (4.10)
10 What is the P/E ratio? (4.17) Why is it significant? (4.18, 4.19)
11 What is the dividend cover? (4.29) What does it indicate? (4.30)
12 What factors should be taken into consideration in a practical approach to dividend policy? (5.22)

Question to try	Level	Marks	Time
23	Examination	20	36 mins

Chapter 23

LONG-TERM FINANCE II

Chapter topic list		Syllabus reference
1	Preference shares	7(a)(ii)
2	Loan stock	7(a)(ii)
3	Convertibles and warrants	7(a)(ii)

Introduction

In this chapter, we continue with the coverage of the sources of long-term finance begun in Chapter 22, looking first at **preference shares** and **long-term debt** and then at **convertibles** and **warrants**.

When sources of **long-term finance** are used, large sums are usually involved, and so the financial manager needs to consider all the options available with care, looking to the possible effects on the company in the long term.

1 PREFERENCE SHARES

KEY TERM

Preference shares are shares which have a fixed percentage dividend, payable in priority to any dividend paid to the ordinary shareholders.

1.1 As with ordinary shares a preference dividend can only be paid if sufficient distributable profits are available, although with cumulative preference shares the right to an unpaid dividend is carried forward to later years. The arrears of dividend on cumulative preference shares must be paid before any dividend is paid to the ordinary shareholders.

1.2 The stated dividend (such as 7%) on preference shares is the cash dividend, not grossed up.

Why issue preference shares?

1.3 From the company's point of view, preference shares have some positive features.

(a) Dividends do not have to be paid in a year in which profits are poor, while this is not the case with interest payments on long-term debt (loans or debentures).

(b) Since they do not carry voting rights, preference shares avoid diluting the control of existing shareholders while an issue of equity shares would not.

(c) Unless they are redeemable, issuing preference shares will lower the company's gearing. Redeemable preference shares are normally treated as debt when gearing is calculated.

(d) The issue of preference shares does not restrict the company's borrowing power, at least in the sense that preference share capital is not secured against assets of the business.

(e) The non-payment of dividend does not give the preference shareholders the right to appoint a receiver, a right which is normally given to debenture holders.

1.4 However, dividend payments on preference shares are not tax deductible in the way that interest payments on debt are. Furthermore, for preference shares to be attractive to investors, the level of payment needs to be higher than for interest on debt to compensate for the additional risks.

1.5 From the point of view of the investor, preference shares are less attractive than loan stock because:

(a) they cannot be secured on the company's assets;

(b) the dividend yield traditionally offered on preference dividends has been much too low to provide an attractive investment compared with the interest yields on loan stock in view of the additional risk involved.

In recent years preference shares have formed a very small proportion only of new capital issues.

2 LOAN STOCK 12/96

KEY TERM

Loan stock is long-term debt capital raised by a company for which interest is paid, usually half yearly and at a fixed rate. Holders of loan stock are therefore long-term creditors of the company.

2.1 Loan stock has a nominal value, which is the debt owed by the company, and interest is paid at a stated 'coupon' on this amount. For example, if a company issues 10% loan stock, the coupon will be 10% of the nominal value of the stock, so that £100 of stock will receive £10 interest each year. The rate quoted is the gross rate, before tax.

2.2 Unlike shares, debt is often issued at par, ie with £100 payable per £100 nominal value. Where the coupon rate is fixed at the time of issue, it will be set according to prevailing market conditions given the credit rating of the company issuing the debt. Subsequent changes in market (and company) conditions will cause the market value of the bond to fluctuate, although the coupon will stay at the fixed percentage of the nominal value.

2.3 Debentures are a form of loan stock, legally defined as the written acknowledgement of a debt incurred by a company, normally containing provisions about the payment of interest and the eventual repayment of capital.

2.4 A debenture trust deed would empower a trustee (such as an insurance company or a bank) to intervene on behalf of debenture holders if the conditions of borrowing under which the debentures were issued are not being fulfilled. This might involve:

(a) failure to pay interest on the due dates;

(b) an attempt by the company to sell off important assets contrary to the terms of the loan;

(c) a company taking out additional loans and thereby exceeding previously agreed borrowing limits established either by the Articles or by the terms of the debenture trust deed. (A trust deed might well place restrictions on the company's ability to borrow more from elsewhere until the debentures have been redeemed.)

Debentures with a floating rate of interest

2.5 These are debentures for which the coupon rate of interest can be changed by the issuer, in accordance with changes in market rates of interest. They may be attractive to both lenders and borrowers when interest rates are volatile, and preferable to fixed interest loan stock or debentures.

(a) **Floating rate debentures** protect borrowers from having to pay high rates of interest on their debentures when market rates of interest have fallen. On the other hand, they allow lenders to benefit from higher rates of interest on their debentures when market rates of interest go up.

(b) The market value of debentures depends on the coupon rate of interest, relative to market interest rates. With floating rate debentures the market value should be fairly stable (and close to par) because interest rates are varied to follow market rate changes. Stable market prices protect the value of the lenders' investment.

2.6 For example, suppose that a company issues 6% fixed rate debentures at par when the market rate of interest is 6%, and the debentures have a term to maturity of 20 years. If interest rates suddenly rise to 12%, the market value of the debentures would fall by half to £50 per cent (that is, per £100 nominal value). However, if the debentures had carried a floating rate of interest, the interest rate would have been raised to 12% and the debentures would have retained their market value at par (£100 per cent).

Deep discount bonds

2.7 **Deep discount bonds** are loan stock issued at a price which is at a large discount to the nominal value of the stock, and which will be redeemable at par (or above par) when they eventually mature. For example a company might issue £1,000,000 of loan stock in 1997, at a price of £50 per £100 of stock, and redeemable at par in the year 2017.

For a company with specific cash flow requirements, the low servicing costs during the currency of the bond may be an attraction, coupled with a high cost of redemption at maturity.

2.8 Investors might be attracted by the large capital gain offered by the bonds, which is the difference between the issue price and the redemption value. However, deep discount bonds will carry a much lower rate of interest than other types of loan stock. The only tax advantage is that the gain gets taxed (as **income**) in one lump on maturity or sale, not as amounts of interest each year. The borrower can, however, deduct notional interest each year in computing profits.

Zero coupon bonds

2.9 **Zero coupon bonds** are bonds that are issued at a discount to their redemption value, but no interest is paid on them. The investor gains from the difference between the issue price and the redemption value, and there is an implied interest rate in the amount of discount at which the bonds are issued (or subsequently re-sold on the market).

(a) The advantage for borrowers is that zero coupon bonds can be used to raise cash immediately, and there is no cash repayment until redemption date. The cost of redemption is known at the time of issue, and so the borrower can plan to have funds available to redeem the bonds at maturity.

(b) The advantage for lenders is restricted, unless the rate of discount on the bonds offers a high yield. The only way of obtaining cash from the bonds before maturity is to sell them, and their market value will depend on the remaining term to maturity and current market interest rates.

The tax advantage of zero coupon bonds is the same as that for deep discount bonds (see Paragraph 2.8 above).

Security

2.10 Loan stock and debentures will often be secured. **Security** may take the form of either a **fixed charge** or a **floating charge.**

(a) **Fixed charge**. Security would be related to a specific asset or group of assets, typically land and buildings. The company would be unable to dispose of the asset without providing a substitute asset for security, or without the lender's consent.

(b) **Floating charge**. With a floating charge on certain assets of the company (for example stocks and debtors), the lender's security in the event of a default of payment is whatever assets of the appropriate class the company then owns (provided that another lender does not have a prior charge on the assets). The company would be able, however, to dispose of its assets as it chose until a default took place. In the event of default, the lender would probably appoint a receiver to run the company rather than lay claim to a particular asset.

Unsecured loan stock

2.11 Not all loan stock is secured. Investors are likely to expect a higher yield with unsecured loan stock to compensate them for the extra risk. The rate of interest on unsecured loan stock may be around 1% or more higher than for secured debentures.

The redemption of loan stock

2.12 Loan stock and debentures are usually redeemable. They are issued for a term of ten years or more, and perhaps 25 to 30 years. At the end of this period, they will 'mature' and become redeemable (at par or possibly at a value above par).

2.13 Most redeemable stocks have an earliest and a latest redemption date. For example, 12% Debenture Stock 2007/09 is redeemable, at any time between the earliest specified date (in 2007) and the latest date (in 2009). The issuing company can choose the date. The decision by a company when to redeem a debt will depend on:

(a) how much cash is available to the company to repay the debt;

(b) the nominal rate of interest on the debt. If the debentures pay 12% nominal interest and current interest rates are lower, say 9%, the company may try to raise a new loan at 9% to redeem debt which costs 12%. On the other hand, if current interest rates are 14%, the company is unlikely to redeem the debt until the latest date possible, because the debentures would be a cheap source of funds.

2.14 Some loan stock does not have a redemption date, and is 'irredeemable' or 'undated'. Undated loan stock might be redeemed by a company that wishes to pay off the debt, but there is no obligation on the company to do so.

How will a company finance the redemption of long-term debt?

2.15 There is no guarantee that a company will be able to raise a new loan to pay off a maturing debt, and one item to look for in a company's balance sheet is the redemption date of current loans, to establish how much new finance is likely to be needed by the company, and when.

Companies that are unable to repay debt capital

2.16 A company might get into difficulties and be unable to pay its debts. The difficulty could be:

(a) an inability to repay the debt capital when it is due for redemption; or

(b) an inability, perhaps temporary, to pay interest on the debt, before the capital is due for redemption.

2.17 When this occurs, the debenture holders or loan stock holders could exercise their right to appoint a receiver and to make use of whatever security they have. Occasionally, perhaps because the secured assets have fallen in value and would not realise much in a forced sale, or perhaps out of a belief that the company can improve its position soon, unpaid debenture holders might be persuaded to surrender their debentures in exchange for an equity interest in the company or possibly convertible debentures, paying a lower rate of interest, but carrying the option to convert the debentures into shares at a specified time in the future.

Tax relief on loan interest

2.18 As far as companies are concerned, debt capital is a potentially attractive source of finance because interest charges reduce the profits chargeable to corporation tax.

(a) A new issue of loan stock is likely to be preferable to a new issue of preference shares.

(b) Companies might wish to avoid dilution of shareholdings and increase their gearing (the ratio of fixed interest capital to equity capital) in order to improve their earnings per share by benefiting from tax relief on interest payments.

2.19 EXAMPLE: PREFERENCE SHARES AND LOAN STOCK

This example illustrates the differing effects of preference shares and loan stock on the profits attributable to the ordinary shareholders.

Company A has in issue £1,000,000 8% preference shares; Company B £1,000,000 of 10% loan stock. Both have profits before tax and interest of £2,500,000. It is assumed that the corporation tax rate is 31%.

	Company A	*Company B*
	£'000	£'000
Profit before tax and interest	2,500	2,500
Less interest	-	100
Profit before tax	2,500	2,400
Less tax (31%)	775	744
Profit after tax	1,725	1,656
Less preference dividend	80	-
Available to equity	1,645	1,656

For the basic rate taxpayer, 8% preference shares will provide the same yield as 10% loan stock. This is because the tax credit on dividends and also the tax credit on debenture/loan interest are based on the lower rate of income tax of 20%.

Mortgages

2.20 **Mortgages** are a specific type of secured loan. Companies place the title deeds of freehold or long leasehold property as security with a lender and receive cash on loan, usually repayable over a specified period, with interest payable at a fixed or floating rate.

Most organisations owning property which is unencumbered by any charge should be able to obtain a mortgage up to two thirds of the value of the property.

3 CONVERTIBLES AND WARRANTS 12/94, 12/96

Convertible loan stock

KEY TERM

Convertible securities are fixed return securities that may be converted, on predetermined dates and at the option of the holder, into ordinary shares of the company at a predetermined rate.

3.1 Conversion terms often vary over time. For example, the conversion terms of convertible stock might be that on 1 April 2000, £2 of stock can be converted into one ordinary share, whereas on 1 April 2001, the conversion price will be £2.20 of stock for one ordinary share. Once converted, convertible securities cannot be converted back into the original fixed return security.

The conversion value and the conversion premium

3.2 The current market value of ordinary shares into which a unit of stock may be converted is known as the conversion value. The **conversion value** will be below the value of the stock at the date of issue, but will be expected to increase as the date for conversion approaches on the assumption that a company's shares ought to increase in market value over time.

3.3 The difference between the issue value of the stock and the conversion value as at the date of issue is the implicit **conversion premium**.

Question 1

The 10% convertible loan stock of Starchwhite plc is quoted at £142 per £100 nominal. The earliest date for conversion is in four years time, at the rate of 30 ordinary shares per £100 nominal loan stock.

The share price is currently £4.15. Annual interest on the stock has just been paid.

Required

(a) What is the average annual growth rate in the share price that is required for the stockholders to achieve an overall rate of return of 12% a year compound over the next four years, including the proceeds of conversion?

(b) What is the implicit conversion premium on the stock?

Answer

(a)

Year	Investment	Interest	Discount factor	Terminal value
	£	£	12%	£
0	(142)		1.000	(142.00)
1		10	0.893	8.93
2		10	0.797	7.97
3		10	0.712	7.12
4		10	0.636	6.36
				(111.62)

The value of 30 shares on conversion at the end of year 4 must have a present value of at least £111.62, to provide investors with a 12% return.

The money value at the end of year 4 needs to be £111.62 ÷ 0.636 = £175.50.

The current market value of 30 shares is (× £4.15) £124.50.

The growth factor in the share price over four years needs to be:

$$\frac{175.50}{124.50} = 1.4096$$

If the annual rate of growth in the share price, expressed as a proportion, is g, then:

$$(1 + g)^4 = 1.4096$$
$$1 + g = 1.0896$$
$$g = 0.0896\text{, say } 0.09$$

Conclusion. The rate of growth in the share price needs to be 9% a year (compound).

(b) The conversion premium can be expressed as an amount per share or as a percentage of the current conversion value.

(i) As an amount per share $\frac{£142 - £(30 \times 4.15)}{30} = £0.583$ per share

(ii) As a % of conversion value $\frac{£0.583}{£4.15} \times 100\% = 14\%$

The issue price and the market price of convertible loan stock

3.4 A company will aim to issue loan stock with the greatest possible conversion premium as this will mean that, for the amount of capital raised, it will, on conversion, have to issue the lowest number of new ordinary shares. The premium that will be accepted by potential investors will depend on the company's growth potential and so on prospects for a sizeable increase in the share price.

3.5 Convertible loan stock issued at par normally has a lower coupon rate of interest than straight debentures. This lower yield is the price the investor has to pay for the conversion rights. It is, of course, also one of the reasons why the issue of convertible stock is attractive to a company.

3.6 When convertible loan stock is traded on a stock market, its *minimum* market price will be the price of straight debentures with the same coupon rate of interest. If the market value falls to this minimum, it follows that the market attaches no value to the conversion rights.

3.7 The actual market price of convertible stock will depend not only on the price of straight debt but also on the current conversion value, the length of time before conversion may take place, and the market's expectation as to future equity returns and the risk associated with these returns. If the conversion value rises above the straight debt value then the price of convertible stock will normally reflect this increase.

3.8 Most companies issuing convertible stocks expect them to be converted. They view the stock as delayed equity. They are often used either because the company's ordinary share price is considered to be particularly depressed at the time of issue or because the issue of equity shares would result in an immediate and significant drop in earnings per share. There is no certainty, however, that the security holders will exercise their option to convert; therefore the stock may run its full term and need to be redeemed.

3.9 EXAMPLE: CONVERTIBLE DEBENTURES

CD plc has issued 50,000 units of convertible debentures, each with a nominal value of £100 and a coupon rate of interest of 10% payable yearly. Each £100 of convertible debentures may be converted into 40 ordinary shares of CD plc in three years time. Any stock not converted will be redeemed at 110 (that is, at £110 per £100 nominal value of stock).

Estimate the likely current market price for £100 of the debentures, if investors in the debentures now require a pre-tax return of only 8%, and the expected value of CD plc ordinary shares on the conversion day is:

(a) £2.50 per share;
(b) £3.00 per share.

3.10 SOLUTION

(a) *Shares are valued at £2.50 each*

If shares are only expected to be worth £2.50 each on conversion day, the value of 40 shares will be £100, and investors in the debentures will presumably therefore redeem their debentures at 110 instead of converting them into shares.

The market value of £100 of the convertible debentures will be the discounted present value of the expected future income stream.

Year		*Cash flow*	*Discount factor*	*Present value*
		£	8%	£
1	Interest	10	0.926	9.26
2	Interest	10	0.857	8.57
3	Interest	10	0.794	7.94
3	Redemption value	110	0.794	87.34
				113.11

The estimated market value is £113.11 per £100 of debentures.

(b) *Shares are valued at £3 each*

If shares are expected to be worth £3 each, the debenture holders will convert their debentures into shares (value per £100 of stock = 40 shares × £3 = £120) rather than redeem their debentures at 110.

Year		*Cash flow/value*	*Discount factor*	*Present value*
		£	8%	£
1	Interest	10	0.926	9.26
2	Interest	10	0.857	8.57
3	Interest	10	0.794	7.94
3	Value of 40 shares	120	0.794	95.28
				121.05

The estimated market value is £121.05 per £100 of debentures.

Question 2

Downon Howett plc is unable to pay the interest on its debt capital, which consists of £5,000,000 of 10% debenture stock. The debenture holders are entitled, under the terms of their trust deed, to appoint a receiver, but the current financial position of Downon Howett plc is so poor that the enforced liquidation of the company would not realise more than a small fraction of the amount owed to the debenture holders. The debenture holders are therefore willing to consider alternatives.

Downon Howett has suggested that either of two options might satisfy them. The debenture holders would surrender their debentures, in exchange for:

(a) 15,000,000 ordinary shares under option 1;

(b) £5,000,000 of non-interest-bearing convertible debentures under option 2. The debentures would be convertible into ordinary shares in two years time at the rate of 200 shares per £100 of stock. Alternatively, the debentures (which would not be secured) would be repayable at par after two years.

Estimates of the net realisable value of Downon Howett's assets in two years time are as follows.

Probability	*Net realisable value*
	£m
0.2	2
0.4	4
0.3	6
0.1	8

If Downon Howett does not go into liquidation, its value as a going concern after two years is estimated to be 150% of the net realisable value of its assets, and the share price will reflect this value.

Downon Howett would not be allowed to issue any additional shares, nor pay any dividend, for the next two years. There are currently 10,000,000 shares in issue.

Which option would the debenture holders prefer, on the assumption that they choose the one that maximises the expected value of their wealth?

Answer

(a) If option 1 is selected, the debenture holders would own:

$\frac{15}{10+15}$ = 60% of the shares.

After two years, the EV of these shares would be as follows.

Break up value	*Market value (going concern) 150%*	*Ex debenture holder's share 60%*	*Probability*	*EV*
£m	£m	£m		£m
2	3	1.8	0.2	0.36
4	6	3.6	0.4	1.44
6	9	5.4	0.3	1.62
8	12	7.2	0.1	0.72
				4.14

(b) If option 2 is selected, the debenture holders could choose to demand repayment of the debentures, out of the proceeds of sale of the assets of the company, or to convert the debentures into shares.

They would own $\frac{10}{10+10}$ = 50% of the total number of shares.

Break-up value	*Going concern value*	*Value of convertibles as equity*	*Value of convertibles as debt*	*Convert? *yes or no*	*Value of debenture holders' securities*	*Probability*	
£m	£m	£m	£m		£m		£m
2	3	1.5	2.0	No	2	0.2	0.4
4	6	3.0	4.0	No	4	0.4	1.6
6	9	4.5	5.0	No	5	0.3	1.5
8	12	6.0	5.0	Yes	6	0.1	0.6
							4.1

* The answer is 'no' if the break-up value or the total debt of £5,000,000, whichever is lower, exceeds the value of 50% of the equity of the going concern. The debenture holders will compare the value of their convertibles as debt and as shares, and opt to use them in the form that gives the greater value.

The debenture holders would prefer option 1 to option 2, but only marginally so (with a difference in expected value of only £40,000).

Warrants

KEY TERM

A **warrant** is a right given by a company to an investor, allowing him to subscribe for new shares at a future date at a fixed, pre-determined price (the **exercise price**).

3.11 **Warrants** are usually issued as part of a package with unsecured loan stock: an investor who buys stock will also acquire a certain number of warrants.

The purpose of warrants is to make the loan stock more attractive.

3.12 Once issued, warrants are detachable from the stock and can be sold and bought separately before or during the 'exercise period' (the period during which the right to use the warrants to subscribe for shares is allowed). The market value of warrants will depend on expectations of actual share prices in the future.

3.13 During the exercise period, the price of a warrant should not fall below the higher of:

(a) nil; and
(b) the 'theoretical value', which equals:

(Current share price – Exercise price) × Number of shares obtainable from each warrant

3.14 If, for example, a warrant entitles the holder to purchase two ordinary shares at a price of £3 each, when the current market price of the shares is £3.40, the minimum market value ('theoretical value') of a warrant would be (£3.40 – £3) × 2 = 80p.

3.15 If the price fell below the theoretical value during the exercise period, then arbitrage would be possible. For example, suppose the share price is £2.80 and the warrant exercise price is £2.20. The warrants are priced at 50p with each entitled to one share. Ignoring transaction costs, investors could make an instant gain of 10p per share by buying the warrant, exercising it and then selling the share.

3.16 For a company with good growth prospects, the warrant will usually be quoted at a premium above the minimum prior to the exercise period. This premium is known as the **warrant conversion premium.** It is sometimes expressed as a percentage of the current share price.

3.17 EXAMPLE: WARRANT CONVERSION PREMIUM

An investor holds some warrants which can be used to subscribe for ordinary shares on a one for one basis at an exercise price of £2.50 during a specified future period. The current share price is £2.25 and the warrants are quoted at 50p. What is the warrant conversion premium?

3.18 SOLUTION

The easiest way of finding the premium is to deduct the current share price from the cost of acquiring a share using the warrant, treating the warrant as if it were currently exercisable:

	£
Cost of warrant	0.50
Exercise price	2.50
	3.00
Current share price	2.25
Premium	0.75

3.19 You may be wondering why an investor would prefer to buy warrants at 50p when this means that it will cost him more to get the ordinary shares than if he bought them directly. The attractions of warrants to the investor are:

(a) low initial outlay - he only has to spend 50p per share as opposed to £2.25. This means that he could buy $4^1/_2$ times as many warrants as shares or, alternatively, he could invest the remaining £1.75 in other, less risky investments;

(b) lower downside potential - his maximum loss per share is 50p instead of £2.25. Of course the risk of the loss of 50p is much greater than the risk of losing £2.25. The share price of £2.25 is below the exercise price. If it remained at this level until the beginning of the exercise period, the warrants would become worthless as it would not be worthwhile exercising them; and

(c) high potential returns - see below.

The gearing effect of warrants

3.20 Warrants offer the investor the possibility of making a high profit as a percentage of initial cost. This is because the price of the warrants will tend to move more or less in line with the price of the shares. Thus, if the share price rises by 50p the increase in the value of the warrant will be similar.

Using the previous prices, a 50p increase in share price is about 22% but a 50p increase in the warrant price is 100%. This illustrates the gearing effect of warrants.

3.21 Let us now recalculate the premium, assuming a 50p rise in the share price and a 50p rise in the warrant price:

	£
Cost of warrant (50p + 50p)	1.00
Exercise price	2.50
	3.50
Current share price (£2.25 + 50p)	2.75
Premium	0.75

The premium has stayed the same.

3.22 Note also that the share price is now above the exercise price. The warrants now have an 'intrinsic' value of 25p (ie 275p – 250p).

3.23 In the short run the warrant price and share price normally move fairly closely in line with each other. In the longer term the price of the warrant and hence the premium will depend on:

(a) the length of time before the warrants may be exercised;
(b) the current price of the shares compared with the exercise price; and

(c) the future prospects of the company.

As the exercise period approaches, the premium will reduce. Towards the end of the exercise period the premium will disappear because, if there were a premium, it would be cheaper to buy the shares directly rather than via the warrant.

Advantages of warrants

3.24 The main **advantages of warrants to the company** are as follows.

(a) Warrants themselves do not involve the payment of any interest or dividends. Furthermore, when they are initially attached to loan stock, the interest rate on the loan stock will be lower than for a comparable straight debt.

(b) Warrants make a loan stock issue more attractive and may make an issue of unsecured loan stock possible where adequate security is lacking.

(c) Warrants provide a means of generating additional equity funds in the future without any immediate dilution in earnings per share.

3.25 The main **advantages to the investor** are as follows.

(a) As warrants provide no income all profits are in the form of capital gains which will be attractive to higher-rate taxpayers who have not used up their annual tax-free allowance.

(b) As we have seen, there is potential for a high, though speculative, profit on a relatively low initial outlay.

Chapter roundup

- **Preference shares** carry priority over shareholders with regard to dividend payments. They do not carry voting rights. They may be attractive to corporate investors, as (unlike interest receipts) dividends received are not subject to corporation tax. However, for the issuing company, dividend payments (unlike interest payments) are not tax-deductible.
- The term **bonds** describes various forms of long-term debt a company may issue, such as loan stock or debentures, which may be **redeemable** or **irredeemable**.
- Bonds or loans come in various forms, including **floating rate debentures, zero coupon bonds** and **convertible loan stock.**
- **Convertible securities** give investors the opportunity to turn their stock into shares at a later date if they wish and, because of this, they usually carry a lower rate of interest than a similar non-convertible security. For the companies issuing them, convertibles may be viewed as a delayed form of equity which does not immediately affect EPS.
- Share **warrants** give their holder the right to apply for new shares at a specified exercise price in the future. They might be issued a an 'add-on' to a new issue of loan stock.

Quick quiz

1. What are the advantages to a company of issuing preference shares? (see para 1.3)
2. What are zero coupon bonds? (2.9)
3. What factors will influence the market price of convertible debentures? (3.6, 3.7)
4. What are warrants? (3.11)
5. What are advantages of warrants (a) to the company? (3.24) and (b) to the investor? (3.25)

Question to try	Level	Marks	Time
24	Examination	20	36 mins

Chapter 24

THE CAPITAL STRUCTURE DECISION

Chapter topic list		Syllabus reference
1	Gearing	7(b), (c), (d)
2	Factors influencing the level of debt financing	7(d), (c), (d)
3	Short-term financing and capital structure	7(a)(iv), (b), (c), (d)

Introduction

In Chapters 22 and 23, we described different methods by which a company can obtain long-term finance, both in the form of **equity** and in the form of **debt**.

This chapter follows on from Chapter 22 and 23, looking now at the question of what a company's **financial structure** should be. A central question here is: What are the implications of using different proportions of equity and debt finance?

1 GEARING — 12/94, 6/96

Principles of capital structure

1.1 The assets of a business must be financed somehow, and when a business is growing, the additional assets must be financed by additional capital.

1.2 **Capital structure** refers to the way in which an organisation is financed, by a combination of long-term capital (ordinary shares and reserves, preference shares, debentures, bank loans, convertible loan stock and so on) and short-term liabilities, such as a bank overdraft and trade creditors.

Matching assets with funds

1.3 As a general rule, assets which yield profits over a long period of time should be financed by long-term funds. In this way, the returns made by the asset will be sufficient to pay either the interest cost of the loans raised to buy it, or dividends on its equity funding. If, on the other hand, a long-term asset is financed by short-term funds, the company cannot be certain that when the loan becomes repayable, it will have enough cash (from profits) to repay it.

1.4 It is usually prudent for a company not to finance all of its short-term assets with short-term liabilities, but instead to finance short-term assets partly with short-term funding and partly with long-term funding.

Long-term capital requirements for replacement and growth

1.5 A distinction can be made between long-term capital that is needed to finance the replacement of worn-out assets, and capital that is needed to finance growth.

1.6 If a company is not growing and only needs finance to maintain its current level of operations, including the replacement of fixed assets, its main sources of funding are likely to be internally generated, provided that the rate of inflation is reasonably low.

1.7 When a company is seeking to grow, it will need extra finance.

Debts and financial risk

1.8 A high level of debt creates financial risk. **Financial risk** can be seen from different points of view.

(a) **The company** as a whole. If a company builds up debts that it cannot pay when they fall due, it will be forced into liquidation.

(b) **Creditors**. If a company cannot pay its debts, the company will go into liquidation owing creditors money that they are unlikely to recover in full.

(c) **Ordinary shareholders**. A company will not make any distributable profits unless it is able to earn enough profit before interest and tax to pay all its interest charges, and then tax. The lower the profits or the higher the interest-bearing debts, the less there will be, if there is anything at all, for shareholders.

When a company has preference shares in its capital structure, ordinary shareholders will not get anything until the preference dividend has been paid.

The appraisal of capital structures

1.9 The financial risk of a company's capital structure can be measured by:

(a) a gearing ratio;
(b) a debt ratio or debt/equity ratio;
(c) interest cover.

A gearing ratio should not be given without stating how it has been defined.

Exam focus point

You need to be able to explain *and calculate* the level of financial gearing using alternative measures.

Gearing ratios

1.10 We introduced gearing ratios in Chapter 14. **Financial gearing** measures the relationship between shareholders' capital plus reserves, and either prior charge capital or borrowings or both.

1.11 As we saw in Chapter 14, commonly used measures of financial gearing are based on the balance sheet values of the fixed interest and equity capital. They include:

$$\frac{\text{Prior charge capital}}{\text{Equity capital (including reserves)}}$$

and $$\frac{\text{Prior charge capital}}{\text{Total capital employed}\star}$$

⋆ Either including or excluding minority interests, deferred tax and deferred income.

1.12 With the first definition above, a company is low geared if the gearing ratio is less than 100%, highly geared if the ratio is over 100% and neutrally geared if it is exactly 100%. With the second definition, a company is neutrally geared if the ratio is 50%, low geared below that, and highly geared above that.

Question

From the following balance sheet, compute the company's financial gearing ratio.

	£'000	£'000	£'000
Fixed assets			12,400
Current assets		1,000	
Creditors: amounts falling due within one year			
Loans	120		
Bank overdraft	260		
Trade creditors	430		
Bills of exchange	70		
		880	
Net current assets			120
Total assets less current liabilities			12,520
Creditors: amounts falling due after more than one year			
Debentures		4,700	
Bank loans		500	
			(5,200)
Provisions for liabilities and charges: deferred taxation			(300)
Deferred income			(250)
			6,770

Capital and reserves	£'000
Called up share capital	
Ordinary shares	1,500
Preference shares	500
	2,000
Share premium account	760
Revaluation reserve	1,200
Profit and loss account	2,810
	6,770

Answer

Prior charge capital	£'000
Preference shares	500
Debentures	4,700
Long-term bank loans	500
Prior charge capital, ignoring short-term debt	5,700
Short-term loans	120
Overdraft	260
Prior charge capital, including short-term interest bearing debt	6,080

Either figure, £6,080,000 or £5,700,000, could be used. If gearing is calculated with capital employed in the denominator, and capital employed is net fixed assets plus **net** current assets, it would seem more reasonable to exclude short-term interest bearing debt from prior charge capital. This is because short-term debt is set off against current assets in arriving at the figure for net current assets.

Equity = 1,500 + 760 + 1,200 + 2,810 = £6,270,000

The gearing ratio can be calculated in any of the following ways.

(a) $\frac{\text{Prior charge capital}}{\text{Equity}} \times 100\% = \frac{6{,}080}{6{,}270} \times 100\% = 97\%$

(b) $\frac{\text{Prior charge capital}}{\text{Equity plus prior charge capital}} \times 100\% = \frac{6{,}080}{(6{,}080 + 6{,}270)} \times 100\% = 49.2\%$

(c) $\frac{\text{Prior charge capital}}{\text{Total capital employed}} \times 100\% = \frac{5{,}700}{12{,}520} \times 100\% = 45.5\%$

Gearing ratios based on market values

1.13 An alternative method of calculating a gearing ratio is one based on **market values**:

$$\frac{\text{Market value of debt (including preference shares)}}{\text{Market value of equity} + \text{Market value of debt}}$$

The advantage of this method is that potential investors in a company are able to judge the further debt capacity of the company more clearly by reference to market values than they could by looking at balance sheet values. A company with high asset values in its balance sheet might have poor profits after tax and low dividends, so that the gearing ratio based on market values might be high (with debt capital worth more than equity) whereas the gearing ratio based on balance sheet values would be lower. The company should find the task of raising new debt capital fairly difficult, because of its low profitability and consequent high gearing ratio based on market values.

1.14 The disadvantage of a gearing ratio based on market values is that it disregards the value of the company's assets, which might be used to secure further loans. A gearing ratio based on balance sheet values arguably gives a better indication of the security for lenders of fixed interest capital.

The effect of gearing on earnings

1.15 The level of gearing has a considerable effect on the earnings attributable to the ordinary shareholders. A highly geared company must earn enough profits to cover its interest charges before anything is available for equity. On the other hand, if borrowed funds are invested in projects which provide returns in excess of the cost of debt capital, then shareholders will enjoy increased returns on their equity.

1.16 Provided that a company can generate returns on capital in excess of the interest payable on debt, introducing financial gearing into the capital structure will enable **earnings per share** to be raised. If the company fails to generate such returns, earnings per share will be reduced, and so gearing increases the **variability of shareholders' earnings**. Gearing, however, also increases the probability of **financial failure** occurring through a company's inability to meet interest payments in poor trading circumstances.

1.17 EXAMPLE: GEARING

Suppose that two companies are identical in every respect except for their gearing. Both have assets of £20,000 and both make the same operating profits (profit before interest and tax: PBIT). The only difference between the two companies is that Nonlever Ltd is all-equity financed and Lever Ltd is partly financed by debt capital, as follows.

	Nonlever Ltd	*Lever Ltd*
	£	£
Assets	20,000	20,000
10% Loan stock	0	(10,000)
	20,000	10,000
Ordinary shares of £1	20,000	10,000

Because Lever Ltd has £10,000 of 10% loan stock it must make a profit before interest of at least £1,000 in order to pay the interest charges. Nonlever Ltd, on the other hand, does not have any minimum PBIT requirement because it has no debt capital. A company which is lower geared is considered less risky than a higher geared company because of the greater likelihood that its PBIT will be high enough to cover interest charges and make a profit for equity shareholders.

Operating gearing

1.18 Financial risk, as we have seen, can be measured by financial gearing.

Business risk refers to the risk of making only low profits, or even losses, due to the nature of the business that the company is involved in. One way of measuring business risk is by calculating a company's **operating gearing** or 'operational gearing'.

$$\text{Operating gearing} = \frac{\text{Contribution}}{\text{Profit before interest and tax (PBIT)}}$$

Contribution is sales minus variable cost of sales, and a contribution/sales ratio represents the amount by which profits will rise or fall per £1 of sales as sales revenue rises or falls.

1.19 The significance of operating gearing is as follows.

(a) If contribution is high but PBIT is low, fixed costs will be high, and only just covered by contribution. Business risk, as measured by operating gearing, will be high.

(b) If contribution is not much bigger than PBIT, fixed costs will be low, and fairly easily covered. Business risk, as measured by operating gearing, will be low.

Interest cover

1.20 **Interest cover** is a measure of financial risk which is designed to show the risks in terms of profit rather than in terms of capital values.

1.21 You will recall that:

$$\text{Interest cover} = \frac{\text{Profit before interest and tax}}{\text{Interest}}$$

The reciprocal of this, the interest to profit ratio, is also sometimes used.

1.22 As a general guide, an interest cover of less than three times is considered low, indicating that profitability is too low given the gearing of the company.

The debt ratio (debt/equity ratio)

1.23 Another measure of financial risk which we introduced in Chapter 15 is the **debt ratio**, which is the ratio of a company's total debts, long-term and short-term, to its total assets: net fixed assets plus total current assets.

Another way of expressing the debt ratio is as the ratio of debt to equity (the **debt/equity ratio**).

(Long-term provisions and liabilities, such as deferred taxation, can be ignored.)

1.24 There is no firm rule on the maximum safe debt ratio, but as a general guide, you might regard 50% as a safe limit to debt. In practice, many companies operate successfully with a higher debt ratio than this, but 50% is a helpful benchmark. If the debt ratio is over

50% and getting worse, the company's debt position will be worth looking at more closely.

2 FACTORS INFLUENCING THE LEVEL OF DEBT FINANCING

Limitations and restrictions

2.1 The gearing ratio and the debt/equity ratio indicate whether a company is likely to be successful in raising new funds by means of extra borrowing. Lenders will probably want a higher **interest yield** to compensate them for higher financial risk and gearing.

2.2 In addition, ordinary shareholders will probably want a bigger expected return from their shares to compensate them for a higher financial risk. The market value of shares will therefore depend on gearing, because of this premium for financial risk that shareholders will want to earn. Directors should bear in mind their responsibility to maximise the value of shares.

2.3 **Business confidence and expectations** of future profits are crucial factors in the determination of how much debt capital investors are prepared to lend. The level of gearing which the market will allow will therefore depend on the nature of the company wishing to borrow more funds, and the industry in which it is engaged.

(a) A company which is involved in a cyclical business, where profits are subject to periodic ups and downs, should have a relatively low gearing.

(b) A company in a business where profits are stable should be able to raise a larger amount of debt.

2.4 There may be restrictions on further borrowing:

(a) contained in the debenture trust deed for a company's current debenture stock in issue; or

(b) occasionally, in the company's Articles of Association.

2.5 A further limitation is that potential lenders may want **security** in the form of legal charge over company assets which the borrowing company is unable to provide.

International differences

2.6 Gearing levels vary between one country and another, largely as a result of differing economic and social histories. For example, in Germany and, to some extent, Japan, the capital markets are dominated by the banks. They are the main providers of both equity and loan finance and they will usually have board representation in all the companies in which they invest. It follows that they will be largely indifferent to the risk aspects of gearing when providing fresh capital to a particular company. Instead, gearing levels will be determined by other factors such as legal requirements, taxation and liquidity.

Inflation, debt capital and interest rates

2.7 The *cost* of any extra finance will reflect investors' expectations about the rate of inflation. Investors will usually want a real return on their investment, that is, a return in excess of the rate of inflation.

(a) If long-term debt finance is issued in an inflationary period the nominal interest rate needs to be high enough to convince potential investors that they will get a real return. Current market interest rates will reflect investors' expectations.

(b) However, if actual rates of inflation subsequently turn out to be lower than expected, market interest rates will probably fall. A company that issues debt capital at a high nominal interest rate would then find itself paying interest charges on its borrowings which are higher than current market rates.

2.8 Both inflation and uncertainty about future interest rate changes help to explain why:

(a) companies are unwilling to borrow long-term at high rates of interest and investors are unwilling to lend long-term when they think that interest yields might go even higher;

(b) companies therefore rely quite heavily for borrowed funds on bank borrowing and short- term borrowing (such as money market borrowing).

2.9 The advantage of short-term borrowing is that the company is not committed to paying a high interest rate for a long period.

The idea of an optimal structure; the cost of capital

2.10 When we consider the capital structure decision, the question arises of whether there is an optimal mix of capital and debt which a company should try to achieve.

Exam focus point

This is a question which we shall just consider briefly here; the topic is covered in more detail in ACCA Paper 14 *Financial strategy*.

2.11 So-called traditional theory maintain that there is indeed an optimal capital mix at which the average cost of capital, weighted according to the different forms of capital employed, is minimised.

2.12 As gearing rises, so the return demanded by the ordinary shareholders begins to rise in order to compensate them for the risk resulting from a larger and larger share of profits going to the providers of debt. At very high levels of gearing the holders of debt too will begin to require higher returns as they become exposed to risk of inadequate profits.

2.13 Briefly, the alternative view of **Modigliani and Miller** is that the firm's overall **weighted average cost of capital** changes in its capital structure. Their argument is that the issue of debt causes the cost of equity to rise in such a way that the benefits of debt on returns are exactly offset. Investors themselves adjust their level of personal gearing and thus the level of corporate gearing becomes irrelevant.

2.14 The Modigliani-Miller view however does contain some debatable assumptions. It assumes that investors operate in a perfect market where full information is equally available to all players, and that transaction costs are irrelevant. Further, companies can often borrow on better terms than private investors, and importantly the effects of taxation are ignored in the original Modigliani-Miller theory.

3 SHORT-TERM FINANCING AND CAPITAL STRUCTURE 12/96

3.1 There are different ways in which the funding of current and fixed assets can be achieved by employing different capital structures with different proportions of long and short-term sources of funding.

3.2 The diagram below illustrates three alternative types of policy A, B and C. The dotted lines A, B and C are the cut-off levels between short-term and long-term financing for each of the policies A, B and C respectively: assets above the relevant dotted line are financed by short-term funding while assets below the dotted line are financed by long-term funding.

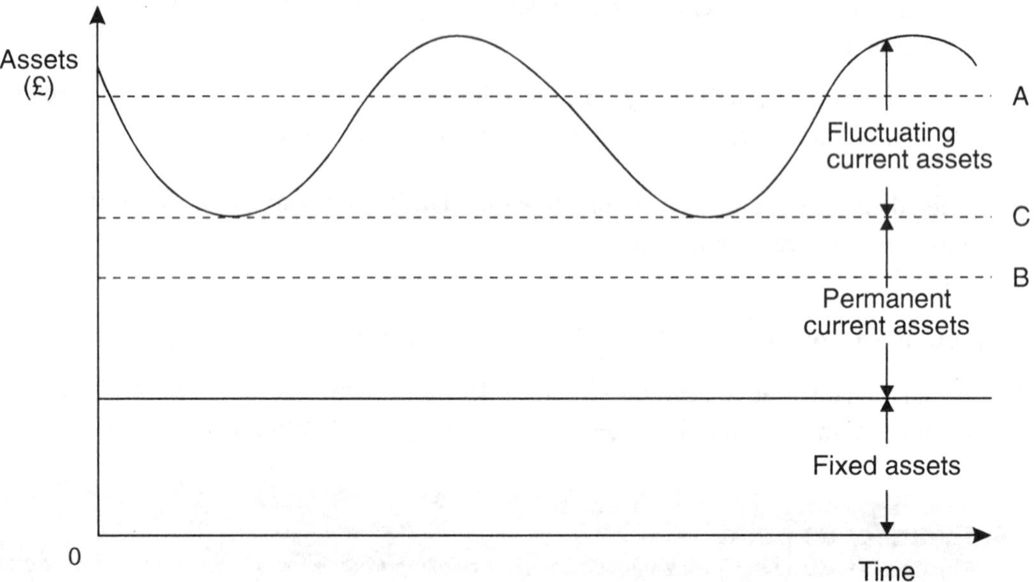

3.3 Fluctuating current assets together with permanent current assets form part of the working capital of the business, which may be financed by either long-term funding (including equity capital) or by current liabilities (short-term funding). This can be seen in terms of policies A, B and C.

(a) Policy A can be characterised as **conservative**. All fixed assets and permanent current assets, as well as part of fluctuating current assets, are financed by long-term funding. There is only a need to call upon short-term financing at times when fluctuations in current assets push total assets above the level of dotted line A. At times when fluctuating current assets are low and total assets fall below line A, there will be surplus cash which the company will be able to invest in marketable securities.

(b) Policy B is more **aggressive** in its approach to financing working capital. Not only are fluctuating current assets all financed out of short-term sources, but also a part of the permanent current assets. This policy presents an increased risk of liquidity and cash flow problems, although potential returns will be increased if short-term financing can be obtained more cheaply than long-term finance.

(c) A **balance** between risk and return might be best achieved by policy C, in which long-term funds finance permanent assets while short-term funds finance non-permanent assets.

Chapter roundup

- **Gearing** must be considered when deciding how to finance a business.
- **Financial gearing** and **operating** or **operational gearing** need to be distinguished.
- If a company can generate returns on capital in excess of the interest payable on debt, an element of financial gearing in the **capital structure** will raise the EPS. Gearing will, however, also increase the **variability of returns** for shareholders and increase the chance of corporate **failure.**
- If shareholders' interests are to be safeguarded, the shareholders must put up a reasonable amount of their own money as equity capital, to ensure that loan interest payments and loan capital repayments do not drive the business into **insolvency**.
- **Gearing** is also limited by the reluctance of lenders to lend to a company which does not have an adequate equity base.
- The way in which a company funds its current and permanent assets through either short-term or long-term finance may be **conservative** at on extreme or **aggressive** at the other.

Quick quiz

1 What is a company's capital structure? (see para 1.2)

2 What is the effect of gearing on earnings? (1.15)

3 What is operating gearing? (1.18)

4 Outline the limitations on further borrowing which a company may face. (2.1 - 2.5)

5 Define interest cover. (1.20)

6 What different ways of financing working capital and permanent (long-term) assets are possible? (3.3)

Question to try	Level	Marks	Time
25	Examination	20	36 mins

Part I
Project appraisal

Chapter 25

INVESTMENT DECISIONS

Chapter topic list		Syllabus reference
1	Investment	8
2	Identification of investment opportunities	8(a)
3	The payback period	8(b)(i)
4	The accounting rate of return method	8(b)(i)
5	The payback and ARR methods in practice	8(b)(i)

Introduction

This chapter introduces **investment appraisal** and covers the manner in which investment opportunities are identified and two investment appraisal methods.

Chapter 26 will look at investment appraisal using the more sophisticated **DCF** methods.

1 INVESTMENT

1.1 Investment is any expenditure in the expectation of future benefits. We can divide such expenditure into two groups.

- Capital expenditure
- Revenue expenditure

Capital expenditure and revenue expenditure

1.2 **Capital expenditure** is expenditure which results in the acquisition of fixed assets or an *improvement* in their earning capacity. It is *not* charged as an expense in the profit and loss account of an organisation: the expenditure appears as a fixed asset in the balance sheet.

1.3 **Revenue expenditure** is expenditure which is incurred for either of the following reasons.

(a) For the purpose of the trade of the business. This includes expenditure classified as selling and distribution expenses, administration expenses and finance charges.

(b) To maintain the existing earning capacity of fixed assets.

1.4 Revenue expenditure is charged to the profit and loss account of a period (provided, of course, that it relates to the trading activity of that particular period).

1.5 Suppose that a business purchases a building for £30,000. It then adds an extension to the building at a cost of £10,000. The building needs to have a few broken windows mended, its floors polished and some missing roof tiles replaced. These cleaning and maintenance jobs cost £900.

1.6 The original purchase (£30,000) and the cost of the extension (£10,000) are capital expenditure because they are incurred to acquire and then improve a fixed asset. The other costs of £900 are revenue expenditure because they merely maintain the building and thus the earning capacity of the building.

1.7 Capital expenditures therefore differ from day to day revenue expenditures for the following reasons.

(a) They often involve a bigger outlay of money.

(b) The benefits will accrue over a long period of time, usually well over one year and often much longer, so that the benefits cannot all be set against costs in the current year's profit and loss account.

Fixed asset investment and working capital investment

1.8 **Investment** can be made in **fixed assets** or **working capital**. Investment in working capital arises from the need to pay out money for resources (such as raw materials) before it can be recovered from sales of the finished product or service. The funds are therefore only committed for a short period of time, say one year.

1.9 Investment in fixed assets, on the other hand, involves a significant elapse of time between commitment of funds and recoupment of the investment. This is because money is paid out to acquire resources which are going to be used on a continuing basis within the organisation.

1.10 Capital investment decisions (that is, investment in fixed assets) are normally the most important decisions that any organisation makes, since they commit a substantial portion of a firm's resources to actions that are likely to be irrevocable. Such decisions are applicable to all sections of society.

Investment by the commercial sector

1.11 Investment by commercial organisations might include investment in plant and machinery, research and development, advertising or warehouse facilities. The overriding feature of a commercial sector investment is that it is generally **based on financial considerations alone.** The various capital expenditure appraisal techniques that we will be looking at assess the financial aspects of capital investment.

Investment by not-for-profit organisations

1.12 Investment by not-for-profit organisations differs from investment by commercial organisations for several reasons.

(a) Relatively few not-for-profit organisations' capital investments are made with the intention of earning a financial return. Certainly, nationalised industries may be expected to earn profits on their investments, but spending on roads, hospitals, schools, the defence forces and the police service, nuclear waste dumps and so on are not made with an eye to profit and return. Investments by organisations such as charities would not be made with profit in mind.

(b) When there are two or more ways of achieving the same objective (mutually exclusive investment opportunities), a commercial organisation might prefer the option with the lowest present value of cost and if a cost-saving capital item is being considered for purchase, the decision might be to buy the item, provided that the present value of savings exceeds the present value of costs. In these ways, capital expenditure decisions by commercial organisations are based on financial considerations alone.

Not-for-profit organisations, however, rather than considering financial cost and financial benefits (if any) alone, will often have regard to the **social costs** and **social benefits** of investments when making capital expenditure decisions.

The social costs of building a new motorway into a city might include the loss of people's homes, more pollution and health hazards whereas the social benefits might include faster travel, the ability of the road to carry a larger volume of traffic and the environmental benefits for the people in the city from reduced traffic congestion.

(c) The **cost of capital** that is applied to project cash flows by the public sector will not be a 'commercial' rate of return, but one that is determined by the Treasury on behalf of the government. Any targets that a public sector investment has to meet before being accepted will therefore not be based on the same criteria as those in the commercial sector.

2 IDENTIFICATION OF INVESTMENT OPPORTUNITIES

Exam focus point

You are expected to have an 'elementary knowledge' of the topics covered in this section of the Chapter for the purposes of Paper 8.

2.1 A company can be offered a number of possible investment projects, each of which might appear attractive in the return it offers as assessed by investment appraisal techniques such as discounted cash flow.

2.2 Igor Ansoff argues, however, that capital investment appraisal is concerned with only the last two steps of a more complex process of strategic decision making. This process has four stages.

(a) Perception of the need for an investment, or awareness of a potential opportunity
(b) Formulation of alternative courses of action
(c) Evaluation of the alternatives identified in (b)
(d) Choice of one of these alternatives for implementation

2.3 **Strategic analysis** deals with the first two steps.

(a) A company needs some mechanism for identifying when it needs to embark on an investment project. For example, a firm may be making substantial profits on its current activities. If its current competitive environment did not change, it could continue on much the same path. The entry of a new competitor to the market, on the other hand, might challenge some of the fundamental assumptions of the company's strategy. It would have to take defensive action to maintain its position in the altered market place.

(b) Furthermore, to continue with the example, a variety of alternatives might suggest themselves. The company could try and undercut the competitor by charging a lower price. The company could spend heavily on advertising. The company could invest to improve its products.

(i) Each suggested option will, if implemented, affect the way in which the competitor responds. Sadly, competitor response is not something that can be predicted with any degree of certainty, and it is hard to include this in investment appraisal techniques.

(ii) At the beginning of the planning period, only a few of the alternatives 'will be known in sufficient detail to permit the construction of cash flows' (Ansoff). Decisions, therefore, are taken in conditions of partial ignorance. This poses two problems.

(1) How do you conduct an active search for attractive opportunities?

(2) How do you allocate resources, when you do not know the entire range of opportunities available?

2.4 Strategic management is a way of coping with these conditions of partial ignorance. This falls into three logical stages.

(a) **Strategic analysis**

(i) **Environmental analysis:** analysing the environment in which the firm operates, encompassing political legal factors, economic factors, socio-cultural factors, technological factors and the competitive environment.

(ii) **Internal appraisal:** analysing the firm's current capacity for dealing with the environment and anticipated changes within it, ie looking at the organisation's past activities and current resources.

(iii) **Mission and objectives:** analysing the firm's objectives, the expectations of its shareholders, in short what is expected of the firm.

(b) **Strategic choice** involves the generation of alternative options, their evaluation, and a selection of a strategy.

(c) **Strategic implementation** involves allocating resources, designing organisation structure and directing the organisation's systems and employees.

Corporate appraisal: SWOT analysis

2.5 Environmental analysis and internal assessment are combined, in the context of the organisation's mission, in a process of corporate appraisal involving a critical assessment of the strengths and weaknesses, opportunities and threats (**SWOT analysis**) in relation to the internal and environmental factors affecting the organisation in order to establish its condition prior to the preparation of the long-term plan.

(a) **Strengths and weaknesses**

From the internal appraisal, a company might find that it has a state of the art production system (a strength) but a very primitive system for assessing the goods customers require (a weakness).

(b) **Opportunities and threats**

A financial services firm might find opportunities in an increased demand for redundancy insurance, but threats in that there are more competitors supplying mortgage finance.

2.6 A cruciform chart is a table listing the significant strengths and weaknesses and opportunities and threats. It can be used to summarise the major conclusions of a SWOT analysis. In the example below, the development of potential strategies from the analysis is illustrated.

Strengths £10 million of capital available. Production expertise and appropriate marketing skills	*Weaknesses* Heavy reliance on a small number of customers. Limited product range, with no new products and expected market decline. Small marketing organisation.
Threats Major competitor has already entered the new market.	*Opportunities* Government tax incentives for new investment. Growing demand in a new market, although customers so far relatively small in number.

2.7 In this simple example, it might be possible to identify that the company is in imminent danger of losing its existing markets and must diversify its products, or its products and markets. The new market opportunity exists to be exploited and since the number of customers is currently few, the relatively small size of the existing marketing force would not be an immediate hindrance. A strategic plan could be developed to buy new equipment and to use existing production and marketing to enter the new market, with a view to rapid expansion. Careful planning of manpower, equipment, facilities, research and development and so on. would be required and there would be an objective to meet the threat of competition so as to obtain a substantial share of a growing market. The cost of entry at this early stage of market development should not be unacceptably high.

2.8 In this example, one individual strategy has been identified from our simplified cruciform chart. In practice, a combination of individual strategies will be required with regard to product development, market development, diversification, resource planning, risk reduction and so on.

2.9 It will help you to get used to the basic thinking that underlies planning if you try a short exercise in SWOT analysis.

Question

Hall Faull Downes Ltd has been in business for 25 years, during which time profits have risen by an average of 3% per annum, although there have been peaks and troughs in profitability due to the ups and downs of trade in the customers' industry. The increase in profits until five years ago was the result of increasing sales in a buoyant market, but more recently, the total market has become somewhat smaller and Hall Faull Downes has only increased sales and profits as a result of improving its market share.

The company produces components for manufacturers in the engineering industry.

In recent years, the company has developed many new products and currently has 40 items in its range compared to 24 only five years ago. Over the same five-year period, the number of customers has fallen from 20 to nine, two of whom together account for 60% of the company's sales.

Give your appraisal of the company's future, and suggest what it is probably doing wrong.

Answer

A general interpretation of the facts as given might be sketched as follows.

(a) *Objectives*

The company has no declared objectives. Profits have risen by 3% per annum in the past, therefore failing to keep pace with inflation but this may have been a satisfactory rate of increase in the current conditions of the industry. Even so, stronger growth is indicated in the future.

(b)

Strengths Many new products developed. Marketing success in increasing market share.	*Weaknesses* Products may be reaching the end of their life and entering decline. New product life cycles may be shorter. Reduction in customers. Excessive reliance on a few customers. Doubtful whether profit record is satisfactory.
Threats Possible decline in the end-product. Smaller end-product market will restrict future sales prospects for Hall Faull Downes.	*Opportunities* None identified.

(c) *Strengths*

The growth in company sales in the last five years has been as a result of increasing the market share in a declining market. This success may be the result of the following.

(i) Research and development spending
(ii) Good product development programmes
(iii) Extending the product range to suit changing customer needs
(iv) Marketing skills
(v) Long-term supply contracts with customers
(vi) Cheap pricing policy
(vii) Product quality and reliable service

(d) *Weaknesses*

(i) The products may be custom-made for customers so that they provide little or no opportunity for market development.

(ii) Products might have a shorter life cycle than in the past, in view of the declining total market demand.

(iii) Excessive reliance on two major customers leaves the company exposed to the dangers of losing their custom.

(e) *Threats*

There may be a decline in the end-market for the customers' product so that the customer demands for the company's own products will also fall.

(f) *Opportunities*

No opportunities have been identified, but in view of the situation as described, new strategies for the longer term would appear to be essential.

(g) *Conclusions*

The company does not appear to be planning beyond the short term, or is reacting to the business environment in a piecemeal fashion. A strategic planning programme should be introduced.

(h) *Recommendation*

The company must look for new opportunities in the longer term.

(i) In the short term, current strengths must be exploited to continue to increase market share in existing markets and product development programmes should also continue.

(ii) In the longer term, the company must diversify into new markets or into new products and new markets. Diversification opportunities should be sought with a view to exploiting any competitive advantage or synergy that might be achievable.

(iii) The company should use its strengths (whether in R & D, production skills or marketing expertise) in exploiting any identifiable opportunities.

(iv) Objectives need to be quantified in order to assess the extent to which new long-term strategies are required.

Product-market mix

2.10 A firm may be faced with a bewildering variety of options, in relation both to product development and the possible markets it sells to. Igor Ansoff developed a tool for analysing these opportunities as follows.

(a) **Market penetration**. Sell more of your existing products in your existing markets.

(b) **Market development.** Sell your existing products to new markets (eg overseas).

(c) **Product development.** Sell new products to existing markets (eg a television company selling hi-fi equipment).

(d) **Diversification**. Sell new products to new markets. Arguably this is the most risky strategy.

2.11 In practice, this tool is an oversimplification. You need not assume that new products are unrelated to existing ones (such as a cheesemaker making and selling chalk), rather than a logical development from them (such as a cheesemaker making and selling butter). The new market may have similarities with the existing ones.

Market share, market growth and cash generation: the Boston classification

2.12 The Boston Consulting Group (BCG) have developed the **Boston matrix**, based on empirical research, which classifies a company's products in terms of potential cash generation and cash expenditure requirements.

2.13 This **growth/share matrix** for the classification of products into cash cows, cash dogs, rising stars and question marks is known as the **Boston classification** for product-market strategy.

(a) **Stars** are products with a high share of a high growth market. In the short term, these require capital expenditure, in excess of the cash they generate, in order to maintain their market position, but promise high returns in the future.

(b) In due course, however, stars will become cash cows, with a high share of a low growth market. **Cash cows** need very little capital expenditure and generate high levels of cash income. The important strategic feature of cash cows is that they are *already* generating high cash returns, which can be used to finance the stars.

(c) **Question marks** are products with a low share of a high growth market. A decision needs to be taken about whether the products justify considerable capital expenditure in the hope of increasing their market share, or whether they should be allowed to 'die' quietly as they are squeezed out of the expanding market by rival products. Because considerable expenditure would be needed to turn a question mark into a star by building up market share, question marks will usually be poor cash generators and show a negative cash flow.

(d) **Dogs** are products with a low share of a low growth market. They may be ex-cash cows that have now fallen on hard times. Dogs should be allowed to die, or should be killed off. Although they will show only a modest net cash outflow, or even a modest net cash inflow, they are 'cash traps' which tie up funds and provide a poor return on investment, below the organisation's target rate of return.

There are also **infants** (products in an early stage of development) and **warhorses** (products that have been cash cows in the past, and are still making good sales and earning good profits even now).

2.14 The idea behind the Boston classification is that a firm should have a mix of cash cows, stars and so on. The cash cows should finance future development.

2.15 There are however various flaws in the Boston classification.

(a) It is not always easy to identify what a 'market' for a product is, as it might be influenced by interdependencies with other markets.

(b) Relative market share may not be a 'good proxy for competitive position and relative costs' (Porter).

(c) Market growth may not be a 'good proxy for required cash investment ... profits (and cash flow) depend on a lot of other things' (Porter).

Organic growth or acquisition ?

2.16 A company which is planning to grow must decide on whether to pursue a policy of 'organic' internal growth or a policy of taking over other established businesses, or a mix of the two.

2.17 **Organic growth** requires funding in cash, whereas acquisitions can be made by means of share exchange transactions. A company pursuing a policy of organic growth would need to take account of the following.

(a) The company must make the finance available, possibly out of retained profits. However, the company should then know how much it can afford, and with careful management, should not over-extend itself by trying to achieve too much growth too quickly.

(b) The company can use its existing staff and systems to create the growth projects, and this will open up career opportunities for the staff. In contrast, when expansion is achieved by taking over other businesses, the company usually acquires and assimilates the staff of those businesses.

(c) Overall expansion can be planned more efficiently. For example, if a company wishes to open a new factory or depot, it can site the new development in a place that helps operational efficiency (eg close to other factories, to reduce transport costs). With acquisitions, the company must take on existing sites no matter where they happen to be.

(d) Economies of scale can be achieved from more efficient use of central head office functions such as finance, purchasing, personnel and management services. With acquisitions, a company buys the head office functions of other companies and there will either be fewer economies of scale, or more redundancies.

2.18 **Acquisitions** are probably only desirable if organic growth alone cannot achieve the targets for growth that a company has set for itself.

Acquisitions can be made to enter new product areas, or to expand in existing markets, much more quickly. Organic growth takes time. With acquisitions, entire existing operations are assimilated into the company at one fell swoop. Acquisitions can be made without cash, if share exchange transactions are acceptable to both the buyers and sellers of any company which is to be taken over.

When an acquisition is made to diversify into new product areas, the company will be buying technical expertise, goodwill and customer contracts and so on, which it might take years to develop if it tried to enter the market by growing organically.

Exam focus point

For the exam, you will be expected to have an appreciation of the advantages and disadvantages of internal *versus* external growth.

3 THE PAYBACK PERIOD 12/95, 6/96, 6/97

3.1 There are a number of ways of evaluating capital projects, two of which we will be examining in this chapter. We will look first at the payback method.

Exam focus point

In both 12/95 and 6/97, candidates were asked about the pros and cons of the payback method.

3.2 Payback may be defined as the time it takes the cash inflows from a capital investment project to equal the cash outflows, usually expressed in years.

3.3 When deciding between two or more competing projects, the usual decision is to accept the one with the shortest payback.

Payback is often used as a 'first screening method'. By this, we mean that when a capital investment project is being considered, the first question to ask is: 'How long will it take to pay back its cost?' The organisation might have a target payback, and so it would reject a capital project unless its payback period were less than a certain number of years.

3.4 However, a project should not be evaluated on the basis of payback alone. Payback should be a *first* screening process, and if a project gets through the payback test, it ought then to be evaluated with a more sophisticated investment appraisal technique.

3.5 You should note that when payback is calculated, we take profits *before* depreciation, because we are trying to estimate the *cash* returns from a project and profit before depreciation is likely to be a rough approximation of cash flows.

Why is payback alone an inadequate investment appraisal technique?

3.6 The reason why payback should not be used on its own to evaluate capital investments should seem fairly obvious if you look at the figures below for two mutually exclusive projects (this means that only one of them can be undertaken).

	Project P	*Project Q*
Capital asset	£60,000	£60,000
Profits before depreciation		
Year 1	£20,000	£50,000
Year 2	£30,000	£20,000
Year 3	£40,000	£5,000
Year 4	£50,000	£5,000
Year 5	£60,000	£5,000

3.7 Project P pays back in year 3 (about one quarter of the way through year 3). Project Q pays back half way through year 2. Using payback alone to judge capital investments, project Q would be preferred. But the returns from project P over its life are much higher than the returns from project Q.

(a) Project P will earn total profits before depreciation of £140,000 on an investment of £60,000.

(b) Project Q will earn total profits after depreciation of only £25,000 on an investment of £60,000.

Disadvantages of the payback method

3.8 There are a number of serious drawbacks to the payback method. It ignores the timing of cash flows within the payback period, the cash flows after the end of payback period and therefore the total project return. Moreover, it ignores the time value of money (a concept incorporated into more sophisticated appraisal methods). This means that it does not take account of the fact that £1 today is worth more than £1 in one year's time. An investor who has £1 today can either consume it immediately or alternatively can invest it at the prevailing interest rate, say 10%, to get a return of £1.10 in a year's time.

3.9 Other disadvantages are as follows.

(a) The method is unable to distinguish between projects with the same payback period.

(b) The choice of any cut-off payback period by an organisation is arbitrary.

(c) It may lead to excessive investment in short-term projects.

(d) It takes account of the risk of the timing of cash flows but not the variability of those cash flows.

Advantages of the payback method

3.10 In spite of its limitations, the payback method continues to be popular, and the following points can be made in its favour.

(a) It is simple to calculate and simple to understand, and this may be important when management resources are limited. It is similarly helpful in communicating information about minimum requirements to managers responsible for submitting projects.

(b) It can be used as a screening device as a first stage in eliminating obviously inappropriate projects prior to more detailed evaluation.

(c) The fact that it tends to bias in favour of short-term projects means that it tends to minimise both financial and business risk.

(d) It can be used when there is a capital rationing situation to identify those projects which generate additional cash for investment quickly.

4 THE ACCOUNTING RATE OF RETURN METHOD 6/95

4.1 The accounting rate of return method (also called the return on capital employed (ROCE) or the return on investment (ROI) method) of appraising a capital project is to estimate the accounting rate of return that the project should yield. If it exceeds a target rate of return, the project will be undertaken. Unfortunately, there are several different definitions of 'return on investment'. One of the most popular is as follows.

$$\text{ARR} = \frac{\text{Estimated average profits}}{\text{Estimated average investment}} \times 100\%$$

The others include:

$$\text{ARR} = \frac{\text{Estimated total profits}}{\text{Estimated initial investment}} \times 100\%$$

$$\text{ARR} = \frac{\text{Estimated average profits}}{\text{Estimated initial investment}} \times 100\%$$

4.2 There are arguments in favour of each of these definitions. The most important point is, however, that the method selected should be used consistently. For examination purposes we recommend the first definition unless the question clearly indicates that some other one is to be used.

4.3 EXAMPLE: THE ACCOUNTING RATE OF RETURN

A company has a target accounting rate of return of 20% (using the first definition in Paragraph 4.1 above), and is now considering the following project.

Capital cost of asset	£80,000
Estimated life	4 years
Estimated profit before depreciation	
Year 1	£20,000
Year 2	£25,000
Year 3	£35,000
Year 4	£25,000

The capital asset would be depreciated by 25% of its cost each year, and will have no residual value.

Required

Assess whether the project should be undertaken.

4.4 SOLUTION

The annual profits after depreciation, and the mid-year net book value of the asset, would be as follows.

Year	*Profit after depreciation*	*Mid-year net book value*	*ARR in the year*
	£	£	%
1	0	70,000	0
2	5,000	50,000	10
3	15,000	30,000	50
4	5,000	10,000	50

4.5 As the table shows, the ARR is low in the early stages of the project, partly because of low profits in Year 1 but mainly because the net book value of the asset is much higher early on in its life.

4.6 The project does not achieve the target ARR of 20% in its first two years, but exceeds it in years 3 and 4. So should it be undertaken?

4.7 When the accounting rate of return from a project varies from year to year, it makes sense to take an overall or 'average' view of the project's return. In this case, we should look at the return as a whole over the four-year period.

	£
Total profit before depreciation over four years	105,000
Total profit after depreciation over four years	25,000
Average annual profit after depreciation	6,250
Original cost of investment	80,000
Average net book value over the four year period $\frac{(80,000 + 0)}{2}$	40,000

The project would not be undertaken because it would fail to yield the target return of 20%.

The ARR and the comparison of mutually exclusive projects

4.8 The ARR method of capital investment appraisal can also be used to compare two or more projects which are mutually exclusive. The project with the highest ARR would be selected (provided that the expected ARR is higher than the company's target ARR).

4.9 EXAMPLE: THE ARR AND MUTUALLY EXCLUSIVE PROJECTS

Arrow Ltd wants to buy a new item of equipment which will be used to provide a service to customers of the company. Two models of equipment are available, one with a slightly higher capacity and greater reliability than the other. The expected costs and profits of each item are as follows.

	Equipment item X	*Equipment item Y*
Capital cost	£80,000	£150,000
Life	5 years	5 years
Profits before depreciation	£	£
Year 1	50,000	50,000
Year 2	50,000	50,000
Year 3	30,000	60,000
Year 4	20,000	60,000
Year 5	10,000	60,000
Disposal value	0	0

ARR is measured as the average annual profit after depreciation, divided by the average net book value of the asset.

Required

Decide which item of equipment should be selected, if any, if the company's target ARR is 30%.

4.10 SOLUTION

	Item X	*Item Y*
	£	£
Total profit over life of equipment		
Before depreciation	160,000	280,000
After depreciation	80,000	130,000
Average annual profit after depreciation	16,000	26,000
(Capital cost + disposal value)/2	40,000	75,000
ARR	40%	34.7%

Both projects would earn a return in excess of 30%, but since item X would earn a bigger ARR, it would be preferred to item Y, even though the profits from Y would be higher by an average of £10,000 a year.

The drawbacks to the ARR method of capital investment appraisal

4.11 The ARR method of capital investment appraisal has the serious drawback that it does not take account of the *timing* of the profits from an investment.

4.12 Whenever capital is invested in a project, money is tied up until the project begins to earn profits which pay back the investment. Money tied up in one project cannot be invested anywhere else until the profits come in. Management should be aware of the benefits of early repayments from an investment, which will provide the money for other investments.

4.13 There are a number of other disadvantages.

(a) It is based on accounting profits and not cash flows. Accounting profits are subject to a number of different accounting treatments.

(b) It is a relative measure rather than an absolute measure and hence takes no account of the size of the investment.

(c) It takes no account of the length of the project.

(d) Like the payback method, it ignores the time value of money.

4.14 There are, however, advantages to the ARR method. It is a quick and simple calculation, it involves a familiar concept of a percentage return and it looks at the entire project life.

5 THE PAYBACK AND ARR METHODS IN PRACTICE

5.1 Despite the theoretical limitations of the payback method, it is the method most widely used in practice. There are a number of reasons for this.

(a) It is a particularly useful approach for ranking projects where a firm faces liquidity constraints and requires a fast repayment of investments.

(b) It is appropriate in situations where risky investments are made in uncertain markets that are subject to fast design and product changes or where future cash flows are particularly difficult to predict.

(c) Most managers see risk as time-related: the longer the period, the greater the chance of failure. The payback method, by concentrating on the early cash flows, therefore uses data in which they have confidence. The justification for this is that cash flows tend to be correlated over time and hence if cash flows are below the expected level in early years, this pattern will often continue.

(d) The method is often used in conjunction with the NPV or IRR method and acts as a first screening device to identify projects which are worthy of further investigation.

(e) It is easily understood by all levels of management.

(f) It provides an important summary method: how quickly will the initial investment be recouped?

5.2 The ROCE (ARR) method is a popular investment appraisal technique despite its drawbacks mentioned earlier in the chapter. Its popularity is probably due to the fact that it is easily understood and that it uses profits rather than cash flows and hence it can be easily calculated from financial statements.

Chapter roundup

- Investment can be divided into **capital expenditure** and **revenue expenditure** and can be made in **fixed assets** or **working capital**.
- **Strategic analysis** aids the identification of investment opportunities and involves **environmental analysis** and **internal appraisal**, which are combined in **SWOT analysis**.
- The **Boston classification** groups a company's products in terms of potential cash generation and cash expenditure requirements. Products may be stars, cash cows, question marks, dogs, infants or warhorses.
- The **payback method** of investment appraisal and the **ARR/ROCE/ROI** methods of investment appraisal are popular appraisal techniques despite their limitations (of which you should be aware). Ensure that you can appraise projects using both methods and are able to explain their advantages and disadvantages.

Quick quiz

1 What are the differences between capital expenditure and revenue expenditure? (paras 1.2 - 1.7)

2 How does investment by not-for-profit organisations differ from investment by the commercial sector? (1.11, 1.12)

3 What is SWOT analysis? (2.5)

4 What are 'cash cows' and 'question marks'? (2.13)

5 Why is the payback method alone an inadequate investment appraisal technique? (3.6, 3.7)

6 List five drawbacks to the ROCE method of investment appraisal. (4.11 - 4.13)

7 Provide six reasons why the payback method is the most widely used investment appraisal technique in practice. (5.1)

Question to try	Level	Marks	Time
26	Examination	20	36 mins

Chapter 26

INVESTMENT APPRAISAL USING DCF METHODS

Introduction

The **payback** and **ARR** methods of investment appraisal were considered in the previous chapter.

This chapter will look at **DCF** methods of investment appraisal.

Chapter 27 will look at how **inflation** and **taxation** can be incorporated into appraisal techniques.

Exam focus point

Investment appraisal is one of the areas designated as a 'major' FM topic which you can expect to be examined in some form in each exam paper. An ability to use DCF is vital - this has been highlighted by the Examiner as a problem area in the past.

1 DISCOUNTED CASH FLOW AND THE COST OF CAPITAL 6/97

1.1 **Discounted cash flow**, or **DCF** for short, is an investment appraisal technique which takes into account both the timings of cash flows and also total profitability over a project's life.

1.2 Two important points about DCF are as follows.

(a) DCF looks at the **cash flows** of a project, not the accounting profits. Like the payback technique of investment appraisal, DCF is concerned with liquidity, not profitability. Cash flows are considered because they show the costs and benefits of a project when they actually occur. For example, the capital cost of a project will be the original cash outlay, and not the notional cost of depreciation which is used to spread the capital cost over the asset's life in the financial accounts.

(b) The timing of cash flows is taken into account by discounting them. The effect of discounting is to give a bigger value per £1 for cash flows that occur earlier: £1

earned after one year will be worth more than £1 earned after two years, which in turn will be worth more than £1 earned after five years, and so on.

Discounting

1.3 Suppose that a company has £10,000 to invest, and wants to earn a return of 10% (compound interest) on its investments. This means that if the £10,000 could be invested at 10%, the value of the investment with interest would build up as follows.

(a) After 1 year £10,000 × (1.10) = £11,000
(b) After 2 years £10,000 × $(1.10)^2$ = £12,100
(c) After 3 years £10,000 × $(1.10)^3$ = £13,310 and so on.

1.4 This is **compounding**. The formula for the future value of an investment plus accumulated interest after n time periods is:

$$FV = PV\,(1 + r)^n$$

where FV is the future value of the investment with interest
PV is the initial or 'present' value of the investment
r is the compound rate of return per time period, expressed as a proportion (so 10% = 0.10, 5% = 0.05 and so on)
n is the number of time periods.

1.5 **Discounting** starts with the future value, and converts a future value to a present value. For example, if a company expects to earn a (compound) rate of return of 10% on its investments, how much would it need to invest now to have the following investments?

(a) £11,000 after 1 year
(b) £12,100 after 2 years
(c) £13,310 after 3 years

1.6 The answer is £10,000 in each case, and we can calculate it by discounting. The discounting formula to calculate the present value of a future sum of money at the end of n time periods is:

$$PV = FV \frac{1}{1+r^n}$$

(a) After 1 year, £11,000 × $\frac{1}{1.10}$ = £10,000

(b) After 2 years, £12,100 × $\frac{1}{1.10^2}$ = £10,000

(c) After 3 years, £13,310 × $\frac{1}{1.10^3}$ = £10,000

1.7 Discounting can be applied to both money receivable and also to money payable at a future date. By discounting all payments and receipts from a capital investment to a present value, they can be compared on a common basis at a value which takes account of when the various cash flows will take place.

KEY TERM

Present value can be defined as the cash equivalent now of a sum of money receivable or payable at a stated future date, discounted at a specified rate of return.

Question 1

Spender Ltd expects the cash inflow from an investment to be £40,000 after 2 years and another £30,000 after 3 years. Its target rate of return is 12%.

Required

(a) Calculate the present value of these future returns.
(b) Explain what this present value signifies.

Answer

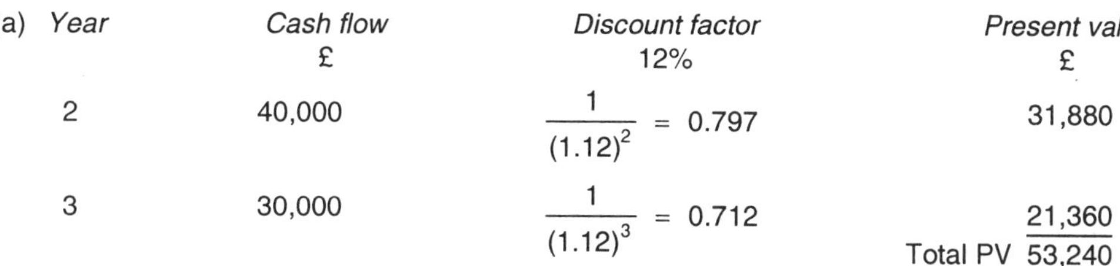

(a) *Year*	*Cash flow* £	*Discount factor* 12%		*Present value* £
2	40,000	$\frac{1}{(1.12)^2}$ = 0.797		31,880
3	30,000	$\frac{1}{(1.12)^3}$ = 0.712		21,360
			Total PV	53,240

(b) The present value of the future returns, discounted at 12%, is £53,240. This means that if Spender Ltd can invest now to earn a return of 12% on its investments, it would have to invest £53,240 now to earn £40,000 after 2 years plus £30,000 after 3 years.

The cost of capital

1.8 The **cost of capital** has two aspects to it.

(a) It is the cost of funds that a company raises and uses, and the return that investors expect to be paid for putting funds into the company.

(b) It is therefore the minimum return that a company should make its own investments, to earn the cash flows out of which investors can be paid their return.

1.9 The cost of capital can therefore be measured by studying the returns required by investors, and used to derive a discount rate for DCF analysis and investment appraisal.

The cost of ordinary share capital

1.10 New funds from equity shareholders are obtained:

(a) from **new issues of shares**
(b) from **retained earnings**

1.11 Both of these sources of funds have a cost.

(a) Shareholders will not be prepared to provide funds for a new issue of shares unless the return on their investment is sufficiently attractive.

(b) Retained earnings also have a cost. This is an opportunity cost, the dividend forgone by shareholders.

1.12 If we begin by ignoring share issue costs, the cost of equity, both for new issues and retained earnings, can be estimated on the assumption that the market value of shares is directly related to expected future dividends on the shares. Different assumptions can be made about whether dividends are expected to grow in the future.

The cost of debt capital and fixed dividend capital

1.13 Estimating the cost of fixed interest or fixed dividend capital (eg preference shares) is much easier than estimating the cost of ordinary share capital because the interest received by the holder of the security is fixed by contract and will not fluctuate. The cost of debt capital already issued is, briefly, the rate of interest (the internal rate of return) which equates the current market price with the discounted future cash receipts from the security.

Computing a discount rate

1.14 It is possible to compute the costs of individual sources of capital for a company, for example in the form of debt or share capital. But how will this help us to work out the **cost of capital** as a whole, or the **discount rate** to apply in DCF investment appraisals?

1.15 In many cases it will be difficult to associate a particular project with a particular form of finance. A company's funds may be viewed as a pool of resources. Money is withdrawn from this pool of funds to invest in new projects and added to the pool as new finance is raised or profits are retained. Under these circumstances it might seem appropriate to use an average cost of capital as the discount rate.

1.16 The correct cost of capital to use in investment appraisal is the marginal cost of the funds raised (or earnings retained) to finance the investment.

The weighted average cost of capital (WACC) might be considered the most reliable guide to the marginal cost of capital, but only on the assumption that the company continues to invest in the future, in projects of a standard level of business risk, by raising funds in the same proportions as its existing capital structure.

Exam focus point

For the Paper 8 exam, you will not be required to produce computations of, or to comment on, a WACC: these more advanced skills form part of the Paper 14 syllabus. In the case of Paper 8, an exam question will give a discount rate as and where appropriate.

1.17 EXAMPLE: WEIGHTED AVERAGE COST OF CAPITAL

Prudence plc is financed partly by equity and partly by debentures. The equity proportion is always kept at two thirds of the total. The cost of equity is 18% and that of debt 12%. A new project is under consideration which will cost £100,000 and will yield a return before interest of £17,500 a year in perpetuity. Should the project be accepted? Ignore taxation.

1.18 SOLUTION

Since the company will maintain its gearing ratio unchanged, it is reasonable to assume that its marginal cost of funds equals its WACC. The weighted average cost of capital is as follows.

	Proportion	*Cost*		*Cost × proportion*
Equity	$\frac{2}{3}$	18%		12%
Debt	$\frac{1}{3}$	12%		4%
			WACC	16%

1.19 The present value of the future returns in perpetuity can be found using the WACC as the discount rate, as follows.

$$\text{Present value of future cash flows} = \frac{\text{Annual cash flow}}{\text{Discount rate}} = \frac{£17{,}500}{0.16} = £109{,}375$$

The NPV of the investment is £109,375 – £100,000 = £9,375.

1.20 Another way of looking at the investment shows how using the WACC as the discount rate ensures that equity shareholders' wealth is increased by undertaking projects with a positive NPV when discounted at the WACC.

The amount of finance deemed to be provided by the debenture holders will be $^1/_3$ × £100,000 = £33,333. The interest on this will be 12% × £33,333 = £4,000, leaving £13,500 available for the equity shareholders. The return they are receiving based on their 'investment' of £66,667 will be as follows.

$$\text{Return to equity} = \frac{£13{,}500}{£66{,}667}$$

$$= 0.2025 = 20.25\%$$

As this return exceeds the cost of equity capital, the project is acceptable.

Weighting

1.21 In the last example, we simplified the problem of weighting the different costs of capital by giving the proportions of capital. Two methods of weighting could be used.

(a) Weights could be based on market values (by this method, the cost of retained earnings is implied in the market value of equity).

(b) Weights could be based on book values.

1.22 Although the latter are often easier to obtain they are of doubtful economic significance. It is, therefore, more meaningful to use market values when data are available. For unquoted companies estimates of market values are likely to be extremely subjective and consequently book values may be used. When using market values it is not possible to split the equity value between share capital and reserves and only one cost of equity can be used. This removes the need to estimate a separate cost of retained earnings.

Argument for and against using the WACC

Arguments for using the WACC

1.23 The weighted average cost of capital is recommended for use in investment appraisal on the assumptions that:

(a) new investments must be financed by new sources of funds: retained earnings, new share issues, new loans and so on;

(b) the cost of capital to be applied to project evaluation must reflect the marginal cost of new capital; and

(c) the weighted average cost of capital reflects the company's long-term future capital structure, and capital costs. If this were not so, the current weighted average cost would become irrelevant because eventually it would not relate to any actual cost of capital.

1.24 It has been argued that the **current weighted average cost of capital** should be used to evaluate projects, because a company's capital structure changes only very slowly over time; therefore the marginal cost of new capital should be roughly equal to the weighted average cost of current capital.

1.25 If this view is correct, then by undertaking investments which offer a return in excess of the WACC, a company will increase the market value of its ordinary shares in the long run. This is because the excess returns would provide surplus profits and dividends for the shareholders.

Arguments against using the WACC

1.26 The arguments against using the WACC as the cost of capital for investment appraisal are based on criticisms of the assumptions that are used to justify use of the WACC.

1.27 The main arguments against the WACC are as follows.

(a) New investments undertaken by a company might have different **business risk** characteristics from the company's existing operations. As a consequence, the return required by investors might go up (or down) if the investments are undertaken, because their business risk is perceived to be higher (or lower).

(b) The finance that is raised to fund a new investment might substantially change the capital structure and the perceived **financial risk** of investing in the company. Depending on whether the project is financed by equity or by debt capital, the perceived financial risk of the entire company might change. This must be taken into account when appraising investments.

(c) Many companies raise **floating rate** debt capital as well as fixed interest debt capital. With floating rate debt capital, the interest rate is variable, and is altered every three or six months or so in line with changes in current market interest rates. The cost of debt capital will therefore fluctuate as market conditions vary. Floating rate debt is difficult to incorporate into a WACC computation, and the best that can be done is to substitute an 'equivalent' fixed interest debt capital cost in place of the floating rate debt cost.

Required returns in the public sector

1.28 For private sector projects, the objective in setting required returns will normally be to match or exceed the returns obtainable from comparable investments by those who subscribe capital (eg ordinary shareholders of a company). In the public sector, on the other hand, the authorities may choose to take account of externalities and the wider social costs and benefits of projects, some of which will not be priced by the market.

Social opportunity cost return

1.29 The social opportunity cost return approach focuses on the opportunity cost to society of undertaking the project. The discount rate chosen reflects the rate of return obtainable from the next best alternative use of public funds, including all externalities.

Social rate of time preference

1.30 Another approach to adopting a discount rate for public sector projects is based on the argument that society has a longer time horizon than private individuals. To reflect this, a lower discount rate is used then would be used for a private sector project.

2 THE NET PRESENT VALUE METHOD 6/95, 12/96

2.1 There are two methods of using DCF to evaluate capital investments.

(a) The net present value (NPV) method
(b) The internal rate of return (IRR) method, or DCF yield method

KEY TERMS

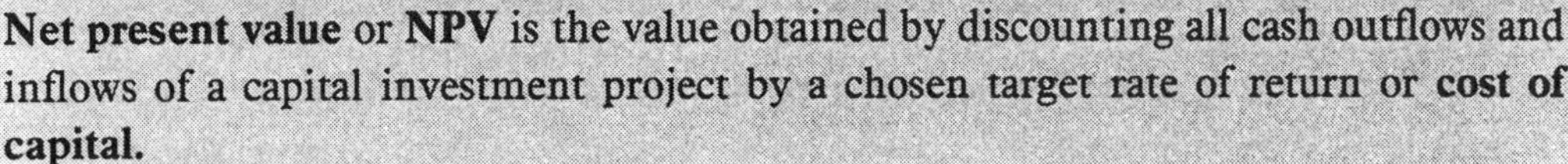

Net present value or **NPV** is the value obtained by discounting all cash outflows and inflows of a capital investment project by a chosen target rate of return or **cost of capital.**

2.2 The NPV method compares the present value of all the cash inflows from an investment with the present value of all the cash outflows from an investment. The NPV is thus calculated as the PV of cash inflows minus the PV of cash outflows.

(a) **If the NPV is positive**, it means that the cash inflows from a capital investment will yield a return in excess of the cost of capital, and so the project should be undertaken if the cost of capital is the organisation's target rate of return.

(b) **If the NPV is negative,** it means that the cash inflows from a capital investment will yield a return below the cost of capital, and so the project should not be undertaken if the cost of capital is the organisation's target rate of return.

(c) **If the NPV is exactly zero**, the cash inflows from a capital investment will yield a return which is exactly the same as the cost of capital, and so if the cost of capital is the organisation's target rate of return, the project will be only just worth undertaking.

2.3 EXAMPLE: NPV

Slogger Ltd is considering a capital investment, where the estimated cash flows are as follows.

Year	*Cash flow*
	£
0 (ie now)	(100,000)
1	60,000
2	80,000
3	40,000
4	30,000

The company's cost of capital is 15%.

Required

Calculate the NPV of the project, and assess whether it should be undertaken?

2.4 SOLUTION

Year	*Cash flow*	*Discount factor*	*Present value*
	£	15%	£
0	(100,000)	1.000	(100,000)
1	60,000	$\frac{1}{(1.15)} = 0.870$	52,200
2	80,000	$\frac{1}{(1.15)^2} = 0.756$	60,480
3	40,000	$\frac{1}{(1.15)^3} = 0.658$	26,320
4	30,000	$\frac{1}{(1.15)^4} = 0.572$	17,160
		NPV =	56,160

(**Note**. The discount factor for any cash flow 'now' (year 0) is always = 1, regardless of what the cost of capital is.)

The PV of cash inflows exceeds the PV of cash outflows by £56,160, which means that the project will earn a DCF yield in excess of 15%. It should therefore be undertaken.

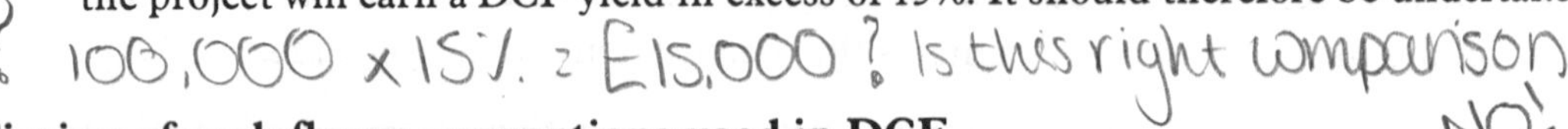

? 100,000 x 15% = £15,000 ? Is this right comparison.
NO!

Timing of cash flows: conventions used in DCF

2.5 It was stated earlier that discounted cash flow applies discounting arithmetic to the relevant costs and benefits of an investment project. Discounting, which reduces the value of future cash flows to a present value equivalent, is clearly concerned with the timing of the cash flows. As a general rule, the following guidelines may be applied.

(a) A cash outlay to be incurred at the beginning of an investment project ('now') occurs in year 0. The present value of £1 now, in year 0, is £1 regardless of the value of r. This is common sense.

(b) A cash outlay, saving or inflow which occurs **during the course of a time period** (say, one year) is assumed to occur all at once at the end of the time period (at the end of the year). Receipts of £10,000 during year 1 are therefore taken to occur at the end of year 1.

(c) A cash outlay or receipt which occurs **at the beginning of a time period** (say at the beginning of one year) is taken to occur at the end of the previous year. Therefore a cash outlay of £5,000 at the beginning of year 2 is taken to occur at the end of year 1.

Discount tables for the PV of £1

2.6 The discount factor that we use in discounting is $\frac{1}{(1+r)^n} = (1+r)^{-n}$

Instead of having to calculate this factor every time we can use tables. Discount tables for the present value of £1, for different values of r and n, are shown in the Appendix to this Study Text. Use these tables to work out your own solution to the following question.

Question 2

LCH Limited manufactures product X which it sells for £5 per unit. Variable costs of production are currently £3 per unit, and fixed costs 50p per unit. A new machine is available which would cost £90,000 but which could be used to make product X for a variable cost of only £2.50 per unit. Fixed costs, however, would increase by £7,500 per annum as a direct result of purchasing the machine. The machine would have an expected life of 4 years and a resale value after that time of £10,000.

Sales of product X are estimated to be 75,000 units per annum. LCH Limited expects to earn at least 12% per annum from its investments.

Ignore taxation.

Required

Decide whether LCH Limited should purchase the machine.

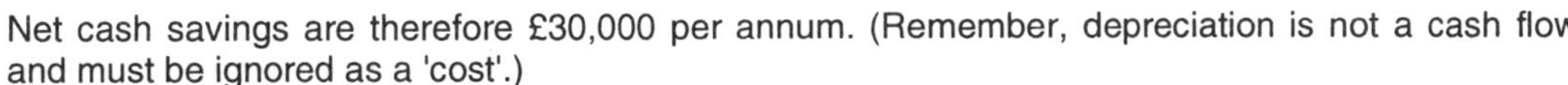

Answer

Savings are 75,000 × (£3 – £2.50) = £37,500 per annum.

Additional costs are £7,500 per annum.

Net cash savings are therefore £30,000 per annum. (Remember, depreciation is not a cash flow and must be ignored as a 'cost'.)

The first step in calculating an NPV is to establish the relevant costs year by year. All future cash flows arising as a direct consequence of the decision should be taken into account.

It is assumed that the machine will be sold for £10,000 at the end of year 4.

Year	*Cash flow*	*PV factor*	*PV of cash flow*
	£	12%	£
0	(90,000)	1.000	(90,000)
1	30,000	0.893	26,790
2	30,000	0.797	23,910
3	30,000	0.712	21,360
4	40,000	0.636	25,440
		NPV =	+7,500

The NPV is positive and so the project is expected to earn more than 12% per annum and is therefore acceptable.

Annuity tables

2.7 In the previous exercise, the calculations could have been simplified for years 1-3 as follows.

$$
\begin{aligned}
& \quad 30{,}000 \times 0.893 \\
& + \ 30{,}000 \times 0.797 \\
& + \ 30{,}000 \times 0.712 \\
& = \ 30{,}000 \times 2.402
\end{aligned}
$$

2.8 Where there is a constant cash flow from year to year (in this case £30,000 per annum for years 1-3) it is quicker to calculate the present value by adding together the discount factors for the individual years. These total factors could be described as 'same cash flow per annum' factors, 'cumulative present value' factors or 'annuity' factors. They are shown in the table for cumulative PV of £1 factors which is shown in the Appendix to this Study Text (2.402, for example, is in the column for 12% per annum and the row for year 3.)

Question 3

If you have not used them before, check that you can understand annuity tables by trying the following exercise.

(a) What is the present value of £1,000 in contribution earned each year from years 1-10, when the required return on investment is 11%?

(b) What is the present value of £2,000 costs incurred each year from years 3-6 when the cost of capital is 5%?

Answer

(a) The PV of £1,000 earned each year from year 1-10 when the required earning rate of money is 11% is calculated as follows.

£1,000 × 5.889 = £5,889

(b) The PV of £2,000 in costs each year from years 3-6 when the cost of capital is 5% per annum is calculated as follows.

PV of £1 per annum for years 1 - 6 at 5% =	5.076
Less PV of £1 per annum for years 1 - 2 at 5% =	1.859
PV of £1 per annum for years 3 - 6 =	3.217

PV = £2,000 × 3.217 = £6,434

2.9 EXAMPLE: NPV INCLUDING USE OF ANNUITY TABLES

Elsie Limited is considering the manufacture of a new product which would involve the use of both a new machine (costing £150,000) and an existing machine, which cost £80,000 two years ago and has a current net book value of £60,000. There is sufficient capacity on this machine, which has so far been under-utilised.

Annual sales of the product would be 5,000 units, selling at £32 per unit. Unit costs would be as follows.

	£
Direct labour (4 hours at £2 per hour)	8
Direct materials	7
Fixed costs including depreciation	9
	24

The project would have a five-year life, after which the new machine would have a net residual value of £10,000. Because direct labour is continually in short supply, labour resources would have to be diverted from other work which currently earns a contribution of £1.50 per direct labour hour. The fixed overhead absorption rate would be £2.25 per hour (£9 per unit) but actual expenditure on fixed overhead would not alter.

Working capital requirements would be £10,000 in the first year, rising to £15,000 in the second year and remaining at this level until the end of the project, when it will all be recovered.

The company's cost of capital is 20%. Ignore taxation.

Required

Assess whether the project is worthwhile.

2.10 SOLUTION

The relevant cash flows are as follows.

(a)	Year 0	Purchase of new machine	£150,000
			£
(b)	Years 1-5	Contribution from new product	
		(5,000 units × £(32 – 15))	85,000
		Less contribution foregone	
		(5,000 × (4 × £1.50))	30,000
			55,000

(c) The project requires £10,000 of working capital at the end of year 1 and a further £5,000 at the start of year 2.

Increases in working capital reduce the net cash flow for the period to which they relate. When the working capital tied up in the project is 'recovered' at the end of the project, it will provide an extra cash inflow (for example debtors will eventually pay up).

(d) All other costs, which are past costs, notional accounting costs or costs which would be incurred anyway without the project, are not relevant to the investment decision.

(e) The NPV is calculated as follows.

Year	*Equipment*	*Working capital*	*Contribution*	*Net cash flow*	*Discount factor*	*PV of net cash flow*
	£	£	£	£	20%	£
0	(150,000)	(10,000)		(160,000)	1.000	(160,000)
1		(5,000)		(5,000)	0.833	(4,165)
1-5			55,000	55,000	2.991	164,505
5	10,000	15,000		25,000	0.402	10,005
					NPV =	10,390

The NPV is positive and the project is worthwhile, although there is not much margin for error. Some risk analysis of the project is recommended.

Annual cash flows in perpetuity

2.11 You need to know how to calculate the cumulative present value of £1 per annum for every year in perpetuity (that is, forever).

When the cost of capital is r, the cumulative PV of £1 per annum in perpetuity is £1/r.

2.12 For example, the PV of £1 per annum in perpetuity at a discount rate of 10% would be £1/0.10 = £10.

Similarly, the PV of £1 per annum in perpetuity at a discount rate of 15% would be £1/0.15 = £6.67 and at a discount rate of 20% it would be £1/0.20 = £5.

Question 4

An organisation with a cost of capital of 14% is considering investing in a project costing £500,000 that would yield cash inflows of £100,000 pa in perpetuity.

Required

Assess whether the project should be undertaken.

Answer

Year	*Cash flow*	*Discount factor*	*Present value*
	£	14%	£
0	(500,000)	1.000	(500,000)
1 - ∞	100,000	1/0.14 = 7.143	714,300
		Net present value	214,300

The NPV is positive and so the project should be undertaken.

3 THE INTERNAL RATE OF RETURN METHOD 12/96

3.1 Using the NPV method of discounted cash flow, present values are calculated by discounting at a target rate of return, or cost of capital, and the difference between the PV of costs and the PV of benefits is the NPV.

In contrast, the **internal rate of return (IRR)** method is to calculate the exact DCF rate of return which the project is expected to achieve, in other words the rate at which the NPV is zero.

If the expected rate of return (the IRR or DCF yield) exceeds a target rate of return, the project would be worth undertaking (ignoring risk and uncertainty factors).

3.2 Without a computer or calculator program, the calculation of the internal rate of return is made using a hit-and-miss technique known as the interpolation method.

3.3 The first step is to calculate two net present values, both as close as possible to zero, using rates for the cost of capital which are whole numbers. Ideally, one NPV should be positive and the other negative.

3.4 Choosing rates for the cost of capital which will give an NPV close to zero (that is, rates which are close to the actual rate of return) is a hit-and-miss exercise, and several attempts may be needed to find satisfactory rates. *As a rough guide*, try starting at a return figure which is about two thirds or three quarters of the accounting return on investment or accounting rate of return (ARR).

3.5 EXAMPLE: THE IRR METHOD

A company is trying to decide whether to buy a machine for £80,000 which will save costs of £20,000 per annum for 5 years and which will have a resale value of £10,000 at the end of year 5.

Required

If it is the company's policy to undertake projects only if they are expected to yield a DCF return of 10% or more, ascertain whether this project be undertaken.

3.6 SOLUTION

Annual depreciation would be £(80,000 – 10,000)/5 = £14,000.

The return on investment would be:

$$\frac{20{,}000 - \text{depreciation of } 14{,}000}{\frac{1}{2} \text{ of } (80{,}000 + 10{,}000)} = \frac{6{,}000}{45{,}000} = 13.3\%$$

Two thirds of this is 8.9% and so we can start by trying 9%.

The IRR is the rate for the cost of capital at which the NPV = 0.

Try 9%:

Year	*Cash flow*	*PV factor*		*PV of cash flow*
	£	9%		£
0	(80,000)	1.000		(80,000)
1-5	20,000	3.890		77,800
5	10,000	0.650		6,500
			NPV	4,300

3.7 This is fairly close to zero. It is also positive, which means that the real rate of return is more than 9%. We can use 9% as one of our two NPVs close to zero, although for greater accuracy, we should try 10% or even 11% to find an NPV even closer to zero if we can. As a guess, it might be worth trying 12% next, to see what the NPV is.

Try 12%:

Year	*Cash flow*	*PV factor*	*PV of cash flow*
	£	12%	£
0	(80,000)	1.000	(80,000)
1-5	20,000	3.605	72,100
5	10,000	0.567	5,670
		NPV	(2,230)

This is fairly close to zero and *negative*. The real rate of return is therefore greater than 9% (positive NPV of £4,300) but less than 12% (negative NPV of £2,230).

Note. If the first NPV is positive, choose a higher rate for the next calculation to get a negative NPV. If the first NPV is negative, choose a lower rate for the next calculation.

3.8 If we were to draw a graph of a 'typical' capital project, with a negative cash flow at the start of the project, and positive net cash flows afterwards up to the end of the project, we could draw a graph of the project's NPV at different costs of capital. It would look like Figure 1.

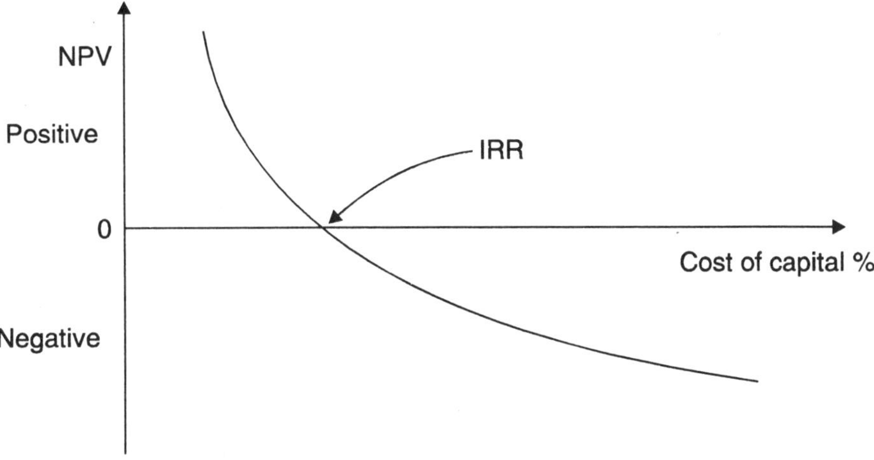

Figure 1

3.9 If we calculate a cost of capital where the NPV is slightly positive, and another cost of capital where it is slightly negative, we can estimate the IRR - where the NPV is zero - by drawing a straight line between the two points on the graph that we have calculated.

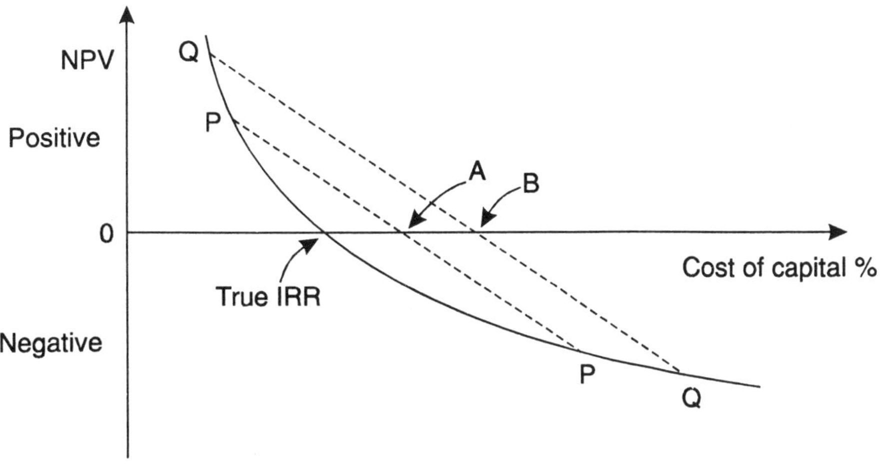

Figure 2

3.10 Consider Figure 2.

(a) If we establish the NPVs at the two points P, we would estimate the IRR to be at point A.

(b) If we establish the NPVs at the two points Q, we would estimate the IRR to be at point B.

The closer our NPVs are to zero, the closer our estimate will be to the true IRR.

3.11 We shall now use the two NPV values calculated earlier to estimate the IRR.

The interpolation method assumes that the NPV rises in linear fashion between the two NPVs close to 0. The real rate of return is therefore assumed to be on a straight line between NPV = £4,300 at 9% and NPV = –£2,230 at 12%.

3.12 The formula to apply is as follows.

$$IRR = A + \left[\frac{P}{P+N} \times (B - A)\right]\%$$

where A is the (lower) rate of return with a positive NPV
B is the (higher) rate of return with a negative NPV
P is the amount of the positive NPV
N is the amount of the negative NPV

3.13 Let us go back to our example.

$$IRR = 9 + \left[\frac{4{,}300}{4{,}300 + 2{,}230} \times (12 - 9)\right]\% = 10.98\%, \text{ say } 11\%$$

0·658

If it is company policy to undertake investments which are expected to yield 10% or more, this project would be undertaken.

Question 5

Find the IRR of the project given below and state whether the project should be accepted if the company requires a minimum return of 17%.

Time		£
0	Investment	(4,000)
1	Receipts	1,200
2	"	1,410
3	"	1,875
4	"	1,150

Answer

The total receipts are £5,635 giving a total profit of £1,635 and average profits of £409. The average investment is £2,000. The ARR is £409 ÷ £2,000 = 20%. Two thirds of the ARR is approximately 14%. The initial estimate of the IRR that we shall try is therefore 14%.

Time	*Cash flow*	*Try 14%* *Discount factor*	*PV*	*Try 16%* *Discount factor*	*PV*
	£	14%	£	16%	£
0	(4,000)	1.000	(4,000)	1.000	(4,000)
1	1,200	0.877	1,052	0.862	1,034
2	1,410	0.769	1,084	0.743	1,048
3	1,875	0.675	1,266	0.641	1,202
4	1,150	0.592	681	0.552	635
		NPV	83	NPV	(81)

The IRR must be less than 16%, but higher than 14%. The NPVs at these two costs of capital will be used to estimate the IRR.

Using the interpolation formula:

$$\text{IRR} = 14\% + \left[\frac{83}{83 + 81} \times (16\% - 14\%)\right] = 15.01\%$$

The IRR is, in fact, exactly 15%.

The project should be rejected as the IRR is less than the minimum return demanded.

4 NPV AND IRR COMPARED

4.1 Given that there are two methods of using DCF, the NPV method and the IRR method, the relative merits of each method have to be considered.

Advantages of IRR method

4.2 The main advantage of the IRR method is that the information it provides is more easily understood by managers, especially non-financial managers. For example, it is fairly easy to understand the meaning of the following statement.

> 'The project will be expected to have an initial capital outlay of £100,000, and to earn a yield of 25%. This is in excess of the target yield of 15% for investments.'

It is not so easy to understand the meaning of this statement.

> 'The project will cost £100,000 and have an NPV of £30,000 when discounted at the minimum required rate of 15%.'

Disadvantages of IRR method

4.3 It might be tempting to confuse IRR and accounting return on capital employed (ROCE). The accounting ROCE and the IRR are two completely different measures. If managers were given information about both ROCE (or ROI) and IRR, it might be easy to get their relative meaning and significance mixed up.

4.4 The IRR method ignores the relative size of investments. Both the following projects have an IRR of 18%.

	Project A	*Project B*
	£	£
Cost, year 0	350,000	35,000
Annual savings, years 1-6	100,000	10,000

Clearly, project A is bigger (ten times as big) and so more 'profitable' but if the only information on which the projects were judged were to be their IRR of 18%, project B would be made to seem just as beneficial as project A, which is not the case.

Non-conventional cash flows

4.5 The projects we have considered so far have had conventional cash flows (an initial cash outflow followed by a series of inflows). When flows vary from this they are termed non-conventional. The following project has **non-conventional cash flows**.

Year	*Project X*
	£'000
0	(1,900)
1	4,590
2	(2,735)

4.6 Project X would have two IRRs as shown by Figure 3.

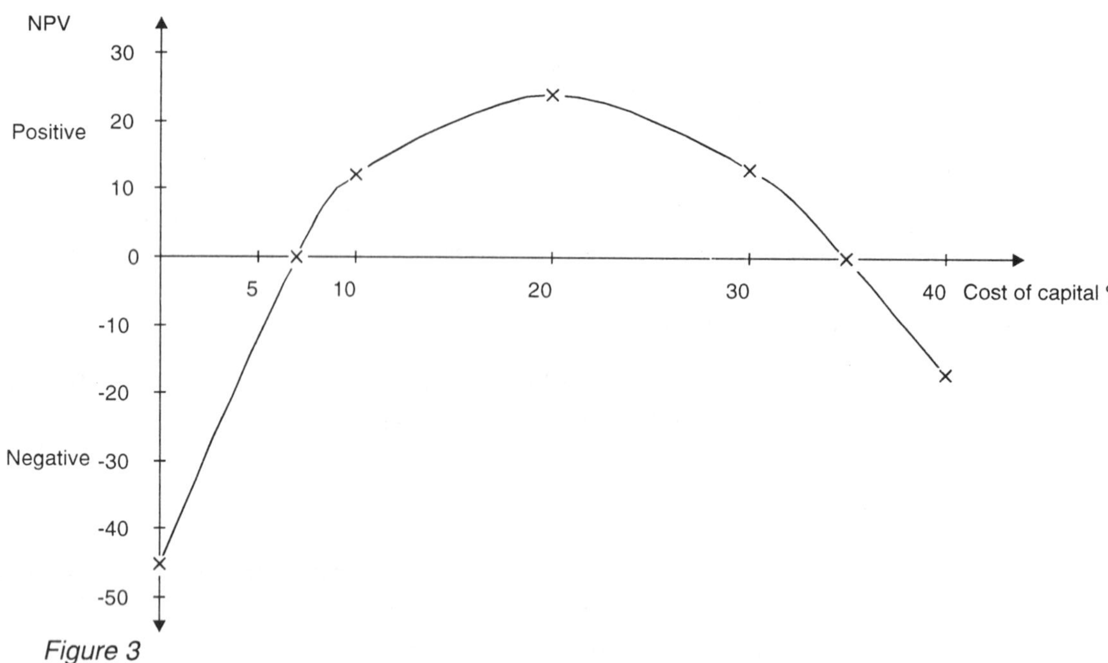

Figure 3

4.7 The NPV rule suggests that the project is acceptable between costs of capital of 7% and 35%. Suppose that the required rate on project X is 10% and that the IRR of 7% is used in deciding whether to accept or reject the project. The project would be rejected since it appears that it can only yield 7%. The diagram shows, however, that between rates of 7% and 35% the project should be accepted. Using the IRR of 35% would produce the correct decision to accept the project. Lack of knowledge of multiple IRRs could therefore lead to serious errors in the decision of whether to accept or reject a project.

4.8 In general, if the sign of the net cash flow changes in successive periods, it is possible for the calculations to produce as many IRRs as there are sign changes.

4.9 The use of the IRR is therefore not recommended in circumstances in which there are non-conventional cash flow patterns (unless the decision maker is aware of the existence of multiple IRRs). The NPV method, on the other hand, gives clear, unambiguous results whatever the cash flow pattern.

Exam focus point

You need to be aware of the possibility of multiple IRRs, but the area is not examinable at a computational level.

Mutually exclusive projects

4.10 Mutually exclusive projects are two or more projects from which only one can be chosen. Examples include the choice of a factory location or the choice of just one of a number of machines.

4.11 The IRR and NPV methods can, however, give conflicting rankings as to which project should be given priority. Let us suppose that a company is considering two mutually exclusive options, option A and option B. The cash flows for each would be as follows.

Year		Option A	Option B
		£	£
0	Capital outlay	(10,200)	(35,250)
1	Net cash inflow	6,000	18,000
2	Net cash inflow	5,000	15,000
3	Net cash inflow	3,000	15,000

The company's cost of capital is 16%.

4.12 The NPV of each project is calculated below.

		Option A		Option B	
Year	Discount factor	Cash flow	Present value	Cash flow	Present value
		£	£	£	£
0	1.000	(10,200)	(10,200)	(35,250)	(35,250)
1	0.862	6,000	5,172	18,000	15,516
2	0.743	5,000	3,715	15,000	11,145
3	0.641	3,000	1,923	15,000	9,615
		NPV =	+610	NPV =	+1,026

The DCF yield of option A is 20% and the yield of option B is only 18% (workings not shown.)

On a comparison of NPVs, option B would be preferred, but on a comparison of IRRs, option A would be preferred.

4.13 If the projects were independent this would be irrelevant since under the NPV rule both would be accepted and the organisation would be indifferent as to the order in which they were accepted. With mutually exclusive projects, however, only one project can be accepted and therefore the ranking is crucial and we cannot be indifferent to the outcomes of the NPV and IRR appraisal methods.

Reinvestment assumptions

4.14 An assumption underlying the NPV method is that any net cash inflows generated during the life of the project will be reinvested at the cost of capital (that is, the discount rate). The IRR method, on the other hand, assumes these cash flows can be reinvested to earn a return equal to the IRR of the original project. In the example in Paragraph 4.12, the NPV method assumes that the cash inflows of £6,000, £5,000 and £3,000 for option A will be reinvested at the cost of capital of 16% whereas the IRR method assumes they will be reinvested at 20%. In theory, a firm will have accepted all projects which provide a return in excess of the cost of capital and any other funds which become available can only be reinvested at the cost of capital. This is the assumption implied in the NPV rule.

Summary of NPV and IRR comparison

4.15 (a) When cash flow patterns are conventional both methods gives the same accept or reject decision.

(b) The IRR method is more easily understood.

(c) NPV is technically superior to IRR and simpler to calculate.

(d) IRR and accounting ROCE can be confused.

(e) IRR ignores the relative sizes of investments.

(f) Where cash flow patterns are non-conventional, there may be several IRRs which decision makers must be aware of to avoid making the wrong decision.

(g) The NPV method is superior for ranking mutually exclusive projects in order of attractiveness.

(h) The reinvestment assumption underlying the IRR method cannot be substantiated.

(i) When discount rates are expected to differ over the life of the project, such variations can be incorporated easily into NPV calculations, but not into IRR calculations.

(j) Despite the advantages of the NPV method over the IRR method, the IRR method is widely used in practice.

5 THE ADVANTAGES OF THE DCF METHOD OF PROJECT APPRAISAL

The time value of money

5.1 DCF is a capital appraisal technique that is based on a concept known as the time value of money: the concept that £1 received today is not equal to £1 received in the future.

5.2 Given the choice between receiving £100 today, and £100 in one year's time, most people would opt to receive £100 today because they could spend it or invest it to earn interest. If the interest rate was 10%, you could invest £100 today and it would be worth (£100 × 1.10) = £110 in one year's time. A sum of money received now is therefore worth more than the same amount of money received in the future.

5.3 There are, however, other reasons why a present £1 is worth more than a future £1.

(a) **Uncertainty.** The business world is full of risk and uncertainty and although there might be a promise of money to come in the future, it can never be certain that the money will be received until it has actually been paid.

(b) **Inflation.** It is common sense that £1 now is worth more than £1 in the future because of inflation. It should be noted that the time value of money concept applies even if there is zero inflation. Inflation obviously increases the discrepancy in value between monies received at different times but it is not the basis of the concept.

5.4 Taking account of the time value of money (by discounting) is one of the principal advantages of the DCF appraisal method.

Other advantages of the DCF appraisal method

5.5 (a) The method uses all cash flows relating to the project.
(b) It allows for the timing of the cash flows.
(c) There are universally accepted methods of calculating the NPV and the IRR.

The use of appraisal methods in practice

5.6 A survey of the use of capital investment evaluation methods in the UK carried out by RH Pike in 1992 produced the following results on the frequency of use of different methods by 100 large UK firms.

Capital investment evaluation methods in 100 large UK firms: frequency of use

	Total	*Always*	*Mostly*	*Often*	*Rarely*
Firms using	%	%	%	%	%
Payback	94	62	14	12	6
Accounting rate of return	50	21	5	13	17
Internal rate of return	81	54	7	13	7
Net present value	74	33	14	16	11

(Source: Pike & Neale, *Corporate finance and investment*)

5.7 Almost two-thirds of the firms surveyed by Pike used three or more appraisal techniques, indicating that DCF techniques complement rather than replace more traditional approaches.

5.8 The following points are worth noting.

(a) The payback method is used in the great majority (94%) of companies surveyed. Although it remains a traditional 'rule-of-thumb method' with limited theoretical justification because it ignores the profile of cash flows and cash flows beyond the payback period, it will provide in practice a fair approximation to the net present value method. Its widespread use is perhaps then not so reprehensible given the uncertainty of future cash flows and the tendency of cash flows following the payback period to be similar in form to earlier cash flows in most cases.

(b) In spite of its theoretical limitations (notably, its failure to take account of the time value of money), the accounting rate of return (ARR) method was used in half of the companies surveyed. This is perhaps to be expected, given the importance in practice of the rate of return on capital as a financial goal.

(c) The data shows a preference for the IRR method over the NPV method. It would appear that, in spite of theoretical reasons for favour NPV, the IRR method is preferred by managers as a convenient way of ranking projects in percentage terms.

6 ASSET REPLACEMENT DECISIONS

6.1 As well as assisting with decisions between particular assets, DCF techniques can be used in asset replacement decisions, to assess *when* and *how frequently* an asset should be replaced.

6.2 When an asset is to be replaced by an 'identical' asset, the problem is to decide the optimum interval between replacements. As the asset gets older, it may cost more to maintain and operate, its residual value will decrease, and it may lose some productivity/operating capability. Consider the following example.

6.3 EXAMPLE: REPLACEMENT OF AN IDENTICAL ASSET

James Ltd operates a machine which has the following costs and resale values over its four year life.

Purchase cost: £25,000

	Year 1	*Year 2*	*Year 3*	*Year 4*
	£	£	£	£
Running costs (cash expenses)	7,500	10,000	12,500	15,000
Resale value (end of year)	15,000	10,000	7,500	2,500

The organisation's cost of capital is 10%.

Required

Assess how frequently the asset should be replaced.

6.4 SOLUTION

There are three basic methods of deciding the optimum replacement cycle.

(a) The lowest common multiple method
(b) The finite horizon method
(c) The equivalent annual cost method

Each method will give the same recommendation, as shown in the paragraphs below.

6.5 All three methods are concerned with the problem that a replacement asset will eventually be replaced itself by an asset which will also in its turn be replaced. Replacements are continuous, and are assumed to occur into the indefinite future. The replacement options in our example are assumed to be to replace the machine as frequently as shown below.

(a) Every year
(b) Every two years
(c) Every three years
(d) Every four years (at the end of its useful life)

To compare these options, given that replacements will be continuous into the indefinite future, it is necessary to assess costs over a comparable period of time.

The lowest common multiple method

6.6 The **lowest common multiple method** works like this.

(a) Estimate the cash flows over a period of time which is the lowest common multiple of all the replacement cycles under consideration. Thus for replacement cycles of one, two, three or four years, the lowest common multiple of time is twelve years. In twelve years there would be the following numbers of replacement cycles.

(i) Twelve complete replacement cycles of one year
(ii) Six complete replacement cycles of two years
(iii) Four complete replacement cycles of three years
(iv) Three complete replacement cycles of four years

(b) Discount these cash flows over the lowest common multiple time period. The option with the lowest present value of cost will be the optimum replacement cycle.

6.7 In our example, we can calculate the annual cash flows as follows.

(a) *Replacement every year*

Year		£	£
0	Purchase		(25,000)
1	Running cost	(7,500)	
	Resale value	15,000	
	New purchase	(25,000)	
			(17,500)
2-11	Same as year 1		(17,500)
12	Running cost	(7,500)	
	Resale value	15,000	
			7,500

The new purchase at the end of year 12 is ignored, because this starts a new 12-year cycle for all four replacement options.

(b) *Replacement every two years*

Year		£	£
0	Purchase		(25,000)
1	Running cost		(7,500)
2	Running cost	(10,000)	
	Resale value	10,000	
	New purchase	(25,000)	
			(25,000)
3,5,7,9,11	Same as year 1		
4,6,8,10	Same as year 2		
12	Running cost	(10,000)	
	Resale value	10,000	
			0

(c) *Replacement every three years*

Year		£	£
0	Purchase		(25,000)
1	Running cost		(7,500)
2	Running cost		(10,000)
3	Running cost	(12,500)	
	Resale value	7,500	
	New purchase	(25,000)	
			(30,000)
4,7,10	Same as year 1		
5,8,11	Same as year 2		
6,9	Same as year 3		
12	Running cost	(12,500)	
	Resale value	7,500	
			(5,000)

(d) *Replacement every four years*

Year		£	£
0	Purchase		(25,000)
1	Running cost		(7,500)
2	Running cost		(10,000)
3	Running cost		(12,500)
4	Running cost	(15,000)	
	Resale value	2,500	
	New purchase	(25,000)	
			(37,500)
5,9	Same as year 1		
6,10	Same as year 2		
7,11	Same as year 3		
8	Same as year 4		
12	Running cost	(15,000)	
	Resale value	2,500	
			(12,500)

6.8 We can now go on to calculate the PV cost for each replacement cycle, over a 12-year period. Discount factors are not shown in the figures below, but check that you can do the calculations yourself, using the discount tables.

Year	Replacement every year Cash flow £	PV at 10% £	Replacement every 2 years Cash flow £	PV at 10% £	Replacement every 3 years Cash flow £	PV at 10% £	Replacement every 4 years Cash flow £	PV at 10% £
0	(25,000)	(25,000)	(25,000)	(25,000)	(25,000)	(25,000)	(25,000)	(25,000)
1	(17,500))		(7,500)	(6,818)	(7,500)	(6,818)	(7,500)	(6,818)
2	(17,500))		(25,000)	(20,650)	(10,000)	(8,260)	(10,000)	(8,260)
3	(17,500))		(7,500)	(5,633)	(30,000)	(22,530)	(12,500)	(9,388)
4	(17,500))		(25,000)	(17,075)	(7,500)	(5,123)	(37,500)	(25,613)
5	(17,500))		(7,500)	(4,658)	(10,000)	(6,210)	(7,500)	(4,658)
6	(17,500))	(113,663)	(25,000)	(14,100)	(30,000)	(16,920)	(10,000)	(5,640)
7	(17,500))		(7,500)	(3,848)	(7,500)	(3,848)	(12,500)	(6,413)
8	(17,500))		(25,000)	(11,675)	(10,000)	(4,670)	(37,500)	(17,513)
9	(17,500))		(7,500)	(3,180)	(30,000)	(12,720)	(7,500)	(3,180)
10	(17,500))		(25,000)	(9,650)	(7,500)	(2,895)	(10,000)	(3,860)
11	(17,500))		(7,500)	(2,625)	(10,000)	(3,500)	(12,500)	(4,375)
12	7,500	2,393	0	0	(5,000)	(1,595)	(12,500)	(3,988)
PV of costs		(136,270)		(124,912)		(120,089)		(124,706)

6.9 The cheapest replacement policy would be to replace the machine every three years, because this has the lowest total PV of cost.

The finite horizon method

6.10 As you will appreciate, the lowest common multiple method becomes a very long and tedious process when the maximum life of the asset is more than about three years. If the maximum life were, say, seven years, there would be seven different replacement options and the lowest common multiple would be 420 years.

6.11 The finite horizon method is to calculate the present value of costs over a 'significant' time period (perhaps 15 or 20 years), because the present values of cash flows beyond this period are unlikely to affect the relative costs of the replacement options.

6.12 In our example, if the PV of costs had been calculated over a finite time period of ten years, the three year replacement option would still have been the cheapest. The finite time horizon method is therefore an approximation method which reduces the figure work needed, in the expectation that in spite of taking a short cut, the result is still the same.

The equivalent annual cost method

6.13 When there is no inflation, the **equivalent annual cost method** is the quickest method of deciding the optimum replacement cycle. To begin, it is necessary to calculate the present value of costs for each replacement cycle, but over one cycle only.

Year	Replace every year Cash flow £	PV at 10% £	Replace every 2 years Cash flow £	PV at 10% £	Replace every 3 years Cash flow £	PV at 10% £	Replace every 4 years Cash flow £	PV at 10% £
0	(25,000)	(25,000)	(25,000)	(25,000)	(25,000)	(25,000)	(25,000)	(25,000)
1	7,500	6,818	(7,500)	(6,818)	(7,500)	(6,818)	(7,500)	(6,818)
2			0	0	(10,000)	(8,260)	(10,000)	(8,260)
3					(5,000)	(3,755)	(12,500)	(9,388)
4							(12,500)	(8,538)
PV of cost over one replacement cycle		(18,182)		(31,818)		(43,833)		(58,004)

6.14 These costs are not comparable, because they refer to different time periods, whereas replacement is continuous.

The equivalent annual cost method of comparing these cash flows is to calculate, for each length of replacement cycle, an annuity (annual cost) which has the same present value, discounted at the cost of capital, as the cost of repeated cycles of the various lengths under consideration.

6.15 In other words, we calculate the cash flows over one replacement cycle, and the PV of these cash flows, and then we turn this PV of cost into an equivalent annual cost.

The equivalent annual cost is calculated as follows.

$$\frac{\text{The PV of cost over one replacement cycle}}{\text{The cumulative present value factor for the number of years in the cycle}}$$

If there are three years in the cycle, the denominator will be the present value of an annuity for three years at 10% (2.487).

6.16 In our example, given a discount rate of 10%, the equivalent annual cost is calculated as follows.

(a) Replacement every year:

$$\text{Equivalent annual cost} = \frac{£(18{,}182)}{0.909} = £(20{,}002)$$

(b) Replacement every two years:

$$\text{Equivalent annual cost} = \frac{£(31{,}818)}{1.736} = £(18{,}328)$$

(c) Replacement every three years:

$$\text{Equivalent annual cost} = \frac{£(43{,}833)}{2.487} = £(17{,}625)$$

(d) Replacement every four years:

$$\text{Equivalent annual cost} = \frac{£(58{,}004)}{3.170} = £(18{,}298)$$

The optimum replacement policy is the one with the lowest equivalent annual cost, every three years. This is the same conclusion reached by the earlier lowest common multiple method.

Exam focus point

The equivalent annual cost method is recommended because it is quicker and less cumbersome than either of the previous two methods described.

Non-identical replacement

6.17 When a machine is to be replaced by a machine of a different type, there is a different replacement problem. The decision has to be made as to when the existing asset should be replaced rather than how frequently it should be replaced.

6.18 The optimum replacement cycle for the new machine may be calculated by one of the methods described previously. This does not resolve the further problem as to whether the old machine should be replaced now, or in one year's time, two year's time, and so on.

6.19 EXAMPLE: NON-IDENTICAL REPLACEMENT

Suppose that James Ltd's machine (in our example in Paragraph 6.3) is a new machine, and will be introduced to replace a non-identical existing machine which is nearing the end of its life and has a maximum remaining life of only three years. The organisation wishes to decide when is the best time to replace the old machine, and estimates of relevant costs have been drawn up as follows.

Year	*Resale value of current machine*	*Extra expenditure and opportunity costs of keeping the existing machine in operation during the year*
	£	£
Now 0	8,500	n/a
1	5,000	9,000
2	2,500	12,000
3	0	15,000

Required

Calculate the best time to replace the existing machine.

6.20 SOLUTION

The costs of the new machine will be those given in Paragraph 6.3, so that the optimum replacement cycle for the new machine will already have been calculated as three years, with an equivalent annual cost in perpetuity of £17,625 (Paragraph 6.16(c)).

The best time to replace the existing machine will be the option which gives the lowest NPV of cost in perpetuity, for both the existing machine and the machine which eventually replaces it.

(a) The present value of an annuity, £a per annum, in perpetuity is:

$\frac{a}{r}$ where r is the cost of capital

(b) This formula may be used to calculate the PV of cost in perpetuity of the new machine. In our example:

$$\text{PV of cost} = \frac{£17,625}{0.1} = £176,250$$

The new machine will have a PV of cost in perpetuity of £176,250 from the start of the year when it is eventually purchased.

The present value relates to the beginning of the year when the first annual cash flow occurs, so that if replacement occurs now, the first annuity is in year 1, and the PV of cost relates to year 0 values. If replacement occurs at the end of year 1 the first annuity is in year 2, and the PV of cost relates to year 1, and so on.

The total cash flows of the replacement decision may now be presented as follows. These cash flows show the PV of cost in perpetuity of the new machine, the running costs of the existing machine, and the resale value of the existing machine, at the end of year 0, 1, 2 or 3 as appropriate.

Year	Replace now	Replace in 1 year	Replace in 2 years	Replace in 3 years
	£	£	£	£
0	(176,250)	–	–	–
	8,500			
1	–	(176,250)		
		(9,000)	(9,000)	(9,000)
		5,000		
2	–	–	(176,250)	
			(12,000)	(12,000)
			2,500	
3	–	–	–	(176,250)
				(15,000)

The PVs of each replacement option are as follows.

	Year	Cash flow	Discount factor	Present value
		£	10%	£
Replace now	0	(176,250)		
		8,500		
		(167,750)	1.000	(167,750)
Replace in one year	1	(176,250)		
		(9,000)		
		5,000		
		(180,250)	0.909	(163,847)
Replace in two years	1	(9,000)	0.909	(8,181)
	2	(185,750)	0.826	(153,430)
				(161,611)
Replace in three years	1	(9,000)	0.909	(8,181)
	2	(12,000)	0.826	(9,912)
	3	(191,250)	0.751	(143,629)
				(161,722)

The *marginally* optimum policy would be to replace the existing machine in two years' time, because this has the lowest total PV of cost in perpetuity.

Chapter roundup

- There are two methods of using DCF to evaluate capital investments, the **NPV method** and the **IRR/DCF yield method.**
- The **NPV method** of investment appraisal is to accept projects with a positive NPV. Ensure that you are aware of the three conventions concerning the timings of cash flows.
- An **annuity** is a constant cash flow for a number of years. A **perpetuity** is a constant cash flow forever.
- The **IRR method** of investment appraisal is to accept projects whose IRR (the rate at which the NPV is zero) exceeds a target rate of return. The IRR is calculated using interpolation.
- The formula to apply is as follows.

$$\text{IRR} = A + \left[\frac{P}{P+N} \times (B-A)\right]\%$$

- There are advantages and disadvantages to each appraisal method. Make sure that you can discuss them.
- **DCF methods of appraisal** have a number of **advantages** over other appraisal methods.

  The time value of money is taken into account.
  The method takes account of all of a project's cash flows.
  It allows for the timing of cash flows.
  There are universally accepted methods of calculating the NPV and IRR.

- DCF techniques can assist **asset replacement decisions**. When an asset is being replaced with an identical asset there are three methods of choosing an **optimum replacement cycle**.

  The lowest common multiple method
  The finite horizon method
  The equivalent annual cost method

- When an asset is being replaced with a non-identical asset the decision is when to replace the asset rather than how frequently.

Quick quiz

1 What is the formula for calculating the future value of an investment plus accumulated interest after n time periods? (see para 1.4)

2 What is the formula for calculating the present value of a future sum of money at the end of n time periods? (1.6)

3 What is the present value of a sum of money? (1.7)

4 List three cash flow timing conventions used in DCF. (2.5)

5 What is the perpetuity formula? (2.11)

6 How is an IRR calculated using the interpolation formula? (3.2 - 3.12)

7 What are the non-conventional cash flows? (4.5)

8 List four advantages of the DCF methods of project appraisal over other appraisal methods. (5.4, 5.5)

9 Explain how the lowest common multiple method assists in asset replacement decisions. (6.6 - 6.9)

Question to try	Level	Marks	Time
27	Examination	25	45 mins

Chapter 27

ALLOWING FOR INFLATION AND TAXATION

Chapter topic list		Syllabus reference
1	Allowing for inflation	6(b)(iii)
2	Allowing for taxation	7(a)(vi)

Introduction

Having covered the more sophisticated of the investment appraisal techniques which are available in Chapter 26, we will be looking in this chapter at how to incorporate **inflation** and **taxation** into investment decisions.

The next chapter will consider how the **risk** associated with a project can be assessed and taken into account.

1 ALLOWING FOR INFLATION 6/94, 12/96

1.1 So far we have not considered the effect of **inflation** on the appraisal of capital investment proposals. As the inflation rate increases so will the minimum return required by an investor. For example, you might be happy with a return of 5% in an inflation-free world, but if inflation was running at 15% you would expect a considerably greater yield.

1.2 EXAMPLE: INFLATION (1)

A company is considering investing in a project with the following cash flows.

Time	*Actual cash flows*
	£
0	(15,000)
1	9,000
2	8,000
3	7,000

The company requires a minimum return of 20% under the present and anticipated conditions. Inflation is currently running at 10% a year, and this rate of inflation is expected to continue indefinitely. Should the company go ahead with the project?

1.3 Let us first look at the company's required rate of return. Suppose that it invested £1,000 for one year on 1 January, then on 31 December it would require a minimum return of £200. With the initial investment of £1,000, the total value of the investment by 31 December must therefore increase to £1,200. During the course of the year the purchasing value of the pound would fall due to inflation. We can restate the amount received on 31 December in terms of the purchasing power of the pound at 1 January as follows.

Amount received on 31 December in terms of the value of the pound at 1 January

$$= \frac{£1,200}{(1.10)^1} = £1,091$$

1.4 In terms of the value of the pound at 1 January, the company would make a profit of £91 which represents a rate of return of 9.1% in 'today's money' terms. This is known as the real rate of return. The required rate of 20% is a money rate of return (sometimes called a nominal rate of return). The money rate measures the return in terms of the pound which is, of course, falling in value. The real rate measures the return in constant price level terms.

The two rates of return and the inflation rate are linked by the equation

$$(1 + \text{money rate}) = (1 + \text{real rate}) \times (1 + \text{inflation rate})$$

where all the rates are expressed as proportions.

In our example,

$$(1 + 0.20) = (1 + 0.091) \times (1 + 0.10) = 1.20$$

Exam focus point

Understanding the difference between a real terms and a money terms analysis was a problem for many candidates in the 12/96 exam.

Which rate is used in discounting?

1.5 We must decide which rate to use for discounting, the real rate or the money rate. The rule is as follows.

(a) If the cash flows are expressed in terms of the actual number of pounds that will be received or paid on the various future dates, we use the money rate for discounting.

(b) If the cash flows are expressed in terms of the value of the pound at time 0 (that is, in constant price level terms), we use the real rate.

1.6 The cash flows given in Paragraph 1.2 are expressed in terms of the actual number of pounds that will be received or paid at the relevant dates. We should, therefore, discount them using the money rate of return.

Time	*Cash flow*	*Discount factor*	*PV*
	£	20%	£
0	(15,000)	1.000	(15,000)
1	9,000	0.833	7,497
2	8,000	0.694	5,552
3	7,000	0.579	4,053
			2,102

The project has a positive net present value of £2,102.

1.7 The future cash flows can be re-expressed in terms of the value of the pound at time 0 as follows, given inflation at 10% a year.

Time	Actual cash flow	Cash flow at time 0 price level	
	£		£
0	(15,000)		(15,000)
1	9,000	$9{,}000 \times \frac{1}{1.10}$ =	8,182
2	8,000	$8{,}000 \times \frac{1}{(1.10)^2}$ =	6,612
3	7,000	$7{,}000 \times \frac{1}{(1.10)^3}$ =	5,259

1.8 The cash flows expressed in terms of the value of the pound at time 0 can now be discounted using the real rate of 9.1%.

Time	Cash flow	Discount factor	PV
	£	9.1%	£
0	(15,000)	1.00	(15,000)
1	8,182	$\frac{1}{1.091}$	7,500
2	6,612	$\frac{1}{(1.091)^2}$	5,555
3	5,259	$\frac{1}{(1.091)^3}$	4,050
		NPV	2,105

1.9 The NPV is the same as before (and the present value of the cash flow in each year is the same as before) apart from rounding errors with a net total of £3.

The advantages and misuses of real values and a real rate of return

1.10 Although it is recommended that companies should discount money values at the money cost of capital, there are some advantages of using real values discounted at a real cost of capital.

(a) When all costs and benefits rise at the same rate of price inflation, real values are the same as current day values, so that no further adjustments need be made to cash flows before discounting. In contrast, when money values are discounted at the money cost of capital, the prices in future years must be calculated before discounting can begin.

(b) The government or nationalised industries might prefer to set a real return as a target for investments, as being more suitable to their particular situation than a commercial money rate of return.

Costs and benefits which inflate at different rates

1.11 Not all costs and benefits will rise in line with the general level of inflation. In such cases, we can apply the money rate to inflated values to determine a project's NPV.

1.12 EXAMPLE: INFLATION (2)

Rice Ltd is considering a project which would cost £5,000 now. The annual benefits, for four years, would be a fixed income of £2,500 a year, plus other savings of £500 a year in year 1, rising by 5% each year because of inflation. Running costs will be £1,000 in the first year, but would increase at 10% each year because of inflating labour costs. The general rate of inflation is expected to be 7½% and the company's required money rate of return is 16%. Is the project worthwhile?

Ignore taxation.

1.13 SOLUTION

The cash flows at inflated values are as follows.

Year	*Fixed income*	*Other savings*	*Running costs*	*Net cash flow*
	£	£	£	£
1	2,500	500	1,000	2,000
2	2,500	525	1,100	1,925
3	2,500	551	1,210	1,841
4	2,500	579	1,331	1,748

The NPV of the project is as follows.

Year	*Cash flow*	*Discount factor*	*PV*
	£	16%	£
0	(5,000)	1.000	(5,000)
1	2,000	0.862	1,724
2	1,925	0.743	1,430
3	1,841	0.641	1,180
4	1,748	0.552	965
			+ 299

The NPV is positive and the project would seem to be worthwhile.

Variations in the expected rate of inflation

1.14 If the rate of inflation is expected to change, the calculation of the money cost of capital is slightly more complicated.

1.15 EXAMPLE: INFLATION (3)

Mr Gable has just received a dividend of £1,000 on his shareholding in Gonwithy Windmills plc. The market value of the shares is £8,000 ex div.

What is the (money) cost of the equity capital, if dividends are expected to rise because of inflation by 10% in years 1, 2 and 3, before levelling off at this year 3 amount?

1.16 SOLUTION

The money cost of capital is the internal rate of return of the following cash flows.

Year	*Cash flow*	*PV at 15%*	*PV at 20%*
	£	£	£
0	(8,000)	(8,000)	(8,000)
1	1,100	957	916
2	1,210	915	840
3 - ∞	1,331 pa	6,709	4,621
		581	(1,623)

The IRR is approximately $15\% + \left[\frac{581}{581 - -1{,}623} \times (20 - 15)\right]\% = 16.3\%$, say 16%

Expectations of inflation and the effects of inflation

1.17 When managers evaluate a particular project, or when shareholders evaluate their investments, they can only guess at what the rate of inflation is going to be. Their expectations will probably be wrong, at least to some extent, because it is extremely difficult to forecast the rate of inflation accurately. The only way in which uncertainty about inflation can be allowed for in project evaluation is by risk and uncertainty analysis.

1.18 We stated earlier that costs and benefits may rise at levels different from the general rate of inflation: inflation may be **general,** affecting prices of all kinds, or **specific** to particular prices. Generalised inflation has the following effects.

(a) Since fixed assets and stocks will increase in money value, the same quantities of assets must be financed by increasing amounts of capital.

   (i) If the future rate of inflation can be predicted, management can work out how much extra finance the company will need, and take steps to obtain it (for example by increasing retentions of earnings, or borrowing).

   (ii) If the future rate of inflation cannot be predicted with accuracy, management should guess at what it will be and plan to obtain extra finance accordingly. However, plans should also be made to obtain 'contingency funds' if the rate of inflation exceeds expectations. For example, a higher bank overdraft facility might be negotiated, or a provisional arrangement made with a bank for a loan.

(b) Inflation means higher costs and higher selling prices. The effect of higher prices on demand is not necessarily easy to predict. A company that raises its prices by 10% because the general rate of inflation is running at 10% might suffer a serious fall in demand.

(c) Inflation, because it affects financing needs, is also likely to affect gearing, and so the cost of capital.

Mid-year and end of year money values

1.19 You might wonder why, in all the examples so far, the cash flows have been inflated to the end of year money prices. Inflation does not usually run at a steady rate. For example, labour costs will often go up on a fixed date in each year in accordance with wage and salary agreements, and prices are likely to be reviewed and put up at regular intervals, perhaps once a year or once every six months. Nevertheless, it might seem reasonable to assume that inflation is more or less continuous and that cash flows in each year should be taken at a mid-year price level. Thus if the expected rate of inflation in year 1 is 10%, say, should year 1 cash flows be inflated by 5% to mid-year price levels?

1.20 In DCF calculations it is more appropriate to use *end of year* money values. This is because by convention, all cash flows are assumed to occur at the end of the year, and a discount factor appropriate to the end of the year is applied. Since end of year discount factors are used, it is only consistent to use end of year money values for the cash flows.

1.21 In an examination question which introduces inflation into the calculation where DCF is *not* required to reach a solution, there might be a greater merit in using mid-year prices rather than end of year prices in your figures, and this is a point on which you might need to exercise some judgement.

2 ALLOWING FOR TAXATION 6/97, 12/97

2.1 So far, in looking at project appraisal, we have ignored **taxation**. However, payments of tax, or reductions of tax payments, are cash flows and ought to be considered in DCF analysis.

2.2 Typical assumptions which may be stated in questions are as follows.

(a) Corporation tax is payable in the year following the one in which the taxable profits are made. Thus, if a project increases taxable profits by £10,000 in year 2, there will be a tax payment, assuming tax at 31%, of £3,100 in year 3.

This is not always the case in examination questions. Look out for questions which state that tax is payable in the same year as that in which the profits arise.

(b) Net cash flows from a project should be considered as the taxable profits arising from the project (unless an indication is given to the contrary).

Exam focus point

The main UK corporation tax rate for financial years 1997 and 1998 is 31%. Check any question involving tax carefully to see what assumptions about tax rates are made.

Capital allowances

2.3 Capital allowances are used to reduce taxable profits, and the consequent reduction in a tax payment should be treated as a cash saving arising from the acceptance of a project.

2.4 Writing down allowances are generally allowed on the cost of **plant and machinery** at the rate of 25% on a **reducing balance** basis. Thus if a company purchases plant costing £80,000, the subsequent writing down allowances would be as follows.

Year		*Capital allowance*	*Reducing balance*
		£	£
1	(25% of cost)	20,000	60,000
2	(25% of RB)	15,000	45,000
3	(25% of RB)	11,250	33,750
4	(25% of RB)	8,438	25,312

When the plant is eventually sold, the difference between the sale price and the reducing balance amount at the time of sale will be treated as:

(a) a taxable profit if the sale price exceeds the reducing balance; and

(b) a tax allowable loss if the reducing balance exceeds the sale price. Examination questions often assume that this loss will be available immediately, though in practice the balance less the sale price continues to be written off at 25% a year as part of a pool balance unless the asset has been de-pooled.

The cash saving on the capital allowances (or the cash payment for the charge) is calculated by multiplying the allowance (or charge) by the corporation tax rate.

2.5 Assumptions about capital allowances could be simplified in an exam question. For example, you might be told that capital allowances can be claimed at the rate of 25% of cost on a straight line basis (that is, over four years), or a question might refer to 'tax allowable depreciation', so that the capital allowances equal the depreciation charge.

2.6 There are two possible assumptions about the time when capital allowances start to be claimed.

(a) It can be assumed that the first claim for capital allowances occurs at the start of the project (at year 0) and so the first tax saving occurs one year later (at year 1).

(b) Alternatively it can be assumed that the first claim for capital allowances occurs later in the first year, so the first tax saving occurs one year later, that is, year 2.

2.7 You should state clearly which assumption you have made. Assumption (b) is more prudent, because it defers the tax benefit by one year, but assumption (a) is also perfectly feasible. It is very likely, however that an examination question will indicate which of the two assumptions is required.

2.8 EXAMPLE: TAXATION

A company is considering whether or not to purchase an item of machinery costing £40,000 in 19X5. It would have a life of four years, after which it would be sold for £5,000. The machinery would create annual cost savings of £14,000.

The machinery would attract writing down allowances of 25% on the reducing balance basis which could be claimed against taxable profits of the current year, which is soon to end. A balancing allowance or charge would arise on disposal. The rate of corporation tax is 31%. Tax is payable one year in arrears.

The after-tax cost of capital is 8%.

Assume that tax payments occur in the year following the transactions.

Should the machinery be purchased?

2.9 SOLUTION

The first capital allowance is claimed against year 0 profits.

Cost: £40,000

Year	*Allowance*	*Reducing balance (RB)*	
	£	£	
(0) 19X5 (25% of cost)	10,000	30,000	(40,000 – 10,000)
(1) 19X6 (25% of RB)	7,500	22,500	(30,000 – 7,500)
(2) 19X7 (25% of RB)	5,625	16,875	(22,500 – 5,625)
(3) 19X8 (25% of RB)	4,219	12,656	(16,875 – 4,219)
(4) 19X9 (25% of RB)	3,164	9,492	(12,656 – 3,164)

	£
Sale proceeds, end of fourth year	5,000
Less reducing balance, end of fourth year	9,492
Balancing allowance	4,492

2.10 Having calculated the allowances each year, the tax savings can be computed. The year of the cash flow is one year after the year for which the allowance is claimed.

Year of claim	Allowance	Tax saved	Year of tax payment/saving
	£	£	
0	10,000	3,100	1
1	7,500	2,325	2
2	5,625	1,744	3
3	4,219	1,308	4
4	7,656	2,373	5
	35,000 *		

* Net cost £(40,000 – 5,000) = £35,000

These tax savings relate to capital allowances. We must also calculate the extra tax payments on annual savings of £14,000.

2.11 The net cash flows and the NPV are now calculated as follows.

Year	Equipment	Savings	Tax on savings	Tax saved on capital allowances	Net cash flow	Discount factor	Present value of cash flow
	£	£	£	£	£	8%	£
0	(40,000)				(40,000)	1.000	(40,000)
1		14,000		3,100	17,100	0.926	15,835
2		14,000	(4,340)	2,325	11,985	0.857	10,271
3		14,000	(4,340)	1,744	11,404	0.794	9,055
4	5,000	14,000	(4,340)	1,308	10,968	0.735	8,061
5			(4,340)	2,373	(1,967)	0.681	(1,340)
							1,882

The NPV is positive and so the purchase appears to be worthwhile.

An alternative and quicker method of calculating tax payments or savings

2.12 In the above example, the tax computations could have been combined, as follows.

Year	0	1	2	3	4
	£	£	£	£	£
Cost savings	0	14,000	14,000	14,000	14,000
Capital allowance	10,000	7,500	5,625	4,219	7,656
Taxable profits	(10,000)	6,500	8,375	9,781	6,344
Tax at 31%	3,100	(2,015)	(2,596)	(3,032)	(1,967)

2.13 The net cash flows would then be as follows.

Year	Equipment	Savings	Tax	Net cash flow
	£	£	£	£
0	(40,000)			(40,000)
1		14,000	3,100	17,100
2		14,000	(2,015)	11,985
3		14,000	(2,596)	11,404
4	5,000	14,000	(3,032)	10,968
5			(1,967)	(1,967)

The net cash flows are exactly the same as calculated previously in Paragraph 2.11.

Taxation and DCF

2.14 The effect of taxation on capital budgeting is theoretically quite simple. Organisations must pay tax, and the effect of undertaking a project will be to increase or decrease tax payments each year. These incremental tax cash flows should be included in the cash flows of the project for discounting to arrive at the project's NPV.

2.15 When taxation is ignored in the DCF calculations, the discount rate will reflect the pre-tax rate of return required on capital investments. When taxation is included in the cash flows, a post-tax required rate of return should be used.

Question 1

A company is considering the purchase of an item of equipment, which would earn profits before tax of £25,000 a year. Depreciation charges would be £20,000 a year for six years. Capital allowances would be £30,000 a year for the first four years. Corporation tax is at 31%.

What would be the annual net cash inflows of the project:

(a) for the first four years;
(b) for the fifth and sixth years,

assuming that tax payments occur in the same year as the profits giving rise to them, and there is no balancing charge or allowance when the machine is scrapped at the end of the sixth year?

Answer

(a)

	Years 1-4	*Years 5-6*
	£	£
Profit before tax	25,000	25,000
Add back depreciation	20,000	20,000
Net cash inflow before tax	45,000	45,000
Less capital allowance	30,000	0
	15,000	45,000
Tax at 31%	4,650	13,950

Years 1 - 4 Net cash inflow after tax £45,000 – £4,650 = £40,350

(b) Years 5 - 6 Net cash inflow after tax = £45,000 – £13,950 = £31,050

Question 2

A company is considering the purchase of a machine for £150,000. It would be sold after four years for an estimated realisable value of £50,000. By this time capital allowances of £120,000 would have been claimed. The rate of corporation tax is 31%.

What are the tax implications of the sale of the machine at the end of four years?

Answer

There will be a balancing charge on the sale of the machine of £(50,000 – (150,000 – 120,000)) = £20,000. This will give rise to a tax payment of 31% × £20,000 = £6,200.

Chapter roundup

- **Inflation** is a feature of all economies, and it must be accommodated in financial planning.
- (1+ money rate of return) = (1 + real rate of return) × (1 + rate of inflation)
- **Real cash flows** (ie adjusted for inflation) should be discounted at a real discount rate.
- **Money cash flows** should be discounted at a money discount rate.
- **Taxation** is a major practical consideration for businesses. It is vital to take it into account in making decisions.
- In investment appraisal, tax is often assumed to be payable **one year in arrears**.
- **Capital allowances** details should be checked in any question you attempt.

Quick quiz

1 What is the relationship between the money rate of return, the real rate of return and the rate of inflation? (see para 1.4)

2 The money cost of capital is 11%. The expected annual rate of inflation is 5%. What is the real cost of capital? (See below)

3 A company wants a minimum real return of 3% a year on its investments. Inflation is expected to be 8% a year. What is the company's minimum money cost of capital? (See below)

4 Summarise briefly how taxation is taken into consideration in capital budgeting. (2.14, 2.15)

Quick quiz: solutions

2 $\frac{1.11}{1.05} = 1.057$. The real cost of capital is 5.7%.

3 1.03 × 1.08 = 1.1124. The money cost of capital is 11.24%.

Question to try	Level	Marks	Time
28	Examination	20	36 mins

Chapter 28

PROJECT APPRAISAL AND RISK

	Chapter topic list	Syllabus reference
1	What is risk and why does it arise?	8(b)
2	Sensitivity analysis. Certainty-equivalents	8(b)
3	Probability analysis	8(b)
4	Decision tree analysis	8(b)
5	Simulation models	8(b)
6	Ways of reducing risk	8(b)

Introduction

This chapter will show some of the different methods of assessing and taking account of the **risk** associated with a project.

The last two chapters of this Study Text will consider two further project appraisal topics - **capital rationing** and **leasing**.

1 WHAT IS RISK AND WHY DOES IT ARISE?

1.1 The terms risk and uncertainty are often used interchangeably but a distinction should be made between them.

1.2 **Risk** can be applied to a situation where there are several possible outcomes and, on the basis of past relevant experience, probabilities can be assigned to the various outcomes that could prevail.

Uncertainty can be applied to a situation where there are several possible outcomes but there is little past relevant experience to enable the probability of the possible outcomes to be predicted.

1.3 A risky situation is one where we can say that there is a 70% probability that returns from a project will be in excess of £100,000 but a 30% probability that returns will be less than £100,000. If, however, no information can be provided on the returns from the project, we are faced with an uncertain situation.

1.4 In general, risky projects are those whose future cash flows, and hence the projects returns, are likely to be variable - the greater the variability, the greater the risk. The problem of risk is more acute with capital investment decisions than other decisions for the following reasons.

(a) Estimates of capital expenditure might be for up to several years ahead, such as for major construction projects, and all too often with long-term projects, actual costs escalate well above budget as the work progresses.

(b) Estimates of benefits will be for up to several years ahead, sometimes 10, 15 or 20 years ahead or even longer, and such long-term estimates can at best be approximations.

Why are projects risky?

1.5 A decision about whether or not to go ahead with a project is based on expectations about the future. Forecasts of cash flows (whether they be inflows or outflows) that are likely to arise following a particular course of action are made. These forecasts are made, however, on the basis of what is expected to happen given the present state of knowledge and the future is, by definition, uncertain. Actual cash flows are almost certain to differ from prior expectations. It is this uncertainty about a project's future income and costs that give rise to risk in business generally and investment activity in particular.

2 SENSITIVITY ANALYSIS. CERTAINTY-EQUIVALENTS 12/96

2.1 **Sensitivity analysis** is one method of analysing the risk surrounding a capital expenditure project and enables an assessment to be made of how responsive the project's NPV is to changes in the variables that are used to calculate that NPV.

2.2 The NPV could depend on a number of uncertain independent variables.

(a) Estimated selling price
(b) Estimated sales volume
(c) Estimated cost of capital
(d) Estimated initial cost
(e) Estimated operating costs
(f) Estimated benefits

2.3 The basic approach of sensitivity analysis is to calculate the project's NPV under alternative assumptions to determine how sensitive it is to changing conditions. An indication is thus provided of those variables to which the NPV is most sensitive (critical variables) and the extent to which those variables may change before the investment results in a negative NPV.

2.4 Sensitivity analysis therefore provides an indication of why a project might fail. Once these critical variables have been identified, management should review them to assess whether or not there is a strong possibility of events occurring which will lead to a negative NPV. Management should also pay particular attention to controlling those variables to which the NPV is particularly sensitive, once the decision has been taken to accept the investment.

Let us consider an example.

2.5 EXAMPLE: SENSITIVITY ANALYSIS

Kenney Ltd is considering a project with the following cash flows.

Year	*0*	*1*	*2*
	£'000	£'000	£'000
Initial investment	(7,000)		
Variable costs		(2,000)	(2,000)
Cash inflows (650,000 units at £10 per unit)		6,500	6,500
Net cashflows	(7,000)	4,500	4,500

The cost of capital is 8%.

Required

Measure the sensitivity of the project to changes in variables.

2.6 SOLUTION

The PVs of the cash flow are as follows.

Year	*Discount factor* 8%	*PV of initial investment* £'000	*PV of variable costs* £'000	*PV of cash inflows* £'000	*PV of net cash flow* £'000
0	1.000	(7,000)			(7,000)
1	0.926		(1,852)	6,019	4,167
2	0.857		(1,714)	5,571	3,857
		(7,000)	(3,566)	11,590	1,024

The project has a positive NPV and would appear to be worthwhile. The changes in cash flows which would need to occur for the project to only just breakeven (and hence be on the point of being unacceptable) are as follows.

(a) *Initial investment.* The initial investment can rise by £1,024,000 before the investment breaks even. The initial investment may therefore increase by 1,024/7,000 = 15%.

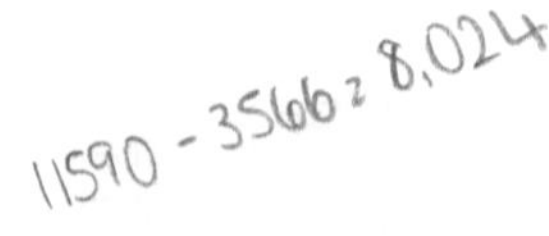

(b) *Sales volume.* The present value of the cash inflows less the present value of the variable costs will have to fall to £7,000,000 for the NPV to be zero.

We need to find the net cash flows in actual values. As the cash flows are equal each year, cumulative discount tables can be used. The discount factor for 8% and year 2 is 1.783. If the discount factor is divided into the required present value of £7,000,000 we get an annual cash flow of £3,925,968. Given that the most likely net cash flow is £4,500,000, the net cash flow may decline by approximately £574,032 each year before the NPV becomes zero. Total sales revenue may therefore decline by £831,930 (assuming net cash flow is 69% (4,500/6,500) of sales). At a selling price of £10 per unit this represents 83,193 units. Alternatively we may state that sales volume may decline by 13% before the NPV becomes negative.

(c) *Selling price.* When sales volume is 650,000 units per annum, total sales revenue can fall to £5,925,968 (£(6,500,000 – 574,032) per annum before the NPV becomes negative. This assumes that total variable costs and sales volume remain unchanged. This represents a selling price of £9.12 per unit, which represents a 8.8% reduction in the selling price.

(d) *Variable costs.* The total variable cost can increase by £574,032, or £0.88 per unit. This represents an increase of 28.6%.

(e) *Cost of capital.* We need to calculate the IRR of the project. Let us try discount rates of 15% and 20%.

Year	*Net cash flow* £'000	*Discount factor* 15%	*PV* £'000	*Discount factor* 20%	*PV* £'000
0	(7,000)	0.870	(6,090)	0.833	(5,831)
1	4,500	0.756	3,402	0.694	3,123
2	4,500	0.658	2,961	0.579	2,606
		NPV =	273	NPV =	(102)

$$\text{IRR} = 0.15 + \left[\frac{273}{273+102} \times (0.20 - 0.15)\right]$$

$$= 18.64\%$$

The cost of capital can therefore increase by 133% before the NPV becomes negative.

2.7 The elements to which the NPV appears to be most sensitive are the selling price followed by the sales volume, and it is therefore important for management to pay particular attention to these factors so that they can be carefully monitored.

2.8 EXAMPLE: MORE SENSITIVITY ANALYSIS

Nevers Ure Ltd is considering a project with the following cash flows.

Year	*Purchase of plant*	*Running costs*	*Savings*
	£	£	£
0	(7,000)		
1		2,000	6,000
2		2,500	7,000

The cost of capital is 8%. Measure the sensitivity (in percentages) of the project to changes in the levels of expected costs and savings.

2.9 SOLUTION

The PVs of the cash flows are as follows.

Year	*Discount factors* 8%	*PV of plant cost* £	*PV of running costs* £	*PV of savings* £	*PV of net cash flow* £
0	1.000	(7,000)			(7,000)
1	0.926		(1,852)	5,556	3,704
2	0.857		(2,143)	5,999	3,856
		(7,000)	(3,995)	11,555	560

The project has a positive NPV and would appear to be worthwhile. The changes in cash flows which would need to occur for the project to break even (NPV = 0) are as follows.

(a) Plant costs would need to increase by a PV of £560, that is by $\frac{560}{7,000} = 8\%$

(b) Running costs would need to increase by a PV of £560, that is by $\frac{560}{3,995} = 14\%$

(c) Savings would need to fall by a PV of £560, that is by $\frac{560}{11,555} = 4.8\%$

Weaknesses of this approach to sensitivity analysis

2.10 These are as follows.

(a) The method requires that changes in each key variable are isolated but management is more interested in the combination of the effects of changes in two or more key variables. Looking at factors in isolation is unrealistic since they are often interdependent.

(b) Sensitivity analysis does not examine the probability that any particular variation in costs or revenues might occur.

(c) It may reveal as critical, factors over which managers have no control, and thus not provide a helpful guide for action.

(d) In itself it does not provide a decision rule: parameters defining acceptability must be laid down by managers.

The certainty-equivalent approach

2.11 Another method is the **certainty-equivalent approach**. By this method, the expected cash flows of the project are converted to riskless equivalent amounts. The greater the risk of an expected cash flow, the smaller the 'certainty-equivalent' value (for receipts) or the larger the certainty equivalent value (for payments).

2.12 EXAMPLE: CERTAINTY-EQUIVALENT APPROACH

Dark Ages Ltd, whose cost of capital is 10%, is considering a project with the following expected cash flows.

Year	*Cash flow*	*Discount factor*	*Present value*
	£	10%	£
0	(9,000)	1.000	(9,000)
1	7,000	0.909	6,363
2	5,000	0.826	4,130
3	5,000	0.751	3,755
		NPV	+5,248

The project seems to be clearly worthwhile. However, because of the uncertainty about the future cash receipts, the management decides to reduce them to 'certainty-equivalents' by taking only 70%, 60% and 50% of the years 1, 2 and 3 cash flows respectively. (Note that this method of risk adjustment allows for different risk factors in each year of the project.)

Required

On the basis of the information set out above, assess whether the project is worthwhile.

2.13 SOLUTION

The risk-adjusted NPV of the project is as follows.

Year	*Cash flow*	*PV factor*	*PV*
	£		£
0	(9,000)	1.000	(9,000)
1	4,900	0.909	4,454
2	3,000	0.826	2,478
3	2,500	0.751	1,878
		NPV =	- 190

The project is too risky and should be rejected.

2.14 The disadvantage of the 'certainty-equivalent' approach is that the amount of the adjustment to each cash flow is decided subjectively.

3 PROBABILITY ANALYSIS 12/97

3.1 A **probability distribution** of '**expected cash flows**' can often be estimated, and this may be used to do the following.

(a) Calculate an expected value of the NPV.

(b) Measure risk, for example in the following ways.

(i) By calculating the worst possible outcome and its probability

(ii) By calculating the probability that the project will fail to achieve a positive NPV

(iii) By calculating the standard deviation of the NPV

Let us look at an example.

3.2 EXAMPLE: PROBABILITY ESTIMATES OF CASH FLOWS

A company is considering a project involving the outlay of £300,000 which it estimates will generate cash flows over its two year life at the probabilities shown in the following table.

Cash flows for project

Year 1

Cash flow	*Probability*
£	
100,000	0.25
200,000	0.50
300,000	0.25
	1.00

Year 2

If cash flow in Year 1 is:	*there is a probability of:*	*that the cash flow in Year 2 will be:*
£		£
100,000	0.25	Nil
	0.50	100,000
	0.25	200,000
	1.00	
200,000	0.25	100,000
	0.50	200,000
	0.25	300,000
	1.00	
300,000	0.25	200,000
	0.50	300,000
	0.25	350,000
	1.00	

The company's investment criterion for this type of project is 10% DCF.

Required

Calculate the expected value (EV) of the project's NPV and the probability that the NPV will be negative.

3.3 SOLUTION

First we need to draw up a probability distribution of the expected cash flows. We begin by calculating the present values of the cash flows.

Year	*Cash flow*	*Discount factor*	*Present value*
	£'000	10%	£'000
1	100	0.909	90.9
1	200	0.909	181.8
1	300	0.909	272.7
2	100	0.826	82.6
2	200	0.826	165.2
2	300	0.826	247.8
2	350	0.826	289.1

Next we set out the possible cash flows and their probabilities.

Year 1 PV of cash flow £'000	Probability	Year 2 PV of cash flow £'000	Probability	Joint probability	Total PV of cash inflows £'000	EV of PV of cash inflows £'000
(a)	(b)	(c)	(d)	(b) × (d)	(a) + (c)	
90.9	0.25	0.0	0.25	0.0625	90.9	5.681
90.9	0.25	82.6	0.50	0.1250	173.5	21.688
90.9	0.25	165.2	0.25	0.0625	256.1	16.006
181.8	0.50	82.6	0.25	0.1250	264.4	33.050
181.8	0.50	165.2	0.50	0.2500	347.0	86.750
181.8	0.50	247.8	0.25	0.1250	429.6	53.700
272.7	0.25	165.2	0.25	0.0625	437.9	27.369
272.7	0.25	247.8	0.50	0.1250	520.5	65.063
272.7	0.25	289.1	0.25	0.0625	561.8	35.113
						344.420

	£
EV of PV of cash inflows	344,420
Less project cost	300,000
EV of NPV	44,420

Since the EV of the NPV is positive, the project should go ahead unless the risk is unacceptably high.

The probability that the project will have a negative NPV is the probability that the total PV of cash inflows is less than £300,000. From the column headed 'Total PV of cash inflows', we can establish that this probability is 0.0625 + 0.125 + 0.0625 + 0.125 = 0.375 or 37.5%. This might be considered an unacceptably high risk.

The standard deviation of the NPV

3.4 The disadvantage of using the EV of NPV approach to assess the risk of the project is that the construction of the probability distribution can become very complicated. If we were considering a project over 4 years, each year having five different forecasted cash flows, there would be 625 (5^4) NPVs to calculate. To avoid all of these calculations, an indication of the risk may be obtained by calculating the standard deviation of the NPV.

3.5 EXAMPLE: STANDARD DEVIATION OF THE NET PRESENT VALUE

Frame plc is considering which of two mutually exclusive projects, A or B, to undertake. There is some uncertainty about the running costs with each project, and a probability distribution of the NPV for each project has been estimated, as follows.

Project A NPV £'000	Project A Probability	Project B NPV £'000	Project B Probability
– 20	0.15	+ 5	0.2
+ 10	0.20	+ 15	0.3
+ 20	0.35	+ 20	0.4
+ 40	0.30	+ 25	0.1

Required

Decide which project should the company choose, if either.

3.6 SOLUTION

We can begin by calculating the EV of the NPV for each project.

	Project A			Project B	
NPV	Prob	EV	NPV	Prob	EV
£'000		£'000	£'000		£'000
– 20	0.15	(3.0)	5	0.2	1.0
10	0.20	2.0	15	0.3	4.5
20	0.35	7.0	20	0.4	8.0
40	0.30	12.0	25	0.1	2.5
		18.0			16.0

Project A has a higher EV of NPV, but what about the risk of variation in the NPV above or below the EV? This can be measured by the standard deviation of the NPV.

The standard deviation of a project's NPV, s, can be calculated as:

$$s = \sqrt{\Sigma p(x - \overline{x})^2}$$

where $\overline{x}$ is the EV of the NPV.

	Project A, $\overline{x}$ = 18				Project B, $\overline{x}$ = 16		
x	p	$x - \overline{x}$	$p(x - \overline{x})^2$	x	p	$x - \overline{x}$	$p(x - \overline{x})^2$
£'000		£'000		£'000		£'000	
– 20	0.15	– 38	216.6	5	0.2	– 11	24.2
10	0.20	– 8	12.8	15	0.3	– 1	0.3
20	0.35	+ 2	1.4	20	0.4	+ 4	6.4
40	0.30	+ 22	145.2	25	0.1	+ 9	8.1
			376.0				39.0

		Project A			Project B
s	=	√376	s	=	√39.0
	=	19.391		=	6.245
	=	£19,391		=	£6,245

Although Project A has a higher EV of NPV, it also has a higher standard deviation of NPV, and so has greater risk associated with it.

Which project should be selected? Clearly it depends on the attitude of the company's management to risk.

(a) If management are prepared to take the risk of a low NPV in the hope of a high NPV they will opt for project A.

(b) If management are risk-averse, they will opt for the less risky project B.

4 DECISION TREE ANALYSIS

Exam focus point

If decision tree analysis comes up in a Paper 8 question, you can expect that it will involve a relatively simple decision tree.

4.1 When appraising a project using the NPV method, it is possible that, of the many variables which affect the NPV, more than one will be uncertain. The value of some variables may be dependent on the values of other variables. Many outcomes may therefore be possible and some outcomes may be dependent on previous outcomes. Decision trees are useful tools for clarifying the range of alternative courses of action and their possible outcomes.

4.2 There are two stages in preparing a decision tree.

Step 1. Drawing the tree itself, to show all the choices and outcomes
Step 2. Putting in the numbers: the probabilities, outcome values and EVs

Drawing a decision tree: the basic rules

4.3 Every decision tree starts from a decision point with the decision options that are currently being considered.

(a) There should be a line, or branch, for each option or alternative.

(b) It helps to identify the decision point, and any subsequent decision points in the tree, with a symbol. Here, we shall use a square shape.

4.4 It is conventional to draw decision trees from left to right, and so a decision tree will start as follows.

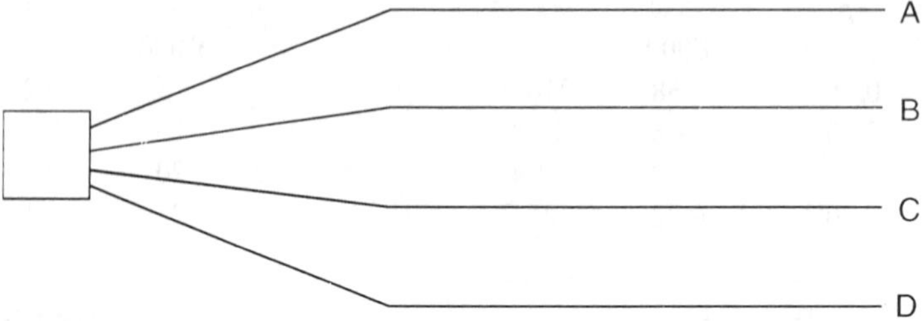

The square is the decision point, and A, B, C and D represent four alternatives from which a choice must be made.

4.5 If the outcome from any choice is certain, the branch of the decision tree for that alternative is complete.

4.6 If, on the other hand, the outcome of a particular choice is uncertain, the various possible outcomes must be shown. We show this on a decision tree by inserting an outcome point on the branch of the tree. Each possible outcome is then shown as a subsidiary branch, coming out from the outcome point. The probability of each outcome occurring should be written on to the branch of the tree which represents that outcome.

4.7 To distinguish decision points from outcome points, a circle will be used as the symbol for an outcome point.

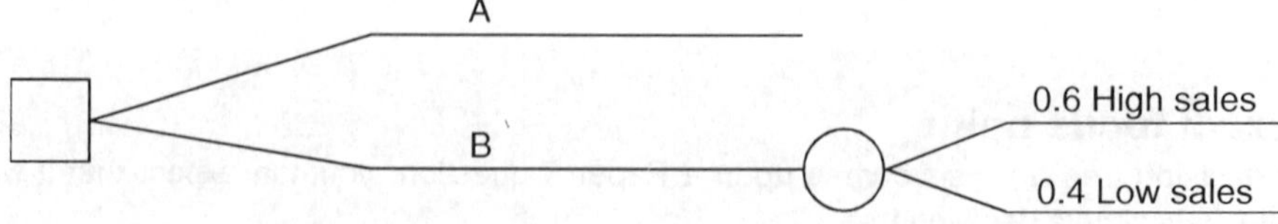

In the example above, there are two choices, A and B. The outcome if A is chosen is known with certainty, but if B is chosen, there are two possible outcomes, high returns (0.6 probability) or low returns (0.4 probability).

4.8 When several outcomes are possible, it is usually simpler to show two or more stages of outcome points on the decision tree.

4.9 EXAMPLE: SEVERAL POSSIBLE OUTCOMES

A company can choose to invest in project XYZ or not. If the investment goes ahead, expected cash inflows and expected costs might be as follows.

Cash inflows	*Probability*	*Costs*	*Probability*
£		£	
10,000	0.8	6,000	0.7
15,000	0.2	8,000	0.3

(a) The decision tree could be drawn as follows.

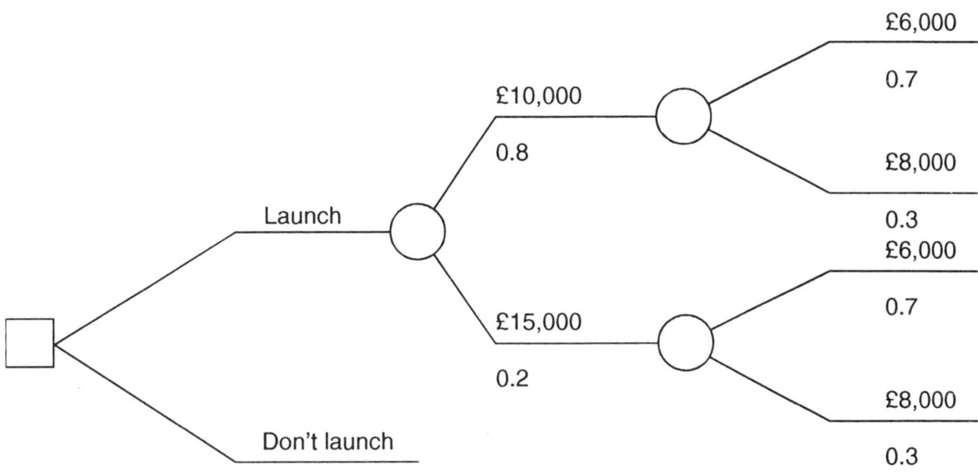

(b) The layout shown above will usually be easier to use than the alternative way of drawing the tree, which is shown below.

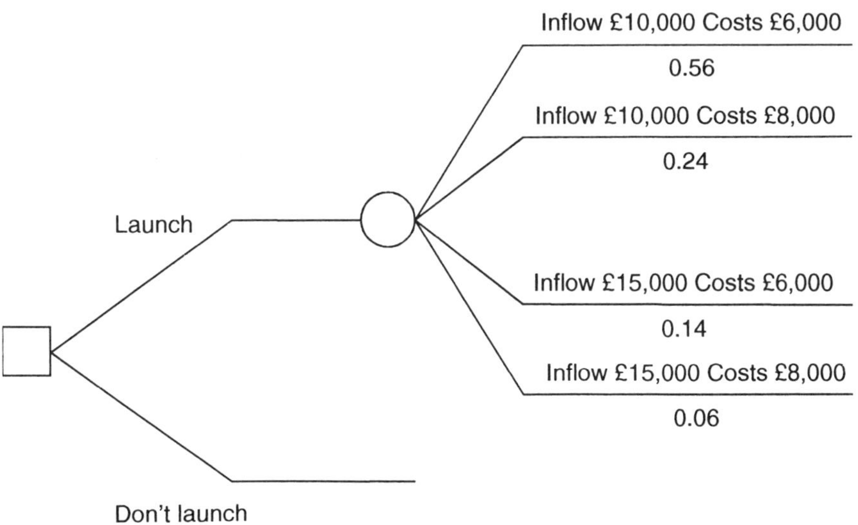

4.10 Sometimes, a decision taken now will lead to other decisions to be taken in the future. When this situation arises, the decision tree can be drawn as a two-stage tree, as follows.

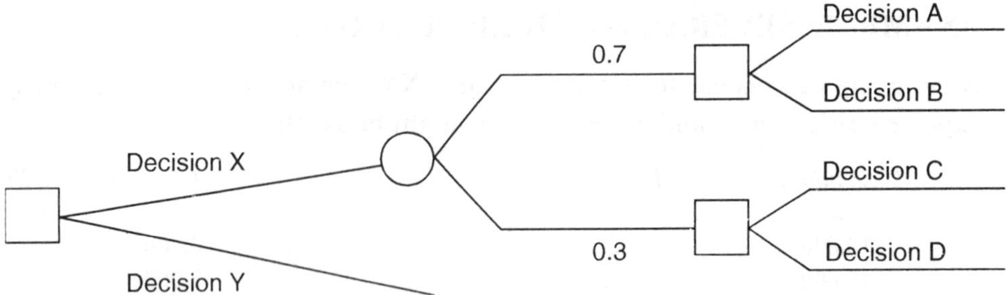

In this tree, either a choice between A and B or else a choice between C and D will be made, depending on the outcome which occurs after choosing X.

4.11 The decision tree should be in chronological order from left to right. When there are two-stage decision trees, the first decision in time should be drawn on the left.

4.12 The project cash flows for the example in Paragraph 3.2 could be shown on a decision tree as follows.

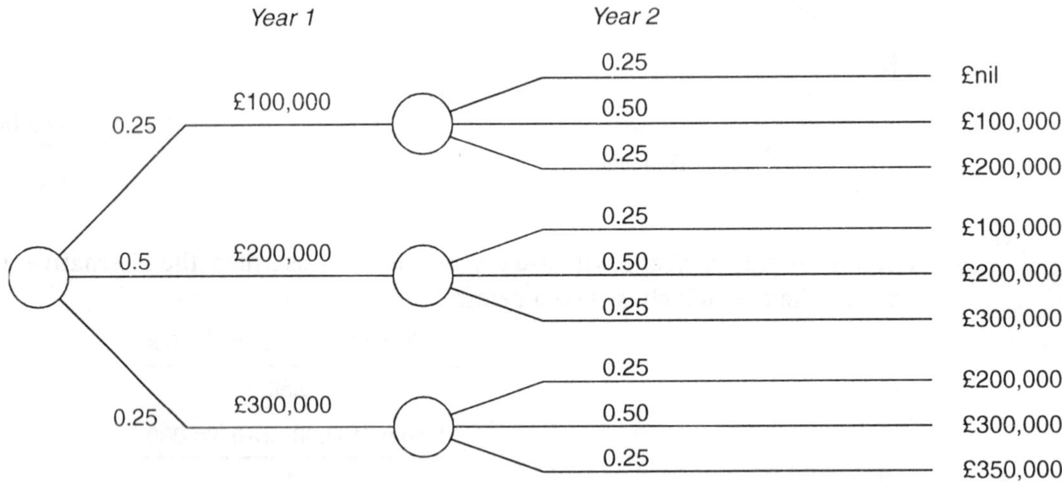

Evaluating the decision with a decision tree

4.13 The EV of each decision option can be evaluated, using the decision tree to help with keeping the logic properly sorted out.

The basic rules are as follows.

4.14 We start on the right hand side of the tree and work back towards the left hand side and the current decision under consideration.

4.15 Working from right to left, we calculate the EV of revenue, cost, contribution or profit at each outcome point on the tree.

4.16 Consider the decision tree below.

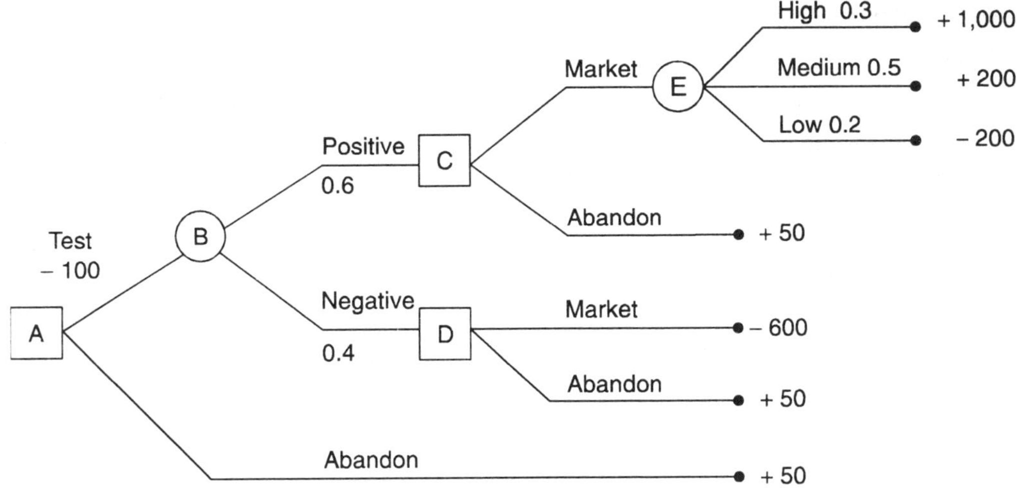

(a) At E the EV is calculated as follows.

	£'000	*Probability*	
	x	*p*	*px*
High	1,000	0.3	300
Medium	200	0.5	100
Low	(200)	0.2	(40)
		EV	360

(b) At C, the choice is an EV of £360,000 or a value of £50,000. The choice would be £360,000 and so the EV at C is £360,000.

(c) At D, the choice is a value of –£600,000 or a value of £50,000. The choice would be £50,000 and so the EV at D is £50,000.

(d) At B the EV is calculated as follows.

$$EV = (0.6 \times £360{,}000)\ (C) + (0.4 \times £50{,}000)\ (D) = £236{,}000$$

(e) At A the choice is between an EV of £226,000 minus costs of £100,000 or a value of £50,000. The choice would be £126,000 and so the EV at A is £126,000.

Question

Elsewhere Ltd is considering the production of a new consumer item with a five year product lifetime. In order to manufacture this time it would be necessary to build a new plant. After having considered several alternative strategies, management are left with the following three possibilities.

Strategy A: build a large plant at an estimated cost of £600,000
This strategy faces two types of market conditions: high demand with a probability of 0.7 or low demand with a probability of 0.3. If the demand is high the company can expect to receive a net annual cash inflow of £250,000 for each of the next five years. If the demand is low there would be a net annual cash outflow of £50,000.

Strategy B: build a small plant at an estimated cost of £350,000
This strategy also faces two types of market conditions: high demand with a probability of 0.7 or low demand with a probability of 0.3. The net annual cash inflow of the five-year period for the small plant is £25,000 if the demand is low and is £150,000 if the demand is high.

Strategy C: do not build a plant initially
This strategy consists of leaving the decision for one year whilst more information is collected. The resulting information can be positive or negative with estimated probabilities of 0.8 and 0.2 respectively. At the end of this time management may decide to build either a large plant or a small plant at the same costs as at present providing the information is positive. If the resulting information is negative, management would decide to build no plant at all. Given positive information the probabilities of high and low demand change to 0.9 and 0.1 respectively, regardless of which plant is built. The net annual cash inflows for the remaining four-year period for each type of plant are the same as those given in strategies A and B.

All costs and revenues are given in present value terms and should not be discounted.

Required

(a) Draw a decision tree to represent the alternative courses of action open to the company.

(b) Determine the expected return for each possible course of action and hence decide the best course of action for the management of Elsewhere Ltd.

Answer

(a) *Decision tree for a possible new plant*

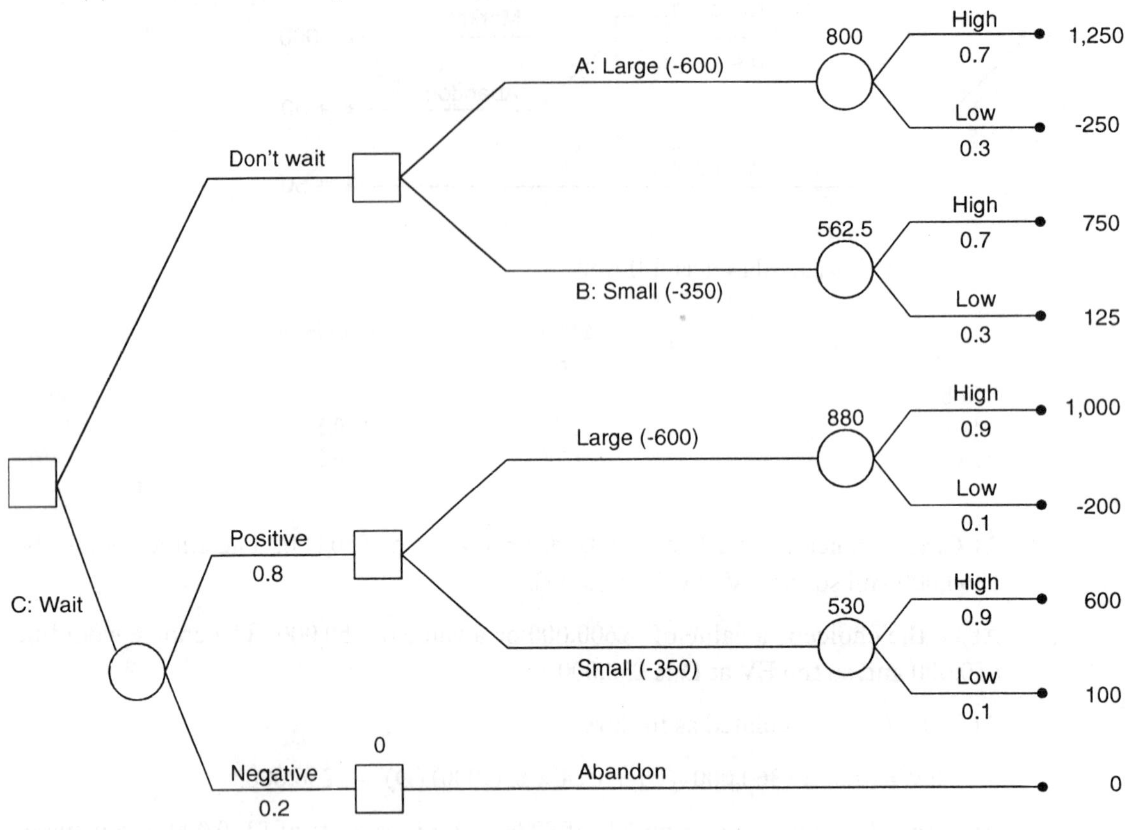

(b) Evaluation of the decision tree (see above) shows that the best course of action is to wait a year, and then build a large plant if positive information is received, but abandon the project if negative information is received.

Expected values (in thousands of pounds) are calculated as follows.

Large plant now (A)	$(0.7 \times 5 \times 250) - (0.3 \times 5 \times 50) - 600$	= 200
Small plant now (B)	$(0.7 \times 5 \times 150) + (0.3 \times 5 \times 25) - 350$	= 212.5
Large plant following positive information		
	$(0.9 \times 4 \times 250) - (0.1 \times 4 \times 50) - 600$	= 280
Small plant following positive information		
	$(0.9 \times 4 \times 150) + (0.1 \times 4 \times 25) - 350$	= 180

Positive information: higher of 280 and 180, ie 280

Waiting (C)	$(0.8 \times 280) + (0.2 \times 0)$	= 224

224 is higher than either 200 or 212.5, hence the recommendation to wait.

5 SIMULATION MODELS

5.1 A decision tree of a simple project stretching over three years, the net cash flow each year being forecast at five different levels, would have 125 different outcomes. In practice, it may be necessary to produce separate probabilities for alternative sales revenue outcomes, different items of costs and different possible life spans. A decision tree could therefore have thousands of different branches. In addition, cash flows may be correlated over time. A new project which is successful in early years is also likely to be successful in later years. When cash flows are correlated over time, the standard deviation calculation (section 3 of this chapter) will not give a correct calculation of the variation in the project's NPV. **Simulation** will overcome these problems.

5.2 EXAMPLE: SIMULATION MODEL

The following probability estimates have been prepared for a proposed project.

	Year	*Probability*	£
Cost of equipment	0	1.00	(40,000)
Revenue each year	1-5	0.15	40,000
		0.40	50,000
		0.30	55,000
		0.15	60,000
Running costs each year	1-5	0.10	25,000
		0.25	30,000
		0.35	35,000
		0.30	40,000

The cost of capital is 12%.

Required

Assess how a simulation model might be used to assess the project's NPV.

5.3 SOLUTION

A simulation model could be constructed by assigning a range of random number digits to each possible value for each of the uncertain variables.

The random numbers must exactly match their respective probabilities. This is achieved by working upwards cumulatively from the lowest to the highest cash flow values and assigning numbers that will correspond to probability groupings as follows.

Revenue				*Running costs*		
£	*Prob*	*Random numbers*		£	*Prob*	*Random numbers*
40,000	0.15	00 - 14	*	25,000	0.10	00 - 09
50,000	0.40	15 - 54	**	30,000	0.25	10 - 34
55,000	0.30	55 - 84	***	40,000	0.35	35 - 69
60,000	0.15	85 - 99		40,000	0.30	70 - 99

* Probability is 0.15 (15%). Random numbers are 15% of range 00 - 99.

** Probability is 0.40 (40%). Random numbers are 40% of range 00 - 99 but starting at 15.

*** Probability is 0.30 (30%). Random numbers are 30% of range 00 - 99 but starting at 55.

For revenue, the selection of a random number in the range 00 and 14 has a probability of 0.15. This probability represents revenue of £40,000. Numbers have been assigned to cash flows so that when numbers are selected at random, the cash flows have exactly the same probability of being selected as is indicated in their respective probability distribution in Paragraph 5.2.

Random numbers would be generated, for example by a computer program, and these would be used to assign values to each of the uncertain variables.

For example, if random numbers 378420015689 were generated, the values assigned to the variables would be as follows.

	Revenue		*Costs*	
Calculation	*Random number*	*Value*	*Random number*	*Value*
		£		£
1	37	50,000	84	40,000
2	20	50,000	01	25,000
3	56	55,000	89	40,000

A computer would calculate the NPV may times over using the values established in this way with more random numbers, and the results would be analysed to provide the following.

(a) An expected NPV for the project

(b) A statistical distribution pattern for the possible variation in the NPV above or below this average.

The decision whether to go ahead with the project would then be made on the basis of expected return and risk.

6 WAYS OF REDUCING RISK

6.1 Only if management know for certainty what is going to happen in the future can they appraise a project in the knowledge that there is no risk. It is, of course, unlikely that such information would be available since the future is uncertain by nature. There are, however, steps that management can take to reduce the riskiness of a project.

(a) A maximum payback period can be set to reflect the fact that risk increases the longer the time period under consideration.

(b) A high discounting rate can be used so that a cash flow which occurs quite some time in the future will have less effect on the decision.

(c) Projects with low standard deviations and acceptable average predicted outcomes can be selected.

(d) Sensitivity analysis can be used to determine the critical factors within the decision-making process. Management effort can then be directed to those factors which are critical to the success of a particular decision.

(e) To ensure that future events are no worse than predicted, prudence, slack and overly pessimistic estimates can be applied.

Chapter roundup

- **Risk** can be applied to a situation where there are several possible outcomes and, on the basis of past relevant experience, probabilities can be assigned to the various outcomes that could prevail.
- **Uncertainty** can be applied to a situation where there are several possible outcomes but there is little past relevant experience to enable the probability of the possible outcomes to be predicted.
- There are a wide range of techniques for incorporating risk into project appraisal.
- **Sensitivity analysis** assesses how responsive the project's NPV is to changes in the variables used to calculate that NPV. One particular approach to sensitivity analysis, the certainty - equivalent approach, involves the conversion of the expected cash flows of the project to riskless equivalent amounts.
- A **probability analysis** of expected cash flows can often be estimated and used both to calculate an expected NPV and to measure risk. The standard deviation of the NPV can be calculated to assess risk when the construction of probability distributions is complicated.
- **Decision tree analysis** clarifies the range of alternative courses of action open and their possible outcomes. Ensure that you know the rules for constructing decision trees and are able to evaluate them.
- **Simulation models** can be used to assess those projects which may have too many outcomes to allow the use of a decision tree or those projects which have correlated cash flows. Simulation models are constructed by assigning a range of random number digits to each possible value for each of the uncertain variables. The numbers are assigned to the cash flows so that when numbers are selected at random, the cash flows have exactly the same probability of being selected as is indicated in their particular probability distribution.

Quick quiz

1 What is the difference between a risky project and an uncertain project? (see para 1.2)

2 Why are projects risky? (1.5)

3 How does sensitivity analysis enable management to control risk? (2.3)

4 What are the weaknesses of sensitivity analysis? (2.10)

5 What is the certainty-equivalent approach to assessing projects? (2.11)

6 In what three ways does the construction of a probability distribution of expected cash flows allow risk to be measured? (3.1)

7 What is the advantage of using the standard deviation of the NPV rather than the EV of the NPV to assess risk? (3.4)

8 How are decisions with a decision tree evaluated? (4.14 - 4.16)

9 Describe the way in which random numbers are assigned to probabilities when using a simulation model. (5.3)

Question to try	Level	Marks	Time
29	Introductory	n/a	30 mins

Chapter 29

CAPITAL RATIONING

Chapter topic list		Syllabus reference
1	Causes of a shortage of capital	8(b)(v)
2	Single period capital rationing	8(b)(v)
3	Multi-period capital rationing	8(b)(v)

Introduction

Having looked in Chapters 24 to 28 at the methods available for appraising projects when funds are available, we will now be considering the procedure for assessing projects when capital is a **scarce** resource. Chapter 30 concludes our study of investment appraisal with a consideration of **leasing**.

1 CAUSES OF A SHORTAGE OF CAPITAL 12/94

1.1 The decision rule with DCF techniques is to accept all projects which result in positive NPVs when discounted at the organisation's cost of capital. If an organisation is in a **capital rationing** situation it will not be able to enter into all projects with positive NPVs because there is not enough capital for all of the investments.

KEY TERM

Capital rationing: a situation in which a company has a limited amount of capital to invest in potential projects, such that the different possible investments need to be compared with one another in order to allocate the capital available most effectively.

Exam focus point

Be prepared to discuss the need for capital rationing as well as to perform calculations of NPVs order to evaluate project under conditions of capital rationing.

Soft and hard capital rationing

1.2 Capital rationing may occur due to internal factors (soft capital rationing) or external factors (hard capital rationing).

1.3 **Soft capital rationing** may arise for one of the following reasons.

(a) Management may be reluctant to issue additional share capital because of concern that this may lead to outsiders gaining control of the business.

(b) Management may be unwilling to issue additional share capital if it will lead to a dilution of earnings per share.

(c) Management may not want to raise additional debt capital because they do not wish to be committed to large fixed interest payments.

(d) There may be a desire within the organisation to limit investment to a level that can be financed solely from retained earnings.

(e) Capital expenditure budgets may restrict spending.

1.4 **Hard capital rationing** may arise for one of the following reasons.

(a) Raising money through the stock market may not be possible if share prices are depressed.

(b) There may be restrictions on bank lending due to government control.

(c) Lending institutions may consider an organisation to be to risky to be granted further loan facilities.

(d) The costs associated with making small issues of capital may be too great.

Relaxation of capital constraints

1.5 Whenever an organisation adopts a policy that restricts funds available for investment (soft capital rationing), such a policy may be less than optimal as the organisation may reject projects with a positive net present value and forgo opportunities that would have enhanced the market value of the organisation. Relaxation of the capital constraints imposed by soft capital rationing, of course, requires a change in management policy for such opportunities to be exploited.

1.6 In the case of hard capital rationing, a company may still be able to exploit new opportunities by limiting the effects of hard capital rationing in the following ways.

(a) It might seek joint venture partners with which to share projects.

(b) As an alternative to direct investment in a project, the company may be able to consider a licensing or franchising agreement with another enterprise, under which the licensor/franchisor company would receive royalties.

(c) It may be possible to contract out parts of a project to reduce the initial capital outlay required.

(d) The company may seek new alternative sources of capital (subject to any restrictions which apply to it) for example:

(i) venture capital;
(ii) debt finance secured on the assets of the project;
(iii) sale and leaseback of property or equipment (see the next chapter);
(iv) grant aid;
(v) more effective capital management.

2 SINGLE PERIOD CAPITAL RATIONING 12/94

2.1 We shall begin our analysis by assuming that capital rationing occurs in a single period, and that capital is freely available at all other times.

2.2 The following further assumptions will be made.

(a) If a project is not accepted and undertaken during the period of capital rationing, the opportunity to undertake it is lost. It cannot be postponed until a subsequent period when no capital rationing exists.

(b) There is complete certainty about the outcome of each project, so that the choice between projects is not affected by considerations of risk.

(c) Projects are divisible, so that it is possible to undertake, say, half of Project X in order to earn half of the net present value (NPV) of the whole project.

2.3 The basic approach is to rank all investment opportunities so that the NPVs can be maximised from the use of the available funds.

Note that ranking in terms of absolute NPVs will normally give incorrect results since this method leads to the selection of large projects, each of which has a high individual NPV but which have, in total, a lower NPV than a large number of smaller projects with lower individual NPVs. Ranking is therefore in terms of what is called the **profitability index,** which is the ratio of the present value of the project's future cash flows (not including capital investment) divided by the PV of the total capital outlays. This ratio measures the PV of future cash flows per £1 of investment, and so indicates which investments make the best use of the limited resources available.

2.4 Suppose that Hard Times Ltd is considering four projects, W, X, Y and Z. Relevant details are as follows.

Project	*Investment required*	*Present value of cash inflows and outflows*	*NPV*	*Profitability index (PI)*	*Ranking as per NPV*	*Ranking as per PI*
	£	£	£			
W	(10,000)	11,240	1,240	1.12	3	1
X	(20,000)	20,991	991	1.05	4	4
Y	(30,000)	32,230	2,230	1.07	2	3
Z	(40,000)	43,801	3,801	1.10	1	2

2.5 Without capital rationing all four projects would be viable investments.

Suppose, however, that only £60,000 was available for capital investment.

Let us look at the resulting NPV if we select projects in the order of ranking per NPV.

Project	*Priority*	*Outlay*	*NPV*	
		£	£	
Z	1st	40,000	3,801	
Y (balance)*	2nd	20,000	1,487	($^2/_3$ of £2,230)
		60,000	5,288	

* Projects are divisible. By spending the balancing £20,000 on project Y, two thirds of the full investment would be made to earn two thirds of the NPV.

2.6 Suppose, on the other hand, that we adopt the profitability index approach. The selection of projects will be as follows.

Project	*Priority*	*Outlay*	*NPV*	
		£	£	
W	1st	10,000	1,240	
Z	2nd	40,000	3,801	
Y (balance)	3rd	10,000	743	($^2/_3$ of £2,230)
		60,000	5,784	

2.7 By choosing projects according to the PI, the resulting NPV if only £60,000 is available is increased by £496.

2.8 Note, however, that the above approach can only be used if projects are divisible. If the projects are not divisible a decision has to be made by examining the absolute NPVs of all possible combinations of complete projects that can be undertaken within the constraints of the capital available. The combination of projects which remains at or under the limit of available capital without any of them being divided, and which maximises the total NPV, should be chosen.

Question

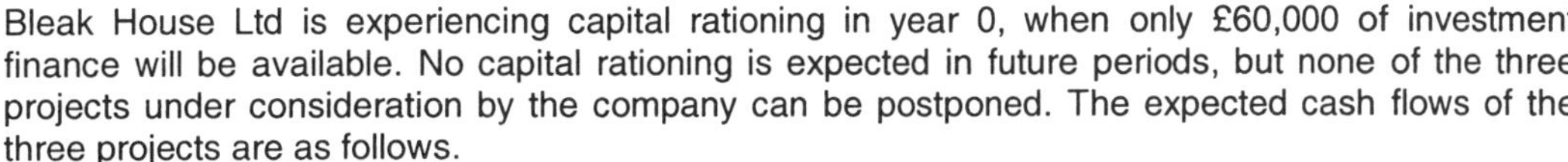

Bleak House Ltd is experiencing capital rationing in year 0, when only £60,000 of investment finance will be available. No capital rationing is expected in future periods, but none of the three projects under consideration by the company can be postponed. The expected cash flows of the three projects are as follows.

Project	*Year 0*	*Year 1*	*Year 2*	*Year 3*	*Year 4*
	£	£	£	£	£
A	(50,000)	(20,000)	20,000	40,000	40,000
B	(28,000)	(50,000)	40,000	40,000	20,000
C	(30,000)	(30,000)	30,000	40,000	10,000

The cost of capital is 10%.

Required

Decide which projects should be undertaken in year 0, in view of the capital rationing, given that projects are divisible.

Answer

The ratio of NPV at 10% to outlay in year 0 (the year of capital rationing) is as follows.

Project	*Outlay in Year 0*	*PV*	*NPV*	*Ratio*	*Ranking*
	£	£	£		
A	50,000	55,700	5,700	1.114	3rd
B	28,000	31,290	3,290	1.118	2nd
C	30,000	34,380	4,380	1.146	1st

The optimal investment policy is as follows.

Ranking	*Project*	*Year 0 outlay*	*NPV*
		£	£
1st	C	30,000	4,380
2nd	B	28,000	3,290
3rd	A (balance)	2,000 (4% of 5,700)	228
NPV from total investment			7,898

Postponing projects

2.9 We have so far assumed that projects cannot be postponed until year 1. If this assumption is removed, the choice of projects in year 0 would be made by reference to the loss of NPV from **postponement**.

2.10 EXAMPLE: POSTPONING PROJECTS

The figures in the previous exercise will be used to illustrate the method. If any project, A, B or C, were delayed by one year, the 'NPV' would now relate to year 1 values, so that in year 0 terms, the NPVs would be as follows.

		NPV in Year 1				NPV in Year 0 Value	Loss in NPV
		£				£	£
(a)	Project A	5,700	×	$\frac{1}{1.10}$	=	5,182	518
(b)	Project B	3,290	×	$\frac{1}{1.10}$	=	2,991	299
(c)	Project C	4,380	×	$\frac{1}{1.10}$	=	3,982	398

2.11 An index of postponability would be calculated as follows.

Project	*Loss in NPV from one-year postponement*	*Outlay deferred from year 0*	*Postponability index (loss/outlay)*
	£	£	
A	518	50,000	0.0104
B	299	28,000	0.0107
C	398	30,000	0.0133

2.12 The loss in NPV by deferring investment would be greatest for Project C, and least for Project A. It is therefore more profitable to postpone A, rather than B or C, as follows.

Investment in year 0:

Project	*Outlay*		*NPV*
	£		£
C	30,000		4,380
B	28,000		3,290
A (balance)	2,000	(4% of 5,700)	228
	60,000		7,898

Investment in year 1 (balance):

Project A	£48,000	(96% of 5,182)	4,975
Total NPV (as at year 0) of investments in years 0 and 1			12,873

3 MULTI-PERIOD CAPITAL RATIONING

3.1 When capital is expected to be in short supply for more than one period, the selection of an optimal investment programme cannot be made by ranking projects according to a profitability index. Other techniques, notably linear programming, should be used.

Solution by graphical linear programming

3.2 You should have already covered the **graphical approach to linear programming** in your earlier studies and so you will be aware that the technique can only be used if there are two variables. The variables in this instance are the individual investment projects and so this method is confined to dealing with those scenarios concerned with a choice between just two investment projects. We will illustrate this particular approach to multi-period capital rationing with an example.

3.3 EXAMPLE: GRAPHICAL LINEAR PROGRAMMING APPROACH

Finch Ltd has the chance to invest in two projects, A and B, details of which are set out below.

Investment project	*Present value of outlay in period 1*	*Present value of outlay in period 2*	*Present value of outlay in period 3*	*Net present value of investment at time 0*
	£'000	£'000	£'000	£'000
A	30	10	10	56
B	20	4	2	8

Capital investment limits, as set by Finch Ltd's parent company, are as follows.

	£'000
Period 1	36
Period 2	8
Period 3	6

It is assumed that the capital investment limits are absolute and cannot be expanded by project generated cash inflows.

Projects are divisible but cannot be repeated more than once.

Required

Formulate and solve the linear programming model which will maximise net present value.

3.4 SOLUTION

(a) *Define variables*

Let x = the proportion of project A accepted.
Let y = the proportion of project B accepted.

(b) *Establish constraints*

$30x + 20y \leq 36$ (period 1 investment)
$10x + 4y \leq 8$ (period 2 investment)
$10x + 2y \leq 6$ (period 3 investment
$x, y \leq 1$ (proportion must be less than or equal to 1)
$x, y \geq 0$ (proportion must be greater than or equal to 0)

The last two constraints ensure that a project cannot be undertaken more than once but allows for a project to be partially accepted.

(c) *Establish objective function*

The objective is to maximise the NPV from the total investment in periods 1, 2 and 3.

Maximise $56x + 8y$.

(d) *Graph the model*

3
2
10x + 2y = 6
x = 1
A
B
1
y = 1
30x + 20y = 36
FEASIBLE REGION
10x + 4y = 8
C
0
1

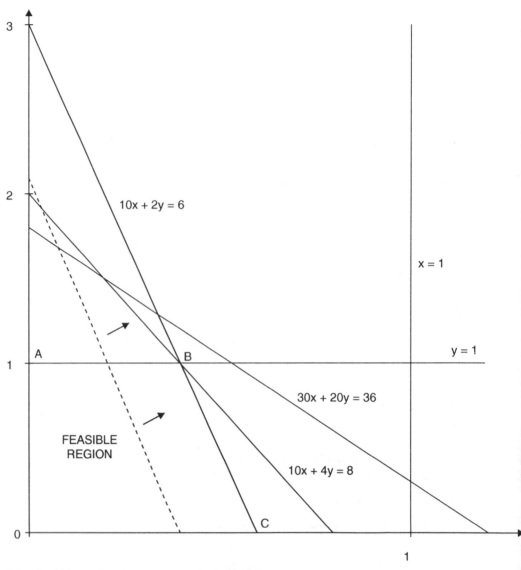

The feasible region is represented by OABC.

(e) *Finding the best solution*

Using the 'iso-NPV line' plotted on the graph, the optimal solution can be established as at point C (0.6,0).

The optimal solution is therefore to invest in 0.6 of project A and to make no investment in project B.

The total NPV available is therefore 0.6 × £56,000 = £33,600.

More than two investments under consideration

3.5 The graphical approach to linear programming cannot deal with situations where there are more than two investments under consideration.

Exam focus point

A method for solving such linear programming problems is called the simplex method. This is outside the scope of your syllabus.

Limitations of the linear programming approach to capital rationing

3.6 When two constraints apply, the graphical approach to linear programming may be a useful method of selecting projects but there are a number of assumptions and limitations which must be kept in mind if the use of the technique is to be considered.

(a) It assumes that variables are linearly related.

(b) It assumes that projects are divisible or that scalar multiples of projects are possible.

(c) It assumes that the returns of the projects are in proportion to the amount invested in each project.

(d) Uncertainty is ignored. It assumes that all future cash flows and available resources are known with certainty.

(e) It assumes that all projects and constraints are independent.

(f) It is possible that other investment opportunities not included in the linear programming model could realise a higher NPV.

(g) Linear programming cannot be used when projects are mutually exclusive in multi-period capital rationing situations. Instead integer programming (not part of your syllabus) has to be used.

(h) No account of risk attached to the projects or the company's attitude to risk is taken.

Chapter roundup

- **Capital rationing** may occur due to internal factors (soft capital rationing) or external factors (hard capital rationing).
- When capital rationing occurs in a **single period**, projects are ranked in terms of **profitability index**.
- When capital rationing occurs in a **number of periods** and two projects are under consideration, the graphical approach to **linear programming** is used to arrive at an NPV - maximising mix of products.
- Although the graphical approach is a useful technique to use for arriving at optimum project mixes, you should be aware of its limitations.

Quick quiz

1 List four reasons why soft capital rationing might occur. (see para 1.3)

2 List four reasons why hard capital rationing might occur. (1.4)

3 How might capital rationing constraints be relaxed? (1.5, 1.6)

4 What is the ranking approach if there is capital rationing in year 0 only but projects are **not** divisible? (2.8)

5 What are the five steps in solving a linear programming problem with graphs? (3.4)

Question to try	Level	Marks	Time
30	Examination	25	45 mins

Chapter 30

LEASING DECISIONS

Introduction

In this chapter, we consider the option of **leasing** an asset.

As well as looking at the advantages and disadvantages of different types of lease compared with **other forms of credit finance**, we shall be discussing the tax and cash flow implications of leasing.

1 LEASING AS A SOURCE OF FINANCE 6/96

The nature of leasing

1.1 Rather than buying an asset outright, using either available cash resources or borrowed funds, a business may lease an asset. **Leasing** has become a popular source of finance in the UK.

1.2 Leasing can be defined as a contract between lessor and lessee for hire of a specific asset selected from a manufacturer or vendor of such assets by the lessee. The lessor retains ownership of the asset. The lessee has possession and use of the asset on payment of specified rentals over a period.

1.3 Many lessors are financial intermediaries such as banks and insurance companies. The range of assets leased is wide, including office equipment and computers, cars and commercial vehicles, aircraft, ships and buildings.

Types of leasing

1.4 In Statement of Standard Accounting Practice (SSAP) 21 *Accounting for leases and hire purchase contracts*, finance leases and operating leases are distinguished for accounting purposes.

1.5 A further type of leasing arrangement is **sale and leaseback**, an arrangement which is similar to mortgaging. A business which already owns an asset, for example a building or an item of equipment, agrees to sell the asset to a financial institution and to lease it back on terms specified in the agreement. The business has the benefit of the funds from the sale while retaining use of the asset, in return for regular payments to the financial institution.

1.6 **Operating leases** are rental agreements between a lessor and a lessee whereby:

(a) the lessor supplies the equipment to the lessee;

(b) the lessor is responsible for servicing and maintaining the leased equipment;

(c) the period of the lease is fairly short, less than the expected economic life of the asset, so that at the end of one lease agreement, the lessor can either:

(i) lease the same equipment to someone else, and obtain a good rent for it; or
(ii) sell the equipment second-hand.

1.7 Much of the growth in the UK leasing business in recent years has been in operating leases. With an operating lease, the lessor, often a finance house, purchases the equipment from the manufacturer and then leases it to the user (the lessee) for the agreed period.

1.8 **Finance leases** are lease agreements between the user of the leased asset (the lessee) and a provider of finance (the lessor) for most or all of the asset's expected useful life.

1.9 Suppose that a company decides to obtain a company car and finance the acquisition by means of a finance lease. A car dealer will supply the car. A finance house will agree to act as lessor in a finance leasing arrangement, and so will purchase the car from the dealer and lease it to the company. The company will take possession of the car from the car dealer, and make regular payments (monthly, quarterly, six monthly or annually) to the finance house under the terms of the lease.

1.10 There are other important characteristics of a finance lease.

(a) The lessee is responsible for the upkeep, servicing and maintenance of the asset. The lessor is not involved in this at all.

(b) The lease has a primary period, which covers all or most of the useful economic life of the asset. At the end of this primary period, the lessor would not be able to lease the asset to someone else, because the asset would be worn out. The lessor must therefore ensure that the lease payments during the primary period pay for the full cost of the asset as well as providing the lessor with a suitable return on his investment.

(c) It is usual at the end of the primary period to allow the lessee to continue to lease the asset for an indefinite secondary period, in return for a very low nominal rent, sometimes called a 'peppercorn rent'. Alternatively, the lessee might be allowed to sell the asset on a lessor's behalf (since the lessor is the owner) and to keep most of the sale proceeds, paying only a small percentage (perhaps 10%) to the lessor.

1.11 Under some schemes, a lessor leases equipment to the lessee for most of the equipment's life, and at the end of the lease period sells the equipment himself, with none of the sale proceeds going to the lessee.

1.12 Returning to the example of the car lease, the primary period of the lease might be three years, with an agreement by the lessee to make three annual payments of £6,000 each. The lessee will be responsible for repairs and servicing, road tax, insurance and garaging. At the end of the primary period of the lease, the lessee might be given the option either to continue leasing the car at a nominal rent (perhaps £250 a year) or to sell the car and pay the lessor 10% of the proceeds.

Attractions of leasing

1.13 The attractions of leases to the supplier of the equipment, the lessee and the lessor are as follows.

(a) The supplier of the equipment is paid in full at the beginning. The equipment is sold to the lessor, and apart from obligations under guarantees or warranties, the supplier has no further financial concern about the asset.

(b) The lessor invests finance by purchasing assets from suppliers and makes a return out of the lease payments from the lessee. Provided that a lessor can find lessees willing to pay the amounts he wants to make his return, the lessor can make good profits. He will also get capital allowances on his purchase of the equipment.

(c) Leasing might be attractive to the lessee:

(i) if the lessee does not have enough cash to pay for the asset, and would have difficulty obtaining a bank loan to buy it, and so has to rent it in one way or another if he is to have the use of it at all; or

(ii) if finance leasing is cheaper than a bank loan. The cost of payments under a loan might exceed the cost of a lease.

The lessee may find the tax relief available advantageous.

1.14 Operating leases have these further advantages.

(a) The leased equipment does not have to be shown in the lessee's published balance sheet, and so the lessee's balance sheet shows no increase in its gearing ratio.

(b) The equipment is leased for a shorter period than its expected useful life. In the case of high-technology equipment, if the equipment becomes out of date before the end of its expected life, the lessee does not have to keep on using it, and it is the lessor who must bear the risk of having to sell obsolete equipment secondhand.

1.15 Not surprisingly perhaps, a major growth area in operating leasing in the UK has been in computers and office equipment (such as photocopiers and fax machines) where technology is continually improving.

Hire purchase

1.16 Another form of credit finance with which leasing can be contrasted is **hire purchase**, which is a form of instalment credit. There are two basic forms of instalment credit, whereby an individual or business purchases goods on credit and pays for them by instalments.

(a) **Lender credit** occurs when the buyer borrows money and uses the money to purchase goods outright.

(b) **Vendor credit** occurs when the buyer obtains goods on credit and agrees to pay the vendor by instalments. Hire purchase is an example of vendor credit.

Hire purchase is similar to leasing, with the exception that ownership of the goods passes to the hire purchase customer on payment of the final credit instalment, whereas a lessee never becomes the owner of the goods.

1.17 Hire purchase agreements nowadays usually involve a finance house.

(a) The supplier sells the goods to the finance house.
(b) The supplier delivers the goods to the customer who will eventually purchase them.
(c) The hire purchase arrangement exists between the finance house and the customer.

1.18 The finance house will nearly always insist that the hirer should pay a deposit towards the purchase price, perhaps as low as 10%, or as high as 33%. The size of the deposit will depend on the finance company's policy and its assessment of the hirer. This is in contrast to a finance lease, where the lessee might not be required to make any large initial payment.

1.19 An industrial or commercial business can use hire purchase as a source of finance. With **industrial hire purchase,** a business customer obtains hire purchase finance from a finance house in order to purchase a fixed asset.

1.20 Goods bought by businesses on hire purchase include company vehicles, plant and machinery, office equipment and farming machinery. Hire purchase arrangements for fleets of motor cars are quite common, and most car manufacturers have a link with a leading finance house so as to offer hire purchase credit whenever a car is bought.

1.21 When faced with an investment opportunity, an organisation may have to decide whether to purchase the equipment, acquire it under a finance lease arrangement or acquire it under a hire purchase arrangement. (Our interest here is in **finance leases,** not operating leases.)

1.22 When a company acquires a capital asset under a hire purchase agreement, it will eventually obtain full legal title to the asset. The HP payments consist partly of 'capital' payments towards the purchase of the asset, and partly of interest charges.

1.23 For example, if a company buys a car costing £10,000 under an HP agreement, the car supplier might provide HP finance over a three year period at an interest cost of 10%, and the HP payments might be, say, as follows.

	Capital element £	*Interest element* £	*Total HP payment* £
Year 0: down payment	2,540	0	2,540
Year 1	2,254	746	3,000
Year 2	2,479	521	3,000
Year 3	2,727	273	3,000
Total	10,000	1,540	11,540

1.24 The tax position on a hire purchase arrangement is as follows.

(a) The buyer obtains whatever capital allowances are available, based on the capital element of the cost. Capital allowances on the full capital element of the cost can be used from the time the asset is acquired.

(b) In addition, interest payments within the HP payments are an allowable expense against tax, spread over the term of the HP agreement.

(c) Capital payments within the HP payments, however, are not allowable against tax.

2 LEASE OR BUY DECISIONS 6/96

2.1 There are several ways of evaluating a decision whether to lease an asset, or to purchase it by another means of finance.

2.2 The traditional method is to take the view that a decision to lease is a financing decision, which can only be made after a decision to acquire the asset has already been taken. It is therefore necessary to make a two-stage decision, as follows.

Step 1. An **acquisition decision** is made on whether the asset is worth having. The present values of operational costs and benefits from using the asset are found to derive a net present value (NPV).

Step 2. A **financing decision** is then made if the acquisition is justified by a positive NPV. This is the decision on whether to **lease or buy**.

2.3 The traditional method is complicated by the need to choose a discount rate for each stage of the decision. In the case of a non-taxpaying organisation, the method is applied as follows.

Step 1. The cost of capital that should be applied to the cash flows for the acquisition decision is the cost of capital that the organisation would normally apply to its project evaluations.

Step 2. The cost of capital that should be applied to the (differential) cash flows for the financing decision is the cost of borrowing.

(i) We assume that if the organisation decided to purchase the equipment, it would finance the purchase by borrowing funds (rather than out of retained funds).

(ii) We therefore compare the cost of borrowing with the cost of leasing (or hire purchase) by applying this cost of borrowing to the financing cash flows.

2.4 In the case of a tax-paying organisation, taxation should be allowed for in the cash flows, so that the traditional method would recommend:

(a) discounting the cash flows of the acquisition decision at the firm's after-tax cost of capital;

(b) discounting the cash flows of the financing decision at the after-tax cost of borrowing.

The tax treatment of finance leases in the UK under Finance Act 1991 rules is:

(a) to allow depreciation as an expense;

(b) to allow the interest element of the finance charge as an expense over the period of the lease.

This treatment leads to some complex calculations, while the result may not be materially different from that obtained if we assume that the lease payments are allowable for tax in full.

Exam focus point
In the exam, it is acceptable to make this latter assumption provided that you state it in your answer and provided that the question does not direct otherwise.

2.5 EXAMPLE: LEASE OR BUY DECISIONS (1)

Mallen and Mullins Ltd has decided to install a new milling machine. The machine costs £20,000 and it would have a useful life of five years with a trade-in value of £4,000 at the end of the fifth year. Additional cash profits from the machine would be £8,000 a year for five years. A decision has now to be taken on the method of financing the project. Three methods of finance are being considered.

(a) The company could purchase the machine for cash, using bank loan facilities on which the current rate of interest is 13% before tax.

(b) The company could lease the machine under an agreement which would entail payment of £4,800 at the end of each year for the next five years.

(c) The company could purchase the machine under a hire purchase agreement. This would require an initial deposit of £6,500 and payments of £4,400 per annum at the end of each of the next five years. The interest part of the payments, for tax purposes, would be £2,100 at the end of year 1 and £1,800, £1,400, £1,000 and £700 at the end of each of years 2, 3, 4 and 5 respectively.

The company's weighted average cost of capital, normally used for project evaluating, is 12% after tax. The rate of corporation tax is 31%. If the machine is purchased, the company will be able to claim an annual writing down allowance of 25% of the reducing balance.

Advise the management on:

(a) whether to acquire the machine;

(b) the most economical method of finance;

(c) any other matter which should be considered before finally deciding which method of finance should be adopted.

2.6 SOLUTION

The traditional method begins with the acquisition decision. The cash flows of the project should be discounted at 12%. The first writing down allowance is assumed to be claimed in the first year resulting in a saving of tax at year 2.

Capital allowances

Year	*Allowance*	
		£
1	25% of £20,000	5,000
2	25% of £(20,000 – 5,000)	3,750
3	25% of £(15,000 – 3,750)	2,813
4	25% of £(11,250 – 2,813)	2,109
		13,672
5	£(20,000 – 13,672 – 4,000)	2,328
		16,000

Taxable profits and tax liability

Year	*Cash profits*	*Capital allowance*	*Taxable profits*	*Tax at 31%*
	£	£	£	£
1	8,000	5,000	3,000	930
2	8,000	3,750	4,250	1,317
3	8,000	2,813	5,187	1,608
4	8,000	2,109	5,891	1,826
5	8,000	2,328	5,672	1,758

NPV calculation for the acquisition decision

Year	*Equipment*	*Cash profits*	*Tax*	*Net cash flow*	*Discount factor*	*Present value*
	£	£	£	£	12%	£
0	(20,000)			(20,000)	1.000	(20,000)
1		8,000		8,000	0.893	7,144
2		8,000	(930)	7,070	0.797	5,635
3		8,000	(1,317)	6,683	0.712	4,758
4		8,000	(1,608)	6,392	0.636	4,065
5	4,000	8,000	(1,826)	10,174	0.567	5,769
6			(1,758)	(1,758)	0.507	(891)
					NPV	6,480

2.7 The net present value (NPV) is positive, and so we conclude that the machine should be acquired, regardless of the method used to finance the acquisition.

2.8 The second stage is the financing decision, and cash flows are discounted at the after-tax cost of borrowing, which is at 13% × 69% = 8.97%, say 9%.

2.9 The only cash flows that we need to consider are those which will be affected by the choice of the method of financing. The operating savings of £8,000 a year, and the tax on these savings, can be ignored.

(a) *The PV of purchase costs*

Year	*Item*	*Cash flow*	*Discount factor*	*PV*
		£	9%	£
0	Equipment cost	(20,000)	1.000	(20,000)
5	Trade-in value	4,000	0.650	2,600
	Tax savings, from allowances			
2	31% × £5,000	1,550	0.842	1,305
3	31% × £3,750	1,162	0.772	897
4	31% × £2,813	872	0.708	617
5	31% × £2,109	654	0.650	425
6	31% × £2,328	721	0.596	430
			NPV of purchase	(13,726)

(b) *The PV of leasing costs*

It is assumed that the tax payments are fully tax-allowable.

Year	*Lease payment*	*Savings in tax (31%)*	*Discount factor*	*PV*
	£	£	9%	£
1-5	(4,800) pa		3.890	(18,672)
2-6		1,488 pa	3.569	5,311
			NPV of leasing	(13,361)

(c) *The PV of hire purchase*

Year	*HP payments* £	*Capital allowances - tax saved* £	*Tax saved due to interest on HP payments at 31%*	*Net cash flow* £	*Discount factor at 9%*	*PV* £
0	(6,500)			(6,500)	1.000	(6,500)
1	(4,400)			(4,400)	0.917	(4,035)
2	(4,400)	1,550	651	(2,199)	0.842	(1,852)
3	(4,400)	1,162	558	(2,680)	0.772	(2,069)
4	(4,400)	872	434	(3,094)	0.708	(2,191)
5	(400)*	654	310	564	0.650	367
6		721	217	938	0.596	559
				NPV of hire purchase		(15,721)

* £4,400 less £4,000 trade-in value

2.10 The cheaper option would be to lease the machine. However, other matters to be considered include the following.

(a) **Running expenses**. The calculations assume that the running costs are the same under each alternative. This may not be so. Expenses like maintenance, consumable stores, insurance and so on may differ between the alternatives.

(b) The **effect on cash flow**. Purchasing requires an immediate outflow of £20,000 compared to nothing for leasing. This effect should be considered in relation to the company's liquidity position, which in turn will affect its ability to discharge its debts and to pay dividends.

(c) **Alternative uses of funds**. The proposed outlay of £20,000 for purchase should be considered in relation to alternative investments.

(d) The **trade-in value**. The net present value of purchase is materially affected by the trade-in value of £4,000 in the fifth year. This figure could be very inaccurate.

2.11 A disadvantage of the traditional approach to making a lease or buy decision is that if there is a negative NPV when the operational cash flows of the project are discounted at the firm's cost of capital, the investment will be rejected out of hand, with no thought given to how the investment might be financed. It is conceivable, however, that the costs of leasing might be so low that the project would be worthwhile provided that the leasing option were selected. This suggests that an investment opportunity should not be rejected without first giving some thought to its financing costs.

2.12 **Other methods** of making lease or buy decisions are as follows.

(a) Compare the cost of leasing with the cost of purchase, and select the cheaper method of financing; then calculate the NPV of the project on the assumption that the cheaper method of financing is used. In other words, make the financing decision first and the acquisition decision afterwards.

(b) Calculate an NPV for the project under each of two assumptions about financing.

(i) The machine is purchased.
(ii) The machine is leased.

Select the method of financing which gives the higher NPV, provided that the project is viable (that is, has a positive NPV). In other words, combine the acquisition and financing decisions together into a single-stage decision. This method is illustrated in the following example.

2.13 EXAMPLE: LEASE OR BUY DECISIONS (2)

In the case of Mallen and Mullins Ltd, the NPV with purchase would be + £6,480. This was calculated above. The NPV with leasing would be as follows. A discount rate of 12% is used here.

Year	*Profit less leasing cost*	*Tax at 31%*	*Net cash flow*	*Discount factor*	*PV*
	£	£	£	12%	£
1	3,200		3,200	0.893	2,858
2	3,200	(992)	2,208	0.797	1,760
3	3,200	(992)	2,208	0.712	1,572
4	3,200	(992)	2,208	0.636	1,404
5	3,200	(992)	2,208	0.567	1,252
6		(992)	(992)	0.507	(503)
				NPV	8,343

Using this method, leasing is preferable, because the NPV is £1,863 higher.

Operating leases

2.14 Since operating leases are a form of renting, the only cash flows to consider for this type of leasing are:

(a) the lease payments;
(b) tax saved: operating lease payments are allowable expenses for tax purposes.

The position of the lessor

Exam focus point

So far, we have looked at examples of leasing decisions from the viewpoint of the lessee. You may, as in the 6/96 paper, be asked to evaluate a leasing arrangement from the position of the lessor. This is rather like a mirror image of the lessee's position.

2.15 Assuming that it is purchasing the asset, the lessor will receive capital allowances on the expenditure, and the lease payments will be taxable income.

2.16 EXAMPLE: LESSOR'S POSITION

Continuing the same case of Mallen and Mullins Ltd, suppose that the lessor's required rate of return is 12% after tax. The lessor's cash flows will be as follows.

	Cash flow	*Discount factor*	*PV*
	£	12%	£
Purchase costs (see 2.9)			
Year 0	(20,000)	1.000	(20,000)
Year 5 trade-in	4,000	0.567	2,268
Tax savings			
Year 2	1,550	0.797	1,235
Year 3	1,162	0.712	827
Year 4	872	0.636	555
Year 5	654	0.567	371
Year 6	721	0.507	366
Lease payments: years 1-5	4,800	3.605	17,304
Tax on lease payments: years 2-6	(1,488)	3.218	(4,788)
NPV			(1,862)

2.17 *Conclusion.* The proposed level of leasing payments are not justifiable for the lessor if it seeks a required rate of return of 12%, since the resulting NPV is negative.

Question

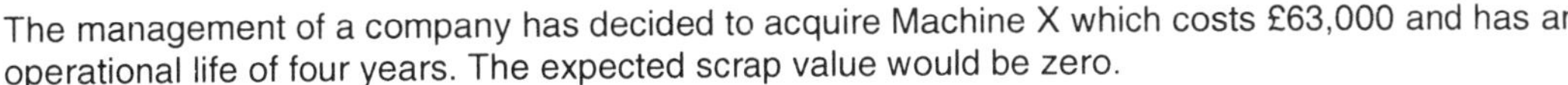

The management of a company has decided to acquire Machine X which costs £63,000 and has an operational life of four years. The expected scrap value would be zero.

Tax is payable at 31% on operating cash flows one year in arrears. Capital allowances are available at 25% a year on a reducing balance basis.

Suppose that the company has the opportunity either to purchase the machine or to lease it under a finance lease arrangement, at an annual rent of £20,000 for four years, payable at the end of each year. The company can borrow to finance the acquisition at 10%. Should the company lease or buy the machine?

Answer

Working

Capital allowances

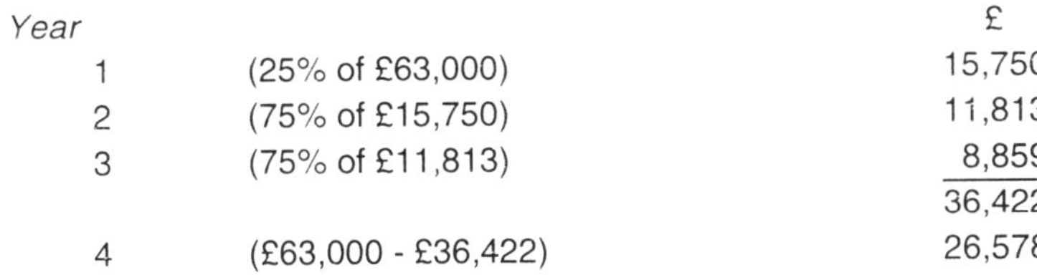

Year		£
1	(25% of £63,000)	15,750
2	(75% of £15,750)	11,813
3	(75% of £11,813)	8,859
		36,422
4	(£63,000 - £36,422)	26,578

The financing decision will be appraised by discounting the relevant cash flows at the after-tax cost of borrowing, which is 10% × 69% = 6.9%, say 7%.

(a) *Purchase option*

Year	*Item*	*Cash flow* £	*Discount factor* 7%	*Present value* £
0	Cost of machine	(63,000)	1.000	(63,000)
	Tax saved from capital allowances			
2	31% × £15,750	4,833	0.873	4,263
3	31% × £11,813	3,662	0.816	2,988
4	31% × £8,859	2,746	0.763	2,095
5	31% × £26,578	8,239	0.713	5,874
				(47,780)

(b) *Leasing option*

It is assumed that the lease payments are tax-allowable in full.

Year	*Item*	*Cash flow* £	*Discount factor* 7%	*Present value* £
1-4	Lease costs	(20,000)	3.387	(67,740)
2-5	Tax savings on lease costs (× 31%)	6,200	3.165	19,623
				(48,117)

The purchase option is marginally cheaper, using a cost of capital based on the after-tax cost of borrowing.

On the assumption that investors would regard borrowing and leasing as equally risky finance options, the purchase option is recommended.

Chapter roundup

- **Leasing** is a commonly used source of finance. We have distinguished three types of leasing: **operating leases** (**lessor** responsible for maintaining asset), **finance leases** (**lessee** responsible for maintenance), and **sale and leaseback** arrangements.
- The decision whether to **lease or buy** an asset involves two steps.
    - The **acquisition decision**: is the asset worth having? Test by discounting project cash flows at a suitable cost of capital.
    - the **financing decision**: if the asset should be acquired, compare the cash flows of purchasing and leasing or HP arrangements. The cash flows can be discounted at an after-tax cost of borrowing.

Quick quiz

1. What is a sale and leaseback arrangement? (see para 1.5)
2. What is an operating lease? (1.6)
3. What is the traditional method for lease or buy decisions? (2.2)
4. What factors other than net present values should be considered when making lease or buy decisions? (2.10)
5. Give two alternatives to the traditional method of making lease or buy decisions. (2.12)

Question to try	Level	Marks	Time
31	Examination	20	36 mins

Appendix
Mathematical tables

PRESENT VALUE TABLE

Present value of 1 ie $(1+r)^{-n}$

where r = discount rate

n = number of periods until payment

Periods (n)	1%	2%	3%	4%	5%	6%	7%	8%	9%	10%
1	0.990	0.980	0.971	0.962	0.952	0.943	0.935	0.926	0.917	0.909
2	0.980	0.961	0.943	0.925	0.907	0.890	0.873	0.857	0.842	0.826
3	0.971	0.942	0.915	0.889	0.864	0.840	0.816	0.794	0.772	0.751
4	0.961	0.924	0.888	0.855	0.823	0.792	0.763	0.735	0.708	0.683
5	0.951	0.906	0.863	0.822	0.784	0.747	0.713	0.681	0.650	0.621
6	0.942	0.888	0.837	0.790	0.746	0.705	0.666	0.630	0.596	0.564
7	0.933	0.871	0.813	0.760	0.711	0.665	0.623	0.583	0.547	0.513
8	0.923	0.853	0.789	0.731	0.677	0.627	0.582	0.540	0.502	0.467
9	0.914	0.837	0.766	0.703	0.645	0.592	0.544	0.500	0.460	0.424
10	0.905	0.820	0.744	0.676	0.614	0.558	0.508	0.463	0.422	0.386
11	0.896	0.804	0.722	0.650	0.585	0.527	0.475	0.429	0.388	0.350
12	0.887	0.788	0.701	0.625	0.557	0.497	0.444	0.397	0.356	0.319
13	0.879	0.773	0.681	0.601	0.530	0.469	0.415	0.368	0.326	0.290
14	0.870	0.758	0.661	0.577	0.505	0.442	0.388	0.340	0.299	0.263
15	0.861	0.743	0.642	0.555	0.481	0.417	0.362	0.315	0.275	0.239

(n)	11%	12%	13%	14%	15%	16%	17%	18%	19%	20%
1	0.901	0.893	0.885	0.877	0.870	0.862	0.855	0.847	0.840	0.833
2	0.812	0.797	0.783	0.769	0.756	0.743	0.731	0.718	0.706	0.694
3	0.731	0.712	0.693	0.675	0.658	0.641	0.624	0.609	0.593	0.579
4	0.659	0.636	0.613	0.592	0.572	0.552	0.534	0.516	0.499	0.482
5	0.593	0.567	0.543	0.519	0.497	0.476	0.456	0.437	0.419	0.402
6	0.535	0.507	0.480	0.456	0.432	0.410	0.390	0.370	0.352	0.335
7	0.482	0.452	0.425	0.400	0.376	0.354	0.333	0.314	0.296	0.279
8	0.434	0.404	0.376	0.351	0.327	0.305	0.285	0.266	0.249	0.233
9	0.391	0.361	0.333	0.308	0.284	0.263	0.243	0.225	0.209	0.194
10	0.352	0.322	0.295	0.270	0.247	0.227	0.208	0.191	0.176	0.162
11	0.317	0.287	0.261	0.237	0.215	0.195	0.178	0.162	0.148	0.135
12	0.286	0.257	0.231	0.208	0.187	0.168	0.152	0.137	0.124	0.112
13	0.258	0.229	0.204	0.182	0.163	0.145	0.130	0.116	0.104	0.093
14	0.232	0.205	0.181	0.160	0.141	0.125	0.111	0.099	0.088	0.078
15	0.209	0.183	0.160	0.140	0.123	0.108	0.095	0.084	0.074	0.065

ANNUITY TABLE

Present value of an annuity of 1 ie $\frac{1-(1+r)^{-n}}{r}$

where r = interest rate

n = number of periods

Periods (n)	Discount rates (r) 1%	2%	3%	4%	5%	6%	7%	8%	9%	10%
1	0.990	0.980	0.971	0.962	0.952	0.943	0.935	0.926	0.917	0.909
2	1.970	1.942	1.913	1.886	1.859	1.833	1.808	1.783	1.759	1.736
3	2.941	2.884	2.829	2.775	2.723	2.673	2.624	2.577	2.531	2.487
4	3.902	3.808	3.717	3.630	3.546	3.465	3.387	3.312	3.240	3.170
5	4.853	4.713	4.580	4.452	4.329	4.212	4.100	3.993	3.890	3.791
6	5.795	5.601	5.417	5.242	5.076	4.917	4.767	4.623	4.486	4.355
7	6.728	6.472	6.230	6.002	5.786	5.582	5.389	5.206	5.033	4.868
8	7.652	7.325	7.020	6.733	6.463	6.210	5.971	5.747	5.535	5.335
9	8.566	8.162	7.786	7.435	7.108	6.802	6.515	6.247	5.995	5.759
10	9.471	8.983	8.530	8.111	7.722	7.360	7.024	6.710	6.418	6.145
11	10.37	9.787	9.253	8.760	8.306	7.887	7.499	7.139	6.805	6.495
12	11.26	10.58	9.954	9.385	8.863	8.384	7.943	7.536	7.161	6.814
13	12.13	11.35	10.63	9.986	9.394	8.853	8.358	7.904	7.487	7.103
14	13.00	12.11	11.30	10.56	9.899	9.295	8.745	8.244	7.786	7.367
15	13.87	12.85	11.94	11.12	10.38	9.712	9.108	8.559	8.061	7.606

	11%	12%	13%	14%	15%	16%	17%	18%	19%	20%
1	0.901	0.893	0.885	0.877	0.870	0.862	0.855	0.847	0.840	0.833
2	1.713	1.690	1.668	1.647	1.626	1.605	1.585	1.566	1.547	1.528
3	2.444	2.402	2.361	2.322	2.283	2.246	2.210	2.174	2.140	2.106
4	3.102	3.037	2.974	2.914	2.855	2.798	2.743	2.690	2.639	2.589
5	3.696	3.605	3.517	3.433	3.352	3.274	3.199	3.127	3.058	2.991
6	4.231	4.111	3.998	3.889	3.784	3.685	3.589	3.498	3.410	3.326
7	4.712	4.564	4.423	4.288	4.160	4.039	3.922	3.812	3.706	3.605
8	5.146	4.968	4.799	4.639	4.487	4.344	4.207	4.078	3.954	3.837
9	5.537	5.328	5.132	4.946	4.772	4.607	4.451	4.303	4.163	4.031
10	5.889	5.650	5.426	5.216	5.019	4.833	4.659	4.494	4.339	4.192
11	6.207	5.938	5.687	5.453	5.234	5.029	4.836	4.656	4.486	4.327
12	6.492	6.194	5.918	5.660	5.421	5.197	4.988	4.793	4.611	4.439
13	6.750	6.424	6.122	5.842	5.583	5.342	5.118	4.910	4.715	4.533
14	6.982	6.628	6.302	6.002	5.724	5.468	5.229	5.008	4.802	4.611
15	7.191	6.811	6.462	6.142	5.847	5.575	5.324	5.092	4.876	4.675

Exam question bank

1 **MANAGEMENT AND FINANCIAL ACCOUNTING (5 marks)** *9 mins*

Distinguish between financial accounting and management accounting.

2 **RYMAN COUPLETS LTD (20 marks)** *36 mins*

Ryman Couplets Ltd is a newly established company which plans to start operations from the beginning of 19X2. During the first two years, it is considered that there will be some build-up of stocks, so that production volumes will normally exceed demand in the year. Budgeted production and sales for the first two years are as follows.

	19X2			*19X3*		
Product	*X*	*Y*	*Z*	*X*	*Y*	*Z*
Production (000's of units)	20	20	10	20	20	10
Sales (000's of units)	14	16	3	14	12	14

From 19X4 onwards, it is expected that annual production levels will be about the same, but that sales demand will rise to these same levels.

The unit sales price and variable costs during 19X2 and 19X3 are expected to be as follows.

Product	*Unit sales price*	*Unit variable costs*
	£	£
X	30	16
Y	35	18
Z	25	12

Fixed production costs will be £560,000 per annum in total.

The products are all manufactured by machine, but some additional direct labour effort is required to finish them. The time required per unit has been measured, by work study techniques, is as follows.

Product	*Machine hours per unit*	*Labour hours per unit*
X	3	2
Y	1	4
Z	2	2

The company's managing director, William Gwilliam, wished to ascertain the expected profitability of each product and the total company profits for 19X2 and 19X3. (You may ignore administration, selling and distribution costs.) His management accountant, Simon Hyman, produced three sets of figures, one using direct costing and the other two using absorption costing, but each with a different basis of overhead recovery. William Gwilliam was somewhat irate, because each set of figures gave differing results, and he demanded to know which figures were right and which were wrong.

Required

(a) Prepare the three standards of total profit in each of the two years, and the profitability of each product individually. (8 marks)

(b) Compare the resulting figures, and comment on how the absorption costing figures might be improved. Advise the managing director which set of figures is 'correct' and which are 'wrong'. (6 marks)

(c) It is decided to increase production quantities in the first year only by a further 25% in order to build up stocks to a higher level. Calculate the following.

   (i) The annual cost to Ryman Couplets Ltd of the stock increase, if the financial cost of holding stocks is 14% per annum

   (ii) The effect this increase would have on reported profits during 19X2 (only) using each of the three costing methods described (6 marks)

3 **TAKE SOME PROFIT (5 marks)** *9 mins*

Explain why it is regarded as desirable for contracting companies to include some profit on uncompleted contracts. Your explanation should contain some reference to prudence.

4 BREEZEBLOCK LTD (20 marks) *36 mins*

Breezeblock Ltd operates a process that makes two joint products, P and Q, and a toxic waste product. The budgeted production mix of inputs and outputs is as follows.

Inputs

7 kg of chemical A
8 kg of chemical B

Outputs

6 kg of P (joint product)
6 kg of Q (joint product)
3 kg of X (toxic waste)

The joint products are separated at the end of the process but the waste product is extracted from a batch of the mixture at an even rate throughout the processing. Products P and Q each require further processing before they can be sold. At present X is disposed of using an outside contractor who charges £3 per kg for his services.

The following details relate to March 19X2.

Main process	kg		£
Opening work-in-progress	2,250	50% processed, costing (Direct material £7,000; waste disposal cost £1,500; processing £1,100)	9,600
Opening stock of X	400		
Closing work-in-progress	2,250	50% processed	
Closing stock of X	600		
Input of A	10,500	cost	42,000
Input of B	12,000	cost	21,000
Process labour	-	cost	11,700
Processing expense	-	cost	8,100
Payments for waste disposal	-	cost	16,500
Transfers to finishing processes:			
P	9,000		
Q	9,000		
Finishing process for P			
Opening work-in-progress	500	50% processed (Direct material £2,378; processing £50)	2,428
Process labour	-		1,100
Processing expense	-		700
Closing work-in-progress	500	50% processed	
Finished production	9,000		
Finishing process for Q	kg		
Opening work-in-progress	800	50% processed (Direct material £4,756; processing £120)	4,876
Process labour	-		1,660
Processing expense	-		1,100
Closing work-in-progress	400	50% processed	
Finished production	9,400		

In the foregoing details the work in progress stocks are fully complete as far as the material content is concerned. The established selling prices are £4.20 per kilo for product P and £5.30 per kilo for product Q.

Required

(a) Write up the three process accounts for the accounting period, using the relative sales value method for the apportionment of the joint costs. The waste disposal expense is to be accrued and charged to the main process account whenever a fresh batch of raw material is fed into the process. (14 marks)

(b) The accountant has received a request for his comments on a proposal that the waste product X should be processed further to give a saleable by-product, Z. You estimate the additional direct processing costs to be as follows.

Process labour	£1.20 per kilo
Processing expense	£3.40 per kilo

He anticipates that Z could be sold for £2.50 per kilo. One kilo of X will produce one kilo of Z.

Comment on this proposal. (2 marks)

(c) Assuming that the proposals are adopted, discuss the procedures that might be adopted for dealing with the new situation in the process accounts. (4 marks)

5 **THE FEEDBACK PROCESS (5 marks)** *9 mins*

'The feedback process is an essential part of a management accounting system.' Discuss the significance and implications of this statement.

6 **FREEWHEEL LTD (20 marks)** *36 mins*

Freewheel is in the process of preparing its master budget for the six months ending December 19X2. The balance sheet for the year ended 30 June 19X2 is estimated to be as follows.

	Cost	*Deprec prov*	*Net book value*
	£	£	£
Fixed assets	140,000	14,000	126,000
Current assets			
Stock	25,000		
Trade debtors	24,600		
Bank	3,000		
Net current liabilities		52,600	
Creditors: Amounts falling due within one year			
Trade creditors	25,000		
Other creditors	9,000		
		34,000	
Net current assets			18,600
Total assets less current liabilities			144,600
Capital and reserves			
Share capital			100,000
Profit and loss account			44,600
			144,600

The budget committee have derived the following trading forecasts for the six months ended 31 December 19X2.

	Sales in units	*Purchases*	*Wages and salaries*	*Overheads excl. deprec*	*Purchase of fixed assets*	*Issue of 20,000 £1 shares*	*Dividends*
		£	£	£	£	£	£
May	4,000	12,000	8,000	7,000			
June	4,200	13,000	8,000	7,000			
July	4,500	14,000	8,000	7,000			
August	4,600	18,000	10,000	7,000			
September	4,800	16,000	10,000	7,000		20,000	
October	5,000	14,000	10,000	8,000			10,000
November	3,800	12,000	12,000	8,000	30,000		
December	3,000	12,000	12,000	8,000			

You are given the following information.

(a) The selling price in May 19X2 was £6 per unit and this is to be increased to £8 per unit in October. 50% of sales are for cash and 50% on credit to be paid two months later.

(b) Purchases are to be paid for two months after purchase.

(c) Wages and salaries are to be paid 75% in the month incurred and 25% in the following month.

(d) Overheads are to be paid in the month after they are incurred.

(e) The fixed assets are to be paid for in three equal instalments in the three months following purchase.

(f) Dividends are to be paid three months after they are declared and the receipts from the share issue are budgeted to be received in the month of issue.

(g) Fixed assets are depreciated 10% per annum on a straight line basis on those assets owned at 31 December 19X2.

(h) Closing stock at the beginning of the period under review was equal to the previous two months purchases. At 31 December 19X2 it was equal to three months purchases.

Required

(a) Prepare the following budgets for the six months ended 31 December 19X2.

(i) Cash budget (6 marks)
(ii) Budgeted profit and loss account (4 marks)
(iii) Budgeted balance sheet (5 marks)

(b) Comment upon the results, highlighting those areas that you wish to draw to the attention of the budget committee. (5 marks)

7 BUDGETING, BUDGETARY CONTROL AND BEHAVIOUR — *15 mins*

(a) State and explain the conditions which ought to be present within an organisation for a system of budgeting and budgetary control to be successful.

(b) Discuss briefly four points related to the behaviour of people which management needs to take into consideration when a system of budgeting and budgetary control is introduced.

8 TERRY HENDSETTER — *25 mins*

Terry Hendsetter is the manager in your company with responsibility for monitoring sales of product XN30. He is convinced that the levels of sales is on a rising trend, but that it is seasonal, with more sales at some times of the year than at others.

He has gathered the following data about sales in recent years. Trend values are shown in brackets.

	Sales (thousands of units of product XN30)			
Year	*Spring*	*Summer*	*Autumn*	*Winter*
19X3			250	340
19X4	186 (281)	343 (285)	263 (289)	357 (293)
19X5	203 (297)	358 (302)	278 (305)	380 (307)
19X6	207 (311)	371 (313)	290 (317)	391 (320)
19X7	222	383		

Required

(a) Show the actual sales level and the trend line on a historigram.
(b) Establish seasonal deviations from the trend.
(c) Estimate what the level of sales might be in the autumn and winter of 19X7.)

9 PPBS (20 marks) — *36 mins*

Various attempts have been made in the public sector to achieve a more stable, long-term planning base in contrast to the traditional short-term annual budgeting approach, with its emphasis on 'flexibility'.

Required

(a) Explain the deficiencies of the traditional approach to planning which led to the attempts to introduce PPBS (programme budgeting).

(b) Give an illustration of how a PPBS plan could be drawn up in respect of one sector of public authority activity.

(c) Discuss the problems which have made it difficult in practice to introduce PPBS.

10 STANDARD COSTS (5 marks) *9 mins*

(a) Outline the benefits which a company may obtain from a standard costing system.

(b) Discuss the problems which may arise in the development and operation of a standard costing system.

11 PAN CO LIMITED (20 marks) *36 mins*

Pan Co Ltd, a manufacturing firm, operates a standard marginal costing system. It makes a single product ZX, using a single raw material VW.

Standard costs relating to ZX have been calculated as follows.

Standard cost schedule - ZX

	£ per unit
Direct material VW, 10 kg @ £15 per kg	150
Direct labour, 5 hours @ £9 per hour	45
	195
Variable production overhead, 5 hours @ £3 per hour	15
	210

During the week ending 9 November 19X1, 1,000 units of ZX were produced, the relevant information regarding actual performance being as follows.

Direct material VW - 4,000 kg was the opening stock
- 10,000 kg were purchased during the week, actual cost being £144,000
- 3,000 kg was the closing stock.

(*Note.* Stocks of the direct material VW are valued at the standard price of £15 per kg.)

Direct labour - 5,200 hours were worked during the week, total wages being £48,360.
Variable production overhead - the actual cost for the week was £16,800.

Required

(a) Compute the cost variances which arose in the week ending 9 November 19X1 under the following headings.

(i) Variable production cost variance
(ii) Direct wages cost variance, and analyse into rate and efficiency
(iii) Direct material cost variance, and analyse into price and usage
(iv) Variable production overhead variance (10 marks)

(b) Prepare a commentary on the variances for the production manager, indicating any additional information which might prove useful in explaining them. (6 marks)

(c) Briefly consider the view that past performance is the best guide to ascertaining standard costs. (4 marks)

12 UMBRELLA PLC (20 marks) *36 mins*

Umbrella plc is a company which has established divisional profit centres. The managers of its divisions are held responsible for the profits earned by their division and they have the authority to establish their own detailed operating budgets within certain policy and profit guidelines laid down by head office.

Each division employs a standard costing system. The Watershed Division makes and sells a single product for which there is an external market at a price of £32 per unit, but which can also be transferred to other divisions within Umbrella plc for £30 per unit.

The standard cost of the Watershed Division's product is as follows.

	£
3 units of material X at £1.50	4.50
4 units of material Y at £2.25	9.00
½ hour of labour at £4 per hour	2.00
Variable manufacturing overhead (£1 per hour)	0.50
Fixed manufacturing overhead (£8 per hour)	4.00
Standard full cost of production	20.00
Head office charge	2.00
Selling overhead	5.00
Total standard cost per unit	27.00

The fixed manufacturing overhead is absorbed on the basis of budgeted monthly production of 15,000 units (or 7,500 hours of work).

The head office charge is a fixed cost of £30,000 per month, and is charged to products sold on the basis of budgeted monthly sales of 15,000 units.

The selling overhead is not charged to units transferred to other divisions, only to units sold externally. This is because selling costs are only incurred on units sold externally.

The budget for a normal month allows for 10,000 units of external sales, and the estimated costs are as follows.

	£
Fixed costs	20,000
Variable costs	30,000
	50,000

Unsold stock is carried forward in the accounts at standard full manufacturing cost.

The actual and budgeted results for the month of September 19X2 were as follows.

		Actual		*Budget*	
		Units	£	Units	£
Sales:	External	7,000	224,000	10,000	320,000
	Internal transfers	7,000	210,000	5,000	150,000
		14,000	434,000	15,000	470,000
Cost of goods manufactured		18,000	363,000	15,000	300,000
Less increase in stocks		4,000	80,000	-	-
		14,000	283,000	15,000	300,000
Head office charge			30,000		30,000
Selling overhead			52,000		50,000
Total costs of sale			365,000		380,000
Profit			69,000		90,000

The actual costs of production of £363,000 can be analysed as follows.

		£
Material X:	52,000 units used at £1.50 per unit	78,000
Material Y:	78,000 units used at £2.25 per unit	175,500
Labour:	9,200 hours	36,500
Variable manufacturing overhead		9,700
Fixed manufacturing overhead		63,300
		363,000

Required

Prepare a statement for the manager of the Watershed Division explaining why the actual profit fell short of budgeted profit in the month by £21,000.

13 GAMMA LTD (16 marks) *29 mins*

A manufacturing company makes a standard product called the alphabeta. Last year the company installed a computer-based costing and accounting system which deals with stock records, standards product costing, planning stock requirements and scheduling work for different departments.

The unit cost for one alphabeta is as follows.

Description	*Quantity*	*Price*	*Cost per unit*
			£
Material alpha	1 kg	£40 per kg	40
Material beta	6 sq metres	£45 per sq metre	270
Machining time	1½ hrs	£10 per hour	15
Total			325

Each time materials are purchased, a purchase price variance is extracted. Materials in stock are held at standard cost.

The following information is available for the accounting period just completed.

The overhead budget for the machining department was £209,000, and the budgeted machine hours were 9,500. 70% of the budgeted overhead are estimated to be fixed. The remaining variable element varies with the number of standard hours of work produced in the department.

1,000 alphabetas were manufactured during the accounting period under consideration. 1,200 kg of material alpha were issued from store for manufacturing alphabetas. The exception report showed that 200 square metres of material beta were issued in excess of the standard quantity specified.

The total purchases of material alpha were 20,000 kg at a price of £44 per kg and 12,900 square metres of material beta was purchased for £619,200. During the period there were issues of 8,500 kg of material alpha and 5,300 square metres of material beta to other products and job orders. There were no opening stocks.

The actual overhead incurred in the machining department was £217,340, and 9,650 standard hours were used to manufacture other products. There was no record of the actual machine hours worked.

Required

(a) Calculate the following variances for the accounting period just completed.

(i) The material usage variance for product alphabeta (2 marks)

(ii) The total price variance for each material (3 marks)

(iii) The total overhead variance of the machining department, analysed as far as is possible (5 marks)

(b) (i) Summarise the purposes of a standard costing system. (3 marks)

(ii) Calculate the value of closing stock of materials alpha and beta.

If the stock value that you have calculated is for published balance sheet purposes, and if the period concerned is the full year, comment on this value given the total price variance for each material. (3 marks)

14 JB LIMITED (25 mins)

JB Limited is a small specialist manufacturer of electronic components and much of its output is used by the makers of aircraft for both civil and military purposes. One of the few aircraft manufacturers has offered a contract to JB Limited for the supply over the next twelve months, of 400 identical components.

The data relating to the production of each component is as follows.

(a) *Material requirements*

3 kilograms material M1 - see note 1 below
2 kilograms materials P2 - see note 2 below
1 Part No 678 - see note 3 below

Note 1

Material M1 is in continuous use by the company. 1,000 kilograms are currently held in stock at a book value of £4.70 per kilogram but it is known that future purchases will cost £5.50 per kilogram.

Note 2

1,200 kilograms of material P2 are held in stock. The original cost of this material was £4.30 per kilogram but as the material has not been required for the last two years it has been written down to £1.50 per kilogram scrap value. The only foreseeable alternative use is as a substitute for material P4 (in current use) but this would involve further processing costs of £1.60 per kilogram. The current cost of material P4 is £3.60 per kilogram.

Note 3

It is estimated that the Part No 678 could be bought for £50 each.

(b) *Labour requirements*

Each component would require five hours of skilled labour and five hours of semi-skilled. An employee possessing the necessary skills is available and is currently paid £5 per hour. A replacement would, however, have to be obtained at a rate of £4 per hour for the work which would otherwise be done by the skilled employee. The current rate for semi-skilled work is £3 per hour and an additional employee could be appointed for this work.

(c) *Overhead*

JB Limited absorbs overhead by a machine hour rate, currently £20 per hour of which £7 is for variable overhead and £13 for fixed overhead. If this contract is undertaken it is estimated that fixed costs will increase for the duration of the contract by £3,200. Spare machine capacity is available and each component would require four machine hours.

A price of £145 per component has been suggested by the large company which makes aircraft.

Required

(a) State whether or not the contract should be accepted and support your conclusion with appropriate figures for presentation to management.

(b) Comment briefly on three factors which management ought to consider and which may influence their decision.

15 CORPORATE OBJECTIVES *20 mins*

Should a quoted company's directors seek only the maximisation of the company's profit?

16 MARKET EFFICIENCY *30 mins*

Explain the implications for market efficiency of the fact that very few financial intermediaries are able to out-perform the market on a regular basis.

17 ECONOMIC POLICY OBJECTIVES *30 mins*

(a) State the main objectives of economic policy.
(b) Why in practice is it difficult to achieve these objectives simultaneously?

18 PSBR *35 mins*

(a) Explain the term *public sector borrowing requirement* (PSBR) and show how it might be financed.

(b) Why might the size of the PSBR change over time?

19 CAUSES OF INFLATION *30 mins*

What is inflation, and what causes it?

20 MIDSOUTH ELECTRIC PLC (20 marks) *36 mins*

(a) Among the industries which have been privatised by the UK government in recent years is the electricity supply industry.

Required

Outline the likely objectives of an electricity supply company:

(i) operating in the public (government-run) sector; (3 marks)

(ii) operating in the private sector (following privatisation). (3 marks)

The information below relates to parts (b) and (c) of the question

Midsouth Electric plc (MSE) is an electricity supply company which was privatised six years ago, in 19X0, having formerly been an authority under government control. On privatisation, the newly issued shares in the company went to an immediate 40% premium on the share market.

As a privatised electricity supply company, MSE is now subject to regulatory controls over prices.

The data given below is available. The 19X0 *proforma* figures reflect the company's performance during its last year under government control adjusted to reflect the accounting conventions applying in the private sector.

Midsouth Electric plc
Summarised financial and operational information

	19X0 Proforma	*19X1*	*19X2*	*19X3*	*19X4*	*19X5*	*19X6*
	£m	£m	£m	£m	£m	£m	£m
Turnover	760	800	850	880	920	955	995
Profit before taxation	37	49	62	74	88	94	99
Profit after taxation	30	47	52	62	74	77	80
Wages and salaries	110	109	108	108	107	106	106
Directors' emoluments	1.2	1.6	1.8	2.4	3.1	3.4	3.6
Dividends	10*	11	12	14	17	20	24
Net assets	120	126	130	150	165	180	205
Capital spending	25	30	35	50	75	82	90
Price earnings ratio	-	7.4	7.5	8.1	8.5	8.7	9.0
Number of employees	14,500	14,200	14,000	13,700	13,600	13,400	13,200
Output of electricity supplied**	100	102.5	105	107.5	110	113	116

* Notional dividend which would be paid under post-privatisation dividend policy.

** 19X0 = 100

The Retail Prices Index for the years shown is set out below.

	RPI
19X0	100
19X1	102
19X2	103
19X3	105
19X4	106
19X5	107
19X6	109

(b) *Required*

Evaluate whether the privatisation of Midsouth Electric has been a positive step from the point of view of:

(i) ordinary shareholders (4 marks)
(ii) employees of the company (3 marks)
(iii) customers (3 marks)

(c) You read a letter in the press which suggests that electricity supply privatisation has, along with other privatisations, been of great benefit to the economy.

Required

Assess whether Midsouth Electric's privatisation appears to have:

(i) assisted with attainment of the government's anti-inflation objective; (2 marks)
(ii) been beneficial to growth in the national economy. (2 marks)

21 WORKING CAPITAL *15 mins*

In an article dealing with company liquidity, the statement was made that 'it is widely accepted that stronger and more profitable companies have a higher proportion of working capital'.

Set out and comment on the various circumstances under which this belief might or might not be true.

22 H FINANCE PLC *30 mins*

H Finance plc is prepared to advance 80% of D Ltd's sales invoicing, provided its specialist collection services are used by D Ltd. H Finance plc would charge an additional 0.5% of D Ltd's turnover for this service. D Ltd would avoid administration costs it currently incurs amounting to £80,000 per annum.

The history of D Ltd's debtors' ledgers may be summarised as follows:

	19X8	*19X9*	*19Y0*
Turnover (£'000)	78,147	81,941	98,714
% debtors at year end	17	20	22
% debtors of 90+ days (of turnover)	1.5	2	2.5
Bad debts (£'000)	340	497	615

D Ltd estimates that the aggressive collection procedures adopted by the finance company are likely to result in lost turnover of some 10% of otherwise expected levels.

Currently, each £1 of turnover generates 18 pence additional profit before taxation. D Ltd turns its capital over, on average, three times each year. On receipt by H Finance plc of amounts due from D Ltd's customers, a further 15% of the amounts are to be remitted to D Ltd.

The cheapest alternative form of finance would cost 20% per annum.

Required

(a) Calculate whether the factoring of D Ltd's debtors ledger would be worthwhile.
(b) Explain how the factoring of sales invoicing may assist a firm's financial performance.

23 HEADWATER PLC (20 marks) *36 mins*

It is now August 19X6. In 19X0, the current management team of Headwater plc, a manufacturer of car and motorcycle parts, bought the company from its conglomerate parent company in a management buyout deal.

Six years on, the managers are considering the possibility of obtaining a listing for the company's shares on the stock market.

The following information is available.

HEADWATER PLC
PROFIT AND LOSS ACCOUNT FOR THE YEAR ENDED 30 JUNE 19X6

	£ million
Turnover	36.5
Cost of sales	(31.6)
Profit before interest and taxation	4.9
Interest	(1.3)
Profit before taxation	3.6
Taxation	(0.5)
Profit attributable to ordinary shareholders	3.1
Dividends	(0.3)
Retained profit	2.8

BALANCE SHEET AS AT 30 JUNE 19X6

	£ million	£ million
Fixed assets (at cost less accumulated depreciation)		
Land and buildings		3.6
Plant and machinery		9.9
		13.5
Current assets		
Stocks	4.4	
Debtors	4.7	
Cash at bank	1.0	
	10.1	
Current liabilities		
Trade creditors	7.0	
Bank overdraft	2.0	
	9.0	
Net current assets		1.1
Total assets less current liabilities		14.6
Creditors due after more than one year: 12% Debenture 19X8		(2.2)
Net assets		12.4
Financed by		
Ordinary £1 shares		
Voting		1.8
'A' shares (non-voting)		0.9
Reserves		9.7
Shareholders' funds		12.4

Average performance ratios for the industry sector in which Headwater operates are given below.

Industry sector ratios

Return before tax on long-term capital employed	24%
Return after tax on equity	16%
Operating profit as percentage of sales	11%
Current ratio	1.6:1
Quick (acid test) ratio	1.0:1
Total debt: equity (gearing)	24%
Dividend cover	4.0
Interest cover	4.5
Price/earnings ratio	10.0

Required

(a) Evaluate the financial state and performance of Headwater by comparing it with that of its industry sector. (8 marks)

(b) Discuss the probable reasons why the management of Headwater is considering a Stock Exchange listing. (4 marks)

(c) Explain how you think Headwater should restructure its balance sheet before becoming a listed company. (5 marks)

(d) Discuss changes in financial policy which the company would be advised to adopt once it has been floated on the Stock Exchange. (3 marks)

24 PRIMULA PLC (20 marks) *36 mins*

Primula plc is a manufacturer of fragrances whose shares are listed on the London Stock Exchange. The company made sales (to distributors and retailers) of £40,000,000 during 19X5. The company's summarised balance sheet as at its last accounting date is set out below.

PRIMULA PLC
SUMMARISED BALANCE SHEET AS AT 31 DECEMBER 19X5

	£m	£m
Fixed assets		
Cost		42.0
Accumulated depreciation		11.5
Net book value		30.5
Current assets		
Stocks	4.2	
Debtors	5.2	
Cash at bank	1.2	
		10.6
Creditors: amounts falling due within one year		
Trade creditors	5.8	
Corporation tax	1.8	
		(7.6)
Net current assets		3.0
Creditors: amounts falling due within more than one year		
Loans		(6.0)
Net assets employed		27.5
Financed by		
Ordinary 25p shares		16.0
Profit and loss account		11.5
		27.5

Currently, Primula sells a range of products which are retailed under the name of Parelle. This year (19X6) it plans to exploit a different market segment by introducing a new range of lower-prices products. A retail name for the range has not yet been decided, but for planning purposes it has been named 'Range X'.

Introduction of Range X is expected to raise the company's annual turnover to £50,000,000 taking account of the effect of introducing the X range on sales of existing products.

The introduction of Range X is expected to require £12 million to be spend on fixed assets. Apart from taxation, all current assets and liabilities are expected to increase proportionately with the increase in sales. The company wishes to maintain cash balances at a level of 8% of sales at least.

The company generated profits before interest and taxation of £6,000,000 in 19X5. The depreciation charge of £1.5 million in 19X5 is expected to rise by 50% in 19X6. Interest is payable on the company's £6m long-term loan at a rate of 11%.

In 19X5, Primula paid £3.84 million in dividends and it plans to increase dividends by 8% each year for the foreseeable future.

The rate of corporation tax is 31%, payable one year after the year in which profits are earned.

Required

(a) Calculate how much further finance Primula plc will need to raise from external sources. (8 marks)

(b) Discuss four sources of long-term finance that the company might use. (12 marks)

You should ignore advance corporation tax (ACT), and you should treat depreciation as a tax-allowable expense.

25 CAPITAL GEARING (20 marks) *36 mins*

A company has the following balance sheet.

	£	£
Fixed assets		35,000,000
Current assets	30,000,000	
Less current liabilities:		
Trade creditors	(10,000,000)	
Bank overdraft	(15,000,000)	
		5,000,000
		40,000,000

Ordinary share capital (50p shares)	10,000,000
8% Preference share capital	5,000,000
Retained profits	10,000,000
	25,000,000
5% Convertible debentures	5,000,000
12% Irredeemable debentures	10,000,000
	40,000,000

Notes

(a) The ordinary shares have a market value of 200 pence.

(b) The rate of return required by the market on fixed interest financial instruments of this company is ten per cent.

(c) The convertible debentures are convertible into 100 ordinary shares for each £100 unit of debentures.

Required

(a) Calculate the capital gearing ratio of the company using three different ratios for this purpose. (10 marks)

(b) Explain the problems involved in the measurement of capital gearing with regard to each of the following.

Treatment of preference shares.
Treatment of convertible debentures.
Treatment of bank overdraft.
Treatment of trade creditors.
Use of book values or market values. (10 marks)

26 **PROJECT APPRAISAL (20 marks)** *36 mins*

(a) A company is considering two capital expenditure proposals. Both proposals are for similar products and both are expected to operate for four years. Only one proposal can be accepted.

The following information is available.

	Profit/(loss)	
	Proposal A	*Proposal B*
	£	£
Initial investment	46,000	46,000
Year 1	6,500	4,500
Year 2	3,500	2,500
Year 3	13,500	4,500
Year 4	(1,500)	Profit 14,500
Estimated scrap value at the end of year 4	4,000	4,000

Depreciation is charged on the straight line basis.

The company estimates its cost of capital at 20% pa.

	Discount factor
Year 1	0.833
Year 2	0.694
Year 3	0.579
Year 4	0.482

Required

(i) Calculate the following for both proposals.

(1) The payback period to one decimal place (4 marks)

(2) The average rate of return on initial investment, to one decimal place (2 marks)

(ii) Give two advantages for each of the methods of appraisal used in (i) above. (4 marks)

(b) D'Arcy Toby Wise Ltd is a private family business of aluminium founders, incorporated in 1949. It makes castings by three processes of pressure die-casting, gravity die-casting and sand casting and serves a variety of customers and trades, though 40% of its output goes to one particular customer who makes do-it-yourself tools.

Profits have always been low, but liquidity has remained high, due to careful cash management. The company has invested its surplus cash in stocks and shares of quoted companies.

A new professional managing director was appointed two years ago after the retirement of the firm's founder. He has proposed to the Board that since the stocks and shares do not provide a satisfactory return and have shown little capital growth, they should be sold to provide funds to exploit other business opportunities. In particular, he has recommended either of the following.

(i) The purchase of a small aluminium foundery
(ii) Diversification into new products and new markets

Required

Describe the main factors to consider in deciding the strategy to be adopted by D'Arcy Toby Wise Ltd. (10 marks)

27 KNUCKLE DOWN LTD (25 marks) *45 mins*

The management of Knuckle Down Ltd are reviewing the company's capital investment options for the coming year, and are considering six projects.

Project A would cost £29,000 now, and would earn the following cash profits.

1st year	£8,000	3rd year	£10,000
2nd year	£12,000	4th year	£ 6,000

The capital equipment purchased at the start of the project could be resold for £5,000 at the start of the fifth year.

Project B would involve a current outlay of £44,000 on capital equipment and £20,000 on working capital. The profits from the project would be as follows.

Year	*Sales*	*Variable costs*	*Contribution*	*Fixed costs*	*Profit*
	£	£	£	£	£
1	75,000	50,000	25,000	10,000	15,000
2	90,000	60,000	30,000	10,000	20,000
3	42,000	28,000	14,000	8,000	6,000

Fixed costs include an annual charge of £4,000 for depreciation. At the end of the third year the working capital investment would be recovered and the equipment would be sold for £5,000.

Project C would involve a current outlay of £50,000 on equipment and £15,000 on working capital. The investment in working capital would be increased to £21,000 at the end of the first year. Annual cash profits would be £18,000 for five years, at the end of which the investment in working capital would be recovered.

Project D would involve an outlay of £20,000 now and a further outlay of £20,000 after one year. Cash profits thereafter would be as follows.

2nd year £15,000 3rd year £12,000 4th to 8th years £8,000 pa

Project E is a long-term project, involving an immediate outlay of £32,000 and annual cash profits of £4,500 in perpetuity.

Project F is another long-term project, involving an immediate outlay of £20,000 and annual cash profits as follows.

1st to 5th years £5,000 6th to 10th years £4,000 11th year onwards for ever £3,000

The company discounts all projects of ten years duration or less at a cost of capital of 12%, and all other projects at a cost of 15%.

Ignore taxation.

Required

(a) Calculate the NPV of each project, and determine which should be undertaken by the company. (17 marks)

(b) Calculate the IRR of projects A, C and E. (8 marks)

28 DINARD (20 marks) *36 mins*

(a) Explain the difference between real rates of return and money rates of return and outline the circumstances in which the use of each would be appropriate when appraising capital projects under inflationary conditions. (6 marks)

(b) Dinard plc has just developed a new product to be called Rance and is now considering whether to put it into production. The following information is available.

(i) Costs incurred in the development of Rance amount to £480,000.

(ii) Production of Rance will require the purchase of new machinery at a cost of £2,400,000 payable immediately. This machinery is specific to the production of Rance and will be obsolete and valueless when that production ceases. The machinery has a production life of four years and a production capacity of 30,000 units per annum.

(iii) Production costs of Rance (at year 1 prices) are estimated as follows.

	£
Variable materials	8.00
Variable labour	12.00
Variable overheads	12.00

In addition, fixed production costs (at year 1 prices), including straight line depreciation on plant and machinery, will amount to £800,000 per annum.

(iv) The selling price of Rance will be £80.00 per unit (at year 1 prices). Demand is expected to be 25,000 units per annum for the next four years.

(v) The retail price index is expected to increase at 5% per annum for the next four years and the selling price of Rance is expected to increase at the same rate. Annual inflation rates for production costs are expected to be as follows.

	%
Variable materials	4
Variable labour	10
Variable overheads	4
Fixed costs	5

(vi) The company's weighted average cost of capital in money terms is expected to be 15%.

Required

Advise the directors of Dinard plc whether it should produce Rance on the basis of the information above. (14 marks)

Notes

Unless otherwise specified all costs and revenues should be assumed to rise at the end of each year. Ignore taxation.

29 MUGGINS PLC *30 mins*

Muggins plc is evaluating a project to produce a new product. The product has an expected life of four years. Costs associated with the product are expected to be as follows.

Variable costs per unit
Labour: £30
Materials:
6 kg of material X at £1.64 per kg
3 units of component Y at £4.20 per unit
Other variable costs: £4.40

Indirect cost each year
Apportionment of head office salaries £118,000
Apportionment of general building occupancy £168,000
Other overheads £80,000, of which £60,000 represent additional cash expenditures (including rent of machinery)

To manufacture the product, a product manager will have to be recruited at an annual gross cost of £34,000, and one assistant manager, whose current annual salary is £30,000, will be transferred from another department, where he will be replaced by a new appointee at a cost of £27,000 a year.

The necessary machinery will be rented. It will be installed in the company's factory. This will take up space that would otherwise be rented to another local company for £135,000 a year. This rent (for the factory space) is not subject to any uncertainty, as a binding four-year lease would be created.

60,000 kg of material X are already in stock, at a purchase value of £98,400. They have no use other than the manufacture of the new product. Their disposal value is £50,000.

Expected sales volumes of the product, at the proposed selling price of £125 a unit, are as follows.

Year	*Expected sales*
	Units
1	10,000
2	18,000
3	18,000
4	19,000

All sales and costs will be on a cash basis and should be assumed to occur at the end of the year. Ignore taxation.

The company requires that certainty-equivalent cash flows have a positive NPV at a discount rate of 14%. Adjustment factors to arrive at certainty-equivalent amounts are as follows.

Year	*Costs*	*Benefits*
1	1.1	0.9
2	1.3	0.8
3	1.4	0.7
4	1.5	0.6

Required

Assess whether the project is acceptable.

30 BANDEN LTD (25 marks) *45 mins*

Banden Ltd is a highly geared company that wishes to expand its operations. Six possible capital investments have been identified, but the company only has access to a total of £620,000. The projects are not divisible and may not be postponed until a future period. After the project's end it is unlikely that similar investment opportunities will occur.

Expected net cash inflows (including salvage value)

Project	*Year 1*	*2*	*3*	*4*	*5*	*Initial outlay*
	£	£	£	£	£	£
A	70,000	70,000	70,000	70,000	70,000	246,000
B	75,000	87,000	64,000			180,000
C	48,000	48,000	63,000	73,000		175,000
D	62,000	62,000	62,000	62,000		180,000
E	40,000	50,000	60,000	70,000	40,000	180,000
F	35,000	82,000	82,000			150,000

Projects A and E are mutually exclusive. All projects are believed to be of similar risk to the company's existing capital investments.

Any surplus funds may be invested in the money market to earn a return of 9% per year. The money market may be assumed to be an efficient market.

Banden's cost of capital is 12% a year.

Required

(a) (i) Calculate the expected net present value.

(ii) Calculate the expected profitability index associated with each of the six projects.

(iii) Rank the projects according to both of these investment appraisal methods. Explain briefly why these rankings differ. (10 marks)

(b) Give reasoned advice to Banden Ltd recommending which projects should be selected. (6 marks)

(c) A director of the company has suggested that using the company's normal cost of capital might not be appropriate in a capital rationing situation. Explain whether you agree with the director. (5 marks)

(d) The director has also suggested the use of linear programming to assist with the selection of projects. Discuss the advantages and disadvantages of this mathematical programming method to Banden Ltd. (4 marks)

31 FLOCKS LTD (20 marks) *36 mins*

The management of Flocks Ltd is trying to decide which of two machines to purchase, to help with production. Only one of the two machines will be purchased.

Machine X costs £63,000 and machine Y costs £110,000. Both machines would require a working capital investment of £12,500 throughout their operational life, which is four years for machine X and six years for machine Y. The expected scrap value of either machine would be zero.

The estimated pre-tax operating net cash inflows with each machine are as follows.

Year	*Machine X*	*Machine Y*
	£	£
1	25,900	40,300
2	28,800	32,900
3	30,500	32,000
4	29,500	32,700
5	-	48,500
6	-	44,200

With machine Y, there is some doubt about its design features, and consequently there is some risk that it might prove unsuitable. Because of the higher business risk with machine Y, the machine Y project cash flows should be discounted at 15%, whereas machine X cash flows should be discounted at only 13%.

Flocks Ltd intends to finance the machine it eventually selects, X or Y, by borrowing at 10%.

Tax is payable at 31% on operating cash flows one year in arrears. Capital allowances are available at 25% a year on a reducing balance basis.

Required

(a) For both machine X and machine Y, calculate:

(i) the (undiscounted) payback period;
(ii) the net present value;

and recommend which of the two machines Flocks Ltd should purchase. (13 marks)

(b) Suppose that Flocks Ltd has the opportunity to lease machine X under a finance lease arrangement, at an annual rent of £20,000 for four years, payable at the end of each year. Should the company lease or buy the machine, assuming it chooses machine X? (7 marks)

Exam answer bank

1 **MANAGEMENT ACCOUNTING AND FINANCIAL ACCOUNTING**

As its name implies, management accounting involves the provision of accounting information for managers to use. This is the main distinction between management accounting and financial accounting.

(a) Financial accounting systems try to ensure that the assets and liabilities of a business are properly accounted for, and provide information about profits etc to shareholders and to other interested parties.

(b) Management accounting systems provide information specifically for the use of managers within the organisation.

2 **RYMAN COUPLETS LTD**

(a)

Product		*Machine hours per annum*	*Labour hours per annum*
		Hours	Hours
X		60,000	40,000
Y		20,000	80,000
Z		20,000	20,000
		100,000	140,000
Budgeted annual overhead costs		£560,000	£560,000
Absorption rate		£5.60 per machine hour	£4 per direct labour hour
Overhead cost per unit	X	£16.80 per unit	£8 per unit
	Y	£5.60 per unit	£16 per unit
	Z	£11.20 per unit	£8 per unit

(i) *Direct costing*

				19X2				*19X3*
	X	*Y*	*Z*	*Total*	*X*	*Y*	*Z*	*Total*
	£'000	£'000	£'000	£'000	£'000	£'000	£'000	£'000
Opening stocks	0	0	0	0	96	72	84	252
Direct production costs	320	360	120	800	320	360	120	800
	320	360	120	800	416	432	204	1,052
Closing stocks	96	72	84	252	192	216	36	444
Variable cost of production and sales	224	288	36	548	224	216	168	608
Sales	420	560	75	1,055	420	420	350	1,190
Contribution	196	272	39	507	196	204	182	582
Overheads				560				560
Profit/(loss)				(53)				22

(ii) *Absorption costing, using a machine hour rate of recovery*

				19X2				*19X3*
	X	*Y*	*Z*	*Total*	*X*	*Y*	*Z*	*Total*
	£'000	£'000	£'000	£'000	£'000	£'000	£'000	£'000
Opening stock	0	0	0	0	196.8	94.4	162.4	453.6
Direct costs of production	320.0	360.0	120.0	800.0	320.0	360.0	120.0	800.0
Overheads absorbed	336.0	112.0	112.0	560.0	336.0	112.0	112.0	560.0
	656.0	472.0	232.0	1,360.0	852.8	566.4	394.4	1,813.6
Closing stock *	196.8	94.4	162.4	453.6	393.6	283.2	69.6	746.4
Full cost of sales	459.2	377.6	69.6	906.4	459.2	283.2	324.8	1,067.2
Sales	420.0	560.0	75.0	1,055.0	420.0	420.0	350.0	1,190.0
Profit	(39.2)	182.4	5.4	148.6	(39.2)	136.8	25.2	122.8

There would be no under- or over-absorbed overhead if actual production volumes are the same as budgeted production volumes.

Per unit: X £(16 + 16.8) = £32.80; Y £23.60; Z £23.20

(iii) *Absorption costing, using a direct labour hour rate of recovery*

	X	*Y*	*Z*	*19X2 Total*	*X*	*Y*	*Z*	*19X3 Total*
	£'000	£'000	£'000	£'000	£'000	£'000	£'000	£'000
Opening stock	0	0	0	0	144	136	140	420
Direct costs of production	320	360	120	800	320	360	120	800
Overheads absorbed	160	320	80	560	160	320	80	560
	480	680	200	1,360	624	816	340	1,780
Closing stock **	144	136	140	420	288	408	60	756
Full cost of sales	336	544	60	940	336	408	280	1,024
Sales	420	560	75	1,055	420	420	350	1,190
Profit	84	16	15	115	84	12	70	166

** Per unit: X (£16 + £8) = £24; Y £34; Z £20

(b) The figures differ because of the overhead content in stock carried forward or stock brought forward in each period, and thus in the valuation of opening and closing stocks.

(i) *19X2*

	Stock b/f	*Stock c/f*	*Stock change*	*Profit/ (loss)*
	£'000	£'000	£'000	£'000
Direct costing	0	252.0	+ 252.0	(53.0)
Full costing - machine hour method	0	453.6	+ 453.6	148.6
Full costing - labour hour method	0	420.0	+ 420.0	115.0

The difference in the stock change between each method explains the difference in profit; for example the difference in the stock change between direct costing and absorption costing with a machine hour recovery rate is (in £'000s) 453.6 – 252 = 201.6. The difference in profit is 148.6 – (–53) = 201.6.

(ii) *19X3*

	Stock b/f	*Stock c/f*	*Stock change*	*Profit/ (loss)*
	£'000	£'000	£'000	£'000
Direct costing	252.0	444.0	+ 192.0	22.0
Full costing - machine hour method	453.6	746.4	+ 292.8	122.8
Full costing - labour hour method	420.0	756.0	+ 336.0	166.0

Once again, the difference in profit is explained by the difference in the value of stock changes; for example, the difference in profit between the two methods of absorption costing (166 – 122.8) = £43,200 is the same as the difference in stock changes (336 – 292.8).

The absorption costing method of stock valuations might be improved if separate departmental overhead absorption rates could be used for machining work (for which a machine hour rate would be applied) and for finishing work (for which a direct labour hour rate would be applied). Total overheads would need to be apportioned fairly between the two departments, so that the more equitable method of recovering fixed costs in product costs would be possible. This system of separate departmental rates is fairer because it would make allowance for both the machine hours and the labour hours worked on each product.

Of the three costing systems, none is more 'correct' than the other. Each is equally 'right' or 'wrong'. Different costing principles have been applied to stock valuations, therefore different (short-term) period profits will be reported.

(c) (i) If production in 19X2 is increased by 25% the extra costs incurred in producing the additional stock would be the *variable* costs of production.

Total direct costs in original budget for 19X2	£800,000
A 25% increase in costs would be	£200,000
Interest rate per annum	14%
Annual interest cost of extra stocks	£28,000

(ii) If the increase in production is budgeted and fixed costs remain unaffected by the higher output, the overhead recovery rates would be reduced, as follows.

		Machine hours		*Labour hours*	
Budget		(125% of 100,000) = 125,000		(125% of 140,000) = 175,000	
Budgeted overheads		£560,000		£560,000	
Recovery rate		£4.48 per machine hour		£3.20 per labour hour	
Unit costs:	X	£(16 + 13.44)	= £29.44	£(16 + 6.40)	= £22.40
	Y	£(18 + 4.48)	= £22.48	£(18 +12.80)	= £30.80
	Z	£(12 + 8.96)	= £20.96	£(12 + 6.40)	= £18.40

	Direct costing		*Absorption costing Machine hour method*		*Absorption costing Labour hour method*	
	£'000	£'000	£'000	£'000	£'000	£'000
19X2						
Opening stock		0		0		0
Production costs:						
Direct (800 x 125%)		1,000		1,000		1,000
Fixed		560		560		560
		1,560		1,560		1,560
Closing stocks						
X (11,000 units)	176		324		246	
Y (9,000 units)	162		202		277	
Z (9,500 units)	114		199		175	
		452		725		698
Cost of sales		1,108		835		862
Sales		1,055		1,055		1,055
Profit		(53)		220		193

The loss in direct costing would be unaffected, but with absorption costing a larger proportion of fixed costs would be carried forward in closing stock values, so that total profits in 19X2 would increase.

3 TAKE SOME PROFIT

Most of the jobs undertaken by contracting companies are of long duration, spanning more than one accounting period. If profits are not taken on contracts until they are complete, then reported profits could be subject to wild fluctuations.

For instance, in one year there may be several contracts completed, so that reported profits are very high. In a subsequent year there may be no contract completed, and an enormous loss would be reported. Such fluctuations would make it very difficult for managers to control the business, and for outsiders to judge the business's performance.

It is therefore the custom to include some profit on contracts as they progress, but for the sake of prudence a profit is only taken when the contract has reached a significant degree of completion and no problems can be foreseen. It is also the custom to reduce the profit, again for prudence, to allow for unforeseen circumstances, and to allow for any monies retained by the customer.

4 BREEZEBLOCK LTD

(a)

MAIN PROCESS

	kg	£		kg	£
Opening WIP	2,250	9,600	Output of P (W5)	9,000	42,800
Material A	10,500	42,000	Output of Q (W5)	9,000	53,500
Material B	12,000	21,000	Closing WIP (W4)	2,250	9,600
Process labour		11,700	X removed from process (W1)	4,500	-
Process expense		8,100			
Disposal costs of X (W1)	-	13,500			
	24,750	105,900		24,750	105,900

FINISHING PROCESS P

	kg	£		kg	£
Opening WIP	500	2,428	Output of P (W6)	400	44,600
Input of P (W5)	9,000	42,800	Closing WIP (W6)	500	2,428
Process labour		1,100			
Process expense		700			
	9,500	47,028		9,500	47,028

FINISHING PROCESS Q

	kg	£		kg	£
Opening WIP	800	4,876	Output of B (W7)	9,000	58,698
Input of B (W5)	9,000	53,500	Closing WIP (W7)	400	2,438
Process labour		1,660			
Process expense		1,100			
	9,800	61,136		9,800	61,136

Workings

1 The amount of X produced should be 3/15 of the input. The quantity input in the period was 22,500 kg. The amount of X should, therefore, be 22,500 × 3/15 kg = 4,500 kg. The appropriate charge to the process account is, therefore, £13,500 (4,500 kilos @ £3).

2 At the beginning of the period, there was 400 kg of X in stock, at the end 600 kg. This simply means that the contractor has yet to remove it from the site (although it has been removed from the process). The full cost is therefore accrued in the process account.

3 *Equivalent units of completed production: main process*
As the opening and closing WIP is only half produced, only half the quantity of X will have been extracted. Over the whole process 15 kg of input should give 3 kg of X and 12 kg of P and Q. Half way through the process its weight should have declined to 13.50 kg, with 50% of 3 kg = 1.5 kg of X already produced.

Thus the opening WIP should yield 12/13.5 × 2,250 = 2,000 kilos of P and Q.

	Units of equivalent completed production	
	Materials	*Labour & processing expense*
Complete opening WIP (50% × 2,000)	-	1,000
Units started and completed (P and Q)(18,000 – 2,000)	16,000	16,000
Started closing WIP (50% × 2,000)	2,000	1,000
Equivalent units of work done	18,000	18,000
Processing costs		
(£(42,000 + 21,000))	£63,000	
(£(11,700 + 8,100))		£19,800
Costs per equivalent unit	£3.50	£1.10

4 *Valuation of closing WIP*

		£
Materials	2,000 × £3.50 (W3)	7,000
Labour and processing	1,000 × £1.10 (W3)	1,100
Disposal costs (3/12 of expected output of P and Q)	3/12 × 2,000 × £3	1,500
		9,600

Tutorial note. The valuation of the closing WIP is the same as for the opening WIP.

5 *Allocation of joint costs*
By balancing the main process account it can be seen that the total joint costs amount to £96,300 (105,900 – 9,600). Since there are no sales values for P or Q at separation

point, the basis to be selected is sales value minus further processing costs. These further costs are the labour and processing expense costs in the completion process for each product. This should be split as follows.

	Product	
	P	*Q*
	£	£
Sales price	4.20	5.30
Further processing costs (see below)	0.20	0.30
	4.00	5.00
Output	9,000	9,000
Adjusted sales values	£36,000 ↘	£45,000 ↙
	£81,000	

Costs allocated to P $\frac{36,000}{81,000} \times$ £96,300 = £42,800

Costs allocated to Q $\frac{45,000}{81,000} \times$ £96,300 = £53,500

6 *Finishing process - P*

	Equivalent units	
	Materials	*Processing*
Complete opening WIP (50%)	-	250
Units started and completed (9,000 - 500)	8,500	8,500
Started closing WIP (50%)	500	250
	9,000	9,000
Process costs		
Materials (see apportionment in W5 above)	£42,800	
Processing and labour		£1,800
Cost per equivalent unit	£4.7555	£0.20
	£4.9555	

Valuation of closing WIP	£
Material 500 @ £4.7555	2,378
Processing 250 @ £0.20	50
	2,428

Value of completed output =	£
Opening WIP	2,428
Opening stock completed (250 × £0.20)	50
Other finished work (8,500 × £4.9555)	42,122
	44,600

7 *Finishing process - Q*

	Equivalent units	
	Materials	*Processing*
Complete opening WIP (50%)	-	400
Units started and completed (9,400 - 800)	8,600	8,600
Started closing WIP (50%)	400	200
	9,000	9,200
Process costs		
Materials (see apportionment in W5 above)	£53,500	
Processing		£2,760
Cost per equivalent unit	£5.9444	£0.30
	£6.2444	

Valuation of closing WIP	£
Material 400 @ £5.9444	2,378
Processing 200 @ £0.30	60
	2,438

Value of completed output =	£
Opening WIP	4,876
Cost to complete opening WIP (400 × £0.30)	120
Other finished output (8,600 × £6.2444)	53,702
	58,698

(b) The joint cost apportionment procedures in (a) are irrelevant to the decision about by-product Z. The decision should be based on the savings or extra loss that producing Z would incur.

	£ per kilo
Sale value of Z	2.50
Additional cost of turning X into Z (£(1.20 + 3.40))	4.60
Loss on sale of Z	(2.10)
Saving on disposal costs of X	3.00
Incremental profit per kg of Z	0.90

Because of savings in disposal costs of X, it would appear profitable to make by-product Z, even though Z will make an accounting loss on sales.

(c) This part of the question appears to call for a discussion of the accounting treatment of the accounting loss of £2.10 per kg that would be incurred on making Z. The two main methods of accounting for the by-product losses are as follows.

(i) Make no charge tc the main process account for the by-product losses. The losses of £2.10 per kg could either be charged directly to the P&L account as a loss, or deducted from revenue from P and Q, to reduce the reported profitability of each product.

(ii) Charge the main process account with the loss of £2.10 per kg of Z produced. The by-product losses would then be one of the costs of the main process, which would then be apportioned between joint products P and Q.

Method (ii) is probably more suitable, since it recognises that the losses on Z are an unavoidable feature of making P and Q, and so these losses should be charged to the costs of production of P and Q, to reflect more fairly the total costs involved in their manufacture.

5 THE FEEDBACK PROCESS

Feedback is the process in a control system which monitors differences between planned and actual results so that corrective action can be taken to achieve the desired results. Feedback is used in control loops in many different management systems. Examples are budgetary control, stock control and production control.

Feedback is an essential part of a management accounting system for the following reasons.

(a) *Control.* Without feedback of actual results managers are unable to control their activities. Feedback reports will highlight the differences between planned and actual performance so that corrective action can be taken if necessary. Effective planning will enable each separate activity to start out in the right direction. To ensure that activities continue in the right direction managers need regular feedback of actual results to exercise control by comparison.

(b) *Regular monitoring.* If a system is not monitored regularly it may drift so far out of control that corrective action becomes difficult or impossible. Effective feedback operates as a continuous process so that managers can identify variances as soon as possible and take early corrective action.

(c) *Attention directing.* Feedback can help management to concentrate their efforts in the most useful areas. By highlighting those activities which are not proceeding according to plan a feedback report can direct management's attention and avoid them wasting time on areas that are under control. This is known as management by exception.

(d) *Motivation.* Feedback of information has been identified by management theorists as an essential component of an intrinsically motivating job. Individuals will not be motivated to achieve their performance targets if they are kept in ignorance of how well or badly they are performing.

6 FREEWHEEL LTD

(a) (i) FREEWHEEL LTD
CASH BUDGET JULY TO DECEMBER 19X2

	July	Aug	Sept	Oct	Nov	Dec
	£	£	£	£	£	£
Receipts						
From sales (W1)	25,500	26,400	27,900	33,800	29,600	32,000
Share issue	-	-	20,000	-	-	-
	25,500	26,400	47,900	33,800	29,600	32,000
Payments						
Purchases (W2)	12,000	13,000	14,000	18,000	16,000	14,000
Wages and salaries (W3)	8,000	9,500	10,000	10,000	11,500	12,000
Overheads	7,000	7,000	7,000	7,000	8,000	8,000
Fixed assets (W5)	-	-	-	-	-	10,000
	27,000	29,500	31,000	35,000	35,500	44,000
Excess of receipts over payments	(1,500)	(3,100)	16,900	(1,200)	(5,900)	(12,000)
Balance b/f	3,000	1,500	(1,600)	15,300	14,100	8,200
Balance c/f	1,500	(1,600)	15,300	14,100	8,200	(3,800)

(ii) FREEWHEEL LTD
BUDGETED PROFIT AND LOSS ACCOUNT
JULY TO DECEMBER 19X2

	£	£
Sales (W7)		177,800
Less cost of sales		
Opening stock	25,000	
Purchases	86,000	
Closing stock	(38,000)	
		(73,000)
Gross profit		104,800
Less expenses		
Wages and salaries	62,000	
Overheads	45,000	
Depreciation (W8)	8,500	
		(115,500)
Net loss		(10,700)
Profit and loss account balance b/f		44,600
Profits available for appropriation		33,900
Less dividends		(10,000)
Profit and loss account balance c/f		23,900

(iii) FREEWHEEL LTD
BUDGETED BALANCE SHEET
AS AT 31 DECEMBER 19X2

	Cost	Provision for depreciation	Net book value
	£	£	£
Fixed assets	170,000	22,500	147,500
Current assets			
Stock	38,000		
Trade debtors (W1)	27,200		
		65,200	
Current liabilities			
Bank overdraft	3,800		
Trade creditors (W2)	24,000		
Other creditors (W9)	41,000		
		(68,800)	
Net current assets			(3,600)
Total assets less current liabilities			143,900
Capital and reserves			
Share capital			120,000
Profit and loss account			23,900
			143,900

Workings

1 *Receipts from sales*

	May	June	July	Aug	Sept	Oct	Nov	Dec	Debtors
	£'000	£'000	£'000	£'000	£'000	£'000	£'000	£'000	£'000
Total	24.0	25.2	27.0	27.6	28.8	40.0	30.4	24.0	NA
Cash	12.0	12.6	13.5	13.8	14.4	20.0	15.2	12.0	NA
Credit	NA	NA	12.0	12.6	13.5	13.8	14.4	20.0	*27.2
Receipts	NA	NA	25.5	26.4	27.9	33.8	29.6	32.0	

*(£15,200 + £12,000)

2 *Purchases*

	May	June	July	Aug	Sept	Oct	Nov	Dec	Creditors
	£'000	£'000	£'000	£'000	£'000	£'000	£'000	£'000	£'000
Purchases	12	13	14	18	16	14	12	12	NA
Payment	NA	NA	12	13	14	18	16	14	*24

*(£12,000 + £12,000)

3 *Wages and salaries*

	June	July	Aug	Sept	Oct	Nov	Dec	Creditors
	£'000	£'000	£'000	£'000	£'000	£'000	£'000	£'000
Total incurred	8	8	10	10	10	12	12	NA
75%	NA	6	7.5	7.5	7.5	9.0	9	NA
25%	NA	2	2.0	2.5	2.5	2.5	3	3
		8	9.5	10.0	10.0	11.5	12	

4 *Overheads*

Creditor at December of £8,000

5 *Fixed assets*

	November	December	Creditor
	£'000	£'000	£'000
Purchase	30		
Payment		10	
Creditor			20

6 *Dividends*

Dividends - declared October and therefore paid in January
creditor at December of £10,000

7 *Sales*

	£
(4,500 + 4,600 + 4,800) × £6 =	83,400
(5,000 + 3,800 + 3,000) × £8 =	94,400
	177,800

8 *Depreciation*

	£
Assets owned at 30 June 19X2	140,000
Additions	30,000
	170,000
Depreciation = £170,000 × 10% × 0.5 =	£8,500

9 *Other creditors*

	£'000
Wages and salaries (W3)	3
Overheads (W4)	8
Fixed assets (W5)	20
Dividend (W6)	10
	41

(b) (i) The cash budget shows that there will be an overdraft at the end of August and at the end of December, despite the share issue in September. Payments in January and February 19X2 for the fixed asset and the payment of the dividend in January will only increase the overdraft. Sufficient overdraft facilities must therefore be arranged or other action, such as a reversal of the decision to purchase the fixed asset, should be considered.

(ii) A reduction in sales quantities in November and December results in a net loss of £10,700. If such a reduction is not part of a plan then ways of either cutting costs or increasing sales must be considered.

(iii) Stock at the end of the period represents three months' purchases whereas stock at the beginning of the period represents two months' purchases. If this is due to the reduction in sales quantities then it may be advisable to reduce purchases if the drop in sales is unavoidable.

7 BUDGETING, BUDGETARY CONTROL AND BEHAVIOUR

(a) The conditions necessary for the success of a system of budgeting are as follows.

(i) Management must have formulated a plan for the future of the organisation.

(ii) That plan must be capable of expression in financial terms.

(iii) The organisation's business must be such that it is possible to make reasonably accurate forecasts, especially of sales, upon which other forecasts are likely to depend. Equally the organisation must not be subject to too rapid change.

(iv) Managers responsible for each area of the organisation must be willing to co-operate both with the budgeting process and with each other.

(v) Some form of 'budget manual' should lay down the responsibilities mentioned in (iv).

(vi) The budgeting process should be led by someone able to liaise between and co-ordinate the input of the various areas of the organisation. This person will need the backing of the most senior management.

Budgetary control involves 'the establishment of budgets relating the responsibilities of executives to the requirements of a policy, and the continuous comparison of actual with budgeted results, either to secure by individual action the objectives of that policy or to provide a basis for its revision'. (CIMA *Official Terminology*).

Thus the conditions required, in addition to those noted above, are as follows.

(i) The organisation must be able to produce regular, timely, accurate financial and production information.

(ii) There must be good channels of communication throughout the organisation.

(iii) The various areas of the organisation must be able to change and improve their performance in line with the plan.

(iv) Conversely the system must not pressurise those given responsibility to achieve unrealistic targets.

(b) Some of the behavioural considerations of budgeting are as follows.

(i) Managers might resent control information coming from the management accountant, which they see as part of a system of trying to find fault with their work. This resentment is likely to be particularly strong when budgets are imposed on managers without allowing them to participate in the budget-setting process. When managers resent control reports they are likely to adopt a hostile and defensive attitude.

(ii) In order to cover themselves against unforeseen circumstances managers may build in 'slack' to their expenditure estimates and lobby for a high allowance. They will then try to make sure that they spend up to their full allowance to ensure that it is not cut in future years. (Zero base budgeting can counteract this tendency.)

(iii) The budget may be seen as a pressure device used by management to force 'lazy' employees to work harder. Employees may fear job losses, or extra pressure if efficiency levels rise and they therefore work more slowly, but this merely increases the *need* for budgetary pressure.

(iv) Achieving the departmental target may come to have paramount importance, encouraging rigidity and discouraging flexibility in operational decision making, and possibly undermining the efforts of other departments. In some cases this could be a deliberate ploy to score points over another departmental manager who is seen as a competitor.

8 TERRY HENDSETTER

(a) *Graph of absenteeism*

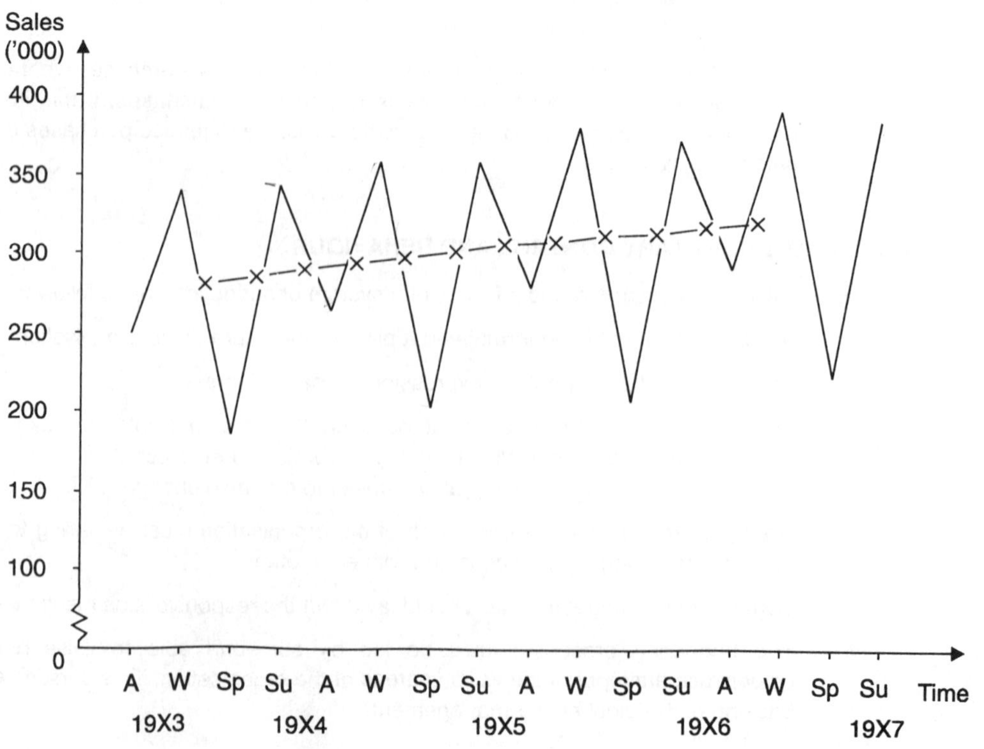

(b) *Seasonal variations*

	Spring	*Summer*	*Autumn*	*Winter*	*Total*
19X4	–95	+58	–26	+64	
19X5	–94	+56	–27	+73	
19X6	–104	+58	–27	+71	
	–293	+172	–80	+208	
Average variation	–97.7	+57.3	–26.7	+69.3	+2.2
Adjust to nil	– 0.5	– 0.5	–0.6	– 0.6	–2.2
	-98.2	+56.8	–27.3	+68.7	0.0
Round to whole number	–98	+57	–28*	+69	0

*Adjusted to keep the total of seasonal variations at zero.

(c) The trend line shows increases in sales of about three thousand per quarter, and so a forecast of sales will be based on this assumption.

			Trend line	*Seasonal variation*	*Forecast*
19X6	Winter	Trend line value	320		
19X7	Autumn	Estimate 320 + (3 × 3)	329	–28	301
	Winter	Estimate 320 + (4 × 3)	332	+69	401

The forecasts of sales, based on the calculations and assumptions here, are 301,000 units of product XN30 in autumn 19X7 and 401,000 units of products XN30 in winter 19X7.

9 PPBS

(a) The shortcomings of traditional approaches to planning which led to attempts to introduce PPB systems include the following.

(i) A lack of clarity as to long-term objectives and their relationship with resource inputs

(ii) An emphasis on inputs to functions and departments rather than on outputs of programmes or related activities

(iii) A tendency to start from last year's budget and plan incremental changes rather than to consider whether activities still met their purposes, or whether alternative activities would be better

(iv) Planning for separate committees, departments or sections with inadequate consideration of overall 'corporate' objectives and requirements of the environment

(v) An inadequate approach to surveys, forecasts, statistical and other analyses to scan the environment, and identify problems and needs for the organisation to consider and to plan to meet

(vi) A lack of consideration of performance and provision of evidence to help decide if plans were adequate and objectives achieved

Traditional approaches represent an inadequate process for rational decision making and consideration of economy, efficiency and effectiveness.

(b) *Illustration: Care of the aged*

A PPBS would involve the following stages and considerations.

(i) Assessing community needs and the nature of problems with care for the aged. How serious are they? How many people are affected? What are the likely future trends and developments? Consideration of how far Council is able and prepared to go in meeting these needs.

(ii) Identifying objectives in tackling problems and a consideration of programme areas. Setting targets against which to assess alternative policies and eventually to provide a basis for measuring performance.

(iii) Grouping current and proposed activities into programme categories that together contribute to an objective or sub-objective, for example domiciliary services and residential services. Sub-dividing categories, say domiciliary into health and home support. Describing and quantifying outputs required, for example house meals per 1,000 aged, ratio of full-time equivalent home helps for 1,000 aged.

(iv) Identifying alternative approaches; consideration of likely costs and effects. For residential accommodation hospitals, hotels, hostels, welfare homes, sheltered housing, private housing or council housing could be considered.

(v) Establishing a medium-term programme budget for each programme area including costs and outputs required, combining all activities regardless of which organisation, department or section carries out the tasks.

(vi) Converting year 1 of all programme budgets into an annual budget.

(vii) Monitoring, reporting and reviewing performance for control purposes, to consider changes to plans or methods of implementation.

(c) The problems that have made PPBS difficult to introduce in practice have included the following.

(i) Expectations were raised too high and the changes were portrayed as 'revolutionary'. Results in practice were disappointing and slow in coming. What was really required at the time was evolutionary change via improvements to current arrangements along the lines of corporate management.

(ii) Objectives are often difficult to define in the public sector and very often activities have multiple objectives and thus multidimensional outputs.

(iii) Policy makers are usually short-term pragmatists who make incremental changes, to meet ever changing circumstances, rather than formal explicit long-term commitments.

(iv) There was resistance to such substantial change from senior officials who were used to departmental arrangements and departmental lines of reporting and accounting.

(v) It is difficult to define costs and allocate them to objectives and then relate them to outputs and the wider community. When activities have several purposes how should whatever costs are identified be split?

(vi) Developing PPBS, or changing traditional systems, is costly and likely to be ineffective where systems and structures are changed but the management processes they should support are not.

(vii) Major change to accounting systems is required, but much of the output of such systems must fit the requirements of government documents, for example Department of Health forms for health authorities.

Despite the problems and experiences of PPBS that have not worked, in practice many aspects of programme budgeting and the corporate approach have been successfully incorporated into traditional approaches since the late 1960s and remain in effective working order.

10 STANDARD COSTS

(a) *The benefits of standard costing*

(i) Standard costing provides a standard base whereby performance may be measured on the basis of what an item should cost or how much should have been produced, on the basis of the expected levels of activity.

(ii) It provides a method whereby labour and overheads can be consistently recovered and charged into stock.

(iii) It provides a basis of control for buying, usage and efficient work levels.

(iv) In setting up standards management can reappraise activities to ascertain if they are being done in the most cost-effective and efficient way.

(v) It creates an atmosphere of cost-consciousness amongst all levels, motivating staff and workers to see if there is a better way of performing a particular task.

(vi) By creating a realistic target it motivates staff and operatives to achieve or better the standard laid down.

(vii) It is a recognisable method of performance monitoring though variance analysis, motivating investigations into causes of shortfall and improving methods and procedures for the future.

(viii) It provides a recognisable basis for budgeting, forecasting and planning.

(ix) Where firms are in similar industries and are willing to compare, a meaningful basis for comparison might be established.

(b) *Problems of standard costing*

(i) If a standard is too easy to attain or impossible to attain it becomes a disincentive and operatives will work at their own pace.

(ii) Operatives may be suspicious of standards and may be reluctant to super-achieve in case the standard is changed. Also, when standards are being set, the operatives may contrive to make the standard easy to beat by working slowly. The result will be a subjective standard.

(iii) Standards or material prices (which are largely uncontrollable) are at best opinions of what is likely to happen. Standards of labour cost should be set as a result of union negotiations. Consequently standards no longer measure buying powers but ability to predict accurately and negotiate hard bargains with the unions.

(iv) The setting of standards and the reporting through variance accounting is now a complicated, laborious, time consuming and costly business. The savings arising from cost control are often eroded by the high reporting cost and any time lapse means that the detailed information is too late in presentation to be of real use.

(v) Standards are considered coercive and as such management and staff may find them a 'big stick' which may be dysfunctional. This may make management liable to 'passing the buck' to keep within standard or to be unadventurous for similar reasons.

(vi) Standards inevitably produce variances. For reasons outlined in (iii) above, many costs are not a 'fait accompli'. The non-recognition of this fact may give rise to there being a substantial amount of time wasting over uncontrollable variances.

11 PAN CO LIMITED

(a) (i)

	£
Variable production cost should be (1,000 × £210)	210,000
but was (W1)	224,160
Variable production cost variance	14,160 (A)

Check	£
Wages (from (ii))	3,360 (A)
Materials (from (iii))	9,000 (A)
Overhead (from (iv))	1,800 (A)
	14,160 (A)

(ii)

	£
5,200 hours should cost (× £9)	46,800
but did cost	48,360
Direct wages rate variance	1,560 (A)

	hrs
1,000 units should take (× 5 hours)	5,000
but did take	5,200
Direct wages efficiency variance	200 (A)
× standard rate (£9)	1,800 (A)

Summary	£
Direct wages rate variance	1,560 (A)
Direct wages efficiency variance	1,800 (A)
	3,360 (A)

(iii) Direct materials

	£
10,000 kg should cost (× £15)	150,000
but did cost	144,000
Direct materials price variance	6,000 (F)

	kg
1,000 units should use (× 10 kg)	10,000
but did use (W)	11,000
Usage variance	1,000 (A)
× standard cost (£15)	£15,000 (A)

Summary

Direct materials price variance	6,000 (F)
Direct materials usage variance	15,000 (A)
Direct materials variance	9,000 (A)

	£
(iv) Variable production overhead should cost (1,000 × £15)	15,000
but did cost	16,800
Variable production overhead variance	1,800 (A)

Workings

1 *Variable production cost*

	£
Total wages	48,360
Variable production overhead	16,800
Direct materials (W2)	159,000
	224,160

2 *Direct materials*

		Standard cost	
	kg	£	£
Opening stock	4,000	15	60,000
Purchases	10,000	-	144,000
	14,000		204,000
Closing stock	(3,000)	15	(45,000)
Production	11,000		159,000

(b) To: Production manager
From: Management accountant
Subject: Commentary on variances arising in the week ending 9 November 19X1

Variable production cost variance

The total variance is an adverse one of £14,160. This represents 6% of total standard production cost. Investigation is clearly warranted to identify what control action is required to bring costs back into line with budget. The total variance may be analysed into its different components to give a clearer idea of where problems are arising, as follows.

Direct wages rate variance

An adverse variance arises because the labour force were paid an average of (£48,360/5,200) = £9.30 per hour instead of the standard cost of £9 per hour. If this is a new agreed rate the standard should be revised. It may, however, be due to a short-term need to recruit temporary labour at rates more expensive than standard or to overtime working or bonus payments. The production manager and/or the personnel department should be contracted for further information.

Direct wages efficiency variance

An adverse variance of £1,800 has arisen because the labour force took 200 hours more to produce 1,000 units than the standard allowance. The production manager should be asked to explain the variance. Possible causes are lack of training or machine breakdown, but the material variances may also offer a clue as to the explanation.

Materials price variance

Materials were purchased for £14.40 per kg in the week, a price £0.60 less than standard giving rise to a favourable price variance of £6,000. However this appears to have been at the expense of quality, to judge from the usage variance.

Materials usage variance

1,000 kg more than standard were used to make 1,000 units. This seems most likely to be because cheaper, poor quality materials were purchased, probably resulting in excessive waste. It is possible that the need for rectification work due to poor materials also explains why the labour force was less efficient than standard.

Variable production overhead variance

An adverse variance of £1,800 has arisen. Variable overhead appears to vary in line with labour costs and thus 200 hours O £3 = £600 of the variance is explicable by reference to the extra labour hours worked. The remainder is due to an increase in variable overhead costs: the actual rate per hour was £16,800/5,200 hours = £3.23, as opposed to the standard rate of £3. For further explanation we need to know what the overhead comprises and who is responsible for the expenditure.

(c) Past performance is one possible guide to the ascertainment of standard costs but it is not necessarily the best guide. For example if it is known at the time when standards are being set that a new labour rate has been agreed, that new more efficient working methods are to be introduced, that materials prices are going to rise or that the materials specification of products is going to change then the standard should be revised accordingly. There is no point in measuring performance against out-of-date standards.

The point should also be made that standards can be used as a psychological incentive by giving employees a realistic but challenging target of efficiency. Standards based on past performance will not have any motivational impact.

The most that can be said, therefore, is that past performance may offer a starting point for ascertaining standard costs, but only in the absence of change will it provide the best available basis for doing so.

12 UMBRELLA PLC

Most of the variance calculations are fairly straightforward. However, there are one or two tricky points worth looking at more closely.

There is a sales volume variance.

	External sales	*Internal transfers*
	Units	Units
Budgeted sales	10,000	5,000
Actual sales	7,000	7,000
Sales volume variance	3,000 (A)	2,000 (F)

These variations must now be converted into pounds, but what standard profit or contribution margin should be used?

One possibility would be to use the net standard profit per unit of £(32 – 27) = £5 for external sales and of £(30 – 22) = £8 for internal transfers. (*Note.* Transfers do not incur any selling costs.)

The drawback to this approach is that by including head office costs (which are fixed) into the standard cost), we must then calculate a *fixed cost volume variance* for these items. This would be a most tedious and unrewarding exercise and should be avoided if possible.

Another possibility is to take the standard full manufacturing cost per unit, and use a standard gross profit to evaluate the sales volume variance.

External sales standard gross profit £(32 – 20) =	£12
Internal transfers standard gross profit £(30 – 20) =	£10

The drawback to this approach is that it ignores the variable selling cost for external sales of £3 per unit. The profit per unit from external sales should be reduced by £3 in order to allow for this directly attributable cost of sale.

It might seem simplest to use marginal costing, and evaluate the sales volume variance using the standard contribution per unit. This approach, although perhaps the easiest and most satisfactory solution, is not recommended for an examination question which includes fixed overheads in standard unit costs, thereby indicating that the examiner probably expects you to use standard absorption costing in your solution.

The best solution under the circumstances would seem to be to use the profit margins shown above, but to reduce the standard profit margin on the external sales by the variable selling cost of £3 per unit:

External sales standard profit £(12 – 3)	£9
Internal transfers standard profit	£10

The variances can now be calculated as follows.

(a) *Sales volume variance*

	£
External sales 3,000 units (A) × £9	27,000 (A)
Internal transfers 2,000 units (F) × £10	20,000 (F)
	7,000 (A)

(b) There is no selling price variance.

(c) There is no materials price variance.

(d) *Materials usage variance*

			Material X		*Material Y*
18,000 units produced	should use	(× £3)	54,000 units	(× £4)	72,000 units
	did use		52,000 units		78,000 units
Usage variance			2,000 units (F)		6,000 units (A)
× standard price			× £1.50		× £2.25
			£3,000 (F)		£13,500 (A)

(e) *Efficiency variances*

18,000 units produced	should take (× 1/2 hr)	9,000 hrs
	did take	9,200 hrs
Efficiency variance		200 hrs (A)
Labour efficiency variance (× £4)		£800 (A)
Variable manufacturing overhead efficiency variance (× £1)		£200 (A)
Fixed manufacturing overhead volume efficiency variance (× £8)		£1,600 (A)

(f) *Labour rate and variable manufacturing overhead expenditure variances*

			Labour		*Variable overhead*
			£		£
9,200 hours	should cost	(× £4)	36,800	(× £1)	9,200
	did cost		36,500		9,700
Variance			300 (F)		500 (A)

(g) *Fixed manufacturing overhead expenditure variance*

	£
Budgeted fixed manufacturing overhead (15,000 × £4)	60,000
Actual cost	63,300
Expenditure variance	3,300 (A)

(h) *Fixed manufacturing overhead volume variance*

Budgeted production volume	15,000 units
Actual production volume	18,000 units
Volume variance in units	3,000 units (F)
× standard absorption rate per unit	× £4
	£12,000 (F)

This can be analysed into an efficiency variance of £1,600 (A) (see efficiency variances above), and a capacity variance.

Budgeted hours of work (15,000 units × 1/2 hr)	7,500	hrs
Actual hours of work	9,200	hrs
Capacity variance in hrs	1,700	hrs (F)
× standard absorption rate per hour	× £8	
	£13,600	(F)

(i) There is no head office cost variance

(j) *Selling overhead spending variance*

This relates to external sales only.

	£
7,000 units of external sales should cost:	
Fixed overhead	20,000
Variable overhead at £3 per unit	21,000
	41,000
Selling overhead actually was	52,000
Variance	11,000 (A)

These variances can now be summarised in an operating statement.

			£	£
Budgeted profit				90,000
Sales volume variances:				
External sales			27,000 (A)	
Internal sales			20,000 (F)	
				7,000 (A)
				83,000
Cost variances:				
		£	£	
		(F)	*(A)*	
Material usage:	Material X	3,000		
	Material Y		13,500	
Labour rate		300		
Labour efficiency			800	
Variable manufacturing o/hd expenditure			500	
Variable manufacturing o/hd efficiency			200	
Fixed manufacturing o/hd expenditure			3,300	
Fixed manufacturing o/hd volume efficiency			1,600	
Fixed manufacturing o/hd volume capacity		13,600		
Selling overhead spending			11,000	
		16,900	30,900	14,000 (A)
Actual profit				69,000

The fixed overhead volume variance was £12,000 (F) because actual production exceeded the budget by 3,000 units. The effect of this excess production was therefore to prevent a further fall in profits, from £69,000 to perhaps as low as £57,000.

13 GAMMA LTD

(a) (i) *Material usage variances for product alphabeta*

Material alpha

1,000 alphabetas did use	1,200 kg
1,000 alphabetas should have used (1,000 × 1kg)	1,000 kg
	200 kg (A)
× standard cost per kg	£40
Variance	£8,000 (A)

Material beta

Adverse usage of material beta was 200 kg (as given in the question).

200kg × standard cost per kg = 200 × £45
= £9,000 (A)

(ii) *Total price variance for each material* (on purchases)

Material alpha

	£
20,000kg should have cost (20,000 × £40)	800,000
20,000kg did cost (20,000 × £44)	880,000
	80,000 (A)

Material beta

	£
12,900 square metres should have cost (12,900 × £45)	580,500
12,900 square metres did cost	619,200
	38,700 (A)

(iii) *Total overhead variance of the machining department*

Total fixed overhead = 70% × £209,000 = £146,300

$\therefore$ Fixed overhead rate per hour = $\frac{146{,}300}{9{,}500}$ = £15.40

Total variable overhead = 30% × £209,000 = £62,700

$\therefore$ Variable overhead rate per hour = $\frac{62{,}700}{9{,}500}$ = £6.60

$\therefore$ Total overhead rate per hour = £15.40 + £6.60 = £22

Standard hours of production = 9,650 + (1.5 × 1,000) = 11,150 hours

Total overhead variance

	£
Overhead recovered (11,150 × £22)	245,300
Actual overhead incurred	217,340
	27,960 (F)

This variance can be analysed into an expenditure variance and a volume variance.

Overhead expenditure variance

	£
Flexible budget [£146,300 + (11,150 × £6.60)]	219,890
Actual overhead incurred =	217,340
	2,550 (F)

Overhead volume variance

Budgeted production volume	9,500	hours
Actual production volume	11,150	hours
	1,650	(F)hours
× standard rate per hour (fixed)	15.40	
	£ 25,410	(F)

(b) (i) *The purposes of a standard costing system are:*

- to assist in the budgeting, forecasting and planning processes;
- to highlight situations which do not confirm to original plans, thereby supporting managerial control;
- to assist in the evaluation of managerial performance;
- to assist in decision-making (eg pricing);
- to provide a method whereby costs can be consistently recovered and charged to stock.

(ii) *Closing stock valuations*

Material alpha: (20,000 – (1,200 + 8,500))	10,300kg
Valued at standard cost per kg	£40
Value of closing stock	£412,000

Material beta: (12,900 – (5,300 + (6 × 1,000) + 200))	1,400kg
Valued at standard cost per square metre	£45
Value of closing stock	£63,000

The system in operation at Gamma Ltd holds stock at standard price, therefore the year-end stock is valued at standard price also. For financial reporting purposes, stock is held at the lower of cost or market value. If a company has favourable material price variances, this indicates that the standard cost is greater than the purchase price of the material. Valuing stock at a value which is above its cost amounts to recording a profit before a sale has taken place, and means that stock is not being valued in the way that is required for financial reporting purposes.

If a material amount of stock with a favourable price variance is held, the standard value of closing stock could be reduced by deducting a proportion of the favourable price variance.

Since both material price variances were found to be adverse, there is no need to reduce the value of the closing stock as described above.

If however, the price variance for material alpha was found to be £80,000 (F) instead of £80,000(A), we may consider valuing the stock as follows (since 10,300kg remain in stock, out of 20,000kg purchased).

$\frac{10,300}{20,000}$ = 51.5% of stock unused at year-end.

51.5% of a favourable price variance (£80,000) = £41,200.

Therefore, we might consider revaluing the stock of material alpha as follows.

£412,000 – £41,200 = £370,800.

14 JB LIMITED

(a) Using replacement costs, the cost per component is as follows.

	£
3 kg of M1	16.50
2 kg of P2	7.20
Part no 678	50.00
Labour	
Skilled × 5 hours	20.00
Unskilled × 5 hours	15.00
Overhead	
Variable × 4 hours	28.00
Fixed-incremental cost $\frac{£3,200}{400}$	8.00
	144.70
Less additional costs of P2 (2 kg × £1.60)	(3.20) (see note)
	141.50

The contract should be accepted, because the unit cost will be £141.50, giving a profit of £3.50 per unit or £1,400 in total.

(*Note:* the cost of P2 materials is calculated as the replacement cost of P4, less the cost of the additional work needed to convert P2 to P4).

If historical costs of material are substituted for replacement costs, the unit profit will be higher.

(b) The calculations in part (a) above merely give an indication of the immediate financial effect of accepting the contract. There are many other factors which management should consider before reaching a decision.

(i) How reliable are the estimated costs of fulfilling the contract? For example, it has been assumed that five hours of skilled labour are required for each component. if it turned out that six hours were required, the additional cost of £4 per unit would more than eliminate the expected profit.

(ii) The company is proposing to take on additional employees to fulfil the contract. There are hidden costs in this course of action, such as the costs of recruitment and the increased administrative burden in the personnel and payroll departments. It should also be considered whether new employees could be used more profitably on other activities.

(iii) There may be long-term factors affecting the decision. For example, successful completion of the contract might lead to new orders from the aircraft manufacturers. On the other hand, specially recruited employees might need to be dismissed at the end of the contract, leading possibly to redundancy payments and certainly to increased administrative paperwork.

15 CORPORATE OBJECTIVES

As a general rule, increases in a company's profits will be in the interests of the shareholders. However, the maximisation of profits should not be the only goal, and it may be beneficial to aim for profits below the maximum possible.

The limitations of profit as a measure of performance

The profits shown in a company's accounts are not a wholly objective measure of the company's performance. The final figure depends on policies chosen on, for example, depreciation and the writing off of development expenditure. In the short term, profits can be increased by capitalising development expenditure, but such policies do not really increase the company's worth.

It is very hard to work out what profit could have been attained. Comparisons with an industry average may be useful, but comparisons with exceptional performers in the industry may be inappropriate. Profits need to be adjusted to reflect the resources used to earn them. A company which doubles its capital and increases its profits by 50% has probably done badly, not well.

Profits are computed annually, with half-yearly interim results. Investments which are highly profitable in the long term but are loss-makers initially could be rejected if management is concerned only with next year's profits.

Alternative financial objectives

A company must ensure its financial stability both in the short term and in the long term. Targets for the reduction of gearing or the retention of profits may therefore be appropriate. Of key importance is the solvency of the company. Profitable investments must be rejected if the expenditure required would leave the company unable to pay its debts.

Non-financial objectives

A company's directors may legitimately take into account a range of non-financial objectives, including the welfare of employees and of society, the provision of a service to the public and environmental goals. In some cases the pursuit of such objectives may lead to increased profits, for example when an environmentally responsible company attracts customers who share such concerns.

16 MARKET EFFICIENCY

The efficient market hypothesis contends that some capital markets (in the UK and US for instance) are 'efficient markets' in which the prices at which securities are traded reflect all the relevant information available. In other words, this information is freely available to all participants in the market and is fully reflected in share prices. Further, it is assumed that transaction costs are insignificant and do not discourage trading in shares, and that no single individual or group of individuals dominates the market.

The theory exists in three forms: weak form, semi-strong form and strong form.

Weak form efficiency contends that prices only change when new factual information becomes available. Thus if a takeover bid is anticipated, the share prices of the participants will not change until the bid is actually announced. Information is in the public domain and equally available to all players in the market, and thus if this form of the hypothesis is correct, no one player should be able to outperform the market consistently. Thus the fact that financial institutions rarely outperform the market on a regular basis lends weight to this form of the theory.

The *semi-strong form* of the theory holds that in addition to responding to information that is publicly available, the market also reflects all other knowledge that is publicly available and relevant to the share valuation. Thus to take the example used above, the share prices of companies involved in a takeover bid will change in advance of the bid being formally announced as the market anticipates the bid. Once again, this form of the theory is based upon the assumption that all the knowledge upon which share price movements are based is in the public domain and freely available. Thus no single player or group of players should be able consistently to outperform the market. This form of the theory is supported by empirical research which suggests that share price movements do anticipate merger announcements. The fact that the neither the financial institutions nor any other group of investors regularly beat the market also supports this version of the hypothesis.

The *strong form* of the theory holds that the market price of securities reflects all information that is available. This includes knowledge of past performance and anticipated events as in the semi-strong form, and also 'insider' knowledge not publicly available. This form can be tested by investigating the effect on the share price of the effect of releasing a piece of information previously confidential to the firm; if the strong form of the hypothesis is valid, then this should already be factored into the share value and a significant price movement should not result. The implication is that this sort of information is only available to specialists who are in regular contact with the company, such as investment trust managers, and that as a result they could use their privileged position to outperform other investors. Empirical work suggests that this form of the hypothesis is not valid, and this is what one would expect since insider dealing is illegal in the UK.

Thus the fact that the financial institutions in general do not consistently outperform the market supports both the weak and semi-strong forms of the efficient market hypothesis. The fact that a number of institutions do consistently perform well is probably more related to the fund managers' understanding of the structure of the industries and markets in which they invest, and their ability to hold a more widely diversified portfolio than the small investor. This means that they are in a better position to avoid the risk of large losses. The fact that they are in daily contact with the markets also means that they are in practice able to react more quickly to new information that becomes available than is the small investor.

17 ECONOMIC POLICY OBJECTIVES

(a) There are four main objectives of macroeconomic policy:

- (i) to achieve a sustained *real* economic growth, measured as growth in national income or GDP after allowing for price inflation;
- (ii) to achieve 'full' employment;
- (iii) to maintain stable prices, or just a low annual rate of inflation;
- (iv) in the long term, to achieve equilibrium in the country's balance of payments on current account.

It can be argued that objectives (iii) and (iv) are simply means towards achieving the prime objectives (i) and (ii).

(b) In practice, it is difficult to achieve all of these objectives simultaneously.

- (i) Measures to control the rate of inflation might be aimed at reducing consumer demand (perhaps through higher taxation or higher interest rates) and the result of this could be a decline in the rate of real growth in the economy, as well as a decline in the 'money rate' of growth. This is because any cutbacks in consumer demand will not just restrain price increases, and some of the cutbacks will lead to a fall in demand for some products and so a decline in the real output of some industries.

  Controlling the rate of inflation through higher interest rates is likely to result in a stronger exchange rate and a consequence of this would be lower exports, higher imports and a worsening balance of payments position on current account.

Measures to control inflation which have the effect of reducing the competitiveness of exports and the real rate of growth in the economy are likely to result in higher unemployment, particularly when current levels of employment are quite high. The Phillips curve is used by some economists to describe the rise in inflation as the level of unemployment falls, and the rise in unemployment as the level of inflation comes down.

(ii) Measures to achieve equilibrium in the balance of payments when a country has a current account deficit could involve lower interest rates and a lower exchange rate. Both of these could be inflationary, and damaging to economic growth in the long run.

If a country tries to tackle a balance of trade deficit by protectionist measures against imports, the lower import volumes would restrict domestic industrial growth (because of imported raw material and components shortages). Retaliatory action by other countries would damage export volumes and so restrict economic growth.

(iii) Economic measures to achieve more economic growth face the problem that the real output of industry will increase if productivity can be improved and if demand in the economy increases to meet the extra supply capacity. In practice, economic policy measures to encourage demand (such as lower taxes) result in a faster growth in demand than in supply, so that the rate of inflation goes up. Higher inflation in turn results in a loss of competitiveness by domestic industries, and a fall in exports. Higher wage demands, provoked by higher prices, will result in higher unemployment.

(iv) It would appear that measures to reduce the level of unemployment can result in lower economic growth partly because lower unemployment can result in cost-push inflation. Without proper training, extra people employed are likely to be less productive, and so production costs will rise. Attempts by a government to reduce unemployment by increasing expenditure in the public sector could result in higher taxation and lower growth in the private sector.

18 PSBR

Tutorial note. Part (a) requires an explanation of the PSBR and the way it might be financed by borrowing from the banking system, the non-bank private sector or overseas, or by issuing notes and coin. Part (b) considers the various aspects of government income and expenditure and why these change in response, for example, to changes in the level of economic activity.

(a) The *public sector borrowing requirement (PSBR)* is the total amount the public sector needs to borrow from the private sector and from overseas for the year. It consists of borrowing by the central government, by the local authorities and by the public corporations, the largest component being the central government borrowing requirement (CGBR). Part of the CGBR is on-lent to other institutions within the public sector, and to this extent reduces the amount that the rest of the public sector needs to borrow. In other words, only that part of borrowing by local authorities and public corporations that has not been on-lent by the central government adds to the PSBR.

There are several methods of financing the PSBR. One of the main methods is by borrowing from the non-bank private sector through the sale of government securities, Treasury bills, local authority bonds and so on, to private companies and individuals. In addition, private sector debt may be bought by the banks. The most publicised aspect of the PSBR is its effect on the money supply. The money supply will not increase when the PSBR is financed by private borrowing as this represents a simple transfer of funds from the private to the public sector, but it will increase when financing comes from the banking system, because this results in an increase in bank deposits. As a result, a government attempting to control the money supply will try to avoid financing the PSBR from the banking sector.

The PSBR may also be financed by borrowing from overseas. Funds made available in this way will be received in foreign currency which must be paid into the Exchange Equalisation Account at the Bank of England in exchange for an equal value of sterling, then paid into the government's account at the Bank of England. Again, this increases the amount of operational deposits within the banking system and, unless offset by sales of debt to the non-bank private sector so as to reduce deposits, there will be an increase in the money supply.

The final method of financing the PSBR is by increasing the issue of notes and coin in circulation. This has a direct effect on the money supply but has had little impact in recent years as it is the least important means of financing the PSBR.

(b) The size of the PSBR essentially reflects the extent to which the expenditure of the public sector exceeds its income. The main component of public sector income is the government's receipts from taxation, and these may fluctuate over time for a number of reasons. There have been a number of changes in the tax system such as reduction in the rates of income and corporation tax, increases in tax thresholds and allowances and replacement of some income tax bands, and these changes will have some impact on the amount of tax revenue generated. In addition, tax receipts will vary with the general level of economic activity: in a recession, incomes and profits will fall and so too will the associated tax revenue while, in an upturn, tax revenues will tend to rise.

Government spending will be affected by changes in the level of economic activity. In a recession, the higher rate of unemployment requires additional spending on social security benefits, exacerbating the loss of potential tax revenue. Government spending will also be affected by changes in other aspects of the welfare system. The ageing of the population, for example, has constituted an additional drain on public sector resources in recent times, as more is paid out in retirement benefits. It also means that the dependency ratio (the economically inactive population relative to the economically active) rises which again compounds the adverse effect on the public sector budget.

The exploitation of North Sea oil provided a substantial boost to the UK's public purse, enabling the government to avoid the dilemma of having either to raise taxes or increase its borrowing requirement to maintain its outlay on public services such as health and education. The benefits from the North Sea oil were only temporary, however, and more recently expenditure on public services has been reduced in an attempt to balance the government's budget. An alternative source of income which the government utilised extensively during the 1980s and 1990s is privatisation. The transfer of assets from the public to the private sector raised revenue which, again, meant a temporary reduction in the PSBR. The disadvantages of the privatisation programme in terms of the PSBR, however, was that it tended to be the more successful industries that were sold. Therefore, the losses of the remaining public corporations were no longer 'absorbed' by the more profitable enterprises but instead translated directly into an increase in the PSBR.

19 CAUSES OF INFLATION

Inflation can be defined in the simplest terms as a rise in the overall price level of goods and services. Normally, this rise would have to continue over a period of time before it would be described as 'inflation'. A one-off rise in the price level would not generally be regarded as inflation.

For example, raising taxes is considered to be a deflationary act on the part of government. However, the immediate impact of an increase in indirect taxes (eg VAT) is to increase prices. The explanation for this paradox is that the policy of raising taxes is expected to reduce demand in the longer term and thereby help to reduce prices. The short-term impact of increasing prices would not be considered to be inflation in a pure economic sense. In practice, however, inflation is measured by means of prices indices which usually include the effect of indirect taxes. Therefore, it can be seen that the practical view of inflation has diverged slightly from the pure economic one.

Inflation is not necessarily either a good or a bad thing in itself. Of more importance is the rate of inflation relative to other factors. For example, individuals would be most concerned with the difference between the rate of inflation and the rate of increase in their wages or salaries because this would determine how much their income would buy and therefore their material standard of living.

On the other hand, companies which rely on exports for a significant proportion of their income would be more concerned with the rate of the country's inflation compared with the rate of inflation in the countries with which they are competing in their international markets since this would affect their overall competitiveness, depending upon the relevant exchange rates.

Economic theorists would generally recognise three potential causes of inflation, although there is much debate as to whether the third cause listed below is a genuine one. The three causes are as follows.

(a) Demand-pull
(b) Cost-push
(c) An increase in the money supply

Demand-pull inflation occurs when demand exceeds supply, leading to a rise in prices in an attempt to restore equilibrium. This can be described in diagrammatic form by considering the demand curves D_1 and D_2 and the supply curve S in the diagram below.

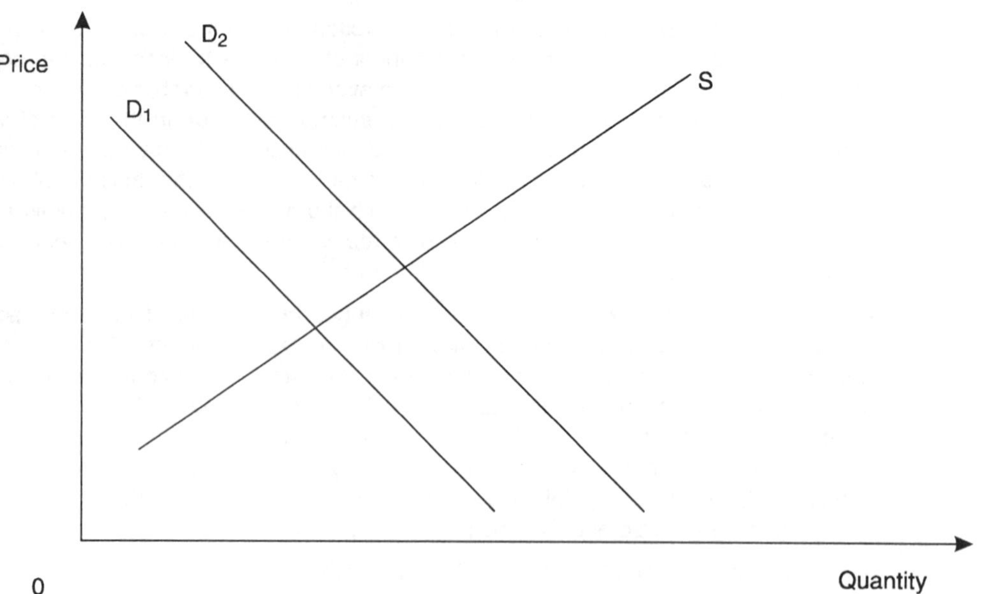

If the demand curve moves from D_1 to D_2 then the price will rise. It is true that supply will rise too, stimulated by the higher prices, but equilibrium will still only be achieved at a higher price level. If forces are at work which keep pulling the demand curve to the right, then the price rise will be sustained.

Examples of things which might lead to demand-pull inflation are excessive government spending and expectation of further inflation. The latter could induce people to buy goods early in order to get them at a lower price, thus creating the already anticipated price rises.

Cost-push inflation occurs when the cost of production of goods and services rises, irrespective of their relative supply. The prices of goods and services are pushed up as companies try to maintain their profit margins. Examples of cost-push demand are increases in wages, possibly caused by the relative power of workers and unions compared with employers, and increases in raw material costs such as the rise in oil prices in the 1970s.

Finally, monetarists would argue that inflation is caused by increases in the money supply on the basis of the equation MV = PT. If T, the number of transactions, and V, the velocity of money in circulation, are constant then the effect of an increase in M, the supply of money, is to increase P, the price level.

20 MIDSOUTH ELECTRIC PLC

> *Tutorial note.* In part (a) you may find it helpful to contrast the primary objectives of public sector and private sector organisations and to use this as a basis for your discussion in the changes in the associated objectives.

(a) (i) The primary objective prior to privatisation is likely to be to serve the public interest in the best possible way. Associated objectives are likely to include:

(1) providing a safe and reliable source of supply to domestic and industrial consumers;

(2) keeping supply and distribution costs as low as possible;

(3) keeping prices to consumers low, often in response to political pressures;

(4) achieving the target rate of return on investment set for public sector organisations;

(5) keeping capital expenditure within limits, particularly during times of restraint on public sector capital investment.

Following transfer to the private sector, the primary financial objective is likely to be the maximisation of the wealth of the ordinary shareholders. Although some of the objectives such as providing a safe and reliable supply of electricity are likely to remain the same after privatisation, the relative importance of the aims is likely to change, and further objectives will be introduced. These are likely to include:

(1) establishing and maintaining a good and reliable stream of dividends;

(2) ensuring that the use of available funds is maximised in order to provide a good return to shareholders and to protect the company against hostile takeover bids;

(3) fulfilling the requirements of the industry regulator.

The demands of the market may mean that there is a greater concern with short-term results to the detriment of long-term investment.

(b) (i) It is assumed that shareholders will demand that the company should operate so as to maximise their wealth accruing from the company. This can be measured in terms of the flow of dividends and the movement in the share price. The figures allow the market capitalisation (in £m) to be calculated. For analytical purposes, we use below the figures for alternate years.

	19X2	*19X4*	*19X6*
Profit after tax (£m)	52	74	80
P/E ratio	7.5	8.5	9.0
Market capitalisation (£m)	390	629	720
Dividends (£m)	12	17	24

The shareholders have seen a rise of 84.6% in the market capitalisation over the last four years together with a doubling in the level of dividends. If it is assumed that this has not involved the raising of additional equity, then this, together with the premium achieved on the first day of trading suggest that the shareholders have done very well out of the issue.

(ii) Sales per employee have risen from £60,700 in 19X2 to £75,400 in 19X6. However, the average salary has risen from £7,714 to £8,030, an increase of 4.1% compared with an increase of 6.8% in the RPI. Over the same period the number employed has fallen by 800, a reduction of 69%. The apparently poor rate of increase in remuneration, particularly when compared with the increase in the level of sales per employee, could partly reflect a move to a less skilled workforce, or perhaps a greater proportion of part-time employees.

The directors' emoluments have trebled since before the privitisation, and have doubled since 19X2. It is not known whether the number of directors has increased, or whether this increase has been solely in order to bring their remuneration into line with that in the private sector in order to retain quality management. It is also not known whether they also hold share options which could be a further valuable benefit.

(iii) Customers, as consumers, are primarily concerned with the quality and consistency of supply and the price that they have to pay for it. Information is not available to assess the service quality performance over the period, but the price levels can be evaluated, given that the output of electricity appears to have increased by an average of 2½% per annum. Figures for alternate years are shown below.

	19X0	*19X2*	*19X4*	*19X6*
Turnover (£m)	760	850	920	995
Projected turnover (£m) taking into account solely the increase in demand (2½%pa)	760	798	839	881
Increase due to price (£m)		52	29	28
Average annual increase in price (%)		3.4	1.8	2.0
Average annual RPI increase (%)		2.5	1.5	1.4

Thus the component of the growth in turnover due to price has been rising at an increasing rate over the period and at a rate in excess of the rate of inflation. At first sight this might appear to be due to weak regulation giving a bad deal to consumers, but there could be two other factors at work, as follows.

(1) The company could be expanding into other unregulated areas which are accounting for the growth in turnover, for example developing its laboratory facilities into a commercial business.

(2) The increase in price could be needed to fund investment in improved service quality and reliability of supply. There is no information available on this area.

(c) (i) The figures above suggest that prices have risen above the rate of inflation, although it is not known whether some of this increase is due to expansion into unregulated businesses. If this is the case then the company could have been attempting to cooperate with the government's desire for low inflation. At the same time, the price of labour as calculated above has been kept very low with increases below the rate of inflation, although the same has not been true for the directors. The effect of this is to transfer value to the directors and the shareholders rather than to society at large.

(ii) The company has demonstrated a rapid rate of growth in both turnover and operating profit over the period. The amount of revenue accruing to the government in the form of corporation tax has almost doubled since 19X2 to £19m in 19X6. Capital investment has increased by 2.57 times compared with 19X2 to £90m in 19X6. This will not only benefit the industry, but also the wider economy through the multiplier effect. (It is assumed that the money has not been spent outside the UK.)

21 WORKING CAPITAL

In order to carry on a business successfully a company cannot just invest in capital projects and fixed assets. It must also invest in and exercise control over working capital: stocks, debtors and creditors. This working capital has an important bearing on a company's cash needs and cash flows, and therefore on its liquidity which is as important as its profitability.

Different companies will have different working capital needs depending on the nature of the company's business. The statement in the question that 'stronger and more profitable companies have a higher proportion of working capital' may well be true for a manufacturing company. A manufacturing company will need substantial levels of stocks and will probably have high levels of debtors and creditors as well. However, an equally profitable service company may have a much lower proportion of working capital because, although it may have debtors and some creditors, a service company is unlikely to have large stocks.

Even in manufacturing companies, a decision to use Just in Time techniques of production, if implemented successfully, would result in lower stocks, with smaller batches being produced and so smaller stocks of finished goods.

So a company need not necessarily have a high proportion of working capital in order to be profitable or strong. Conversely companies with high proportions of working capital are not necessarily profitable, well managed companies. It may be that in some companies the reason for high working capital is bad management. Stock control and credit control may be lax whilst not enough advantage is being taken of available trade credit. A much more profitable company may have lower levels of working capital due to an efficient stock-holding policy, tight credit and minimum cash holdings.

22 H FINANCE PLC

(a) Assuming that the historical data presented is a reasonable guide to what will happen in the future, we can calculate whether the factoring of the debts on the debtors' ledger of D Ltd would be worthwhile as follows. The 19Y0 figures are assumed below to be typical.

The cost of the finance provided by the factor is 5% of sales, since 80% and then a further 15% is remitted by the factor. This is equivalent to around 23% of debtors ($5 \div 0.22$) based on the 19Y0 year end debtors' figure. However, it should be borne in mind that 15% of the finance is only received when the amounts due are received by the finance company: this delay of course makes the finance less attractive than if 95% were received straight away.

In addition, there would be administration costs of $0.5\% \times 98.7\text{m} = £0.5$ million which amounts to considerably more than the amount of £80,000 saved in D Ltd's own administration costs.

There may be some saving through a reduction in bad debts, which in 19Y0 amounted to 0.6% of turnover (£0.6m). However there is against this a loss of contribution amounting to $18\% \times 10\% \times £98.7\text{m} \approx £1.8\text{m}$ as a result of the factor's aggressive collection procedures. This will outweigh any savings in the cost of bad debts.

Considering:

(i) the cost of the finance provided;
(ii) the higher administration costs; and
(iii) the loss in contribution from lost turnover;

it would appear that factoring is not justified on the basis of any of these three elements.

(b) The three main aspects of factoring are as follows.

(i) Administration of the client's invoicing, sales accounting and debt collection service.

(ii) Credit protection for the client's debts, whereby the factor takes over the risk of loss from bad debts and so 'insures' the client against such losses. This service is also referred to as 'debt underwriting' or the 'purchase of a client's debts'. The factor usually purchases these debts 'without recourse' to the client, which means that in the event that the client's debtors are unable to pay what they owe, the factor will not ask for his money back from the client.

(iii) Making payments to the client in advance of collecting the debts. This might be referred to as 'factor finance' because the factor is providing cash to the client against outstanding debts.

The benefits of factoring for a business customer include the following.

(i) The business can pay its suppliers promptly, and so can take advantage of any early payment discounts that are available.

(ii) Optimum stock levels can be maintained, because the business will have enough cash to pay for the stocks it needs.

(iii) Growth can be financed through sales rather than by injecting fresh external capital.

(iv) The business gets finance linked to its volume of sales. In contrast, overdraft limits tend to be determined by historical balance sheets.

(v) The managers of the business do not have to spend their time on the problems of slow-paying debtors.

(vi) The business does not incur the costs of running its own sales ledger department.

Factoring of sales invoicing leads to a reduction of debtors and therefore of assets employed in the business, accompanied by a reduction in profit as a result of the costs involved. Part of these 'costs' are generally reflected in the fact that less than 100% of the debt is paid to the company by the factor. The effect on the return on assets employed will depend upon the cost of factoring and the level of profits without factoring relative to assets employed.

Since they reduce assets, the funds advanced by the factor do not show up as borrowings in the balance sheet. The apparent gearing will therefore improve. Factoring is attractive to some companies as a method of avoiding borrowing limits or covenants being breached. It provides a means of financing debtors, which are otherwise unsuitable for secured lending because of their volatility.

The main disadvantage of factoring is that it is a relatively expensive form of finance compared to loan finance. Some businesses will also find it undesirable for customer relations if the administration of debt collection is passed to a third party.

23 HEADWATER PLC

Tutorial note. In part (a) it is helpful to tabulate a comparison of Headwater's ratios with the industry averages. These can then form the basis for a discussion of the profitability, liquidity and financial security of the company. Define clearly the way in which the ratios are calculated.

In part (c) you can discuss the ways in which Headwater could seek to remedy the deficiencies revealed by your earlier analysis. Take into account the effect of your suggestions on *all* the performance indicators since changes in one area can impact on reported performance in others.

(a) The performance and financial health of Headwater in relation to that of the industry sector as a whole can be evaluated by comparing its financial ratios with the industry averages, as follows.

Headwater plc	*Industry average*
Return on (long-term) capital employed	
Operating profit (PBIT): Equity + long-term debt	
£4.9m: (£12.4m + £2.2m) = 33.6%	24%
Return on equity	
Profit attributable to ordinary shareholders: Equity	
£3.1m: £12.4m = 25%	16%
Operating profit margin	
Operating profit : Sales	
£4.9m: £36.5m = 13.4%	11%
Current ratio	
Current assets: Current liabilities	
£10.1m: £9.0m = 1.12:1	1.6:1
Acid test	
Current assets excluding stock: Current liabilities	
£5.7m: £9.0m = 0.63:1	1.0:1
Gearing	
Debt: Equity	
(£2m + £2.2m): £12.4m = 33.9%	24%
Dividend cover	
Profit attributable to equity: Dividends	
£3.1m: £0.3m = 10.3 times	4.0
Interest cover	
Profit before interest and tax (PBIT): Interest	
£4.9m: £1.3m = 3.77 times	4.5

These ratios can be used to evaluate performance in terms of profitability, liquidity and financial security.

Profitability

Headwater's return on capital employed, return on equity and operating profit margin are all significantly above the industry averages. Although the first two measures could be inflated due to assets being shown at low book values, the profit margin indicates that Headwater is managing to make good profits, which could be due to successful marketing, a low cost base or to its occupation of a particularly profitable niche in the market.

Liquidity

Both the current and the quick (acid test) ratios are well below the industry averages. This suggests that Headwater is either short of liquid resources or is managing its working capital poorly. Three key working capital ratios are:

Debtor days:	365 × 4.7/36.5	=	47 days
Stock turnover:	365 × 4.4/31.6	=	51 days
Payment period:	365 × 7.0/31.6	=	81 days

Although the industry averages are not known, these ratios appear to be very good by general standards. It therefore appears that Headwater has become under-capitalised, perhaps through the use of working capital to finance growth.

Financial security

Gearing is high in comparison with the rest of the industry, and 48% of the debt is in the form of overdraft which is generally repayable on demand. This is therefore a risky form of debt to use in large amounts. The debenture is repayable in two years and will need to be refinanced since Headwater cannot redeem it out of existing resources. Interest cover is also poor, and this together with the poor liquidity probably account for the low payout ratio (the inverse of the dividend cover).

In summary, profit performance is strong, but there are significant weaknesses in both the liquidity and the financial structure. These problems need to be addressed if Headwater is to be able to maintain its record of strong and consistent growth.

(b) A company such as Headwater may seek a stock market listing for the following reasons.

(i) To allow access to a wider pool of finance: companies that are growing fast may need to raise larger sums than is possible privately. Obtaining a listing widens the potential number of equity investors, and may also result in an improved credit rating, thus reducing the cost of additional debt finance.

(ii) To improve the marketability of the shares: shares that are traded on the stock market can be bought and sold in relatively small quantities at any time. This means that it is easier for existing investors to realise a part of their holding.

(iii) To allow capital to be transferred to other ventures: founder owners may wish to liquidate the major part of their holding either for personal reasons or for investment in other new business opportunities.

(iv) To improve the company image: quoted companies are commonly believed to be more financially stable, and this may improve the image of the company with its customers and suppliers, allowing it to gain additional business and to improve its buying power.

(v) Growth by acquisition is easier: a listed company is in a better position to make a paper offer for a target company than an unlisted one.

(c) Restructuring its balance sheet prior to flotation will help to make Headwater appear a sounder prospect to potential investors who know little about its past performance. Methods available include the following.

Disposal of surplus assets. This will improve both gearing and liquidity.

Fixed asset revaluation. Land and buildings may well be shown in the accounts at values that are significantly below the current market valuation. Adjustment to market values will improve the gearing ratio and the value of shareholders' funds, although the effect of this will be to depress the reported return on capital employed and return on equity. However, since these are currently well above industry averages this should not present too much of a problem.

Liquidity improvement. Although there does not appear to be much scope for tightening the control of working capital, Headwater may be able to improve its cash flow by other means, for example by reducing overheads and delaying the purchase of additional fixed assets.

Sale and leaseback. If Headwater owns valuable freehold premises it may be able to release cash by selling them and exchanging the freehold for an operating lease. This would improve both the liquidity position and the reported return on capital employed although the gearing would be little affected.

Elimination of non-voting 'A' shares. These are not permitted by the Stock Exchange for companies newly entering the market.

Share split. On the basis of the industry average P/E of 10, the shares would be priced at £11.48 (= 10 × 3.1m/(1.8m + 0.9m)). A highly priced new issue is likely to deter potential small investors. This problem could be overcome by reducing the nominal value of the shares by means of a share split.

(d) Following the flotation Headwater is likely to come under pressure to improve the payout ratio and dividend performance of the shares. If it wishes to maintain a good share price and the ability to raise further finance in the future then it would be well advised to consider this seriously. It could also work towards lowering the gearing ratio, perhaps by using a part of the issue proceeds to redeem some or all of the debentures. However this should not appear to be the prime reason for the float or the attractiveness of the issue will be diminished.

24 PRIMULA PLC

Tutorial note. In part (a) the approach is to calculate the amount of additional working and fixed capital required, and then to compare this with the level of internally generated funds in order to establish the external financing requirement. You will need to make an assumption about the operating margin for 19X6.

In part (b) take into account the size and status of the company (ie listed) as well as the funds required when deciding on the appropriate financing alternatives.

(a) The first step is to calculate Primula's total additional financing requirement.

	£m
Existing working capital:	
Current assets	10.6
Creditors	(5.8)
	4.8
Additional working capital (+25%)	1.2
Additional fixed capital	12.0
Total	13.2

This can be met in part from internal sources as follows. It is assumed that the margin before depreciation will remain unchanged. The profit in 19X5 before depreciation was £6m + £1.5m = £7.5m.

	£m
19X6 profit before depreciation (£7.5m × 125%)	9.38
Less outflows:	
Interest (£6m × 11%)	(0.66)
Corporation tax (19X5)	(1.8)
Dividends (£3.84m × 1.08)	(4.15)
Net additional internal funds generated	2.77

Internally generated funds are therefore inadequate to finance the costs of expansion, there being a shortfall of £10.43m (£13.2m – £2.77m) which will have to be raised externally.

(b) Financing options include the following.

(i) *Leasing capital equipment*

Some of the new capital equipment could be acquired using some form of leasing agreement. This would have the added benefits that rental payments qualify for tax relief, and that the cost of the assets is spread more evenly over their useful life. Alternatively Primula could consider a sale and leaseback agreement on some of the assets that it already owns.

(ii) *Raising additional debt*

Since the gearing level at present is low at 21.8% (£6m/£27.5m) and the interest cover is good at 9.1 times (£6m/£0.66m), Primula could take on significant amounts of additional debt without too much risk. This could be in the form of a debenture or medium-term bank loan. It is likely that the rate of interest would have to be higher than that on the existing debt.

(iii) *Venture capital*

Primula is of a sufficient size and with growth prospects that should make it appropriate for some form of development capital from an organisation such as 3i. However, the venture capital company is likely to require an equity stake and a seat on the board in return for its investment and the directors must therefore accept that there is likely to be some loss of control.

(iv) *Raising additional equity*

Since Primula is already listed it has access to a wide range of investors. Given the size of the sum required this should be possible to attain by means of a rights issue at a discount to the current market price of the shares. Although the effect of this would be to reduce EPS and hence the market price, the wealth of the ordinary shareholders would be unaffected providing that the issue was well subscribed.

Other methods include:

(i) regional assistance, if available;
(ii) mortgage on property.

25 CAPITAL GEARING

(a) (i) $\frac{\text{Book value of prior charge capital}}{\text{Book value of equity}}$

Book value of prior charge capital:

	£
Bank overdraft	15,000,000
Preference shares	5,000,000
5% Convertible debentures	5,000,000
12% Irredeemable debentures	10,000,000
Total	35,000,000

Book value of equity:

	£
Ordinary share capital	10,000,000
Retained profits	10,000,000
Total	20,000,000

Gearing ratio = 35/20 × 100% = 175%

(ii) $\frac{\text{Prior charge capital}}{\text{Total capital employed}}$ (Book values)

Book value of prior charge capital (from (i)) = £35,000,000

Total capital employed = £40,000,000

Gearing ratio = 35/40 × 100% = 87.5%

(iii) $\frac{\text{Market value of prior charge capital}}{\text{Market value of equity}}$

It is assumed that the convertible debentures can be redeemed at any time. If this is the case, then they will be valued assuming conversion has taken place since with the share price at 200p, this would give the maximum return to a holder of the convertibles, all other things being equal.

Since the rate of return required by the market is known (10%), it is possible to calculate the market value of the loan stock by using the expression:

MV = D/i

where: MV = Market value of stock
D = Actual rate of return
i = Required rate of return

	£
Market value of prior charge capital:	
Bank overdraft	15,000,000
Preference shares (5m × 8/10)	4,000,000
5% Convertible debentures (at 200p)	10,000,000
12% Irredeemable debentures (10m × 12/10)	12,000,000
Total	41,000,000
Market value of equity:	
Ordinary share capital (at 200p)	40,000,000
Retained profits	10,000,000
Total	50,000,000

Gearing ratio = 41/50 × 100% = 82%

(b) (i) *Treatment of preference shares*. These are normally included as part of the prior charge capital since they carry a fixed percentage return which is payable before any dividend is paid to the ordinary shareholders. However, in some ways they are more similar to equity than to prior charge capital since the preference dividend can only be paid if sufficient distributable profits are available, although with cumulative preference shares the right to an unpaid dividend is carried forward to later years. Also, a preference dividend, unlike loan interest, is not allowable for corporation tax. Thus if there is a high proportion of preference shares, the company will appear to be highly geared although it may have more potential to raise further debt than if the prior charge capital consisted of other forms of loan stock.

(ii) *Convertible debentures.* These are generally included with the prior charge capital in the gearing ratio. However, if conversion is imminent, whether due to the date or to the prevailing market price of the shares, a case may be made for including the convertibles with the equity since they are more similar to equity capital than to debt.

(iii) *Bank overdraft.* A case could be made for excluding the bank overdraft from the prior charge capital on the grounds that it is only a short term loan and therefore not part of the capital structure of the firm. However, in practice, a company will often maintain an overdraft as part of its financing policy, and this is also often secured on the assets of the firm. In this situation it seems appropriate to include the overdraft as part of the prior charge capital in the capital gearing calculation.

(iv) *Trade creditors.* Prior charge capital is capital which has a right to payment of interest before there can be any payment to the ordinary shareholders and which also has a prior claim on the assets in the event of a winding up. Although the trade creditors qualify in the latter respect, they are not entitled to interest payments and are a short term form of finance. Neither are they secured on the assets of the company. On these grounds they are therefore excluded from the capital gearing calculation.

(v) *Book or market values.* The advantage of a gearing ratio based on market values is that potential investors in a firm are able to judge the further debt capacity of the firm more clearly than by looking at book values. A firm which has a large asset base may have poor profit and dividend performance, giving rise to a higher gearing ratio when calculated from market values, and it is also likely to find it harder to raise further debt. However, the use of market values ignores the value of the assets which may be used as security for future loans. It can also be argued that the use of a gearing ratio based on book values relates more directly to the last-resort security available to fixed interest lenders.

26 PROJECT APPRAISAL

(a) (i) Depreciation must first be added back to the annual profit figures, to arrive at the annual cash flows.

$$\text{Depreciation} = \frac{\text{Initial investment £46,000 – scrap value £4,000}}{\text{4 years}}$$

$$= \text{£10,500}$$

Adding £10,500 per annum to the profit figures produces the cash flows for each proposal.

	Proposal A		*Proposal B*	
Year	*Annual cash flow*	*Cumulative cash flow*	*Annual cash flow*	*Cumulative cash flow*
	£	£	£	£
0	(46,000)	(46,000)	(46,000)	(46,000)
1	17,000	(29,000)	15,000	31,000
2	14,000	(15,000)	13,000	(18,000)
3	24,000	9,000	15,000	(3,000)
4	9,000	18,000	25,000	22,000
4	4,000	22,000	4,000	26,000

Proposal A / *Proposal B*

(1) Payback period =

$$2 + \left(\frac{15,000}{24,000} \times 1 \text{ year}\right)$$

= 2.6 years

Payback period =

$$3 + \left(\frac{3,000}{25,000} \times 1 \text{ year}\right)$$

= 3.1 years

(2) The average rate of return is calculated using the accounting profits given in the question.

Proposal A Average profit $= \dfrac{£(6,500 + 3,500 + 13,500 - 1,500)}{4}$

$= \dfrac{£22,000}{4}$

$= £5,500$

Accounting rate of return on initial investment $= \dfrac{£5,500}{£46,000} \times 100\%$

$= 12.0\%$

Proposal B Average profit $= \dfrac{£(4,500 + 2,500 + 4,500 - 14,500)}{4}$

$= \dfrac{£26,000}{4}$

$= £6,500$

Accounting rate of return on initial investment $= \dfrac{£6,500}{£46,000} \times 100\%$

$= 14.1\%$

(ii) Two advantages of each of the methods of appraisal can be selected from the following.

Payback period

(1) It is simple to calculate.
(2) It preserves liquidity by preferring early cash flows.
(3) It uses cash flows instead of more arbitrary accounting profits.
(4) It reduces risk by preferring early cash flows.

Average rate of return

(1) It uses readily available accounting profits.

(2) It is understood by non-financial managers.

(3) It is a measure used by external analysts which should therefore be monitored by the company.

(b) A general interpretation might be as follows.

(i) *Objectives.* The company does not have any stated objectives. In view of the probable high (100%) shareholding by the family, it may be that a high level of liquidity is required to meet future dividend expectations. There is a clear necessity to agree stated objectives with regard to earnings and dividend payments.

(ii)

Strengths	*Weaknesses*
High liquidity. A wide range of products and markets.	Low profits due to poor returns from investments and possibly high unit costs, low sales or low prices. Family business, therefore possibly weak management. Heavy reliance on one customer. Poor growth due to limited markets or poor R & D.
Threats Unknown future for the market for aluminium products.	*Opportunities* Investment in stocks and shares. Purchase of a small foundry. Product-market diversification. Major customer involved in the do-it-yourself industry, which still has buoyant markets.

(iii) *Strengths*. The high liquidity is the clearest source of strength. Although the company offers a wide range of products to a variety of customers, growth is poor.

(iv) *Weaknesses*. Low growth and profitability in current markets and with current products should be a matter of some concern. The reasons for poor performance might range from high variable costs, low output (therefore high unit fixed costs), sluggish demand, weak marketing, high prices, inadequate R & D, ageing machinery and out-of-date technology, poor management, inefficient purchasing and so on. Weaknesses need to be identified more specifically.

(v) *Threats*. None are known, and the future for the aluminium products market may be reasonable if the managing director is correct in his assessment that the purchase of a new foundry would be a viable proposition.

(vi) *Opportunities*

(1) *Stocks and shares*. The return from existing stocks and shares has been poor, which might be the result of poor investment management which should be dealt with. There should be a prospect of improvement in the future, especially if professional advice is taken to sell parts of the existing portfolio and to re-invest in securities offering a higher return or better capital growth. If high liquidity remains a top priority, this strategy has clear merits.

(2) *Purchase of an aluminium foundry*. This policy of market penetration through the acquisition of a competitor offers several advantages:

- increased market share (and new customers);
- perhaps improved technology;
- joint fixed costs of administration and marketing, therefore lower unit costs of output;
- rationalisation of production and distribution;
- possibly, management expertise will be acquired.

The purchase consideration might be for cash only, although it might be possible to obtain agreement to a share exchange deal, or a shares plus cash deal. Because the company is a private company, a share exchange arrangement is unlikely to be attractive (and the poor profit record of the company makes a launch on to the AIM an unlikely prospect).

Although the company already has knowledge of the aluminium industry, a close investigation of the past performance and history (and the future prospects) of the new foundry would be required.

(3) *Diversification into new products and markets*. This would be a difficult step into the unknown, especially in view of the lack of management experience in the company. It is not recommended strategy, unless clear opportunities for profits and growth present themselves since the company has no obvious strengths to exploit apart from its cash. However, there is a possibility of vertical integration,

by attempting the acquisition of the do-it-yourself tools manufacturer. Leisure industries are prospective growth markets and a closer investigation of this possibility may be worthwhile.

(vii) *Conclusion.* No recommendation is possible, except that a strategic planning exercise should be carried out to recommend a long-term strategy. It is perhaps significant that in a comparison of the three opportunities mentioned the following conclusions can be drawn.

(1) The continued investment in stocks and shares promises high liquidity and returns in the long and short term.

(2) The acquisition of the aluminium foundry offers the prospect of a timescale for achieving profits which might be relatively short.

(3) Diversification offers no clear prospects, and the timescale required to earn profits might be long. Carefully chosen acquisitions, however, might yield the greatest long-term profits.

27 KNUCKLE DOWN LTD

(a) (i) *Project A*

Year	*Cash flow*	*Discount factor*	*Present value*
	£	12%	£
0	(29,000)	1.000	(29,000)
1	8,000	0.893	7,144
2	12,000	0.797	9,566
3	10,000	0.712	7,120
4	11,000	0.636	6,996
		Net present value	1,826

(ii) *Project B*

Year	*Equipment*	*Working capital*	*Cash profit*	*Net cash flow*	*Discount factor*	*Present value*
	£	£	£	£	12%	£
0	(44,000)	(20,000)		(64,000)	1.000	(64,000)
1			19,000	19,000	0.893	16,967
2			24,000	24,000	0.797	19,128
3	5,000	20,000	10,000	35,000	0.712	24,920
					Net present value	(2,985)

(iii) *Project C*

Year	*Equipment*	*Working capital*	*Cash profit*	*Net cash flow*	*Discount factor*	*Present value*
	£	£	£	£	12%	£
0	(50,000)	(15,000)		(65,000)	1.000	(65,000)
1		(6,000)		(6,000)	0.893	(5,358)
1-5			18,000	18,000	3.605	64,890
5		21,000		21,000	0.567	11,907
					Net present value	6,439

(iv) *Project D*

Year	*Cash flow*	*Discount factor*	*Present value*
	£	12%	£
0	(20,000)	1.000	(20,000)
1	(20,000)	0.893	(17,860)
2	15,000	0.797	11,958
3	12,000	0.712	8,544
4-8	8,000	2.566	20,528
		Net present value	3,170

Discount factor at 12%, years 1 to 8	4.968
Less discount factor at 12%, years 1 to 3	2.402
Discount factor at 12%, years 4 to 8	2.566

(v) *Project E*

The cumulative discount factor for a perpetuity at 15% is 1/0.15 = 6.667.

Year	*Cash flow*	*Discount factor*	*Present value*
	£	15%	£
0	(32,000)	1.000	(32,000)
1-∞	4,500	6.667	30,000
		Net present value	(2,000)

(vi) *Project F*

		£
1	Present value (at 15%) of £3,000 a year from year 1 in perpetuity	20,000
	Less present value of £3,000 a year for years 1 to 10 (× 5.019)	15,057
	Present value of £3,000 a year from year 11 in perpetuity	4,943
2	Discount factor at 15%, years 1 to 10	5.019
	Less discount factor at 15%, years 1 to 5	3.352
	Discount factor at 15%, years 6 to 10	1.667

3

Year	*Net cash flow*	*Discount factor*	*Present value*
	£	15%	£
0	(20,000)	1.000	(20,000)
1-5	5,000	3.352	16,760
6-10	4,000	1.667	6,668
11-∞	3,000	See above	4,943
		Net present value	8,371

(vii) Projects A, C, D and F have positive net present values and should be undertaken. Projects B and E should not be undertaken.

(b) (i) The IRR of project A is above 12% (where the NPV is £1,826). We will calculate the NPV at 15%.

Year	*Cash flow*	*Discount factor*	*Present value*
	£	15%	£
0	(29,000)	1.000	(29,000)
1	8,000	0.870	6,960
2	12,000	0.756	9,072
3	10,000	0.658	6,580
4	11,000	0.572	6,292
		Net present value	(96)

The IRR is between 12% and 15%. By interpolation, we can estimate the IRR as about

$$12\% + \left[\frac{1,826}{(1,826 - -96)} \times (15 - 12)\right]\%$$

$= 14.85\%$

(ii) The IRR of project C is above 12%, where the NPV is £6,439. Try 20%.

Year	*Net cash flow*	*Discount factor*	*Present value*
	£	20%	£
0	(65,000)	1.000	(65,000)
1	(6,000)	0.833	(4,998)
1-5	18,000	2.991	53,838
5	21,000	0.402	8,442
		Net present value	(7,718)

The IRR is approximately $12\% + \left[\frac{6,439}{(6,439 - -7,718)} \times (20 - 12)\right]\% = 15.6\%$

(iii) The IRR, r, of project E is found as follows.

PV of cost = PV of benefits

$$(32{,}000) = \frac{4{,}500}{r}$$

$$r = \frac{4{,}500}{32{,}000} = 0.140625$$

IRR = 14.0625%.

28 DINARD

(a) The real rate of return is the rate of return which an investment would show in the absence of inflation. For example, if a company invests £100, inflation is 0%, and the investment at the end of the year is worth £110, then the real rate of return is 10%.

In reality however, there is likely to be an element of inflation in the returns due to the change in the purchasing power of money over the period. In the example above, if inflation was running at 5%, then to show a real rate of return of 10%, the investment would need to be worth £115.50 at the end of the year. In this case the money rate of return is 15.5% which is made up of the real return of 10% and inflation at 5%.

The relationship between the nominal ('money') rate of return and the real rate of return can be expressed as follows:

(1 + nominal rate) = (1 + real rate) × (1 + inflation rate)

The rate to be used in discounting cash flows for capital project appraisal will depend on the way in which the expected cash flows are calculated. If the cash flows are expressed in terms of the actual number of pounds that will be received or paid on the various future dates, then the nominal rate must be used. If however they are expressed in terms of the value of the pound at year 0, then the real rate must be used.

(b) *Workings*

	Year 1	*Year 2*	*Year 3*	*Year 4*
Sales volume	25,000	25,000	25,000	25,000
Unit price (£)	80	84	88	93
Variable material cost (£)	8.00	8.32	8.65	9.00
Variable labour cost (£)	12.00	13.20	14.52	15.97
Variable overhead (£)	12.00	12.48	12.98	13.50

Notes

(i) Development costs of £480,000 are sunk costs and will be excluded from the calculations.

(ii) Depreciation does not involve any movement of cash and will be excluded from the fixed overheads (£600,000 in year 1).

(iii) All figures have been adjusted for the appropriate rate of inflation. The investment will therefore be evaluated using the WACC expressed as a nominal rate of 15%.

Evaluation of investment
(All figures £'000)

	Year 0	*Year 1*	*Year 2*	*Year 3*	*Year 4*
Capital outlay	(2,400)				
Sales		2,000	2,100	2,205	2,315
Direct costs					
Materials		(200)	(208)	(216)	(225)
Labour		(300)	(330)	(363)	(399)
Overhead		(300)	(312)	(324)	(337)
Fixed overheads		(200)	(210)	(221)	(232)
Gross cash flow	(2,400)	1,000	1,040	1,081	1,122
Discount at 15%	1.000	0.870	0.756	0.658	0.572
Present value	(2,400)	870	786	711	642
Cumulative PV	(2,400)	(1,530)	(744)	(33)	608

The investment yields a net present value at the end of four years of £608,000. In the absence of other factors such as a capital rationing situation, production of the Rance should be undertaken.

29 MUGGINS PLC

Certainty-equivalent cash flows

	Year 1	*Year 2*	*Year 3*	*Year 4*
	£'000	£'000	£'000	£'000
Sales (W1)	1,125	1,800	1,575	1,425
Material X (W2)	50	230	248	280
Other variable costs (W3)	517	1,100	1,184	1,340
Management salaries (W4)	67	79	85	92
Rental: opportunity cost	135	135	135	135
Other overheads (× 1.1, 1.3, 1.4, 1.5)	66	78	84	90
	835	1,622	1,736	1,937
Sales less cash costs	290	178	(161)	(512)
Discount factor at 14%	0.877	0.769	0.675	0.599
Present value	254	137	(109)	(303)

The net present value is -£21,000, so the project is not acceptable.

Workings

1 *Sales*
Year 1 10,000 × £125 × 0.9
Year 2 18,000 × £125 × 0.8
Year 3 18,000 × £125 × 0.7
Year 4 19,000 × £125 × 0.6

2 *Material X*
Year 1 £50,000 opportunity cost
Year 2 18,000 × 6 × £1.64 × 1.3
Year 3 18,000 × 6 × £1.64 × 1.4
Year 4 19,000 × 6 × £1.64 × 1.5

3 *Other variable costs*
Per unit: £30 + (3 × £4.20) + £4.40 = £47
Year 1 10,000 × £47 × 1.1
Year 2 18,000 × £47 × 1.3
Year 3 18,000 × £47 × 1.4
Year 4 19,000 × £47 × 1.5

4 *Management salaries* Year 1 £34,000 + £27,000 = £61,000 x 1.1
Year 2 £61,000 × 1.3
Year 3 £61,000 × 1.4
Year 4 £61,000 × 1.5

5 Apportioned costs are irrelevant because they are not incremental cash flows.

30 BANDEN LTD

(a) The profitability index will be calculated as the ratio of the PV of net cash inflows to the year 0 capital outlay.

	Year	*Cash flow* £	*Discount factor* 12%	*Present value* £	*Profitability index*
Project A	1-5	70,000	3.605	252,350	6,350
	0	(246,000)	1.000	(246,000)	246,000
				NPV = 6,350	= 0.026
Project B	1	75,000	0.893	66,975	
	2	87,000	0.797	69,339	
	3	64,000	0.712	45,568	
				181,882	1,882
	0	(180,000)	1.000	(180,000)	180,000
				NPV = 1,882	= 0.010
Project C	1	48,000	0.893	42,864	
	2	48,000	0.797	38,256	
	3	63,000	0.712	44,856	
	4	73,000	0.636	46,428	
				172,404	(2,596)
	0	(175,000)	1.000	(175,000)	175,000
				NPV = (2,596)	= (0.015)
Project D	1-4	62,000	3.037	188,294	8,294
	0	(180,000)	1.000	(180,000)	180,000
				NPV = 8,294	= 0.046
Project E	1	40,000	0.893	35,720	
	2	50,000	0.797	39,850	
	3	60,000	0.712	42,720	
	4	70,000	0.636	44,520	
	5	40,000	0.567	22,680	
				185,490	5,490
	0	(180,000)	1.000	(180,000)	180,000
				NPV = 5,490	= 0.031
Project F	1	35,000	0.893	31,255	
	2	82,000	0.797	65,354	
	3	82,000	0.712	58,384	
				154,993	4,993
	0	(150,000)	1.000	(150,000)	150,000
				NPV = 4,993	= 0.033

Ranking	*NPV*	*Profitability index*
1st	D	D
2nd	A	F
3rd	E	E
4th	F	A
5th	B	B
6th	C	C

The rankings differ because the project's capital outlays differ. NPV shows the absolute benefit from a project, while profitability index scales that benefit according to the project's size.

(b) Project C comes sixth and last in the ranking according to both NPV and profitability index. It has a negative NPV and should not be undertaken.

Banden Ltd cannot afford to undertake more than three projects, given the maximum available capital of £620,000. It should not undertake project C, and it cannot undertake A and E simultaneously. The various feasible options are as follows.

Projects	*Capital outlay in total*	*NPV in total*
D, F, E	£510,000	£18,777
D, F, A	£576,000	£19,637
D, F, B	£510,000	£15,169
D, E, B	£540,000	£15,666
D, A, B	£606,000	£16,526
F, A, B	£576,000	£13,225
F, E, B	£510,000	£12,365

Banden Ltd should not invest any funds in the money markets, because the return would only be 9% pa and the cost of capital for Banden is higher, at 12% pa.

It is assumed that the company does not have to use more funds than it needs to, and so there will not be any surplus funds which have to be invested somewhere.

Recommendation. The company should use £576,000 and invest in projects D, F and A.

(c) When there is capital rationing, there is not enough capital to invest in all the projects which have a positive NPV, when their NPVs are calculated by discounting the estimated cash flows at the company's cost of capital. The financial director is correct in theory to say that the company's cost of capital is inappropriate. The marginal opportunity cost of capital, which will be higher than the company's cost of capital, would be more appropriate for calculating project NPVs and deciding which projects would yield the best returns, given the shortage of capital.

However, the marginal cost of capital cannot be calculated easily, and a practical way of making decisions in a capital rationing situation is to calculate the NPV of each project using the company's normal cost of capital, and then to rank the projects in order of desirability, as in parts (a) and (b) of this solution.

(d) Linear programming has the advantages of helping management:

(i) to identify the optimal capital expenditure programme in a capital rationing situation;

(ii) to establish the opportunity cost of capital, from the shadow price for capital in the solution to the linear programming problem.

Once the model has been set up, it can be used for sensitivity tests, for example by varying the estimated cash flows of any projects.

Linear programming has the very serious drawback, however, that projects are assumed to be divisible, and so the optimal solution obtained from a model might be to undertake fractions of one or more projects. This is often unrealistic and impractical.

A second disadvantage of linear programming is that although sensitivity analysis is possible, the data used in the model are initially treated as being certain and the constraints as fixed. In reality, neither of these is the case. For example, when capital is a constraint, management will often be able to raise some extra capital from one source or other.

For Banden Ltd, linear programming seems unnecessarily complex, since there are only seven sensible combinations of projects. A simpler mathematical approach, as illustrated in part (b) of this solution, would seem to be suitable for making the investment decision.

31 FLOCKS LTD

(a) *Workings*

(i) *Capital allowances*

Year		Machine X allowance	Year		Machine Y allowance
		£			£
1	(25% of £63,000)	15,750	1	(25% of £110,000)	27,500
2	(75% of £15,750)	11,813	2	(75% of £27,500)	20,625
3	(75% of £11,813)	8,859	3	(75% of £20,625)	15,469
		36,422	4	(75% of £15,469)	11,602
4	(£63,000 - £36,422)	26,578	5	(75% of £11,602)	8,702
					83,898
			6	(£110,000 - £83,898)	26,102

(ii) *Taxable profits and tax liabilities*

Machine X

Year	Cash profits	Allowance	Taxable profits	Tax at 31% (one year later)
	£	£	£	£
1	25,900	15,750	10,150	3,147
2	28,800	11,813	16,987	5,266
3	30,500	8,859	21,641	6,709
4	29,500	26,578	2,922	906

Machine Y

Year	Cash profits	Allowance	Taxable profits	Tax at 31% (one year later)
	£	£	£	£
1	40,300	27,500	12,800	3,968
2	32,900	20,625	12,275	3,805
3	32,000	15,469	16,531	5,125
4	32,700	11,602	21,098	6,540
5	48,500	8,702	39,798	12,337
6	44,200	26,102	18,098	5,610

NPV and payback calculations

Machine X

Year	Machine cost	Working capital	Cash profits	Tax	Net cash flow	Discount factor	Present value	Cumulative cash flow
	£	£	£	£	£	13%	£	£
0	(63,000)	(12,500)			(75,500)	1.000	(75,500)	(75,500)
1			25,900		25,900	0.885	22,922	(49,600)
2			28,800	(3,147)	25,653	0.783	20,086	(23,947)
3			30,500	(5,266)	25,234	0.693	17,487	1,287
4		12,500	29,500	(6,709)	35,291	0.613	21,633	
5				(906)	(906)	0.543	(492)	
						NPV =	6,136	

The NPV for machine X is + £6,136, and the payback period is about three years.

Machine Y

Year	Machine cost	Working capital	Cash profits	Tax	Net cash flow	Discount factor	Present value	Cumulative cash flow
	£	£	£	£	£	15%	£	£
0	(110,000)	(12,500)			(122,500)	1.000	(122,500)	(122,500)
1			40,300		40,300	0.870	35,061	(82,200)
2			32,900	(3,968)	28,932	0.756	21,873	(53,268)
3			32,000	(3,805)	28,195	0.658	18,552	(25,073)
4			32,700	(5,125)	27,575	0.572	15,773	2,502
5			48,500	(6,540)	41,960	0.497	20,854	
6		12,500	44,200	(12,337)	44,393	0.432	19,178	
7				(5,610)	(5,610)	0.376	(2,109)	
						NPV =	6,682	

The NPV for machine Y is + £6,682 and the payback period is about four years.

Machine X would appear to be the preferable option.

(b) The financing decision will be appraised by discounting the relevant cash flows at the after-tax cost of borrowing, which is 10% × 69% = 6.9%, say 7%.

(i) *Purchase option*

Year	*Item*	*Cash flow*	*Discount factor*	*Present value*
		£	7%	£
0	Cost of machine	(63,000)	1.000	(63,000)
	Tax saved from capital allowances			
2	31% × £15,750	4,827	0.873	4,214
3	31% × £11,813	3,662	0.816	2,988
4	31% × £8,859	2,746	0.763	2,095
5	31% × £26,578	8,239	0.713	5,875
				(47,828)

(ii) *Leasing option*

Years	*Item*	*Cash flow*	*Discount factor*	*Present value*
		£	7%	£
1 - 4	Lease costs	(20,000)	3.387	(67,740)
2 - 5	Tax savings on lease costs (× 31%)	6,200	3.165	19,623
				(48,117)

The purchase option is marginally cheaper, using a cost of capital based on the after-tax cost of borrowing.

On the assumption that investors would regard borrowing and leasing as equally risky finance options, the purchase option is recommended.

Lecturers' question bank

1 FLEXIBLE BUDGETS

Bearing in mind the wide discrepancies that could occur when comparisons of actual results are made with a fixed budget, the use of a flexible budget can be recommended. Describe the factors that should be taken into account at the planning stage of flexible budgets and also why they are an essential part of budgetary control.

2 JOBBING ENGINEERING COMPANY (20 marks) *36 mins*

You have just taken up the position as the first full-time accountant for a jobbing engineering company. Previously the accounting work had been undertaken by the company's auditors who had produced the following summarised profit and loss statement for the financial year which ended on 31 March of this year.

	£	£	£
Sales			2,400,000
Direct material		1,000,000	
Direct labour - Grinding Department	200,000		
Direct labour - Finishing Department	260,000		
		460,000	
Production overhead - Grinding	175,000		
Production overhead - Finishing	208,000		
		383,000	
Administration costs		118,500	
Selling costs		192,000	
			2,153,500
Net profit			246,500

The sales manager is currently negotiating a price for an enquiry for a job which has been allocated number 878 and he has been given the following information by his staff:

Preferred price to obtain a return of $16^2/3$% on selling price	£22,656
Lowest acceptable price	£18,880

These prices have been based on the following estimated costs for proposed job 878.

	£	£
Direct material		9,000
Direct labour - Grinding department: 400 hours @ £5	2,000	
Direct labour - Finishing department: 300 hours @ £6	1,800	
		3,800
		12,800
Add 47.5% to cover all other costs		6,080
Total cost		18,880

The sales manager seeks your advice about the validity of the method he is using to quote for Job 878.

The company is currently busy with a fairly full order book but the Confederation of British Industry has forecast that a recession is imminent for the engineering industry.

Required

As the accountant:

(a) criticise the method adopted for estimating the costs which are used as the basis for quoting prices for jobs; (6 marks)

(b) suggest a better method of estimating job costs and calculate a revised job cost and price, based on the information available, to give to the sales manager; (6 marks)

(c) suggest how you would propose to improve the accounting information to assist with controlling costs and providing information for pricing purposes. (8 marks)

3 THE INTERRELATIONSHIP OF VARIANCES (5 marks) *9 mins*

To what extent may standard costing variances be interrelated?

4 ROUNDABOUT LTD

Roundabout Ltd sells three products, P, Q and R. It operates a standard marginal costing system, and budgeted and actual results for 19X9 were as follows.

	Standard sales price per unit	*Standard marginal cost per unit*	*Budgeted sales*	*Actual sales price per unit*	*Actual marginal cost per unit*	*Actual sales*
	£	£	Units	£	£	Units
P	10	6	4,000	11	6	4,200
Q	6	3	10,000	5	3	9,000
R	20	15	5,000	20	15	5,200

The company's management believes that they can influence the sales mix of P, Q and R through advertising and sales promotion.

Required

Reconcile the budgeted and actual contribution in 19X9, by means of a sales price, sales mix and sales quantity variance, using the units method for calculating the mix variance.

Prove that the mix and quantity variances add up to the total sales volume (contribution) variance.

5 PROCESS COSTING (20 marks) *36 mins*

Process costing, unlike individual job costing, contract costing and batch costing is not specifically related to individual items, but to the volume of 'throughput' during a particular period of time. Define process costing and show how you would account for incomplete production, process losses and joint accounts.

6 PRODUCTION SHORTFALL (20 marks) *36 mins*

A company is preparing its production budget for the year ahead. Two of its processes are concerned with the manufacture of three components which are used in several of the company's products. Capacity (machine hours) in each of these two processes is limited to 2,000 hours.

Production costs are as follows.

			Component	
		X	*Y*	*Z*
		£/unit	£/unit	£/unit
Direct materials		15.00	18.50	4.50
Direct labour		12.00	12.50	8.00
Variable overhead		6.00	6.25	4.00
Fixed overhead -	Process M	6.00	6.00	4.50
	Process N	10.50	10.50	3.50
		49.50	53.75	24.50

Requirements for components X, Y and Z for the following year are as follows.

Component X	300 units
Component Y	300 units
Component Z	450 units

Fixed overhead is absorbed on the basis of machine hours at the following rates.

Process M	£3.00 per hour
Process N	£3.50 per hour

Components X and Z could be obtained from an outside supplier at the following prices.

Component X	£44.00 per unit
Component Z	£23.00 per unit

Required

(a) Demonstrate that insufficient capacity is available to produce the requirements for components X, Y and Z in the year ahead, and calculate the extent of the shortfall. (6 marks)

(b) Determine the requirements for bought-in components in order to satisfy the demand for components at minimum cost. (7 marks)

(c) Consider briefly any other factors which may be relevant to decisions regarding these components in the longer term. (7 marks)

7 **SCARCE RESOURCES**

Scarce resources restrict a firm's growth at a particular point of time, which results in management having to take limiting factor decisions in order to achieve maximisation of profit. Examine the various factors that must be taken into account when considering such decisions.

8 **FINANCIAL INTERMEDIATION**

Explain in detail the various functions performed by financial intermediaries in the financial markets.

9 **SUPPLY SIDE (20 marks)** *36 mins*

What policies might a government adopt when attempting to improve the 'supply side' of an economy?

10 **THE TREASURY FUNCTION (20 marks)** *36 mins*

P & Q plc is a UK-based manufacturing company having subsidiary companies in the USA and various European countries and also a number of overseas agencies.

The company has been growing rapidly and the finance director has recently put in hand a major reorganisation of the finance department, including the setting up of a separate treasury function.

Required

Draft a report from the finance director to the board:

(a) describing the proposed responsibilities of the treasury function; (12 marks)

(b) stating the advantages to the company of having such a specialist function. (8 marks)

11 **MORIBUND (20 marks)** *45 mins*

(a) Explain the term 'operating cycle'. (6 marks)

(b) Calculate the operating cycle for Moribund plc for the years 19X1 and 19X2 on the basis of the following information.

	19X2	*19X1*
	£	£
Stock: raw materials	150,000	130,000
work in progress	60,000	50,000
finished goods	200,000	150,000
Purchases	500,000	450,000
Debtors	230,000	180,000
Trade creditors	120,000	90,000
Sales	900,000	800,000
Cost of goods sold	750,000	650,000

(8 marks)

(c) Advise Moribund plc on the steps which might be taken in order to improve the operating cycle. (6 marks)

12 **KNOSSOS LTD (20 marks)** *36 mins*

It is now the end of 19X0. Knossos Ltd is a small manufacturing company which is experiencing a short-term liquidity crisis. The company accountant has estimated that by the end of February 19X1, a further £200,000 of funds will be required. Since the company already has a large overdraft, its bank will not advance any more funds. Three solutions to the problem have been put forward.

(a) *Option 1.* A short-term loan of £200,000 could be raised for six months from 1 January 19X1 at an annual interest rate of 18%. This would be obtained through a finance company, but there would be no costs involved in raising the funds.

(b) *Option 2.* The company could forgo cash discounts of 2% which are obtained from suppliers of raw materials for payment within 30 days. The maximum credit which could safely be taken is 90 days. Monthly purchases of raw materials amount to £100,000, before discounts. Knossos Ltd would forgo the discount for six months before reviewing the position again.

(c) *Option 3.* The company could factor its trade debtors. A factor has been found who would be prepared, for a period of six months from 1 January 19X1, to advance Knossos Ltd 75% of the value of its invoices less factoring charges, immediately on receipt of the invoices. (You may assume that all invoices are sent out at the end of the month of sale). The factoring charges would be:

(i) an interest charge of 15% a year on the amount of money advanced, calculated on a day-to-day basis, and estimated and deducted in advance;

(ii) a fee for taking on the task of collecting Knossos Ltd's debts, amounting to 2% of the total invoiced and deducted in advance.

Monthly sales are expected to be £300,000. The factor would pay the balance owing on the invoices to Knossos on receipt of the money from the debtors. On average, debtors pay at the end of the month following the month of sale. As a result of using the factor, Knossos Ltd estimates that there would be savings in administration costs of £4,000 a month.

Any surplus funds in excess of the £200,000 required would be used to reduce the bank overdraft, which costs 1% a month.

Required

(a) Show which of the three options is cheapest. (13 marks)

(b) If the factoring arrangement is the option preferred, what would be the cash receipts for the first eight months of 19X1? (4 marks)

(c) Briefly describe the other considerations which should be taken into account when choosing between the three options. (3 marks)

Ignore taxation.

13 THEORIES (20 marks) *36 mins*

The financial manager of a medium-sized listed company has recently completed an MBA specialising in finance. At his first board meeting after completing his degree he is anxious to put his newly acquired knowledge into effect and makes the following arguments.

(a) It has been proved in the theory of finance that dividend policy has no impact upon share price. If the company were to retain all of its profits this would save the transaction costs involved in other methods of capital-raising and would not harm the price of the company's shares.

(b) It has been demonstrated that the London Stock Exchange is efficient. He believes that this means that resources are allocated efficiently by the Stock Exchange with the result that funds throughout the economy are made available to those companies which can make the most efficient use of them.

Required

Write a report which explains whether or not his arguments are correct both in theory and in practice.

14 DUCEY (25 marks) *45 mins*

Ducey plc has decided to acquire some new plant and machinery and is now considering whether to buy or to lease it. The machinery in question has a useful life of four years and is expected to have no residual value at the end of that time. It would cost £176,000 to buy which would be financed by borrowing. Alternatively it could be leased for four years at an annual rental of £55,000 payable annually in advance.

The corporation tax rate is 31%. If purchased the machine would attract a writing down allowance of 25% (reducing balance basis) per annum. A balancing allowance or charge would be made on disposal. If leased, the rental would be allowed fully against corporation tax. Tax is paid (and allowances received) one year in arrears.

The before tax cost of borrowing to Ducey plc is estimated to be 19%.

Required

(a) Advise Ducey plc whether to buy or to lease the machine on the assumption that the company has sufficient taxable profits to fully absorb all tax allowances rising from the buy or lease decision. (18 marks)

(b) Advise Ducey plc whether to buy or to lease the machine on the basis that the company is in a permanent non-tax paying position. (2 marks)

(c) Outline briefly any other factors which the company should take into account when making the lease or buy decision. (5 marks)

15 CAPITAL RATIONING

(a) Describe capital rationing and indicate ways in which it may arise.

(b) Explain the extent to which the following require modification under conditions of capital rationing.

  (i) Project selection techniques
  (ii) The discount rate

(c) Comment on the merits and limitations of the following when selecting projects under conditions of capital rationing.

  (i) Ranking by the ratio of NPV to capital laid out
  (ii) Linear programming

List of key terms and Index

These are the terms which we have identified throughout the text as being KEY TERMS. You should make sure that you can define what these terms mean; go back to the pages highlighted here if you need to check.

ORDER FORM

To order your ACCA books, you can phone us on 0181 740 2211, email us at publishing@bpp.co.uk, fax this form to 0181 740 1184 or cut this form out and post it to the address below.

To: BPP Publishing Ltd, Aldine House, Aldine Place, London W12 8AW

Tel: 0181-740 2211
Fax: 0181-740 1184

Forenames (Mr / Ms): ______________ Surname: ______________________________

Daytime delivery address: ____

____

Post code: ________________ Date of exam (month/year): ____________________

Please send me the following books:	*Price* 6/98 *Text* £	1/98 *Kit* £	1/98 *Passcards* £	*Quantity* *Text*	*Kit*	*Passcards*	*Total* £
Foundation							
The Accounting Framework	18.95	8.95	4.95	....	....	....	....
The Accounting Framework (Int'l)	18.95	8.95*		....	....		....
The Legal Framework	18.95	8.95	4.95	....	....	....	....
Management Information	18.95	8.95	4.95	....	....	....	....
The Organisational Framework	18.95	8.95	4.95	....	....	....	....
Certificate							
Information Analysis	18.95	8.95	4.95	....	....	....	....
The Audit Framework	18.95	8.95	4.95	....	....	....	....
The Audit Framework (Int'l)	18.95	8.95*		....	....		....
The Tax Framework FA 98 (7/98 Text, 8/98 P/c, 8/98 Kit)	18.95	8.95	4.95	....	....	....	....
Managerial Finance	18.95	8.95	4.95	....	....	....	....
Professional							
Information for Control and Decision Making	19.95	9.95	5.95	....	....	....	....
Accounting and Audit Practice A: Accounting	15.95	9.95	5.95	....	....	....	....
Accounting and Audit Practice A: Accounting (Int'l)	15.95	9.95*		....	....		....
Accounting and Audit Practice B: Auditing	13.95			....			....
Accounting and Audit Practice B: Auditing (Int'l)	13.95			....			....
(Kit and Passcards cover both accounting and auditing)							
Tax Planning FA 98 (7/98 Text, 8/98 P/c, 8/98 Kit)	19.95	9.95	5.95	....	....	....	....
Management and Strategy	19.95	9.95	5.95	....	....	....	....
Financial Reporting Environment	19.95	9.95	5.95	....	....	....	....
Financial Reporting Environment (Int'l)	19.95	9.95*		....	....		....
Financial Strategy	19.95	9.95	5.95	....	....	....	....
Postage and packaging:							
UK: Texts £3.00 for first plus £2.00 for each extra				....	....	....	....
Kits and Passcards £2.00 for first plus £1.00 for each extra				....	....	....	....
Europe (inc ROI & CI): Texts £5.00 for first plus £4.00 for each extra				....	....	....	....
Kits and Passcards £2.50 for first plus £1.00 for each extra				....	....	....	....
Rest of the World: Texts £20.00 for first plus £10.00 for each extra				....	....	....	....
Kits and Passcards £15.00 for first plus £8.00 for each extra				....	....	....	....
(Single Kits/Passcards are airmailed. All other parcels are sent by courier and should arrive in not more than six days.)							

*** International Stream Kits will be published in Autumn 1998** Total ________

I enclose a cheque for £ _________ or charge to Access/Visa/Switch

Card number | | | | | | | | | | | | | | | | | | | |

Start date (Switch only) ________ **Expiry date** ____________ **Issue no. (Switch only)**___

Signature ________________________

REVIEW FORM & FREE PRIZE DRAW

All original review forms from the entire BPP range, completed with genuine comments, will be entered into one of two draws on 31 January 1999 and 31 July 1999. The names on the first four forms picked out on each occasion will be sent a cheque for £50.

Name: ______________________ **Address:** ______________________

____

____

How have you used this Text?
(Tick one box only)

☐ Home study (book only)
☐ On a course: college ______________
☐ With 'correspondence' package
☐ Other ______________

Why did you decide to purchase this Text?
(Tick one box only)

☐ Have used BPP Texts in the past
☐ Recommendation by friend/colleague
☐ Recommendation by a lecturer at college
☐ Saw advertising
☐ Other ______________

During the past six months do you recall seeing/receiving any of the following?
(Tick as many boxes as are relevant)

☐ Our advertisement in *Students' Newsletter*
☐ Our advertisement in *Pass*
☐ Our brochure with a letter through the post

Which (if any) aspects of our advertising do you find useful?
(Tick as many boxes as are relevant)

☐ Prices and publication dates of new editions
☐ Information on Text content
☐ Facility to order books off-the-page
☐ None of the above

Your ratings, comments and suggestions would be appreciated on the following areas

	Very useful	*Useful*	*Not useful*
Introductory section (Key study steps, personal study plan etc)	☐	☐	☐
Chapter introductions	☐	☐	☐
Key terms	☐	☐	☐
Explanations	☐	☐	☐
Case examples and examples	☐	☐	☐
Questions and answers	☐	☐	☐
Chapter roundups	☐	☐	☐
Quick quizzes	☐	☐	☐
Exam focus points	☐	☐	☐
Exam question bank	☐	☐	☐
Exam answer bank	☐	☐	☐
List of key terms and index	☐	☐	☐
Icons	☐	☐	☐

	Excellent	*Good*	*Adequate*	*Poor*
Overall opinion of this Text	☐	☐	☐	☐

Do you intend to continue using BPP Study Texts/Kits? ☐ Yes ☐ No

Please note any further comments and suggestions/errors on the reverse of this page.

Please return to: Edmund Hewson, BPP Publishing Ltd, FREEPOST, London, W12 8BR

REVIEW FORM & FREE PRIZE DRAW (continued)

Please note any further comments and suggestions/errors below

FREE PRIZE DRAW RULES

1 Closing date for 31 January 1999 draw is 31 December 1998. Closing date for 31 July 1999 draw is 30 June 1999.

2 Restricted to entries with UK and Eire addresses only. BPP employees, their families and business associates are excluded.

3 No purchase necessary. Entry forms are available upon request from BPP Publishing. No more than one entry per title, per person. Draw restricted to persons aged 16 and over.

4 Winners will be notified by post and receive their cheques not later than 6 weeks after the relevant draw date. Lists of winners will be published in BPP's *focus* newsletter following the relevant draw.

5 The decision of the promoter in all matters is final and binding. No correspondence will be entered into.